VIETNAM

VIETNAM

THE COMPLETE STORY OF THE AUSTRALIAN WAR

BRUCE DAVIES
WITH GARY McKAY

ALLEN&UNWIN
SYDNEY · MELBOURNE · AUCKLAND · LONDON

First published in 2012

Allen & Unwin
Sydney, Melbourne, Auckland, London

83 Alexander Street
Crows Nest NSW 2065
Australia
Phone: (61 2) 8425 0100
Email: info@allenandunwin.com
Web: www.allenandunwin.com

Cataloguing-in-Publication details are available
from the National Library of Australia
www.trove.nla.gov.au

ISBN 978 1 74175 028 7

Internal design by Lisa White
Index by Geraldine Suter
Set in 11/16 pt Minion by Midland Typesetters, Australia
Printed and bound in Australia by Griffin Press

10 9 8 7 6 5 4 3 2 1

MIX
Paper from
responsible sources
FSC® C009448

The paper in this book is FSC® certified.
FSC® promotes environmentally responsible,
socially beneficial and economically viable
management of the world's forests.

The Vietnamese hate the Americans.
The Americans hate the Vietnamese.
The Americans hate the Americans.
The local Chinese are hated by the Vietnamese and the Americans.
The Australians hate everybody.

Lynn Ludlow
San Francisco Examiner
9 April 1968

CONTENTS

———

LIST OF MAPS

———

FOREWORD

As well as costing the lives of nearly 500 Australians, 3000 physically wounded and many more with psychological injuries, the Vietnam War defined the adult lives of tens of thousands of Australians.

Younger Australians see Vietnam not so much as a war but as a destination for tourists or as a conference venue. The war for these touring Australians consists only of the titillation of visiting the Cu Chi tunnels on a day trip from Saigon. They are fed the line by young tourist guides, many of whom are the children of ex-South Vietnamese soldiers, that 'The American War' was fought by the Vietnamese people against foreign aggression, forgetting the sacrifice of millions of South Vietnamese people, perhaps even the bravery of their fathers and uncles. It is always healthy to remember that the tanks which knocked down the gates of the Independence Palace on 30 April 1975 were part of a war of northern aggression. Each generation must see history from its own perspective and that applies as equally to young Australians as it does to today's Vietnamese living in what was once South Vietnam.

It is said that the victor writes the history but Bruce Davies assisted by Gary McKay MC, both veterans of this war, prove once again that we, the defeated, can and should have a voice. Indeed, Australian voices have been heard many times since our troops left Vietnam. Australians have written on battles and on operations, and most recently, the last volume of the official history has been published.

Bruce Davies is eminently qualified to add to the voices on Vietnam, having seen extensive combat in South Vietnam and been recognised for his gallantry and his service. He has written before on Vietnam, in the form of a history of the Australian Army Training Team Vietnam, which almost spans the entire conflict, and the brilliantly told story of a small but vicious battle on a hill known as Ngok Tavak, where the North Vietnamese fought and defeated an Australian-led company of Nungs and a US Marine artillery detachment.

In this book, *Vietnam: The complete story of the Australian war*, Davies applies the forensic approach to history that he demonstrated in his previous books, but in a style which, while being both readable and academic, does not disguise his own, somewhat cynical view of the big political issues that shaped the war, and particularly the war's ignominious end.

I joined the Australian Army at the height of Australia's involvement in this war, but finished my training too late to fight there. I read voraciously about the war from 1968 to 1971 as I prepared, but then only on and off over the next few decades. Vietnam was 'someone else's war'. In the early seventies I served in Australia with Bruce Davies, at a time when his achievements and those of his comrades from Vietnam had still not become general knowledge.

As I served in units that had battle honours from Vietnam, I was exposed to our Veterans as they and I grew older. I still stand in awe of the type of tactical military operations that they conducted, and Davies' book reminds us of these achievements. Regardless of who won or lost in Vietnam, it is fair to say that the Australian soldier, regular and conscript, fought well. The Australian soldier has never lost any war in which we have been involved. Wars are lost by civilian and military 'generals'. Despite this, Davies has a balanced and realistic view of exactly how well our soldiers fought and our generals commanded, and is not overcome by the inevitable myths and legends that all wars produce.

As time went on after Australia's withdrawal, Australia, its military and its government focused on other conflicts. Vietnam might have been for later generations someone else's war, but it still holds many critical lessons relevant to today's conflicts. I worked for a US general in Baghdad whose father, the commanding general of a US division, was killed in Vietnam. General George Casey took over in Iraq as the war deteriorated severely around us, and for the initial few months in the US Embassy in the Green Zone in Baghdad, the word on our lips was: 'This will not be another Tet.'

The way that the US fought the war in Iraq, another militarily successful war with dubious strategic outcomes, was strongly and beneficially influenced by the US realisation that they had been soundly defeated in Vietnam. US generalship, the courage and professionalism of the US soldier and the ethics of how they prosecuted that war, benefitted immensely from the acceptance of failure in Vietnam. It was a shame that US political leadership did not learn as much as the military.

Over forty years of military service, I gained the impression that my army and certainly successive Australian governments and influential bureaucrats, did not learn the lessons of Vietnam. Our approach was coloured by the view that it was all the US's fault—they had lost the war. The popular lesson from Vietnam has now become, erroneously, that such wars were unwinnable, we should never again become involved in them, therefore there is no need to maintain a modern independent military in Australia.

But Australia's involvement in Iraq and Afghanistan shows that, regardless of what popular critics might think of involvement in foreign wars as an ally of the US, Australian governments continue to see value in doing so. If Australian governments are going to remain aggressive and their soldiers continue to pay in blood, then we had better learn which are the right wars in which to become involved, and how to win them once involved. The real benefit of this book is not just as a well-written and researched history offered in a more concentrated form than the official histories, but as an object lesson in how to win and lose wars, especially from the point of view of a small ally in a big war. This book is a superb vehicle for learning the lessons.

I have found that most governments, their civilian advisers and active duty military officers are too busy for the kind of deliberate study of history that is required to give a Australia a fighting chance of not repeating our failures. Davies' history, because of its brutally honest treatment of the Australian involvement in a previous unsuccessful war, is frighteningly similar to the situation that Australia now finds itself in at this final stage of the Afghanistan

War. Because of where we are in Afghanistan, this book has immense relevance. This history of Australia's involvement in Vietnam should have been studied ten years ago, when we had a real chance to win in Afghanistan.

A. J. (Jim) Molan AO, DSC
Major General (Retired)

PREFACE

The story of Vietnam began well before the war that seared the country into Australian consciousness. In *Vietnam: The Complete Story of the Australian War*, the narrative first sets out the region's origins—its civilisation, wars, colonial domination, a search for freedom and its subsequent loss. These events and preoccupations form the backstory of the people living in the region that we now identify on a map as Vietnam.

The history of Vietnam also speaks to an Australian anxiety, that of a very small population on an extremely large island continent, far away from the centre of an Empire to which it was firmly committed. Australian fears were compounded by the rise of Japan and the War in the Pacific followed by a new conundrum: the post-colonial independence of the peoples of Southeast Asia, the mercurial influence of Ho Chi Minh and the possible rise of monolithic communism prosecuted by China and the USSR.

The book leads readers inevitably to the 1960s war and Australia's commitment of forces to counter the perceived communist aggression threatening Southeast Asia's security and economic stability. Subsequent chapters document the challenges Australians faced in this war, not only against a dogged and determined enemy, but also the difficulties faced by the allies to cooperate in their quest to establish a united counterinsurgency infrastructure.

While Australian sentiment and political and diplomatic decision makers were willing to deploy forces to the defence of South Vietnam as part of an allied contribution, Australian commanders soon expressed a strong desire to fight as an independent command. This wish to be a distinct force was bolstered by a belief that Australians were tactically superior to the American and South Vietnamese forces. However, an examination of Australian, American and Vietnamese archival sources and the reinterpretation of previous accounts give rise to questions about that perception. In addition to political and diplomatic manoeuvrings, reports on operational performance are discussed in detail in this book—and some of the conclusions are challenging.

Newly available documents and publications from the former enemy now provide a better understanding of their strategies and motivations. It would be a mistake on behalf of readers to reject all of this information as propaganda. In particular, recently found detail about some of the major battles fought against the Australians provides a strong insight into the enemy's tactical thinking, and it was not all as the intelligence agencies reported.

Vietnam: The Complete Story of the Australian War offers valuable new insights on the historiography of why Australia went to war in South Vietnam and the difficulties of fighting the battles of the war. Some of the information in this book can overlay current operations in Afghanistan, and may even provide a prescient view of the probable end to commitments there. Readers might also find relevance in this book that matches observations by distinguished author Susan Jacoby on 'why history matters' as western leaders attempt to steer a course of cooperation with but containment of an expanding Chinese military into the region once dubbed by US President Dwight D. Eisenhower as being the 'falling dominoes'.

1

IN THE BEGINNING

*Two men are talking in a bar after the 9/11 attacks on America in 2001.
'This is just like Pearl Harbor,' says one. 'What is Pearl Harbor?' says the
other. 'That was when the Vietnamese dropped bombs in a harbour and
it started the Vietnam War,' comes the reply.*

Attributed to Susan Jacoby, commenting on why history is important[1]

Dragons and elephants

Fifty male descendants of the water-dragon king and a supernatural mother,
who had laid 100 eggs in the terrestrial highlands, followed their father to
the river delta where they established a cantonment. The mother, Au Co,
kept the other 50 sons in the high plateaux, where fable tells us that they
formed ethnic tribes. Montagnards? Perhaps. The dragon king shielded his
sons from the hordes in the north and his protective barriers—caused by
the fire of his tongues—remain evident in the geographic forms of Ha Long
Bay, the Mekong Delta and the S-shape of current-day Vietnam. In 1960,
excavations at the Dong-son archaeological site south of Hanoi, near the
current city of Thanh Hoa, unearthed pieces of pottery which supported
the legend that an early kingdom existed in the Red River Delta (in the
north of modern-day Vietnam). It was here that the peoples thought to
be a homogeneous grouping formed from the mixing of early adventurers from Indonesia, Thai and Mongol stock cleared the lands and took up

Chinese methods of agriculture, governance and religion. They were known as 'Viets'.

With the decline of the Chinese Qin Empire to which the Viets had submitted during one of that empire's expeditions, the Viet province was conquered by disaffected Qin generals and named 'Nam Viet', the 'Viets of the South'. After a Chinese civil war in 210 BCE, the Chinese Han pushed the Viets out of the southern Chinese land known as Kwang Tung into an enclave which remained a Chinese colony for almost a thousand years. There were rebellions, one of the most celebrated being that in which the Viet Trung sisters led a series of sieges against a lazy and careless Chinese force which had not fought a battle in Nam Viet for 150 years. Trung Trac and Trung Nhi were decreed queens for three years between 40 and 43 AD. The Chinese reaction was venomous. The Trung army was routed and the sisters committed suicide by drowning in the Day River. Two further uprisings, one in 248 and another between 544 and 547, were crushed. Under the powerful Chinese Tang Dynasty (618–907), Vietnam became known as 'Annam, the Pacified South', a derogatory term denoting subjugation for the Viets. Strong Chinese garrisons were deployed to keep the contemptuous natives in check while Chinese administrators continued the Han policies of assimilation through education, religion and the use of the Chinese writing script. The language, however, remained Vietnamese. Development in the Red River Delta also expanded as the population increased, with emigrants coming from the central provinces of China. Vietnam was 'Sino-cised' and this overwhelming Chinese influence appeared to suffocate Viet culture.

Although Chinese culture permeated Annamese society, it was not China. Despite the long and strong cultural links between the two, the Vietnamese fought the Chinese over the centuries for an independence that perversely required the approval of the Chinese Court. When the power of the vast Chinese Empire fractured, the Vietnamese took control of their own Red River Delta state in 940. Now the Vietnamese began to fight among themselves. Petty local chieftains fought each other until Dinh Bo Linh won out and proclaimed himself emperor of the Dinh Dynasty that lasted from 968 to 980. Relations with China were bound through customary tributary payments. However, one of Dinh's generals threw him out of office and it was not until around 1009 that the stable Ly Dynasty was established. Although Emperor Ly continually looked over his shoulder at the northern hordes with suspicion, his new state started to develop. Once the habitat of 'wild beasts and crocodiles', this land 'that consisted mostly of swamps and forests' became a new agricultural centre. The Ly Dynasty was to 'provide the new state with public revenues, with an army and with an administrative service, while the draining and settlement of the Red River Delta was completed, dykes constructed, and the capital moved to Thang Long (Hanoi)'.[2]

That fiefdom—known as 'Dai Viet'—was no more than a small heel print at the northern end of a 1650-kilometre-long, S-shaped area of land, which at its narrowest point was no more than 50 kilometres wide. To the east was the sea, to the west formidable mountains, some of them 3000 metres high, and to the south were the Chams, a people thought to be of Indonesian stock but heavily influenced by Indian culture. A further attempt by the Chinese to invade the Red River region was defeated and the Vietnamese expanded their coastal redoubt to the vicinity of the 17th parallel. This delimitation was to come to the fore again in 1954 at Geneva, where the Chinese exercised old-fashioned suzerainty over their former subjects and 'advised' the Vietnamese to draw a line across their country against the modern colonialists at that spot.

In the 13th century the Ly Dynasty fell to the Tran, and Mongol armies attacked the Red River enclave three times between 1254 and 1287. They were defeated because of a lack of supplies, sickness and attacks by the Vietnamese Army. The Chinese tried again in 1406, and were finally defeated in 1427 by an army led by Le Loi, a wealthy landowner. Le Loi immediately despatched an emissary to pay homage to the Chinese Emperor. He then resumed tribute payments in the hope of discouraging any future Chinese invasion and the Vietnamese Army was reduced to 100,000 men. Le Loi also recognised that Annam remained culturally dependent upon China.

. The next few hundred years were pivotal centuries in the formation of the region that was to become Indochina. The Funanese—Indian seafarers—had established a trading state in the Mekong Delta, probably around the beginning of the Christian Era. The Chams centred their kingdom on Fai Fo, modern-day Hoi An. The Southern Khmers (Cambodians) had a thriving society along the Mekong River and Tonlé Sap that extended southeast into lands near Prey Kor (pre-Saigon). Siamese (Thai) and Lao chieftains also made efforts to extend their frontiers, generally at the expense of the Cambodians, although they were involved in clashes with the Vietnamese as well.

This was a war cauldron that boiled and bubbled from China in the far north to the swamps of the Cau Mau Peninsula in the Gulf of Siam (Thailand). Funan disappeared, but the Southern Khmers survived for the time being. 'What happened next'—historian and war correspondent Bernard Fall wrote— 'was as thorough a job of genocide as any modern totalitarian state could have devised'.[3] Historian Donald Lancaster agreed: the Vietnamese 'engaged in a succession of wars which ended in the annexation of the Cham kingdom and the destruction of the Cham race'.[4] The recorded mid-15th century conquest of the Champa centre at Vijaya (Binh Dinh) is also evidence of Vietnamese expansion without assimilation. According to accounts by scholars Jean Chesneaux and Georges Maspero, between 40,000 and 60,000 Chams were massacred there when they could not escape the attacking Vietnamese army.[5]

The Vietnamese dynasty then imploded. Success in battle and annexation of enemy territory inversely affected the morals and competence of the Vietnamese monarchs. General Mac Dang Dung usurped the throne. The Chinese Emperor was not happy about this, 'but doubts about the legitimacy of the [Mac] dynasty were finally laid at rest, after the distribution of bribes, cession of certain frontier districts, and . . . the usurper to accept the rank of "Governor" instead of . . . "Vassal King"'.[6] Despite his title, the local populace was reluctant to kowtow to the new governor and revolution followed, splitting the Vietnamese kingdom into two major territories divided in the vicinity of the 17th parallel at Dong Hoi. The Nguyen family led those who moved south while the Trinh held sway in the northern Red River Delta. Both sides then prepared for battle.

The Mac had made themselves unpleasant in the Cao Bang region, a natural fortress of jungle and mountains in the far northwest, with the assistance of the Chinese. This activity sapped the military power of the Trinh. Something very similar was to happen around 275 years later when a new tribe, the French, ventured there.

The mutually ruinous battles between the Trinh and the Nguyen continued for 50 years. After seven failed attacks upon the Nguyen fortifications, the last one being in 1673, the Trinh gave up their efforts and a truce prevailed. The Trinh then concentrated on their northern realm, occasionally attacking Laos. The Mac were defeated and the Trinh and the Nguyen continued to bang their drums and threaten the elephants and the infantry of the other with the help of their Dutch (Trinh) and Portuguese (Nguyen) advisers who had arrived in the early 1600s. The line of fortifications built at Dong Hoi by the Nguyen held them apart during their 100-year 'truce', but the power of the Portuguese artillery probably helped as well. This stalemate was unfortunate for the other peoples who remained in the coastal lowlands, the land the Vietnamese preferred. They did not like the highlands: the jungle was cold and wet, and the savages (Montagnards) who lived there frightened them. The savages were a useful barrier against the Lao, the Khmer and the Siamese. This allowed the Nguyen to turn their attention south, away from the provinces of Quang Tri, Thua Thien and Quang Nam. With the paddy fields of the Chams now in their possession, they looked covetously at the Mekong Delta.

Thrusting the Khmers aside, the Vietnamese moved south towards the Gulf of Siam. By the 1750s, Cambodian provinces in the Mekong Delta region surrendered to—'were colonised by' is a polite term—the Vietnamese in less than pleasant circumstances. Khmer (Cambodian) land in an arc that reached to Tonlé Sap was temporarily annexed in the early part of the 19th century, an annexation that was only stopped by war between Siam and Vietnam. This created a continuing enmity between Cambodia and Vietnam, as Vietnamese Lieutenant General Lam Quang Thi recorded in 1953 when, as a lieutenant, he was to take command of the 3rd Battery, 1st Vietnamese Artillery Battalion. The battalion was moving from Can Tho in southern Vietnam to Laos via Cambodia, a trip that took five days.

Surprisingly, we were neither harassed nor attacked by the Viet Minh ... [Communist-led, anti-French organisation] however, a regrettable incident took place at Kratie, located on the Mekong River. Some Cambodian officers, learning that we were a Vietnamese artillery unit, wanted to encircle and attack our battery. Obviously, they were upset that a unit of the Vietnamese Army, *their historic enemy* [emphasised], had entered their country without authorization, and, for them, this was equivalent to an act of war.[7]

The European religion and more war

The early European sailing ships brought not only merchant adventurers and foreign military to Vietnam but Jesuit missionaries who had been expelled from Japan. The religious proselytisers of Catholicism established their first mission in 1616 at Fai Fo (Hoi An). Ten years later, Alexandre de Rhodes, a Frenchman and a father in the Jesuit domain of the Superior of the Order located in Macao, was sent to Hanoi. To make matters difficult for the missionaries, the ladies of the Vietnamese Court in the north expressed their misgivings about the Christian belief in monogamous marriages. Court officials were also displeased by the clash of precepts between Catholicism and Confucianism.

Soon after Rhodes was deported from Tonkin in 1645, he went to France in an attempt to raise funds for the protection of the clergymen in a land called Cochin China. This appealed to the French, as such religious matters were controlled by the duopoly enjoyed by the Portuguese and the Spanish. Money was raised, but approval was not given for the appointment of vicars 'and the maintenance of their dignity' until 1658. Rhodes died in 1660, but his translation of the Vietnamese language into Romanised script lived on. Even though there was a lack of money for religious expeditions and 'in spite of recurrent and on occasion severe persecution, the Vietnamese Christian community was estimated by the middle of the [18th] century to number 300,000'.[8] The French had won control from the Portuguese over the Catholic missionaries, a decision that was to have ramifications far beyond the 18th century.

Another war, the Tay Son revolt, began in 1773. Military forces led by three brothers who had changed their family name from 'Ho' to the more esteemed 'Nguyen' came down from the foothills in the central region of the future South Vietnam and captured Qui Nhon, a pleasant seaside village with a naturally protected harbour that would be valuable in another war, many years hence. Tay Son was a canton centred on Binh Khe located on the eastern lowland side of the Central Highlands along modern-day Route 19, which connected the coast to Pleiku via An Khe.

The Trinh invaded from the north and captured Hue, while the Tay Son Nguyen and the ruling Nguyen Dynasty fought each other for control of the southern regions. The Tay Son Nguyen were victorious and then took the battle to the northern Trinh, defeating them, too. After this victory, Nguyen Hue from Tay Son declared himself emperor. That forced Nguyen Anh—the survivor of the vanquished ruling Nguyen Dynasty—to hide out in the swamps of the Cau Mau Peninsula and in the Gulf of Siam, where Monsignor Pigneau de Behaine, the French Apostolic Vicar, protected him. This meeting changed the future of the region. Although the monsignor had been based in Pondichery, in India, within the French settlements, he had moved to Ha Tien, in what is now the extreme southwestern corner of Vietnam. Following some shenanigan between the vicar, the French governor-general of their Indian settlements and the Court of Louis XVI of France, de Behaine believed that he had the French Court's approval to restore Nguyen Anh to the throne.

That did not happen because a bankrupt French government advised its military commander he need not continue if he thought an expedition impracticable. Not to be deterred, de Behaine gathered about 100 French volunteers to train the army and navy of Nguyen Anh. The volunteers then marched north and captured Hue. Following this victory, Nguyen Anh named himself 'Gia Long'—a combination of 'Gia Dinh' meaning 'Saigon' and 'Thanh Long' meaning 'Hanoi'. In 1801, he was emperor of a united land from Saigon to Hanoi. Gia Long immediately sent an envoy to China to request he be granted the title 'Vassal King'. This was approved and the capital was moved to Hue where the Citadel sits today. In 1802, Gia Long named his kingdom 'Viet Nam'. In an historical context, the Vietnamese takeover of the lands south of the 17th parallel was still underway when the first English colony of what was to become the United States of America was established in Virginia in 1607, when Lieutenant James Cook claimed the east coast of Australia in 1770 for the British, and in 1789 when the French Revolution began.

De Behaine failed in his efforts to have a Catholic invested as the leader of the Vietnamese and died in 1799. He would have been appalled when Minh Mang, Gia Long's son, decreed that 'the perverse religion of the Europeans corrupts the heart of man'. Minh Mang later demanded that all Catholic churches be destroyed, as Christianity was a crime that deserved the death penalty. This caused a few skirmishes between some Vietnamese Catholics in the south and the central government. The Catholics were defeated. The country, except the city of Danang (French Tourane), was closed to Europeans.

In 1858, the Treaty of Tientsin probably had an unintended effect upon Vietnam's fortunes. The end of the Anglo-Chinese Opium Wars freed up French and Spanish troops, more accurately Filipinos, commanded by

Spanish officers, to return to Vietnam with a mission of establishing a base there. After an unsuccessful occupation of Danang, the French commander moved his force to Saigon from where he could control the large rice harvest in the Mekong Delta. Although this move was successful, the Vietnamese put Saigon to the siege but they were overwhelmed by French reinforcements. Subsequently the military power of the French coerced the Vietnamese Court at Hue to cede administrative power to them in 1862. After that, Vietnam was broken into three regions: Cochin China, soon to be a French colony, in the south; Annam in the middle; and Tonkin to the north. Annam and Tonkin became protectorates of France.

There were several battles against the remnants of the Chinese Taiping Rebellion during 1882 and 1883, and as a result the French sent 3000 troops to Vietnam. That military power swept over the Vietnamese Court, which was in disarray, as were the Chinese. The Chinese fleet was sunk at Keelung and Formosa was attacked, leading to a second Treaty of Tientsin in 1885, in which China relinquished the great seal of suzerainty over Vietnam to the French. The European colonial offices recognised Vietnam's strategic importance to the region, and the Chinese warlords knew it, too. Vietnam was the land that would be nominated as a strategic essential by both East and West. It was a battleground about which a future American president, John F. Kennedy, was to say: 'Now we have a problem in making our power credible, and Vietnam is the place'.[9]

A spark of nationalism

There are many reasons recorded in the 1900s for the growing resentment by the Vietnamese against the French. Heavy taxes, exploitation of the mineral wealth in the north and rubber and rice in the south, a lack of industrial development for ethnic Vietnamese companies, limited employment opportunities and the usury of the Bank of Indochina all added to the groundswell of discontent that some would call nationalism, and others, communism.

At the same time, there were great improvements within Vietnam. Although financially burdensome to the country, roads, a railway link from Hanoi to Saigon and ports were built and improved. The great financial benefits, however, were restricted to privileged Vietnamese. These very wealthy Vietnamese were often absentee landlords, probably schooled in France, people who lived with the trappings of high style, both in Vietnam and France. When their voices were coupled with those of the administrative class of Vietnamese—the few who had made it through to the upper echelons of the French administration—they were heard as 'the Vietnamese'. In fact they were just as isolated from a real understanding of the Vietnamese people as the French or other foreign parties were.

After the 1905 Japanese victory over the Soviets at Port Arthur in Manchuria, a small group of Vietnamese set up the Association for the Restoration of Vietnam in 1913. Two leading members of the group, Phan Boi Chau and Phan Chau Trinh, had been incited to take action, not only by the Japanese naval victory, but also by an earlier French effort in 1891 to defeat resistance fighters on the border with China. The 1891 military and administrative actions were known as *pacification*, a concept which continued to reverberate through counterinsurgency actions to the present. The French plan dictated that:

> Military action was to be limited to establishing military garrisons at communications and supply centres with orders to restrict punitive action to the minimum and to neglect no opportunity to acquire the confidence of the local people. When . . . conditions improved the population were entrusted with the organization of their own defences . . . and the garrisons then moved forward to the edge of the pacified area.[10]

Some among the fragmented nationalist leadership within Vietnam, believed that the Eastern revolution—*Meiji* in Japan—came from western powers. As a result, they thought that France was the model for the development of Vietnam. Surprisingly, the English model did not attract them, even when Phan Boi Chau felt great freedom when he first travelled through Hong Kong, which at that time was a British colony. Both Phan Boi Chau and Phan Chau Trinh were imprisoned in French jails. Phan Boi Chau was betrayed and arrested by the French in 1925. Many commentators believe the person who informed the police special branch (Sûreté) of Phan's whereabouts was a man called Ho Chi Minh. Eminent biographers Sophie Quinn-Judge, William Duiker and Pierre Brocheux disagree with that charge. They consider the most likely culprit to have been Lam Duc Thu, a former associate of Ho's

and a known police informer.[11] Another fact supporting the view that Ho
Chi Minh had not betrayed him, was that Phan Boi Chau wrote favourably
of Ho in his autobiography *Overturned Chariot*.[12] The suspicion that Ho Chi
Minh played a part in Phan's betrayal in order to obtain the large reward—
HK$10,000—and to remove a potential threat to his leadership was never
erased, however. Some writers said that Ho's perfidious conscience was salved
by the fact that Phan was not a communist.

During World War I there was an attempted armed uprising against the
French in Vietnam, but some executions and the banishment to the god-
forsaken island of Réunion in the Indian Ocean of the royal leader Duy Tan
put a stop to those ideas. (The former emperor went on to become a respected
French air force officer.) With approximately 45,000 Vietnamese troops sent
to serve on the Western Front for the Allies, Vietnam was kept under control
by less than 10,000 French troops.

In 1922, Australia entered this strategic arena when Senator George Pearce,
Minister for Home and Territories, signed the Nine-Power Treaty as Australia's representative on 6 February in Washington. The Treaty's goal was:

> To adopt a policy designed to stabilize conditions in the Far East, to safeguard the
> rights and interests of China, and to promote intercourse between China and the
> other Powers upon the basis of equality of opportunity.[13]

Australia must have sneaked in under the 'Powers' heading as a corollary
to the United Kingdom of Great Britain and Ireland and the British Dominions beyond the Seas.

Later, in 1934, John G. Latham, Minister for External Affairs, led an
Australian Far East Trade Mission through the area, which included French
Indochina. As an advocate for the 'Near East', Latham stressed its importance
to Australia and wrote many reports about his beliefs for the region.

> From our childhood we have been accustomed to read, think and speak of the
> 'Far East'. But we must realise that it is the 'Near East' to Australia. Therefore,
> it is important that we should endeavour to develop and improve our relations
> with our near neighbours, whose fortunes are so important to us, not only in
> economic matters, but also in relation to the vital issues of peace and war.[14]

Agitation against the French in Vietnam became violent in the 1920s. In 1927 a small party was formed called the Viet Nam Quoc Dan Dang (VNQDD), whose aim, according to historian Joseph Buttinger, was to get rid of the French. Some said that the VNQDD had a close connection with the Chinese Kuomintang—Chinese Nationalists—while others saw it as an informal meeting of minds between the two parties, both having nationalism as an ideal. Other views held that the VNQDD derived its ideology from the Chinese Communists who, until 1927, operated in concert with the Kuomintang. Whatever the underlying political theory, armed struggle was an approved means of achieving political objectives.

In 1929, the director of the French Bureau for Labour was murdered, probably for good reason. The bureau had been despatching Vietnamese labourers—*slaves*—to islands in the Pacific, where many perished. In 1930, a Vietnamese force mutinied at Yen Bay and killed their French officers, non-commissioned officers and some Vietnamese. The rebellion was defeated and the VNQDD party's headquarters was bombed. Some of the mutineers were guillotined at Yen Bay to set an example, but other members escaped into China. After the Yen Bay incident, there was a series of riots and anti-colonial actions throughout Vietnam but the anti-French insurrection was savagely crushed. One of the leaders of the anti-French group was an absentee communist revolutionary, a man of a hundred faces.

Nguyen Tat Thanh, a man of a hundred faces

Nguyen Sinh Cung, Nguyen Tat Thanh, Nguyen Ai Quoc, Tran Dan Tien—biographer, in reality autobiographer—and Ho Chi Minh are some of the aliases by which the Vietnamese leader was known throughout his life. There are reportedly many other assumed names, some say 100 or more, which means that there is much conflicting evidence about who he was. His travels and political activities also elicit points of view that are diametrically opposed.

Some of the plausible variations mentioned here challenge some commonly accepted tales about Ho's early years. Dates given for Ho's year of birth range from 1890 to 1895, and his place of birth is also uncertain. In his application for admittance to the French Colonial School in 1911, Nguyen Tat Thanh said that he was born in 1892 at Vinh and was the son of Nguyen Sinh Huy.[15] That application raises questions about why he travelled to France. Did he go there to set the groundwork for a rebellion against France? Or did he intend to gain access into the colonial administrative system as an official? Alexander Woodside, a political historian, wrote in *Community and Revolution in Modern Vietnam* that Ho Chi Minh thought France was an expanding power. His application to enter the school was, therefore, a request to join with them, not fight them.[16] Furthermore, Phan Boi Chau, the man betrayed to the French by an associate of Ho's, was running a nationalist organisation that was gathering anti-French recruits to send to Japan and China for revolutionary training. Ho did not join with him, but his siblings did and were jailed for their efforts. Ho Chi Minh's 1911 application was more in line with Phan Chau Trinh's Francophile philosophy. However, this attempted association with the French administration was allegedly a plan of deceit to destroy the enemy from within.

Ho Chi Minh used so many aliases between 1911 and 1941 that they cast a shadow of disbelief over segments of his personal history. Many of the stories are distractions intended no doubt to steer inquisitors along false paths of information and to create an air of mystery about the man. The tales may have been a form of propaganda, or a method of protection from the Sûreté and other intelligence agencies. When Ho arrived in Marseilles in September 1911, did he stay in France, or go back to sea, having failed to gain entry to the Colonial School? Perhaps. Did he then travel to and work in America? Maybe. Did he come ashore and work as a kitchen hand at the Carlton Hotel in London? Possibly.

Many writers have addressed these questions and more, and each has drawn a conclusion slightly at odds with the others. For example, Donald Lancaster outlined Ho's story:

> Nguyen Ai Quoc ... who was born in 1890 ... had signed on as a galley boy on ... a French merchant ship in 1911. He ... visited ports in Europe, Africa and America. During the winter of 1913 he [reportedly] came ashore in London, where [he worked] at the Carlton Hotel. Five years later [1918–19] he moved to Paris ... sharing lodgings with Phan Chau Trinh.[17]

This was not his first connection with Phan Chau Trinh, as Ho had worked as a young teacher at a Phan Thiet school established by a Trinh associate.

He had obtained his educational credentials by attending the Quoc-Hoc school in Hue, which had been established by Ngo Dinh Kha, the father of Ngo Dinh Diem, the future president of South Vietnam. Both Vo Nguyen Giap, the future commander of the North Vietnamese Army, and Ngo Dinh Diem were later students at Quoc-Hoc.

Sophie Quinn-Judge writes in her book *Ho Chi Minh: The Missing Years 1919–1941* that 'Ho Chi Minh's passage to America in 1917–18 remains in the realm of conjecture—the next confirmed sighting of Nguyen Ai Quoc/ Nguyen Tat Thanh is in Paris in 1919'.[18] Quinn-Judge agrees that Ho Chi Minh, using one of his aliases, settled in London in either 1913 or 1914, although there was no evidence that he worked at the Carlton Hotel. The conjecture is irrelevant. At this stage in his burgeoning career as a revolutionist, Ho was a minor functionary. The important location and date is Paris 1919, as it is from here that he began his serious journey within the socialist and then communist clique. The 1919 Paris date may also be wrong; he might have returned to France during 1917 and it is also possible that he went back to Vietnam in 1911 for a brief period.[19]

Known now as 'Nguyen Ai Quoc'—although Ho's detractors point out that 'Nguyen Ai Quoc' was the pseudonym of Phan Van Truong, the leader of the Group of Viet Patriots—Ho 'rented a black suit and a bowler hat' to prowl the corridors of the World War I Paris Peace Conference at Versailles. He did not gain an audience with any of the main leaders, nor get the chance to present an eight-point plan on behalf of the Viet Patriots. Disillusioned by the failure of the Versailles Conference to address the 'colonial issue', Ho became a 'founding member' of the French Communist Party in December 1920. The light of world revolution espoused by the Moscow 'Comintern' and the Nationalist/Communist ideals of China would guide his pathway back to Vietnam.

Ho's first step in that journey was his election to the Krestintern—Red Peasant International—in 1923 at Moscow. After this he worked with Michael Borodin, a Soviet arms agent at Canton, then he was actively involved with the Vietnam Revolutionary Youth Association, the South Seas (Southeast Asia) Communist Party. At Hong Kong in 1930, Ho Chi Minh was an original member of the Vietnamese Communist Party. This party was fragmented, but it eventually became the Indochinese Communist Party. Along the way

Ho would be arrested by the British in Hong Kong and saved from probable execution by the French through the action of the British Privy Council who prevented his extradition.

Ho became the consummate Communist Party apparatchik who avoided the Stalin purges that sent many of his comrades before the firing squad. He was also adept at eliminating his political rivals, or those he considered to be unreliable communists following their training in China, by simply slipping their names to the French authorities inside Vietnam. Ho always kept one foot on each side of the bamboo fence in an effort not to upset either the Chinese or the Soviets. But his star became somewhat tarnished because of the failure of his communist enterprises. The capture of his files in Hong Kong, the desertion of the Vietnamese Nationalist Party efforts at Yen Bay— which the Vietnamese communists vehemently denied—and the collapse of the Nghe An revolt in July 1930, during which Vo Nguyen Giap was captured and jailed, did not auger well for the future leader.

Ho Chi Minh reportedly spent four years in the Soviet Union attending 'Party schools' before returning to China in early 1938 during the war between Japan and China. He deployed with the 8th Route Army (Chinese Communist) before becoming the political commissar to Chinese General Yeh Chien Ying who was Mao Zedong's most capable guerrilla expert. He disappeared for a short period after Yeh Chien Ying's mission was withdrawn, and then entered Vietnam, supposedly for the first time in 30 years, at Cao Bang Province. It was either at Pac Bo (Vietnam) in May 1941 or nearby Jingxi (China) that the Indochinese Communist Party formed the organisation called the League for the Independence of Vietnam, *Viet Nam Doc Lap Dong Minh Hoi*, the Viet Minh.

Another Vietnamese present during these meetings was Vo Nguyen Giap. Giap was a known firebrand from his school days at the National Academy in Hue. He had been jailed for two years following the Nghe Tinh revolt in 1931 for taking part in 'revolutionary demonstrations', but after his release he obtained a degree from the University of Hanoi and went on to teach history at a private school in that city. In the mid-1930s, Giap married Nguyen Thi Minh Giang, the younger sister to Nguyen Thi Minh Khai, who was supposedly Ho Chi Minh's wife. No one knows with certainty whether Khai was married to Ho or not; even the acknowledged experts differ in variously describing her as wife, mistress and girlfriend. When Vo Nguyen Giap was warned to leave Tonkin for China in 1938, he was told that he would probably meet Ho Chi Minh (Nguyen Ai Quoc) whom he had not met before, and that, as an ardent student of military history, he should prepare himself for the potential of guerrilla warfare. There was nothing prescient about this statement; almost every force in the Asian strategic region had—or would soon have—some type of unconventional group that operated as guerrillas. When Giap left Vietnam, he was not to see his wife or daughter again.

The members of the Indochinese Communist Party were now embroiled in a Chinese region best described as a seething political and military can of worms. The Communist Chinese were ensconced at Yenan in northeastern China while the Nationalist Chinese were headquartered around Kunming and Chungking in the southwest. Ho Chi Minh, Vo Nguyen Giap and Pham Van Dong—a future prime minister of North Vietnam—manipulated the resources of both the Chinese Nationalist and the Communist camps to obtain aid for the Indochinese communists. Although each side displayed some willingness to help, there was always a degree of suspicion, even among friends, and as will be seen later that included the western allies. Later the Chinese Nationalists incarcerated Ho Chi Minh because he was a communist and a French spy. He was released allegedly through the help of American Office of Strategic Services (OSS) personnel then based in Kunming.[20] But there were also more mutterings that Ho was a self-preservationist who obtained his freedom through cooperation with the British and the French by reporting on his political rivals, or those whom he considered poor communists.

A Japanese shadow and Pacific alliances

The entry of America into the war against Japan brought a whole new multifaceted diplomatic dimension, the magnitude of which was to change Australia's security relationships from a dependence upon the United Kingdom to the brash but powerful United States of America. America was a more sympathetic ally to Australia's potentially dire circumstances because the Pacific Ocean was also its backyard. No doubt the underpinning usefulness of Australia to the Americans and the Pacific War was its size and location that would allow US forces the respite and succour needed to take the battle forward and defeat the Japanese. The real prizes sat to the north among the then sought-after raw materials and the potential of the huge populations of Asia. The strategists might have turned back the pages of their history books and heeded the words of Leon Trotsky when he spoke of the road to London and Paris lying via the towns of Afghanistan, Punjab and Bengal, to which Lenin had added the towns of China and Tsarist Russia.

Before America's entry into World War II, many commentators referred to the Atlantic Charter as an eight-point blueprint for the future fortunes of British and French colonies. Australia later subscribed to the common principles of the charter in what became the Declaration of the United Nations. America was not in the war when Winston Churchill and Franklin Roosevelt met in August 1941 at Newfoundland, but that meeting exuded an air of great confidence that presaged defeat for Germany, Italy and Japan, the Axis Powers. Of the Charter's eight points, two are continually mentioned in the never-ending debate about the 20th-century wars in Vietnam.

> They [USA and UK] desire to see no territorial changes that do not accord with the freely expressed wishes of the peoples concerned. They respect the right of all peoples to choose the form of government under which they will live; and they wish to see sovereign rights and self-government restored to those who have been forcibly deprived of them.[21]

The Charter appeared to underline the rather vitriolic thoughts later expressed by President Roosevelt against the French possessions in Indochina and Noumea. Prime Minister Churchill was not enthused by the possibility that he would oversee the dismantling of the British Empire, saying that he had not been appointed as 'the King's first minister in order to preside over the liquidation of the British Empire'.[22]

A little over a year before the Churchill–Roosevelt meeting, expansionist Japan was uppermost in the minds of those countries that bordered the Pacific. At Batavia (Jakarta) in February 1940, Mr Saito, the Japanese Consul General, told Erle Dickover, the Consul General for the United States, that there was no need to be suspicious of the Japanese, as they had no territorial designs on the Netherlands Indies (Indonesia). Saito believed that the Japanese government was 'prepared to give "any assurances" desired in regard to the security' of this archipelago. He also added that the same factors applied to the Philippines. When asked by Dickover what Japan expected in return, the consul general replied, 'Nothing but cooperation'.[23] This referred to Japan's desire to have 'free access to raw materials', especially the petroleum in the Netherlands Indies.

Naturally Japan's ideas about 'protecting' this region concerned Australia. Richard G. Casey, DSO, MC, Australia's Minister to the United States, visited Adolf Berle, the Assistant Secretary of State, at his house and asked what advice he should give the Australian War Cabinet if the Japanese moved against the Dutch East Indies. Casey wanted advice on whether Australian troops and ships should be moved to Darwin, a clear indication that Australia's leaders had turned, or were turning, towards America as their strategic bulwark. Berle subsequently discussed the question with Secretary of State, Cordell Hull, on the croquet ground at Woodley Park. Hull's view was that 'the information was not sufficient to justify us in giving the Australians any particular advice; further, that the Australian forces were not sufficient to have any real effect in defending the Dutch East Indies'.[24]

Meanwhile Japan and the Chinese warlords engaged in a vicious series of incidents that had developed into a full-scale war, albeit undeclared. The Soviet Union and the western powers provided supplies, including war stores, to the Chinese in an effort to prevent the full power of the Japanese being deployed against them. The West did this by using the Burma Road and the Indochinese rail route from Haiphong to Kunming. That did not please the Japanese who had bombed the railway route in 1939 and now assembled a force on the island of Hainan that was capable of a move towards Indochina or the Netherlands East Indies in the event of an Allied collapse in Europe. Tokyo then requested the French to close the border between Indochina and China before the morning of 21 June 1940.

During this period the Japanese kept a close eye on American intentions, which at this stage were being played out in the arcane world of words among the diplomats. As the French Ambassador to Washington enquired: 'Does the State Department see its way to give friendly advice to the Japanese government to refrain from such aggression?'[25] No answer was given and Indochina's French Governor-General, Georges Catroux, in concert with the French ambassadors in Japan and China closed the frontier on 20 May 1940. The closure attracted a flurry of diplomatic apologies from the French officials involved—to the Americans, in particular—and threats from the Chinese to invade Indochina if the Japanese used it as a base. With the collapse of France before the advancing Germans on the European Front there was no other option for General Catroux, who was dismissed by the Vichy government for his acquiescence. The new Governor-General Admiral Decoux's expressed intention to defend Indochina at all costs was a hollow gesture. He lacked a substantial fighting force and his war stores were limited.

The use of the Burma Road was also 'suspended' by the British for several months on the demand of the Japanese. Diplomatic protestations continued, but these complaints centred on trade and the delivery of goods approved by previous pacts, one of which was the 1922 Nine-Power Treaty that supposedly safeguarded China's interests. The prospect of further military expansion by Japan loomed like a dark cloud across the horizon. The oil fields of the Dutch East Indies beckoned, causing Australian Minister Casey to make frequent visits to officials at the US Department of State.

Australian anxiety

In September 1940, following considerable diplomatic brouhaha and a Japanese attack against French positions on the border with China and the bombing of Haiphong, an agreement was concluded with the Vichy French that permitted Japanese forces to be stationed inside northern Vietnam (Tonkin). Subsequently, many stinging claims and counter-claims were aired about America's efforts, or lack thereof, to dissuade the Japanese from their creeping expansionism, and the lack of support given to the French effort during this period of crisis. Bernard Fall, for example, laid the blame for the war in the Pacific and the subsequent woes of Indochina at the feet of President Franklin Roosevelt. In his book *The Two Viet-Nams*, Fall wrote:

Indochina became the watershed that separated peace from war in the Pacific ... Washington had clung to its noncommittal attitude ... but ... when it became obvious that the Vichy would no longer resist Japanese demands, the President ordered the freezing of all Japanese assets ... and an embargo on petroleum exports to Japan. F.D.R. [Roosevelt] proposed the complete neutralization of Indochina in exchange for a guarantee of Japan's 'right of acquisition . . . of supplies and raw materials therefrom on a basis of equality'.[26]

He went on to say that this did not solve Japan's need for oil, nor did it shut down the railway between Haiphong and the Chinese Yunnan Province, which carried American equipment that sustained the Chinese Nationalists in their efforts against the Japanese. Furthermore, the Japanese Navy hardened its 'insistence upon an attack on Southeast Asia before its petrol supplies were totally exhausted'. He also made an acerbic observation about President Roosevelt's attention to matters in Indochina.

President Roosevelt's preoccupation with Indochina and the attitude of the French there did not abate to his dying day. And, considering the negligible role that Viet Nam, Laos, and Cambodia played throughout World War II, they probably absorbed more of the President's attention than they deserved. Indochina thus became the object of several high-level decisions of fateful importance to its postwar development—decisions that might perhaps have been better adapted to local realities had they been made at a lower level.[27]

Roosevelt's criticisms of French colonialism and the British efforts were terse and barbed as the *Foreign Relations of the United States* (records of the Department of State) show. Marshal Stalin, the Soviet leader, told Roosevelt at their Tehran conference in 1943 that 'the Allies should not shed blood to restore Indochina to the old French colonial rule'. Roosevelt said that he was '100 per cent in agreement . . . and remarked that after 100 years of French rule in Indochina the inhabitants were worse off than they had been before'. In reply to Winston Churchill's opinion about France's reconstruction as a strong nation, Roosevelt made this biting retort: 'The first necessity for the French, not only for the Government but the people as well, was to become honest citizens'.[28] Did this cutting assessment come from a strong personal dislike of the French, a disapproval that was so strong as to influence his presidential duties? This note from Bernard Fall's book suggests that it did.

At least one French authority on the history of Indochina, George Taboulet, expressed to this writer [Fall] the interesting theory that Roosevelt's particular hatred for the French in Indochina stemmed from his maternal grandfather, Warren Delano [Delaneau], who had lost a great deal of money in 1867 in prematurely selling two parcels of real estate at the entrance of the 'Chine Arroyo' into the Saigon River. Today, the area is still one of the choice spots in Saigon and is owned by a French industrial concern. The French consulate is also located there. There is no evidence that Roosevelt was ever informed of his grandfather's interests in the area, but Taboulet's information provides additional evidence of the United States' century-old interest in Viet Nam.[29]

Japan's manoeuvres in 1940 continued to worry Australia and at a meeting in Minister Casey's house in Washington on the evening of 27 September 1940, Casey speculated aloud, 'in the event that war resulted', whether America would 'immediately assist by going to war with Japan'. Although Casey did not ask Berle to comment, he did say that Dr Stanley Hornbeck, the Political Adviser to Cordell Hull, was 'belligerent'. This probably was an attempt to influence Berle to commit himself. Casey went on to say that he had 'cabled his government about the possibility of supplying some arms to Indo-China, but they had replied that they could not, because they needed all they had for themselves'. Berle replied that such decisions were difficult and pondered: 'Is the greatest usefulness obtained by keeping arms close to home, or by letting them go elsewhere, so as to prevent the conflict from coming nearer to home?' Berle's comment highlighted the coming strategic dilemma associated with the security of Southeast Asia as well as Australia and New Zealand. Even though there was the possibility of a smokescreen of distance around the activities of Vichy France, to suggest an offer of arms to a colonial administration of a state whose standing with Britain was icy, to say the least, should have raised a question within the corridors of the Australian government. No matter, the United States recognised the Vichy state, and they just might fight the Japanese even though neither Australia nor America was at war with Japan at this stage. As Berle left Casey's house, the minister again asked about war with Japan. Berle would not comment, but he did say: 'There would be . . . very great reluctance to become involved in hostilities in the Far East until defenses in the Atlantic were considered entirely safe. This . . . was a purely personal opinion.'[30]

Berle's reasoning also highlighted the future strategy of Europe first, which was to influence the next phase in Vietnam's history. Australia attempted to juggle its Asian regional diplomatic difficulties by opening a legation in Japan in 1940. A second post was established in 1941 at Chungking, China, where Keith Waller, a future Secretary of External Affairs, was second secretary. One of his tasks was military intelligence liaison and the Vichy French were among the contacts that he developed, although according to the Minister at Chungking, Sir Fredric Eggleston, Canberra showed no interest in their reports. Eggleston wrote in one report to Canberra that it was like dealing with an unechoing void.

War in the Pacific

'December 7, 1941—a date which will live in infamy.' This was the opening of President Roosevelt's speech to the US Congress on 8 December and referred to Japan's surprise attack upon Pearl Harbor. Further into his address the president told the assembled politicians that six other locations around the Pacific and the Pacific rim had also been attacked. Bombers flying out of Saigon supported the invasion fleet that carried the Japanese 25th Army from Hainan Island off southern China, and Cam Ranh Bay in Indochina. This force began its landings into Thailand and Malaya and bombed Singapore on 8 December—7 December Hawaiian time—just several hours before the Pearl Harbor attack.

The president requested Congress to declare that a state of war existed between the United States and the Japanese Empire. Australia followed suit a day later, on 8 December, Australian time. On 10 December the loss of the British battleship *Prince of Wales* and the battle cruiser *Repulse* off the coast of Malaya was the cause of a considerable shock to the morale of not only the British, but also Australia. Churchill said that in all of the war he never got 'a more direct shock' and that, as he had turned in his bed, the full horror of the sinking had fallen upon him. The Japanese force quickly rolled over the defenders on both the east and west coasts of Malaya. Despite some spirited defence by British and Australian forces at Kampar and Muar, the Japanese were soon sitting on Singapore's doorway in the Malayan state of Johore.

The rapid Japanese advance obviously unnerved many people. John Curtin, the Australian Prime Minister, sent a personal plea to President Roosevelt that was passed by Casey to the Secretary of State and immediately to the president on 23 December 1941. In that telegram, Prime Minister Curtin underlined the importance of Singapore to regional security and acknowledged that the 'amount of resistance to the Japanese ... will depend directly upon the amount ... provided by the governments of the United Kingdom and the United States'. Curtin explained that Australia had three divisions fighting in the Middle East and had sent 'great quantities of supplies to Britain, the Middle East and to India', which meant resources at home 'were very limited indeed'. He acknowledged, 'It is in your power to meet the situation' and ended his telegram with a telling statement: 'Should the Government of the United States desire, we would gladly accept an American Commander in the Pacific area'.[31]

Historians continue to argue whether there was a threat to Australia from invasion by the Japanese or not, but often, tangled within their arguments, is the question of Australian–US–Anglo relations. Was this series of attacks in 1941 the turning point for the firming of a stronger alliance by Australia with the United States? When the prime minister lobbied for an American commander in his own backyard in 1941 that single message of intent must have carried a potent signal of realignment. Curtin all but admitted this in November 1942 when he wrote to Churchill that Australia had 'surrendered part of our sovereignty' by placing its forces under American command.[32]

Even though there was no formal alliance between Australia and the United States, there was an obvious hope that a new partnership would develop that would swing a strong America behind—or more correctly in front of—Australia, regardless of the hurt to Australia's British family connections. The Australian government transmitted an update to the president on the desperate situation in Malaya on 24 December 1941, summarising the immediate need for large numbers of the latest fighter aircraft and reinforcements in divisions, not brigades. Any effort that was not powerfully modern and immediate was considered futile. In the mind of the Australian Prime Minister, the fall of Singapore was only a matter of weeks away and the need for 'decision and action is a matter of hours, not days'.

The telegram was also made available to Prime Minister Churchill and the British chiefs of staff. The telegrams preceded a prime-ministerial statement in the Melbourne *Herald* on 27 December 1941 that annoyed Churchill immensely and allegedly attracted a criticism from President Roosevelt, who thought it smacked of panic. Australians were astonished when, in his end-of-year message, Curtin said: 'Without any inhibitions of any kind, I make it clear that Australia looks to America, free of any pangs as to our traditional links or kinship with the United Kingdom'.[33] Troubled by the Australian Prime Minister's pragmatic statements, Churchill wrote to Curtin on 29 December:

> I now read in the American Press your reported statement . . . for the 'Melbourne Herald'. Such a statement will cause resentment throughout the Empire and had a very poor reception in high quarters in the United States.[34]

Churchill sent a memo to the Lord Privy Seal and Dominions Secretary on the same day in which he directed that a firm attitude be adopted in the House of Commons.

> You should take a firm stand against this behaviour, which certainly does not represent the brave Australian nation. I hope . . . there will be no weakness or pandering to them at this juncture, while at the same time we do all in human power to come to their aid. You should call Earle Page [Australian minister at London] to account in Cabinet for it and ask what is the meaning of this sort of language.[35]

Curtin's urgent pleas received a mundane reply from Roosevelt on 30 December along the lines we'll see what we can do and thanks for your magnificent contribution. Simultaneously, plans for Australia were already being deliberated upon at the First Washington Conference that was underway in the United States, a war planning conference between Roosevelt and Churchill and their staff. The America British Dutch Australia (ABDA) command was approved at this meeting, with General Archibald Wavell named as the first commander, although even at this stage General Douglas MacArthur was also being considered. Roosevelt thought it would be better to have an American commander of the area 'because he believed an American would be accepted more readily by the Australians and the Dutch than any Britisher'.[36] Interestingly, Indochina was not part of the ABDA area; it belonged to Chiang Kai Shek's China Theatre of War.

Curtin's forecast that, without reinforcements, Singapore would fall within weeks soon proved tragically correct. The Japanese crossed the Johore Strait on 8 February and at 8.30 p.m. on 15 February General Edgar Percival, the British commander, capitulated. Australia lost nearly 2000 killed, with more than 1000 wounded, and 15,000 became prisoners of war. In controversial circumstances the commanding general of the 8th Australian Division, Major General H. Gordon Bennett, escaped and made his way back to Australia. Vivian Bowden, the Australian government's official representative in Singapore, led several diplomats, including John Quinn, in an attempted escape, but they were caught by the Japanese Navy and put ashore in Sumatra. After an angry argument over what might have been a protestation by Bowden of his diplomatic status, two Japanese guards took him outside and shot him. Quinn remained incarcerated until the end of the war.

The Japanese military pushed on and Darwin was bombed twice on 19 February 1942. More than 250 people, both military and civilian, were killed. President Roosevelt ordered General MacArthur from the Philippines to Australia in February, although he did not arrive in Melbourne until 21 March. In April he was appointed Supreme Commander South West Pacific Area. This replaced Wavell's ABDA command and the land boundaries were altered so that Sumatra, Singapore and Malaya, as well as Thailand and Indochina, were outside the responsibility of the South West Pacific Area. Later there were deliberate attempts by British Admiral Louis Mountbatten—with approval of the British Foreign Office and the prime minister—to bring Indochina into his Southeast Asia Command (SEAC) sphere of operations. Mountbatten believed that Indochina was an important objective in the defeat of Japan and to get Indochina he needed the French.

Even though the Australians feted MacArthur on his arrival, the military resources available to him were slim because of the Europe-first strategy approved by Roosevelt and Churchill. Opinions vary as to whether Australia surrendered its strategic circumstances to the United States at this stage, but the notes of the Washington conferences of December 1941 – January 1942 resolve any uncertainty as to who was driving strategic planning with regard to Australia's future fortunes. According to historian Gavin Long's *The Six Years War: Australia in the 1939–45 War*, America had the power that the British had lost and the Australian political leaders turned to General MacArthur in the hope that he could influence the deployment of resources to the Pacific. Every country was scrabbling to either protect its homeland from a perceived invasion, or taking action to place its national interests to the fore after the war. The embroilment was inextricably linked to the other end of the Pacific Basin where China carried the hopes of America, first as a stable enemy of Japan, and then as a possible post-war ally and trading partner. The American President and his senior generals saw Britain and France as colonialist troublemakers in the fight against Japan, and as a result Indochina was a diplomatic hot potato.

What to do with Indochina

US Navy Captain Milton Miles who commanded the little-known Sino America Cooperative Organization (SACO) that equipped, trained and operated as guerrilla forces against the Japanese inside China—and who for a time was the 'Director of O.S.S-Far East'—wrote an assessment of Indochina in his 1942 memoirs:

> In addition to having certain responsibilities in China, I had others . . . to do with 'activities in Indo-China'. General Tai [head of China's intelligence organisation] could do almost nothing so far as Indo-China was concerned. The region had many different groups . . . but the trouble was they did not like each other [and] . . . they did not like the Chinese. General Tai made it clear to me . . . there were French, British and Chinese groups, as well as several different native stocks [with] individual aims and ideas. The French were . . . divided. There were the Fighting French . . . one group was sympathetic to General Giraud and another to General de Gaulle. Then there were the Vichy French. The British . . . in Chungking were supporting the French Mission, which was outspokenly De Gaullist. The Chinese . . . objected to the French Mission . . . the French Mission was angry at General Tai. Then there were the people of Indo-China, among whom all shades of political feeling are to be found, from conservative to revolutionary . . . all were afraid of the Chinese who lived . . . to the north, but they also heartily disliked the French.[37]

SACO made contact with nationalist Indochinese well before the much more celebrated link-up between Archimedes Patti of the Office of Strategic Services (OSS) and Ho Chi Minh later in the war. Unfortunately, the

SACO chance failed. Miles and Brigadier William Donovan, the Coordinator of Information—later the OSS—did not see eye to eye on matters regarding China and Indochina, but there was nothing unusual about that. The powerful US General George Marshall detested General Tai who was a close ally of SACO, which meant Miles had to watch his back during inter-service rivalry power games in China. For every plan or idea there was a counterplan or a different concept of what to do in the Far East. It was fair to say that the allied agencies in the region were arguing more among themselves than fighting the Japanese. This permitted politically astute local aspirants to obtain the stamp of approval from one government agency while another department within the same government would have banned that person from negotiations. At one stage the Communist Chinese were in favour with the Americans, which was probably accentuated by Lieutenant General Joseph 'Vinegar Joe' Stilwell's dislike of the nationalist Generalissimo Chiang Kai Shek. Stilwell was Chiang's chief of staff and commanded the China–Burma–India theatre. Despite claims to the contrary, Indochina—while not a principal battleground—got a lot of attention at major conferences among the western leaders during World War II. It was an anti-French subject that President Roosevelt seemed very happy to pursue, even when he did not wish to make a decision about its many diplomatic challenges.

From the altruistic Atlantic Charter through a variety of discussions at conferences, presidential dictums, off-the-record analyses and talks with members of the administration and influential persons, President Roosevelt's objective for Indochina was quite clear: the French should not get it back. Why did the objective change? It changed because of security and trade. President Roosevelt's death before the end of the war did not change the inevitable. President Harry Truman picked up the pieces of Roosevelt's anti-colonial policies and discovered a hidden strategy that would see America and China become the policemen and trading partners of the Asia region, which implied military forces and bases in the area. That envisaged strategic region included Australia.

This was very different from the selfless expressions uttered at the meeting that had drafted the Atlantic Charter and the ill feeling about France's administration of Indochina that Stalin, Chiang Kai Shek and Churchill discussed at the conferences in Cairo and Tehran in 1943. President Roosevelt also discussed with Chiang Kai Shek the possibility of a system of trusteeship for Indochina, which would have the task of preparing the people for independence in perhaps 20 to 30 years' time. In a later conversation with Edward Stettinius, Secretary of State, Stettinius recorded that the president had indicated that Stalin had said Indochina should be independent, but that it was not ready for self-government. Stalin said the idea of a trusteeship was excellent. When Churchill objected, the president told him he was outvoted three to one—Roosevelt, Stalin and Chiang Kai Shek against Churchill.[38]

Before this, an American political adviser at Algiers, Robert Murphy, told French General Henri Giraud: 'It is thoroughly understood that French sovereignty will be re-established as soon as possible throughout all of the territory, metropolitan or colonial, over which flew the French flag in 1939'.[39] Murphy had exceeded his authority, Roosevelt said. He had grave doubts that Indochina would be returned to French control. According to another source, The Pentagon Papers (Gravel Edition), Murphy's statement that the territories would be returned was not an isolated proclamation of intent by members of the US administration.

Somewhere along the way the mood of noble-mindedness began to dissipate. There were rumours that the British wanted to create a Southeast Asia federation of Burma, Malaya, Thailand and Indochina under British guidance and protection. The military operations of the British SEAC were often scathingly referred to as 'Save England's Asian Colonies'. Roosevelt reportedly told Sumner Welles, Under Secretary of State, that America would have more trouble with Great Britain after the war than they were having with Germany now. Another idea was to return Indochina to the French so long as the United States could have bases there. The British were alarmed; they could see that Roosevelt's plans meant the dismantling of their Asian holdings—especially India—in other words, a loss for Britain of raw materials and the potential of the Asian markets. Within the American administration, there was also factious squabbling over the right for all Asian peoples to choose the form of government under which they would live after the war.

Throughout 1944, Roosevelt's trustee plans for Indochina began to unravel. Henry Stimson, the US Secretary of War, and the secretaries for all the US armed services opposed the Department of State's plans for a trusteeship; they wanted to keep the Mandated Islands in the Western Pacific as

US bases. The Japanese had governed the Mariana, Caroline and Marshall islands under a League of Nations mandate, but the Americans had captured them during the war and now did not want to give them back. Australia and the United States also exchanged robust diplomatic cables about matters in the South West Pacific that included opinions on the Mandated Islands and the security of Australia and New Zealand. Dr Herbert Evatt, Australia's Minister for External Affairs, complained that decisions about war in the Pacific had been taken at the Cairo Conference in 1943 to which Australia had not been invited.

Evatt argued about convening a South West Pacific conference to follow on from an Australia New Zealand Agreement in 1944, but the Americans were unimpressed. Dr Evatt was a much-disliked man in Washington and London. In their opinion, the war was not yet won. Both countries were worried about the devil in the detail that they thought might emerge from the proposed Australian discussions. The Chinese Embassy in Washington was informed:

> That frankly we do not take the Australian–New Zealand Agreement too seriously . . . it probably reflects . . . the desire of Australia and New Zealand as small countries to participate . . . on a plane of equality with the Great Powers.[40]

The American minister at Canberra reported that 'Australia is under a deep obligation to a Fighting France. It is publicly pledged . . . to maintain the sovereignty of France in [the] South Pacific'.[41] Australian support to the French would become much more than words, as we will see. To confuse matters even more, the hollow man in Roosevelt's post-war plans was Chiang Kai Shek. The China Theatre looked as if it might implode and fragment into Kuomintang fighting Kuomintang, with the Japanese and the Communists watching from the sidelines. Then the Chinese mainland lost its importance in the plans for the defeat of Japan when the American military's Pacific island-hopping strategy got underway. Then de Gaulle defeated Henri Giraud to lead the Free French and the Americans knew that they would need the French for the future security of Europe. General de Gaulle wanted Indochina.

By 1945, words and actions were still a long way apart. As a letter shown by presidential naval adviser Vice-Admiral Willson to the Secretary of the

Navy before the pre–United Nations San Francisco Conference in April–June 1945 suggested: '[the Navy needed to send] representatives to San Francisco in order to protect themselves against "the international welfare boys"'.[42] The navy objected to the idea of giving up strategically important islands to satisfy the utopian visions of self-government by the natives. Roosevelt thought that all the holding of the Mandated Islands would do 'would be to provide jobs as governors of some insignificant islands for inefficient Navy and Army officers or members of the civilian career service'. Stimson argued with the Secretary of State that the Mandated Islands obtained by the United States would not be 'colonized' but would be 'outposts', even though 'they must belong to the United States to rule and fortify them'. Hypocrisy comes to mind. At the Yalta Conference in February 1945, the five governments who would form the Security Council of the United Nations agreed that trusteeship would apply to territory that 'may *voluntarily* [emphasised] be placed under trusteeship'.[43] France was one of the five members of the council and that meant that Indochina would not go into a trusteeship.

On 9 March 1945, the Japanese took full control of Indochina by ousting the Vichy regime, which was only a façade because Japanese military power dictated the rules for the region. General de Gaulle called upon the American Ambassador in France to ask why American military aid was not being provided to the French troops fighting in Indochina. He wanted to know, 'What are you driving at?' 'Do you want us to become, for example, one of the federated states under the Russian aegis?' A series of diplomatic cables between the countries followed. Evasive American answers included statements like 'military assistance will be provided dependent upon . . .', and 'an appreciable number of tactical missions have been flown in support' and 'further assistance is the subject of active negotiations'.

Although Chiang Kai Shek was the theatre commander, he played the politics of don't answer, don't get involved and don't move troops as requested. Many years later, Australian diplomat Keith Waller said: 'The fact is the Chinese were not fighting. They would go through the motions . . . announce great victories and then withdraw. It was a pretty shameful performance, and their eventual admission to the role of a great power was not justified'.[44] The other three—France, Britain and America—trashed each other's morality. Each senior commander pushed his nation's barrow, in some cases with bitter personal enmity. President Roosevelt died on 12 April 1945. On 9 May 1945, Washington advised its ambassador in France that the American government was not questioning 'even by implication, French sovereignty over Indo-China'.[45] Regardless of any further posturing on the subject, France would be permitted to return to take possession of what she considered to be legally and rightfully her territory.

In the remaining days of World War II, the political battle for the future of Indochina was severely fragmented. There were many foes and apparently not many friends. The proverb 'An enemy of my enemy is my friend' appeared to prevail. The Chinese Nationalists wanted information about Vietnam, so they turned to the Viet Minh who operated as guerrillas against the Japanese. They were a mix of nationalists and communists led by Ho Chi Minh, known in Nationalist China by the alias 'Tong Van So' who was not identified as a communist. With their removal of the Vichy establishment, the Japanese permitted Emperor Bao Dai to form a government; there was strong support for Ngo Dinh Diem to be premier, but he declined. In the same period, famine caused the deaths of an untold number of Vietnamese—perhaps several million—in Tonkin. The famine was a result of the Japanese war levy policy and the fact that they had jailed the French technicians who operated the crop irrigation systems.

A French column that had fought its way out of Vietnam after the Japanese takeover in March had moved into southern China where it caused American Lieutenant General Albert Wedemeyer concern. Wedemeyer, formerly Admiral Mountbatten's chief of staff, advocated very strongly against allowing the British and the French to come back as imperialist rulers. He was now Chiang Kai Shek's chief of staff and commander of the American forces in the area, General Stilwell having been recalled. Wedemeyer had a French force of 5000—made up of 2000 Europeans and 3000 Indochinese—that he was reluctant to equip or use in any action that might upset the Chinese as well as his political masters at home, but everyone wanted access to the French networks inside Indochina. For the time being it did not appear to matter what a group's ideology might have been; to utter the word 'nationalist' was sufficient to obtain acceptance into the allied fold.

Meanwhile the Viet Minh had grown in numbers, especially in the north, but they had done little in battle other than harass the Japanese. When they wished, they were a helpful intelligence agency. In the south the Viet Minh were not as strong, but bands of belligerents and bandits who were either anti-French, pro-Japanese, pro-communist, religious sects, or just thugs also roamed the countryside. With the obvious defeat of the Japanese looming, the scramble for recognition by regional leadership aspirants began. Ho Chi Minh did this very well. The Viet Minh leader's efforts to court favour with the Americans were assisted by America's policy confusion in the field. Much is written about the OSS helping Ho Chi Minh and his oaths of loyalty to nationalism and the American way. If only the Americans had taken him under their influence, the claimants of a lost opportunity write. But nothing surrounding the puzzle of international affairs that existed in this region during 1945–46 was that simple.

Paul Helliwell—the OSS chief in China at the time—later denied that the OSS had managed Ho Chi Minh in any way. Helliwell did not use Ho Chi Minh because Ho was a communist and that meant post-war trouble. Additionally, the Viet Minh would not pledge to use the arms and ammunition given to them only against the Japanese and not against the French as well. Helliwell did give Ho Chi Minh six .38 revolvers and some ammunition, which was simply gratitude for bringing in several downed American pilots. These revolvers and a previously obtained autographed photograph of US General Claire Chennault were used cunningly by Ho Chi Minh to convince Vietnamese disbelievers that America backed him. Several OSS teams deployed into northern Indochina in mid-1945 went with a directive to treat all resistance groups on an equal footing because every action against the Japanese was to the advantage of the American war effort. Those teams did arm and train forces under the command of Vo Nguyen Giap. At the same time, allegedly any French returning to Indochina would be shot and get no food because the natives hated them. This appeared to be accepted with delight by the Americans, as it matched their dislike for French imperialism.

Later, the French would complain that without the arms and ammunition supplied by America the Viet Minh would not have been able to take control of as much of the countryside as they did after the Japanese surrender. The fact that Japanese weapons were easy to obtain was not mentioned. This ill feeling between the French and the Americans continued to percolate from this war into and through the next. When OSS Major Patti travelled to Hanoi with Ho Chi Minh on 2 September 1945 to hear him declare the establishment of the Democratic Republic of Vietnam (DRV) in the paraphrased words of the American Declaration of Independence, the visibility of the American officers convinced the people that Ho Chi Minh had approval from the mighty United States of America.

In August, when the Viet Minh front came into the open with its well-established 'political network' to establish a 'government', Bao Dai abdicated. His resignation was also allegedly influenced by perceived support from the United States for the Viet Minh. Bao Dai then became Ho's supreme political adviser under his family name of 'Vinh Tuy'. Ho had played them all off against each other and, even though he opted for American power, he didn't really like the Americans. He told Bao Dai: 'They [US] are only interested in replacing the French ... they are capitalists to the core. All that counts for them is business'.[46] To paraphrase Ho's remarks about past Chinese and French overlords, maybe a bit of American shit might not taste too bad and it might be more palatable than Chinese shit. When Ho Chi Minh's letters to President Truman were ignored, it soon became clear that the French were on their way back. They would return behind the shields of the Chinese and British forces that were approved to take the surrender of the Japanese in Indochina.[47]

The French return

When the Japanese surrendered, the Chinese plundered and ate their way south to the 16th parallel while the British moved the 20th Indian Division—that included some attached French personnel—into Saigon in September 1945. The division, commanded by Major General Douglas Gracey, had responsibility for the area south to north up to the 16th parallel. Gracey's orders included the disarming of the Japanese, releasing prisoners of war, and maintaining law and order without getting involved in the local political situation.

When the Communist Provisional Executive Committee in Saigon staged a very large demonstration to show that the people did not want the French to return, the display turned nasty and several people were killed. The British and the French blamed the Viet Minh, who in turn blamed the British and the French. General Gracey judged that, if he did not act, total chaos would follow. In effect, he proclaimed martial law. Two days later Gracey backed a French coup d'état in Saigon. The French General Philippe Leclerc was most grateful, telling Admiral Mountbatten, 'Gracey has saved Indochina'. Later, when the British used Japanese troops to assist suppress any further 'civil disturbances', Mountbatten worried that the British would be seen as a force there only to keep the 'Viet Minh Independence Movement in check'. When some houses were burnt down in Saigon, Mountbatten cabled Gracey: 'Could not such unsavoury jobs be left to the French?' Gracey replied: 'The French do not understand minimum violence and would have burnt not twenty but two thousand huts'.[48] As an aside, when Richard Kirby of the Australian War Crimes Commission went to Kandy—Mountbatten's headquarters—to argue for leniency towards the Japanese, Mountbatten replied: 'If I had my way I'd shoot about twenty of them . . . to satisfy the bloodlust . . . then I'd officially kick about 200 or 300 of them in the arse in front of all the rest . . . and that would be the end of the whole show, old man'.[49]

On 4 March 1946, Indochina was removed from Mountbatten's SEAC responsibility. The French were back, but a large number of Chinese troops remained in the north and the Viet Minh prepared for war. Then, in Bernard Fall's words, 'Ho made a 180-degree policy switch and began to advocate cooperation with France'. Fall questioned whether Ho's pro-western feelings ever actually existed. While Ho Chi Minh was in France, Fall described what happened behind the scenes.

> While Ho was negotiating with [the] French government . . . his ablest deputies [that included]—Vo Nguyen Giap—were liquidating the internal enemies of the regime: leaders of religious sects, mandarins (such as Ngo Dinh Khoi [Diem's brother]), intellectuals, Trotskyites, and anti-Communist nationalists. The outbreak of the Indochina War greatly simplified Ho's political problems.[50]

Liquidating the enemy was called 'crab fishing'. People were bundled together, alive, and thrown into the rivers. Following an extended period of discussions—which unbeknown to most had started in November 1945—and plain old horse trading among the French, the Viet Minh, the Chinese, the Americans and the British, open war between the French and the Viet Minh began in earnest in Tonkin and Annam in December 1946. The Democratic Republic of Vietnam was thrown out of its Tonkin office by French force.

Monolithic communism and its implications

The new fear for the West was a rampaging, monolithic communist organisation controlled by Moscow, or so many of the government agencies thought. Soon after the end of World War II, most people in Australia believed that another war was not far off and would be fought against the Soviet Union. When President Harry Truman addressed members of Congress on 12 March 1947, he announced plans to assist Greece and Turkey, which became his interventionist line in the sand against 'outside pressures' (communism). His announcement was the mother of the famous 'falling dominoes' statement later made by President Eisenhower about the protection of Indochina. If it were to fall, the others (Southeast Asia) would follow, like a line of dominoes.

> When the Chinese communists took control of Mainland China in 1949, western strategists thought a fault line of instability stretched across Europe and through Asia along which communism, Moscow in particular, had gained a strong foothold from which they could threaten the interests of the West. Indonesia, Indochina, Thailand, Malaya the Philippines and Burma were all experiencing communist-inspired insurgencies by 1950. The Chairman of the [US] Joint Chiefs of Staff [wrote to the Secretary of Defense], South East Asia is a vital segment in the line of containment of communism stretching from Japan southward and around to the Indian Peninsula.[51]

In Australia, a rail strike in Queensland in 1948 and a number of other disruptions to the economy were blamed on communist-influenced unions. In 1949, a crippling coalminers' strike was broken by the use of Australian troops. During the strike, Arthur Calwell, a later leader of the Labor Party, said 'the reds must be taught a lesson', and by the middle of August 1949 the strike was finished. Whether the communists were responsible for the disruptions or not, they bore the blame. At around the same time, the Soviet Union exploded its first atomic bomb and when Nationalist China collapsed, taken over by the communists, the fear of war was palpable. Robert Menzies, who had resigned his commission as prime minister in 1941, campaigned relentlessly during the 1949 elections, using strikes and whipping up fear of communism to full effect. The Liberal and Country parties won that election with a large margin of seats. In office again, Menzies was concerned by the instability in Asia. British battalions had been deployed to Malaya to fight in an action called 'the Malayan Emergency' and Australian diplomats studied the Indochina clash. Their reports raised the likelihood of disturbing consequences, if the French were to fail against the Viet Minh.

The Australian Commissioner for Malaya reported to External Affairs in April 1949 the possibility of a 'French withdrawal either from the whole country or from the northernmost province of Tonking [Tonkin]'. The information appeared to come from rumours from Paris that were picked up by the British government, but the UK Consul General in Saigon did not support the information. The Australian commissioner went on to say: 'The deterioration on the Tonking border . . . and the indubitable evidence of collaboration by Chinese, *who may or may not be communist* [emphasised], has given point to this UK anxiety'. The French High Commissioner for Indochina was hopeful that Bao Dai would be able to hold Annam and Cochin China, the central and southern regions. Bao Dai had initialled an agreement with the French in June 1948 that recognised 'the independence of Vietnam [qualified by] its adherence to the French Union as a state associated with France'.[52]

By the end of 1949, the military situation in the north had deteriorated; arms were being smuggled across the border with China, and 'Chinese bandits' were assisting the Viet Minh. All the reports indicated that a major offensive by the Viet Minh to push the French out of the north would soon be attempted. Bao Dai's effectiveness as a national leader was also heavily criticised. He was seen as a French puppet whose administration lacked the ability to counter the Viet Minh. In February 1950—just four months before hostilities erupted in Korea—the Associated States of Indochina—Cambodia, Laos and Vietnam—were recognised by a number of countries, including the United States and Australia. In a parallel move, China and the Soviet Union recognised Ho Chi Minh's Democratic Republic of Vietnam, which he had proclaimed in 1945. The deteriorating situation in China and its southern regions influenced the US Congress to approve the *Mutual Defense Assistance Act, 1949*, which permitted President Truman to deploy a military advisory mission to Vietnam in 1950.

America, the French War and SEATO

America was in the fight; although their advisers had little impact at this stage, the American dollar kept the French in the field. On 15 October 1950, the French Minister of Finance announced that the United States would provide more than US$2 billion (two thousand million) in aid, which would include assistance for the war in Indochina. In some estimates, 'the United States paid for at least 50 per cent of the French War, but others say at least 75 per cent was funded by the US'.[53] The collapse of Nationalist China not only raised the perception that Communist China was ready to roll through Indochina, it also brought Indonesia into the picture. In the United States, a Policy Planning Staff Paper No. 51 analysed the challenges in the Southeast Asian region, calling in part for 'developing, in collaboration with the Philippines, Australia and New Zealand, as well as India and Pakistan a plan for wider cooperation in Southeast Asia, leading . . . to one or more associations of non-Communist nations'. The UK Foreign Secretary, Ernest Bevin, supported the concept and added in a memorandum to Dean Acheson, the US Secretary of State: 'If a common front can be built up from Afghanistan to Indochina inclusive, then it would be possible to contain the Russian advance southwards'.[54]

These were the first rumblings of what went on to become the South East Asia (Collective Defence) Treaty Organisation (SEATO). In the meantime there was discussion between Australia and America about Japan's economic re-emergence, which concerned Australia. America was also relieved that Percy Spender had replaced Dr Evatt as Minister for External Affairs and that Spender saw the security threat as 'being inherent in communist advances in Asia', and not coming from Japan. Australia also wanted to see a stronger US military presence in the Pacific.

When Richard Casey became Australia's Minister for External Affairs in 1951, both he and the Secretary of the Department of External Affairs, Alan Watt, toured Southeast Asia. 'It was 17 years since Latham had made a Cook's tour through the East', Casey wrote in his diary. 'My trip must be the first of regular visits of this sort', he added.[55] After this trip, Casey believed that if Indochina and Burma were lost to the communists it would be impossible for Thailand to resist heavy communist pressure. He concluded that it was essential for Australia to have its own posts in the region to report 'directly and quickly to Australia'.[56] Alan Watt travelled back to the region in 1952, accompanied by diplomat John Rowland, who established an Australian legation in Saigon in March and Rowland became Australia's first diplomat in the country as Chargé d'Affaires. Soon after, in November 1952, John Quinn arrived to present his credentials as Australia's Saigon Minister. Quinn was one of the three diplomats who had attempted to escape from Singapore in February 1942. In one of life's unjust quirks of fate, Quinn was killed in an Air France crash near Rabat, Morocco, on 12 September 1961. He was just 42.

The military situation in Vietnam, especially in the northern regions, now worried the West. French General Jean de Lattre de Tassigny swept into command in late 1951 with a dynamic flair and declared he would win the war in fifteen months. His son, Bernard, was killed in 1951 and the general was forced by illness to return to France, where he died in 1952. Australia may have found some relief to its worries about the possibility of an expanding conflict in the region when the ANZUS Security Treaty was agreed between Australia, New Zealand and the United States at San Francisco on 1 September 1951. Subsequent criticisms of the Treaty have highlighted its perceived weakness, contained within Article III, which called for the parties to *consult together* whenever, in the opinion of any of them, they were threatened in the Pacific. Dean Acheson, the Secretary of State, explained why he disagreed with that assessment to the US Secretary of Defense in 1952: 'Neither Australia nor New Zealand . . . had any reason to believe that the Treaty . . . did not provide for both a security guaranty and an effective consultative relationship with the United States'.[57]

The British were petulant at their exclusion from ANZUS, with Foreign Secretary Anthony Eden challenging the validity of the reasoning behind not letting them join. He claimed that one of Britain's primary responsibilities was the defence of Singapore and Malaya, after the Middle East, and that ANZUS overlapped with the Anglo, New Zealand, Australia and Malaya 1949 'consultative' arrangement (ANZAM) for defence of the Malayan region.[58] Eden went on to say: 'If either Australia or New Zealand is attacked, the United Kingdom will at once and without question be at war with the aggressor'. All of that, he explained, would make it very difficult for him to tell Parliament why the United Kingdom was excluded from ANZUS.[59] Australia might have been surprised by this statement, given its understanding that the United Kingdom planned to withdraw its maritime forces from the region should a global war erupt.[60]

Diplomatic reports back to Australia from Vietnam were now being couched in terms of a deteriorating military situation. At Paris, new political leaders entered and exited the National Assembly with a frequency that defied good government. There were rumours of a possible armistice and a reducing number of French troops in Vietnam. Other information had the Chinese providing advisers and secure training bases for the Viet Minh, which increased the West's concerns for regional security. Australia's William McMahon, Minister for Navy and for Air, paid a short visit to Tonkin in mid-December 1952. He was flown to a northern battlefront at Na San, a camp that had been attacked during the night of 1–2 December, but poor weather prevented the aircraft from landing. The Viet Minh had suffered heavy casualties during the assault and it was claimed that 565 were killed against 15 French dead. Radio contact had been lost with Dien Bien Phu, 100 kilometres to the west, and it was assumed that the garrison and airstrip there had been overrun. A major enemy attack hit Dien Bien Phu eighteen months later and this increased the worry that the big powers of the West held for the region.

During this period, December 1952, President Truman was in the throes of handing the presidential baton to General Dwight Eisenhower, who made it clear that he planned to continue US opposition to communism in Indochina. John Foster Dulles, the incoming Secretary of State, declared that Indochina was important not only as a containment line against communism in Asia, but because a loss there would have serious repercussions on the 'mood of France' and its willingness to be part of a united and secure Europe. Even though France was needed as an ally in Europe, American commanders criticised the timid nature of French tactics in Vietnam. Admiral Arthur Radford, Commander in Chief Pacific, found fault with the French and said they needed to 'adopt a much more aggressive spirit'. In one of history's great military ironies, Radford sent a Marine colonel to review the situation in

Vietnam. On his return, the colonel reported, 'Two good American divisions with the normal American aggressive spirit could clean up the situation in the Tonkin Delta in 10 months'.[61] France's Lieutenant General Henri Navarre now commanded in Vietnam, but American military opinion believed he lacked aggression as well as organisational ability and was prone to vacillation. 'One general even believed that Navarre had been appointed to give the French government a scapegoat for anticipated failures in Indochina.'[62]

Australian arms to the French

In January 1953, Richard Casey, the Australian Minister for External Affairs, wrote to two fellow ministers expressing his thoughts about assisting the French in Indochina. He explained that reports from the Australian Legation at Saigon stressed that the French felt they were fighting a 'lonely battle' and would welcome any assistance Australia could give them. Casey's draft submission to Cabinet highlighted, once again, the communist threat in Southeast Asia, emphasising that if Indochina were to fall, the whole of Southeast Asia would be imperilled. Casey added that the French had made it clear that in the absence of *overt* Chinese intervention they did not seek assistance in the form of troops. Casey's worry and that of the government were reinforced by an Australian Defence policy review, approved in January 1953, that concluded by saying in part: 'ensure . . . action is taken to bolster the French in Indo-China . . . all possible action must be taken by the Allies to hold Indo-China and to ensure stable democratic government'.[63]

Casey's letter set off a chain of events that ultimately saw Australia 'gift' a variety of arms and ammunition to the French force in Indochina. The French Quartermaster General, Far East, also purchased Australian live sheep to be shipped to Indochina for French Muslim troops. Joseph Stalin died on 5 March 1953 and General Giap wrote in a publication called *The People's Army*:

> Stalin's theory concerning the armed struggle and the development of the army has illuminated the path of our Party and our Army. We are using the experiences of the Chinese Army of Liberation and the military thinking of Mao Tse Tung. Comrade Stalin is dead but his theory, the doctrine of Marx, Engels, Lenin, Stalin,

will always light the revolutionary path of the entire world, the path of victory. We must always unite ourselves around the Soviet Union; always follow [their] ... doctrine.[64]

No doubt General Giap's article further increased Richard Casey's grave doubts about the security of the region, doubts that he felt were already justified by the Korean War.

It took a little over a year for the Australian arms to be identified, inspected and shipped to Indochina. The equipment included millions of rounds of small-arms ammunition, several thousand machine guns of .50 and .30 calibre as well as 1000 Thompson .45 guns, several thousand 250 pound and 500 pound bombs, 75 mm howitzers and shells, clothing, parachutes and sundry other items, and was despatched on board the ships *Nellore*, *Radnor* and *Eastern*. Two of the ships sailed immediately, but the Waterside Workers' Federation objected to some working conditions and that stopped the loading of the *Radnor* in Sydney. The federation objected to an insufficient number of lavatories; the workers wanted ten to serve the 80-odd men working the ship, but only four were available. Harold Holt, the Minister for Labour and National Service, explained in a press statement on 7 April 1954 that 'the ship's loading was being hindered as a result of obvious Communist policy applied through the officials of the Waterside Workers' Federation'.[65] Eventually the ship sailed and General Ely, Commander in Chief Indochina, acknowledged receipt of the equipment by letter dated 17 July 1954. In a wry course of events, a few days later, at midnight on 20 July 1954, a cease-fire agreement signed by the military commanders of the French forces and the Viet Minh came into effect.

The Geneva Armistice, 1954

In Berlin on 18 February 1954 a joint communiqué issued by the United States, Great Britain, the Soviet Union and France—Communist China was named in a later, final list—declared that they and 'other parties concerned' would meet at Geneva 'to seek a peaceful solution of the eight-year-old war in Indochina'.

A battle raging at Dien Bien Phu now became 'an urgent matter' for the Chinese and the Viet Minh. They wanted to achieve a decisive victory there to put themselves in a position of strength at the coming negotiations. The Chinese had a copy of General Navarre's plan, which the Chinese senior adviser to Vietnam, General Wei Guo Qing, had taken to Mao Zedong personally. The French plan was to establish a major base in the remote northwestern valley of Tonkin (North Vietnam) that would cut the Viet Minh's access to Laos and at the same time draw them into a battle in which they would be destroyed.

> The French parachuted and airlifted 10,000 men into the valley in an operation that started on 20 November 1953. A further 4277 would parachute into the valley after 13 March 1954. Three quarters of the force were not French, 25 per cent were from the Foreign Legion, mostly Germans; nearly as many were Africans and more than 30 per cent were Vietnamese. Against all expectations the Viet Minh gathered 50,000 men and a powerful and unsuspected artillery into a tight ring around the valley.[66]

In April 1954, Mao Zedong urged the Chinese advisory team to wrap up the Dien Bien Phu campaign. He ordered that artillery pieces and anti-air-craft guns were to be supplied by China and that training could be done in either Vietnam or China, using Korean War veterans and equipment. Mao Zedong took a personal interest in the tactics of the battle and in several cases the Chinese directed that General Giap change his methods of attack. In particular, Giap was told to stop futile and expensive frontal assaults and concentrate on isolating and destroying the camp's outposts. By April, when a cease-fire looked probable, Mao cancelled China as a training location, but directed that the artillery pieces were to be shipped as early as possible. As the battle entered its final phase, the possibility that America would attack the Viet Minh with aircraft made some of its officers reluctant to occupy Dien Bien Phu.[67]

In the United States, President Dwight Eisenhower was not so eager to commit American troops. In a private meeting upstairs in the White House on 4 April, Eisenhower met with a few of his principal advisers and agreed 'to send American forces to Indo-China under certain strict conditions. It was to be . . . a joint action with the British . . . Australia and New Zealand troops, and, if possible . . . units from Far Eastern countries . . . so that the forces would have to continue to fight . . . and bear a full share of responsibility until the war is over'. He was also concerned that 'American intervention . . . might be interpreted as protection of French colonialism'.[68] The Dien Bien Phu bastion collapsed on 7 May 1954 after 170 days of occupation and a 57-day battle.

The total French casualties and captured are not known in detail. The references show the following statistics: killed and died from wounds, 1571; that included Colonel Charles Piroth, the French commander of artillery, who committed suicide because he was outgunned by the enemy's artillery. Missing, 1606 and wounded, 4436. Some 9000 to nearly 11,000 fighters and one nurse—Geneviève de Galad—were marched more than 500 kilometres into captivity, of whom perhaps more than half died or just disappeared. The official history site of the battle recorded 10,863 prisoners, of whom only 3290 returned four months later. De Galad had arrived on the last medevac flight, her 40th into Dien Bien Phu. She—and a few hundred seriously wounded— was released within several days of the surrender. The Viet Minh paid dearly with the loss of an estimated 10,000 dead and 15,000 wounded.[69]

Other less well-known battles in the first half of the year also weakened France's military power significantly. Operation Atlante conducted between January and July in the Phu Yen–Qui Nhon coastal region had fizzled operationally. Worse than its lack of results, it had split the French military power and taken away the capability to reinforce Operation Castor at Dien Bien Phu. The Groupment Mobile 100 was decimated in June during a withdrawal from An Khe to Pleiku along Route 19 in the southern Central Highlands. With these devastating defeats and the loss of control over great tracts of the country, France's negotiating power at Geneva all but evaporated.

The kerfuffle over which interested parties would attend the Geneva Conference and who could be seen talking face-to-face made for an entertaining sideshow, but not for effective diplomacy. Bao Dai and later Ngo Dinh Diem were persistent in their claims that they represented the legitimate government of Vietnam and that the Viet Minh forces were merely armed rebels. These claims had some substance, considering that Vietnam's application for membership of the United Nations in 1952 had been supported by ten nations, but was vetoed by the Soviet Union.[70] US Secretary of State Dulles commented that the only way he and Zhou Enlai, the Chinese negotiator, 'could possibly meet was if their cars collided'. The chief negotiators who sat in the first session came from the United Kingdom, the Soviet Union, the United States, France, the People's Republic of China, the State of Vietnam (South), Cambodia and Laos, and included the Viet Minh. The Democratic Republic of Vietnam was not a member, although obviously it controlled the Viet Minh delegation. Coincidentally, the meeting was on 8 May, the day after the fighting stopped at Dien Bien Phu.

At the conference there were secret meetings and scheming between friends and foes. Australia was there, behind the scenes, and in President Eisenhower's eyes Australia, among others, would be required to provide a favourable response to the idea of American military intervention in Vietnam to protect the Red River Delta region after the loss of Dien Bien Phu, if America was invited by France to do so. President Eisenhower was insistent that collective action was necessary; America should not go it alone. He understood the British would not commit themselves and that Australia was facing a general election later in May that would only allow them to show a willingness to participate. That was in May 1954, and then in June the Australian Chief of Staff travelled to Washington where he met with French General Valluy and British and New Zealand chiefs, to be told that the Red River Delta would not hold without prompt intervention from the allies.

The possible surrender of further territory in Vietnam exhausted the patience of all the parties at Geneva. China was concerned that continued fighting in the full Indochina region would push the western powers further towards their idea of a collective security grouping for Southeast Asia. Zhou Enlai, with Mao Zedong's agreement, persuaded the Viet Minh to accept a partition at the 17th parallel, even though many in the Democratic Republic of Vietnam thought this was selling out their powerful position after their military victories. Mao Zedong pushed for the agreement when he emphasised the following at Liuzhou, southern China, in July 1954:

The Indochina issue was different from the Korean issue and that Indochina could affect all Southeast Asia (including Burma, Thailand, Malaya, Indonesia, the Philippines), Pakistan, India, Australia, New Zealand and Ceylon. 'If we are not careful, we will affect 600 million people in ten countries. We should make necessary concessions. In this way, we can isolate the minority (the United States), win over the majority' and reach a final agreement.[71]

His words also mirrored the strategic worries that the West held at the time. The French promised the (South) Vietnamese that the French government did not intend to seek a settlement based on the partition of Vietnamese territory—a dreadful lie. While France formally recognised only one Vietnam diplomatically, their former 1946 negotiator, Jean Sainteny, was back in Hanoi dealing with the Democratic Republic of Vietnam to preserve French economic interests throughout the country. South Vietnam was the lone voice in the wilderness. Premier Ngo Dinh Diem warned against a partition of the country in his investiture speech on 7 July 1954 when he said, '[This solution] can only be the preparation for another more deadly war'.[72] A cease-fire solution was agreed—although no nation signed a final declaration—when Brigadier General Delteil of the French Union Forces and Ta-Quang Buu, Vice-Minister of National Defence of the Democratic Republic of Vietnam, signed an armistice. The signing by the French general bypassed the many objections of the South Vietnamese Bao Dai government, which had argued against the legality of the settlement. The Vietnamese believed that the French did not have the right to commit their government to an arrangement with which they did not agree.

The splitting of Vietnam

Everyone except the South Vietnamese believed that dividing the country into two parts was the only way to separate the combatants and to settle their widely disparate political and military demands. An addendum to the main document of the agreement prescribed that a provisional military demarcation would be at the 17th parallel, but was not to be construed as a political or territorial boundary. The consensus of the negotiators was that 'reunification' would be achieved by a general election to be held in 1956. However, no definitive date was set in the Geneva Articles. The elections did not go ahead. It was a foregone conclusion that the North would win the elections easily based on their capability to subvert the larger population and South Vietnam simply did not submit to the proposal. As Pham Van Dong, the North's negotiator, told a visitor to his villa in 1954, the North was not overly concerned because '[they] did not expect elections ever to take place. Victory would be achieved by default of the ineffectual southern government'.[73] In rejecting the elections, the South Vietnamese emphasised that no political solution had been determined by the agreements for the divided Korea and Germany following their wars.[74]

Throughout this turbulent period, Australia was always sitting in the shadows. Australia supported France, the United States and the nationalist South Vietnamese, as well as the wider community of Southeast Asia, in the belief that a communist expansion would be to the detriment of the region. The Democratic Republic of Vietnam, on its own admissions, was beholden to the giants of communism and Indochina was a strategic location that neither side of the ideological divide could give up. The fear was if communism were to flood the countries of Southeast Asia, an economic tragedy would follow. The western leaders believed that if this were to happen it had the potential to cause loss and misfortune not only to the emerging colonial nations but also to the world's economic post–World War II redevelopment.

The risk of further war, especially against China, was great. Eisenhower had been at odds with his Secretary of State, John Dulles. When the crisis in northern Vietnam had worsened, Dulles had wanted independent action. Eisenhower argued that 'direct Chinese aggression would force him to go all the way with naval and air power (including "new weapons" [atomic])'. He went on to say that this 'action would need more than Congressional approval . . . other nations, such as Australia would have to give their approval'.[75] In a letter to General Alfred Gruenther, Supreme Allied Commander Europe, the president complained about the lack of inspirational French leadership which had been shown up in Indochina. He suggested that if Gruenther learnt to speak French he might qualify and Eisenhower could get him a suit of nice shiny white armor! In a more serious vein, Eisenhower went on to explain that the loss of Dien Bien Phu did not mean the loss of the war and that 'we should all (United States, France, Thailand, United Kingdom, Australia, New Zealand et al) begin conferring at once on means of stopping the Communist advances in Southeast Asia'.[76]

A crucial year

Nineteen fifty-four was a pivotal year; this was the year for the West to either cut and run or make a stand. The perceived risk of a detrimental loss caused by doing nothing was too great. Even though there were differences of opinion about how to prevent a regional loss, the western leaders agreed that communism must be stopped. The peoples of Southeast Asia, the resources of the region, and the future economic health of the countries within its broad span warranted action. Mao Zedong spoke of influencing 600 million people, while others wrote of the Southeast Asian region 'as an integral part of that great crescent formed by the Indian Peninsula, Australia and Japan'. Communism was seen to be pecking away at that crescent. The Soviet Union had tested an atomic bomb, China was lost to communist forces, war in Korea was at an uneasy cease-fire, British troops and Royal Australian Air Force bombers were deployed to the fight in the Malayan Emergency, and the communist-influenced Huk Rebellion in the Philippines were all cogent evidence of the communist threat.

Even though 1954 was a year of crucial importance—with the defeat of the French at Dien Bien Phu—the western leaders had analysed the Vietnam problem over several years. America was a strong proponent for collective action, but found stumbling blocks appeared in the form of the bogey words, racism, colonialism and new imperialism and, according to the British, American impulsiveness. For a short period, Robert Menzies sided with Britain's objection to 'united action' until the United States reminded Australia that this response did not accord with the ANZUS spirit of solidarity. The real fear was China and behind China stood the Soviet Union. Some western military commentators thought that the Soviet Union was just as anxious for the West to kill the Chinese as it was for the Chinese to kill them. An analysis of the use of tactical nuclear weapons put great fear into the British, not because of what might happen in Southeast Asia, but because of what they believed would happen in Europe by way of retaliation from the Soviets.

The senior and respected military commanders of the day, men such as UK Field Marshal Sir William Slim, US General of the Army Omar Bradley, French General Alphonse Juin and US General Lawton Collins discussed and analysed what they saw as the recognised threats to Southeast Asia, which always came back to China and the Soviet Union acting either through overt invasion, or by subversion. US Department of State personnel also joined the debate and on one occasion added a disrespectful comment that it would be difficult to hold Malaya and Indonesia; the people there have very weak knees.

An ambassador asked if it would be necessary to land forces in Indochina if there were to be a mass Chinese attack by the Chinese. Admiral Radford answered by saying: 'What we have there now [in 1952] is pretty much what can be absorbed, as *Europeans could hardly live and fight successfully there* [emphasised]'!⁷⁷

Was war with the Soviet Union inevitable if Southeast Asia was lost? Did Stalin's philosophy—'that when a country is at war it builds strength'—mean that he did not want to see the United States and China at war because the United States would grow in strength? The United Kingdom, France and the United States agreed that further studies were an ongoing necessity and that Australia and New Zealand should be invited to join in the strategic discussions about the region. Not only were the opinions of the countries' leaders being canvassed, but the possible isolation of the countries—particularly Australia—was also a concern, and prevention of that was a prerequisite in the planners' considerations.

War alone was not the focal point of these discussions. The advisers were asked: would a type of Marshall Plan—a large-scale economic initiative—work here?⁷⁸ Another question pursued the collective agreement potential: could deterrence be achieved by establishing 'a western oriented complex in Southeast Asia incorporating Indo-China, Thailand, Burma, Malaya, Indonesia, and the Philippines'? That question involved a big worry for Australia: Indonesia and Netherlands West New Guinea. Australia wanted the Dutch to remain in control as a shield for their territory, the next door Papua New Guinea, which led to Australia's northern front door. The battles fought against the Japanese there during World War II were still fresh in the minds of Australians. When Richard Casey attended the first meeting of ANZUS in 1952 he said that 'the repercussions in a sovereignty change in Netherlands New Guinea . . . would be explosive . . . whatever the merits of the case. The Australian Government would fall if Indonesia gained control of this vital approach to Australia'.⁷⁹

The United States believed that it was better to have Indonesia on side, but also thought that the strength of communism within Indonesia could put the island chain in a precarious position if Indochina were to fall to communism. As with Thailand and Malaya, the menace went beyond a military threat. Economic welfare was a major worry for a region that contained much sought-after supplies of rubber, tin, surplus rice—which was important for Japan and

India—and Indonesia was a strong secondary source of petroleum. Expanding the ANZUS Treaty was considered an option as a preventative measure, but ran up against an Occidental versus Oriental argument (racism). President Eisenhower said that a grouping of nations suitable to assist the Associated States (Indochina) would need to be confined to those in or near Southeast Asia. To include Japan and Korea would encounter the problem of the hostility that existed between those nations. He went on to say that it would be better 'to consider Australia, New Zealand, the Philippines, Formosa, the free nations of Southeast Asia, the British and the French. That was enough, wasn't it?' Secretary Dulles said the real problem was France. The difficulty with either option was the European Defence Community and France's involvement in it, or not.

The diplomatic desire to seek a silver bullet solution for the containment of communism continued throughout 1954. A suggestion that the first grouping of nations, mentioned above, might be expanded by the addition of the 'Colombo Powers'—India, Burma, and Ceylon—did not eventuate. Before the formal agreement that established SEATO, Casey told a counsellor from the US Department of State that he wished to advise the Secretary of State that Prime Minister Menzies had told Australia that the country would commit troops in 'advance of hostilities, under the SEATO concept'.

On 8 September 1954, America, Australia, France, New Zealand, Pakistan, the Philippines, the United Kingdom and Thailand signed the SEATO Treaty, with ratification completed in February 1955. A separate protocol added Cambodia, Laos and South Vietnam as 'protocol states' covered by Articles III and IV of the Treaty. Although what was expected of the Treaty varied according to the nation concerned, Australia and some others wanted a committed SEATO force; the Americans did not agree. The United States said that their response 'would probably be with mobile forces', as desired by their Joint Chiefs of Staff. The Treaty also dictated 'that the common danger' would be met in accordance with each signatory's constitutional processes. In the negotiations the 'common danger' had started as communist aggression, but that was abbreviated to aggression, which was not defined and for which there were many explanations.

Several noteworthy events took place over the next several years. First, a transmigration of Vietnamese between the two 'administrative areas' of

North and South was completed in May 1955. A large group of migrants—said to number more than one million and primarily Catholics—went to the Saigon side of the 17th parallel. Ngo Dinh Diem was a staunch Catholic and in the early 1950s had resided in a seminary in America where Cardinal Francis Spellman, the Archbishop of New York, befriended him. This connection undoubtedly assisted Diem's efforts to get the Catholics out of the North where it was feared they would be persecuted.

This fear was well justified if only to escape the continuing land reform campaign being pursued in a deadly and vigorous manner by Ho Chi Minh's Democratic Republic of Vietnam. Land was confiscated, peasants were labelled landlords, purges were conducted and to be tagged a landlord or an agent of a landlord meant death. Large numbers of people, thought to be between 50,000 and several hundred thousand, were executed. The *Vietnamese Economic History: 1945–2000*, printed in Hanoi in 2005, admitted to a very exact 172,008 deaths.[80]

Eventually the Party realised it had made a mistake; its Chinese advisers had got it wrong! Ho apologised and supposedly added a quaint 'but we cannot awaken the dead'. Xuan Vu, a war correspondent who went to the North in 1954, heard a rumour that Uncle Ho had cried in a Central Committee meeting that discussed the executions, but was unsure about this tale, as he thought Uncle Ho was an 'awfully foxy guy'.

A Menzies win, 1954

In Australia, the Menzies-led coalition was returned to power in May 1954 with 64 seats to 59, a victory helped no doubt by the defection of Vladimir Petrov, the head of Soviet Intelligence in Australia. Menzies told Dr Evatt, Leader of the Opposition, that nothing important was planned for Parliament on the eve of the last day of sitting before the coming election, so Evatt did not attend. In Parliament, Menzies then dropped the defection bombshell and announced a Royal Commission into Espionage. All the flustered Evatt could do next day was to agree with the government's proposals; he had been outfoxed. Petrov was whisked away, but his beautiful wife was photographed being dragged across the tarmac at Mascot airport by two 'Slavic gorillas'. 'This was a durable visual image of what most Australians thought the cold war to be about—the struggle between the forces of evil and good.' "'Somehow or other . . . we reckon we learned more about the Soviet system in these pictures than in all the things about Russia we've ever read or heard", Melbourne *Herald* columnist Bill Tipping said.'[81]

Evatt believed that Menzies had set up the whole affair so that the defection would help his chances of re-election. After the event, Evatt's behaviour became erratic to the point that he was banned from a Royal Commission into the defection. Evatt was also convinced of a conspiracy against him. He railed against the anti-communist group within the party led by B. A. Santamaria, which eventually split the Australian Labor Party (ALP) into groups that consisted of the ALP, the Anti-Communist Labor and the Democratic Labor Party (DLP). The effects of this split were seen at subsequent elections in 1955 and 1958, when the balance of seats in the House of Representatives was ALP 49, and the Liberal/Country Party Coalition 77. Menzies' winning margins were boosted by gaining the preferences of the anti-communist arms of the Labor Party.

A win for Ngo Dinh Diem and the French depart

In Vietnam in 1955, Diem had established unexpectedly firm control over the Hoa Cao and Cao Dai religious sects and the Binh Xuyen gangsters who controlled the underworld districts of Saigon and Cholon. Regardless of his methods of winning, Diem confounded the critics and strengthened his power as a result. In October 1955, he was elected president to replace the 'Baccarat prince', Bao Dai, but a result of 98 per cent of the ballot in Diem's favour did not impress the people.

In the same year, Australia's regional military involvement was activated with the deployment of the 2nd Battalion, Royal Australian Regiment (2RAR), to Penang Island, Malaya, and in early 1956 it began anti-communist operations on Malaya's mainland. Coincidentally the last of the French troops left Vietnam in February 1956. Their war was over, but French diplomatic, economic and general nuisance interference was not. With this final departure of the French, the United States now held the Vietnamese steering wheel but the pathway to success had already proved to be long and winding, and some thought it never-ending.

There were numerous questions to be answered. How many personnel was the US Military Advisory and Assistance Group (MAAG) permitted to have in Vietnam? (Restrictions were imposed by the Geneva Agreement.) What economic development and agrarian reform could be planned and implemented? What was to happen with the Civil Guard and the Self Defence Corps? What size was the Army of the Republic to be? How was it to be trained? Who would pay? How effective were the armed forces of Vietnam? What was the latest intelligence on the insurgency in Vietnam? There were many comprehensive answers. They had been well recorded previously, but the answers lacked a common acceptance and that affected their countrywide implementation.

Australia's defence resources and regional unrest

Australia was also undergoing a change in its defence planning. According to 1957 reports, the government thought that full-scale war was unlikely but that regional tensions would need a balanced regular force, which could be deployed overseas at short notice. This was summarised in the *1957 Year Book Australia*:

> The emphasis is no longer so much on numbers as on mobility, equipment and firepower. Equipment used by Australian forces will be standard or compatible as far as possible with that used by United States forces, with whom they are likely to be associated in war. The Defence programme provides for the acceleration of . . . the building up of a Regular Army brigade group . . . [which] will be additional to the infantry battalion in Malaya. [82]

Certain unnamed squadrons of the RAAF would be re-armed with the latest fighter and transport aircraft. A naval construction program designed to produce ships of the appropriate types would be accelerated. The estimated cost for 1957–58 was £190 million ($380 million). National service would continue, but from July 1957 the intake would be for training in the Army only, at 77 days full-time and 63 days over two years with the Citizen Military Forces (CMF). Previously all three services had trained national servicemen who were required to perform 176 days of full- and part-time duty. The last intake was in August 1959. The strengths of Australia's permanent forces as at 31 December 1956 were Navy 12,238, Army 22,409, and Air Force 14,570, for a total of 49,217.[83] As some jokesters would say, this was less than a decent crowd at an Australian Rules football grand final.

Minister Casey was back in Saigon where he had talks with American Lieutenant General Samuel Williams about Williams' plan for raising guerrilla units in the South Vietnamese Army, a concept with which Casey agreed. Regardless of Vietnam's importance, Australia's immediate concern continued to be Indonesia. A 1959 strategic paper concluded that Indonesia could pose a threat to Netherlands New Guinea as well as a small threat to Australia. There was a concern that 'Indonesia could also provide bases from which external communist forces could operate against Australia . . . in particular an air and submarine threat could develop very quickly'.[84] One interesting item in the study was the mention that Indonesia might risk 'an adventure' against Netherlands New Guinea 'as a means of achieving national unity'. Here was an echo of Joseph Stalin's idea of war to make the nation stronger.

In April 1961, Indonesian President Sukarno made his move against the Netherlands West Guinea, and warned that Indonesia would use force if necessary to bring the province under its control. Sukarno was supported by both the Soviet Union and China. The beat of rumbling war drums reverberated down to Canberra where it merged with the Soviet leader, Nikita Khrushchev's, 1956 'We will bury you' threat against the West.[85] The anticommunist policy planners went to work once more.

2

DIFFICULT DECISIONS
1960–1965

---

*Modern wars are not internecine wars in which the killing of the enemy
is the object. The destruction of the enemy in modern war, and, indeed
modern war itself, are means to obtain that object of the belligerent which
lies beyond the war.*

US War Department, General Orders No. 100
24 April 1863

A turbulent decade

During these early years of what was to become a turbulent decade, Australia's
military planning was not focused exclusively upon Indonesia and Vietnam.
Another little known, landlocked entranceway to Southeast Asia was thrust
into the limelight: Laos. Topographic tentacles snaked out of Laos into the
north and south of Vietnam, China, Burma, Thailand and Cambodia, which
meant western politicians and their generals slept a little uneasily if there
was any turmoil in its jungles. Military staff at SEATO and ANZAM continually upgraded plans to protect the regional peoples against communism,
particularly Thailand, whose location was described as being the end of a
spear. The Malay Peninsula with its point at Singapore was the lance and it
aimed south.

A series of SEATO plans was developed to protect the region if there
were to be an outbreak of communist insurgency. In Plan 5C of 1959, for

example, Australia's task was to provide a force that would deploy with Task Force Bravo to counter communist insurgency in Laos. The force would operate in southern Laos with British and New Zealand troops; US and Thai forces would cover northern Laos. Australia's initial offer of troops to be used in the plan was an infantry battalion. This unit would come from the Far East Strategic Reserve (Malaya/Singapore), which was controlled by the ANZAM Defence Committee. That meant, if deployment were necessary, a very complex process of request and approval through SEATO and ANZAM would be required to get the force into action. Defining, to the satisfaction of each contributing state, an acceptable definition of a 'communist insurgency' was just the initial hurdle.

The Task Force Bravo sector was to be based on Seno, an airfield 20 kilometres northeast of the city of Savannakhet in Laos on the banks of the Mekong River. It was to be secured by the French.[1] In 1961 Australian Brigadier Francis Hassett, commander of the 28th Commonwealth Brigade in Malaya and later to become a general and Chief of the Defence Force Staff, conducted a reconnaissance of both South Vietnam and Seno. Hassett wanted to get into Seno because no one from SEATO had previously conducted a reconnaissance of the area. At first, Hassett was denied an entry visa to Laos. However, with the help of the Australian Ambassador in Thailand a story was concocted that he was a lieutenant colonel returning to Australia and wanted to visit a friend who happened to be the Australian services attaché in Vientiane. This allowed him to get to Seno and walk around the airfield and its surrounds so that he could plan the Australian brigade's arrival and defences should Plan 5C be enacted.

The History of the [US] Joint Chiefs of Staff: The Joint Chiefs of Staff and the War in Vietnam recognised that the communists were causing great disruption to the country where the guerrilla war of 1957–59, 'though not of great magnitude, played havoc with the social, political and economic rehabilitation of the countryside'.[2] 'Equally regrettable, Diem felt impelled to exercise steadily more authoritarian attitudes and measures.' The report continued: The 'damage inflicted by [the] enemy . . . seemed to indicate the current strength and fullest reach of the communists'.[3]

On 26 January 1960, a North Vietnamese surrogate military force known as the Viet Cong launched a 300-man attack against a South Vietnamese army regiment's command post at Tay Ninh, near the South's border with Cambodia. The US Joint Chiefs of Staff declared this was the start of a new phase of warfare by the Viet Cong. The attack 'gained additional symbolic importance ... by occurring on the eve of Tet [Chinese New Year]'. America's reply was to commit to the aid of South Vietnam with an expressed goal of 'developing a viable economy and government' and to build and train 'armed forces capable of assuring internal security and providing limited initial resistance to aggression from the North'.[4] These ideals were underpinned by the US National Security Council document NSC 5809, which stated that the United States would seek to prevent the free nations of Southeast Asia from passing into or becoming economically dependent on the Communist Bloc whether that was by overt aggression, subversion, or a political and economic offensive.

After the January attack at Tay Ninh, it was clear that North Vietnam was actively directing an insurgency against the South. On 20 December 1960, Radio Hanoi announced the establishment of the National Front for the Liberation of South Vietnam (NLF). The NLF was an all-encompassing political organisation that held absolute power over the proposed political and military efforts to seize power in the South. Radio Hanoi called for the 'overthrow of the disguised colonial regime of the U.S. imperialists and the dictatorial Ngo Dinh Diem administration, lackey of the United States'.[5]

How to train, what type of war

In their major challenges of training and equipping the South Vietnamese, US military advisers faced a challenge: what type of warfare should they prepare the Vietnamese for? Renowned Brigadier General Edward Lansdale, assigned to the CIA station in Saigon in the mid-1950s, had assisted the Philippines in their successful fight against the Huk rebellion. He now provided personal advice on politics and warfare to South Vietnamese President Ngo Dinh Diem. Lansdale recommended guiding the Vietnamese away from an emphasis on a threat based upon the clashes of the Korean War. Lansdale thought that Ho Chi Minh and Vo Nguyen Giap would not attack the South in a conventional sense.

Lieutenant General Samuel Williams—a Korean War veteran and the then Chief of the Military Assistance and Advisory Group (MAAG)—was not so sure and the training of the South Vietnamese concentrated upon the possibility of an invasion. In 1962, General Paul Harkins commanded American efforts in Vietnam. He appointed Major General Richard G. Weede as his chief of staff. United Press International commented upon the importance of this appointment:

> Military circles ... thought ... [the] selection of a marine general was particularly significant. They felt that Weede as Harkins' deputy will have a firm grasp of the entire situation, if a Korean-type war broke out—and military authorities are not ruling out that possibility.[6]

Years later, Lansdale admitted that when Williams questioned his prediction, he 'had to admit honestly that I might be wrong'. 'The Vietnamese are not that predictable and . . . I didn't know how hard Giap and other Communist military leaders were listening to the advice of Soviet officers.' Lansdale also criticised the armchair experts who based their opinions on hindsight; they did not have to look across the border where troops were forming for 'what looked suspiciously like an invasion'.[7]

As well as training the Army of the Republic of Vietnam (ARVN), the Americans also had to train the Civil Guard (CG) and the Self Defence Corps (SDC). Authorised manning of the Civil Guard was 50,000 personnel and the Self Defence Corps, 40,000. These were the troops that Australia would soon be called upon to assist. To put the size of Australia's force in perspective, Australia had a Regular Army of around 24,500 of whom about half were allocated to the operational forces, but not all of these were ready for deployment.[8]

Under normal circumstances, the Civil Guard's task was 'to provide for the internal security of the country while the regular military establishment concentrated on the conventional threat from outside the country'.[9] The duty of the Self Defence Corps was to protect the villages. However, training, equipment and organisation of the two groups did not match the rhetoric. The Civil Guard answered to the Department of Interior, which put it outside the US Military Assistance Program's weapons and finance support. At the end of 1960, these arrangements changed and it came under the control of the Ministry for Defence.

General Lyman Lemnitzer, the US Army Chief of Staff, wrote to the Joint Chiefs of Staff in March 1960 emphasising that 'the "critical situation" in South Vietnam required definite action'. 'He agreed with the Commander in Chief Pacific (CINCPAC) that an anti-guerrilla capability could be developed ... by changing the emphasis in training from conventional to anti-guerrilla warfare, but ... additional support in specialized fields was warranted.'[10] President Diem was adamant that there were two threats: one external and one internal and wanted to increase his total force to 170,000. This idea was rejected totally by the US Ambassador and the US military advisers. The Americans said he had enough men under arms already, but they needed to be used more efficiently. At the same time Diem was told he must introduce some political reform to win the confidence of the people.

Although Diem was considered the right man for the job, the American Ambassador Elbridge Durbrow cabled the Department of State to advise, rather ominously, that if Diem did not adopt some measure of reform, the United States should consider alternative courses and leaders.[11] During an attempted coup in November, Diem kept the US Ambassador out of his presidential palace for several weeks because he thought he had had prior knowledge of the attempted takeover and refused to talk to him. Relations between the two countries were now extremely strained. President Kennedy had all but approved Edward Lansdale to become the new ambassador, but this raised 'a storm in the Pentagon' because of his CIA background, so Lansdale was not appointed.

The problem of South Vietnam

Throughout 1961 there were numerous discussions among Australian External Affairs and Defence officials, and many messages were sent between the embassies at Saigon, Washington and London on the growing problem of increased communist activity in South Vietnam. Questions about what Australia could do to help SEATO countries and its protocol states were formulated on the continuing basis that the immediate threat to Australia's strategic interests and security stemmed from the Southeast Asian mainland. South Vietnam was seen as a lynchpin in this equation; if it were to fall to communism, other countries would soon follow.

In May 1961, the questioners began to form options, which then required something more than hypothetical answers. Australia had committed £200,000 ($400,000) under SEATO funds to assist the Civil Guard with such items as tents and telecommunications equipment. The possibility of using the Jungle Training Centre at Canungra in Queensland was canvassed, but was thought too expensive. Facilities in Malaya were closer and had been used by Vietnam for some years. Frederick J. Blakeney, Assistant Secretary at External Affairs, amended a departmental memorandum, headed 'Counterinsurgency—Possible Australian Contribution', with the following note: 'If we were requested to send to Vietnam instructors who have experience in Malaya, probably only a small number could be spared'. He also highlighted a possible problem for training, by noting that Australian jungle-fighting methods were dissimilar to those of the United Kingdom—an incorrect assessment—and the United States and Australia used different weapons.[12] As expected, there were opposing points of view on the use of Canungra, and whether the difference in techniques used by Australia would bother the Vietnamese. The different weapons argument was brushed aside on the basis that the Vietnamese used a variety of weapons and this had not influenced their training in Malaya.

In June 1961, the British High Commission in Canberra advised Australia that the United Kingdom had considered certain proposals, including one to create a civilian advisory group that would be attached to the British Embassy in Saigon. Sir Robert Thompson, DSO, MC, an expert on guerrilla warfare from Malaya who had also served on both Chindits operations in Burma during World War II, would lead the group of no more than four or five. The Chindits operated deep behind the Japanese lines in North Burma during 1943 and 1944. Other proposals put forward by the British included enlarged training programs for ARVN officers and the Civil Guard in Malaya and extended training for the police and other security services, as well as assistance with administrative matters and medical teams.

In November 1961, Sir Howard Beale, Australia's Ambassador to the United States, reported that it would be advantageous to advise the United States promptly of Australia's general support for America's proposals in South Vietnam. Beale said this would encourage the United States to persist with its efforts on the Southeast Asian mainland, which would be essential to ensuring the area was not lost by default. He reported that the Kennedy administration was unhappy about the efforts its allies were prepared to make when it was their vital interests, as well as those of America, that were at stake.

America stressed that no combat forces would be involved in their assistance to Vietnam at this stage and that their involvement would 'fall far short of intervention'. The United States told Beale 'that the steps proposed would not be dangerous and would not provoke reaction from Communist China'. American officials did admit privately that there was some risk of upsetting China. The Australian Ambassador also reported that Dean Rusk, US Secretary of State, was unsympathetic towards and had rejected the French Ambassador's concern that the United States should not do anything in Vietnam to upset the Geneva Laos negotiations that had been convened earlier that year in May. Menzies cabled Beale in reply:

> Glad if you would pass following message to Rusk. I have put under immediate study your proposals for action to help South Vietnam counter Viet Cong insurgency. In general, they seem admirably adapted to meeting a very difficult situation. I am also examining the possibility of Australia increasing its assistance to Vietnam and hope to be able to make a decision on this after the elections next month. 27 November 1961.[13]

Assistance for South Vietnam

The Australian federal election held on 9 December 1961 was a close-run thing. Treasurer Harold Holt had imposed a credit squeeze in late 1960 that caused major dissatisfaction. Holt's decision had been influenced by a drop in the price of wool—a major contributor to Australia's prosperity at the time—drought, inflation and rising prices. The increased loan interest rates and a big increase in sales tax on vehicles saw car manufacturers General Motors–Holden and Ford sack more than 2000 workers in less than six months. Public opinion swung against the government and the election result saw the two major parties with 62 seats each in the House of Representatives. Menzies' party remained in government because two ALP members—those for the Northern Territory and the Australian Capital Territory—had restricted voting rights in the chamber, but he lost control of the Senate where he needed the support of the Democratic Labor Party or independent senators to have a majority.

With the political question decided, departments got on with assessing what assistance could be provided to South Vietnam. At a meeting held at the Department of External Affairs on 14 December 1961, Ralph Harry, a senior officer in the department, identified two issues: 'the supply of aid and its co-ordination with efforts of other countries concerned'. Harry stated that 'the motivation for Australia providing assistance as far as the ambassador at Washington, and the United States were concerned was predominantly political'. At this stage in the planning discussions the SEATO pact was the principal authority against which funds and assistance would be approved. Other aid, such as the possible provision of .303 rifles, had been considered earlier in the year for the Self Defence Corps, which was not being armed by the United States. It was agreed that Australia's training contribution would be limited, and doubts were expressed about the value of such an involvement. Indeed, Brigadier Tim Cape felt that 'the Army might be embarrassed by the need to produce the appropriate people and believed this would represent an unrewarding dissipation of its limited resources'.[14] It was agreed that Australia could do no more than provide a token contribution to training.

Australia had also imposed a restriction on itself, based on the 1954 Geneva Agreement, not to introduce arms and servicemen to South Vietnam. During the meeting a question was asked on whether Australia continued to have a moral obligation to observe the Geneva agreements given the military violations, such as the 1960 Tay Ninh attack, committed by the communists. The Americans and the North Vietnamese were locked in a shadow war inside Laos, but this was extremely secret information and not available to the members at this meeting.[15] The question remained unanswered. The talks continued on what surplus weapons and ammunition might be available to give to the Vietnamese. Answers ranged from 5000 9 mm Austen submachine guns to 600 .303 Bren guns as well as large stocks of revolvers; .303 rifles got another mention because there were 10,000 of them (but no ammunition). Various other options, such as medical supplies, air photo units and an army construction unit, were suggested. The RAAF said that they did not have an aerial photographic unit and the Army had no medical dressing stations that could be supplied. In conclusion, the meeting agreed that Washington should 'authorize MAAG to discuss with the Australian Embassy in Saigon possible forms of Australian assistance'.[16] Sterling Cottrell, the director of the American

Inter-Departmental Task Force on Vietnam, said that he would advise the US Embassy in Saigon so that MAAG would be ready for an approach by the Australian Attaché. Cottrell also replied 'that the Department was most grateful for and took great comfort from Australia's prompt and unequalled moral and practical support of US efforts in South Vietnam'.[17]

The worsening situation in Vietnam

Away from diplomatic and political circles, the situation in Vietnam was getting worse. Lieutenant General Lionel McGarr in Saigon wrote a strongly worded letter to the Chairman, Joint Chiefs of Staff, on 12 October 1961 briefing him on the basic causes of the worsening situation and expressing his grievance about the interference by the Department of State in the military's plan. As the new Chief of MAAG, McGarr's letter was a powerful complaint on several fronts. The letter highlighted the urgent military, political, psychological and economic actions required to win a counterinsurgency confrontation that had now developed into battles against more conventional-type enemy units coming down from the North and across the Laotian border into South Vietnam.[18]

In December 1961, the Australian Joint Planning Committee received a report from Colonel Stuart Graham, the director of Australian Military Intelligence, on the inadequacy of the Vietnamese command structure, which mirrored some of the problems General McGarr had identified. Early in the New Year, Robert Thompson briefed personnel in Australia's Department of External Affairs on his activities in Vietnam and the challenges South Vietnam faced, particularly the hatred the people in Saigon felt towards Diem and Nhu, his brother. The British High Commission later amended the notes of the meeting by inserting after 'hatred'—'now for the first time appearing'. Thompson said that 'the possibility of a further coup could not be excluded'.[19]

Australian Colonel Francis P. 'Ted' Serong, who had been on loan to the Burmese Army equivalent of a training command for just over two years, wrote to Lieutenant General Sir Reginald Pollard, the Chief of the General Staff (CGS), in February 1962 outlining the potential for an Australian team to be attached to the American MAAG in Saigon. Serong had a friendly relationship with Pollard that had been established during their service together as divisional staff officers in New Guinea during World War II. The letter, written in Serong's inimitable and unabashed style, detailed some of his thoughts about counterinsurgency and his own capabilities.

> We [Australia] have been out of operations now for nearly two years. At the moment, the only Australian shooting is me [an exaggeration]. We must keep in the act, or we'll become also-rans. The Americans are hard at it in Vietnam, with a conspicuous lack of success. They acknowledge that they are raw hands . . . but they'll soon become the fount of all knowledge, and that could be dangerous. The proposal is to offer the Americans a small Australian contingent. I would lead them myself. The advantages are obvious—continued operational experience, prestige, a gesture of allied solidarity—and all for minimal expense. Later, if we wish, it could be developed to a larger integrated effort. Or, if events took a different turn, the group is on the ground to act as a forward headquarters for a more massive intervention in that zone.[20]

Third-country involvement

Amid this concern about conditions in Vietnam, there were reservations about what Australia could do. First and foremost, General McGarr didn't want foreign troops to be intermingled with his force. He was aware that the Department of State had applied pressure to get British assistance into South Vietnam, as well as other third-country nationals, such as Australia, Malaya and the Philippines. The US Presidential Task Force had discussed possible contributions from other countries in May 1961 when Australia was mentioned almost as an afterthought; it was believed that Australia had a useful capability. The use of third-country nationals would be an administrative bugbear, but if the United States could get Britain involved it would be worthwhile.

The Department of State's desire was to have more Free World countries committed to the cause in South Vietnam to manifest a strong political alliance against communism. McGarr was concerned that there would be too much confusion if the American military doctrine and training were to be diluted by methods used by other countries such as Australia. He had written to General Lyman Lemnitzer, Chairman of the US Joint Chiefs of Staff, in June 1961, to express a strong opinion against the introduction of third-country trainers. President Diem had assured him that they were not needed. McGarr also wanted to obtain a copy of the qualifications of the British Advisory Mission 'experts' headed by Thompson before *he* would approve their coming to Vietnam.

McGarr made it clear in his correspondence that the introduction of other forces would be counterproductive, but, if introduced, they were to be controlled by MAAG. McGarr took exception to the Delta Plan written by Robert Thompson for President Diem. He thought the report exceeded Thompson's terms of reference, and, furthermore, he objected to being told things he already knew.[21] This and the arguments over a conventional army structure versus 'irregular operations', in which regular forces supposedly had little importance, caused quite a deal of concern at very senior levels of the military that flowed through to the president. Kennedy told Secretary of Defense Robert McNamara that the effort devoted to the challenge of communist-directed subversive insurgency and guerrilla warfare should be comparable in importance to the preparations for conventional warfare. Subsequently, in February 1962, Major General Victor Krulak, US Marine Corps, was designated to head the Office of Special Assistant for Counter Insurgency and Special Activities (SACSA).

The previously strong objections lodged by the American MAAG and others against permitting third-country nationals, such as Australians, to deploy troops into Vietnam was toned down to a reluctant acceptance. At meetings in Honolulu in January and February of 1962, McNamara said 'that if it were politically wise to accept Australian help we should do so'. McGarr replied that he 'would be glad to have small numbers of Australians if they were willing to serve under the MAAG'. The Department of State had won the debate. Acceptance of third-country nationals was reinforced during the February meeting in this assessment:

It will probably be necessary to assign considerable numbers of American and possibly third-country NCOs to work with the Vietnamese in organizing defense and civic action in the villages. This will a difficult decision since good NCOs who could fit into the Vietnamese way of life are hard to find in large numbers and it will present the political problem of increasing American casualties. The Australians, Malayans, Filipinos, and even the Koreans and ChiNats [Nationalist Chinese] might also be asked to supply some of their NCOs.[22]

Australia enters the fray

In a letter written to Sir Garfield Barwick in March 1962, Athol Townley, Australia's Minister for Defence, summarised his thoughts on the 'possible availability of suitable Australian forces to participate in the training program in Vietnam'. He recognised that the initial reaction from the Americans in Saigon 'was rather unenthusiastic', as they had sufficient troops of their own. The United States had also advised him of the difficulties of integration and accommodation—an aspect that would influence where the Australians would eventually deploy—and the possibility that President Diem would play nationalities off against each other.

In America, the Department of State had convinced the Pentagon to accept an Australian offer and a request by Admiral Harry Felt, CINCPAC, was to be submitted through military channels. The Australians did not have much to offer. 'The Army could make available a group of some ten officers with ranks from *Lieutenant Colonel to Lieutenant* [emphasised] who could be attached to MAAG in such positions as the United States Commander might require.' Townley suggested that these officers should have either war or Malayan Emergency experience. He said that some warrant and non-commissioned officers (NCOs) could also be provided. He also addressed the perceived difficulty of differences in training methods. The Australians, he wrote, would have no difficulty 'adapting themselves to American doctrine'. 'It would not be practicable to teach Australian techniques to a small proportion of a large [Vietnamese] army.'[23]

A strange series of events then unravelled that involved the travels of Colonel Serong on his way back from Burma and a meeting of the ANZUS parties in May 1962 that culminated in the deployment of the Australian Army Training Team Vietnam (AATTV) to South Vietnam in July. When Serong realised that the Burmese Directorate of Military Training probably would not extend his cut-off date beyond a second year, he knew it was time to leave, and extricated himself from Burma. On his way back to Australia,

Serong planned an eight-week official tour of Southeast Asia to 'wrap up in one parcel the latest of all S. E. Asian insurgency'. This entailed travel to Bangkok, Saigon, Hong Kong and Manila before arriving at Singapore on 30 April, and then home by sea. Lieutenant General Pollard did not agree with such a long itinerary and restricted Serong's public-purse travels to 30 days from 1 April to 1 May, with an approved return to Australia by air, not sea. Serong was in Singapore by then and on his way home. Pollard added a note to a letter about the revised itinerary that 'Serong would be high on the list if a senior officer is required for service in Vietnam or some similar area'.[24]

On his return, Serong was debriefed by Allan Loomes, an Assistant Secretary at the Department of External Affairs. Serong, like others, criticised the Vietnamese command structure and the American system of training, which he said lacked confidence in the Vietnamese soldier to do the job. He also wrote a personal dot-points list summarising the general situation and the problems that existed, as he saw them. He said the situation was worse than he had been led to believe and was worsening. The border problem with Cambodia and Laos was not appreciated. General Paul Harkins (the new commander of the MACV) had not grasped the nature of his task, and the Strategic Hamlet system was not a plan because if all hamlets were strategic, none was.

Serong's comment pedantically misinterpreted the term 'strategic hamlet' (which he misnamed as villages) by applying a strict military definition to 'strategic'. The purpose of the strategic hamlets was to separate the people from the Viet Cong, placing them in protected communities that the government could control and into which they would provide services to enhance living conditions. These pacified areas would eventually link together like ink blots to force the Viet Cong out of the selected regions completely. What really happened was different to the theory because some people were forced from their land and the program expanded too quickly. The forced resettlements angered some of the rural communities and turned them against the government while the fast expansion created additional security problems. The program was a just a new name for an old concept known as 'Agroville' in Vietnam in 1959 and a similar system had been used in Malaya during its communist insurgency battles (1948–60). In January 1964, the name was changed to 'New Life' hamlet and the settlements attracted strong enemy military action because a secure area prevented communist influence over the inhabitants.[25]

Serong also stated in his debriefing that his experience in Burma 'would enable him to infuse a much more realistic element into the training programme'. While his observations were fundamental to the background on how Vietnam was faring, at the time, he was uninformed. The French and the Americans had addressed these issues in detail, and the lessons had been written in Vietnamese, French and English long before Colonel Serong's visit.[26]

Who was Colonel F. P. 'Ted' Serong?

Who was this officer who wrote in his personal notes 'These people need me', and who had the confidence of the CGS? Ted Serong had been estranged from the mainstream of Australian military activity by his two years as a tactical trainer and adviser to the Burmese Director of Military Training. In Burma, before his interest in Vietnam, he had proposed an Australian Training Team Burma composed of six staff from the Jungle Training Centre in Canungra, where Serong had been commandant between 1955 and 1957. Major Ben O'Dowd and Lieutenant Colonel George Warfe, principal instructors in jungle warfare on Battle Wing at the centre, were the proposed frontrunners for his Burma Training Team concept.

Major General Hugh G. Harlock—the General Officer Commanding Northern Command—was unimpressed by the colonel and castigated him severely in a special confidential report on his command ability in February 1957. Harlock wrote that Serong did not have the balance or sense of responsibility appropriate to his command and ended with an assessment that he did not recommend him for promotion. Harlock also noted that Colonel Serong had not served with troops since 1945, during his deployment with the 35th Infantry Battalion in New Guinea.

During World War II, the then Major Serong served as a staff officer with Headquarters New Guinea Force for two months during December 1942 and January 1943. Later, he travelled from Australia for a few weeks to observe the amphibious landings at Morotai in September 1944, and then in June 1945 he returned to New Guinea for service with the 4th and 35th battalions. This period was his only recorded regimental service with troops in a combat zone. During his service with the 35th Battalion Serong, who commanded one of the battalion's administration echelons, was given the task on 22 July 1945 of destroying a previously discovered Japanese ammunition dump. The dump turned out to be two piles of approximately 80 (artillery?) rounds. There was no contact with the enemy during this task other than some occasional unaimed rifle shots. A subsequent attachment to the 2nd/3rd Battalion to gain experience in deep patrolling was cancelled. World War II in the Pacific ended soon afterwards and Serong returned to Australia in September 1945 where he filled a variety of instructor and staff positions in the post-war Army. He did not serve in Korea or Malaya.[27]

ANZUS, MACV and nuclear weapons

At a time when regional security was focused on SEATO, a meeting of the ANZUS partners in Australia on 8–9 May 1962 was the venue for America's anticipated request through military channels for some Australian involvement in Vietnam. At this meeting, American Admiral Harry Felt, the Commander in Chief Pacific, briefed the ANZUS members on the military challenges they faced on the Southeast Asian mainland. These included the continuing problems in Laos which was stumbling towards another Geneva accord that would supposedly guarantee a state of neutrality for the land-locked kingdom. Fourteen countries eventually signed the International Agreement on the Neutrality of Laos on 23 July 1962.[28] At the meeting, Sir Garfield Barwick, Australia's Minister for External Affairs, questioned Dean Rusk, the US Secretary of State, about the possibility of American troops going into Laos and/or Vietnam. Rusk replied 'that South Vietnam was not an alternative effort to Laos'. He made the point that committing troops into a landlocked battle reduced the power of the US military to hit hard from the sea and the air. 'In simple terms, the U.S.A. was more inclined to back the play in South Vietnam than Laos.'[29]

Rusk and Barwick had a robust discussion on the suitability of Diem to continue as leader, and, more importantly, whether a 'political–military decision had been made to stand in South Vietnam. How far and deep did United States resolution go?' One can deduce from Rusk's reply that he bristled somewhat at the question, making the point that the United States had 8000 men in Vietnam. 'It [the USA] might well ask what other S.E.A.T.O. powers thought!' What were you prepared to do, was his challenge. He went on to say 'that Southeast Asia was vital to America, but the US should not be obliged to stand alone'. Barwick declared that Southeast Asia was also a vital area to Australia, particularly because of the increasing dangers in Indonesia. 'We were committed'—Barwick said—'and thought we were pulling our weight'.

A zestful head-to-head followed about full commitment by the United States, even if China were to become involved. Based on Rusk's reply, Barwick concluded that 'no ultimate United States political decision had been made'. Rusk then asked if Australia had made such a decision. Australia had not, was the reply. This meant 'that no one had decided that the area was vital', Barwick added as a personal conclusion. Rusk made the point that a decision on general war was a matter for an exchange between the prime minister and the president, as he was not in a position to give such an assurance. He again reminded Barwick of America's commitment and added with a little sarcasm: 'If Australia brought its commitment up to the [US] level, we could consider the next stage'. The note taker prefaced the next part of their conversation with the entry 'Following an interchange'—probably diplomatic shorthand for a shouting match—Rusk said 'he had referred to the degree of political commitment, rather than . . . material commitment'.[30]

From the Australian point of view, Indonesia was the demon in all of this. In April Barwick had presented his concern to Cabinet that 'communist activity could extend into Eastern New Guinea and in due course the Pacific Islands'. The West New Guinea–Indonesia question had pulled Australia through a 180-degree arc of diplomacy. At first, Australia supported the Dutch in the hope that their staying in the region would prevent a communist takeover of Indonesia. This proved unsustainable when the Dutch made moves to leave the territory. Barwick explained, 'it was a painful movement round the compass to the position where we would not be standing with the Dutch'.

Dean Rusk replied pragmatically that Indonesia with its large population was more important than West New Guinea and he and Barwick agreed it was better to negotiate rather than have warfare over an insignificant West New Guinea population. The United States was not willing to act 'as a gendarme' for the Dutch although they would assist protect their citizens if Indonesia attacked West New Guinea, something for which the Dutch had not expressed any appreciation, Rusk added. Rusk's comments on Indonesia were assiduously recorded even though he had specifically asked that 'notes not be taken of them'. Australia, Barwick commented, 'now had to face up to the fact that instead of a friendly power to our north we had the prospect of an Indonesian West New Guinea and an Indonesia under communist control'.[31]

More talks on Australia providing military aid to South Vietnam took place on 9 May 1962, without the presence of the New Zealand Prime Minister, Keith Holyoake. During the meeting it was agreed that a request for Australian assistance with military training in Vietnam could now be made. The delay in making the request, caused by reluctance within MAAG, had been 'overridden by higher American authority'. Rusk said it would be 'most valuable to have Australians in Vietnam flying the Australian flag'. The most important part of this decision-making process was the lack of a request from the Government of South Vietnam. Admiral Felt was to travel to Saigon on 10 May where he would discuss the 'possible form and extent' of the Australian involvement with General Harkins.

Military Assistance Command Vietnam (MACV) was activated on 8 February 1962 with responsibility for all military policy, operations and assistance; it absorbed MAAG under its military umbrella. President Diem had agreed to its establishment, but 'insisted that it be made clear that a civilian remained the head of the US mission in South Vietnam'. US ambassadors held the full responsibility for the coordination and supervision of agencies in their respective countries including, at this stage, the military. Following strong discussions within the American administration, both sides—the ambassador and the military commander—were approved to make representation to Washington through their respective chains of communication should there be a major disagreement. Diem's request for a civilian head was made to avoid the impression that America had taken over the direction of the war effort, as this would provide the enemy with propaganda advantages that could be exploited throughout the region. The many subsequent suggestions to appoint a supreme commander, in the Malayan image, ignored the message of subjugation or new colonialism that such an appointment would have unleashed, especially when the allied officers did not see the position as a suitable command for a Vietnamese officer.

After his 10 May arrival in Vietnam, Admiral Felt was to provide Air Marshal Sir Frederick Scherger, the Australian Chairman of the Chiefs of Staff Committee, with any additional information that would allow a case to be submitted to the Australian government. It was also suggested that an Australian delegation should go to Vietnam. The remainder of the meeting on 9 May was taken up with the most serious deliberations of all—the use of nuclear weapons. Felt and Rusk admitted that nuclear weapons were part of some of their SEATO planning documents, but their use was 'not automatic' should those plans be implemented. If such weapons were used it would be for tactical purposes such as 'closing passes', Felt said. When Barwick asked how the use of nuclear weapons 'could be made to appear justifiable', Rusk replied that 'at a certain point . . . it would be necessary to override Asian opinion which [he believed] would not greatly increase the "agony of decision" which fell upon the United states in these matters'. In other words, the United States would bomb the area whether the Asian nations assented or not. It was agreed that further talks would be necessary on the use of such weapons in the Pacific area.[32]

After the meeting Barwick held a press conference at Parliament House. He began by speaking of matters that a Minister for External Affairs might be expected to cover: unity, comfort in not standing alone, security, disarmament, and Soviet secrecy. These rousing sentiments led into the issue of Vietnam:

> There is no question . . . about Vietnam being the subject of infiltration and aggression. Thousands of men are deployed there terrorizing villages, massacering [sic] people, and these are inspired, trained, receive their supplies, from North Vietnam.[33]

He went on to explain that because the South Vietnamese had shown they were willing to stand up for themselves, both the United States and Australia would provide 'aid and assistance' that 'will enable them to carry on their defence'. He made the point that this was not 'military participation', but assistance to help in the security of village life. He then took questions. The reporters immediately latched on to what type of assistance Australia would provide to Vietnam—would it be military training?

Questions and answers developed into a cat and mouse game, with some very hazy and dubious replies. If asked for assistance, Australia would meet the request, Barwick answered one questioner. 'Asked by whom, Sir?' 'By the Vietnamese', came the reply. 'Have you been asked yet?' 'Not by the Vietnamese.' Had Australia been asked by the Americans? Barwick deftly sidestepped this with his technically correct reply: 'No, the Americans *haven't asked us at this conference* [emphasised]'. And one questioner humorously enquired: 'Who will tell the Vietnamese to ask us?'

The reporters had warmed to their task and were trying now to sniff out anything that would give them a lead on what was going on. Some answers given deliberately manipulated the facts and the minister might have lied. For example, when asked whether an offer to assist the Vietnamese had arisen from the ANZUS Council meeting, the minister said: 'Oh, no . . . it is not an ANZUS decision, really'. The meeting which had finished only a short time earlier had just agreed on procedures to start a request process for assistance from Australia.

Australia's first military commitment

Eventually a journalist asked how many people might be sent to Vietnam. Barwick's reply is instructive because it is the start of a body of evidence about how many and who would go to Vietnam in Australia's first deployment to that country. He said: 'I mean something in the order of three or four'. He saw a distinct difference in the deployment of troops that went to Malaya for combat; he did not 'see any immediate possibility of a like move in regard to Vietnam'. This did not accord with the Australian Cabinet's approval in April of the possible use of an infantry battalion in South Vietnam in SEATO Plan 7. Barwick went on to emphasise that he saw Australia's possible contribution being more towards assistance to the 'Civil Guard, . . . not an army organisation in the ordinary way'.[34]

Many years later in 1995, Barwick wrote in his autobiography *A Radical Tory* that he had met Rusk in 1963 at the ANZUS meeting and they had discussed the need to upgrade the American troops' performance in jungle warfare. As Australia maintained a jungle warfare training school commanded by Colonel Serong, Rusk allegedly said: 'It would be a distinct advantage if Australia would lend America Colonel Serong and a few of his trainers'. Barwick added that he had discussed this matter with Townley and they both thought of the possible effects that such an agreement might have on any future request for combat troops. They both then agreed to make the men available.[35] The book is sub-titled 'Garfield Barwick's Reflections and Recollections', recollections that were obviously blurred by time. The meeting with Rusk was in 1962 and Serong had relinquished command of the Jungle Training Centre in 1957.

The use of the term 'jungle warfare' intimated counterinsurgency operational skills, but at this stage in Canungra's lifespan Australian soldiers were being taught how to fight a conventional war in a jungle environment. Furthermore, the American commanders in Saigon would have rejected the suggestion that Australians might be brought in to train MAAG personnel in jungle warfare. Harkins and McGarr had just reluctantly accepted the introduction of third-country personnel into their bailiwick by direction of a higher authority. To be told that MAAG personnel were to be trained by Australians would have caused a blast of military anger that would have reverberated all the way back to Washington. In fact the opposite was proposed. According to a briefing for a staff-level discussion in Canberra in May 1962, it was assumed that the Australians would conform to US training doctrine and methods. This was highlighted in an Australian Joint Planning Committee memo that stated: 'It will probably be necessary for the detachment to receive instruction from US personnel before they are committed to their training role'.[36] Also, the available notes of the ANZUS meetings show that Admiral Felt would prompt a request for Australians during his 10 May 1962 visit to Saigon, but the detail of what might be requested had not been cleared with the American commander in Saigon. When the deployment plan did begin to unfold, the numbers of Australians to go changed quickly from three or four to 30, but an Australian commander was not named until 5 July 1962.

The Australian administration now closed its book on ANZUS and Vietnam; it was as if the meeting had not taken place. After this, the planning and discussions were all driven by the SEATO Treaty, but, to be historically correct, the beginning of Australia's *defence* commitment to South Vietnam was stirred along by the May 1962 ANZUS meeting. The military advisers at SEATO had drawn up a new plan 'to deal with any major insurgency in South

Vietnam'. This was Plan 7, and it had obtained Australian Cabinet approval on 30 April 1962 (Decision 195). Australia's military commitment in Plan 7 was similar to its role in the Laos Plan 5C, which was to deploy an infantry battalion group from the 28th Commonwealth Brigade, plus Navy and Air Force assets from the Malaya/Singapore area. Plan 7 expected the Australian troops would be sent into South Vietnam—not Laos—as part of a SEATO three-regiment combat team, equivalent to a division—with the task of securing key strategic areas.

SEATO problems

Cabinet continued its discussion about the country's contribution to the maintenance of stability in Southeast Asia in its next meeting that was held on 15 May. This meeting started with a reference to the recent ANZUS conference, in particular the possible use of nuclear weapons. These weapons, it was noted, would be useful for 'smashing airfields and blocking passes', but the United States 'had no intention of using this weapon against centres of population'! Did they really understand nuclear weapons? Cabinet then agreed that the use of an Australian military unit in the region should be as part of a SEATO operation. Military assistance was justified 'because we would not wish to be involved in a conflict in Asia which would be almost exclusively between white and coloured and the use of a nuclear weapon would be diminished' if it were a SEATO operation. In addition, Cabinet noted, deployment of the Australian force would be at 'the request of the government of the country into which our forces were to enter'. If Australia were to provide instructors to assist the South Vietnamese, its justification might be explained in these terms: 'South Vietnam is among the protocol countries associated with SEATO . . . and Australia is willing to discharge the obligations she has accepted in this area'.[37]

Again the focus was upon the strategic power of SEATO, which supposedly emanated from its title 'South East Asia Treaty Organisation' but its true epicentre lay thousands of kilometres away in the cities of London, Paris and Washington. Britain was playing its part in South Vietnam, albeit its Advisory Mission was very small. However, Rusk was grateful that London was in SEATO to a greater degree than Paris. Events in Laos in the preceding years, where communist forces supported by both the Soviet Union and North Vietnam had not been matched by all of the SEATO nations, had diminished morale in the organisation. Thailand's position on voting procedures had caused some difficulties and had the potential to cause the Europeans to split from SEATO. That would be a problem because Paris and London held sufficient diplomatic and economic power to influence defence strategies elsewhere. France was an irreplaceable piece of the European bulwark, and its commitment to SEATO was based on its assertion of no military commitment. Rusk understood that this 'was the filter through which we must analyse French attitudes'. 'We must find ways of circumventing the empty chair and go ahead with what had to be done.'[38]

Alarm bells

In the middle of May, alarms bells started to ring in the Department of Defence at Canberra. A preliminary list of possible military assets that Australia could send to Vietnam had been discussed in a meeting between Admiral Felt and the Australian Chiefs of Staff Committee before Felt travelled to Saigon. That list had now found its way into the hands of the formidable Secretary of the Department of External Affairs, Sir Arthur Tange. Felt had not heard Barwick's press conference and his staff clearly lacked an understanding of Australia's capabilities when they put together a suggested military assistance proposal package. The list included two radar-equipped ships, jungle-trained troops to act as a training cadre within army (South Vietnamese) battalions or to act as instructors, engineer units or engineer instructors, signals units, and an aircraft to support the Australian Embassy—later upgraded to a squadron of Dakotas. These items were well beyond what was politically acceptable, and it was a list that could not be filled militarily.

The difference between the Australian and American lists was at least amusing and no doubt the Americans had a few derisive chuckles when the details became known. Felt also made it clear to Scherger that he 'would talk over the *possibility* [emphasised] of some Australian forces coming into South Vietnam with General Paul Harkins' before a formal request was made. Felt reminded the Australians that it would be advantageous to send a 'small group of service officers to discuss the details with Harkins'. Keith Brennan, the Assistant Secretary, Defence Liaison Branch, recorded on 17 May that the Joint Planning Committee (JPC) would recommend that the delegation be led by (Navy) Captain Stevenson of the JPC and that he be joined by an Army colonel from Australia and an Air Force officer from Butterworth. During the Defence Committee meeting Brennan's report was noted, but Pollard proposed that Scherger should go to Saigon. It was decided to defer the decision on the delegation until the 'views of ministers were known'.

Matters now began to move probably more quickly than the committees and the two principal departments—External Affairs and Defence—anticipated. Admiral Felt dined with President Diem and Robert McNamara, the US Secretary of Defense, on 10 May at Dalat, a pleasant mountain retreat in the southern Central Highlands. During this dinner, Felt told the president and Nguyen Dinh Thuan, the Assistant Minister for Defence and the Minister at the Presidency, of the 'Australian government's preparedness to provide some training personnel for Vietnam'. Athol Townley, the Minister for Defence, announced on 24 May 'that up to some 30 Australian Army Personnel will be sent [to Vietnam] . . . *at the invitation of the Government of the Republic of Vietnam* [emphasised]'.[39] The minister did not have a large pool of Defence personnel from which to draw.

Australia's defence force before the Vietnam commitment

In the late 1950s, Australia's Regular Army had been based on a brigade group and strategic thinking that any larger commitments would be met by using the Citizen Military Forces (CMF), much as it had in the two world wars. The senior officers in the Australian Regular Army were mostly World War II veterans, and a good number of the field officers—major and above—had seen active service in the Korean conflict. Most of the officers and men had decided to make the army their career. The Korean experience was not lost on those who now served as regulars. As noted historian David Horner wrote:

They quickly learned that it was a far cry from the world wars when they were supported by almost the entire nation. Now they were largely out of sight and out of mind in a lonely war. As in the AIF [Australian Imperial Force], they relied on mateship, but they also learned to draw strength from their professionalism—from a pride in achievement. Their ethos was summed in their motto of the Royal Australian Regiment: 'Duty First'.[40]

The NCOs were men who often spent a decade rising to the rank of corporal or section commander and the sergeants were generally experienced men in their late thirties and early forties. George Mansford was a young 17-year-old from Western Australia when he enlisted and served in Korea a few years later with the 1st Battalion of the Royal Australian Regiment (1RAR). There were some pretty 'tough old bastards' serving in the line infantry in those days, as Mansford pointed out: 'Our [rifle] section included a former pilot with a DFC, another with the DFM [who] had been a tail gunner, and two [others] who had fought in the Middle East'. He recalled his infantry training after Korea as 'rudimentary', but effective.

The officer corps was largely made up of men trained at Duntroon, the Royal Military College. The course took four years to complete and graduates were seen as career men and future senior commanders of the army. In June 1950, the Korean crisis erupted and Australian troops—3RAR who were in Japan—were deployed to the war zone in September of that year. This placed an additional demand on all echelons of the Army which was ramped up another notch with the introduction of a national service training program in April 1951. The officer corps needed more flexibility to meet the expanding demands and this led to the introduction of the Officer Cadet School (OCS) at Portsea, Victoria, in January 1952. OCS trained officer aspirants in a shorter course, which at first was six months duration but it eventually ran for 44 weeks before a graduate earned one pip. As a second lieutenant, the new officer was at the bottom of the officer totem pole and some said treated with disdain by their two-pip Duntroon cousins. Many of the more than 3000 OCS graduates, nonetheless, would go on to fill senior command positions and serve with distinction and courage in all aspects of army life.

A new Pentropic system of organisation for the Army was introduced in 1960. Based upon Pentropic battalions which were established on a system of fives, it was an idea adopted from the US Pentomic division that was designed for atomic warfare in the fields of Europe. This dramatically changed the structure of the whole Army. The influence and strength of the CMF declined markedly. No longer were citizen soldiers the mainstay of the Army. The new Pentropic infantry battalions, each commanded by a colonel, had an establishment of 1300 but there were only two in the Regular Army: 2RAR at Holsworthy and 3RAR at Enoggera. Australia also had a smaller Tropical Warfare battalion (1RAR) in Malaya. This battalion had about 800 in total. National service was also cancelled in November 1959, which some commanders thought a godsend because they believed it was a drain on resources for minimal return. Although small, the Army was well trained and would increase in size over the coming years to a ceiling of 21,000 in July 1962. That limit was raised to 24,500 in September and then raised again to 28,000 in May 1963, which was to be achieved by 1967.[41] The overall plan was to have an Army of 33,000. These projected targets subsequently could not be achieved through standard recruitment.

The Royal Australian Navy (RAN) was tiny compared to the navies of Australia's main allies. One American battle group contained more than the entire complement of seagoing RAN personnel. The RAN totalled approximately 13,000 personnel—some 13 per cent below establishment with less than 5000 in the fleet—and a handful of ships whose main role was keeping the sea lanes open, anti-submarine warfare and providing support to the Army.[42] The first Fleet Air Arm operations flew off HMAS *Sydney*—formerly HMS *Terrible*—and the ship was the first Dominion carrier to see active service in the Korean War where air strikes were flown off her on 5 October 1951. HMAS *Melbourne*—formerly HMS *Majestic*—arrived in Australia on 10 May 1956 after conversions that provided an angled flight deck and other improvements that allowed improved flight operations. HMAS *Sydney* was too old to undergo a facelift and retired gracefully to a training role. *Melbourne* then became the sole operational carrier in the Australian Fleet. At 20,000 tons when loaded, with a crew of just over 1000 sailors, it was a small aircraft carrier by international standards. In 1962 HMAS *Sydney* was converted into a fast troop transport, a ship that many soldiers deployed to South Vietnam came to call the 'Vung Tau ferry'. The Australian Navy had no submarines of its own. This capability was provided by the Royal Navy's 4th Submarine Flotilla, which was based in Sydney until 1969.

The Royal Australian Air Force (RAAF) was also small, with a primary strike force of three fighter squadrons that operated Australian F-86 Sabres made under licence. Two squadrons were deployed operationally to the RAAF base at Butterworth on the west coast of the Malay Peninsula and the other was based at Williamtown near Newcastle, in central New South Wales. The Sabres did not have an all-weather capability. There were three squadrons of Canberra jet bombers, but they were limited by the lack of a night-bombing system. Hercules C-130 medium range transport aircraft and Dakotas made up the transport element. In 1962 there were only eight Iroquois helicopters in the RAAF, used primarily for search and rescue, casualty evacuation, light liaison duties and limited troop training. The maritime element consisted of one squadron of Neptunes and one squadron of Lincoln maritime patrol aircraft. The RAAF had eight operational flying bases in Australia and a personnel complement of 15,459 service personnel, supplemented by 2837 civilians.[43] Australia's population in 1962 was 10,743,000.

Sir Garfield Barwick goes to Vietnam, 1962

Not long after Minister Townley made his announcement on the commitment of Army personnel, Barwick travelled to South Vietnam for two days in late May 1962 for a first-hand inspection. When he finished his tour and got to Hong Kong, he wrote a personal note to Townley in which he told the Defence Minister that President Diem had provided him with his personal Dakota so that he could travel around the country and see as much as possible. Robert Thompson, now advising Diem, had travelled with him and they had had useful conversations during the flight. He described the strategic hamlets as analogous to English walled towns of the Middle Ages. He thought the Strategic Hamlet concept was improving the morale of the people in the countryside and, if pursued efficiently, felt it would 'materially assist to turn back the insurgency'. A few years later, the VC command in the South emphasised action to destroy these hamlets because they had become a serious hindrance to their efforts.[44]

Barwick had obtained the very strong impression from the Vietnamese and the American Ambassador that an Australian group would be well received. During talks with Nguyen Dinh Thuan, the Assistant Defence Minister, it was suggested that a jungle training school should be established near Quang Ngai City, located 100 kilometres south of Danang on Highway 1. Barwick thought there was some merit in having a separate unit, although he acknowledged there could be logistical problems. The Vietnamese, through Thuan, promised to provide the buildings and the administrative staff. Barwick was flown around Quang Ngai and then on to Danang, which he saw as being the main point of entry for a resupply effort if Quang Ngai were to be established. At this point in his letter, Barwick suggested that Townley might like to 'talk this over with your Military wallahs'. The use of such a generic term at this stage in the planning confirmed that a commander of the Australian group had not yet been appointed. Barwick added that if Australia were to set up its own camp he would favour channelling all of the SEATO aid for village defence into the same area. Brian Hill, the Australian Ambassador in Saigon, had earlier sent a recommendation to concentrate Australian aid in Vinh Long Province, in the Mekong Delta, well to the south.

Barwick also made it clear to Townley: 'I have made no commitments of any kind'. The minister noted that Thuan's proposal—read President Diem's—was first for the centre to train the Civil Guard, not the Regular Army, and second for a 'home guard' element to be established in the villages. Barwick thought this a good idea and finished by saying: 'There is a degree of urgency here. This place should be regarded as our present frontier'. He wanted something done as quickly as possible. Australia had just sent a squadron of RAAF Sabres to Ubon in Thailand and the delay in getting the squadron there did not benefit Australia, Barwick said. He wanted to get the training group into position quickly, preferably as an Australian unit and 'not peppered through the American forces'. He signed off with an ominous warning: 'I hope you'll watch the climate in relation to Indonesia. I still might have to reconsider my position'.[45]

Serong in Saigon and Quang Ngai, 1962

On 3 June 1962, the American Embassy at Saigon reported to the Department of State that Australia was sending a military officer to Saigon for discussions. Subsequently, the Department of External Affairs advised the Australian Embassy that the US Defense Department had authorised an Australian military visit. Colonel Ted Serong, who had lobbied the CGS to lead a team to Vietnam in February 1962 and who had travelled through Saigon in April on his way home from Burma, now got his wish to be involved. Before his departure he had a meeting with Sir Walter Cawthorn, head of the Australian Secret Intelligence Service (ASIS). Over coming years this link with ASIS was to develop an air of mystique that will be slightly unravelled as this book progresses.

Wing Commander Brinsley accompanied Serong and they got to Saigon on or about 3 June 1962. Keith Brennan from Defence Liaison sent a note to Ambassador Hill explaining the purpose of Serong's visit. 'He will be trying to find out facts rather than conveying formal Australian positions. Things for example like the command of the ground forces and liaison with other people involved are to be determined upon the basis of Serong's report.'[46] One of the problems that had been aired previously was the limited administrative support that the embassy could provide to the defence services. The embassy did not have the staff and Canberra was reluctant to increase staff numbers. Brennan told Hill that Serong was under explicit instructions to keep in very close contact with him.

Ambassador Hill had carefully read Serong's brief, which he thought was fine 'except that my position here as Ambassador is not properly recognised'. Although he declared he was not especially worried, 'But it must be spelt out. E.g. it must be clear that I have control overall in respect of relations with the Vietnamese and also with the Yanks [underlining in original]'.[47] The same argument had occurred when the Americans had established MACV and in this instance, too, it would settle down into the same pattern of command and control in which the ambassador was responsible for the political, and the military for operations. It was highly desirable that each kept the other well informed, of course.

Back in Australia signals were being despatched around the country to alert military units that selected personnel were to prepare for service in South Vietnam. Married men could expect a tour of less than twelve months so that their families could not travel with them, but single soldiers would be required to serve up to eighteen months. There was nothing secret about these preparations; Barwick and Townley had announced the task publicly earlier in the month. The gathering of the required number of officers and men was just another routine task in getting those selected up to Defence Preparedness Level 1, which would permit them to be deployed overseas.

Now it was Serong's turn to complain. In a personal letter sent to General Pollard, CGS, and marked 'Top Secret', he attacked Barwick's actions during his trip that had finished three days before Serong arrived. In his back-channel letter, he wrote: 'It appears that Barwick has committed us up to the gills, and claims he has the support of Minister Townley'. This is a damning observation, considering that the colonel would not have had any confirmation of what Barwick had written to Townley in his letter of 1 June, in which Barwick had specifically said: 'I have made no commitments of any kind'.

The concept of a separate Australian training establishment at Quang Ngai, which Serong saw as a Robert Thompson plot, caused him some angst at first. But he went on to tell the CGS: 'Actually, the thing is quite all right, provided: Thuan can provide . . . Barwick doesn't . . . force it to grow, and it doesn't foul our relations with the US'. Jealousy may have caused Serong's expressed feeling of unease about Thompson's involvement. Thompson was respected as an acknowledged pre-eminent counterinsurgency expert, an officer with a great deal of experience, and now an adviser gaining more attention than Serong.[48]

Over the years, the selection of Quang Ngai as a possible training centre has been the subject of much conjecture. One claim declared that putting Australians there was a trap to have them killed by the enemy. Allegedly, this ploy was predicted and avoided by the Australian reconnaissance party. In other words, the Australians assessed Quang Ngai as too dangerous for them, a quite different proposition to the bragging tone in which Serong wrote to the CGS in February when he wanted to lead a team to Vietnam. In that letter he said: 'We should take over one sector—the dirtiest they have, if they wish—and work that for them'.[49] The Australian archives also tell a different story. In a discussion with Minister Thuan, Colonel Serong accepted the projected facility at Quang Ngai on the grounds that all Australia had to provide was 30 men. The Vietnamese were to provide the 'physical aspects—buildings, staff, logistics, interpreters' and so forth. A few weeks of rice and little else would have soon changed the minds of the Australians about those responsibilities.

As the centre was not ready, Serong planned to integrate the Australian team into the American MAAG establishments so that the men could obtain experience in the tasks they would perform at Quang Ngai. 'Meanwhile'—he wrote—'we provide advice on layout, programming, etc., for the Quang Ngai project'. If Quang Ngai did not work out, he added, the team was out in the field doing what was expected of them. Always one to thrust himself forward, Serong mentioned in his letter that Major General Richard Weede, USMC, the MACV Chief of Staff, said to him 'that his people were all hoping I'd be available to join them as leader of the group. It was a bit garbled . . . but obviously their hearts were in the right place'.[50]

Over the next two weeks cablegrams sped back and forth between Saigon and Canberra in an attempt to finalise what was to be done with the Australians. President Diem had a special interest in Quang Ngai Province because the Viet Minh had assassinated his brother there and he thought it a likely location for a thrust by the Viet Cong coming from the mountains down to the sea. Subsequently, the newly formed ARVN 25th Division was to be located there, thus providing protection for the training establishment where the Australians would be located. As General Pollard noted: 'Quang Ngai must be classed as a zone of high Vietcong activity, and one in which Australian personnel would be quite likely to become involved', but contact with the enemy in other regions could not be discounted either.[51] In these years, it was more dangerous in the south around Saigon and in the Mekong Delta. In his cable of 7 June, Serong mentioned that it would be necessary to put two Australian personnel with the Special Forces training establishment at Danang.

This was the first indication that Serong was not going to abide by the political mantra that Australia was going to South Vietnam to train the villagers in self-protection, particularly the Civil Guard. There was no comment on this from Canberra. Serong now reported that the Quang Ngai task was within capacity, the nearby airstrip could handle Dakotas all year round and he anticipated the building would be finished by December 1962. All in all it was a difficult but challenging project whose success would produce some responses from the Viet Cong. Serong believed that the MACV had not considered this possible development , but that his own 'presence at MACV will help [overcome this lack of foresight]'.

Ambassador Hill and Serong got a serve of military Realpolitik from General Harkins early on in their fact-finding mission when he told them that the Quang Ngai proposal was off the rails. He believed that the ANZUS meeting in Canberra had envisaged integration of Australian personnel with US personnel. He would have to seek fresh instructions from Admiral Felt if a separate operation were to go ahead in Quang Ngai. The general implied that if Australia went it alone it should not expect any logistical support from America. He also made it clear that the United States had just established an expensive jungle-training centre at Duc My near the central coastal town of Nha Trang and did not believe that there was a priority for the Civil Guard to be trained in jungle-fighting techniques. The concept was for the Civil Guard to relieve the ARVN from internal security tasks, which would allow them to undertake jungle combat duty. After this, the fate of a separate Australian training facility was doomed and the Australians now hurried to be integrated into the MAAG facilities.

Serong submitted his report to General Pollard on 21 June 1962 telling the CGS that he had reached agreement with General Harkins and the staff of MACV. The agreement provided for US operational control of the Australians, integration of the Australian team into MAAG, and the provision of logistical support by the United States against a per capita payment. Pollard concurred and recommended to the Defence Committee that the Australians be deployed in two ten-man contingents at Hiep Khanh and Dong Da training centres; four would go to Duc My; the Special Forces training centre near Danang got two; three went to the MAAG headquarters; and Serong was attached to MACV.

Serong's appointment was only resolved after the Australian CGS asked the commander of MACV (COMUSMACV) directly about the need for a colonel to command such a small group. General Harkins replied he would be delighted to have Colonel Serong serve as the commander of the Australian component and as an adviser to him on counterinsurgency. If Serong was too senior for the task, he would be happy to have another fine Australian officer serve in his stead. Bruce White, Secretary of the Department of the Army, advised the Secretary of the Department of Defence that the Minister for the Army had approved the appointment of Colonel F. P. Serong, OBE, as commander of the Australian Army Component, Vietnam on 5 July 1962.[52] During the inter-departmental discussions on his appointment, Serong requested his family accompany him. External Affairs, citing 'special considerations', granted the request. However, his suggestion that families should accompany all officers was quickly refused.

The Australian Army Training Team Vietnam

The officers and men selected to go to South Vietnam now started to get the orders that would permit their movement to the Intelligence Centre at Middle Head on Sydney Harbour where they sat through an introduction and familiarisation briefing on the current situation in Vietnam. As one participant said: 'At least it was better than the briefing before I went to Korea when the fellow held up a copy of *National Geographic* and told us there were tigers in Korea'.[53]

There were 37 in the group, including Colonel Serong, and they came from a wide variety of units. For example, the warrant officers and sergeants came from the Royal Military College, the Recruit Training Battalion, battalions of the Royal Australian Regiment, Special Air Service (SAS), and the Infantry Centre. The officers also were posted from a diverse range of employment such as Army Headquarters, the Divisional Intelligence Unit, the Divisional Signal Regiment, an engineer field squadron and Headquarters Northern Command. When the final 30 were named, three officers had not served overseas, but the other 27 were experienced campaigners from World War II, Korea, Malaya or the British Commonwealth Occupation Force in Japan, or a combination of the wars. Three had served in World War II, Korea and Malaya.

The army bureaucracy now set in motion the myriad orders and instructions to raise the new unit and place it on to the Australian Order of Battle. It was to be known as the 'Australian Army Component Vietnam' (1 July 1963), which was soon amended to 'Training Component'. However, that title suggested it might be a component of the American force, so on 12 July the title was changed again to its now famous name: the 'Australian Army Training Team Vietnam' (AATTV).[54]

After the course at Middle Head had been completed, the unit was directed to move to Canungra in Queensland, where *the instructors*—members of the AATTV—would be refreshed in the tactics and techniques of tropical warfare up to platoon level! It was a naïve program. The training centres in Vietnam were churning through companies and battalions in what really was a rest cycle between operational deployments. This was a training schedule of six days that spent more time on lines inspection and an introduction to naviga-tion for officers and warrant officers, than it did on counterinsurgency, which was no time at all. Other subjects of no more than 40 minutes' duration included an introduction to tropical warfare, countering a vehicle ambush, a demonstration of fire and movement and the dreaded muscle toughening and confidence course. Ian Gollings remembered that everyone was amused when Colonel Serong turned up on the last day of the course and jumped from the tower into the creek to show his empathy with the troops.[55]

Additionally, the AATTV members were to undergo training arranged by the MACV in US weapons, doctrine and techniques. This training was neces-sary General Pollard told the Secretary of the Department of Defence as 'our instructors would be using American doctrine and techniques, so as not to confuse the Vietnamese'.[56] But the MACV training did not happen.

As they got closer to leaving for the conflict, the instructions became more detailed and slightly comical. Among their personal clothing, officers of field rank and above were directed to take their Sam Browne belt and medals. Everyone was required to have a white mess kit, which could be bought in Singapore if necessary. The team were reminded that they would be required to pay for their US ration packs as well as any meals consumed in the static (bachelor) quarters in which they would be lodged, but their allowances had yet to be approved by Treasury. All members were advised to take with them an ample supply of Australian five-penny stamps for their personal mail, which could be sent through the embassy bag for posting in Australia.

Twenty-eight men departed Sydney on Qantas flight 739 for Singapore via Perth on 29 July 1962. Lieutenant Peter Young had gone ahead on 22 July and Colonel Serong had left on the 27th. From the date of departure, the AATTV were on active service in an operational zone that had not been declared a war. Three members travelled on British passports, which became an embar-rassment to the British Embassy in Saigon later in the year. Their passports were quietly replaced with Australian documents.

The group reassembled in Singapore to sort out final administrative matters before heading on to Saigon. The Australian Army element of the Far East Land Force (FARELF) was the AATTV's superior headquarters for matters of administration and Major Leo Fitzpatrick and Warrant Officer Joe Vezgoff went there to obtain a cash advance of US$15,000 to cover the unit's pay. They were surprised to be told that they did not have American dollars, the only useful currency in Vietnam. The problem was solved by a trip to the notorious 'Change Alley' where an Indian moneychanger thought he had hit the jackpot. As Vezgoff commented years later, what a sight—an Indian with a bag stuffed full of US dollars and two Australian soldiers on their knees counting out the transaction, oblivious to the pedestrian traffic around them.

Active service, 31 July 1962

As the contingent commander Serong was able to go ahead and became the first Australian to land in Vietnam on active service on 31 July.[57] This was the beginning for Australia of more than ten years of military involvement in the conflict. The remainder of the unit, led by the commanding officer, Lieutenant Colonel Joe Mann, boarded Pan Am flight 808 on 3 August in civilian clothes.[58] The senior Australian diplomat in Singapore was nervous that a group of uniformed Australian soldiers seen heading off to Vietnam might create a messy diplomatic situation. Other passengers on the flight were amused as the men trooped to the toilet to change from civilian clothes to their uniforms during the flight. The team arrived in Saigon at 12.30 pm the same day.

In Saigon, Australian Ambassador Brian Hill was also worried about the status of the force, which he was trying to sort out with the Department of External Affairs after he had received a draft suggestion in a message on 6 August on how to approach the Vietnamese. Part of that suggestion read: 'I have the honour to refer to recent discussions concerning the status of Australian service personnel sent by the Australian Government to Vietnam at the invitation of the Vietnamese Government'. The ambassador answered on 7 August, 'Assume you have received "invitation" for AATTV through the Viet Namese Embassy in Canberra'. He added that no official discussions had taken place in Saigon. The lack of diplomatic and lawful arrangements for the AATTV continued for three more months when the ambassador sent an additional notification to Canberra. 'By the time you receive this letter AATTV will have been in Viet Nam about three and a half months and nothing has been done to establish their legal status. I must say that this is a situation that causes some concern.'[59] External Affairs eventually advised the Secretary of the Department of Defence on 30 July 1963—almost twelve months later—

that a status of forces agreement for the AATTV had been resolved. The privileges, advantages and immunities granted by Vietnam to the personnel of the United States of America under the 'Pentilateral Agreement' signed on 23 December 1950 would be extended to the Australians. Before this, the men of the AATTV had no special privileges or exemptions from prosecution under Vietnamese law other than a quick flight out in the dark of night.

Another diplomatic matter that required attention was Article 16 of the Geneva Agreement of 1954, which prohibited the entry of any additional military personnel into Vietnam. Even though Australia had not signed the Agreement it felt morally obliged to respect the spirit of the articles. Should Australia inform the International Control Commission (ICC), the body overseeing the implentation of the Geneva Accords that established the partition of Vietnam into North and South, that they had despatched advisers to South Vietnam? The Minister for External Affairs decided not, that this was 'a matter for the South Vietnamese Government', and any formal notification would attract a citation from the ICC as evidence of a violation without serving a useful purpose, 'and it would cut across the established policies of America and South Vietnam'.

North Vietnam had lodged a complaint with the ICC in early June about Australia's intention to send troops. The fact that this was known and the troops were now in Vietnam could be handled by some diplomatic public relations. Australia's overseas posts were advised to argue that it was for Saigon to advise the ICC that they had permitted the troops to come, and the posts should repeat that the North had already put troops in the South, an earlier violation of the armistice.[60]

American troop numbers in Vietnam had crept up a little during the year and by the end of 1962 stood at just over 11,000, compared with 30 Australians who supposedly were designated 'priority targets and to be shot on sight'. This came from a low grade and very doubtful intelligence report that quoted a Cambodian newspaper, but sounded dramatic in Serong's monthly report for September.

A year of optimism

Australia settled its advisers into the MACV–MAAG system, somewhat to the bemusement of the Americans at Hiep Khanh. When the group of ten

Australians arrived at this isolated training camp northwest of Hue, they doubled the size of the advisory team, and the Americans didn't really understand why they were there. This confusion later bubbled into open conflict between an American major and Australian Captain Barry Tinkler over the fundamentals of counterinsurgency warfare. The Australians thought the Americans lacked basic infantry skills. The clash was calmed soon after by a natural rotation of American personnel, but the disagreement was indicative of the differences between a big army with worldwide responsibilities, whose strategies were governed by conventional warfare, and a small army that prided itself on an operational technique—jungle warfare—that matched its recent limited operational experiences in Southeast Asia.

Most of Vietnam's 'big picture' problems had been examined many times over by the American Country Team, later the US Mission Council, a select group of officials from the American Embassy staff, the military and other agencies in their development of the 1961 counterinsurgency plan.[61] This plan had three objectives: 'to suppress and defeat the communist guerrillas while maintaining a capability to meet overt aggression; to establish political stability, improve economic conditions, and instil a sense of unity among the people; and to interdict aid flowing to the insurgents across South Vietnam's borders'.[62] Military force was considered the immediate threat to Vietnam. The 234-page plan reasoned that terrorism could be eliminated by the presence of conventional armed forces. Thomas L. Ahern, Jr, later described the report in an analysis on pacification for the Center for the Study of Intelligence as being superficial and incoherent, with recommendations that amounted to nothing more than a compendium of program preferences from each of the agencies represented.[63]

Reports submitted in 1962, from both the Australian Embassy and through the American military chains of command, told of improvements by South Vietnam's armed forces. The Vietnamese were better trained, better equipped, more flexible in deployment, and more aggressive than in previous years. Overall intelligence methods had also improved. In a personal letter to the CGS, Serong declared that in twelve months 'September of this year [1962] . . . will be seen as the point at which this war turned in the Government's favour'. His conclusion was based upon increases in the numbers of ARVN operations, the logistical problems of the Viet Cong, the considerable increase in intelligence material coming from the local people and 'the stature and growth of the strategic hamlet program and the failure of the Viet Cong to block it'.[64]

Nonetheless considerable debate continued about the effectiveness of the hamlet program and the control of Vietnam's western borders with Laos and Cambodia. Robert Thompson's Delta Plan was absorbed into the Strategic Hamlet operation, which abandoned the aim of pacification in a previously agreed high priority region in favour of building lots of protective hamlets across the country. The Americans thought Thompson's plan was one of too many, too fast. All the agencies believed that much could be accomplished if specific step-by-step objectives were met in a less rushed time frame, and their gains were consolidated.

Training the Civil Guard and the Self Defence Corps to take over the static role of protecting villages and hamlets was making a tremendous demand on the American advisory and training capabilities, as was the provision of weapons and equipment under the Military Assistance Program. Both these Vietnamese forces now had strengths in excess of 60,000 and the Vietnamese wanted to increase those numbers still further. At one point, Diem asked for American agreement to a plan to bring in several thousand Special Forces personnel from Taiwan. The American Department of State rejected the idea for fear of antagonising Communist China. Unknown to most officials, there were some Nationalist Chinese already in Vietnam and they had been there for several months. They were providing support to covert operations under OPLAN 34A and 'special technical operations' with the *Sea Swallows*, an anti-communist village militia force led by the 'fighting priest' Father Nguyen Lac Hoa in the Ca Mau Peninsula area.[65]

Although there were some discussions about a possible increase to Australia's commitment, the detachment remained at 30. Colonel Serong told General Pollard in a series of 1962 reports that both the Civil Affairs Minister and the Interior Minister had asked him to make himself 'available on request . . . to discuss such aspects . . . [that] they might need my help on'. Serong added that he had told General Harkins, the US COMUSMACV, who thought it was a good thing and had encouraged him to take up the offer and had then come to him so that they could provide agreed-upon advice. Pollard told Serong to watch his step, as any advice that he offered had to be in accord with Australian government policy, not only with General Harkins' ideas. Australia's CGS also warned him to be careful in discussing SEATO plans; it would be a catastrophe, he advised, if Serong expressed views contrary to Defence thinking.

Pollard directed that 'the Ambassador must not only be kept fully in the picture, but concur in your actions and advice'. Once again Serong mentioned the potential for Australians to be deployed with the US Special Forces on village defence projects, which he said they could do because 'our good infantry NCOs are superior to the US SF [Special Forces] NCOs'. Furthermore he believed that it would be a wise move to get more senior Australian officers up to Vietnam into positions such as division senior adviser and deputy corps adviser. 'To have me'—he wrote in October 1962—'as the only authority on counterinsurgency for the Australian Army is quite intolerable'. The Americans were disturbed that they had to turn to Australia to provide essential guidance in the counterinsurgency program, he said, 'but I did not enlighten them that I was Australia's one and only'.[66]

The Australians who had served in Malaya during the Emergency, which Serong had not done, and Brigadier Hassett of the 28th Commonwealth Brigade would have disagreed with his sentiments. His comments were exaggerated. Many years later, in a filmed interview for the Australian Army Training Command, Serong recalled that the AATTV:

> Was going there [to Vietnam] to support the army that was a fact. We were doing that, but what occupied us much more was the support, advisory support and functional support, to what the CIA was doing. The CIA was really running the war.[67]

AATTV and the CIA

Contrary to Serong's assertion, the majority of the Australians were operating in army establishments that provided support for army-approved training programs. This was in accordance not only with the directive to Serong signed by the Deputy Chief of the General Staff on 25 July 1962 but also with the demands of Cabinet ministers, frequently expressed in correspondence between government departments.[68] The Team only had two officers deployed with a CIA program in Danang, which also had a training centre nearby at Hoa Cam. The CIA was not running the war; Robert McNamara, the American Secretary of Defense, and his generals were. The ultimate authority was the president, but all major items such as training, equipment, expansion of the Vietnamese armed forces, and strategic hamlet kits required McNamara's endorsement. McNamara even cancelled some tactical operations.

The much-maligned CIA's counterinsurgency role in the war grew out of a 1961 clash between Defense and the Department of State over the development of US policy in Vietnam. Following the Bay of Pigs fiasco in Cuba in April 1961, McNamara was directed by the president to come up with a plan to prevent communist domination of Vietnam.[69] Roswell Gilpatric, a Defense Deputy Secretary, and Edward Lansdale, now back in an air force uniform as a major general, did the heavy staff work to get an action program of 33 points approved by the president. The program designated the political, economic, military and psychological actions necessary 'to create . . . a viable and increasingly democratic society and to keep Vietnam free'. Included in the list was a supporting program of a 'covert character', which was approved by President Kennedy in National Security Action Memorandum 52, dated 11 May 1961.

Coincidentally, exactly one year earlier Vice-President Lyndon Johnson had arrived in Saigon, carrying a personal message from the president that assured Vietnam of more than moral support in their battle against communist aggression. When Johnson returned home, he reported that the introduction of combat troops into South Vietnam was unnecessary and undesirable. President Diem 'categorically rejected' even a consideration of introducing ground combat troops, but said that trainers and advisers were welcome. It was amid this build-up of support for a 170,000-man South Vietnamese force with attendant increases in support and advice for the Civil Guard and the Self Defence Corps that a special element was activated to concentrate on border control.

On 26 October 1961, John McCone, the Director of Central Intelligence, had authorised the start of a defence program among the Montagnard villages of the Central Highlands. Two Australian AATTV officers were attached to this program in August 1962, which also had a training centre near Danang at Hoa Cam. From November 1961, Special Forces teams from Okinawa were deployed to support the CIA's program which was now known as the Civilian Irregular Defence Group (CIDG). Buon Enao in Darlac Province was the first Montagnard village to get assistance from a CIA–Special Forces team. Captain Barry Petersen of the AATTV joined this group in September 1963 and extended its capabilities through the CIA–Combined Studies Division, his foster agency.

The Special Forces–CIA mix stirred a few rumbles of discontent from some of the generals. They believed that although the CIA operation was a very successful pacification program, it was not the type of operation to which Special Forces should be committed. Brigadier General William Yarborough, commander of the US Special Warfare Center, and Brigadier General William Rosson, Special Assistant to the Chief of Staff for Special Warfare, both reported that the Special Forces teams were being used incorrectly. They were disappointed that the teams were not being deployed in a more offensive role such as operations into Laos or North Vietnam. Three US National Security Action Memorandums (NSAM) were in play here. The first to be activated was NSAM 52, which was applied by Allen Dulles, who was replaced by John McCone at the CIA, to start the CIDG. Memorandums 55 and 57 transferred the balance of power back to the military, and some theorise that the president used them—especially Memorandum 55—to rein in the CIA's activities. When the AATTV arrived in Vietnam in August 1962, Operation Switchback had been triggered by Memorandum 57, which stipulated, in part, that:

Any large paramilitary operation wholly or partly covert which requires significant numbers of militarily trained personnel, amounts of military equipment which exceed normal CIA-controlled stocks and/or military experience of a kind and level peculiar to the Armed Services is properly the primary responsibility of the Department of Defense with the CIA in a supporting role.[70]

Several programs remained with the CIA, who made valiant efforts to extend their concept of pacification through several worthwhile concepts and one idea named the Phoenix Program that attracted more derision than compliments.

The real significance from these very high level studies and powerful arguments about winning in Vietnam was Australia's lack of military clout.

Diplomatically, the United States needed to have another flag flying to show support from the Free World, and the Americans were pleased with Australia for that. Militarily, the small group of highly experienced men of the AATTV disappeared into the amorphous green-clad mob. Despite a handful of remarkable personal achievements, size mattered. The Vietnamese knew where the big guns were. Even if their cultures were an ocean and a thousand years apart, the Vietnamese knew their survival came in dollars, ships and planes marked United States of America.

The battle at Ap Bac

All was going well, the optimism of 1962 had gained some momentum and the planners were now looking at a program of withdrawal for the US military to leave Vietnam, a plan that would see only minimal numbers remaining by 1965. Suddenly, Ap Bac crashed into centre stage. The hamlet was nestled among paddy fields to the west of My Tho, about 65 kilometres southwest of Saigon. A South Vietnamese Army and Civil Guard operation set out on 2 January 1963 to destroy a VC force and a radio station located near Ap Bac. According to Lieutenant Colonel John Vann, then senior adviser to the ARVN 7th Division, the enemy unit was bigger and more powerful than anticipated and the operation was a failure.

The advisers and the Vietnamese commanders exchanged insults about who was to blame. It mattered little. By now the international press had reported the battle as a debacle, a battle that was 'one of the most costly and humiliating defeats of the South Vietnamese army and its United States military advisers'.[71] The *Washington Post*'s damning indictments ran hot around the world's news services. Five US helicopters had been shot down. Three US advisers and 80 Civil Guard and ARVN had been killed and 100 wounded, against 20 enemy dead, although the figures were never agreed. Colonel Serong reported to Canberra that the press had exaggerated the results of the battle, nevertheless it was a mess. The Americans identified the main reasons, among a litany of complaints, as poor training, a complete lack of discipline in battle and, above all, a lack of a will to win. Colonel Daniel Porter, senior adviser at the headquarters of IV Corps, endorsed these 'many glaring weaknesses' when he made his report.

More reporters began to wonder what other war stories could be uncovered. Unfortunately for members of the American administration, there was more to be revealed. The administration had championed the lines that no US combat personnel were committed to the conflict, and that only the Vietnamese were fighting this war. When Farm Gate—a US–Vietnamese air operation—was discovered running around 1000 sorties a month and that they had taken casualties, it looked very much like Americans were in combat. They were. The Americans were told not to talk; no interviews were to be given on the subject. With more than 12,000 personnel in Vietnam, this was an impossible directive to control.

Diplomatic relations between Vietnam and the United States now fell into the language of expressing displeasure and were further exacerbated by the impression that Vietnam was becoming a US protectorate, as many junior advisers insisted on overriding Vietnamese officials in the completion of their day-to-day duties. Behind the scenes, the Vietnamese muttered that the Americans were impatient, overbearing bullies who paid little or no respect to the Vietnamese officials and, even worse, to the people. When Vice-President Johnson had visited, President Diem had said that they were not used to being asked what they wanted. The tales of resentment became stronger and both Diem and his brother Ngo Dinh Nhu complained that there were too many Americans in Vietnam. Diem told the American Ambassador, but Nhu told the *Washington Post* that half of them could be sent home and 'the other half exposed themselves too readily to enemy fire'. At this point, the numbers of US personnel exceeded 13,000 and another 1900 were on the way.

No hunting in the hills

Australia's contingent of 30 had no such problems; they were bored. Not long after they had arrived in 1962, some of the officers were annoyed that they were not permitted to go hunting in the hills and now, in 1963, they felt inadequate because they were not permitted to engage in combat operations. Sir Wilfred Kent-Hughes, a distinguished former Australian soldier and politician, took up their case, after a personal visit to Vietnam in March. He asked the Australian government why experts were being sent to Vietnam when they were prohibited from going into the jungle, thus restricting their operations to basic training. If this directive was considered wise, why were the men being sent for such long periods of duty? In reply, the Minister for the Army stated that the men were there at the invitation of the government of Vietnam. They were there to guide the efforts of the South Vietnamese instructors in training establishments where their expertise could best be employed. Predictably, he denied that they were prohibited from going into the jungle.

This was true, but they were banned from going into the jungle on combat operations. This argument was a silly word association between 'jungle' and 'combat', as if battles only took place in the jungle. The minister did acknowledge the difficulty associated with such a ban when he said that a Vietnamese company had been ambushed on their way home from a training area. Luckily the Australian instructor had departed before the ambush occurred, a comment that displayed a lack of empathy for the Vietnamese troops killed. As for the length of duty, it was considered appropriate considering the need to acclimatise and allow the men 'to become fully conversant with the weapons, doctrines and techniques used by the Vietnamese [emphasised]'.[72] Unbeknown to the politicians, a few of the AATTV had been permitted to observe some combat operations near Danang and in the Central Highlands at Kontum. Ray Simpson—later awarded a Victoria Cross and a Distinguished Conduct Medal—was detached to the US Special Forces village defence program at Lao Bao, very close to the border with Laos along Route 9, and then at the village of Khe Sanh.

Sergeant Bill Hacking: The controversy

Perversely, it was during a detachment to observe how a Vietnamese battalion operated in the jungle that the Team took its first casualty when Sergeant Bill Hacking died on 1 June 1963. His death has been the subject of a lot of speculation and misleading comment ever since.[73] Captain Bob Hagerty and Sergeant Hacking were patrolling with an ARVN battalion in the mountains well to the northwest of Hue. The battalion was moving in extremely difficult terrain along a high narrow ridgeline where they had stopped, not only to rest, but also to allow the ridge to be cleared ahead. Soon after, a shot was heard and Hagerty turned immediately to where Bill Hacking was lying on his back with his head on his pack and found him dead. There were no enemy nearby and no Vietnamese had fired a shot. A court of inquiry in Vietnam investigated his death and concluded that 'while handling his weapon [Hacking] was killed by the accidental discharge of that weapon'.[74]

During the inquiry and over subsequent years, numerous rumours about Hacking's death circulated among members of the Australian Army. One rumour claimed that an ARVN soldier had murdered Bill Hacking. This gossip was supported by so-called undeniable information that Hacking was shot in the back. A post-mortem report clearly showed that the claim lacked credibility. The position of his carbine after the shot, the angle of the bullet's penetration and powder burns on Sergeant Hacking's forehead did not support the court's conclusion.[75] Why was such a bad verdict allowed to stand? The answer to that question is in the realm of speculation. Australia had always described this group of 30 soldiers as handpicked, highly trained and war-experienced jungle experts. The possibility of one of them taking his life was unthinkable. This would be seen as the act of a soldier unfit for combat duty and that would be a slight against the commander who had said he personally selected each man. Sadly, Sergeant Hacking was an unhappy man whose anxieties—expressed in letters to his girlfriend—may be traced back to his service in Korea. It was possible that he carried mental scars from Korea that might have precluded him going to Vietnam if a better selection procedure had been in place. But two arms, two legs, two eyes and cough were sufficient to be stamped fit; traumatic war-stress and the brain remained an unknown.

Sergeant Hacking's body was returned to Australia and he was interred at Springvale Cemetery in Victoria. This was approved at Commonwealth expense, which does not seem exceptional, but after this death others who were killed in Vietnam were not returned home at public expense until a change in policy was enacted in January 1966.

Serong meets Diem and goes to America

Following Robert McNamara's personal takeover of 'command' in November 1961, a stream of high level US officials visited Vietnam to analyse and report on the most effective ways and means to win this ever-increasing and worrying conflict. Roger Hilsman from the Department of State was impressed by Robert Thompson's ideas and his report to President Kennedy echoed many of Thompson's concepts. According to Hilsman, the president was also impressed by them.

Colonel Serong got his chance to present his thoughts on a counter-insurgency plan in May 1963 when he was invited to Fort Bragg, the home of the American Army's Special Forces. Before Serong travelled to the United States, President Diem invited Ambassador Brian Hill and Colonel Serong to the presidential palace for discussions. This drawn-out visit to the palace, which took place over two days, 4–5 May 1963, is the only meeting between Colonel Serong and President Diem recorded in the AATTV commander's reports.[76] Serong told the president that the successful operations of the ARVN's 25th Division at Quang Ngai were the result of the AATTV's efforts. This was an overly boastful claim considering that South Vietnam had sent several hundred of its officers and NCOs through a continuing cycle of training courses at the British Jungle Warfare School at Kota Tinggi in Malaya, which specialised in jungle warfare. Furthermore, the Australians in Vietnam did not control the program of instruction for the ARVN at the Vietnamese training centres. Although there may have been some minor tweaking of a local training base's program and some improvement in the methods of instruction, the overwhelming tactical emphasis was American. Serong also told the president that Vietnam was in a 'favourable position', but warned against prematurely extending the Strategic Hamlet Program, a recommendation that the Americans made frequently as well.

In reply, Diem provided a detailed explanation of every province in Vietnam that included his strategic view as well as his belief that he could raise more troops to increase his resources and achieve his vision. The problem was one of focus; Diem's plans called for simultaneous actions that would weaken the total plan and the United States would not support the raising of more troops, Serong said later in a written report.[77] Diem's request to talk with the Australians appeared to be a means by which he could send an informal message to Washington for its continued support to, in his words, 'maintain and extend the machinery of democracy [South Vietnam] against communism'.

The Americans believed that the manpower barrel was almost empty. Although South Vietnam had 500,000 under arms, they were scattered between the ARVN, Civil Guard, Self Defence Corps, CID Group, Hamlet Militia, Montagnard Commandos, Force Populaire, Republican Youth, Catholic Youth, independent groups controlled by Catholic priests, and an army controlled by a businessman in Vung Tau. Diem also expressed his disappointment at not having an Australian training school at Quang Ngai. He wanted 'to give us that task, comparable to the effort at the Dardanelles', Serong reported.[78]

In a different context later on—the colonel wrote in his report—the president mentioned that a disaster at Quang Ngai would have led to massive third-nation intervention. According to Serong this meant a deployment like the Dardanelles was code for a planned treachery against the Australians. As mentioned earlier, the Quang Ngai proposal had had Australian support but General Harkins' strong objections saw it shelved. No one saw the proposed training centre as a trap, even if that is what Diem had in mind. The only trap the Australians recognised was the one that would have them provide all the administrative support without American assistance if they wished to pursue an independent operation in the province. That was beyond Australia's capabilities. Interestingly, the successful 25th Division was the unit that had been raised and stationed in Quang Ngai in June 1962 to provide protection for the proposed training base.

A few days later, a Buddhist demonstration in Hue was the first indication of serious internal trouble that lay ahead for Diem's regime. The self-immolation of Thich Quang Duc, a Buddhist monk, on 11 June 1963, attracted worldwide attention. Journalist and photographer Malcolm Browne's image of a monk all but engulfed by flames, rigid in the lotus position, without expressions of pain or fear, mesmerised and troubled millions. Shortly afterwards, near Nha Trang, Warrant Officer Don Dalton of the AATTV witnessed a ritual suicide at close quarters.

> I was coming back from the Swamp Camp [a training facility] one day and we had to go through the little town of Ninh Hoa. As we got to the village square, there were a whole lot of people standing around and I decided to stop and have a look at what was going on. My little driver did not want me to do this. Now, in the middle of the square, a Buddhist monk was sitting down he got a can of petrol, he opened it, tipped it across himself and set himself alight. I was speechless!

I was absolutely speechless! I didn't know what to say. I had never seen anything like it before, nor have I since, and it torments me to this day, just watching that happen.[79]

Serong left for his visit to Fort Bragg on 6 May 1963, but just before his departure Lieutenant General John Wilton, who had replaced General Pollard as the CGS in January 1963, directed that Serong's reports also go to the Australian Army element located with the British Far East Land Force. Although this Singapore-based headquarters was the AATTV's senior administrative unit, Serong rarely told them what he was doing. He certainly didn't send them a copy of the demi-official notes that he wrote to the CGS. Wilton's directive brought about a detectable change of tone in the relationship between the CGS and his commander in Vietnam, especially when Serong's visit to the United States got underway. Wilton and some officials in the diplomatic corps were nervous about letting Serong loose in an environment where a few ill-chosen comments could have severe repercussions that would affect not only the US–Vietnam relationship, but also the SEATO and ANZUS networks.

According to Anne Blair in her biography *Ted Serong*, Serong's tactical presentations on counter-ambush techniques and saturation patrolling went well at Fort Bragg. (His comments about Americans in Vietnam 'making themselves notoriously vulnerable' by moving in single file appear to have been added well after the event, since there were no US ground combat troops in Vietnam in 1963.) After his Fort Bragg visit, Serong went to Washington where the Defense and State departments were making arrangements for him to meet a group of officials that included Governor Averell Harriman, the Assistant Secretary of State for Far Eastern Affairs. The Australian Embassy told Canberra that the ambassador would be present during any meeting with Harriman and they would have an officer present at any other discussions arranged with the Department of State. There is no evidence in the correspondence from the Australian Embassy in Washington, or in the pages of the president's diary, to support later claims that Serong met with President Kennedy.[80]

On 23 May Serong met with the Special Group for Counterinsurgency. Members of this group included Averell Harriman, who chaired the meeting; John McCone, CIA Director; Robert Kennedy, the Attorney General; Michael

Forrestal, a White House adviser; William Bundy, Defense Assistant Secretary; and Major General Victor Krulak, USMC. Serong told them that 'we are winning the war', that the trends were favourable but there were problems with the press. He said the big success story was the Strategic Hamlet Program, although there were problems with it being overextended, which would allow the Viet Cong to penetrate areas already cleared. The matters pertaining to the hamlet program were not his views alone and had been discussed with others including President Diem and General Harkins, but there were some differences of opinion in those discussions, Serong said later. The minutes of the Special Group's meeting convey nothing out of the ordinary. Nonetheless, according to David Halberstam in *The Best and the Brightest*, General Krulak 'violently' challenged Serong's supposed doubts about the hamlet program. Krulak was the Special Assistant for Counter Insurgency and Special Activities, a position President Kennedy had directed be designated within the Joint Staff.[81] Krulak was not a man to have on your dark side.

Serong had also commented on the strategic hamlets in an interview with the *Times of Vietnam* in March, just two months before the Special Group meeting.

> The Viet Cong had no answer to the Strategic Hamlet Program, and . . ., besides, they were being challenged by a growing South Vietnamese Army bolstered by American personnel and equipment. . . . the ordinary Viet Cong province and hamlet guerrilla . . . are simply what we call in many countries juvenile delinquents that the Viet Cong had lured . . . in the countryside with an aura of romantic adventure.[82]

All in all, the Washington visit went well and the American civilians (Department of State) thought that Serong's explanations were most helpful but as Howard Beale, the Australian Ambassador at Washington, reported on his return to Saigon, Serong might 'find that his relations with his American service colleagues may not be as harmonious as in the past'.[83] Many commentators believe that his statements about the hamlet program would have caused this, but Serong's assessments were no more critical than what the Americans already understood and with which most agreed. The danger came from his providing Washington critics of the military establishment with comments that supported their view that the military didn't understand the political objectives of the war. Although supportive of Serong, Beale tarred him with the same brush when he reported that Serong had acquitted himself very ably on professional matters, but was less impressive when questioned about matters of policy.

General Wilton read about the next leg of Serong's long absence from Vietnam in a newspaper cutting that said Serong was in Munich. Wilton asked his aide: 'What on earth is that bloody man up to now?'[84] Serong did not return to Saigon until 6 June, after an absence of 31 days.

Indonesian sabre-rattling

General Wilton's elevation to the top Army job in 1963 came at a time when Australia's defence nervousness was wound up a notch or two. His first task was to save and strengthen the Australian Army as the regional future looked somewhat bleak. Indonesia kept declaring its dislike of the proposed Malaysian Federation, and that meant a potential for problems in New Guinea. Not only did these perceived threats mean a need for more money and equipment across the three Australian services, but more manpower was needed, especially for the Army. National service was considered in April 1963, but Cabinet was advised against adopting a selective service program.

At this stage, Australian forces were deployed in Malaya and forces were also earmarked for a possible SEATO commitment, a separate obligation to the group in Malaya. The inappropriateness of the Army's Pentropic organisation must have been obvious when 3RAR was nominated to replace 2RAR in Malaya. The battalion had to reduce in size from a large five-company unit to a lighter Tropical Warfare establishment before its deployment. Although Wilton was involved with the introduction of the Pentropic organisation, he later said that he had not agreed with the concept. (The US Army's 21 June 1963 reorganisation of its 'cumbersome' Pentomic divisions into a modified triangular division structure may have influenced Australian Defence planners as well.) The need for fewer men was an advantage that favoured Tropical Warfare battalions and, with the current manpower shortage, allowed the savings from 3RAR to go to 4RAR, a new battalion to be raised in South Australia in February 1964.

The sabre-rattling by Indonesia turned nasty in September 1963 when President Sukarno declared the Malaysian Federation illegal. Britain asked for Australian forces to join with them to protect the new federation when rioters attacked diplomatic posts in Jakarta. At first, a mixture of troops was recommended. This included 3RAR, which was in the country now known as Malaysia. That meant that this battalion was not available for any SEATO request. Nevertheless, Australia declared it would provide military help if needed. However, with one battalion overseas and only one of the two regular battalions at home classified as deployable, the commanders would run short of manpower very quickly. A deteriorating situation in South Vietnam refocused the attention of the Australian Defence chiefs and their political masters away from Malaysia, but Australia's limited military resources posed a critical question on what could be provided.

Buddhist unrest

In Vietnam, the earlier displays of unrest by the Buddhists in Hue and increasingly hard-handed actions being used against them by Diem, his brother Nhu and Nhu's wife, the infamous Madame Nhu, had damaged the reputations of the South Vietnamese leadership group in the eyes of the West. British expert Robert Thompson said that without Diem the South would lose the war. Henry Lodge, the American Ambassador, held a contradictory opinion when he told Washington, 'There is no possibility, in my view, that the war can be won under a Diem administration'. Australia also joined the anti-Diem bandwagon with messages transmitted through the External Affairs network that expressed a lack of support for Diem. In a cable to Washington and London on 26 August 1963, the department conveyed a view that 'we [Australia] should seek a leadership in South Vietnam, which will command respect internally and internationally, but Diem, in recent months, had not lived up to these requirements'.[85] Some support still existed for Diem but only if he got rid of the Nhu family, which was highly unlikely. Then there was the other unanswered question of who would replace him.

Serong reported to Australia that South Vietnam was in a 'state of siege' during August 1963 when he advised the CGS not to come on a visit. By now rumours about a possible coup were circulating; many thought the coup was being encouraged by either the US Department of State officers or the CIA, or even by some of the most senior officials of Kennedy's inner circle. Several former Australian External Affairs officers have suggested that the Catholic Church had indicated a lessening in their support for Diem, which would have severely damaged his chance of retaining the presidency. This anecdotal evidence was supported in their opinion by an article in the *Milan Catholic Weekly*, circa August 1963, which referred to Diem's Catholic government 'and the difficulty of the Buddhist'. It was 'not possible to be on the side of the former', the article concluded.[86]

The diplomatic wire services were rife with suggestions that a feeler had been put out for rapprochement between the North and the South. Thompson met with Serong in September to discuss the current political power grouping within Vietnam, which Thompson said would have difficulty surviving over the next few months. He also expressed a rather startling point of view that 'we [the West] are forcing them to fight'. Serong disagreed and reported to Australia that 'there had been an improvement in the US–VN relations', which in his opinion would see the current dispute simmer down to minor dimensions.[87] Meanwhile the war in the provinces was running hot. The basic rural infrastructure of the South was under sustained attack. North of Saigon, many houses were destroyed in a battle that caused nearly 200 casualties and the loss of more than 100 weapons.

The coup of 1963

In September 1963, an article in the *Times of Vietnam* accused the CIA of financing a coup. The accusation was dismissed as preposterous by senior officials in Vietnam. But, unbeknown to many, a small group of second-rank officials at Defense and the Department of State had drafted a crucial message to Ambassador Lodge that sealed Diem's fate. Assistant Secretary for Far East Affairs Roger Hilsman released the so-called 'green light' message of 24 August, which was seen as the signal that the US government would not continue to support Diem if improvements were not made to relations with the Buddhists. Nhu also had to go. There were misgivings and some powerful arguments among the senior members of the US administration that split the president's advisers into two distinct groups of coup and anti-coup. Even their latter-day memories still conflict.

Following the 'Hilsman cable', President Kennedy convened a number of meetings at the White House specifically to thrash out whether the United States should support a coup or not. The Australian Ambassador rated a mention in a record of these events made by John Prados at the National Security Archive. He wrote that there was no mention in Hilsman's summary of the 27 August meeting about Frederick Nolting's (the immediate past US Ambassador to Vietnam) account that the Australian Ambassador had been asked to invite Madame Nhu to his country to get her out of South Vietnam.

Notes and tape recordings of the White House meetings up to and including 29 August 1963 provide some insight into the president's decision-making process on the support or otherwise for a coup. On the 29th, Kennedy approved a message be sent to Ambassador Lodge in Saigon that said what had previously been conveyed by CIA officers now represented the policy of the US government. General Harkins was to obtain more details of the plot and the Vietnamese generals were to be told the coup would get US support if it had a good chance of succeeding, but no US forces were to be involved.[88]

Serong and Thompson met again on 29 October to discuss the latest information in an analysis that Thompson had done on how to live with the Diem regime. According to Washington, a coup was imminent on 30 October. On 31 October, Serong left Saigon on a visit to Nha Trang and then to Ban Me Thuot in the Central Highlands. The coup was activated on 1 November. Much to the embarrassment of the United States, General Harkins allegedly sent a message 40 minutes before the attack, saying that MACV has no information from advisory personnel which could be interpreted as clear evidence of an impending coup. In other words, MACV had no information that a coup was about to take place.

Colonel Serong was also caught out; he was stuck in Ban Me Thuot, more than mildly agitated by his lack of knowledge about the events. He managed to get back to Saigon on a mail plane, and from there reported that the coup was 'quite a smooth operation' with the Military Council headed by General Duong Van Minh in firm control and a carnival atmosphere evident in Saigon.

Unexpectedly, Major Nguyen Van Nhung—who was executed in 1964—assassinated Ngo Dinh Diem and his brother Ngo Dinh Nhu during the coup on 2 November 1963. This shocked President Kennedy, who only survived them by three weeks before he was killed in Dallas, Texas, on 21 November 1963. His death shocked the world.

Australians were provided with the opportunity to change their government through the ballot box. An early election was called for the House of Representatives on 30 November 1963, which the Liberal/Country Party Coalition won with an increased majority by 72 to 52 seats.

Serong gets a reprimand

Earlier in 1963, General Harkins had complimented 'Colonel Sarong [*sic*]' on the AATTV's impressive achievements over the past year. Nonetheless a November 1963 memorandum from Serong that involved the American Ambassador angered Harkins. He was extremely annoyed by Serong's statement that Harkins' large headquarters was nothing more than a group of professional data gatherers. He was so incensed that he censured Serong:

> [Your statement was] a gross and unsoldierly affront, to me, to my staff, and to my superiors and I must insist, that you, as Senior Officer, Australian Army Training Team Vietnam (AATTV), attached to my staff, operate in accordance with the spirit of the reference in the future.[89]

Several points of interest arise from this exchange. First, Serong's monthly report implies that he briefed the American Ambassador *personally* [emphasised] on 10 December. Harkins' letter refers to 'your memorandum *delivered* [emphasised] to the U.S. Ambassador, 10 Dec 1963'. In his letter of explanation to the Australian Ambassador, Serong explained that 'in some extraordinary fashion, he [Harkins] *was shown a memorandum record of the points of conversation* [emphasised]', which supposedly came out of his meeting with the American Ambassador. In 1994, Serong mentioned this episode in an interview with Anne Blair. 'I was already under some surveillance for rocking the MACV boat and contributing to the removal of Harkins', he told her.[90] If that was so, it was a rather nasty betrayal of his senior officer, as he had told the Australian Ambassador twice that 'having said his piece he reverts to being a loyal servant of General Harkins'.[91]

Someone did not tell the truth about how the information was provided to Ambassador Lodge. Furthermore Serong's assessment of the war had now altered from 'we are winning the war'—in May 1963—to telling the ambassador that the war would be over in 1964. On that point he was almost prophetic. The coming year would be politically and militarily messy. Major General Nguyen Khanh led another coup against the leaders of the 1963 rebellion in January 1964. Khanh believed a group of rabidly pro-French generals in the Military Council was talking about neutralism. Many others believed that he did not get a fair share of the spoils last time around and had decided to counter-balance the scales in his favour. The Australian commander reported to Canberra that the advisers had no knowledge of this coup at all, which was not correct. The Americans knew; he did not.

Back in Australia, the Defence Committee faced increasing demands for their advice on the use of Australian troops in Malaysia. At first, the Menzies government thought that there was no need for help, but then Indonesia attacked a Malaysian police station in Sabah in December 1963. This prompted Malaysia to ask for assistance from the British Far East forces, in particular for the use of the Australian 3RAR for duty on the Thai border. The Australian Cabinet approved the request and the battalion operated on the border between February and April 1964.

Disobedient combat duty

In South Vietnam Sergeant Ray Simpson was attached to the Village Defence project at Khe Sanh village in October 1962. Soon after, in May 1963, Australian advisers were authorised to 'cooperate and participate in operations' at company level with the 1st Infantry Division, ARVN. The only restriction imposed was one from the Vietnamese that required US advisers to be present also.[92] Serong pushed more of his advisers out into likely combat locations in 1964. Men from the recently closed Hiep Khanh training centre were sent to the US Special Forces at Danang, and the more dangerous camps at An Diem, Khe Sanh, A Shau and Kham Duc. As a result, there was an immediate increase in contacts with the enemy.

In March 1964, Captain Noel De La Hunty used strike aircraft and armed helicopters to hold back VC attacks while he extracted his patrol from an area near the border with Laos. A few weeks later, he was wounded slightly while out with a CIDG patrol from An Diem when the group came under enemy fire over seven separate days. De La Hunty was awarded a Military Cross for his courage and professional ability under dangerous and exhausting conditions. Also in April 1964, Warrant Officer George Chinn and Captain Rex Clark were attached to 32 Ranger Battalion on an operation in the Ba Long Valley, southwest of Quang Tri. Chinn was awarded a Distinguished Conduct Medal for his courage, calmness and devotion to duty during this operation.

Serong had previously indicated in his reports that he intended to get the men out and into more active roles, contrary to the political directive that the Team be involved in training only. Army knew this but did not stop it, which was very risky, particularly if some of the advisers were to be killed in combat. There was clearly a distinct difference in understanding between Defence, Army and the politicians about what the AATTV was doing and what the real conditions were in Vietnam. There is little doubt that Canberra-based officers viewed Vietnam through a Malayan Emergency prism and to them the picture was one of a tactically challenging counterinsurgency problem, but not an overly dangerous duty. No medal had been created for service in South Vietnam and there was no approved scale of awards for gallant and distinguished service. In the big scheme, perhaps this was meaningless but as an element of morale it left much to be desired, as did the imbroglio over foreign awards that followed. Bitterness among veterans about these things remains today.

It is not well known that a few Australians were attached to the CIA to operate within some of their programs. Barry Petersen's time in the Central Highlands is detailed in his book *Tiger Men* and Frank Walker's *The Tiger Man of Vietnam*, which tell of the continuation and improvement on an earlier CIA–Special Forces effort around Buon Enao in Darlac Province.[93]

The Australians who served with the CIA–Combined Studies Division (CSD) (men such as Peter Young, John Healy, Guy Boileau, Ian Teague and Jim Devitt) have been labelled irreverently as spooks and assassins. In reality while their tasks were a little more exotic than the ordinary soldier's and in some cases more adventurous, in most instances, by necessity, they were involved in the mundane gathering of information about and taking action against the NLF's infrastructure. Their efforts were seen as controversial because they attempted to ferret out the 'political' arm of the Viet Cong, which attracted greater secrecy. Contrarily, everyone knew them and most knew what they did. None of the Australians crossed the borders on clandestine operations, and it is extremely doubtful that any conducted a personal assassination, although they may have identified people who were killed by others later. The Australians did operate successfully within several CIA programs such as the People's Action Teams (PAT). It was this program that attracted an anonymous Australian major general, described as 'impressive and intelligent' by Peer de Silva, the CIA Station Chief, when they met in mid-1964, who arranged for some Australians to be attached to it. They came from the AATTV. The major general was probably Sir Walter Cawthorn, the head of ASIS.

Civic action programs were not new. Brigadier General Edward Lansdale had gone searching for social action committees in the back alleys of Saigon-Cholon in the mid-1950s. They were part of a concept initiated by the Vietnamese to help themselves to improve their living conditions. The committees concentrated upon trying to establish the staples of a satisfied community: security, health and education. Civic Action Teams followed. The teams came from Michigan State University's training centre for government administration, which ran a course that emphasised service in rural communities. It included an effort to improve the rural police, but it was extremely difficult to entice government workers away from Saigon.

President Diem had seen a ready answer with the influx of refugees from the North. They were strongly anti-communist and he got them to join the program on a promise of work within the southern administration. Subsequently, a training centre for civic action was established and a variety of social action methods was attempted in some rural communities. In one undertaking, a good drivers course was conducted for the army. However, it proved to be a hopeless endeavour. As soon as they graduated, the drivers sped off down a narrow village track, oblivious to the mayhem they left behind them. In another effort, teams of wandering minstrel–like groups performed a variety of playlets that told the people about their good government and the bad communists. Lansdale also used the Chinese Communist 8th Route Army's 'eight noteworthy points' that emphasised such things as to buy and sell fairly, to return anything borrowed, and not to bathe in view of women but lamented that not many on the southern side understood that adherence to such rules would unite the army with the people.

After Operation Switchback in August 1962, the CIA did not really want to get back into rural pacification. It was an intelligence agency, argued those against the organisation's involvement in pacification. By 1964 in the Tu Nghia district of Quang Ngai Province, a very successful propaganda and political action program begun in 1963 convinced de Silva to increase CIA support alongside the agencies of the United States Information Service (USIS) and the United States Operations Mission (USOM). Captain Ian Teague (AATTV) was deployed to a 'commando team' in 1964. US Army Major Haskell, the province's senior military adviser, later reported it was the only Popular Force unit of any worth in the province. The Civil Guard and the Self Defence Corps had been respectively renamed the 'Regional Force' and 'Popular Force' or, more facetiously, the 'Ruff-Puffs'. After an orientation period with Teague's group, Captain Jim Devitt established a similar operation in Binh Dinh Province in early 1965.

1964: Doom and gloom

The year 1964 turned into something of a doom and gloom chapter. Behind the scenes, Serong's behaviour was under an External Affairs spotlight. The United States had expressed reservations about some of his talk and Sir Arthur Tange, head of External Affairs, asked Ambassador David Anderson in Saigon and Alan Renouf who was at the embassy in Washington to report on these concerns. Both men agreed that there was no question of Serong's recall, but advised his tour should not be extended. Anderson added: 'There should be no question of any trace of blame attached to an officer who has the courage to voice unpopular truths'.[94]

In a postscript to their report, Anderson said that he had a hint that demands for a bigger Australian effort might soon be forthcoming. Furthermore a paper by Serong entitled 'Formation of a Federation—Vietnam, Laos [and] Cambodia' found its way to the CGS in April. In the paper's introduction, Serong wrote that we are on the defensive: philosophically, against Chinese-inspired Communism; politically, against French-inspired neutralism; tactically, against VC aggression; and spiritually, against the commercialism of the Saigon bourgeoisie. He fleshed out the document with statements on the following themes: We are reactive, We need room, We have tremendous power but lack the room to use it, The leadership of Vietnam is inadequate, and We face a lowering public morale. 'In short'—he wrote—'we need a new deal, a bigger deal', one that would lift our effort from a 'dirty little war' to a 'Grand Challenge'.[95]

There is something disturbing in the tone of that excerpt. Was it his wish to wage war against China, or to establish a new imperial regional sphere? The central theme of his paper was the formation of a federation, 'a new sovereign state, to comprise: Laos, Cambodia, South Vietnam and Montagna [the highlands for the Montagnards] [and] on our terms North Vietnam'. No wonder the CGS scribbled across the bottom of the page: 'I wonder what EA [External Affairs] reaction to a document like this would be?' He also wanted to know who else had a copy of the document. (One who did was General Harkins, COMUSMACV.) Serong recognised that the concept of a federation would require 'a greater display of diplomatic skill than has yet been revealed in South East Asia'. The Australian diplomats were extremely worried; there were suggestions that the minister (unnamed) should speak to Serong, or that he should be 'approved' to be out of the country during a planned Australian parliamentary delegation's visit later in 1964. In his note upon the paper, the Deputy Chief of General Staff wrote 'interesting and I believe original'.[96]

Given that Serong was friendly with Major General Cawthorn (ASIS), who had been the Deputy Chief of General Staff of Pakistan's army between 1948 and 1951, and later Australia's High Commissioner to Pakistan, the Serong paper read very much like the formation of Pakistan. In brief, Pakistan was intended as the grouping of P̲unjab, A̲fghania, K̲ashmir and I̲ndus-Sind with addition of 'stan' ('land'). The Pakistan vision was for a country that would have strategic depth, or room to fight against India. This proposed Southeast Asian Federation in fact sounded like nothing more than rehashed French colonialism or worse.

In one paragraph Serong wrote that the war 'was too complex and difficult a matter to leave in the hands of the Vietnamese, Cambodians, Laotians or Montagnard'. In another he suggested that such a federation would encourage Vietnam's dreams of reviving the glories of the past, something he admitted would need to be played softly. Statements like these were diplomatic poison.

If the contents of the paper were to be revealed, these and other high risk phrases made the paper a piece of psychological-warfare dynamite for the enemy and the western political opponents of the war. The fact that the North Vietnamese leadership saw Indochina as the battlefield and had continually flouted the 1962 Agreement on Laos would be immaterial. The magic words 'American neo-colonialism' coloured western images and would draw attention away from the North Vietnamese Army's movement along Laos's highways 7, 8 and 12 into the Plain of Jars and around Tchepone as well.

More troops and the Gulf of Tonkin incidents

As Ambassador Anderson had predicted in April, a cable from the United States did arrive in which the Americans suggested what additional troops Australia might be capable of providing to their efforts in Vietnam. As a result, the Defence Committee recommended that 30 more advisers be sent to the AATTV, cautioning that this might result in casualties—a point Serong considered would be humorous, if it were not so stupid. During the committee's deliberations, an official from Defence noted that the initial directive to AATTV was an edict for them to be engaged in training and not to go on operations. Although Serong had continued to push for them to be released to go out with their units and he had sent some out, formal approval had not yet been granted for him to do so.

The government approved the increase in the number of advisers and Senator Paltridge, the Minister for Defence, announced on 8 June 1964 that the Team had been increased to 60 and that the training personnel would now be employed in the field at battalion and lower levels. AATTV's politically disobedient combat deployments now had the stamp of approval. Interestingly, at a Honolulu conference held over 1–2 June 1964, the United States also allowed their field advisers to be assigned permanently to battalion and provincial levels, with the agreement of the Vietnamese. Vietnamese concurrence was not mentioned in the Australian approval process. A flight of six RAAF Caribou aircraft was also authorised to go to Vietnam and they started to arrive in August 1964. In accordance with the recommendation to Arthur Tange by his diplomats that Serong's tour not be extended, the Military Secretary told Serong in May that Colonel David Jackson would replace him as commander of the AATTV and that he would go to the Director of Infantry's position.

Serong was not happy. He wrote to Major General Hassett, DCGS, to tell him that Australia's success in Vietnam was the result of his 'prestige in this field'. To remove him from the scene would take away from both the Vietnamese and the United States their only guide. He added that there were plenty of 'bright young men' who could be the Director of the Infantry Corps. 'Unfortunately, there is no one else who can do this job. Once I go you can fold up the map of Vietnam, because however tenuously, inadequately and indirectly (and fruitlessly!) the only strategic direction this war gets is from me.'[97] There are several self-confessed good reasons in that sentence for him to be replaced.

A little later in the year, General Wilton had had enough and told Hassett to place Serong *under command* COMUSMACV. This was done in the revision of the Directive to the Commander AATTV, dated 27 July 1964. The directive raises an interesting point of military law: did that order place the AATTV under command of the American general? This was a question neither asked nor tested.

Earlier in the month, on 6 July, Warrant Officer Kevin Conway was killed immediately at the start of a battle at the Nam Dong Special Forces camp, an isolated base located 50 kilometres west-northwest of Danang. Ambassador Anderson and Colonel Serong visited the camp the next day and the AATTV commander noted that some of the enemy dead were in regular uniform. He reported that they appeared to be from the recently infiltrated PAVN (North Vietnamese Army) *304th Division*. Although Serong placed a question mark after the unit's identification in his notes, elements of the *304th Division* were not found in the South until 1965.

Around the same time Australia was still in difficulties over the commitment of an infantry battalion to Borneo, but an engineer squadron was sent to Sabah in June 1964. Not long afterwards, in August, North Vietnamese torpedo boats reportedly attacked the US warships USS *Maddox* and *C Turner Joy* in the Gulf of Tonkin. Although there is no doubt that the *Maddox* was attacked on 2 August—the North Vietnamese admitted that—a second encounter on 4 August during which the *C Turner Joy* engaged targets '*seen on radar only*' in a two-hour-long battle, proved false.[98]

These clashes were complicated by the fact that a South Vietnamese commando force had raided the North Vietnamese islands in the Gulf of Tonkin known as Hon Me and Hon Niem on 30 July. Arguments among historians persist that the American destroyers were providing electronic intelligence support for the raids by detecting such things as North Vietnamese radar and radio transmissions, although *Maddox* was 120 miles away on 30 July. The US Joint Chiefs of Staff vehemently denied that there was a connection between the two. One line of the argument discussed in *The Pentagon Papers* had it that the raids and the warship deployment were provocation so that a proposed bombing campaign against the North would gain more support among Johnson's advisers.[99]

As a result of the clashes, President Johnson approved 'a one-time maximum effort against petrol, oil and lubricant facilities at Vinh and the north's patrol boat bases'. Only carrier-based aircraft were to be used and the strikes were known as Operation Pierce Arrow. Johnson then requested the Congress to approve a resolution that permitted him to take all necessary steps, including the use of armed force, to assist any member or protocol state of the Southeast Asia Collective Defence Treaty (SEATO). The resolution was known as the Gulf of Tonkin Resolution and the House of Representatives passed it on 7 August by a vote of 416:0 and the Senate approved it 88:2. The resolution permitted the president to wage war beyond the constraints previously applied to a president by the checks and balances of Congress.[100]

These events brought the Australian Defence Committee's attention back to Vietnam, but this refocus did not last long.

The dominoes start to wobble

Indonesia parachuted guerrilla troops into the Malaysian state of Johore on 17 August 1964. In early September, when more Indonesian troops were deployed in an abortive sea raid near Malacca, Indonesia and Malaysia were nearly at war. Indonesia had demonstrated it was backing up its rhetoric with physical actions. The threat of Indonesian forces crossing into Papua New Guinea was now quite real. This caused Australian Defence chiefs to examine what resources were available for fighting on several fronts at once. There were not many but enough; however, once again, national service had to be considered.

In Vietnam, the political scene had worsened with another coup. General Khanh deposed General Minh and the South Vietnamese suffered some heavy losses in battle. This prompted Serong to request that the Caribou flight be put under his command, as the country appeared to be deteriorating to the point at which an evacuation might be necessary. His request was refused; the onus was placed upon the ambassador to request a combined command in the case of an emergency. Matters did not improve through September when Air Force Colonel Nguyen Cao Ky emerged as a political powerbroker. At the same time, Ambassador Anderson and Colonel Serong were in disagreement because Serong had written and sent off a report on the political situation—about the General Minh coup—without consulting the ambassador. Anderson discussed the matter informally with Serong who told him that he felt he had an obligation to report directly to Army Headquarters because it was an incident of an unusual nature that might have affected the safety of Team members. The ambassador was obviously annoyed, but, always the diplomat, asked External Affairs for their views.[101]

At this stage in 1964, although Australia could probably provide a round-one deployment of forces into Southeast Asia, replacing them was a problem. Realistically replacement could not be done in a manner that would maintain a battle-efficient force. Defence strategists now saw Vietnam as a basket case and that implied the domino effect would begin soon. Indonesia remained the main threat for Australia, which meant Australia had to be ready for that menace but at the same time be capable of committing to Vietnam, or to other regional countries to help prevent the collapse of the dominoes. This commitment, it was hoped, would put pressure on the United States to remain in Southeast Asia.

The question was who was pressuring whom to do what in the three regional domains of Malaysia, Indonesia and Vietnam? For example, Indonesian forces continued to cause alarm with their aggression against Malaysia and Australian troops were involved in capturing some of them in October, near Malacca. At the same time the United States was providing aid to Indonesia in the hope of stopping it from succumbing to communism. The British circled their wagons in Malaysia and wanted Australian help. Australia would provide support, but if they were attacked wanted US backup under the ANZUS treaty. America agreed reluctantly but felt Malaysia was a British

Commonwealth thing. Nonetheless, Averell Harriman and Dean Rusk had provided assurances to Menzies during his trip to the USA in July 1963 that America would help Australia, as had President Kennedy. But the Americans didn't really want the ANZUS card to be played over Malaysia. Their attention was fixated on their involvement in South Vietnam. Even though they said they would help the Australians if they got into difficulty, the unwritten rules were that the Australians and the British would handle that bit over there (Malaysia) and the Americans would finish this off over here (Vietnam).

A destructive battle at Binh Gia on Route 2 in Phuoc Tuy Province brought a deadly end to 1964 for South Vietnamese forces. Two regiments that later formed the *9th Viet Cong Main Force Division* as well as several VC local force units fought a pitched battle over the final days of 1964 and into January 1965 against a South Vietnamese Ranger battalion group that was later reinforced by a marine battalion. South Vietnamese casualties were very high, with at least 200 killed and many wounded, while VC casualties were light.[102] The battle also sent a disturbing signal to those paying attention. This was a substantial stand-and-fight engagement, not the hit-and-disappear activity of a guerrilla force. Despite the size of the battle, Serong wrote in his monthly report for January 1965 that he had advised an agitated British Embassy that 'there wasn't going to be any enemy Phase III [conventional warfare]'. The Central Military Party Committee of North Vietnam held a completely different opinion.

National service manpower

Australia's army manpower needs continued to be examined both inside Defence circles and among the politicians. There were as many dissenters as there were supporters for conscription, but an extremely difficult political decision was needed if all the previous security assessments were anywhere near being correct. General Wilton did not like conscription because he believed that the scheme in 1950 did not enhance the Army's capabilities. If a program was to be introduced, he advised that it would need to run for at least two years, with an obligation for overseas service. However, there was a downside. National service tended to suck skills away from the Regular Army through extra training commitments and possibly through reduced voluntary enlistment.

Nevertheless, Australia needed more men in army uniforms and on 10 November 1964, Prime Minister Menzies told Parliament that national service was to be introduced and that the Defence budget was to be increased substantially. Extra infantry battalions would be raised; new weapons and systems were to be purchased that included the M-113 armoured personnel carrier (APC) and, for the infantry signallers, the new AN-PRC 25 tactical FM radio.

The Army's manpower-hungry Pentropic formations were discarded and with the introduction of the lighter scale Tropical Warfare establishment approval was given to form eight battalions. Although classified as regular battalions, the additional manpower necessary to fill them would come from the proposed national service scheme. The current battalions would split to provide the nucleus of the new units: 1RAR and 5RAR, 2RAR and 6RAR, 3RAR (Tropical Warfare) was in Malaysia, 4RAR had recently formed but it would replace 3RAR. When 3RAR returned to Australia it would be the guide for 7RAR, and an 8RAR would be constituted in August 1966.

Between January 1965 and 1972, there were 154,517 men called up for national service; 90,782 failed the medical. The remaining 63,735 were conscripted to serve in the Army only. Of those, 19,450 eventually served in Vietnam.[103] For many, registration for national service was a personal watershed. Some protested against conscription by burning their registration cards or failed to register. The vast majority simply registered as required under the National Service Act and waited until the ballot was due. There were two registration periods: January–June and July–December. Only men who turned twenty in either of those periods were required to register and, as the number of men exceeded the number needed, a ballot that had been used in the earlier national service scheme was used to decide who would be called up.

Numbered marbles, each representing two birth dates, were placed in a barrel. A predetermined number of marbles were drawn randomly by hand, one at a time. Within a month, all affected by the ballot knew if they were 'balloted in' or 'balloted out'. The former received a letter informing them of their rights to apply for exemption or deferment; the latter were told they were under no further obligation and were indefinitely deferred.[104]

For many young Australians the receipt of the 'balloted in' envelope was a sobering and unwanted moment. For the next two years of their young lives they would be known as 'nashos' and they would soon start off on their journey of recruit and specialist training.[105] Gordon Hurford was one of the first men drafted for national service. He was in the first intake of approximately 3000 men called up. After selection for officer training, he graduated from the Officer Training Unit (OTU) at Scheyville, New South Wales, and was allotted to the Royal Australian Infantry Corps. He recalled his conscription as a 20-year-old:

I lived in Ipswich and worked in the State Treasury Department as a records clerk. My initial reaction to being drafted was that at the time of registering it was all a bit of fun or people didn't take much notice of it. But at the time there was a group of about seven of us who were always knocking around together, taking out girls, all in the same rugby team and we all had to register as we were the same age. And I was the only one out of the whole group that actually got papers to say go and report for a medical; the others got papers to say that they were indefinitely deferred, indicating they hadn't been called up. That was when I first reacted to the draft. I thought this is bloody nonsense: why should it be me, why was I singled out? Why aren't the rest of you buggers going, the same as I had to go?[106]

Hurford had not given much thought to the war in Vietnam, but soon found out what it was all about.

Until this time I hadn't really thought about Vietnam. I remember one afternoon as I was coming out of the Treasury and picked up a *Telegraph*. I remember seeing the headlines that 1RAR were going to be deployed to Vietnam, and I thought, 'Gee, this is starting to get a bit serious'. Of course having no military experience then, apart from a stint in school cadets, thinking, 'where is this Vietnam, what's it all about?' Here we are sending a whole battalion of 750 or 800 men, and I guess that is when it dawned on me that something was going on. My Mum was rather distraught, although I think my Mum was rather a tough nut in that it took a fair bit for her to show her emotions. I don't remember Mum saying very much about me being drafted. I know my uncles had all served in the Second World War and all said it would do me 'good' and so on. Not that I think I needed anything that was 'good' for me.[107]

Similar sentiments were expressed about conscription from the other side of the fence. Phan Thanh Long, an NVA sergeant, recalled the day he received his draft notice in 1965.

When the draft notice did reach my hands, I wasn't happy, but I wasn't upset either. I didn't feel anything at all. They were calling on everyone to enlist in order to save the country. But I had a girlfriend. When I got my notice she told me, 'If you can think of a way to stay behind the lines it would be much better'. My oldest sister also got very upset. When I picked up my knapsack . . . she broke into tears . . . both of us were crying. A recruitment cadre showed up . . . and told my sister she should be encouraging me to go. My sister let him have it. She really put this guy in his place. Of course I had to leave anyway. But not everyone had to go. Nguyen Duy Trinh's [a politburo member] two sons were both sent overseas to study instead of doing military service. The chairman of every one of Hanoi's precincts also got their sons out of the country to study.[108]

Strategic challenges and US combat troops

Serious considerations about Australia's increase in its commitment in Vietnam were also underway. The discussions by Australian defence committees in December 1964 and the cables and letters from the United States provide the basis for a good conspiracy, according to some of Australia's military historians.[109] Although Prime Minister Menzies did not announce the introduction of a battalion into Vietnam until 29 April 1965—obviously plans were made before then—some analysts believe that the decision had been made in December 1964 and kept secret. Others say that what was discussed in December was not a firm decision but more a girding-of-the-loins, a preparation for riding out the difficult political and military hazards that would come if combat troops were sent to Vietnam.

Regardless of the debate, the Australian military and political system had already shown a willingness to commit an infantry battalion to either Laos or Vietnam under SEATO Plan 5C or Plan 7 (the latter was approved in April 1962).[110] All this was kept secret and it is argued that the latest consideration was nothing more than a SEATO contingency plan by another name, although in the 1964–65 plan the troops would be sent from Australia, not Malaysia.

Indeed, the command arrangements for the 1965 deployment quoted the 1962 SEATO Plan 7.[111] In the cables and papers of December 1964, a battalion is mentioned among the Australians, even when the talk from Washington and Saigon was for more advisers and sundry forces that included some naval craft, but not combat troops.

A cable sent by Ambassador Waller at Washington on 4 December 1964 reported on a conversation that he had had that day with William Bundy, US Assistant Secretary for the Far East. An unknown reader had marked several small parts for emphasis on the five-page report. The first mark indicated that President Johnson had only approved assistance to a South Vietnamese bombing effort north, between the 17th and 19th parallels, if there was further dramatic action by the Viet Cong. Bundy also revealed that the United States had some additional measures in mind for a second phase, should the South Vietnamese bombing not deter the enemy. Phase 2 proposals—underlined in pencil—included 'a ground force . . . with such ground forces as Australia and New Zealand might be able to provide'. This force would be put near the border (DMZ)—based on and supplied out of Danang—and possibly used into southern Laos.[112]

Not everyone agreed with Bundy's reported comments; there were still many within the American administration who argued against the deployment of combat troops. President Johnson also wrote to Prime Minister Menzies on 12 December 1964, detailing the urgent requirement in the military field: 200 additional combat advisers, as well as some naval assets. The president added: 'Down the road in the future, if the situation in Saigon should require and justify it, there may be a need for organized allied combat units', but he emphasised 'that is not the immediate problem'.[113]

Menzies sent a reply on 18 December in which he explained that Australia 'was unlikely to have any significant number of instructors to spare [because of conscription]', and none of the naval assets that the president had listed in his letter were available either. Menzies added that Australia was 'examining other ways in which we might be able to make a contribution'.[114] The Chiefs of Staff Committee had done that on 16 December and on the basis that they believed America would expect Australia to make an offer should American combat troops be sent, the committee recommended that the Australian offer could be an infantry battalion. The committee paper stated that 'the proposal by the United States to introduce sizeable ground forces [was] an important one revealing a major policy change'. That comment was only an assumption based on Bundy's discussion with Waller and the president's 'down the road in the future' comment.[115] The subsequent claims that a deployment decision had been made to send combat troops in 1964 is not supported. Latter-day commentaries place a great deal of faith in the nuances purportedly detected by diplomatic staff and senior Defence officials, who supposedly decoded the subterfuge that covered the real decision. There is little doubt that staff in Johnson's administration, diplomats and Defense personnel, were discussing and planning for a possible future deployment of combat troops, but in December 1964 the United States was not going to commit ground combat troops into South Vietnam.

Both US Ambassador Maxwell Taylor at Saigon and General William Westmoreland—who had assumed command of MACV on 24 June 1964— agreed that there was no need for American battalions. Taylor, a previous Chairman of the Joint Chiefs of Staff and a four-star general, said: 'White-faced soldier armed, equipped and trained as he is, is not [a] suitable guerrilla fighter for Asian forests and jungles'.[116] Taylor pondered how the foreign soldier could distinguish between the Viet Cong and a friendly farmer, but he had a slight change of heart following two attacks against US personnel and installations in central Vietnam. At the American facility at Pleiku on 7 February 1965, 20 aircraft were destroyed or damaged, 8 US service personnel were killed and over 100 men were wounded. Then on 10 February, a US billet (a hotel) at Qui Nhon was destroyed, with 23 Americans killed and another 22 wounded. The Pleiku attack also created a potential diplomatic threat. At the time of the attack, the Soviet Prime Minister Alexi Kosygin was in Hanoi and McGeorge Bundy, Special Assistant for National Security to the US President, was in Saigon. In his book about his experiences as Soviet Ambassador in Washington for 24 years, Anatoly Dobrynin said that Hanoi had 'done their utmost to foster enmity between Washington and Moscow', a claim denied by Hanoi.[117]

General Taylor remained reluctant to commit men to battle and said so in a cable to Washington on 22 February. He believed that once the Vietnamese saw that the United States was willing to take on these responsibilities, they would seek to unload other ground force tasks upon the Americans. He reluctantly agreed to the deployment of one battalion of Marines for base security at Danang. Westmoreland, CINCPAC, and the Joint Chiefs of Staff disagreed; they wanted two battalions. President Johnson approved the two-battalion request on 26 February; their task was to provide a close-in protective enclave around the Danang air base, a vital base for the conduct of air strikes against the North, which the president had approved in retaliation for the attack on Pleiku. (Combined South Vietnamese–US reprisal air attacks against targets in the North were launched on 7 February 1965.) However, the two battalions were not to undertake counterinsurgency combat operations.

When Bundy arrived back in Washington after the VC attack on the American facility at Pleiku, he immediately advised the president 'that unless the United States did something soon, it was going to lose in Vietnam and it could not afford to lose'.[118] He felt there was no way of unloading the burden on the Vietnamese or of negotiating a way out at present. A negotiated withdrawal would mean surrender on the instalment plan.[119] A series of discussions between the president and his advisers, as well as the Joint Chiefs of Staff, concluded that the most important thing was to establish an improved and broadened pacification program. Bundy told the president: 'The energy and the persistence of the Viet Cong is astonishing . . . but the weary country does not want them to win'.[120] He then recommended a policy of sustained reprisals against North Vietnam, with a warning that the struggle would be long and one that must be made clear to the people of both South Vietnam and America.

Reprisals were to be conducted in partnership with the South Vietnamese and linked to specific acts of violence such as the Pleiku incident. Once the program was launched, it could continue without relating it to any specific enemy act. On 8 February 1965, President Johnson approved that concept of operations. An eight-week bombing program was developed against lower risk targets in the southern part of North Vietnam, with two or three attacks planned each week. On 13 February, Johnson approved 'measured and limited' air actions—Operation Rolling Thunder—to be carried out jointly with the South Vietnamese against selected military targets in North Vietnam. No B-52 bombers were used in these strikes.[121]

Coincidentally, on 7 February in Australia, Lieutenant Colonel Lou Brumfield, the Commanding Officer of 1RAR, was told by Major General John

Andersen, the General Officer Commanding the 1st Division, that 1RAR might be deployed to Vietnam in a few months. This advice was based upon General Wilton's intuition of what he thought would happen and he wanted to be prepared. It was not a specific directive from the government. Officially, Australia had been told that the United States would bomb selected targets in North Vietnam, but did not yet know about the introduction of ground troops. However, the flow of information matches the dates too closely for this to be merely coincidental. There is an almost detectable air of inevitability in the archival files that a battalion might be sent and that little would stand in the way of such a decision. Andersen's information to Brumfield was top secret. This restriction caused great frustration for Brumfield who had to prepare for the possibility of a combat deployment without it being general knowledge.[122] This preparation tested the quartermaster system as the battalion could not draw on its war stores because they were not going to war.

On 8 March 1965, the first elements of the US 3rd Battalion/9th Marines Battalion Landing Team crossed Red Beach just northwest of Danang. Vietnamese girls with garlands of flowers greeted them. A Chinese general, infiltrated from North Vietnam, also watched the landing.[123]

A changing of the guard in Saigon

In Saigon, on 1 February 1965, Colonel David Jackson replaced Serong as commander of the AATTV. This was not the end of Serong's time in Vietnam, however. He made his way back to Vietnam on 'special duties'. His return to Saigon was at the request of the Americans and arranged by ASIS with the Australian Army, in which Serong remained in the rank of colonel. The exchange was a convoluted exercise that placed Ted Serong with the USAID–Public Safety Directorate program for the Vietnamese Police Field Force which also got funds from the CIA. Serong moved their training facility to Tri Mot, near Dalat, where he gathered a motley crew of experienced instructors to teach the police his brand of counterinsurgency tactics. Colonel William 'Pappy' Grieves, who had been the deputy commander of the Special Warfare Center at Fort Bragg under General Yarborough, was also hired by USAID to add his unconventional warfare experience to the group.

Grieves was unimpressed by Serong's activities and he tried to have him removed, without success. A change in attitude came when John Manopli was appointed Director of Public Safety; he told Grieves that 'he had a directive to get rid of Serong'. Grieves said, 'I supplied the ammunition' [for Serong's dismissal] and 'his services were dispensed with', probably late in 1966 or in early 1967.[124] Bill Robertson, Deputy Director of ASIS at the time and the person involved in the detailed exchange arrangements with the Australian Army, said many years later, 'It really was a very difficult thing to do, he did not work for us and I was very annoyed when we were told to take him back'.[125]

Meanwhile, on 22 January 1965 the Malaysian government had made a formal request for Australian assistance in the form of the SAS, 3RAR and another battalion to go to Borneo to help secure the border with Kalimantan. Because there weren't enough troops, only 3RAR and an SAS squadron could be deployed. On 1 May 1965, the 1st Squadron SAS was permitted to operate across the border into Indonesian territory. Other British Commonwealth forces—not Australian—had conducted these operations, codenamed Claret, since October 1964. Two Australian battalions conducted Claret operations in 1965 and 1966. The first 3RAR patrols clashed with Indonesian troops four times between May and July 1965. Later, in April 1966, 4RAR also conducted operations on both sides of the border with Indonesia. Malaysia and Indonesia signed a treaty to end the conflict on 11 August 1966 and 4RAR returned to Terendak camp in Malaysia on 30 August. The details of Operation Claret were kept secret for over 30 years.

In the same time frame, the Australian Labor Party recognised Vietnam's tribulations. A resolution unanimously adopted by the Federal Parliamentary Labor Party Executive on 18 February 1965, just three months before Australia committed a battalion group to the conflict, included the following statement of support for South Vietnam:

The demand of the Soviet Government for the immediate departure of all American and other foreign forces from South Vietnam would be in the interests neither of the people of South Vietnam nor the people of Australia. Its immediate consequences must be a communist takeover of South Vietnam, snuffing out the hope of freedom and the democratic independence in that country and extending the area of communist control closer to this country.[126]

National service was now well underway. Instructors were needed to train the recruits, and as more battalions came online good NCOs and officers were also needed to form the backbone of those units. The better of these soldiers were the ones the AATTV wanted. General Wilton was none too pleased when the Defence Minister announced in January 1965—against his advice—that the Team had been authorised to increase its establishment strength to 100.[127] There was a lag time between approval and actually getting the men on the ground.

Australia's first combat battalion

In June 1965, the AATTV had 92 officers and warrant officers in Vietnam. Air Marshal Scherger went to Honolulu for a conference (31 March–1 April) with Admiral Ulysses Sharp, CINCPAC, at which they were to discuss the possibility of an Australian contribution of combat troops. Controversy has surrounded what was offered by Australia at the Honolulu meeting, and how it was proposed, ever since. Some said that Scherger offered an Australian battalion; others said that Sharp suggested a battalion; even more records allege that the officers discussed prospects in which the possibility of a battalion was proposed. In any case, Admiral Sharp advised the US Joint Chiefs of Staff to accept a battalion from Australia.

On Wilton's directive, Army Headquarters staff in Canberra had been working on the deployment planning for some weeks. No matter what Australia thought about the counterinsurgency task that Scherger brought back from Honolulu, the sending of Australian troops and what they would do was not yet a done deal. Nothing had been discussed with the South Vietnamese, although that nicety would be overcome by US pressure, even though the South Vietnamese Premier Phan Huy Quat was still smarting from the Marine landing in March, which he had been pressured to approve as it was taking place. At a National Security Council meeting in Washington on 1 April 1965, the president told the Secretary of State to see what could be done to induce Australia (and others) 'to deploy rapidly significant combat elements'.[128] In the same memorandum, the president also approved that US Marines conduct operations beyond their defensive enclaves. On 5 April, the US Joint Chiefs of Staff 'concurred' with the introduction of one

Australian infantry battalion with supporting units.[129] This was a necessary agreement, as the Australian contribution would need to be brigaded with a larger American formation for both logistical and operational support, which was a part of the Australian planning process.

Matters must have been moving rapidly because Australia's Defence Committee recommended to Cabinet—in a minute dated 5 April—that a battalion be sent to Vietnam; the recommendation was approved. All that remained to be done was for military staff to complete the detailed planning. The 1st Battalion of the Regiment previously nominated by the CGS for deployment would gain a few extra units to flesh it out into a 'bigger battalion', although at this stage it was not designated a battalion group. This was probably something General Wilton decided without government knowledge. It is interesting to note that the US Joint Chiefs of Staff had agreed to a battalion and supporting units on 5 April, the same day that the Australian Cabinet approved a battalion deployment.

The 1st Battalion scrambled to recover from the split from one Pentropic battalion into two Tropical Warfare battalions, 1RAR and 5RAR, and at the same time gear up for an operational deployment. It is worth repeating that the formal political approval to send the combat battalion to Vietnam was announced in Parliament late on 29 April, the same day South Vietnamese Premier Quat authorised the deployment of the battalion. The approval was a craftily worded, single-page document—guided by Australian Ambassador Anderson—that included the word 'request' in an effort to appease the sceptics.[130]

Quat's letter stated: 'I wish to confirm my government's acceptance of this offer and to request the dispatch of this force to Viet Nam on the basis which we discussed'.[131] Clearly the offer came before the request, and other cables between the Australian embassies at Washington and Saigon confirm this.[132] For instance, part of a cable from the Australian Ambassador at Washington, Keith Waller, to Sir Paul Hasluck, the Minister for External Affairs, on 13 April 1965 disclosed: 'I asked Rusk whether I could inform the Australian Government that it was the President's desire that Australia should supply a battalion for use in South Vietnam at a time and place to be fixed. Rusk said that I could so inform you and that as regards timing, the sooner the battalion was supplied the better'.[133]

Elements of the battalion together with a troop of M-113 APCs from the 4th/19th Prince of Wales' Light Horse and the 1st Logistic Supply Company sailed in the early hours of 27 May on board HMAS *Sydney*, the converted aircraft carrier. Neil McInnes was a 20-year-old able seaman gunner when he first sailed to South Vietnam aboard HMAS *Sydney* in 1965. He had been in the RAN since October 1959 and now he was on his way to war. For the next two years he would find himself steaming to and from the Vietnam 'Special Zone', ferrying soldiers, ammunition, trucks, cannons and armoured vehicles.

> I was on the very first deployment on the HMAS *Sydney* with 1RAR on board. We were in Garden Island and the *Sydney* was under very heavy guard by the civilian and dockyard police. We worked right through the day and night loading all types of army vehicles including APCs, trucks, etc. The next day was the day the First Battalion was to go on board.[134]

The author remembers embarking on the *Sydney* on 26 May—'we sailed in the dead of night around 1 or 2 a.m. on the 27th of May'. Bob Breen captured the moment when he wrote in his book *First to Fight*: 'There had been no emotional farewells—no scenes of soldiers kissing tearful wives, mothers, sisters or girlfriends in the midst of a noisy crowd of well-wishers. The group had embarked in an almost stealthy move by buses and closed trucks from Holsworthy'.[135]

Not to be cheated out of a goodbye, cars full of wives and relatives of the troops crowded to 'Lady Macquaries Drive, overlooking the warship, despite official attempts to keep the departure secret', the *Australian* reported on 27 May. When she sailed at 1.39 a.m. on the 27th, not many people remained on the vantage points to watch the men depart. HMAS *Sydney* was as good as blacked out as she moved down the harbour, with minimal navigation lights on only.

For the soldiers, the days en route to the war zone were filled with training. Physical fitness programs were drawn up, which involved circuit training around the limited passageways of the ship. Lessons were given on the language and culture of South Vietnam and information on the conflict the soldiers were about to enter was discussed. At the rear of the flight deck the infantrymen practised shooting at clusters of floating coloured balloons to keep their reflexes and battle shooting skills tuned. Short courses were conducted in first aid, radio communications, booby trap identification, and helicopter landing zone drills.

The remainder of 1RAR flew in to join the US 173rd Airborne Brigade (Separate) as its third infantry battalion. The brigade was activated on 25 June 1963 as an independent airborne force consisting of two infantry battalions and an artillery battalion with a support battalion, an engineer company, a cavalry troop and a company of armour. The brigade was deployed to protect the major airfield at Bien Hoa, 30 kilometres north of Saigon. After some strongly worded negotiations between Major John Essex-Clark, who commanded the battalion's reconnaissance party, and the American brigade commander, Brigadier General Ellis 'Butch' Williamson, 1RAR was permitted to settle into its perimeter on the northern side of the eastern end of the airstrip called the 'prairie'. The brigade's other battalions, the 1st and the 2nd of the 503rd, were set up in 'neat rows of tents which were being replaced by permanent huts' inside the still-standing rubber trees.[136]

Pat Burgess was a special correspondent with the Australians and described the Australians' position in an article for the *Sun-Herald* headlined '"Mad-dog" Diggers dig in'.

> There is almost no shade and no relief from the sun, except for the daily rainstorm. If there was ever any thought of giving up the traditional Digger hat it has gone now; the slouch hat is as effective here as it was on the kunai plains of Wau [New Guinea]. The nearest American outfit to the Australians—the Second Airborne Battalion of the 503rd Infantry—were surprised that the traditionally resourceful Diggers should choose, like mad dogs and Englishmen, to bake in the Vietnam sun.[137]

But there was a method to the madness. Essex-Clark had laid out the position in the shape of a slightly squashed star, an arrangement that permitted well-sited machine guns to cover a perimeter that was a series of interlocked triangles. This would allow enfilade fire to cover the flanks of each triangle behind which lay in-depth fighting positions. This layout was one favoured by the French during their war against the Viet Minh. At night, the quiet and dark segment of the Australians on the Bien Hoa perimeter amused the Americans and probably confused the enemy.

After the arrival of the last group by air, there was a period of acclimatisation. The brigade commander expected the battalion to be ready for action on 20 June 1965. But no combat could precede a traditional parade, and the soldiers were bussed into Saigon to be welcomed by Vietnamese ladies with flowers, as well as a speech of welcome from Major General Nguyen Van Thieu, later the President of South Vietnam.

As at 1 June 1965, there were approximately 34,000 Americans in Vietnam with approval for that figure to go to 82,000. Australia's force, including the advisers, was around 1400.

Meanwhile, a few months before the Australian combat battalion arrived, Wilfred Burchett and Madeleine Riffaud had been crawling around the countryside with the Viet Cong. Burchett was a controversial Australian journalist who had been branded a traitor by some of his critics for his reporting on the Korean War. His Australian passport had been withdrawn in 1955, and was not returned until 1973. Madeleine Riffaud was a writer with *L'Humanité*, a French paper with strong connections with the French Communist Party. Riffaud recorded their activities for the paper in a series of articles.

> Date line 14 February 1965, it was only last month . . . W. [Wilfred] Burchett and I were crawling, one moonlit night, between two enemy posts [South Vietnamese]. Accompanying a small unit of National Liberation Front [Viet Cong] fighters. For two months we lived this way in the midst of the . . . fighters . . . and never leaving them.[138]

3

MORE THAN GUERRILLA WARFARE
1965–1966

In waking a tiger, use a long stick.
Mao Zedong

The big battles start

Had the Vietnam conflict developed from guerrilla warfare into a limited conventional war? Nineteen sixty-five began badly for South Vietnamese troops who suffered high casualties in the Binh Gia battle in Phuoc Tuy Province when a conglomerate of VC units that included two main force regiments hit them hard in an excellently planned series of ambushes. French journalist Madeleine Riffaud reported on the battle for *L'Humanité*, a newspaper with strong links to the French Communist Party:

> On 4 January 1965, not far from Binh Gia, under the shelter of a hevea [rubber] plantation, an officer of the army of the National Liberation Front of South Vietnam gave a press conference, at which W. [Wilfred] Burchett and I were the only foreign war correspondents. The battle of Binh Gia had ended the day before. It had lasted one month, and the same unit of the army of the Front had fought it successfully . . . under the fire of 20 Sky Raiders [propellor-driven attack aircraft] and 80 helicopters . . . The Americans had to admit that they had just suffered their greatest defeat since the beginning of their war of aggression in South Vietnam.

One of the results of the battle of Binh Gia was the annihilation of some of the enemy's elite reserve troops . . . on several occasions, the liberation soldiers have ignored the puppet units [local force South Vietnamese], whose morale is so low that they can be ignored, in order to attract and strike the shock troops [ARVN].[1]

On 11 May, Song Be, 70 kilometres north of Bien Hoa in Phuoc Long Province, was overrun by a large enemy group who held the ground for over seven hours before heavy air strikes, coupled with an ARVN counterattack, forced them to withdraw. Much further north in I Corps Tactical Zone, the outpost at Ba Gia northwest of Quang Ngai City suffered a major blow on 29 May with ARVN casualties of over 100 dead, 123 wounded and more than 350 missing. An Australian infantryman, WO2 Eric Miller, was advising the 1st Battalion, 4th ARVN, when they went to the rescue of the outpost and joined up with the remnants of the 39th Ranger Battalion.

The enemy attacked in force again on 10 June when they hit the military camp at Dong Xoai, 20 kilometres east of Song Be. Although they overran the camp, this time they suffered heavy casualties due to the strength of the allied air power. During this battle, the Viet Cong showed an improved anti-aircraft capability with many of the Skyraiders and jet aircraft struck by .50-calibre ground fire. It was a deadly duel. Survivors of the attacking force argued that the South Vietnamese and the Americans had known about the attack in advance. When a telephone line to the force on the airport side of town was cut, General Hai Chan, the VC commander, hit the table, saying 'They know the plan'. According to an enemy defector, hardly anything had gone to plan. When one element of the enemy force reported they had gained control of Dong Xoai, Colonel Nam Thuc shouted:

'We've won!' Suddenly there were explosions all over the place. Nam said, 'My God! It's brutal, brutal.' A fleet of jets had come in to bomb the whole area. The bunker was shaking, its lights swaying back and forth. Colonel Nam said, 'Oh my God, what's happened to Q761 [one of the attacking regiments]?'[2]

More enemy positions were hammered when American B-52 bombers flew out of the US Air Force base in Guam and dropped 300 tons of bombs

HMAS *Hobart* (D39) was a *Perth* class guided missile destroyer. *Hobart* was the first RAN destroyer deployed on the gun-line of the US 7th Fleet when she relieved a US destroyer off Chu Lai, Quang Tin Province, I Corps, 15 March 1967. *Hobart* was hit by friendly fire from a US Phantom on 17 June 1968. Two sailors were killed and 7 wounded. *Courtesy National Vietnam Veterans (NVV) Museum, Phillip Island*

During an operation into War Zone 'D' in June 1965, 1RAR was allocated fifty 'Slicks' (troop-carrying helicopters) for their movement. In Australia, the battalion had four helicopters to use during their final field exercise before going to Vietnam. Here US Army helicopters fly into a staging area 50 miles northeast of Saigon in January 1966. *AP Photo/Henri Huet*

Caskets arriving home. The bodies of two Australian soldiers killed accidentally at Bien Hoa, on 29 June 1965, are unloaded at Mascot Airport on 6 July 1965. A private donation paid for their return home. Government policy on soldiers killed in action directed their remains be interred at the nearest Commonwealth War Graves cemetery (Terendak, Malaysia). This policy changed in January 1966; after that date, all bodies were returned home at Commonwealth expense. *Courtesy NVV Museum; photograph Trevor Dallen*

A haul of enemy weapons captured at the battle of Long Tan, 18 August 1966. A .30-calibre machine gun is in the foreground beneath what appears to be the breach of a 75 mm recoilless rifle. Semi-automatic rifles form the next line in front of AK47s with a mix of older weapons at the rear. *Courtesy NVV Museum*

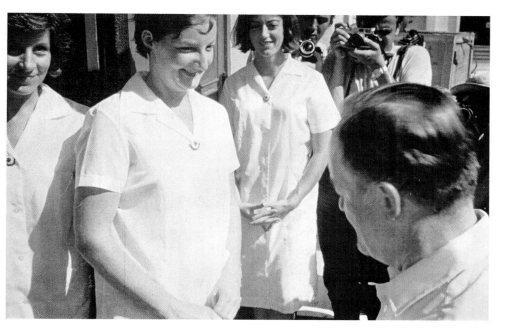

Sisters Barbara Phillips, Canny Rigg and Heather Beveridge welcome Hubert Humphrey, Vice-President of the United States, to the Bien Hoa Provincial Hospital, February 1966. Under a SEATO request for aid, Australia contributed a surgical team from the Alfred Hospital, Melbourne, to assist the civilian populace, followed by other teams located in different provinces. *Courtesy NVV Museum*

Two Caribou aircraft from 35 Squadron, RAAF, 'Wallaby Airlines', at Luscombe Field, Nui Dat. Luscombe was named after Captain Bryan Luscombe, Royal Australian Artillery, who was killed in action flying an observation mission in Korea. *Courtesy NVV Museum*

Contact 5RAR, October 1966. *Background*: Russell Quinn. *Left*: Ian Foran, on radio, Robert Farrell. *Foreground*: Douglas J. Bishop. *Courtesy NVV Museum*

Left: Robert Box is carried to the waiting Dustoff helicopter (Medevac). *Courtesy NVV Museum*

Below: Note the surround of the landing site: Dustoff helicopter pilots were renowned for their ability and willingness to fly into tight situations. *Courtesy NVV Museum*

Australian advisers deployed in I Corps, the northern five provinces of South Vietnam, gather to commemorate Anzac Day in 1965. As is the custom, the advisers then participated in the time-honoured pastime of a game of two-up. *Courtesy of Barbara Pitkunigs, daughter of Keith Rudd, AATTV (deceased)*

In November 1967, a 9 Squadron Iroquois lands to pick up members of 7RAR during Operation Santa Fe, a gruelling three-week-long operation through inhospitable country some 23 kilometres from the Task Force Base at Nui Dat. *AFP/AWM* [neg no. COL/67/1127/VN]

The Commander in Chief Pacific Headquarters, located at Camp Smith, Hawaii, plays host to (from left to right) Secretary of Defense Robert McNamara, Prime Minister Nguyen Cao Ky of South Vietnam, President Lyndon B. Johnson and Lieutenant General Nguyen Van Thieu (South Vietnam) on 8 February 1966. *AFP Photo/National Archives*

An attack on the US Embassy in Saigon, Vietnam, 30 March 1965. The explosion killed two Americans and several Vietnamese. *AP Photo/Horst Faas*

Sergeant Bill O'Donnell, 6RAR, D Company's cook, holds a small puppy found in an abandoned village in 1967. The puppy became D Company's mascot. *Courtesy Dennis Gibbons Collection, NVV Museum*

3RAR Tactical Headquarters Group en route to FSB Coral, 12 May 1968. 1RAR was attacked at Coral during the night of 12–13 May. Nine Australians were killed and a further 28 wounded. The enemy lost at least 51 killed. *Courtesy 104 Signal Squadron Web Site; photograph by Bobby Ellis*

FSB Coral command post, May 1968. *Courtesy 104 Signal Squadron Web Site; photograph by Ralph Bilsby*

An APC from B Squadron, 3rd Cavalry Regiment, grinds its way out of a bog in eastern Phuoc Tuy Province. Sergeant Peter Edwards mans the machine gun. Trooper Mick Chinnick is the driver. *Courtesy NVV Museum*

on VC targets near Ben Cat, 40 kilometres north of Saigon on 18 June 1965. This was the first use of the strategic bombers in a tactical support role inside South Vietnam and ironically they bombed around the area of an Australian dairy farm provided to Vietnam under the Colombo Plan in the early 1960s.

Another possible form of enemy activity was investigated on the edge of Bien Hoa air base among the bars that flourished to cater for American servicemen. The Viet Cong were reported to have planted girls in the bars to poison the drinks of the Americans. American Army Intelligence checked the bars and a source reported, 'There have been no instances of this actually happening . . . but we can't take chances and so eight of the bars have been put off limits'.[3]

Political timidity

The Australians were wrapped in political cotton wool for the first few months after their arrival in Vietnam; they could go no more than 35 kilometres from Bien Hoa. Although there are several versions of this restriction, General Westmoreland believed that General Wilton had set the distance at 30–35 kilometres. The Australian government also insisted that the battalion not be used in 'offensive or reaction operations except in conjunction with the defence of Bien Hoa air base'.[4] The selection of where the Australian battalion would be deployed inside South Vietnam had caused Australian politicians and planners considerable angst. At first it was thought that 1RAR would join with American Marines in an enclave around Hue, Phu Bai or Danang. Further talks canvassed the possibility of operational zones near Chu Lai, south of Danang, again with the Marines, and then at Qui Nhon, a central coastal area of Vietnam, where they would operate as an independent battalion. Sir James Plimsoll, Secretary of the Department of External Affairs, made the following comments at a Defence Committee Meeting on 20 April 1965:

> Australian troops should not be used on their own in exposed positions. If Australia's only battalion in Vietnam was completely lost, our presence there would be gone . . . The expressions of this to the Americans would need careful handling, and we must avoid any suggestion of mollycoddling our forces, but something could be said orally between the relevant commanders.[5]

According to Lieutenant Colonel Alex Preece, an Australian commander in Vietnam during 1965–66:

> Nothing was written but one had the feeling that our tactical deployments were more to the conservative side of the operation; for example, we would be the blocking force and the Americans the attackers. This didn't always work as planned of course, and a good example was the operation where we landed on top of the enemy's tunnels [Operation Crimp, 8–14 January 1966].[6]

In early June 1965 Australian newspaper headlines also asked what the Australians' role was to be: 'Combat or Defence?' Prime Minister Robert Menzies was in Washington at the time and *The Sun*, a Melbourne paper, reported:

> Sir Robert Menzies will outline today [9 June] the combat role of Australian troops in Vietnam. He [is] expected to announce a role parallel to that of American troops. The State Department announced that American troops in future would fight alongside South Vietnamese units, if the Saigon Government sought 'combat support'. In Canberra, Defence officials said that Australian soldiers probably would go into combat if US troops did. In Sydney, the Defence Minister, Senator Paltridge, said that Australian troops had a 'static Defence role' at present.[7]

In the same article, US Senator Morse, a critic of America's combat involvement in Vietnam, described Australia as 'an outlaw nation'.

The Diggers themselves had another complaint. The *Sun*'s 16 June headline told of angry Diggers who claimed they were victims of a 'Canberra Swindle'.

> Angry Australian soldiers . . . claim that they are the 7/6-a-day [seven shillings and sixpence or 75 cents] victims of a Canberra 'swindle'. They say that the daily allowance is less than half that paid to Australian troops in Malaya and Borneo.
>
> In Canberra, the Minister for the Army Dr Forbes ordered an immediate investigation into the complaints.
>
> 'Even the soldiers at Woomera get a better deal than we do', said an irate sergeant at Bien Hoa today.
>
> 'It's just a swindle.'

An officer confirmed the Vietnam allowance as 7/6 a day for privates to corporals; 9/- for sergeants . . . 15/- for Lt. Colonels.

The officer said: 'The basic allowance . . . in Malaya and Borneo starts at between 15/ [$1.50] and 16/6 [$1.65] for a private and goes up.[8]

War Zone D

General Westmoreland was given the green light to start independent combat operations—not linked to those of the South Vietnamese—in late June. His first plan was to challenge the enemy in a VC stronghold called War Zone D, which was north of Saigon in Binh Duong Province near Ben Cat. Now it was time for the Australians to show the Viet Cong and the brash Americans what jungle fighters could do. To find its combat feet, the Australian battalion conducted a two-day test run airmobile operation in an area southeast of Bien Hoa between the main Highway 1A and Route 15. The manoeuvre was on a scale that was previously fantasyland for the Australians. It was a grand display of helicopters, artillery, attack aircraft and gunships, but not much action.

In an unfortunate incident, the battalion took its first casualties at the end of the operation when they were coming back to their base in 'cattle trucks' provided by an American support unit. An Australian soldier leapt over the side of a truck and snagged a grenade attached to his webbing. The resulting explosion caused carnage, killing and wounding Australian and American soldiers. Alan Ramsey, an AAP correspondent who was nearby, recorded what happened:

> The Australian troops had just returned from their first 'search-and-destroy' mission in Vietnam. They were tired and wet after 30 hours in the field. But they laughed and joked . . . some huddled around a radio relaying the Springbok–Australia rugby test. Then came the explosion, a dull, heavy crump. Soldiers began running from everywhere . . . and I ran with them. What we saw was shocking. Two Australians and one American lay dead. Ten Australians and two Americans lay wounded. Groaning, crying, injured lay where they fell. Some did not move.[9]

Don Petersen, another reporter who was in Saigon, reported that hundreds of Americans offered blood for the wounded Australians.

Hundreds of Americans flooded Saigon's US Navy hospital with offers of blood for the 10 Australians wounded in the grenade explosion at Bien Hoa yesterday. Calls for special blood groups were made over the Armed Forces Radio. Queues immediately began to form outside the hospital. A doctor said that they had all the blood needed in 10 minutes. One of the Australians killed was Private William 'Billy' Carroll who was the father of a six-month-old son, David.[10]

Grim reality hit home for the Australian battalion. The puppy fat of peacetime blanks and gas rattles to simulate rifle and machine-gun fire had been stripped away. This wasn't an exercise, a rehearsal; this was for real, even though some American operation orders continued to use the word 'exercise'.

General Westmoreland's War Zone D attack was a combined American, Vietnamese and Australian force of nine battalions that hit the zone in the last week of June 1965. The 173rd Brigade ordered Lieutenant Colonel Ivan 'Lou' Brumfield's 1RAR to be at Bien Hoa airfield on 29 June by 1410 hours and to plan on 50 'slicks' (a helicopter without external armaments) for their lift. In another example that underlined the vast difference between the Australian and US armies, during the battalion's last field Exercise Sky High Two (conducted in April in Australia), 1RAR had just four helicopters in support. Second Lieutenant Adrian Roberts recalled an exercise in Australia where no aircraft were available and commanders had to use some imagination to train their soldiers:

> I had not lost my sense of the ridiculous at that time and there were many ridiculous things on that exercise (from a second lieutenant's perspective). In an absurd attempt to engender realism, troops in Studebaker trucks (simulating Caribou aircraft) circled the airstrip that had been built in the exercise area, while SAS troopers in Land Rovers (simulating helicopters) drove onto the airstrip to remove logs placed to stop the Studebaker trucks from 'landing'. It was a script worthy of the 'Goons'.[11]

But now the soldiers lined up alongside the airstrip in Bien Hoa known as 'the Snake Pit' and shuffled themselves into loads almost with unconcern. Some of the officers and senior NCOs were worried by the nonchalant actions of the soldiers but more troublesome were the range of factors—heat, weight, different models of Iroquois and mechanical gremlins—that affected how many soldiers each different model helicopter could carry.

Clashes with the enemy on this operation were light and the troops returned to base the next day. The Australians' battle procedures had settled into a good routine, even though they were being constantly improved, but the kill or be killed instinct vital to an infantryman's life and success in battle had not yet struck. That soon changed. Private William 'Billy' Nalder from Delta Company was fatally wounded on the next operation into War Zone D when the battalion faced more substantial enemy resistance. On the same operation, elements of Bravo Company hit a section-sized group of enemy and Lance Corporal David Munday was wounded twice in his efforts to help another wounded soldier. He was awarded a Military Medal for his gallantry, the battalion's first. Lance Corporal Kim 'Slob' Benier, a machine gunner in Alpha Company, later played out a black pantomime when he punched his fingers into his chest in a series of staccato thumps to emphasise how he had 'stitched up' a Viet Cong. The operation marked a changed mood within the battalion.

The tempo of operations began to crank up and the Australians attracted visits from several high-ranking officials during their first months at Bien Hoa. General Westmoreland came first, then the Australian Chief of the General Staff, Lieutenant General Sir John Wilton. They were followed by a steady stream of generals, politicians and officials. During a visit by Dr James Forbes, the Minister for the Army, on 10 July 1965, Lou Brumfield took him aside to demonstrate the inadequacy of some Australian equipment. Later, the press took up this private complaint and it attracted a lot of publicity back home. Bob Breen wrote in *First to Fight* that Brumfield 'was reprimanded and . . . his career [possibly] suffered because of it'.[12] Robert McNamara, the US Secretary of Defense, and General Earle Wheeler, the US Chairman of the Joint Chiefs of Staff, accompanied by General Westmoreland, followed Forbes. Not long after, also in July, Admiral Grant Sharp, the Commander in Chief US Forces in the Pacific, visited with Lieutenant General John Throckmorton, Deputy Commander MACV. The Australian soldiers were not star-struck by their high-ranking visitors. In inimitable fashion, two cooks complained to Westmoreland about the quality of American food that they had to use in preparing meals.

It was obvious that there were differences in procedures and combat attitudes between the Australians and the American 173rd Airborne Brigade, their operational controller. The American unit's combat arrogance echoed around the province: here we are—come and get us if you dare! The brigade was on a temporary duty station for 60 days and supremely confident of their combat skills; they intended to finish the war and get back to their family base on Okinawa (Island) in Japan. Tactically there was an enormous difference between the more conventional and plentiful firepower of the up the guts 'Sky Soldiers' and the Malayan jungle techniques of the Diggers. Each side thought the other a bit strange, and not quite as good as themselves in the art of jungle anti-guerrilla warfare. Americans were noisy, poor at patrolling, wore colourful unit patches that did not suit jungle operations, and, in the minds of some Australians, used their firepower, especially the B-52 bombers, indiscriminately. This assessment of how the bombers' targets were approved was inaccurate. Tactical targets to be bombed inside South Vietnam by B-52 bombers were only permitted after analysis at the highest levels within the Johnson administration that included the military chiefs as well as diplomats at the Department of State. Strikes inside North Vietnam by the strategic bombers were still not authorised.

The Americans criticised the Australians, too, although not openly, for being too cautious in their sneaking around the jungle; they looked as if they had dressed for an African safari rather than a war; they were pussyfooters. The potential danger of battles against a company, a battalion or a regiment had not yet filtered through the Australian ranks and their confidence, possibly tinged with disdain, against the communist guerrillas was high. In common, both the Australians and the Americans wanted to restrict the numbers of their casualties. The Americans intended to achieve this by rapid mobility into and out of danger zones using an increasing number of helicopters and their powerful arsenal to not only destroy the enemy, but also to keep him tactically off-balance. The Americans sought the big clash, a battleground of grand manoeuvres on which the peasant army would be smashed if it had the nerve to join in battle against the Americans. The Australian battalion's operational consciousness was guerrilla warfare, something a bit more hectic than Malaya, but still 'contact front' style with the Australian infantry's immediate action drills ready to overwhelm a lesser enemy.

Political and military restrictions weakened the battle flexibility of the allies. When 1RAR was not given authorisation to go on an offensive operation with the 173rd Brigade from 28 July to 2 August, the American brigade had to have another battalion attached from the US 1st Division to maintain its combat balance. Ironically this operation was into Phuoc Tuy Province, a place that would become synonymous with the Australians. Earlier, when the Australian battalion had made an effort to train their soldiers to operate long-range reconnaissance patrols, the plan was cancelled, allegedly by General Wilton who was on a visit to the battalion. It was feared that Australians might be taken prisoners of war. Such events added strength to softly muttered American claims that the Australians were pussyfooters.

Walk softly or carry a big stick

An ongoing tactical disagreement between the Australian and American forces that began during these early operations was the argument over how to defeat the guerrilla army. Some Australians disagreed with the American search-and-destroy concept, especially the shooting at anything that looked like an enemy soldier or an enemy position, but could turn out to be an innocent civilian or a rice-paddy bund. The other option, pacification, a people-oriented approach with an aim of protecting the villagers and their way of life, was a concept that appealed to the Australians and probably matched their ideas on how to defeat an insurgency. However, that argument is somewhat deflated when we learn that the Australian force was offered to the Vietnamese and accepted by them with several provisos attached, one being that the battalion was not to participate in pacification or military operations in populous areas. As Patrick Shaw, Deputy Secretary in Defence, wrote on 7 April 1965:

> We see a lot of difficulty in giving foreign forces the job of winkling out Vietcong terrorists and safeguarding hamlets and policing highways. In our view, only Vietnamese can effectively undertake the task of pacification proper and the use of white forces for this work could be turned to the advantage of the Vietcong.[13]

Senior South Vietnamese officers agreed with this approach and Premier Quat referred to it obliquely in his acceptance letter of 29 April by his use of the phrase, 'on the basis which we discussed'. Nguyen Van Thieu, then Minister of Defence, stressed to Australian Ambassador David Anderson that 'the Battalion should not be committed to pacification work'.[14] Nonetheless, the reality contrasted starkly with the political and military ideals, as an article written by reporter Gerald Stone on why Australia was sending troops to Vietnam illustrated. Stone was an American-born Australian reporter who was with 1RAR.

> Vietnam: Why are our boys fighting? THEY DON'T KNOW! Very few of the Australian soldiers in Vietnam claim to know—or even care—what the war is all about. Instead, they admit to coming here for a variety of personal motives completely unconnected to those grand theories of strategic defence now being so hotly debated in Parliament. A number of soldiers told me, for example, that they volunteered for duty simply to qualify for war service homes. Many were prompted by a young man's sense of adventure. The orientation programme for the Australians has fallen considerably short of the mark. In very few cases have I found anyone—either officer or other rank—who is able to discuss in any depth the type of government in South Vietnam, the names of its leaders, the nature of its people or the history of its conflicts. Many of them admit they don't even have a clear idea why their own government decided to send them here. 'To help the Yanks,' is the most frequent answer. The troops at Bien Hoa are spoiling for action. But one cannot help being dismayed at the sight of so many good men so willing to fight in a country they know nothing about to support the policies they aren't sure of.[15]

And fight the Australians did. Hidden away from the headlines on Vietnam were occasional stories about another place of combat, Malaysian Sarawak, bordering Indonesia. On 17 June 1965, an ambush laid by 3RAR killed at least 17 Indonesians but the toll was probably higher, possibly as many as 50. Several of the Australians who were wounded and evacuated to Singapore for treatment said, 'It was just like shooting ducks. The Indonesians went over like ninepins . . . we couldn't miss them'.[16] This graphic description of the battle in the words of Lance Corporal Jack Ezzy and Private Alby Kyle, while not as politically correct as one expected of today's 'strategic corporals', leaves no doubt about the ferocious effectiveness of the ambush.

An increased Australian commitment

A flurry of activity in the offices of Defence and External Affairs followed a personal letter of 26 July from President Johnson to Prime Minister Menzies.

In that letter, the president provided a 'frank assessment of the situation in South Vietnam', and then asked Menzies to 'give most earnest consideration to increasing that [military] assistance in ways which will give a clear signal to the world . . . of the solidarity of international support for resistance to aggression in Vietnam and for a peaceful settlement in Vietnam'.[17]

Gordon Jockel, First Assistant Secretary at the Defence Liaison Branch, wrote a hasty note to the Minister for External Affairs on 16 August in which he discussed Johnson's letter and the Defence Committee's response. He concentrated on the diplomatic implications if Australia were to announce an increase in troops to be deployed to Vietnam. The handling of any trouble in Papua New Guinea and recent developments in Malaysia/Singapore and Indonesia were matters that 'would seem to make it more desirable that we do not give a formal indication to the Americans that we are planning to make a second battalion available for service in Vietnam in 1966'. He also commented upon objections to the use of the Thailand-based RAAF Sabres over Vietnam, and the movement of any navy asset from the Strategic Reserve, because it might be interpreted as a declining interest by Australia in the defence of Malaysia/Singapore.[18]

The Australian battle area was also expanded in August 1965 when 1RAR was permitted to operate in Bien Hoa and the contiguous provinces of Binh Duong, Long Khanh and Phuoc Tuy.[19] On 17 August, the Foreign Affairs and Defence Committee of Cabinet 'decided to increase the Australian force in Vietnam by the addition of ancillary and supporting units totalling some 350 personnel'.[20] This would build the battalion into a battalion group.

The additional 350 men who would make up the Australian battalion group were to consist of 105 Field Artillery Battery, a troop of engineers, a flight of Cessna fixed-wing aircraft and Sioux helicopters, a signals troop and extra personnel for the headquarters and the logistics company. Until now the battalion had obtained its direct fire support from the American brigade and the New Zealand four-gun 161 Battery, which had guns ready in July 1965. The New Zealand L5 pack howitzers were ideal for quick airmobile deployment and their link with the Australian battalion reinforced the traditional ANZAC spirit, which was made known when General Westmoreland wanted to move the guns north to Cam Ranh Bay to support the 101st Airborne Brigade, even after a New Zealand diplomat said that conditions of life at Bien Hoa were grim, while the 101st Airborne was currently on a large island, secure and right beside a beautiful beach. As a base area, he reported, it offered immensely better conditions over the bleak, inhospitable and noisy Bien Hoa.

During the exchange of cables that outlined what additional Australian troops would be provided, there was a request for a mounted horse unit of 100 horses. Canberra may have been amused, but one point was clear, and that was to avoid any implication 'that Australian horses [would be] used for repressive purposes'. 'Meanwhile', the cable concluded, 'it would be undesirable to encourage expectation of a positive response'.[21]

The message that went to Australia's embassies at London, Washington, Wellington and Saigon instructed the ambassadors to inform their host governments of the proposed increase in the Australian force by 350 personnel. The government would keep the national service intake during 1966 at 8400 per annum instead of a previously planned 6900. The prime minister would announce this in Parliament the next day, 18 August 1965. In addition, some embassies were warned very strongly that if they had received Defence Committee Minute 46/65 dated 2 August they 'should not—repeat—not mention in any way the matters covered in paragraph 37(d) regarding still further forces'.[22] These related to a much larger increase. The Defence Committee paper recommended to 'have available by February/March 1966 an additional infantry battalion with combat and logistic support units to provide an Australian Army task force in South Vietnam of 3500 personnel should this be required'.

The Defence Committee had concluded in its Cabinet submission that there would be some merit in all three services being represented in South Vietnam, but the only practicable contribution from the Navy would be from the Strategic Reserve and it was better employed on that task. Before this, other than the troopship *Sydney* and her escorts, the only other Navy involvement had been a goodwill visit by two Australian warships *Vampire* and *Quickmatch* to Saigon in 1962. There appeared to be no justification for an increased RAAF contribution—a flight of six Caribou was deployed in 1964—but four Iroquois helicopters could be provided if required. Some Canberra bombers could be sent, but these aircraft were considered inefficient for the types of warfare being waged in Vietnam. As expected, the Army would bear the brunt of any increase in numbers; after all, it was a ground war, an anti-guerrilla fight across the paddy fields and into the mountains where no ship could go and air was at the mercy of the weather. Jungle also made a wonderful hide from technology.

Surprisingly, there was no mention during the decision-making of the armoured personnel carriers (APCs) of 4th/19th Prince of Wales' Light Horse (PWLH) (or as one American military order put it, the Prince of Whales Light Horse). The troop had sailed with the battalion and was then put under the command of 1RAR on 15 June 1965. Captain Bob Hill commanded the troop. He would later engage in hand-to-hand fighting with two Viet Cong, receive a grazing wound and for his gallantry be awarded a Military Cross.[23]

In 1965 the APCs were very basic and poorly equipped. As Sergeant 'Blue' O'Reilly stated:

> They did not have (gun) shields . . . They went across with just the pintles . . . They soon realised for obvious reasons—standing up behind a machine gun—that it is not good business . . . if they give you all this heavy firepower you are going to draw the crabs. It just seems amazing to me that they could produce a weapon system [platform] that didn't have protection for the operator . . . They went to shields because that's what the Americans had.[24]

The Americans had learnt a lesson from the South Vietnamese in the battle of Ap Bac in 1962 and when the US 11 Armored Cavalry Regiment (ACR) was employed in 1965 they added shields to those vehicles that hitherto did not have them. They also learnt another lesson from the same battle: do not dismount from an amphibious APC onto swampy terrain. While mounted the infantry had the advantage of the APC's mobility and could also see over the reeds, thus helping them to detect the enemy. Their adviser's mindset was locked into training for European battlefields and when he dumped the infantry into a swamp, the South Vietnamese had lost their tactical advantage.

Additionally, the Task Force would require logistical support from US resources. 'From the military point of view'—the Defence paper commented—'the positioning of an Australian task force in South Vietnam in March, 1966, would have advantages should the current operations escalate to limited war'.[25] It did not elaborate on what those advantages were.

Manpower headaches

The first battalion to fight in Vietnam was a fully regular force. It contained no national servicemen; the first intake had been called up and was undergoing training when 1RAR went off to the war.[26] Before the battalion returned home in mid-1966, a handful of national servicemen joined the unit as reinforcements, but generally served out the majority of their time with other units of the Australian Task Force (ATF).

The national servicemen provided by conscription were the additional manpower lynchpin, without which there could be no increased Australian commitment in Vietnam. The 4th Battalion (4RAR) was to go to Malaysia in late 1965 to relieve 3RAR after a two-year tour, but needed to take over 100 soldiers from 3RAR to bring it up to strength. To send 4RAR to Vietnam would have caused considerable administrative disruption as well as manning problems. If 3RAR were kept in Malaysia, the future 7RAR raising plans would be severely disrupted. On their return to Australia, 320 soldiers from 3RAR were to be posted to 7RAR. If those soldiers did not arrive, it would be impossible for 7RAR to absorb 350 national servicemen in December 1965, as planned. The raising of 3 Training Battalion at Singleton, NSW, by January 1966 would be extremely difficult, as half the warrant officers and non-commissioned officers were to come from 3RAR. The other battalions in Australia—2, 6 and 5RAR—each had strengths of around 550, of whom about 100 were ineligible for overseas service. These three battalions were to take 250 national servicemen each from the first conscription intake and then conduct infantry training from September to December 1965. One idea was to produce one regular battalion from the three understrength units. National service problems also soured this plan, as the percentage of national servicemen in the battalions would then be out of balance with the numbers of Regular Army personnel.[27]

Thus, five of the planned eight infantry battalions were dependent upon the national service intake. These personnel difficulties indicated the scrabbling effort needed to get just one additional infantry battalion into the line. The endeavours revealed the limits of Australia's military strength and capability as well as its lack of capacity to take anything but light casualties.

Combat deaths

In the paddy fields, rubber plantations and jungle, 1RAR's soldiers kept up their harassing patrols and operations, but most actions were inconclusive, fleeting affairs with small numbers of casualties on both sides. Mines and booby traps caused most of the casualties during an operation in October 1965 into an enemy area known as the Iron Triangle, near Ben Cat. These casualties provoked a clash between two majors in the battalion when Ian McFarlane accused John Essex-Clark 'of being responsible for his battle casualties'.[28] They almost came to blows and the claim was withdrawn. Also in October 1965, the 350 additional Australian troops arrived and got ready for action.

Operation Hump in November hurt the Australians. Major John Healy's Alpha Company hit an enemy force in the Gang Toi hills 15 kilometres northeast of Bien Hoa that was well entrenched and too big for them to handle. It was a serious clash and they eventually stopped fighting the next day, following a harrowing night surrounded by enemy. Sadly, they had to leave behind two dead men whose bodies they could not recover. This was a bitter experience for everyone in the battalion and plans were underway to go back, and, in Essex-Clark's words, 'smash the Viet Cong and recover the bodies', but the operation was not approved. In 2007, the remains of Lance Corporal Richard Parker and Private Peter Gillson were found and returned to Australia. The Viet Cong had buried the two together after the battle.

Another loss to the battalion occurred when commanding officer Lou Brumfield had to retire from the battlefield. An old injury from his rugby days put him in considerable pain and he was not fit to go into the field on the next operation. Major H. Malcolm 'Mal' Lander, the battalion second-in-command, took charge of the battalion group on 16 November, initially for a few days, but then the battalion was told that Brumfield would not return. He had to go home and departed Vietnam on 25 November. This caused a nervous flutter among the officers: who would replace him? Surely the second-in-command, they thought.

Mal Lander commanded for the start of Operation New Life, which was conducted around the villages of Vo Dat and Vo Xu northeast of Xuyen Loc in Long Khanh Province, but his period of command was cut short when he was told that he must return to Australia to attend Staff College. Finally the shuffling of officers was settled and Lieutenant Colonel Alexander 'Alex' V. Preece from the AATTV took command of the 1RAR group at midnight on 3–4 December 1965. There was a palpable standoff between the 1RAR 'old family' and the new man. Essex-Clark thought that Preece was 'tired and tetchy' and 'in stamping his authority ... shows that his leadership style is ... quite authoritarian'. 'I chafe at his strict, unyielding and dogmatic style and I find it difficult to like him.'[29] Preece chuckled when reminded of these comments years later. 'There were two officers in the battalion that needed to be reminded that they did not command it; John was one of them,' he said.[30]

Australians killed in action during these early operations brought to light what appeared to be a callous government policy: the bodies were not to be returned to Australia at public expense. This happened because Australia was a signatory to the Imperial War Graves Commission—now the Common-wealth War Graves Commission—that had an established policy prohibiting the repatriation of World War I remains to their homeland. The Commission policy was for personnel killed in war to be buried in the nearest War Graves Commission Cemetery. This policy remained in place after World War II and was still current during the early deployments to Vietnam.

Sergeant Bill Hacking was the first Australian soldier to die in Vietnam in June 1963, but his death was not in combat and his body was returned to Australia at public expense. A subtle difference in the regulations permitted this. WO2 Kevin Conway of the AATTV was the first Australian soldier killed in action on 6 July 1964. Canberra directed that Conway be interred in Saigon, a decision with which his family agreed. Colonel Serong, the Commander of AATTV, did not and protested that it was a bad directive. However, Canberra did not relent and after a period of deliberate obfuscation Conway's body was laid up in Mausoleum 50, Mac Dinh Chi Cemetery, Saigon, on 22 July, sixteen days after he was killed.

There are several interesting side issues to this story. First, it is debatable whether Mac Dinh Chi was a Commonwealth War Grave site, so the directive might have been incorrect. There had been a Commonwealth cemetery in Saigon to accommodate World War II deaths but it appears that these bodies were moved after the war. Second, Canberra was misled by information that Conway had been buried as directed and the 22 July interment was a hurried affair to cover this up. Finally, Conway's remains were placed in a mausoleum because, under Vietnamese law and custom, burial meant exhumation would not be allowed for three years. Subsequently, Conway's body was moved to Ulu Pandan Cemetery in Singapore on 17 October of the same year. But more unrest for his body followed and Conway was finally laid to rest in Kranji Military Cemetery in Singapore when Ulu Pandan was resumed by the state in 1975. In 1964 there was little public disquiet about these arrangements and the two AATTV deaths over twelve months passed largely unnoticed.

As a result of the arrival of 1RAR with its attendant gaggle of press and the increase in the number of soldiers killed in action, unease about the policy started to ripple through both the military and civil communities. When WO2 Ronald Scott died from wounds at Chu Lai in September 1965, US Army Master Sergeant Eugene Jordan brought his body home to Australia. WO1 Stan Kent, the Regimental Sergeant Major of AATTV at Danang, members of the AATTV, and an unknown US Army colonel at HQ MACV made this possible.[31] Jordan's highly publicised arrival and a filmed interview told Australians that the return of Scott's body had been achieved through donations collected in Vietnam. Two more AATTV men were killed in action in November near Tra Bong Special Forces camp, northwest of Quang Ngai, and Pat Burgess, an Australian journalist, led a campaign to bring the bodies of warrant officers 'Dasher' Wheatley and 'Butch' Swanton home. The fact that Australian bodies were returned solely on the goodwill of donations stirred the public and political consciences of the nation and the policy was changed in January 1966. The change allowed for the repatriation of remains if the next of kin wanted this.[32] Some did not because the soldier had expressed a desire to be buried elsewhere.

A Morgan Gallup Poll in September 1965 showed an emerging unease in the Australian community about the war. Twenty-eight per cent were in favour of a withdrawal while 56 per cent supported the war and 10 per cent were undecided. What the remaining 6 per cent thought is not shown. There is little doubt that the potential for a national serviceman to be killed in the future hastened the change to the rules. In addition to the repatriation ruling, families who had previously paid for transhipment were reimbursed for the costs they had incurred to get the bodies home. All other funeral costs had been borne by the government. Not one body was returned to Australia in a 'body bag' as was erroneously reported later; human remains were embalmed and shipped in a hermetically sealed container. Terendak, Malacca, in Malaysia, was classified as the nearest active Commonwealth War Grave to Vietnam and 24 Australians from the Vietnam War are buried there; some were interred after the 1966 policy change either because of a family request or a personal desire expressed in a will.

The tunnels of Cu Chi

Meanwhile battles against the Viet Cong went on. Six months into their twelve-month tour of duty, the Australians of 1RAR were now in the second half of their tour, over the hump, and heading towards going home. Lieutenant Colonel John 'Wingy' Warr, commanding officer of 5RAR, was on a reconnaissance in January 1966 when he visited the 1st Battalion during Operation Crimp in the Ho Bo Woods near Cu Chi, northwest of Saigon. He arrived just after an airborne assault that was more frenetic than most. The enemy was intensely active and dangerous because unknown to the battalion at the time 1RAR had landed almost on top of the enemy's Saigon-Cholon-Gia Dinh Regional Libera-tion Army Headquarters, established in a network of underground tunnels. Even the friendlies were dangerous when Bravo Battery, 3/319 US Artillery, dropped nine 105 mm rounds within 150 metres of the battalion's command post.

In one of combat's more humorous moments, Colonel Warr appeared through the dust in a polyester dress uniform, complete with black shoes and peak cap. He also carried a briefcase. Dressed as if visiting a field exercise at Holsworthy Training Area, the soldiers almost expected him to slip on a white armband to indicate that he was an umpire on this exercise and begin to tap soldiers on the backside and tie a killed or wounded tag on them. However, the humour of the situation evaporated quickly and radios went into over-drive to stop the artillery firing again.

Today these tunnels are a popular tourist stopover, but for the Austra-lians in January 1966 the sinister tentacles of the tunnels were immediately beneath the battalion's defensive position. It was a traumatic time for both sides. At first the Australians were baffled as to how some enemy were inside their perimeter until 'Quiet!' was ordered. The perturbing noises of scurry-ing enemy beneath their feet solved the puzzle, although they added to the nervousness of those in the battalion command post who had set up inside a VC bunker with a tunnel entrance in one corner.

After smoke and/or tear gas was pumped into the tunnels, members of 3 Field Troop, Royal Australian Engineers, who became known as the 'Tunnel

Rats', went down inside the labyrinth in search of the hiding enemy, a terrifying task given that their only weapons were a 9 mm Browning pistol and a torch. The tunnels were just over half a metre each wide and high (approximately 2 feet wide and 2 feet 6 inches high) and allegedly extended for 350 kilometres.[33] Corporal George Wilson remembered going down into the tunnels the day after he arrived in the Ho Bo Woods:

> Late the next day I had my first taste of tunnels. Even at an early stage we realised we had a major complex on our hands. An American engineer, who was working with our troop, and I had just finished handing up a lot of food, clothing, papers and so on and 'Bingo!' we found another, lower level to the tunnel complex. This lower level of tunnels yielded a cache mainly of weapons, ammunition and the like. Included in the [final] haul was a Chicom 12.7 mm anti-aircraft, heavy machine gun including the tripod and sights.[34]

Some of the troop passed out from the lack of oxygen and a brave Corporal Bob Bowtell died when he fell from one level inside a tunnel to another and was unable to recover, despite huge efforts to dig him out. Three other sappers—Peter Ash, Alan Christie and Bill Coolburra—were medically evacuated out of the woods as a result of their desperate efforts to save Bowtell.[35] As Wilson explained, 'The smoke and CS gas together burn oxygen and made our gas masks useless'. The engineers mapped out several kilometres of tunnels and, as Wilson wrote years later, 'It really hurt and went against the grain to seal those tunnel entrances and leave the area'.[36]

The Australian Headquarters in Saigon sent a record of the tunnel experience to the School of Military Engineering back in Australia and many years later John Hooper and Alexander 'Sandy' MacGregor wrote 'Operation "Crimp": The First Penetration of Vietcong Tunnels', an article about Ho Bo woods and its tunnels. Hooper was the second-in-command of the battalion and MacGregor was the commander of 3 Field Troop, the engineers responsible for the searches. Their article explained how the method of searching tunnels changed during Operation Crimp.

> The standard practice when any tunnels were discovered was to blow smoke down them and then look for the telltale signs of other entrances. Once the

entrances were secured, tear gas was blown down . . . and then the entrances were destroyed with explosives. I [MacGregor] suggested after smoking the tunnels . . . rather than seal them up, we should blow fresh air down them, and send men wearing gas masks down to investigate. We had developed a tunnel search kit . . . just for such an occasion. Over six days, the 'tunnel rats' investigated tunnels for 700 metres in one direction and 500 metres across that line and we still had no idea how far the tunnels extended.[37]

Operation Crimp was the battalion group's most costly battle during its year-long deployment. Eight Australians were killed and 29 wounded during the clashes, but their efforts uncovered a good swag of weapons and other military paraphernalia, including four 12.7 mm machine guns. Of greater significance was a veritable goldmine of intelligence information gleaned from more than 7000 documents found in the tunnels. In one of the recovered letters, dated 5 December 1965, Comrade Hung who was appointed to protect some Chinese visitors, had been sick. Although he had recovered, he could not travel, so was sent back to his unit. Another document, dated 16 September 1965, advised on how to neutralise the effects of B-52 bombers. Their bombing patterns had been studied, even though B-52 bombers had only been used in South Vietnam from 18 June 1965. More sophisticated techniques appeared in later years with the help of Soviet trawlers in the South China Sea, but at this stage the fact that the bombing was in continuous lines, generally along the edges of forests and clearings, was identified as a weakness that could be exploited. Combat trench lines should be set up 500 metres from the outer defence line, the document directed, with communication trenches leading to the edge of the forest. This meant, even though the effect of the bombs was considerable, good communication trenches within the target area would enable individuals to evacuate safely.

Another directive ordered the sabotage of land and water to cause the shortage of rice in Saigon and various neighbourhoods to become more serious. The rice shortage would motivate the people to rise up against the enemy (South Vietnamese) government, a method that had been used successfully to lead the people's uprising to seize the Japanese rice storage in 1945. The directive did not mention the famine that followed in 1945 in which vast numbers of their countrymen died.

A more ironic VC memorandum, dated 8 May 1965, reported on various accidents caused by improperly hanging grenades on belts by the levers. The memo advocated the use of string to tie the levers prior to transport. 1RAR, too, suffered another grenade accident on 27 February 1966 when Lance Corporal Thomas Suter was killed while returning grenades to an ammunition bunker in Alpha Company lines at Bien Hoa.

Suddenly, Operation Crimp was over and the troops moved back to Bien Hoa on 14 January 1966. Soldiers in the battalion wondered why they had been pulled out. Various explanations were given: to secure an area for the arrival of the 25th US Division, and the more sophisticated political and strategic issues regarding a possible cease-fire with the North was another. And the Diggers of 1RAR added their own: the Australians had been too successful and if the enemy's main headquarters had been fully routed by them it would have been too much of an embarrassment for the Americans. MacGregor believed that if the search had continued for a few more days they would have discovered and ultimately destroyed the Viet Cong's underground city.[38] That was an extravagant boast if the tunnels did indeed extend for 350 kilometres.

Medical aid

By the time 1RAR returned from Operation Crimp, another group of Australians, non-combatants, had arrived in the provincial capital Bien Hoa. As a result of a request for aid through SEATO, Australia and several other nations responded to an urgent plea from South Vietnam for help with surgeons in their civilian provincial hospitals. Most of the available South Vietnamese surgeons had been drafted into military duty, leaving the civilian populace in desperate need. A surgical team from the Alfred Hospital in Melbourne had arrived under the stewardship of Dr Bill McDonald, and it wasn't long before the two Australian groups interacted. As 1RAR's commanding officer wrote:

> Our respective roles gave us little time for socialising, but we did keep contact as far as possible. We established a liaison with our battalion medical officers, Major Mike Naughton and Captain Peter Haslam. My 2IC, Major John Hooper,

arranged for members of the Surgical Team to join us for lunch occasionally. Our interpreters, Sergeant Ivan Welsh and Corporal Lex McAulay, helped out at the hospital when they could.[39]

The support 1RAR extended to the surgical team foreshadowed the relationship the Australians would develop later in Phuoc Tuy Province with their support for orphanages and hospitals. An Alfred Hospital team anaesthetist Bob Gray also reflected on the rapport that developed between the teams and 1RAR:

> We had a great relationship with 1RAR and they used to invite us over there to just go and relax, and did we ever. And they gave us Ivan Welsh their interpreter and they said we could have him and they had a Sergeant Nanh who was a Vietnamese interpreter . . . I was tremendously impressed with the 1RAR soldiers who came and painted the kids' ward inside and out and they used to bring presents and gifts to the kids.[40]

Other Australian surgical teams were located in Long Xuyen in An Giang Province in the Mekong Delta, and another was later established at Vung Tau, the municipality to the south of Phuoc Tuy Province.

A 1965 review

This chapter began by asking if the war had gone to the third phase of insurgency warfare. An answer can be found in an end-of-year review. The 173rd Airborne Brigade had conducted twelve operations in the July–December period of 1965; not all those operations included the Australian battalion 1RAR. A major deployment in August by the brigade to Pleiku-Kontum in the Central Highlands did not use the Australians when the brigade went to relieve Duc Co, only 5 kilometres from the Cambodian border. This was too close for comfort for Australia's politicians and not that far away from the future battleground (November 1965) of Ia Drang.[41]

MACV recorded in its *Command History* that at the start of 1965 the Viet Cong were winning the war.[42] VC manpower had increased to between 93,000 and 113,000 and they were standardising weapons. Although the terms 'battalion' and 'regiment' were used in the enemy order of battle, their units were less than half the strength of an American or Australian equivalent. For example, at this stage in the war, on average a VC battalion was around 350 personnel and a regiment about 1500. Regular North Vietnamese Army (NVA) elements also started to appear on the battlefield.

A highly effective use of mortars by the Viet Cong indicated an improved state of training not experienced previously and NVA units were judged as being better disciplined in battle. A VC special mission team supported by mortars and 57 mm recoilless rifles destroyed two C-130 and two F-102 aircraft at Danang in July. A two-battalion VC force attacked Bu Dop in Phuoc Long Province, 25 kilometres northwest of Song Be, in late July. American air power again caused heavy casualties to the enemy. In the 1RAR area, a 75 mm howitzer and mortars were used in a harassing attack on Bien Hoa airfield on 24 August 1965 that damaged some aircraft, probably about ten. The 173rd was in the Central Highlands at the time, but 1RAR was at the base. How ironic if the 75 mm ammunition used in that attack had come from the batch Australia sent to the French in 1954.

Multi-battalion attacks recurred in September when the Viet Cong engaged the ARVN 23rd Ranger Battalion with two battalions, and several battalions also attacked the 2nd Battalion, 41st ARVN Regiment. These clashes took place in Binh Dinh Province, a coastal area immediately south of Quang Ngai. Enemy casualties were reportedly severe, again caused by air power. The enemy's ability to take heavy losses, yet continue to conduct large tactical operations drew the conclusion that an accelerated infiltration of men and supplies was underway from North Vietnam.

Two VC regiments used an attack on the Special Forces camp at Plei Me, 75 kilometres southwest of Pleiku, in late October as bait for an ambush. The Special Forces commander recognised the ploy, but in the subsequent battle to relieve the camp the ARVN lost 95 killed, 222 wounded and 19 missing. Enemy losses were listed as over 200 killed and more than 100 weapons captured. Two VC battalions also attacked the 2nd Battalion, 1st ARVN Regiment, in the Ba Long Valley area of northern Quang Tri Province during October. Australian WO2 Ronald 'Butch' Swanton was one of their advisers. He was killed in action a month later at Tra Bong, south of Danang, along-side another warrant officer, Kevin 'Dasher' Wheatley, who was awarded a posthumous Victoria Cross for his valour in this battle by not deserting his wounded mate.

Although most of these far-flung place names were unfamiliar to the Australians based in the southern Bien Hoa Province, they were well known to the Australian advisers who had been deployed in the north since August 1962. WO1 George Chinn was awarded a Distinguished Conduct Medal (DCM) for his courage, calmness and devotion to duty during his attachment to 32 Ranger Battalion in the Ba Long Valley in 1964. WO2 Ray Simpson, another soldier of renown, was awarded a DCM for his courage during a battle in 1964 at Ta Ko, an extremely isolated Special Forces camp on the border with Laos, well to the west of Hoi An. Closer to 1RAR's base, the 7th ARVN Regiment was decimated at the Michelin rubber plantation in Binh Duong Province, immediately west of Bien Hoa, on 27 November 1965 with over 600 casualties. Sixty VC bodies were counted.

The Viet Cong had used a new tactic during this battle that saw them get in close and hug the perimeter of those they were attacking to nullify the effects of attack air and artillery. These battles had gone well beyond guerrilla warfare as Australians knew it in Malaya, and within the war there were several fronts raging, at different levels of combat intensity. Ten of South Vietnam's 44 provinces were to become much more dangerous than the others. The war was four times more active than anywhere else in Vietnam in the five following provinces (within corps tactical zones (CTZs)): Quang Tri (I), Quang Nam (I), Binh Dinh (II), Quang Ngai (I) and Dinh Tuong (IV). The next most deadly areas were: Tay Ninh (III), Thua Tien (I), Kontum (II), Kien Hoa (IV) and Quang Tin (I). Six of these lethal regions bordered North Vietnam, Laos or Cambodia, from where enemy artillery was a frequent combatant. These were also the battlefields in which the French had fought hardest against the Viet Minh in what was to become South Vietnam, which should not be confused with the French battles in North Vietnam.

The question of what type of warfare was now being fought was answered by the victors of the Binh Gia campaign in Phuoc Tuy Province in January 1965:

This was the first full-fledged campaign conducted by COSVN main force units on the battlefields of Cochin China [the southern region of South Vietnam].

Although the scale of the operations was small, the campaign was strategically important because it marked the beginning of a new era in our revolutionary war, the era of combining guerrilla warfare with conventional warfare.[43]

Le Duan, First Secretary of the Party Central Committee, added his assessment, saying: 'After the Binh Gia Campaign the enemy realized that he was in the process of being defeated by us'.[44]

By December 1965 the *MACV Command History* reported that:

There had been a number of successes and failures . . . well-planned operations and incredible blunders . . . But the ARVN had begun to seek out the Viet Cong and although often rebuffed, sometimes disastrously, he was never subdued.[45]

With the arrival of American air power and ground troops, the morale of the ARVN improved. The increased combat power provided a much-needed fillip to the South Vietnamese who suffered 11,243 hostile action deaths in 1965.[46]

Diplomatic and tactical pressures

The Australian presence in Vietnam was warmly welcomed by the United States because the war did not have United Nations sanction and many people saw it as an ideological conflict, with colonialism and other political motives as its driving forces. The other allies who fought with the South Vietnamese included New Zealand, Thailand, South Korea and the Philippines. The United States provided the bulk of the outside support to the conflict; the 1968 estimated cost for the United States was about half of its US\$71 billion annual defence spending.[47]

In the world of political and strategic issues changes were afoot and much was being discussed about Australia's efforts in Vietnam. US Secretary of Defense Robert McNamara told President Johnson in a December 1965 memorandum that Australia had been 'requested to increase their present deployment of one combat battalion to two combat battalions before October 1966'. Ambassador at Large Averell Harriman also wrote to the president that talks with the Australian Ambassador in Washington and the US Embassy

Map 1: The provinces of South Vietnam

South Vietnam was divided into 44 provinces that were responsible to the central government in Saigon. In the main, province chiefs were military officers and held dual responsibilities for public administration and military affairs. Military operations were controlled by a sector that mirrored the provincial area.

in Canberra confirmed that 'Bob Menzies plans to undertake to increase the Australian contribution'.[48] But Menzies resigned on 20 January 1966, handing the reins to Harold Holt who formed a new ministry on 26 January. Allen Fairhall replaced Senator Shane Paltridge as the Minister for Defence. (Paltridge had resigned due to ill health on 19 January and died two days later.) Malcolm Fraser became Minister for the Army. While this did not mean a change in Australian policy, the studies about an increased Australian commitment in Vietnam were dusted off as the serious business of what Australia could do and where it should do it inside Vietnam now came up for serious discussion.

Some Australians expressed their misgivings more openly in general military discussions against the American fight-and-crush approach. They preferred a more 'Softly, softly, catchee monkey' technique. However, not all the commanders supported the (prohibited) pacification. An age-old saying 'grab them by the balls and their hearts and minds will follow' became a new piece of dark humour among the soldiers. Although low-key Civic Action tasks to assist the civil community, such as digging a well, or providing schoolbooks were permitted, they were not to be misinterpreted as pacification. 1RAR's Major Essex-Clark had reservations about the techniques carried over from Malaya, saying 'Perhaps the methods . . . which still influence our thinking, are unsuitable. Perhaps our sensitive style is dangerously foolish'.[49] However, the use of unobserved artillery fire missions by Australians against 'voices' and the chastisement of a platoon that would not destroy a machine gun in a house with an M-72 anti-tank rocket because the house contained women and children also undermined the expressed Australian 'more softly' approach.

The Americans held similar discussions, too. *A Program for the Pacification and Long-Term Development of South Vietnam* (PROVN, March 1966) was an American Army study of more than 1000 pages, more comprehensive than any document produced by the Australians, which set out the problems of the pacification approach and some means of alleviating them.[50] The arguments about what was to come first—enemy destruction or closer support for friendly infrastructure—and who was responsible for what continued. Command issues in Vietnam became an issue again when the Americans planned to use 1RAR in an operation near Cambodia. Australian commander David Jackson rejected the idea and the battalion did not deploy. It was now clear that a larger Australian force would not fit comfortably within an American division.

In the same week that 1RAR was stopped from that deployment, in Australia the Defence Committee analysed the case for an increased commitment to South Vietnam. Air Chief Marshal Scherger highlighted the challenges for Australia and its Vietnam force and in his 10 February 1966 paper stated why the Australians should be independent. Scherger was considering the loss of national identity, the loss of valuable experience, especially in command appointments, and subjection to tactical doctrines to which Australia might not subscribe.[51]

Back in Vietnam this last statement appeared to hold true when the Australian battalion's next task was to protect American engineers building a major road bordered by War Zone D and the Iron Triangle, both well-known VC fighting areas. For this operation, codenamed Rolling Stone, the battalion was attached to the US 1st Infantry Division, the 'Big Red One'. The Australians carried out intensive patrolling, which worried the engineers because they could not see the Diggers sitting behind coils of barbed wire to their immediate front. The Australians found the engineers incredibly noisy and tactically appalling, but recognised that their job was to build a road, while the infantry did the fighting. One naïve soldier from the engineer battalion went for a night bike ride into Ben Cat; he was found shot dead in the morning of 19 February. Tragically, no one had stopped him leaving the perimeter to go and check out the local nightlife.

Lieutenant Colonel Preece and his staff were worried; their patrols told them something was up and they warned the American infantry—the 1st Brigade—to be prepared, according to John Essex-Clark.[52] In the early hours of 24 February 1966, the night was shattered when a large VC force assaulted the American position. After the battle, MACV reported total losses of 15 Americans killed and 101 wounded, against an enemy toll of 148 killed and 16 captured. The Australian battalion was credited with killing 17 enemy; they had one man wounded who remained on duty. As a result, the Australians felt that their patrolling methods had been justified. The American brigade had not been idle either, though their patrolling may have been a little more extravagant.

The Americans again saw the Australians as 'pussyfooting', as did some Australians, when an ambush was not sprung during Operation Silver City in the late hours of 18 March 1966. Essex-Clark dismissed the incident as a 'mistake in battle practice'.[53] However, the decision was more than that because the enemy force exceeded 200. They moved with a fully alert advance guard that cleared the way for the main body, which took half an hour to move through the ambush, a platoon-sized position of 30 men. If the ambush had been detected, it would have been one hell of a firefight. One can never know what the outcome might have been, but the company's mindset was not one prepared for a battle with an enemy force of at least a battalion. Although several soldiers were disciplined over the incident, 1RAR should be grateful for their actions; it was a sensible tactical decision. The call not to spring the ambush was the correct one.[54]

Phuoc Tuy Province

Earlier in the year on 8 March, in a Radio Australia broadcast, 1RAR heard that it would be replaced by 5RAR and that Australia's commitment would be increased to a task force of approximately 4500. For the second time in Australia's history, the force would include conscripted men who could be sent to fight overseas.[55] Soon after this announcement, the Australian generals headed for Vietnam to find a location for the bigger force. The Australian government had embargoed the western provinces because they bordered Cambodia with whom Australia maintained diplomatic relations. Areas further north had been proposed before the deployment of 1RAR and rejected, and to go into the Central Highlands would have required a much more powerful force than two battalions.[56]

Once again, national military pride became part of the decision-making process. 'Our two-battalion task force was worth any US three-battalion brigade', General Wilton said.[57] General William Westmoreland, COMUS-MACV, and Wilton sorted out the command arrangements for the soon-to-be-deployed task force. Brigadier David Jackson would command 1 Australian Task Force (1ATF) and would be under the operational control of Lieutenant General Jonathan O. Seaman, US Commanding General of II Field Force Vietnam. Jackson would answer in the Australian chain of

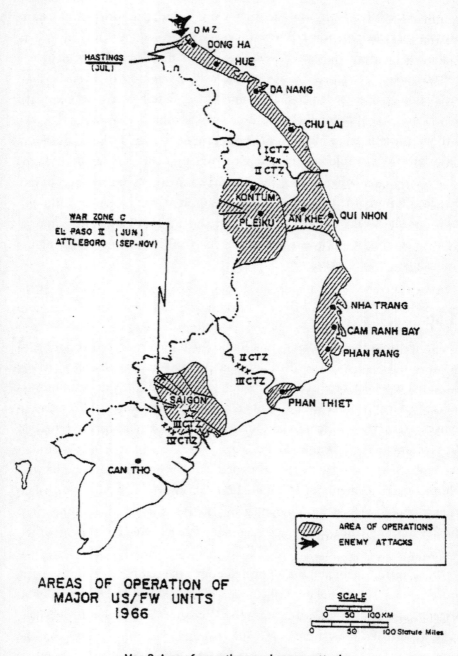

AREAS OF OPERATION OF MAJOR US/FW UNITS 1966

Map 2: Area of operations and enemy attacks

A US MACV diagram that shows areas of operation during 1966 that emphasised the protection of main areas of population. The Central Highlands wedge from Kontum-Pleiku to Qui Nhon via An Khe was long thought to be a possible route for a major thrust by the enemy to split South Vietnam into two.

command to Major General Ken Mackay who came in as the Commander Australian Force Vietnam, on 3 May 1966. Mackay would be the Australian link to General Westmoreland.

The area of operations was also resolved: the Australians would be responsible for a tactical area in Phuoc Tuy Province, but this did not include the control (pacification) of the towns. Australian troops could be used throughout the III CTZ and in the most southeastern sector of II Corps, Binh Thuan Province, if required. The III Corps zone consisted of the ten provinces that surrounded the Capital Military Region of Saigon City and Gia Dinh Province.[58] Phuoc Tuy was slightly smaller than the Australian Capital Territory. The terrain is generally flat, with mountains located in the southern, southwestern and northeastern areas of the province. Dense vegetation covered the entire province, except for small areas along the coast.

Westmoreland tentatively decided to employ the Australian force 'in the area of Route 15'. This was the main road from Vung Tau at the southern tip of Phuoc Tuy Province to Saigon. He considered it 'a priority LOC [line of communication]', he told the Australians on 12 March.[59] His aim was to improve the capacity of the Vung Tau port, which would relieve the stress upon the Saigon docks. For that plan to be realised, Route 15 would need to be safe. According to MACV papers, the Australian Chief of General Staff and COMUSMACV reached an agreement on an area of Australian operations on 17 March 1966.

[The COMUSMACV] agreement called for employment of the ATF in Phuoc Tuy province with a mission of operating in the province, along Highway 15, and in the eastern portion of the Rung Sat Special Zone (RSSZ). On 26 March, a financial working arrangement was signed by both countries, providing for reimbursement . . . by Australia for support provided in RVN.[60]

The agreement appeared to place a greater emphasis on Route 15 security than Air Chief Marshal Scherger's directive to Major General Mackay on 17 May 1966 implied. That document put the security and domination of a tactical area of responsibility in Phuoc Tuy as the number one priority, while operations related to Highway 15 were as required.[61] Scherger also told Mackay 'to make every effort to employ as many members of the AATTV as possible in Phuoc Tuy Province'.[62] Although this request was also mentioned in AATTV documents, no wholesale movement of the advisers took place. For example, in March 1967, only 12 of 87 advisers were deployed in Phuoc Tuy Province. Apparently there were too many complaints from the Vietnamese about moving the Australians out of the I Corps area.

As expected, Wilton, Mackay and Jackson looked over Phuoc Tuy Province, an area that suited Wilton's desire to get away from the stifling American stockade at Bien Hoa. Its topography would permit the Australians to fight their war as they believed it should be done. Furthermore, the Vung Tau peninsula was an ideal site for a logistics base. But the Australians also deployed with the possibility of defeat in mind, a little-known point of discussion in the decision-making process. Several officials raised the need for a potential retreat in the planning process and any geographic region that had a border with the sea would be useful, they wrote. Wilton had this idea too: 'If the war went really bad and some frightful disaster was impending, we could look after ourselves'.[63] Spectres of Gallipoli! However, looking back, many commentators think it was an Australian mistake to go to a little hill named Nui Dat to establish a base. This was a location that required a major engineering and logistics effort to build a camp from scratch. The argument against said that, in addition, the infantry spent a great part of its energy just protecting the base.[64] Others claim it displayed a barrier mentality, that it was an attempt to put a wall between the enemy and the main population centres to the south.

How to provide territorial security without pushing aside the South Vietnamese who were responsible for pacification was the Australian commanders' dilemma. There was no real argument against the selection of Phuoc Tuy Province as an area of operations, but it was a tactical and allied force integration challenge. Westmoreland's priority was Route 15 and the eastern Rung Sat zone, which was an enemy 'docking point' for materiel resupply, as well as an avenue to their Hat Dich base in western Phuoc Tuy. A range of hills dominated the Route 15 coastal strip and available land for a new camp, say around Phu My, was very limited. Indeed, Phu My 5 would have been an ironic choice, 'as some 200 Australian prisoners of war assisted in the airfield's construction . . . from February 1945'.[65]

There were known to be other docking points where the enemy had attempted to land supplies from the sea along some of the beaches in the southeastern sectors of III Corps, that would also need to be blocked if the main enemy threat was to be defeated. To conduct combat operations in the eastern fringe of the province was beyond the Australian capability at this stage. It was not possible for the Australians to provide a constant ring of protection for the 22 villages and 115 hamlets spread across the five districts of Phuoc Tuy Province, which had an area of approximately 2000 square kilometres. Looking after the people and local security was a Vietnamese responsibility; whether they were capable of this was a different question. These considerations influenced the commanders to establish a tactical area of responsibility centred upon a new foreign village to be built at Nui Dat. Keeping a large force of Australians away from Vung Tau was probably sensible for more than operational reasons. One former SAS officer remembered that there was some consideration about placing the first SAS squadron to be deployed at Vung Tau, but in his words: 'I doubt some of us would have survived the high life if we had been based in Vung Tau'.[66]

The Australians faced many challenges in maintaining population security in Phuoc Tuy, including local agreements between villages and the enemy. Although not in the Australian area of responsibility, there was an agreement between the Vinh hamlet chief in Xuan Loc District and his VC foe.

> The hamlet chief in Vinh was a man named Thuan. We had an agreement together that if he did nothing to hurt us we [the Viet Cong] would let him alone. There would have been no problem killing Thuan, but there was no real reason for it either. Maybe the new one would be tougher and more effective than Thuan . . . it was much better to compromise. In addition to keeping a truce of sorts with Thuan, I also did business with him.[67]

When Thuan later refused to sell rice at less than the black market rate, the Viet Cong killed him. 'In Thuan's case this was an easy decision to make. He was a greedy self-serving individual . . . had he been well liked, it would have been harder for us,' VC official Trinh Duc concluded.[68]

In early 1965, the *Central Office for South Vietnam (COSVN)*—the Viet Cong's controlling headquarters in the south of South Vietnam—directed that Baria Province (Phuoc Tuy) was to be a secondary theatre of operations. The importance of the Phuoc Tuy and Binh Thuan sectors to the Viet

Cong and their northern controllers at that time stemmed from the resupply routes that fed their base locations, which provided rest and training facilities. *COSVN* directed that South Vietnamese troops were to be blocked and isolated by fighting battles along routes 1, 2 and 15, the provinces' main roads. This would also prevent concentrated interference against the Viet Cong's primary theatre over on the western border with Cambodia. Strategic hamlets were to be destroyed.[69]

Dangerous territory

'The decision about locating the Australian Task Force in Phuoc Tuy Province and specifically at Nui Dat within the province reveal Wilton's determination not to place the lives of Australians at risk in more adventurous American operations', according to historian David Horner.[70] Although this was a noble nationalistic motive, without the Americans the Australians were vulnerable and the Australian 'light brigade' lacked the combat power to take on the enemy in his main backyard.

Immediately after Operation Silver City, 1RAR was deployed once more with the US 1st Infantry Division on Operation Abilene into Phuoc Tuy Province around the Courtenay rubber plantation at Cam My village. Preece, the battalion commanding officer, took on a $100 bet with the Deputy Commander of the 1st Division who had wagered that their logistics base, which the Australians were responsible for protecting, would be mortared. Preece accepted the bet, believing that his constant patrol plan would deter the enemy. He won. He also displayed a previously unrecognised skill when he assisted the wounded pilot of his helicopter to land just south of Binh Gia, the scene of the major battle in January 1965. Two regiments that later formed the *9th Viet Cong Division*—supported by *800 Battalion* and a perennial local force unit then known as *445 Company*—had fought that battle, but the allies were now looking for the *5th Viet Cong Division* which had a reported strength of less than 4000. The *800 Battalion* went on to form the nucleus of *274 Regiment, 5th Viet Cong Division*, so it had some experience of operations in the province.

It was clear that the enemy was active in the area, but the Australian patrols made only frequent fleeting contacts with members of what appeared to be the local force *C-20 Company*, while the 1st Battalion, 4th Cavalry Regiment, of the US 1st Division lost an APC to enemy recoilless rifle fire at a place called Long Tan. These low level contacts may have lulled Australian planners into a false sense of security about Phuoc Tuy Province. Was sufficient notice being taken of the operational reports and intelligence forecasts? Australian Intelligence Summary No. 12 dated 29 March 1966 provided a stark contrast, with some ominous warnings of the enemy's capabilities:

> The enemy can attack any target in Phuoc Tuy province with up to two main force regiments supported by company size local force units . . . [and] he could reinforce with two main force regiments within four days. Heavy losses have not deterred him and a large-scale attack . . . against friendly forces in Phuoc Tuy province remains a possibility.[71]

Two days after the Australian battalion left Binh Ba and returned to Bien Hoa, an estimated enemy battalion known as *D800*, a unit from the *Viet Cong 274 Main Force Regiment*, surrounded C Company of the US 2nd Battalion, 16th Infantry Brigade. It appears that the company of 134 men made an initial contact during which they killed a small number of Viet Cong. This first clash was to the east of southern Cam My, a village approximately 16 kilometres north of Nui Dat. Charlie Company immediately pursued the retreating enemy but were not aware that the Viet Cong had sucked them into a battalion position, a favoured VC isolate-and-destroy tactic.

The subsequent battle during the night of 11–12 April 1966 was bloody and costly. American artillery fired 1086 rounds in support and this weight of firepower probably prevented the Viet Cong annihilating C Company. As it was, the company suffered heavy losses with 39 killed and 70 wounded—81 per cent of its strength. The 1st Division's report on Operation Abilene is deceptive, as it does not specify in its operational paragraph how many Americans were killed. The information is well down in the report, under Administrative Matters, immediately after Laundry Services, where a small paragraph on Graves Registration shows that 39 remains were processed on 12 April.[72] Claimed enemy losses were 41 dead by body count; possibly 50 more may have been killed. The Viet Cong reported a total of 80 casualties, both wounded and dead.

Press agencies reported the battle in terms that are more graphic:

Binh Gia, Viet Nam (AP). 'It was horrible', said Private Ronald Haley, as he stood in the tiny clearing blasted from the jungle so that the dead and wounded could be evacuated. 'I've never heard such screaming in my life. Many of the wounded were yelling for their mothers. Some of the kids were calling for God', Haley said. Haley . . . was dirty and unkempt after his unit had been in the jungle for two weeks searching for the Viet Cong. The 1st Division infantrymen found them Monday afternoon and in the bitter fighting perhaps a third or more of their number were killed or wounded.

The company . . . was moving through the jungle northeast of Binh Gia on a routine patrol. At noon sniper fire began. 'After a while', [Captain] Nolan said, 'heavy fire started coming in. The Viet Cong withdrew and we called in artillery fire.'

'But suddenly we started receiving fire from all round. There were mortars coming in, heavy-machinegun fire. We were completely surrounded.'

An estimated battalion of the enemy from a main force regiment was involved.[73]

Another piece of intelligence on the enemy that disappeared among the after action words was the detection of a high level VC headquarters north of Long Tan on 3 April. It was written in the innocuous language that was used for signals intercept intelligence, SIGINT. The area was pounded by heavy firepower—tactical airstrikes, artillery and naval gunfire, and helicopter gun-ships—but no casualties were recorded. We now know that a *5th Viet Cong Divisional* tactical command post and the headquarters of *274 Regiment* were in the vicinity of this action. Also, large base camps and over 500 tons of rice were found in an arc to the north and east of Long Tan. That these discoveries and the battle happened so close to the intended Australian base should have alarmed the Australians.

Cyrus Vance, the US Deputy Secretary of Defense, visited 1RAR during Operation Abilene and reported to the president that 'the morale and com-petence of our Korean, Australian and New Zealand allies are outstanding. They are proud to be fighting with us in this common cause'.[74] Harold Holt, the Australian Prime Minister, travelled soon afterwards to see the battalion group at Bien Hoa on 23 and 25 April for an Anzac Day parade. Holt also went down to Vung Tau on 24 April to meet with the RAAF Transport Flight

Vietnam and members of the AATTV who were advising at the Combined Studies Division (CSD) training centre, a CIA program.

Operation Hardihood, the changeover

Another allied operation called Denver was launched into and around Song Be in Binh Long Province near Cambodia during April, when the soldiers of 1RAR could taste the spirit of going home. Paperwork began to flow: administrative instructions, parade directives, dress and behaviour edicts for soldiers going home and 'Q' (stores accounting) dictums on equipment write-off and transfer to the incoming forces. The 5th Battalion and 6RAR and the supporting arms were on their way; they would arrive in May and June respectively by HMAS *Sydney*. Qantas charter flights also brought in the new arrivals.

Frank Amy was a 26-year-old flight engineer when he started flying Qantas Boeing 707 charter flights into South Vietnam. He recalled that 'In those days it was considered to be a "hush-hush" operation and on 707 type 138s—the early series of the Boeing 707'.[75] The first two trips Frank did were with Qantas's chief pilot, Ron 'Torchy' Uren, a pilot veteran of World War II. Frank recalled how he became involved in the charter flights:

> In those days the charter operation was voluntary and you weren't supposed to tell your family where you were going. The operation departure time was mapped out for 11 o'clock at night. The first one they operated was Sydney–Richmond–Townsville–Manila, and contrary to the normal patterns, you didn't stay in the hotels that the normal commercial crews would stay at. Manila was a staging place for the early flights but in later days they went via Singapore. There was some diplomatic problem with Malaysia and there was also a problem flying over Indonesian air space with what was considered to be a military operation. There were no hostesses on board. It was interesting flying over at night from Manila to Saigon because all the USAF aircraft out of their bases operated without lights at night. As we got closer to Saigon we switched off all automatic lights and internal lights, which I am sure had an effect on the passengers.[76]

The *John Monash*, an army ship, and the AV *Vernon Sturdee* also took part in movement of supplies for the Task Force. An attempt to use a chartered vessel the *Boonaroo* was blocked at first by the Seamen's Union who would not crew the vessel, but the ship was commissioned into the Navy and sailors replaced the crew. She sailed for Vietnam on her one and only trip on 17 May 1966. All movements of supplies and personnel and the tactical clearance of Nui Dat, were conducted under an operational plan called Hardihood. The plan stumbled at the first hurdle.

The 5th Battalion's advance party reached Bien Hoa on 20 April, expecting to find the 1st Battalion on an operation in Phuoc Tuy and planning to relieve them in the field at Baria. They were not there; instead, 1RAR was two provinces away to the northwest in Phuoc Long. Lieutenant Colonel Warr arrived at Bien Hoa on 29 April while the transfer of stores and personnel from Australia continued. His interim base for 5RAR began to take shape at Vung Tau, on the beach, 2 kilometres south of the airfield and a little over a kilometre to the east of the main town. Roger Wainwright, a 22-year-old platoon commander, was one of the first in to Vung Tau. He recalled the time and the scene:

> There was a certain amount of excitement, expectation ... We spent the next couple of days essentially putting up wire for the rest of the battalion so they could put up their hoochies [tents] ... stinking hot and no shade, in the full sun on the sand.[77]

The area, known as Back Beach, was inhospitable. The Diggers found it very hot as they tramped through the sand dunes on their way to practise contact drills and weapon training. It was a far cry from the rubber plantations, jungle and monsoonal conditions they would soon endure.

Administratively, 5RAR was to come in complete and get established with a little help from 1RAR. Tactically, those who met up with the outgoing veterans at Bien Hoa absorbed and learnt as much as they could while they had the chance. This allowed a few tales of battle exuberance to be mixed with reality in the time-honoured fashion of soldiers everywhere. By the middle of May, 5RAR was on the ground at Vung Tau and almost ready to enter the fray. They underwent refresher training in ambush techniques and, when some helicopters arrived, some airborne assault drills. However, before the real combat began, an astonishing event took place at Vung Tau: an Officers' Mess dining-in night at the Pacific Hotel.

The dinner event does raise a question of whether the Australian military had really come to grips with this war and the power of their enemy, even when Australian intelligence summaries listed the movement of enemy regiments. For the first few months of 1966 there were strong enemy actions of battalion size or larger in an arc of provinces around Phuoc Tuy. There were attacks from Dinh Tuong in the south around to Long Khanh, immediately adjacent to Phuoc Tuy. These actions were not guerrilla attacks; allied—ARVN and US—casualties numbered several hundreds dead and large numbers wounded. Further north, in the A Shau Valley, for example, an enemy regiment attacked the Special Forces camp with devastating results. Two hundred and sixty-one inside the camp were killed or went missing, 103 were wounded, 375 individual weapons were lost, 43 crew-served weapons were seized by the enemy, as well as 30 radios. The enemy's casualties were not known, in other words, insignificant.[78]

In late May 1966, 5RAR was set to join a 173rd Airborne Brigade clearing operation around Nui Dat. Elements of Delta Company, 1RAR, commanded by Major Ian Fisher were also involved. Fisher had drawn the short straw for this tactical manoeuvre as 1RAR was soon to move back to Sydney, but he got 55 volunteers to go with him. Inexplicably, the Hardihood Operation Order J1 released by Headquarters Australian Army Force Vietnam on 20 April 1966 did not mention the deadly battle at Cam My just nine days earlier in which the Viet Cong savagely attacked an American rifle company. Instead, the Australian Headquarters cited local force resistance, adding, 'These ops may have forced Viet Cong main force units to withdraw to more secure bases'.[79]

Constant warnings about the enemy's potential to launch regimental-sized attacks inside Phuoc Tuy continued to reverberate through the allied network, especially among the Special Forces' teams operating in adjacent provinces. Maybe the dramatic language of the intelligence summaries had worn thin with the Australians and the urgency of the warnings was diluted by the fleeting nature of their recent contacts. For all the disapproval of the Americans' tactics, it was reassuring to be behind that very powerful firepower screen and their Vietnam force of 252,000 and a building armada at sea.

Following close on the heels of the 5RAR advance party was the 6RAR group. They also went through Bien Hoa on the way to Vung Tau where they staged through the sand dunes that would become the base for the Australian

Logistic Support Group. The changeover between 1RAR and 6RAR was to be along the format that units had experienced when going to Malaysia. The incoming unit would arrive light and take over the stores and equipment of the unit in location, but in this case they had to take everything except the tentage and personal weapons 75 kilometres to Nui Dat. Similar exchanges would happen with the Prince of Wales' Light Horse—unimaginatively renamed 1APC Troop—and 105 Field Battery would soon lose its coveted independent status and move to Nui Dat too.

The 6th Battalion was expected to arrive with an anticipated strength of 650 men against an approved level of 850. There were restrictions on eligibility for active service that played havoc with the unit's organisation. Not only did a soldier need to be fit, he also had to be nineteen years old and have six months' residual service remaining on his enlistment for deployment. National servicemen with six months' service or less remaining were not to go. The battalion would be topped up with 120 recent arrivals from 1RAR, which would bolster its strength to a more respectable level. Only a handful of 1RAR soldiers went to 5RAR.

The 6th Battalion had been stationed at Enoggera Barracks in Brisbane and conscripts from the first intake of national servicemen boosted their Regular Army strength. As a result of the army's rapid expansion, initial employment training—courses between recruit and unit training—was now to be completed at the unit. Normally this happened at the Infantry Centre at Ingleburn near Sydney. One of the disadvantages for the unit was that it disrupted their collective sub-unit training, but on the other hand the new Diggers were instilled with the battalion's operating procedures from Day 1.

Were the new Australian units prepared mentally for deployment into an increasingly more dangerous war zone? Major Harry Smith, the officer commanding D Company, 6RAR, wondered if the decision-makers thought they were going off to fight a war like the one they had experienced in Malaya. He was told to pack his trunk, which led him to speculate:

I recall wondering why officers were required to pack their formal white summer Mess kit jacket, starched white shirt with bow tie and blues trousers. And we were all given an allowance to buy minimum summer civilian clothes for leave periods. This sounded just like Malaysia all over again—periods on patrol, followed by leave and barrack festivities, right down to the traditional formal Mess dinners, black coffee, port and all—typically in the best English tradition.[80]

The tactical area of responsibility at Bien Hoa now belonged to the 173rd Airborne Brigade. All that was to be left after 28 May were the main bunkers, the perimeter wire and the accommodation tentage that was removed as each contingent went home between 31 May and 12 June 1966. During their travel back to Australia, it was stressed that soldiers' dress was to be of the highest order. Hat puggarees were to be correctly positioned, all badges, buckles and boots were to be highly polished and the badges of rank for NCOs were to be neatly sewn to the shirt sleeve in the correct position as laid down in the Dress Manual. The first Australian battalion (1RAR) to fight in this war had completed its twelve months of duty; the group (including the New Zealand battery) had lost 29 killed and 130 wounded, both in action and non-battle incidents. They had accounted for 128 enemy dead, or more. Some historians claim Australians never counted bodies as a measure of success. That is not the case, as the reading of any commander's diary from World War II New Guinea to Vietnam will prove.

A Sydney parade, 1966

Although the battalion was aware that demonstrations and protests against the war had increased back home, any doubts that the soldiers may have felt about the war were washed away by a grand parade through Sydney on 8 June 1966. More than 500 veterans from 1RAR and other units, including the AATTV, marched before a crowd of 300,000–500,000. Soldiers who had gone from the unit on posting were brought back for the day. Lieutenant Colonel Preece who commanded the parade specifically requested that the parade's Regimental Sergeant Major be WO1 J. D. 'Macca' McKay, MM, who had had to come home early from Vietnam. AAFV personnel formed a company to the rear of the battalion, led by Lieutenant Colonel Russell McNamara, who had been commanding officer of the AATTV in 1965 and 1966. The Governor-General Lord Casey took the salute from the steps of the Sydney Town Hall. People cheered and clapped and whistled and jostled for the best view. An elderly lady hit a protester and old Diggers shredded anti–Vietnam War banners, but one protester made it through to confront the marchers. Nadine Jensen had daubed herself in red paint and grappled Preece briefly before standing in the centre of the road in front of the oncoming marchers. They marched on without breaking step. It was a proud, gut-wrenching, emotional day for the returning soldiers.

Troop rotation

The rotation of battalions after a twelve-month tour of duty was to become the norm for the remainder of the war. Except for the infantry battalions, the artillery batteries in direct support and the SAS squadrons—whose main bodies were ferried to South Vietnam aboard HMAS *Sydney*—the supporting arms and services interchanged their personnel in an individual trickle flow system. This allowed the smaller specialist units to maintain a high level of competence during their deployments, prevented a loss of combat and command knowledge, and allowed mentoring of newer men into the war zone. Charter aircraft were also used extensively throughout the war to move people to and from Vietnam.

A year-long tour of duty was not what some units particularly wanted—especially the SAS squadrons—who believed that a six-month tour would better suit their demanding role. The British SAS, who had much more experience and history to call on in these matters, believed six months was the optimum period for sustained operations. Australian Troop commander Peter Schuman admitted that 'after six months I started to get run down . . . I started to hide my fear and every patrol became harder and harder'. Schuman, a Military Cross winner from his outstanding tour of duty, was typically direct and honest when he admitted:

> I was shaking so much I'm not sure it wasn't just straight fear because I was buggered . . . I think your courage starts to ebb away after a while after you have a few hairy contacts and you just get out by the skin of your teeth.[81]

A unit designated as 1 Australian Reinforcement Unit (1ARU) was raised on 28 March 1966 with the arrival in Brisbane of a second lieutenant administration officer. The officer commanding, Major Robert Sinclair, did not join the unit until 10 April. Reinforcements and replacements would eventually flow through 1ARU in a process that allowed soldiers to acclimatise and undergo orientation training before they moved to their units. The reinforcement unit's first task on arrival in Saigon on 19 April 1966 was to get down to Vung Tau and set up a staging area for the arrival of 1ATF. It was a shambles. No one knew they were coming; the area was not prepared; they had no tentage; when it did arrive there were no tent poles; and they had to borrow a vehicle from the Americans but it could not get through the sand. By 29 April, the unit still lacked a workforce, which restricted the preparation of its allocated area, and within two days 90 members of 5RAR had arrived. On 3 May, a further 106 personnel from 5RAR arrived. 1ARU had one tarpaulin, two 11 × 11 feet (3.35 metre) tents and two incomplete stoves. This episode was the result of a poorly conceived and implemented plan of raising a new unit and deploying to Vietnam. The then staff at Army Headquarters, Eastern Command and Northern Command should blush with embarrassment at that effort.[82]

A little hill in a dangerous place

At Nui Dat (meaning 'little hill'), an anxiously intense and physically demanding settling-in period now got underway. The new occupants—5RAR on 24 May, Task Force headquarters on 5 June and the guns of 1 Field Regiment on 6 June 1966—had to try and make their living conditions reasonably comfortable. Before the move to Nui Dat from Vung Tau, the Americans offered the artillery regiment 1800 rounds of 105 mm ammunition, as long as the Australians could move them. The response from artillery commander Lieutenant Colonel Richmond 'Dick' Cubis, a gregarious, eccentric officer, was sardonic: 'Our present establishment is designed for airborne operations but we move by road 99.95 per cent of the time and we have an inadequate capacity to provide sybaritic luxuries like water, food and ammunition'.[83]

Recent enemy activity around Nui Dat made it a dangerous place. The force on the hill had to protect itself through a constant program of patrolling and at the same time build a defensive perimeter, to get ready for the arrival of more military equipment, and come to grips with their new environment. Who was friend? Who was foe? What was good information and what was bad? The first tentative steps of command, control and coordination began to take shape as practical standard procedures. The Australian Task Force was a grouping of disparate units gathered together for the first time at Nui Dat. Its main fighting arms came from camps 1000 kilometres apart: 5RAR had been in Sydney and 6RAR in Brisbane. Brigadier Jackson, the commander, now a veteran of Vietnam, was in Saigon. He cobbled together his staff and during the first few months they managed to get a headquarters functioning on a shoestring budget of tents, radios, and practical experience. This was a distinct disadvantage for a combat force that had to hit the ground and be operationally effective immediately. To add discomfort to the challenges, the rain poured down as the wet season took hold.

Although clashes with the enemy were light, 5RAR suffered their first men killed in action in late May and early June. Private Errol Noack, a national serviceman, died of his wounds on 24 May. His death was an unenviable first for national servicemen in the war. From a political point of view, the prime minister and the ministers for Defence and the Army knew that they would have to gird their loins against a concerted attack by the anti-conscription movement over this death, and the others that would inevitably follow. In a small saving grace, the policy for the return of bodies had been changed in January and Private Noack's remains were returned home at public expense. Four warrant officers—Ron Lees, Jim MacDonald, John Andrews and Tom Phillips—and Captain Graham Belleville, all from the AATTV, were killed between January and March 1966, all in I Corps. Graham Belleville was killed on the Hai Van Pass with its spectacular views across the South China Sea.

Two soldiers—Brendan Coupe and Leslie Farren—were killed in a mortar attack upon Delta Company, 5RAR, on 10 June. At first 5RAR told Task Force that friendly artillery had hit Delta Company, but the artillery replied that they had fired on the enemy mortars that had hit the company position. In the after action report there was speculation that 82 mm and 120 mm mortars were fired in this attack. The possible use of 120 mm at this stage of the war in this tactical zone was significant, because it did not match any other reports on the enemy's weapons in this region at the time. If the report was correct, this should have raised serious intelligence questions. This mortar was first used in January 1966 against Khe Sanh, a camp far away in the northwest; it was not the weapon of a regional VC unit. The commanders knew that this was a prelude of more to come. They had anticipated that the Australian presence in the middle of the province would not go unchallenged and warnings that a major clash was anticipated flowed unabated.

The 6th Battalion moved to Nui Dat and dug in on 14 June 1966; reliable intelligence indicated an enemy attack by four battalions against the hill was likely but nothing happened. This lack of action might have influenced thinking about the enemy's capabilities. Earlier in June, eight Iroquois helicopters from 9 Squadron RAAF had arrived at Vung Tau. They were to become operational before the end of the month, but the Army–RAAF relationship was prickly. Army wanted infantry-style support while the RAAF wanted to use the more secure Vung Tau as a refuelling and maintenance base. Task Force headquarters officers also thought that the RAAF system was slow and cumbersome. The differences in thinking between the two services would get worse before they got better.

3 Squadron SAS arrived in the middle of a monsoonal downpour on 17 June and must have wondered why they were there, as they dug the first of their shell scrapes. As Trevor Roderick, one of the troop commanders, remembered many years later:

We departed RAAF Base Pearce on 15 June by Qantas 707 for Saigon via Adelaide [Edinburgh], Richmond, Townsville and Manila. We moved from Saigon to Vung Tau by C130 and then by road to Nui Dat, where we arrived around 1245 hrs on 17 June to be greeted by a tropical downpour. Great pain in the bum, as the layout of Sqn HQ [Squadron Headquarters] and Troop [platoon equivalent] areas was sorted out during this time when you were flat out seeing the limits of the area allocated. Still pissing down when digging shell scrapes, which became swimming pools. Some areas became lakes and shell scrapes vanished. Hoochied up but still stayed wet, welcome to Nui Dat! David Horner in *Phantoms of the Jungle* answers what we were doing there, 'The Sqn OC recalled the final words from Lieutenant Colonel East from AHQ, "We do not know what you are going to do but we do know that you are not going to be the Palace guard"'.[84]

Gradually the disparate units began to form an operational task force, but it lacked the toughness of battle experience and did not yet measure up to General Wilton's boast that it was better than a standard US three-battalion brigade. Two battalions did not have the flexibility and power of a triangular establishment. A comparison between brigades also needed to take into account that some American battalions had only three rifle companies, which the 9th US Infantry Division said was a miserable organisation. A US Army observation about a brigade's combat power was directly relevant to 1ATF's size.

> In our opinion, a two-battalion brigade in Vietnam was of marginal usefulness. A three-battalion brigade handled reasonable well (from the brigade commander's point of view). From occasional experience, a four-battalion brigade seemed the most effective arrangement.[85]

Basic logistical oversights also reduced the Australian force's operational effectiveness: tentage arrived without poles; provisions were in short supply; the SAS did not have radios and security codes and so were unable to conduct their primary mission of reconnaissance patrols; the APC troop that had come from Australia arrived without radio harnesses. As Ron Shambrook, the 5RAR quartermaster, observed: 'The battalion was complete in May 1966 but it wasn't until October that we got the final tent equipment, electricity and floorboards'.[86] Nevertheless, troops got on with the principal tasks of patrolling and clearing an area out to a designated Line Alpha. This line was just beyond the range of enemy mortars and an area from within which the local province chief agreed to remove all civilians. This meant the complete destruction of the Long Phuoc hamlet whose inhabitants were moved to Hoa Long, 5 kilometres south of Nui Dat—a pacification failure, if ever there was one. An additional aim in clearing this area was to provide early warning of 'enemy major offensive operations'.

Early days at Nui Dat

Clashes against the enemy in the Australian area of responsibility within Phuoc Tuy Province remained light during the early days. At the end of June, 16 local force guerrillas had been killed, and 23 weapons captured. Other efforts had destroyed tunnels, and discovered and recovered caches of rice, salt, and medical and dental supplies, while at the same time denying the enemy access to the area, which improved security around the village of Hoa Long. During the Australian settling activities, there was an ongoing consciousness of the possible presence of main force enemy units. Intelligence summaries continued to note the enemy's potential to mount a two-regiment attack, and placed the *5th Viet Cong Division*'s two regiments—known to them as *274* and *275*—in the northwest and northeast of the province.

The reports did not specifically mention the major loss of Americans during Operation Abilene, referring to it in a general sentence about ambush in a paragraph headed 'Analysis and Discussion'. Perhaps this was a deliberate omission, so as not to alarm the Australian troops. It is difficult to understand why this deadly fight was not highlighted and discussed. There was another clash on 29 June when a company of the US 2nd Battalion, 503rd Infantry, engaged elements of the *274 Viet Cong Regiment* in southern Long Khanh Province, just across the border from northwest Phuoc Tuy. The Viet Cong defended their position vigorously. At Nui Dat, although troops were on the ground and nervously alert, the Australian Task Force base was in a precarious situation. Plugging the defensive perimeter on Nui Dat with artillery batteries and the SAS Squadron raised a few military eyebrows. The decision attracted another biting observation from the artillery commander that Australia's Army continued to labour under the delusion that a field regiment was an infantry battalion with too many officers armed with guns. He hoped that when the infantry in Vietnam was educated the lesson would flow back to Canberra.[87] The SAS were there to conduct long-range patrols under conditions that should have precluded them from local security tasks on the perimeter.

A great deal of faith was placed in reports that the recent operations had pushed the enemy's main force regiments away, encouraging the hopeful belief that the Task Force would have time to dig in and be well prepared against a possible attack. By the end of June, apart from the contacts by the battalions, there was some niggling activity by the enemy around the edges of the Task Force position. As well as confusion about the mortar fire that had caused the casualties in 5RAR, only the artillery noticed other mortar firings by the enemy. A battery target called against 'three prowlers' by 5RAR did not endear the battalion, or the artillery, to Brigadier Jackson. He ordered that artillery fire be reserved for serious targets and not to blaze away thoughtlessly, which disturbed people causing them to suppose that the war was more acute than it is!

The pace intensified in July as infantrymen searched and fought in the surrounding districts on three major and three minor operations. Lessons were being learnt. One was that the World War II vintage Owen submachine gun was unsatisfactory because it lacked the power to penetrate and kill and should be replaced immediately with the American M-16. In another lesson, 6RAR experienced the difference in battle quality between a guerrilla and the *D445 Local Force Battalion* soldier, a much more skilful fighter, capable of 'quick offensive reaction and rapid manouvre'. Sergeant Bob Buick remembered, 'It was the first time everyone used the procedures and drills we had trained for and practised in Australia'. Platoon commander Second Lieutenant David Sabben added:

> Operation Hobart was our initiation onto the Viet Cong battlefield, and what an initiation it was. On Day 2, and this was our very first field operation, the battalion had more casualties than it was to suffer in any single day for the rest of the tour other than for the Battle at Long Tan and Operation Bribie.[88]

The loss of two killed and seventeen wounded in action was made more difficult to accept because, although several enemy soldiers were reported as possible casualties, no Viet Cong were confirmed killed in action that day. By the end of the operation enemy losses totalled thirteen killed and nineteen wounded. Operation Hobart prompted an examination of the Australian policy of only shooting when a target was visible. As the most recent contacts had been in dense bush, whenever someone stood up to observe they attracted more enemy fire. Permission was granted to fire in the general direction of the enemy, as long as 'junior leaders [did not] lose fire control'.[89]

This higher level of operations meant greater mental and physical demands on the force. After a road clearing operation to Long Hai on the southern edge of the province, 5RAR went for a swim at the former holiday resort, while their band played for the local villagers during lunch. Jackson also arranged for men to have 48-hour rest periods at the Rest and Convalescent Centre in Vung Tau. He recognised the problem of fatigue that stemmed from having only two battalions in the force.

Army and the RAAF continued to argue over the command and control of the helicopters. Jackson complained that the Air Force lacked a sense of urgency and that an order was taken by the RAAF as something up for discussion rather than a directive to get on with it. There was a chasm between Army's desire to have the RAAF contingent forward and the RAAF's demand to be based in Vung Tau and fly to their restrictive—peacetime style—instructions. However, whenever the fighting men got away from Nui Dat or the more comfortable surrounds of Vung Tau, they performed extremely well together. Hidden behind their cloak of secrecy, the SAS now conducted extensive and successful patrolling; the fighting efficiency of the force was good and increased daily.

Disturbingly, requests for spare parts, clothing, and an operational demand to get more machine guns took far too long to fill. During July 1966, fourteen APCs were unserviceable because they were awaiting spare parts. Defence stores such as star pickets and barbed wire were in short supply. When a battalion left the base to patrol they took their machine guns, leaving a serious gap in defensive firepower. Requests for machine guns took more than a month to be filled.

At the end of July 1966, plans were released for Operation Holsworthy, a mission to begin the pacification of Binh Ba with a view to opening Route 2. This task was to be conducted in conjunction with Phuoc Tuy Sector, the province's Vietnamese military command. Binh Ba village, set in a large rubber plantation, was 8 kilometres north of Nui Dat and only 15 kilometres south of the provincial border. Route 2 was the main north–south arterial road that cut the province into two not quite equal parts; the greater part and less inhabited region was to the east of the road. At its northern end, Route 2 intersected with Highway 1 near Xuan Loc and finished in the south at Phuoc Le (Baria). The Holsworthy plan concluded that it was unlikely that the enemy's *5th Viet Cong Division* would be encountered in strength in or near Binh Ba. Everything went smoothly and the Task Force removed the 'Viet Cong influence from Binh Ba without a shot being fired'.[90]

Although the *5th Viet Cong Division* did not bother the Australians, the US 5th Special Forces Detachment C-3, located at Bien Hoa, advised that the division was planning 'to initiate a series of attacks in Binh Tuy, Long Khanh and Phuoc Tuy, beginning in early August'. The report was dated 6 August 1966.[91]

It was also a busy time for visiting Australian parliamentarians and many staff officers in Saigon and Nui Dat. Gough Whitlam, Deputy Leader of the Opposition, met with US Ambassador Henry Cabot Lodge who reported to the American President that:

> [Whitlam] does not think that his party will elect the Prime Minister at the forth-
> coming elections. I also sense that he is favourably impressed with the effort here,
> and I would be surprised indeed to hear him attack what Americans and Austra-
> lians are doing in Vietnam.[92]

All was calm and Major General Mackay travelled to Vung Tau with his family and then made a brief visit to 1ATF with Whitlam, who left for Singapore on 11 August. The Commander Australian Force Vietnam departed two days later to attend the Chief of the General Staff's Exercise in Australia.

Tran Minh Tam, the Chief of Staff and Deputy Division Commander of the *5th Viet Cong Division*, and senior officers who included Dang Huu Thuan, commander of the *Viet Cong Baria Province Group*, met at their base near Lo O—a stream near Long Tan—on 10 August 1966.[93] They had sent out reconnaissance elements of *D445* and the *5th Viet Cong Division* to study the area around Long Tan and Long Phuoc, and were now ready to determine the fighting tactics to destroy an Australian battalion in the Long Tan region.[94]

4

TO LONG TAN AND ITS AFTERMATH
1966

Old-fashioned Australian courage.
General Westmoreland, COMUSMACV

Rolling Thunder and the bombing pause

The American bombing of North Vietnam that had started on 7 February 1965 and continued as Operation Rolling Thunder on 2 March was put on pause during the 1965–66 Christmas and Chinese Lunar New Year (Tet) truce period. The United States had decided to reduce the military pressure—particularly upon the North—and try a diplomatic path to resolve the growing conflict. Although the hiatus in the bombing may not have been for entirely altruistic reasons, as the *History of the Joint Chiefs of Staff* records:

> During 1965 the cost of the war had risen sharply in dollars and casualties . . . it was clear that the . . . bombing in NVN, was also costing the United States dearly in prestige and good will . . . even among its allies.[1]

The battlefield had taken its toll in 1965 with 1369 Americans killed in action, but the cost in dollars was not easily defined. Arguments raged over how much should be extracted from the total budget for standing expenses, the money that would have been spent on defence anyway. In 1966, one billion—

one thousand million—US dollars per month was being discussed as the real cost of the war.[2]

During a conversation with Robert McNamara about the bombing of North Vietnam, President Johnson suddenly asked: 'Tell me about the women out there, Bob'. The press had said that McNamara would not let any of the Women's Army Corps or Navy females go to Vietnam, even though there were nurses, Red Cross girls and female government and contractor employees there already. 'You reckon we can sprinkle any of them out there?' the president asked. McNamara opposed the idea: 'I think it would just cause a tremendous amount of unrest and trouble'. 'They don't add anything in the way of efficiency to the operation', he added. There were further disadvantages such as the need for separate quarters and special handling and the morale problems with wives. McNamara used Australian diplomats as an example to emphasise his point of view.

> The wives of foreign diplomats allied with us, for example, the Australian diplomats, are allowed in Saigon and they take pictures of young American women in the area and they [US wives] wonder what their husbands are doing.[3]

Correlated with the bombing pause, US emissaries were despatched worldwide to discuss a statement of fourteen points 'as a basis for peace negotiations in Vietnam', which had been announced on 28 December 1965.[4] Australia had been kept fully informed on the Peace Offensive and had made no complaint about the American efforts. Vice-President Hubert Humphrey would visit Australia in February 1966 for briefings and consultations, a cover for his real purpose of lobbying for unflinching support for the war effort in Vietnam. On his return he reported to Johnson that the 'Australian Government is with us 100 per cent [and] . . . studying ways to increase [its] aid to Vietnam'.[5]

Serious protests against the war had begun in the United States, led by respected leaders from academia and religious groupings voicing their dissent. Some of the leaders complained about the use of defoliants, while others expressed discontent about 'the horrors that your [US] planes and massive firepower are inflicting on the people of Vietnam are beyond any moral or political justification'.[6] Herbicides were first used in 1961 to defoliate areas along roadsides, powerlines, railways and other lines of communication.

Crop destruction was not permitted, but an initial operation against crops was approved in July 1961. This was stopped for fear of potential repercussions if a claim of chemical warfare were to be laid against the United States. In October 1962, both the Department of State and Defense approved crop destruction with limitations that emphasised maximum damage to VC crops and minimum exposure for non-communist peasants. It was an impossible delineation to enforce.[7]

Political critics were worried that the fighting in Vietnam would cause a war with China or the Soviet Union. Senate Majority Leader Mike Mansfield led such a group that met with President Johnson in January 1966. During the meeting, Mansfield discussed the prospect that continued fighting might lead to a general war on the Asian mainland. But the diplomatic efforts stalled. Neither the Soviet Union nor China supported the negotiations. Hanoi branded the efforts deceitful, and the halt in bombing to be a trick. General Charles de Gaulle of France had sneered at the American efforts in a private conversation with the British Ambassador in Paris, prompting McGeorge Bundy, the US National Security Advisor, to comment that 'we have not asked the French for anything. This was wise'.[8]

Jack Valenti, Johnson's Special Assistant, wrote to the president on 25 January summarising some of the problems America faced: to 'capsule some thoughts on the problem confronting you'. He provided succinct notes on 'Why Resume?' and 'Dangers to the Resumption', and stated clearly what would happen if the United States allowed 'the Hanoi "Liberation Front"' to win in Vietnam: 'The loss of S. Vietnam will lead to the loss of Malaysia and Singapore, restore the subserviency of Indonesia to China . . . and cause the Australians to live precariously'.[9]

But Rolling Thunder remained on pause. Militarily, the senior US officers responsible for prosecuting the war were concerned that Hanoi was using the cease-fire period to repair bomb damage as well as to hasten reinforcements and resupply to the South. This prompted them to press for the bombing to start again. An American diplomatic message went out on 28 January that was widely construed as a notice of imminent intention for the bombing to resume. Australia was 'solidly aboard' with the bombing to start again. Dean Rusk, the Secretary of State, wrote to the president on 29 January with a recommendation to convene the Security Council at the United Nations as a means to 'demonstrate that we want to stop not just the bombing, but the whole war', although he admitted that he felt that at this stage 'the UN cannot be involved in the conflict'.

> The Soviets and French whom we consulted as well as the British, Australians, and New Zealanders were decidedly negative. The unfavourable reactions have been based primarily on the fact that Hanoi and Peking [Republic of China; Taiwan held UN membership], because they are not UN members, have explicitly and repeatedly rejected any UN jurisdiction in the Viet Nam problem, and would therefore refuse to participate.[10]

Presidential approval was given for the bombing of the North to start again on 31 January 1966. Contrary to popular belief, at this stage B-52s were not being used in the bombing of North Vietnam, nor were Hanoi and Haiphong being hit. Rolling Thunder used fighter-bomber aircraft only against a Joint Chiefs of Staff list that was discussed weekly with the Secretary of Defense. 'Substantive changes to the original [target] proposals were the rule rather than the exception, with both State [Department] and DOD [Department of Defense] officials, and on occasion the President's personal staff, prompting changes in targets.'[11] At first the strikes were limited to just beyond Vinh at latitude 19° north, then Thanh Hoa and Ninh Binh at 20° and 20°30' north, respectively. Approximately 55,000 sorties (a sortie is one aircraft) had been flown in 1965. Most of these were armed reconnaissance missions, which permitted local commanders some flexibility of action. Few strikes were approved in the northeast sector at 21° north, and east of longitude 106°. Hanoi is just north of 21° and 105°50' east. De facto sanctuaries applied to 30 kilometres out from the centre of Hanoi, 10 kilometres from Haiphong, and between 25 and 30 kilometres from the border with China.

The tactical bombing of infiltration routes rather than a powerfully destructive bombing campaign of strategic targets in the North created a stong division of opinion within the Johnson administration. Aircraft losses were mounting as well—408 aircraft had been downed in North Vietnam by the end of October 1966. North Vietnamese air defence batteries had fired 890 surface-to-air missiles (SAM), but the greater danger was from ground fire because the missiles forced the pilots to fly at lower altitudes. The strategic

B-52 bombers were used inside North Vietnam for the first time on 11 April 1966 to bomb the Mu Gia pass that joined North Vietnam to Laos. Mu Gia is south of 18° and almost due west of the coastal city of Dong Hoi.[12]

Combat troops pour in

Tactically, 1966 was a frenetic year. Although the consensus of military opinion was that the previously deteriorating battle situation had slowed at the end of 1965, the tide had not been turned and more troops were needed to defeat a growing enemy force. At the beginning of 1966, there were 780,000 troops deployed to fight the war for the South with 193 manoeuvre battalions. Of these, approximately 580,000 were South Vietnamese and were deployed in 149 battalions. America had moved 184,000 personnel into the theatre to fight in Vietnam with 2 infantry divisions, 2 independent brigades, and just over 13 Marine Corps battalions, a total of 34 manoeuvre battalions. Twenty-two engineer battalions, 24 field artillery battalions, 4 air defence battalions and 46 helicopter companies and/or squadrons—approximately 1700 heli-copters—supported them, as well as more than 500 strike aircraft.[13] Under the banner of the Free World Military Assistance Forces (FWMAF), South Korea had sent nine battalions and Australia one. Thailand deployed non-combatant troops in 1964, but did not send combat troops until 1967. Spain allowed a small number of medical advisers to serve, alongside 29 countries who sent technical and economic aid to the South.[14]

America had been uncomfortable with the Stars and Stripes flying alone in the Southeast Asian crusade against a perceived expanding communist threat, and persisted in constant diplomatic efforts to obtain more support from firm allies and other friendly nations. In its desire 'to make the Free World support "concretely evident"', the United States was prepared 'to pay all costs incurred by other countries in providing units to South Vietnam'.[15] Australia paid its own way and New Zealand also reimbursed the United States the costs of logistical and administrative support. The Philippines had been pressured diplomatically to send a force to Vietnam, but did not do so until later in 1966. Subsequent to a 1965 operational concept known as KANZUS (Korea, Aus-tralia, New Zealand and the United States), a proposal to deploy a brigade-size force in support of the 1st ARVN Division south of the DMZ, the Adjutant

General of the British Army had a talk with the US Army Attaché in London during which the fate of the Ghurkha Brigade was mentioned. If the Ghurkhas were to be phased out of the British Army, the Adjutant General enquired, what was the desirability of their deployment to Vietnam? General Westmoreland at MACV had indicated that the brigade would be used in operations similar to Malaya, if its use was accepted. But Britain decided not to dismiss the brigade before 1970 and the KANZUS force also did not eventuate. MACV forged ahead with a program to field 264 manoeuvre battalions—162 Vietnamese, 79 US and 23 FWMAF—by January 1967.[16]

Intelligence reports and arguments

Allied intelligence reports—although imprecise and in conflict between agencies—indicated an enemy order of battle in Vietnam that included eight confirmed and two possible NVA regiments in the South at the start of 1966. Furthermore, VC regiments were confirmed at thirteen for a possible total of 129 battalions, or about 230,000 personnel.[17] There were many arguments over these figures, which eventually led to a notable libel case by General Westmoreland against a 1982 CBS News broadcast, in which CBS had allegedly accused Westmoreland of manipulation and conspiracy about the size of the enemy's total force. A complicated legal battle followed that was settled out of court.[18] Regardless of the overall debate, there was general agreement in 1966 that the NVA figures were about 15,000 and that the VC main force had approximately 60,000, with irregular (guerrilla) forces of around 120,000. These figures excluded political cadres and support troops. US command was adamant that the penetration of NVA units into the South continued unabated in 1966 and that they were well trained and well armed with the new family of 7.62 mm weapons. This included the K-50 submachine gun that 'far surpassed in firepower an opposing friendly unit equipped with . . . the US M1 rifle or the M-14 rifle'. 'Also in 1965 RVNAF [South Vietnamese] . . . had lost 16,915 weapons to the enemy'.[19]

The Buddhist dilemma

Political and religious troubles were also brewing in the northern provinces of the South and a large demonstration by 20,000 Buddhists in Hue in late

March 1966 spread to Danang in April. This caused military problems for the advisers who had to sit aside while the potential for an armed clash against the protesters looked imminent. Vietnamese marines were flown in to Danang to confront the anti-government demonstrators and the commander of the 1st ARVN Division declared his support for the struggle against the government. AATTV personnel were ordered to evacuate Australia House in Danang on 9 April when the 2nd ARVN Division moved towards the city. Although the plan of evacuation was to move by helicopter to East Danang, the advisers eventually drove through the city in 'borrowed' vehicles, one of which was a white Cadillac.

Premier Nguyen Cao Ky flew in two Ranger battalions, and the scene appeared set for a South Vietnamese versus South Vietnamese battle when the 1st ARVN Division troops denounced the Ky government, but pledged to continue fighting against the communists alongside US and FWMAF troops. By the middle of May, after some armed clashes, the dissent had fizzled out and each side withdrew to positions of serious disagreement that they hoped would be resolved by statements of grievances through the Peoples and Armed Forces Political Congress in Saigon. This did not happen, much to the delight of the French, some said. Strangely, the enemy did not take advantage of this period of political and social fragmentation to launch major attacks that would have been extremely difficult to counter under the restrictions imposed on American and Australian troops, especially the advisers. When the Australian advisers returned to Australia House, they found that it had been looted. (More disappointment followed when they had to return the white Cadillac.)[20]

Throughout this period that had started at the end of 1965, the enemy were thought to be avoiding clashes that would cause them heavy losses but they continued to carry out terrorism, sabotage and ambushes to unnerve the population as well as to unsettle the allied forces. Continuous studies by the Americans and the South Vietnamese on enemy activities identified increased action along the DMZ where extensive fortifications for anti-aircraft and artillery pieces were found. The Ho Chi Minh Trail through Laos had expanded to include not only foot tracks, but 500 miles (805 kilometres) of road trafficable by trucks, of which 200 miles (320 kilometres) were capable of use all year round. These vehicles carried most of the combat resupply for operations in the South.[21]

Australian adviser Barry Rust recalled the extreme difficulty he and the Special Force Montagnards experienced trying to track the enemy's movement in the A Shau Valley on the border with Laos, well to the west of Danang.

I joined a new group to be called the Mobile Guerrilla Force, which was intended to operate independently in remote regions for up to 60 days. Resupply was by air, and one trick was to use modified napalm canisters to drop supplies. In late October 1966, we did our first long-range operation to A Shau. It would have to be the most physical and mentally demanding operation I have done. For the first time, I had to use my rifle as a crutch on the muddy mountains [which ranged from 500 to 1500 metres]. It was the middle of the monsoon and it rained heavily. It was very cold and everything was wet. Because of the rain and fog, we could not get our resupply and then the North Vietnamese Army found us. We were forced to move out and to leave behind several bodies in quick burials, which were recovered in December.[22]

Lessons learnt

Allied after action reports were scoured to find those gems of tactical information that can provide field commanders with an edge in battle. One series of MACV accounts—from February through to June 1966—highlighted a valuable lesson about the enemy's main method of attack against allied units.

The enemy tended to attack when he had overwhelming superiority of numbers. The Viet Cong avoided attacking large Allied units of regiment or brigade size, but he did attack isolated battalions and companies using sufficient strength to insure great numerical superiority. It was typical of the enemy to attack with one-third of his available force and to employ the remaining two-thirds of the units to set up an ambush of the Allied relief team. During attacks the NVA/Viet Cong used a hugging tactic as a means of protecting themselves from Allied artillery and air strikes. The enemy then withdrew by small squad-sized increments, using multiple routes . . . moved frequently, and made use of darkness and periods of low visibility.[23]

In the Australian Area of Operations in III Corps, this assessment was borne out by the two earlier main battle actions conducted by the Viet Cong in Phuoc Tuy Province. These battles—December 1964/January 1965 and

April 1966—saw the enemy attack Vietnamese and American units along or in the vicinity of Route 2 in battles of ambush, or the isolate-and-destroy technique. Had the Australians studied these battles, and made a mental note that the destruction had happened just up the road from Nui Dat?

The enemy and the Australian area of operations

In the early part of 1966, VC strength around Saigon was about 5000, with nearly 40,000 located within an 80-kilometre radius of the capital. The encirclement had the potential to isolate the seat of government from its already

Map 3: III Corps Tactical Zone (later Military Region 3)
III CTZ consisted of ten provinces that surrounded the Capital Special Zone (Saigon City and Gia Dinh Province). 1ATF was located in this CTZ. There were four CTZs throughout South Vietnam, numbered I–IV from north to south. Each CTZ was commanded by a senior South Vietnamese officer (major general/lieutenant general).

harassed and wavering rural population. It also placed the newly estab-lished Australian Task Force in Phuoc Tuy Province within the politically and militarily sensitive Delta–Saigon zone, one that the enemy identified as 'the originating point of new political organisations sent out to support the offensive in the highlands'. The Central Highlands region was classified as the 'killing zone', an area in which the war would be won. It was a priority area with secure bases close to Cambodia and Laos. The mountains and jungle of this region favoured NVA/VC operations.[24]

Since the days of the war against the French, Vietnam had been divided into geographical enemy command zones. These military regions were dictated by the high command in Hanoi and did not match the provinces of South Vietnam; nor did they mirror the South's CTZs. South of the 17th parallel, Vietnam was known as *Trung Bo* and *Nam Bo*. The nine Hanoi command regions changed several times throughout the war. The Central Highlands (*Trung Bo*) was *Military Region 5* (central and north) and *Military Region 6* (lower southern), while regions 7, 8 and 9 made up *Nam Bo*. The Australian Nui Dat base was located in the enemy's *Military Region 7*, which covered the provinces in a north-erly arc from Hau Nghia to Tay Ninh to Phuoc Tuy, but excluded Binh Long, Phuoc Long and Binh Tuy. *Military Region 7* was also known as *Eastern Nam Bo*. Regions 8 and 9 included Long An Province. All the provinces down into the Mekong Delta were known as *Central* and *Western Nam Bo*. The *Central Office for South Vietnam* (*COSVN*), also known by the codename '*R*' and '*Cuc R*' com-manded all of *Nam Bo*. *Nam Bo* was also known as the *B2 Military Front*.[25]

Hanoi understood that control of the more heavily populated coastal districts was essential to its military tactics for the Highlands. Hanoi's plans for Saigon—which had a special district status for both sides—included the domination of the routes that led into the city so that they could isolate it and create an atmosphere of insecurity in and around the Capital Military District. The feeling of fearful isolation in the Phuoc Tuy provincial region came from this constant presence of a lurking enemy main force division.

The *5th Viet Cong Infantry Division*

On 3 February 1965, *T7*, also known as *Military Region 7*, established its first main force regiment. At first, the regiment, known as *4*, had only two battal-

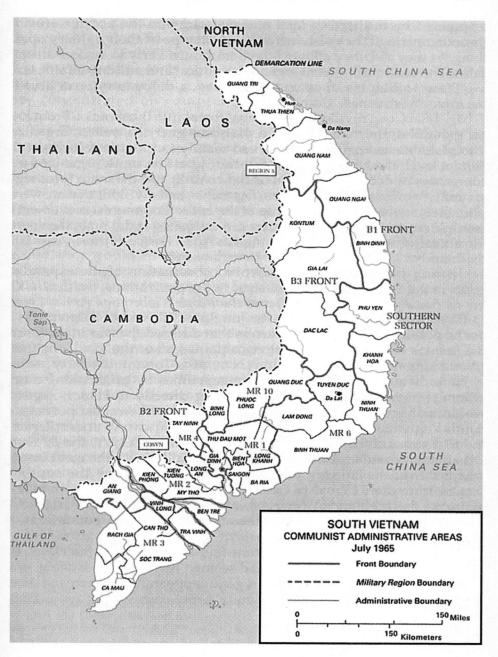

Map 4: South Vietnam communist administrative areas July 1965
North Vietnam divided the South into military fronts and regions that changed throughout
the course of the war. A front was the equivalent of an army corps command. The *COSVN*
area was also the *B2 Front* that covered Phuoc Tuy Province. The province names also
differed from the South Vietnamese titles; for example, Ba Ria (1965) was Phuoc Tuy.

ions, with a combat support company and a reconnaissance platoon. Allied intelligence called it *274 Viet Cong Regiment*. During its early military operations the regiment ranged across several provinces northeast of Saigon and carried the battle honour *Dong Nai Regiment*. In May, *274* ambushed two ARVN convoys on Route 20 in Long Khanh Province. Route 20 connected with Route 1, 15 kilometres west of Xuan Loc, and was the main road to the Southern Highlands city of Dalat. These roads were at the northern end of Phuoc Tuy Province which was split north–south by Route 2, which joined coastal Route 15, which led directly back to Saigon.

Soon afterwards, in early June 1965, *274 Viet Cong Regiment* and the *240th Company* of Xuan Loc attacked the Gia Ray training centre on the rail axis Xuyen Loc to Phan Thiet and captured a large quantity of weapons that included two 81 mm mortars. They followed this with an ambush of an ammunition convoy near Phu My on coastal Route 15. In September 1965, *274 Viet Cong Regiment* was strengthened by the incorporation of *265 Battalion* and moved to the Xa Bang base, reported to be near Le Mountain (Nui Le), east of Highway 2 and south of the provincial border with Long Khanh. The *274 Regiment* and the Baria local force *D445 Battalion* were then given the tasks to organise resistance and to defend the Long Phuoc, Long Tan and Hat Dich base areas within Phuoc Tuy.[26] The local force *D445* was well versed in operations and ambushes around Long Tan, Tam Phuoc and Duc Thanh, and was able to guide the main force strangers through their province.[27] In November 1965, *274 Viet Cong Regiment* attacked ARVN installations at Phuoc Hoa on Route 15 and, in February 1966, hit camps at Ba Ta and Xo Xu (Vo Xu). These battles were 100 kilometres apart over the provinces of Phuoc Tuy and Binh Tuy and epitomised an NVA/VC operational objective:

> To fight without a clear cut front-line, without an objective set once and for all, operating rapid concentration and dispersal, appearing up and fading away unexpectedly, fielding now a big force, now a minor one and attacking the enemy in many places at the same time.[28]

A second regiment known as *5*—called *275* by the allies—was formed in May 1965, with 850 personnel from the Mekong Delta region, and ordered to operate on the Baria (Phuoc Tuy) battlefield in September 1965. Illness took a heavy toll on the new regiment.

> They were unfamiliar with the climate, life was difficult and the unit had to urgently build bases and organize training, while at the same time, finalize the re-organization and pay attention to the health of the cadre and soldiers, which was declining.[29]

There were days when 100 per cent of a battalion suffered malaria, with no one to prepare and cook the rice, and the regiment was required to undergo an extensive period of reorganisation, study and training.

Subsequently, *274* and *275* regiments became the body of the *5th Viet Cong Division*. At a divisional conference held at the May Tao base in Phuoc Tuy Province, the *Division's Party Committee* declared 23 November 1965 as the '*5th Division's Traditional/Heritage Day*'. Some allied military agencies briefly confused this division with the *5th NVA Division* that was operating much further north inside South Vietnam's Phu Yen Province. It is interesting to note that the headquarters was at May Tao, but the regiments were not.

In addition to the two regiments, the *5th Viet Cong Division's* other combat support units were *22 Mountain Artillery Battalion*, *12 Anti-Aircraft Company*, *95 Reconnaissance Company*, *23 Mortar Company*, *25 Engineer Company*, *605 Communications Company* and *96 Medical Company*. At this stage, late 1965 to early 1966, the personnel field strength of the division was probably less than 3000, but it is difficult to determine how many men each regiment had in the field. The Viet Cong admitted that the battalions in *275 Regiment* were seriously understrength in early 1966. A company in the *3rd Battalion* only had 40 weapons and the *1st Company* of the *1st Battalion* had just 45 soldiers, forcing the commander to amalgamate his troops into a two-battalion 500-strong regiment.[30]

The *5th Division's* battlefield was much larger than Phuoc Tuy Province, as *COSVN* grouped Bien Hoa and Baria provinces into a renamed region called Ba-Bien. Later they added parts of Long Khanh Province and occasionally the division went over the eastern border into Binh Tuy Province. But in the first six months of 1966 their operations abided by the directive of the Viet Cong's *B-2 Front*—the military arm of *COSVN*—to isolate Saigon and to create insecurity. The *274 Viet Cong Regiment* created a feeling of danger through mobile operations along routes 1, 2 and 15, centred on the southern and western districts of Phuoc Tuy Province.

In a major action away from that triangle, *274 Regiment* attacked Vo Xu, east of Xuan Loc, in February 1966. They had *275 Regiment* in support; it was tasked to ambush any allied relief forces. The first attacks failed and they tried again in March 1966, with *275 Regiment* as the leading force. There were shortcomings; 'the element of surprise was lost and the *5th [275] Regiment* . . . did not yet have the experience to organize a concentrated battle and was still weak'.[31] The regiment was ordered to return to the Suoi (stream) Ma Da, in Long Khanh Province, across the Dong Nai River and to the west of Route 20. There the unit was to reorganise and retrain, and then come back to do battle in the area north of Route 1, along Route 20 which went to Dalat.

When the Australian Task Force began to establish its base at Nui Dat (1), which was on Route 2, the VC command directed the regiments of the *5th Viet Cong Division* to prepare to defend against and strike the new enemy. During June 1966, *274 Regiment* was ordered to redeploy to the Chau Pha – Hat Dich region to protect *84 Rear Services Group*. Before this, their headquarters might have been located in the area 10 kilometres east of Binh Gia on Route 2 in the vicinity of the Suoi Tam Bo, or east of Dat Do, along Route 23 near Nui La. The *Division*'s documents reveal that the movement to the Hat Dich was achieved under duress from battle losses and difficulties associated with the changing of their responsibilities and combat zone.

Chau Pha – Hat Dich was named after the two streams in an area approximately 15 kilometres northwest of Nui Dat (1). To add to the confusion with place names, there was another Nui Dat (2), 5 kilometres east of the Australian base and 2 kilometres north of the deserted Long Tan village.[32] The Hat Dich was a densely forested, jungle-type terrain that assisted a guerrilla force to hide and move undetected and it was close to the borders of two other provinces, Bien Hoa and Long Khanh. This location was useful for another battle technique the Viet Cong used—they liked to move close to provincial boundaries. Crossing provincial boundaries meant that the allied forces needed additional coordination and approval measures to engage in battle, which could delay any offensive action and that delay often helped the enemy to escape unmolested.

On 29 June 1966, the US 173rd Airborne Brigade reported a clash with elements of *274 Regiment* in Phuoc Tuy's neighbouring Long Khanh Province. The brigade report said that it had threatened VC base areas and in doing so the enemy opposition intensified. This supported information published in the *5th Viet Cong Division*'s history that the regiment had moved into the area. A separate US Special Forces' (USSF) intelligence summary, dated 16 July 1966, also reported that a VC battalion identified as *D800* had been told by the VC *Eastern Committee* to gather coolies for transportation work. The battalion, listed as a unit of *274 Regiment*, was then directed to take weapons from the Tan Uyen area of Bien Hoa Province to supply the Hac (Hat) Dich Secret Zone in Phuoc Tuy Province, some time in late June or early July.[33]

The *275 Viet Cong Main Force Regiment* also moved in June to the east of Route 2, where it was to protect divisional headquarters and prepare forces for striking against the enemy. Again, in the Special Forces' report, an enemy regiment with 1000 personnel was said to be in the vicinity of the provincial borders of Phuoc Tuy and Bien Hoa. The group was supposedly a newly identified regiment with a task to attack the Quyet Thang—a slogan meaning 'Determined to Win'—Training Centre, which might have been the Long Thanh centre on Route 15. The USSF reports show that the G-2 Intelligence at AAFV—Australian Army Force Vietnam, renamed Australian Force Vietnam—was included on the USSF distribution lists. The sighting was classified 'F-6', which meant its reliability and truth could not be judged.[34]

Enemy activities, July 1966

Enemy activity around the Australian base in early July 1966 remained at a low level, with fleeting contacts and light casualties on both sides. Active patrolling by the two battalions continued to clear the area inside Line Alpha. The Task Force area had been split into two, with 5RAR responsible for the northern arc and 6RAR for the southern sector. On 1 July, an air strike hit a target 2 kilometres northeast of Long Tan with 6500 pounds (3000 kilograms) of napalm and 3000 kilograms of general-purpose bombs as well as 2100 rounds of 20 mm cannon. The target was not described, but the hit was reportedly 100 per cent on target. This was a significant and costly strike without a bomb damage assessment or an explanation in the Australian records on what they were bombing.

A further air strike on a VC village just west of Long Tan on 4 July with three 500-kilogram bombs damaged one hoochie; one bomb was a dud. The patrolling Australians continued to find old camps, graves, rice and tunnels, as well as small parties of enemy who generally fled after contact.

A more dangerous enemy force reportedly appeared on 15 July in the western region of the province, north of Route 15 near Phuoc Hoa in the rugged Dinh and Toc Tien hills. This location was not that far from the VC Hat Dich Zone. Operation Brisbane was mounted quickly by 6RAR to sniff out and make contact with the large force, but found nothing. From their foray into the Nui Dinh Valley, the Australians learnt that this was extremely difficult country, even for the infantry. On 18 July, more information about possible enemy forces came in from the 10th ARVN Division's headquarters at Xuan Loc. Their reports said that between 800 and 3000 enemy troops had been seen in an area adjacent to Phu My on Route 15, northwest of the Nui Thi Vai.[35] This information agreed with the earlier Special Forces' report that an enemy regiment was there, but it is doubtful that it was a new regiment; more than likely it was the *274 Viet Cong Regiment*.

American sources evaluated the suggestion that 3000 VC troops had recently arrived in the province as 'F-3', which meant the report's reliability could not be judged but it was possibly true. The more difficult problem was to determine whether this force was additional to the *5th Viet Cong Division* that previous reports had indicated was in the province. The Australian Headquarters in Saigon had already concluded in their Operation Hardihood plan that regiments *274* and *275* were in the northwest and northeast of Phuoc Tuy Province, even though they had downplayed their threat to the Task Force. The numbers disturbed Brigadier Jackson and his staff at Nui Dat beyond the worries they already had, but once again searches by the Australian troops found nothing of substance to support the claim that such large numbers had massed nearby.

More information received from the 10th ARVN Division on 21 July reported that 300 Viet Cong had been seen moving near Long Tan on 18 July and that they had moved off in a northeasterly direction, towards Nui Dat (2).[36] Another force, or maybe the same group, had been seen on 17 July east of Binh Ba. This group was also about 300–500 men, carrying a large number of anti-aircraft guns, but this report had not been evaluated. The Austra-

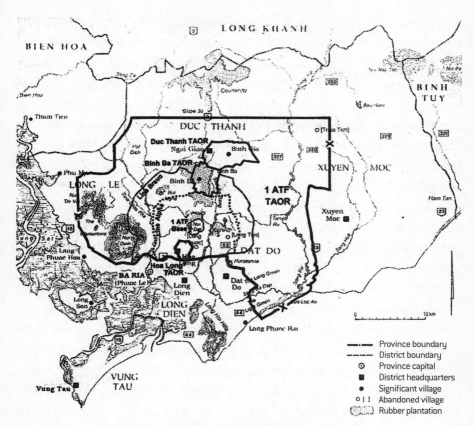

Map 5: Australian Tactical Area of Responsibility 1967
1ATF Tactical Area of Responsibility within Phuoc Tuy Province. Line Alpha was drawn just
beyond the range of enemy mortars. Line Bravo was the range of Australian artillery. The South
Vietnamese province chief maintained responsibility for civilian districts such as Binh Ba.

lian 5th Battalion was several kilometres away near the Suoi Nghe hamlet on
the 17th, which may have caused the Binh Ba enemy to move on. It is also
possible that the locals might have reported them to be the VC force.

Although the trend of contacts with the enemy during the first weeks of
July remained at a low level, some of the enemy equipment and uniforms
indicated that there were main force units in the Australian tactical area of
operations. More reports also came through from Vietnamese agents, telling
the Americans and the Australians that there was possible enemy movement
in the northwestern and northeastern sectors of Phuoc Tuy Province.

These reports were followed by another account on 24 July 1966 that 1000
Viet Cong were digging-in approximately 8 kilometres east of Long Tan and

out towards Xuyen Moc. The next day, 6RAR made contact with an estimated enemy company just east of Nui Dat (2) and 3 kilometres northeast of Long Tan. The units broke contact at 1830 hours, although the Australian force continued to receive sporadic mortar fire up to an hour later. Charlie Company, 6RAR, reported that the enemy used bugles during the action and that when they split into two groups to withdraw, one group stayed in position to cover the getaway of the others. This was an ominous sign that these troops came from a well-disciplined and dangerous enemy unit.

Major John Rowe, the Task Force Intelligence Officer, analysed the action and concluded that the probable intention of the Viet Cong was an attempt to prevent the Australians from interfering with a known VC supply and infiltration route, but he did not have sufficient information to identify which units had been contacted. He did refer to the two regiments of the *5th Viet Cong Division* as well as the *D445 Battalion*, which agents had indicated 'were operating on the eastern fringe of the 1ATF TAOR'.[37]

They were, in fact, a reconnaissance team from *1 Company, D445 Battalion*, who were swiftly reinforced by the remainder of the battalion and they admitted using bugles to coordinate their attack. *D445* claimed that heavy casualties were inflicted upon the Australians, but the artillery fell like rain and *D445* was unable to attack the Australian infantry. The enemy battalion also thought that it had learnt from this encounter and they had 'the capability to deploy and apply our combat techniques swiftly' even though 'we suffered a number of wounded and To Dung, a political officer, died during the withdrawal'. *D445* added a warning:

> From this first test of strength, the battalion confirmed that it could not underestimate the Australian forces—particularly their application of artillery fire to break up attacks and their ability to flexibly redeploy their own forces for counterattacks.[38]

Clashes with the enemy continued and on 26 July 1966, 6RAR again made contact with VC elements to the east of Long Tan. An armed Chinook helicopter was used to attack the force, estimated to be around 120 men, which was trying to move south, just southeast of the destroyed village. When the Chinook fired upon this large group of troops it received concentrated small-arms fire in reply. Documents found on a body after the firefight indicated that he was an officer from the *D445 Battalion*. Another document revealed that the local VC forces operating east of Long Tan were forcing civilians to dig tunnels in an area possibly east of that village. In a follow-up, 6RAR found an extensive VC base area and campsites all close to and in an arc on the northeastern side of Long Tan. Some of the camps had been evacuated within the previous 72 hours.[39]

The Chinook gunships returned on 28 July and again were fired upon by small arms. These heavily armed and ungainly giant dragonflies swooped and strafed and looked as if they might fall out of the sky, without having to be shot down. A standard load for a 'hook-gunship' included 20 mm cannon, a 40 mm grenade launcher, .50 calibre (12.7 mm) machine gun(s) and 2.75 inch (70 mm) rockets. Four of the helicopters returned on 29 July and again were engaged by 'intense small arms and automatic weapons fire'. An observation post on Nui Dat reported that during this firefight the helicopters were getting more fire than they were giving. The Chinooks had stirred an ants' nest of activity. This time the action was to the west of the base and only a few kilometres away, just south of Nui Nghe.

In the aftermath of that action, no bomb damage assessment was made even though an air strike and artillery fire counterattack was called to suppress the enemy's efforts. It all ended with a brief entry in the Task Force log: 'enemy probably well dug in'! Major Rowe reported that the contacts to the east were with *D445*, therefore the battalion to the west was a main force unit. Rowe added that as agents had reported the arrival of 3000 Viet Cong into the province, this battalion might be part of that larger force. He wrote that the threat in the west did not lessen the one recorded earlier in the east.[40]

Intelligence reports, or statements of the bleeding obvious

At this stage, the Australian intelligence summaries deteriorated into platitudes and discrepant advice. Local force guerrillas did not stand and fight against heavily armed Chinooks. This action indicated that a disciplined and well-trained enemy force was in the Task Force area and that was acknowledged by the Australian intelligence summaries (INTSUMS) in the latter part of July. However, previous Australian intelligence papers had downplayed the potential danger that the two main force regiments known to be in the provincial region posed for the Nui Dat base.

Major Rowe's INTSUM No. 58 for 29 July 1966—although not signed by him—warned of a worst-case, multi-regimental assault that might be made up from elements of *274* and *275* regiments as well as *D445 Battalion* in an attack from the east or west, or simultaneously from both directions. To add to the drama, a National Police report dated 26–28 July said that '1000 Viet Cong had moved through YS265584 [Long Son Island]' and 'in a day period 3000 Viet Cong will have arrived in Phuoc Tuy Province'.[41] It sounded like a rehash of information from INTSUM No. 47 released on 18 July.

Captain Mike Wells of the AATTV, an adviser located in the province, said that he had passed information about the movement of a 1000-strong group of enemy to Brigadier Jackson on 26–27 July.

> The earlier reports emanated firstly from a paid agent, via our province Police Chief and then in discussion to my counterpart–Dai Uy [Captain] Quanh, Chief of Staff. It was believed they had moved east to Long Son Island from the 'Rung Sat' zone and rested. [They] then [moved] north through the foothills of the Nui Dinh's eastern edge up to Nui Nghe [where] they had left elements on the Nui Dinh feature as well as digging into the area between both features. I passed this personally to BRIG Jackson. His Aide de Camp LT David Harris was also present. I suggested that on information gathered that they were elements of 274 Main Force Regiment.[42]

Was the newly detected group the same force reported by the 10th ARVN Division? Where had it come from? Was it a redeployment of the *5th Viet Cong Division*, which had a recorded strength of 3500? If so, how did they get to the Hat Dich area? The information from agents that the entire group, or a large part of it, had come out of the Rung Sat Zone, a swampy area west of Phuoc Tuy, is an implausible explanation. The *274 Viet Cong Regiment* had operated in Phuoc Tuy since 1965, according to the VC history. Elements of the regiment—*D800 Battalion*—had mangled an American rifle company in April 1966, an action that attracted scant attention in the Australian operational summaries. Furthermore sub-units of the regiment had been reported in contact in Long Khanh Province in late June 1966 against the American

173rd Airborne Brigade. In addition, the Rung Sat Special Zone, known as *D10*, was outside the *5th Viet Cong Division*'s tactical territory. This new group therefore had to be a new formation. But the *5th Viet Cong Division* did not have a third regiment in 1966. All the confirmed reports on the division said that it had two regiments, each with three infantry battalions. Behind the front-line troops, or intermingled with them for some operations, were the support echelons such as signals, medical, and headquarters staff.

The Rung Sat had also been under recent attack during April by US Marines on Operation Jack Stay. Although they only encountered local force guerrillas and rudimentary defences, the Marines demonstrated that they could operate in the swampy terrain and unleash devastating firepower from naval guns and bombing by B-52.[43] In addition to this operation, the US Navy had established a Rung Sat Special Zone River Patrol Group that patrolled the area's main waterways. The patrol reported that July 1966 was a very quiet month, but two contacts were detected on the Soirap River at the western edge of the Rung Sat on 18 August. Two sampans with six occupants were engaged and the boats were abandoned but a rifle, a carbine, 120 pounds (55 kilograms) of food and a small quantity of medicine were left behind. The action was evaluated as a local force VC attempt to run supplies into the Rung Sat Zone.[44]

The enemy knew now that the Rung Sat was under surveillance because of their attacks against shipping that sailed through the confluence of the many waterways that led to the Saigon River. The waterways were also a known resupply route, especially for rice out of the Mekong Delta. It would have been a tactically dangerous move for a large number of troops—the reported 1000—to come out of the swampy Rung Sat and then across Long Son Island, which was not connected by road to the main peninsula. If they were to be caught with their backs to the sea, there was no escape.

The Australian intelligence officers were obviously flustered by the numbers of enemy now presented to them in a plethora of written and verbal reports. They didn't know who or what to believe and attempted to cover all the bases with a statement of the obvious: that VC forces posed a direct threat to the Australian Task Force. This information posed a tactical dilemma for Brigadier Jackson and his staff. In their western hand, they had a force of 3000 reportedly in the Hat Dich area; doubtful as that number was, there was at least a battalion out there. The *D445 Battalion* was known to be on the eastern side and there was a high probability that there was a stronger force on that side too, which might have been the *275 Viet Cong Regiment*.

There were reportedly large numbers of enemy apparently encircling the base. Did that enemy manoeuvre signal an intention to attack? There was sufficient information—albeit speculative—for Jackson to get his battalions back into the Nui Dat base and send 'Captain Robert Keep to II Field Force Vietnam [IIFFV] with a special request to send reinforcements, as at least an enemy regiment was lurking close by ready to attack'.[45] The Americans 'almost laughed them out of court', Australian Major Alec Piper, an assistant planning officer at the IIFFV Headquarters, said. The Americans saw no threat to the Task Force and, even if there was an attack, they would come in and finish off the retreating enemy, Piper mentioned in a later interview.[46]

Following this embarrassing episode, Task Force headquarters sent out a new summary for the period 31 July, which stated that agent reports (all types) relating to the presence of elements of *275 Viet Cong Regiment* in the general area of the Task Force had been discredited. The cancellation did not make it clear if that meant the supposed recently arrived force of 3000 were phantoms or not. The Task Force Intelligence Summary No. 60 advised that the enemy within or immediately adjacent to the Australian tactical area of responsibility numbered approximately 100 guerrillas, two district companies, one provincial battalion and one possible main force battalion, possibly from *274 Viet Cong Regiment*. A menacing sub-note said that the enemy was capable of attacking 1ATF elements up to battalion size, if those forces appeared vulnerable. This mirrored the earlier 1966 MACV lesson that the enemy could prey upon isolated battalions and/or companies and ambush them. The elusive nature of the larger VC main force regiments continued to be a concern to the Australians, although their program of saturation patrolling was apparently keeping the enemy at bay. It was like chasing main force shadows, and the pace of operations was taking its toll on the infantry. Even the SAS could not find the enemy. The defence of Nui Dat also remained precarious, especially when the infantry was out patrolling.

Some peacetime cobwebs had not been completely swept away, either. Claymore mines were not approved for use on the perimeter of the Task Force base until 25 July 1966—nearly seven weeks after arrival—which, when coupled with the shortage of base-defence machine guns and other defensive stores, was an astounding tactical deficiency. The 5th Battalion authorised the use of claymores in ambushes and harbour positions on 5 August 1966, with a warning that great care should be exercised in the use of the weapon. To add further aggravation to the mix of command and administrative challenges, RAAF helicopter controls and Army demands remained in conflict.[47]

Who owned the Hueys?

The American Army system of using their helicopters, the symbolic workhorse of the Vietnam War, was vastly different to the RAAF's procedures. The helicopter derived its 'Huey' name from the nomenclature of the Bell machine, the Helicopter Utility-1B (HU-1B changed to UH-1B) and later models such as UH-1D and UH-1H. Obviously, the 1700 helicopters deployed by America in 1966 swamped Australia's contribution of eight Hueys, but the differences in operational control were significant. The American Army owned the troop-carrying 'slicks' and the gunships, and up until 1966 they owned the Caribou.[48] Some American commentators said that in trading off the Caribou to the US Air Force the Army negotiated a hands-off deal on the helicopters. Whatever the case, the Army made sure that the Air Force would not get a single force of helicopters by keeping the aircraft in independent operational companies or squadrons. Some suggested this was a lesson the Army had learnt from the days of its loss of the Army Air Corps that went on to become the USAF.

To the American Army commanders, slicks were aerial trucks that moved the infantry quickly over inhospitable terrain to close with the enemy, or to outflank him. Warrant officers mainly flew them.[49] To the Australians, the American system was more laid back when it came to flying troops into battle. Doors were left open; some soldiers dangled their legs outside the aircraft while others who grabbed the side jump seat, where the gunner normally sat, hung on grimly when their pack pushed them that little bit beyond the edge. More importantly, the American helicopters were deployed near the infantry and, although there were probably many arguments, they flew into the heat of battle and landed the infantry where they wanted to go. For the members of 1RAR who arrived in June 1965, the previously prohibitive and impractical RAAF rules were quickly discarded.[50]

Rightly or wrongly, the RAAF's control over its meagre number of Hueys established a mindset among the infantry that the RAAF was reluctant to fly into harm's way. In fairness to 9 Squadron, in the first weeks of its deployment, most of the RAAF Huey seats did not have armoured plate protection and the crews did not have body armour. Stultifying Australian regulations designed to protect aircraft also created a dilemma for the senior RAAF officers in Vietnam. This frustration was evident in Brigadier Jackson's reports. What is often lost in the overall analysis of Australian helicopter operations is the undoubted skill and courage of the crews. What was to happen in a coming battle would have long-term implications for the ownership of these aircraft within the Australian Defence Force.

Wolves at the door

Australian patrolling continued into August with 5RAR operating in a general arc northeast and west, while 6RAR patrolled to the east and south of the base. Reports from Vietnamese agents, police and allied military resources indicated that there had been considerable enemy movement from east to west in the first week of August and an estimated two companies of enemy had concentrated in the vicinity of Nui Dat (2). A lot of attention was given to the Binh Ba rubber plantations in preparation for Operation Holsworthy, which was to be a cordon and search of the village area and then a search of the fields beyond. Binh Ba was just 6 kilometres north of Nui Dat. Once again, the intelligence picture appeared confused. The 1ATF order for Holsworthy provided a threat assessment that noted a potential for a major quick attack against the Binh Ba village security force by the main force regiments operating in Phuoc Tuy. A possible third regiment had been added to the previously identified *274* and *275* regiments. There was no third regiment; it was a phantom enemy formation. Operation Order 1-6-66 (Operation Holsworthy) was released on 31 July 1966, one day before INTSUM No. 60 that said the *275 Regiment* was *not* in the general area of the Task Force. The commander of 5RAR repeated the Task Force assessment of 31 July verbatim in his OPORD 11-66 of 6 August 1966, which implied that a swarm of regiments might threaten the Binh Ba force.[51]

Operation Holsworthy began in earnest on 8 August when 5RAR and two companies of 6RAR moved into their assembly areas and started to establish a cordon. The security of the Task Force base area was now the responsibility of 6RAR minus two companies and the supporting arms based there; in other words, not very much. Operation Holsworthy continued through to 18 August with only minor contact with the enemy. During this period, external warnings that the *5th Viet Cong Division* was going to attack continued. On 6 August 1966, a US Special Forces' Intelligence Summary No. 27 advised that a high level rallier—a soldier who had changed sides—had reported that the *5th Viet Cong Division* would initiate a series of attacks in the contiguous provinces of Binh Tuy, Long Khanh and Phuoc Tuy. It appeared— the report continued—that there was to be a strong effort to interdict the lines of communication in these provinces and the new campaign might open within the next two weeks, that is, *by 20 August.*[52]

The thorough search of the Binh Ba stronghold revealed nothing significant. A lot of suspects were gathered and sent off for interrogation and a few were confirmed as being part of the VC infrastructure for the village. Some documents and medicines were also found. Anyone who looked like an enemy soldier soon fled from the Australian patrols and shots between combatants were infrequent, although on 14 August one Australian was killed in a clash with three Viet Cong. On 16 August, Alpha Company, 6RAR, started what was to be a two-day company patrol to cover Nui Dat (2) and Long Tan village. An agent at Phuoc Tuy Sector reported on the 17th that a possible VC battalion with two mobile guns was moving to a position 4 kilometres southeast of Nui Dat (2) and east of Long Tan. By then, the doom reports must have sounded very hollow indeed.

Defection of a senior VC officer

The extreme difficulty of gathering information against the enemy and providing timely intelligence analysis on their activities was highlighted when another piece in the *5th Viet Cong Division* jigsaw puzzle was told by Lieutenant Colonel Le Xuan Chuyen, Chief of the division's Operations Section. Chuyen surrendered to the South on 2 August 1966. Before giving himself up, he had been ill and not on full-time duty for four months. He had also recently married a southerner. Le Xuan Chuyen told his interrogators that the *5th Viet Cong Division* had a strength of approximately 3500 and was equipped with 75 mm recoilless rifles, medium mortars—81 and 82 mm, 12.7 mm anti-aircraft machine guns, rocket-propelled grenades (B40 RPG), light machine guns and an assortment of rifles and submachine guns, such as AK-47s.

Although he had left his headquarters to go for treatment in March 1966, he was told that the division headquarters was still located in Xuyen Moc District, Phuoc Tuy Province. Officers from the division visited him during his convalescence at Suoi Kiet village, 40 kilometres due east of Xuan Loc along the transnational railway line. The division's two infantry regiments consisted of three battalions apiece, and each regiment also had three service companies: combined artillery—recoilless rifles and light mortars, as well as signals and reconnaissance. Three other main units in the division were a sapper/reconnaissance battalion, a signal battalion and an engineer company, none of which was at full strength. The signal battalion had three 15-watt radio sets, five AN/PRC-10 radios, 40 kilometres of phone wire and 25 field telephones. He gave the location for *275 Regiment*, in July, as 2 kilometres southeast of Phu Mountain, near the boundary of Binh Tuy and Long Khanh provinces, east of Xuan Loc. The *274 Regiment* and other elements of the division were located in Xuyen Moc District of Phuoc Tuy Province (25 kilometres due east of the Task Force base). Considering the known activities that occurred during June and July in western Phuoc Tuy this information highlighted the enemy's outstanding mobility under extremely demanding combat conditions. If this were not true, the intelligence pictures bore no resemblance to reality.

More importantly, Chuyen provided an analysis of the combat efficacy of both regiments. Two battalions in *274 Regiment* were good in combat; these were the 1st and the 3rd. The *2nd Battalion* was very poor. Chuyen said that a large-scale operation for them was of battalion size and they had the capability to attack weak installations. His general observations on *275's* operations were: lack of combat experience, *no capacity for attacking installations*, many sick and weak troops, and little capability for sustained operations. The new recruits, he said, were young—some were sixteen years of age—and in battle they scattered and were difficult to control. The majority of troops in the regiment were recruits. He added that within the *3rd Battalion* of *275 Regiment* there were a lot of North Vietnamese who had been recalled to active duty and infiltrated at a time when he was at the command headquarters—*Central Office for South Vietnam*—so he knew little about them.[53]

The number of North Vietnamese with the division was not confirmed. Several subsequent reports indicated that the only formed NVA unit in the *5th Viet Cong Division* was an anti-aircraft machine-gun battalion that was equipped with approximately fifteen 12.7 mm machine guns.[54] Some of the senior officers in the division were North Vietnamese, as Chuyen was. These cadre officers reportedly came from the *308th NVA Division* to establish and command the new VC division in 1965. The *308th Division* was still tucked away well inside northern North Vietnam at the time—inside *Military Region Bac Viet*—so it could afford to provide a nucleus of support in the South. Chuyen came from the *304th Division*, in *Military Region 3*, south of Hanoi. He was 37 years old and wore a Dien Bien Phu insignia, indicating that he was from the old school of experienced officers. The *275 Regiment* was understrength, with each company having only 70 troops; this would put a battalion at less than 300. Chuyen did not mention a plan to attack the Australians at Nui Dat.[55]

Many comments have been made about the North Vietnamese–VC mix within the *5th Viet Cong Division*. Although it was known that there were northerners in the division, they may not necessarily have been all North Vietnamese. While that sounds like a contradiction, there are several clues which might explain who some of the troops were. During the war against the French, Baria Province (Phuoc Tuy Province) was a Viet Minh stronghold. Under the rules of the 1954 Armistice, the Viet Minh soldiers were permitted to go north, which many from Baria, and various other locations around the South, did. As Le Xuan Chuyen mentioned in his debriefing, 'there were a lot . . . recalled to active duty and infiltrated'.[56] The soldiers and political personnel who came back were known as 'regroupees'—southerners who went north after 1954—and they can be traced back into diverse VC units in the South in the mid-1960s. MACV estimated that most of the 30,000 troops that came from the North between 1959 and December 1963 were 'regroupees'. That intelligence picture is confirmed by the North's official history, which described the preparations for war after 1959.

The 338th Division, which was composed of southern regroupees, and a number of our infantry regiments were converted into training groups for cadre and soldiers who would be sent to perform their duties in South Vietnam. [These soldiers] were natives of South Vietnam or were familiar with the battlefields of South Vietnam gathered for training . . . before being sent off to the [southern] battlefront.[57]

The *3rd Battalion* of *275 Viet Cong Regiment* was probably raised as the *4th Battalion* of the *32nd North Vietnamese Regiment*. Two-thirds of the battalion were southerners who had fought against the French and the plan was to move them back to the South into *Military Region 6*, which bordered Phuoc Tuy Province to the east. Although Chuyen said that the battalion was good, its initial establishment training was not and the order to move south was repealed. After additional training and reinforcement, the battalion was reactivated and redesignated as *Group 605* and directed to move south in September 1965. They arrived somewhere in the Central Highlands region on 22 October 1965. 'They were ordered to stop there for a while [after which] they were given one ton of weapons and ammunition to carry, and . . . 18-day rice ration for the journey to MR6.' The total journey covered '2000 kilometres in 112 days', which meant that *Group 605* probably arrived in *Military Region 6* in late January 1966.[58] Considering the ordeals of infiltration and subsequent battles, its field strength was probably around 350–400 personnel.

It made good military sense to bring back local North Vietnamese to fight the new enemy, as the adding of North Vietnamese into a VC (southern) organisation was not a guaranteed formula for combat success. A document found in Phuoc Long Province in 1968 described examples of friction between Northern and Southern Vietnamese. A directive issued by *Military Region 7* pointed out the assistance that the northerners were providing and emphasised that it was the duty of the people to 'extend assistance and protection to these comrades'. Within the Australians' area, the 'disenchantment between the two factions was highlighted by some NVA soldiers who considered themselves to be elite . . . [and this was] . . . the subject of many an argument, order and counter order within the ranks'. An Australian training information document said that the VC units 'suffered to a degree from the integration of NVA reinforcements'. Although this document referred to their relegation to local force VC units, such as *D445*, the theme is supported by anecdotal evidence that similar problems had been experienced in a mixture of VC units across the South.[59]

During his interrogations, Chuyen also provided details of medical support planning conducted by the *5th Viet Cong Division* before a battle. The Operations Section determined civilian labour requirements using a general rule that four to six civilian labourers were required for each estimated casualty. Chuyen said that it was difficult to judge the effectiveness of the planning because the division had not been involved in a major engagement. Malaria was the major debilitating illness for the division with 80 per cent of *275 Regiment* immobilised in December 1965. Five per cent of those were acutely ill. In June 1966, the malaria rates were 10 per cent for *274 Regiment* and 25–30 per cent for *275 Regiment*. Several operations had to be cancelled because of the sickness, and in February 1966, *275 Regiment* was forced to break contact when its malaria rate rose 10 per cent in the first three days of an operation. Chuyen said that a projected casualty rate of 25–30 per cent was planned for an operation and that was broken down into an expected 80 per cent wounded and 20 per cent killed. Chuyen said that, in his experience, a rate of 50 per cent wounded to 50 per cent killed was closer to reality. He added that the recovery of bodies had a high priority, because of the psychological and propaganda effects, and strong efforts were made to make sure all dead bodies that could be found were recovered and hidden. The numbers recovered were dependent upon the result of the battle.[60] The casualty ratio for the American Army during the war was 5.6 wounded to 1 killed. The Australian Army scale of battle casualties was 316 killed in action to 2348 wounded in action or injured accidentally (1 KIA to 7.43 WIA/injured).[61]

Operation Toledo

To muddy the intelligence picture even further, on 10 August 1966 the 173rd Airborne Brigade at Bien Hoa deployed on Operation Toledo into the area of Phuoc Tuy Province known as the May Tao Mountain—Nui May Tao—approximately 45 kilometres northeast of Nui Dat. The operational title 'Toledo' brings to mind the falcata, or swords, created in Toledo, Spain, since the 5th century BCE by Spanish blacksmiths. These swords had an interior iron blade, designed to increase the blunt slash the weapon made. This operation was to be a powerful, blunt slash at finding and destroying the *5th Viet Cong Division*.

The Toledo operational area was a 500 square kilometre box centred on May Tao Mountain and bounded by Highway 1 to the north. The May Tao straddled the eastern border between Phuoc Tuy and Binh Tuy provinces. It was a region of thick jungle and rugged mountains that held many caves ideal for hides as well as being good protection from artillery and air strikes. The sea was 30 kilometres to the south, which is where the 1st Battalion, 26th Marines (regiment), landed on 16 August. Pre D-day Marine Corps' intelligence also located the units of the *5th Viet Cong Division* in the eastern provincial region along the Phuoc Tuy border with Binh Tuy Province.[62] Approximately the same distance away to the west of the May Tao was Route 2, with the Australian battalions at its southern end, although they were not involved in Operation Toledo at this stage.

The US 173rd Airborne Brigade's enemy situation analysis released before the operation said:

> The operational area was believed to contain elements of the 274th Viet Cong MF Regiment, the 275th Viet Cong MF Regiment, the 5th Viet Cong Division Head-quarters, and the 860th Local Force Battalion. The 274th Regiment was believed to be in the vicinity of YS 5586. [From the village of Cam My, 10 kilometres east of Route 2. For comparison Nui Dat (1) was at YS 4367.] And the 275th Regiment in the vicinity of YS 5473 with the 5th Viet Cong division in the vicinity of YS 6779.[63]

This analysis placed the *274 Viet Cong Regiment* about 30 kilometres east of where the Australians thought they were in the Hat Dich and approximately the same distance away from where the 173rd Brigade had fought them in late June 1966. As an interesting side note, Lieutenant Colonel Chuyen's information about the location of the *275 Viet Cong Regiment* being near Phu Mountain put the regiment 10 kilometres north of Highway 1. Obviously information channels flowed slowly.

Between 10 and 12 August 1966, the American brigade's battalions moved into the operational area by road along Route 1 and by helicopter to establish a main base northeast of the May Tao near the Rung La hamlet. From there they cleared in a general southwesterly direction. Two ARVN Ranger battalions—33 and 35—joined the operation on 14 August in an area of operations just west of the Americans' main position across Route 331 that ran to the south off Route 1. The trap, in the mind of the 173rd Brigade's commander, Brigadier General Paul Smith, had been set and sprung with modern-day power that no Toledo sword could match.

Brigadier General Smith's artillery fired nearly 50,000 shells from 105 mm to 175 mm in size to smash the enemy's impregnable hides. Incredibly, the after action analysis of this intense bombardment recorded that 'at no time was artillery reported as falling among VC forces', and this firepower had no 'effective determination of actual damage to the enemy'. Three B-52 missions struck twelve target areas and 332 tactical strike aircraft sorties were flown against pre-planned targets. Army aviation flew 6951 sorties that included command and control flights, combat assault and armed helicopter attacks.

The 404th Radio Research Detachment, who listened on the enemy radio frequencies, provided information on 90 enemy locations; many of these were hit by artillery. Considering the enemy division's meagre quantity of radios, this is a remarkable number of intercepts. A later study conducted

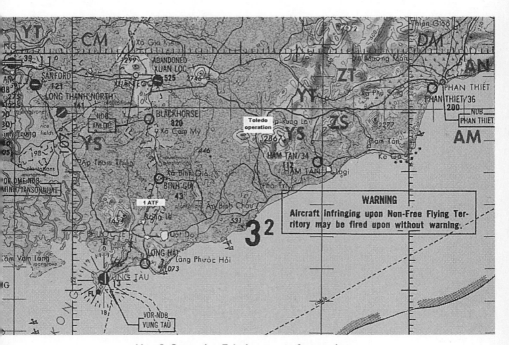

Map 6: Operation Toledo—area of operations
The 173rd Airborne Brigade's Operation Toledo near the May Tao mountains, south of Highway 1, approximately 45 kilometres northeast of the 1ATF base at Nui Dat. American Marines landed to the south near the village of Thuan Bien, west of Ham Tan.

in 1967 by the US-MACV Combined Intelligence Center confirmed that the enemy was aware of electronic warfare throughout the Vietnam conflict and had increased its dedication to this sophisticated art. If the enemy was aware of this eavesdropping what were the real targets and what deceptive procedures did they use during the period of Operation Toledo?[64]

The Viet Cong did not fight. They melted away. In this battle, according to the US tally, their losses were 8 killed in action, 11 captured and 80 suspects detained. American casualties were 7 killed in action, 45 wounded, 4 accidental deaths and 23 non-battle injuries. They also suffered 121 cases of malaria. The Marines who came ashore at Beach Brown, near the coastal village of Thuan Bien, also reported that there was no substantial contact with the enemy; resistance consisted of sporadic sniper fire. They had one killed and seven wounded.[65]

In terms of the much-maligned body-count equation, the Americans lost. Despite the numbers, General Smith's final analysis concluded that the most significant aspect of the operation was the large-scale capture and destruction of vast quantities of weapons, ammunition, equipment and foodstuffs. Although they captured 52 weapons, 5 of which were crew-served, the weapons were a mix of mainly old American-made carbines with a handful of modern AK-50s. The loss of food would have hurt the Viet Cong severely, with more than 50 tons of rice destroyed. General Smith concluded that his brigade had disrupted the plans and movement of the VC units within the Toledo area of operations. And, although some personnel from the *250th NVA Infiltration Group* were discovered in the area, he believed that the *5th Viet Cong Division* did not have a fixed installation in the May Tao region.[66]

This intended combat aimed at an enemy formation that was barely one year old. It was not an overly powerful organisation. The division only had 3500 troops who were equipped with basic infantry weapons and they had suffered badly from malaria in recent times. When he was asked in 1990 if the *5th* was a hard-luck division, NVA Colonel General Tran Van Tra admitted the division was not as strong as the *9th*, the other VC division under his command. General Tra commanded the *B-2 Front*, all of the enemy to the south of a general east–west line drawn through Dalat in the southern Central Highlands.[67] In August 1966, the *5th VC Division* was fighting on two widely dispersed flanks and it had generally evaded its enemies in major battle while they continued to cause the allies tactical problems with their locations and intentions. The *5th VC Division* had suffered losses in personnel and logistics, but their tenacity was obviously unbroken when the commander and his staff developed their plan to confront the Australians.

The enemy plan for Long Tan

According to Lieutenant Colonel Chuyen, Colonel Truyen who commanded the division was patient and able to draw out the strong and weak points from each engagement. He was very resolute in his dealings and had the confidence of his staff. By contrast, Chief of Staff Lieutenant Colonel Nam Tam (also known as Tran Minh Tam) was young and determined, drank and argued, and had little capability in tactics or staff work. More importantly, Senior Captain (later Lieutenant General) Nguyen Thoi Bung, known as Ut Thoi, who commanded the *275 Regiment*, was combat-experienced but still lacked a good knowledge of tactics and a complete knowledge of command.

In August 1966, the command group had decided on a plan, and the Deputy Commander of the division, Tran Minh Tam, met with Dang Huu Thuan, commander of the *Baria Unit*, to discuss the tactics that should be used against the Australians. (The *Baria Unit*, which had overall responsibility for military operations within the province, should not be confused with *D445 Battalion* that was commanded by Bui Quang Chanh who answered to the *Baria Unit*.) The command group agreed that the battle was to be an area ambush over 2–3 kilometres along a stretch of Route 52 in the rubber plantation area of Long Tan. The *5th Viet Cong Division*'s history described the plan:

> The *2nd Battalion* of the [*275*] Regiment and a company of *445 Battalion*-reinforced with B40s [RPG-2] and a 57 mm rocket launcher [recoilless rifle], were located in the south and the northwest of the Bo road and Route 52 with the task of blocking the forward elements of the enemy. *3rd Battalion* was deployed about 800 metres northwest of Route 52 with the task of attacking into the main killing zone at the That Pagoda [location not known]. The *1st Battalion* was reinforced with two companies from *445 Battalion* and deployed about 800 metres north of Route 52 with a rear blocking task and the role of coordinating with *3rd Battalion* to destroy the enemy in the decisive area of battle. To guarantee

support for the battle, we deployed a transport element comprising 80 comrades from the company led by Vo Thi Sau and a forward surgical team from Division led by Comrade Hai Phong and Comrade Nguyen Dinh Kinh to directly support *Regiment 5*. On 15 August, all preparatory tasks to conduct the battle had been completed.

It is essential to understand here that the enemy troops were not yet in the proposed ambush position.[68]

Signals intelligence

Contacts by the Australian patrols remained light to none at all during the first two weeks of August 1966. Reports that Viet Cong were moving in the Phuoc Tuy area continued to flow into the Task Force headquarters, and the Task Force INTSUM No. 69 for 9 August warned that the enemy forces

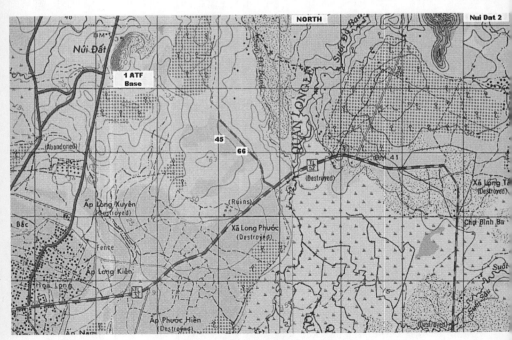

Map 7: Long Tan battlefield
The Long Tan battle was around the grid intersection YS 4867—inside the rubber plantation at the northern end of the track that runs in a north-northeasterly direction off Road 52 (TL 52). The village of Long Tan is shown in the southeast (Xa Long Tan).

were capable of 'attacking up to company-size 1 ATF elements . . . (if the 1 ATF forces appear vulnerable)'.[69]

An enemy battalion attacked Phu My camp along Route 15 on 11 and 12 August. This action confirmed that *274 Viet Cong Regiment* was in the western district of Phuoc Tuy. The Australians mistook the attackers as *265 Battalion*, but this unit belonged to a previously unlisted *221 Regiment*. The problems of enemy unit identification were aggravated by aliases: *274 Regiment* was known to have twenty false names, *275 Regiment* had seventeen, and *D445 Battalion* had at least fifteen disguises. This meant that unit names were often meaningless, as author and historian Douglas Pike wrote in 1986.

> The PAVN [NVA] employed over the years an almost endless variety of troop unit names . . . many only used for a few months . . . some are highly descriptive . . . and some so vague as to be meaningless.[70]

Brigadier Jackson released additional information on enemy activity in a soldiers' newsletter that identified the provinces of Binh Long, Phuoc Long and Tay Ninh as the most likely areas for large-scale enemy attacks. This surprisingly contradicted the intelligence summary distributed by the US Special Forces' INTSUM No. 27 that identified Phuoc Tuy, too, as a probable target.

Behind the scenes, on 29 July and known only to a select few officers, radio intercepts by the Australian 547 Signal Troop indicated that the enemy regiments had changed from a period of rest and retraining to something more active. Captain Trevor Richards, the troop's commander and later a brigadier, informed those in the Task Force headquarters authorised to be told, but Brigadier Jackson apparently took little notice of his information and Major John Rowe, the senior intelligence officer, was sceptical. Captain Bob Keep was the understudy to Rowe and he and Richards pondered the ramifications during the days ahead when the dot on the radio-intercept map suggested that *275 Viet Cong Regiment* was marching inexorably towards Nui Dat. At least some in the command group said that all they had detected was the radio that had a *275 Viet Cong Regiment* call sign. Information of all kinds was flowing through the intelligence network at the time and this was just another piece in the puzzle. None of the Australian patrols made contact with an enemy force that indicated impending tactical doom.

The value of the signals intercept information has long been debated as the key to the battle at Long Tan. The enemy's forces, both Viet Cong and NVA, were aware of intercepts and often used the technique as a two-edged sword. In the *3rd NVA Division*, Binh Dinh Province, in 1966, for example, the signal battalion had a 'secret maintenance section'. NVA signals officer Lieutenant Anh said that he had heard 'of the division talking to US aircraft in order to divert them from the division's area'. 'The function of this section was to monitor American radio frequencies . . . this section monitored all types of American communications.' The NVA signals intelligence people seemed to operate with the same amount of secrecy as the Australians and also tightly controlled their release of information to a select few. Another example of VC electronic warfare was uncovered in January 1966 when a prisoner told how they were able to understand American code words by listening to conversations. From this interception, the Viet Cong were able to detect in advance the planned artillery concentrations and take evasive action.[71]

In addition, the pounding of the detected high level VC headquarters on 3 April 1966 during Operation Abilene and the 90 signals-detected artillery targets during Operation Toledo would have alerted the *5th Viet Cong Division* that signals intercept was being used against them. On 17 August, Alpha Company, 6RAR, 'experienced complete deliberate jamming of C/S 1 [call sign] transmissions every time C/S 1 began to speak'.[72] Further evidence of the enemy's understanding of electronic warfare was apparent when a VC observer was captured in the Nui Dinh in October 1966. Captain Richards said that the radio operator had used very professional methods, such as codes and short times on air, to make the transmissions unreadable.[73]

In March 1967, US intelligence reports and analyses concluded that the *5th Viet Cong Division* was known to have had a technical intelligence detachment to improve their interception, jamming and imitative deception techniques.[74] Given the combat knowledge that the North Vietnamese and the Viet Cong had about signals interception and their ability to at least attempt to deceive and jam allied broadcasts, it is difficult to believe that methodical daily broadcasts by a *275 Viet Cong Regiment* radio were anything other than a test of the Australian capabilities and procedures. Furthermore, the approach march plotted by the signal intercepts at a plodding kilometre a day was completely at odds with the rapid deployment marches used by the Viet Cong in which they covered 15–20 kilometres in a day.[75]

17–18 August 1966

For Brigadier Jackson and his senior staff, there must have been the nagging worry that the Australians had hounded the dreaded main force regiments around Nui Dat but had not made contact with them. Maybe it wasn't as bad as the reports had indicated after all. Then, at 0243 hours on 17 August, this tactical anxiety was seemingly justified when the Task Force base was mortared by 82 mm mortars and shelled by what was thought to be a Japanese 70 mm light howitzer, which could be fired over a short distance at high angles like a mortar. Its maximum range was 2800 metres. A Task Force report, supported by crater analysis, said that a total of approximately sixty-three 82 mm mortars and five 70 mm shells hit the base, wounding 24 and causing minor materiel damage. There were other reports that said 75 mm recoilless rifle fire hit the base, too. Firing debris and a recoilless rifle site were found later.[76] Counter-battery fire began after about seven minutes but there was no follow-up attack by the enemy. That must have soothed a few nerves.

Alpha Company, 6RAR, was out near Nui Dat (2) in the midst of what probably appeared to be fireworks from hell with the artillery counter-battery fire falling nearby. Bravo Company left the Task Force base and started a search for the enemy baseplate position at 0630 hours, just four hours after the mortaring. They soon found a firing position that had five baseplate positions and pits for about 35 personnel almost due east of the base and mid-way between Nui Dat and the Long Tan rubber. A platoon from Charlie Company, 6RAR, was also searching for another enemy position thought to be for a recoilless rifle. This platoon was to the south of Bravo Company, while Alpha Company was still over near Nui Dat (2). Not one of the patrols encountered any enemy. Major Noel Ford's Bravo Company had only anticipated being out for a few hours and were without bedding and rations when their patrol duty was extended. Later in the day they got a resupply of rations, but not their sleeping gear.

The next day, 18 August, Alpha Company was directed to go back towards Bravo Company's position and to search along the Suoi Da Bang that flowed

north–south, about a kilometre to the west of the Long Tan rubber. Bravo
Company had sent men back to base who were to go on Rest and Convalescence leave at Vung Tau. The company was now down to 32 men as they
patrolled east towards the rubber plantation. They found evidence that the
enemy mortar teams had come though the area and that the Task Force artillery had hit the location with its counter-battery fire. There were plenty of
tracks and bloodstains and bits and pieces of equipment, but no enemy. Ford
reported later that he believed the mortaring and the tracks were a ruse to
draw the Australians out of the base, a possibility rejected by Lieutenant
Colonel Townsend, his commanding officer.[77]

Colonel Townsend told Major Smith's Delta Company to go out and
replace Bravo Company and to continue the search for the enemy. Smith's
company met up with Ford's men on the western fringe of Long Tan rubber
at YS473674 around 2.30 p.m. on the 18th, where the two companies
exchanged information on what they had found and speculated on what the
enemy might be doing. Ford then took his men back towards Nui Dat. At
approximately 3 p.m., Delta Company moved off on a northeasterly track
into the rubber plantation. By now the feeling was the enemy had done the
usual 'shoot and scoot', and the chances of finding them and bringing them
to battle were remote.[78]

However, unbeknown to all the Australians, the battle had already started.
Tran Minh Tam's men, *D445* and the *Divisional Reconnaissance Cell*, had fired
the mortars into Nui Dat and placed mines to block Route 52 to force the
Australians to mount a sweeping operation to clear the area of Long Tan. The
5th Division's history tells the story.

At 2am on 17 August, elements of Regiment 5 [275] that had been operating in
the base area began to advance ready to strike the enemy. On 18 August, from
6am to 3pm, our observation element—who had not been detected—noted signs
that the enemy was organizing a sweeping operation. The battle commander,
Tran Minh Tam, concluded that the enemy did not have the capability to launch
a sweeping operation on 18 August—so he directed the observation element to
temporarily withdraw to the 2nd Battalion position, and ordered the forward
attack elements to continue to maintain their formation. However, at 3.30 pm
[Note the time of D Company's move, above], the 2nd Battalion's reconnaissance

cell reported that an enemy company had secretly advanced to within 650 metres of the battalion's battlefield.[79]

Did Tran Minh Tam's decision about the enemy not having the capability to launch a sweeping operation mean that the detected movement of Bravo Company with only 32 men was not a worthy target for a regimental ambush?

All hell breaks loose

Not long after moving off through the rubber, 10 Platoon, commanded by Second Lieutenant Geoff Kendall, came across a fork in the track where the pathway divided into two parallel tracks that headed generally east-southeast about 300 metres apart. At the junction, YS475675, Major Smith recorded that 'there was evidence of 82 mm mortar ammo being prepared for firing, and signs that the enemy fled EAST in a hurry to escape CB [counter-battery fire]'.[80] Discarded grenades, sandals, and pieces of equipment were found over a wide area, giving the impression of a hasty retreat. However, this location was just beyond the range of the Chicom 82 mm mortar that hit the Task Force base.[81] Was the scattering of this debris part of a plan of deception?

> Major Harry Smith made radio contact with his CO and told him that all was quiet and that we were going to 'go east young man', almost as though at the toss of a coin we decided on which track to follow. This track would take them past a hut where 11 Platoon had been a few days earlier and to which B Company had patrolled that morning.[82]

Sergeant Frank Keen had led a Bravo Company section patrol out to the hut at YS481671 with a time out shown as 1100 hours on 18 August, according to Major Ford's after action report written on 23 August 1966. The 6RAR operations log recorded a directive to Bravo Company not to go beyond the track at YS473660. The order was issued at 0635 hours. As B Company had patrolled in the grid squares YS4666 and 4767 before this directive, it is possible that the directive was not recorded in full and should have read: 'Do not go beyond the track that *started* at YS473660', and then cut through the rubber in a northeasterly direction. It would have been an ideal boundary, but that is an assumption by the author. There was a secondary track at YS475670 about 200 metres west of the main track and closer to the B Company patrol location. There is no report recorded in the 6RAR main log that Bravo Company sent a section-sized patrol east into the rubber.[83]

When he changed the company's direction of patrol, Smith also altered his formation to two platoons up, with 10 Platoon on the left and 11 Platoon on the right. Company headquarters was in the centre and 12 Platoon followed to the rear. The distance between soldiers was about 10 metres, which meant the company covered an area of about 400 metres by 400 metres. The plantation was 'mainly clean with some undergrowth in places, visibility was about 150 metres, but fell to 100 metres [or less] when the heavy rain started'.[84] There has been speculation that the platoons were too far apart but, ironically, if they were, that might have been one of the saving graces for them during the coming battle. For example, Major General Peter Abigail (Retd) wrote in a review in 2008:

> The battle began with a minor skirmish that quickly led to a major engagement involving a series of platoon actions against potentially overwhelming odds in which each of the platoons of D Coy had to fight isolated defensive battles and was separately threatened with annihilation.[85]

Private Allen May was the forward scout of the section from 11 Platoon that moved off down the right-hand track:

> When we moved off . . . we travelled a few hundred metres and I saw what I thought was a bunch of kids sitting around a fire having lunch, and then I realized that these kids had weapons. Doug Fabian and myself both opened up on these people. We wounded two and they took off through the rubber.[86]

The 6RAR log recorded the time of the contact as 1540 hours and the location as grid reference YS478673. The report continued: 'probably local—dress Khaki trousers and shirts . . . doubt any casualties due to range, but they got 1 AK [Kalashnikov assault rifle] that had 1 in 2 tracer loaded'. The enemy headed east. Bravo Company asked battalion if they should remain nearby until D Company got sorted out. They were still near the southwestern edge of the rubber at YS458662.[87]

There was disagreement in later years over who fired the first shots at the enemy, but Doug Fabian, the soldier with Allen May, confirmed that the contact was as May had described. Fabian thought that the men were not eating but just squatting, as if they were unaware of the Australians.[88] In the overall analysis of the battle, who fired first is not a major point, but for the soldiers involved and the battalion's historical record it is very pertinent. What happened next is of great significance. Gordon Sharp, the commander of 11 Platoon, requested a hot pursuit and Major Smith agreed.

> There were five or six Viet Cong, at least one of whom was at least wounded and a platoon should have been able to handle the task. With 11 Platoon pushing ahead, I ordered 10 Platoon to maintain its direction and rate of advance.[89]

The Australians obviously saw this episode—from the mortaring of the Task Force base, up to and including this encounter—as the standard 'shoot-and-scoot' drill used by the Viet Cong in many of their contacts. As author Lex McAulay recorded in his book *The Battle of Long Tan*, one officer (Geoff Kendall) also revealed a slightly worrying attitude—he did not recognise the danger:

> 'Sharp, you lucky so-and-so!' It was every platoon commander's dream: a platoon attack, bowling over an enemy section or squad—and picking up an MC on the way through. 'This is it', Sergeant Bob Buick reacted, 'Let's get into them, and hope they don't bug out the way they've always done.'[90]

As the chase began, 11 Platoon was well outside a zone of comfortable mutual support between the platoons, with 10 Platoon at least 400 metres away to their northwest through the rubber trees. Company headquarters and 12 Platoon were about 500 metres away; both these call signs were immediately to the west of 10 Platoon. Eleven platoon then fanned out into an extended line, with a single-line frontage of 250–300 metres and walked quickly into a withering, deafening and deadly fusillade of enfilade fire.[91] This was not a chance encounter; this was a trap, with all the hallmarks of known enemy tactical technique. It was exactly what the enemy wanted. It was 1610 hours; twenty minutes later mortars fell in the Delta Company area. Soon after that, Bravo Company was mortared as well, although the company reported that the nearest mortar exploded about 100 metres away. The ferocity of an initial engagement by an enemy force in an ambush had been reported in February 1965 by MACV:

> As in all their offensive actions, the Viet Cong conduct the ambush violently. Heavy and intense firepower is delivered at the outset to obtain the maximum from surprise and shock action.[92]

The battle that followed lasted almost three and a half hours (although the fear of fighting lasted much longer, until daylight), and claimed the lives of 263 warriors—245 Viet Cong and 18 Australians—and an unknown number of wounded. In a fight to the death, the balance was tipped by the artillery's quick and accurate fire from both Australian 105 mm and American 155 mm howitzers. The arrival of the cavalry in the form of Alpha Company, 6RAR, mounted in APCs, and an ammunition resupply by RAAF Hueys under extremely dangerous and challenging flying conditions turned the battle to the advantage of the Australians, as did the return of the understrength B Company.

It was a near-run thing and the outcome came frighteningly close to a major tactical defeat for the Australians. If 50 or more Australians had been killed, this would have had a major impact upon the Australian people. As an analogy, General Harold Johnson, US Army Chief of Staff, told the commander of the US Army's 1st Division in April 1966, the American public would stop supporting the war if such high casualties of Operation Abilene continued (48 KIA and 135 WIA).[93]

An objective assessment of the battle

This analysis is not a blow-by-blow account of the Long Tan battle. There is a wide coverage of this available in books, newspapers and magazines, as well as on the World Wide Web.[94] Unfortunately, however, an objective judgement of this engagement which disagrees with the perception that it was a chance encounter with several thousand enemy resting on their way to attack the Task Force base—and any suggestion of an ambush—is a view said to be influenced by VC propaganda. To admit an ambush would possibly taint the military reputations of those who fought, without considering that most would have fallen for the trap. Despite all the reports before the battle of a regiment here, a thousand or more VC soldiers there, the threats always appeared to fade away. Saturation patrolling kept the enemy at bay and their numbers were down at manageable levels, or so the intelligence summaries said. However, there was always a nagging worry that something bigger was out there and the commanders emphasised that any main patrols were to be company-sized, and to stay within the range of artillery known as Line Bravo. The mortaring of the Australian base on 17 August appeared to be a bombardment to entice a reaction, although several Australian commanders rejected this view. The counter-battery fire proved that the artillery were on the ball and accurate, and the patrols that followed up initially found only the signs of a hurt enemy thought to be on the run.

Battle experience

Even though the Australians had experienced some strong contacts in their short time in Phuoc Tuy, the more disastrous battle lessons of this war had not yet filtered down to the Australian infantrymen. Did the Australians in this first batch of battalions know of and analyse the 1964–65 slaughter of the ARVN at Binh Gia, just north of Nui Dat? That bloody battle cost the ARVN and its American advisers at least 200 killed, including 5 Americans. More than 190 were wounded, and 68 went missing in action, including 3 Americans. The VC battalion *D445*—then a company—was also involved in the battle. One of the attacking regiments had hidden in and around Nui Nghe, and then rapidly moved 8 kilometres cross-country to ambush an armoured relief column that drove north on Route 2.

In February 1965, MACV distributed a paper highlighting some of the Viet Cong's tactics. One piece of advice aptly described the information quandary for the Australians:

> All Viet Cong attacks endeavour to achieve surprise, and hit the enemy [ARVN] at a time, place and in a manner which is not anticipated. It is not necessarily

dependent on misleading the enemy. The enemy [ARVN] may know from the attendant situation that he will be attacked, but, if the Viet Cong efforts are effective, he will not know how, when, where or in what strength.[95]

Although the Americans and Australians had not deployed their battalions to the battlefield when that report was written, the intelligence gatherers and the planners trawled the system for every piece of detail available on the war. The extensive distribution list for that release included SEATO Headquarters, where Australia had a representative. Even though no Australian organisation was mentioned specifically in the list, it is unlikely that the information did not make it back to Canberra.

Other information on how the enemy fought was also available to the allied forces. The distribution lists on intelligence summaries, for example, show that the Australian Force Vietnam received these messages. Up to and including May 1966, the Headquarters Australian Force Vietnam files mainly show the masses of administrative details concerned with the end of 1RAR's tour and the planning detail for movement of the new ATF units from Australia. Did the information papers on operational intelligence—the battles—receive the attention they should have? Apparently not, if the US Operation Abilene action in April 1966 was any indication. That clash was a strong example of the Viet Cong's mobility and firepower. The battle tactic of isolate and destroy was a pertinent lesson.

> The Americans killed five [enemy] soldiers, [and then] pursued the fleeing survivors toward [southern] Cam My in heavy jungle, not realizing that the Viet Cong platoon was falling back on its battalion base. The Viet Cong reacted in late afternoon with heavy mortar and automatic weapons fire (including 50 calibre) and mounted three successive human-wave assaults. US artillery fired 1086 rounds during the night [preventing the company being overrun].[96]

For the better part of May 1966, the soon-to-be sharp-end of action for the headquarters, 1ATF, was rewriting its Standard Operating Procedures to reflect 'theatre orientation', as well as trying to find tentage and staff, and to get its means of communications established. There were many 'growing pains', but the commander confidently predicted that the headquarters 'will be capable of controlling operations effectively . . . on 5 Jun'.[97] This sounded confident, but in reality everyone was struggling. The Australians had put an ill-prepared force into a new, demanding and dangerous environment with no time for them to acclimatise to the enemy's methods.

One of the principal lessons learnt in the first half of 1966 was the enemy's propensity to suck a force away from its protected environment through a variety of ruses and then ambush it. MACV and the Australians had issued warnings about this. Another piece of deception associated with ambushes, but not as well known, was bait for a trap—the apparently unconcerned enemy soldier. In their 1967 pamphlet *Vietnam Primer*, Americans Brigadier S. L. A. Marshall and Lieutenant Colonel David Hackworth highlighted this danger.

> If you come upon a jungle clearing and you see two or three or even one enemy soldier with back turned, or you are moving fairly in the open, and you see a few NVA or Viet Cong moving at distance with backs turned, never facing about watch out! The chances are very good that you are being led into a trap. The effect is to nourish the hope that the manoeuvring formation has caught the enemy unaware and is on track of something big.[98]

The first contact by Delta Company that prompted 11 Platoon's hot pursuit could have been this type of trick.

What happened?

The clarity of more than 40 years of available research tells us that the *Viet Cong 5th Infantry Division* manoeuvred the Australian Task Force into fighting on a battlefield of the VC commander's choosing. The division's official history is disarmingly open, especially in admitting errors of judgement. This is the *Viet Cong 5th Infantry Division* statement of what happened.

> The first battle was to ambush the Australian force—a new combat objective on the battlefield. We had committed an error in our observation of the enemy and in arranging our formations to start an attack from a far distance—because of this, we were unable to surround and destroy the enemy battalion. Our forces

suffered large casualties—32 were killed and 80 comrades were wounded. [This figure does not include *D445 Battalion*.] However, the battle against the Australians at Long Tan had a very important significance: it was the first time that we had destroyed an Australian company [Note the change in the size of the force.] on the battlefield—a force that had been regarded as the most highly effective of the specialists in counter-guerrilla warfare and which the enemy often lauded. The battle had been conducted very close to the combat headquarters of the Royal Australian Regiment and greatly surprised the enemy.[99]

For those who see such a statement as a rhetorical claim of destruction, consider the report from Bravo Company to headquarters, 6RAR, at 1855 hours on 18 August 1966: 'Now with C/S 1 [A Coy] in C/S 4 [D Coy] Loc. D Coy is now none [*sic*] effective, estimate 25 KIA & 40 WIA.' The operational order for Smithfield—the Vendetta title was changed for the battle and the post-battle search of Long Tan—showed 'D Coy, heavy casualties—two effective platoons', with a note added in the CO's after action report recording that even these were at a much-reduced strength.[100]

Was the battle initiation a failing by the Australians, or an acceptable fortune of war? It was still early in Australia's main deployment and imbued lessons of war still reflected the Malayan Emergency, even though 1RAR had fought in clashes during its year in Vietnam that should have put that mindset to rest. The first contacts of the Task Force in 1966 were also far more dangerous than the Malayan firefights. Possibly, a training image persisted, which saw communist terrorists with a rusty shotgun and antiquated carbines running off through the jungle chased by Diggers in aggressive pursuit. This sort of tactical picture had faded quickly for members of the AATTV in earlier years:

> The road-bound units became easy marks for the Viet Cong, who were expert at the annihilation ambush. Yet the first time that the Australians tried to introduce their method of countering a vehicle ambush, the attempt misfired. The Australian drill, based on small-scale ambushes, was to debus on the opposite side from the ambush and charge back at the enemy. 'Yes, that's very good', said an experienced old ARVN lieutenant, 'but what happens if you've got two companies of Viet Cong on one side of the road and two companies on the other'.[101]

The battle at Long Tan almost mirrored the ARVN lieutenant's hypothetical question, except in this case the target was a company and the deployed enemy force was battalions. Historians for the *5th Viet Cong Division* and the *D445 Battalion* recorded that Dang Huu Thuan, the Baria military commander, and Tran Minh Tam, the division's chief of staff, commanded the 1966 battle. They set up a command post 2 kilometres north of Long Tan in the Lo O stream base. A forward tactical headquarters was probably located on Nui Dat (2), although there is disagreement between the senior enemy officers in later interviews about who actually commanded the battle and where the headquarters was located. There is little doubt that senior commanders were located nearby in several pockets somewhere north and east of Long Tan rubber.[102] Their main means of contact was via field telephones over which the two senior officers warned their groups that an Australian force was advancing into 'our battle zone'.

Dang Huu Thuan contacted the forward blocking force and Tran Minh Tam told the tail:

Comrades must strive to maintain complete secrecy. Wait until the order is truly close, and only open fire when the headquarters gives the order. . . . if there are any difficulties with the communication system, then automatically open fire on the enemy when they are 30 metres from the battle zone's forward blocking position.[103]

The *2nd Battalion* of *Regiment 5 [275]* and the *445 Baria Battalion* then engaged in close combat with the Australian troops.

We waited until the enemy was close and only opened fire when they were 10 metres from our fighting trenches. Eight enemy were killed on the spot. We used sub-machine guns and B40 grenade launchers—and the Australians withdrew in panic into the edge of the rubber . . . abandoning the bodies of almost ten Australians. After 30 minutes of combat, the 2nd Battalion had inflicted heavy casualties in an enemy platoon.[104]

D Company found the fighting line of trenches after the battle. Major Smith assumed incorrectly that they had been dug during the battle, something that D Company was unable to do. But the manoeuvring elements of the ambush, the other two battalions that were to sweep around and encircle Delta Company—much like the old Zulu 'horns-of-a-buffalo' attack—suffered immediate difficulties caused by accurate artillery. As the *5th Division*'s documents revealed:

> Meanwhile at the *3rd Battalion* and the *1st Battalion*, our assault troops moved towards the sound of the battle—but at that time there was very heavy rain and the forward elements encountered difficulties. The enemy began to fire artillery and their rear elements split into two wings along the axis of Route 52 to concentrate on striking and rolling up the *2nd Battalion*. At 4pm, the *3rd Battalion* and an element of the *1st Battalion* attacked the enemy in the decisive area of the battlefield. The Australian troops regrouped and resisted while calling intense artillery fire into our vanguard elements and the blocking elements of the *1st Battalion* and *445 Battalion*. At the same time, the firepower of their armoured vehicles was decisively target against the *3rd Battalion*. At 4.30pm, the situation of our leading elements was difficult due to the enemy's artillery and firepower that blocked us, and we were unable to achieve an encirclement of the enemy battalion. The *1st Battalion* and the *3rd Battalion* suffered high casualties. At 5pm, the battlefield headquarters ordered our units to withdraw to the regrouping position.[105]

The *D445 Battalion* history also detailed the planned ambush, emphasising the activities of the battalion's three companies:

> The ambush configuration for the battle was almost three kilometres long. The battle became close combat, fought in groups and by areas—it was difficult for our infantry and artillery [mortars] to support one another. Rain began to come down in buckets. After the first few minutes . . . our forward position was able to force the enemy into the killing zone. Our rear element began to storm into the killing zone [and] our flank-attacking group advanced. The enemy regrouped . . . and called in artillery fire. We were unable to move even a half-metre to finish off the enemy because of their rain of artillery [referred to as 'the New Zealand orchestra'].[106]

That information explained why a battlefront force of around 1200 could not swamp a company of 108.[107] The *275 Viet Cong Regiment* lacked heavy weapons and was the weaker of the two regiments in the division. Its parent division, the *5th*, was a light division, highly foot-mobile but lacking artillery. In this tactical clash, the VC killing power was too far away to get in quickly and encircle D Company. The *2nd Battalion* with a company from *D445* that hit 11 Platoon and attacked them was probably 350–400 strong and would have been spread out as well. They were held back at first by an infantry fire-fight and then by the artillery that exploded among them. The wide spread of Delta Company probably confused the VC commanders about the size of the Australian force. As the battle progressed, and the other two battalions raced to join in, the weight of artillery fire caused them to falter. Then 3 Troop with Alpha Company blocked the enemy's southern flanking attempt to get to the rear of Delta Company. Alpha Company subsequently dismounted and deployed to protect the eastern and southern sectors and Bravo Company guarded the west while D Company collected their casualties and prepared for their evacuation. When the power of the Australians got into full swing, it was too much for the basic infantry VC regiment and they were forced to retreat.

Was there a reserve NVA infantry battalion?

After the battle, the subsequent identification of an NVA formation known as *45 Regiment* came about because of the lack of general knowledge on the enemy's use of deceptive names for units. The number '45' was a disguise for *275 Regiment*, and this led to some enemy being misidentified as coming from a *reserve* NVA battalion. They were probably from either the *3rd Battalion* of *275 Regiment* or the division's air defence battalion. Latter-day records confirm that *COSVN* had approved an increase of reinforcements for the Nam Bo military regions in June 1966 that included 'a machine gun battalion each' to the *5th* and *9th* VC divisions.[108] Some of these guns might have supported *275 Regiment* during the Long Tan battle by firing from a position on the southern knoll of Nui Dat (2). If anything had been captured from that unit it would have indicated an NVA involvement in the fight.

In trying to trace where the enemy personnel had come from, several subsequent allied reports included links to *33, 66* and *250 NVA* regiments, as well as *605* and *C860* battalions. The *33* and *66 NVA* regiments were not in

Phuoc Tuy, or nearby. They were well to the north in the Darlac–Pleiku provincial areas. There were two known *250* regiments and an infiltration group with the same designation. There were also two *5th* divisions in the enemy's line-up in 1966; the *NVA 5th* was in Phu Yen Province well to the north. Elements of a *250th Infiltration Group* were found by the US 173rd Airborne Brigade during Operation Toledo (I), but their report did not make clear whether they were from an administrative station or a combat unit. The label 'infiltration group' was also a name used by the Viet Cong to conceal a unit's true activity.

Of the infantry regiments titled '*250*', one was an alias for the *88th NVA Regiment* that operated to the north in II CTZ. The other was listed briefly in the *MACV Command History* as a formation under the *7th NVA Division*. The *7th NVA Division* was raised on 13 June 1966 and was active in the provinces of Tay Ninh, Binh Long and Phuoc Long, 125 kilometres west of Phuoc Tuy. Before this, a *250th Regiment* was listed as an independent formation under the direct control of *COSVN*. An officer who claimed to be a senior captain in the *250th Regiment* was captured by 1RAR during the 173rd Airborne Brigade Operation Denver in mid-April 1966 in Phuoc Long Province. Soon after that, the '*250*'-titled unit disappeared from the MACV documents. It was probably another temporary name.[109] Pseudonyms, such as *C860 Battalion* for *D445*, appear to have confused some of the Long Tan analysts also.

In this puzzle of enemy identification a few analysts were inclined, mistakenly, to put the *D445 Battalion* at the head of the attacking force. It was a subordinate unit to *275 Viet Cong Regiment* for this battle. Retired Lieutenant Colonel Nguyen Van Kiem, who commanded *D445* after the battle but not during the action, provided the previously misleading information on the battalion's part during the battle. Bui Quang Chanh commanded the battalion and had done so from May 1965 but it had suffered a bit of a hammering in recent times and its numbers were probably down to something around 350, if that many.[110] In this battle, they would do as they were told. The feeling between the two VC fighting elements was not one of mutual admiration, more sufferance for the cause, something like the Regular Army–CMF niggles in Australia. Even senior NVA generals—Vo Nguyen Giap, the Defence Minister, and Nguyen Chi Thanh, *COSVN*—argued over the coordinated use of main force units and VC guerrillas.[111]

Intelligence reports and the North's official history corroborate the deployment of an NVA air defence battalion to the *5th Viet Cong Division* in May or June 1966, as well as the regroupee infantrymen to bring the regiment back up to strength. This really was an urgent operational need because *275 Viet Cong Regiment* had been reduced to a sickly and badly understrength formation of two battalions in the early part of 1966. Just before May 1966, *275 Viet Cong Regiment* was only 500-strong with two battalions until it was reinforced with the regroupee *605th Battalion* that was absorbed into the regiment as its *3rd Battalion*.

The puzzle over what enemy units fought at Long Tan was amplified by this northerner/regroupee mix, which convinced some of the Australians that the attacking unit was more than a VC regiment. Irrespective of the statements made in the Australian after action reports, no substantive information supported the claim that a reserve NVA infantry manoeuvre battalion was added to the *5th Viet Cong Division* for the Long Tan battle.[112]

There is no reason to doubt the *5th Viet Cong Division*'s admission about what units were involved in this attack. Their telling of what happened is within a reasonable sequence of events when correlated against the Australian reports, with some expected but discounted pieces of hyperbole. One example cited in their history is this action by Le Huu Nghia, the VC Reconnaissance Platoon Commander. Nghia 'advanced into the hail of enemy fire and used a B40 [RPG] to destroy the leading armoured vehicle'. We know that the APC call sign 39M was engaged by what was reported as a '57 RR [recoilless rifle] team from 15–20 yards to his right front', but the vehicle was not destroyed. Corporal John Carter killed the recoilless rifle team members with his Owen gun, a much-maligned weapon of World War II vintage.[113] If the weapon fired was a Chicom B40, the weapon was not very effective against armour as a US survey showed that out of 194 tracked vehicles disabled only 16 were damaged by the B40 and Viet Cong in the field had demanded to have them replaced by the more powerful Soviet B41 (RPG-7).[114]

COSVN also provided tactical directives to its armed forces in March 1966 that included the order to 'pull the enemy out of his lair to fight him'. To counteract Westmoreland's operations in the hectic months from January to May 1966 that targeted the VC base areas and the VC *5th* and *9th* divisions, *COSVN* ordered:

Our troops were to utilize mobile attacks to annihilate enemy forces *outside of their defensive positions as the principal tactic* [emphasised], in combination with shelling attacks and raids by sappers.[115]

COSVN only had two main force divisions—the *5th* and *9th*—in its military regions at the time this directive was issued and their commanders did not dare disobey General Nguyen Chi Thanh. In August 1966, NVA Lieutenant General Hoang Van Thai, Commander *Military Region 5*, also chaired a conference which reviewed the lessons from their main force operations from September 1965 through to the northern summer of 1966. Among the many lessons learnt and directives on how to fight the new enemy was a set of standards for designating 'expert' regiments:

The standard for an expert regiment was to fight a regiment-sized battle that destroyed an American or a puppet battalion operating in the open or to overrun a strong point held by two or three puppet companies.[116]

This tactical detail strengthens the information provided by the *5th Viet Cong Division*'s history and the information obtained through the interrogation of Lieutenant Colonel Chuyen, the defector. The *275th Regiment* did not have the combat power or the tactical approval to attack the ATF base at Nui Dat. However, the battle did adhere to the enemy's combat sequence known as 'one slow and four fasts'—slow preparation, fast advance, fast assault, fast mop-up, and fast withdrawal. Their plan was to ambush an Australian force at Long Tan, but it turned into a deadly battle from which *275 Regiment* was forced to retreat.

Counting the dead

The Australians withdrew from the battle site during the night to establish a stronger defensive position that would permit the evacuation of their casualties by Dustoff helicopters. The next day, the 19th, they advanced back into the rubber. Sergeant Buick described what he found.

The landscape now appeared as if a giant had walked through it, flattening the trees with his footsteps. In one area about 100 metres square all of the trees had been totally smashed and broken. An overpowering stench of death from the bodies and rotting flesh now wafted through the still, cool morning air.[117]

As they advanced cautiously through the devastated landscape, the Australians were extremely wary of anything or anyone who looked like an enemy soldier. They found unimaginable numbers of dead and wounded and, to their surprise, several wounded Australians who had survived the night. Buick remembered getting back into 11 Platoon's position.

> Now the full impact of the carnage of the fighting struck me as I arrived back at our original platoon battle position. The 11 Platoon dead were all facing the front, still holding their rifles, having been killed firing their weapons. Vic Grice, the platoon radio operator, was sitting with a grin on his face, facing the sun and looking quite peaceful. I wasn't expecting to see any of the missing 15 men alive and now Jim [Richmond] and Barry [sic] [John Robbins] had beaten the odds twice.[118]

Buick was disturbed by the arrival of 'shiny-bums from various headquarters' and 'after he punched an officer', Regimental Sergeant Major George Chinn sent him off to count the dead:

> I grabbed Peter Dettman . . . and the two of us went to the area to the east and southeast of 11 Platoon's position. After an hour of walking, sometimes over mangled bodies and having counted about 130 [sic] whole or almost complete Viet Cong we had to give it away. It became sickening after a while and neither of us was in the mood to continue.[119]

The body count, the gruesome task of counting the dead, was a controversial method of measuring success or failure in combat, and has been the subject of continuing debate. In battle, the most demanding of human endeavours, it is a natural reaction to ask 'How many did you get?' Australians were not averse to the counting of bodies and keeping score. They had done so in World War II and they did it in Vietnam as well. The Australian Task Force had directed that a VC scoreboard was to be included in the *Newsweek*, an information letter for the troops.[120] Following the dramatic Long Tan battle, those beyond the battle site thirsted for details. Senior commanders needed something to quieten the politicians; others needed powerful proof to hand on to the press that the Viet Cong were shattered, while still others wanted the information because it was their job to record such things. And deep down, the numbers made for a good boast between the generals, a bit of rubbing it into the noses of the Americans.

At Long Tan, there was no single pit to which bodies were delivered and counted. As Harry Smith, commander of D Company, 6RAR, said:

> There were public relations people and correspondents walking around the area, and I personally wasn't involved other than the couple of bodies that I turned over myself. It was a battalion thing, and reports were coming in from all over the area of body counts. Eventually a body count of 245 was arrived at. I personally never saw 245 bodies in a heap anywhere, but that was the count of bodies located.[121]

The 6RAR diary recorded incrementally increased numbers of dead up to 245. Major Brian McFarlane, commander of C Company, reported that his company buried 50 bodies in the battle location YS485671 and later a grave for 14 bodies was found at YS5067. No other company recorded burying bodies after the battle, although fresh graves were found in other places during the post-battle search. A few of the Australians thought that there were Chinese troops among the dead, but ethnic Chinese came from Cholon, Saigon's Chinatown. *COSVN* had a Chinese department—the *Hoa Van Committee*—that recruited, trained and allocated the Cholon Chinese to VC units in *Military Region 7*.

The number of weapons found helped with body counts. With large counts there had to be a good quantity of weapons, too. In this case, 58 weapons were collected. The enemy had been hurt, but it wasn't clear how badly. The North Vietnamese and the Viet Cong have always been extremely reluctant to discuss their casualty figures. For the battle at Long Tan they admitted there were 33 dead and 80 wounded, but added that they suffered heavy casualties. These figures were well below the Australian claims.[122] Captain Tran Van Tieng from the *275th Viet Cong Regiment*, who was captured in February 1969, said that the regiment had suffered 'over 200 casualties including both

KIA and WIA'.[123] Although it is unlikely that positive proof will ever be found on how many enemy died and were wounded at Long Tan, it is interesting to do a little arithmetic. Enemy casualties reported by Major Smith were 245 killed in action by body count, 150 more possibly killed, 500 possibly wounded, and 3 captured. Smith also believed that the 'artillery did untold damage to the enemy in depth', but that was a guess. Lieutenant Colonel Townsend reported a body count of 245, 3 captured and an estimated 350 casualties evacuated.[124]

Battlefield casualty clearance

The strength of the *275th Viet Cong Regiment* was around 1200 at the front and that included *D445 Battalion*. The immediate assault force, which took the brunt of the attack and probably the most casualties, was probably around 600 strong. Standard reserve and support elements were deployed in the immediate vicinity on the fringe of the battle. Lieutenant Colonel Chuyen, the defector, told his interrogators that in his previous battle planning the staff expected a casualty rate of 25–30 per cent with a split of 80 wounded to 20 killed. In Chuyen's opinion, the number of wounded matched the number of dead. He did not plan the Long Tan engagement, but he also said that collection of the dead and wounded was an important aspect of any battlefield clearance.

The VC divisional planners estimated that four to six labourers would be needed for every wounded soldier requiring evacuation. A 30 per cent casualty rate at Long Tan would mean a force of 1200 would take 360 casualties. Using an 80:20 split for the casualties, 288 would be wounded and 72 killed. To get the seriously wounded and dead off the field, a labour force of something like 800 would be needed. If the casualty figures were increased to 245 dead, the wounded would be 980. Under the 30 per cent rule that would mean an attacking force of just over 4000, plus a clearance labour force of 3500.[125] These are unimaginable numbers for the enemy's organisation at the time.

MACV staff used an overall enemy wounded to killed ratio of 1.5:1—not specific to Long Tan—which meant that by their calculations the Long Tan 245 dead would equal 367 wounded. A MACV general formula showed the number of the wounded that would die, or be permanently disabled: 10 per cent (37) would die during evacuation; thus, 330 would reach hospital. Two per cent (7) of those getting to hospital would die. The total loss to death would then be 289. Of the 323 alive but wounded, 13 per cent (42) would be permanently out of action.[126] Opinions varied between American agencies over what the casualty ratio might be; the CIA used 1.62 wounded to 1 killed after studying the same overall general battle data used by MACV.

A subsequent case study conducted by Project RAND on an operation fought by the 4th US Marine Regiment in July 1968, in I Corps, provided additional information on how the enemy reacted to casualties in a battle. The clash in 1968 involved two NVA companies. The NVA suffered badly in the attack, one in which they used 82 mm mortars and 130 mm artillery in support. They stopped the attack to reorganise when the casualties were at approximately 23 per cent and broke off the attack when casualties reached 30 per cent. Although these figures could not be verified they were said to be a good estimate. In addition, when the NVA retreated from the battle they did so in small groups.[127] This was the same tactic used in the clashes against the Australians.

After the war, the past Australian commanders of 1ATF were interviewed to record their experiences for future generations of commanders and warriors. In the words of Major General Stuart Graham who commanded 1ATF as a brigadier from January to October 1967:

The 18th ARVN Division narrowly missed capturing the commander of 275 Regiment [Ut Thoi] in an operation way up north [assumed to mean Long Khanh Province; it was not the northern region of South Vietnam], but they did capture his diary and a lot of personal documents. We were never able to get a copy of his diary but I saw translations of some bits of it up at 18th Div Headquarters [Xuyen Loc]. He recorded the battle of Long Tan in which, I forget how many Viet Cong we claimed to have killed, I think there were 200 odd or something. But in his diary he listed his losses at 500.[128]

Unfortunately, the diary or parts of it have never been produced. It is also difficult to understand why such an important document was not sent to the Combined Document Exploitation Center, from where translated copies would have been despatched to all interested commands.[129] Also, contrary to rumours, Ut Thoi, the regimental commander at Long Tan, was not killed; he finished the war as a lieutenant general.

The need for a large labour force to clear the battlefield—no matter which set of casualty figures is used—would have meant many of the labourers would themselves have been killed or injured. This raises another question: how many of the bodies counted and buried might have been non-combatants? Those deaths, if in large numbers, would have been difficult to keep quiet in a provincial population of approximately 104,000, the majority of whom were clustered in the southern villages along routes 2, 23 and 15 around Hoa Long, Dat Do, Long Dien and Baria (Phuoc Le). The Dat Do District population, which covered Long Tan village, was 25,000 and Xuyen Moc District had 2000.[130] The other option was that one of the battalions might have been used as the labourers. That seems unlikely, however, because the regiment was not that powerful and could not afford to take manpower away from the battlefront.

Assuming that up to 500 of the enemy were dead—as recorded by Brigadier Graham—the *275th Viet Cong Regiment* would have been wiped off the battle map. In an action just over three months later on 2 December 1966, units of *275 Regiment* ambushed the US 11ACR on Route 1, south of Gia Ray to the east of Xuyen Loc in Long Khanh Province. Before this fight, *274 Viet Cong Regiment* (not at Long Tan) had also fought the US 11ACR troops on 27 November along Route 1 near Xuan Loc. A raid against the Van Kiep rifle range followed this action on 9 December. The raiding party—a battalion from *274 Regiment* and some Chau Duc guerrillas—came from the Hat Dich base, crossed over the Dinh River and turned the ARVN training into a two-way rifle range. It was an embarrassing defeat for the South Vietnamese with at least 70 weapons lost and around 180 recruits captured. Two battalions of *275 Regiment* also fought a major engagement around Suoi Long-Suoi Ben Nom, northwest of Xuyen Loc and west of Highway 20 in the first half of 1967. This action was in Long Khanh Province and is probably the action referred to by Brigadier Graham. Although the regiments remained dispersed, with *274* in the Hat Dich triangle and *275* off to the west of Route 20, the *5th Viet Cong Division* was still combat active.[131]

The high casualty claims against the enemy do not provide a reasonable explanation as to how the seriously damaged units reinforced, re-equipped and got back to an acceptable standard for battle. By comparison, during February 1967 the Australian Task Force with two infantry battalions of approximately 1600 men suffered 24 killed and 72 wounded. Brigadier Graham complained in his commander's diary that 'The reinforcement system was not able to replace our manpower losses for several weeks and this placed a considerable burden on those units affected'.[132] (Note the ratio of wounded soldiers to killed.)

After the battle at Long Tan, the Australians withdrew to the western end of the rubber plantation with their casualties. They had the advantage of APCs to carry their litter patients and 4 dead; subsequently the 21 dead and wounded were lifted out by helicopters. Around the battle site, the Viet Cong gathered as many as they could of their dead and all except three wounded, and escaped while being harassed by artillery fire. How did they do it?

The Australian story

The surviving officers of Delta Company and some of the men believe ardently that their action prevented an intended attack upon the Task Force base. Major Harry Smith and platoon commander Dave Sabben have expressed their points of view on this matter, frequently. Bob Buick, the platoon sergeant of 11 Platoon, and Colin Townsend, the former commanding officer of the battalion, have supported them. But, adding fuel to the debate, the 1ATF INTSUM for 17 August stated that an attack on the Task Force base area was unlikely. Major Noel Ford, the commanding officer of B Company, also was not convinced that the plan was to attack the base.

> It seems unlikely that Viet Cong would alert 1ATF with a Mortar and Recoilless Rifle attack <u>before</u> an infantry assault. 1ATF could be expected to call in all forces (as it did with 5RAR) and to look to its defences. A fairly clear trail was left, leading to the 'trap' sprung by D Coy. This trail was admittedly broken for about 500 yards, but Viet Cong could expect that it would be found in fairly short time. A 445 Bn POW stated that his unit was in Long Tan on 18 Aug and that its orders were to march to the 'sound of the shooting'. This sounds like part of a plan to close a trap.[133]

Major Ford's belief that a trap was expected must raise the question: 'Why did he approve the extremely risky task of sending a section patrol 800 metres to his east, inside the rubber and into the most suspect area of enemy withdrawal after the mortaring of Nui Dat?' He supposedly did this before Delta Company relieved his company.

Although Lieutenant Colonel Townsend disagreed with Ford, he praised Bravo Company's performance in finding the enemy mortar and recoilless rifle firing positions under adverse conditions. At this stage Bravo Company was down to 32 men, which must have sent a subliminal message to those infantrymen left in the field that the area was not that dangerous. They probably thought, why would leave have been allowed if a strong enemy force was thought to be in the area. Townsend believed that the enemy deliberately tried to confuse any follow-up force by breaking numerous trails in the hope that the pursuing force would abandon its attempts to track them down. That effort, Townsend wrote, 'destroyed any theory that the enemy arranged the bombardment to draw a follow-up force into a trap for destruction'. In his commander's analysis, he stated:

> Intelligence obtained from VCC [captured personnel] and documents that D Coy contacted 275 Regt plus elements of D 445 Bn, which was moving to attack 1ATF base on the night 18/19 Aug 66. At least one North Vietnamese battalion was attached to 275 Regiment for their operation.[134]

Bravo Company had performed quite well and the commanding officer had arranged for Delta Company to take over the task of finding any enemy who remained in the area because of the small number of men now left in the field at B Company. All the same, Colonel Townsend chastised Major Ford, rebutting his idea of a trap.

> I believe that follow-up could have been pursued more aggressively and more quickly. B Coy is a slow-moving company, which needs to exhibit more speed and aggressiveness in its cross-country tactical movement.[135]

In a sad postscript, Major Ford's personal belongings and car were found near a beach in Sydney in December 1967 and it was presumed that he had drowned.

Polka dots and reflections

In conjunction with the search and clearing of the Long Tan battlefield, Operation Toledo was extended westwards in the hope that the enemy might have attempted to escape to the north. Lieutenant Colonel Richmond 'Dick' Cubis recorded some personal comments about this period in 1974. He and Brigadier Jackson wrongly believed that General Westmoreland had 'ordered a gaggle of battalions to be dropped in pockets over a large area to try and surround and capture the survivors of Long Tan'. 'Utterly futile', Cubis wrote. He was indebted to Jackson for the perfect description of this and similar actions as 'polka dot strategy'.[136] Unfortunately, comments such as this displayed Australian ignorance of what was happening around them. They should have known that Toledo, a major operation, had been going on since 10 August. Admittedly it was well to their east, but it was still inside Phuoc Tuy Province. The Americans, too, had been trying to flush out the *5th Viet Cong Division*, and slipping the American and South Vietnamese force across to cover the northern sector of Phuoc Tuy on 22 August was the good use of a large force conveniently located nearby. Lost in this reflection on who was tactically stupid and who was smart was the fact that no one found the VC soldiers before Long Tan. Nor did they track them down after the battle. Perhaps the wisest of all was the *5th Viet Cong Division*.

As the artillery commander, Cubis had a particular gripe about the recording of numbers of enemy killed in the battle. There was a board, mounted at Headquarters 1ATF, that recorded the number of enemy dead. There was no column for the artillery. However, listed down one side were all the other units, the battalions, the SAS, the APC squadron and so on. Cubis later wrote:

> I never remarked on this obvious nonsense, as I had no particular pride in expecting to see a list of men destroyed by my guns in a disgraceful war. But my sense of irony was amused when, after Long Tan, the hundreds of Viet Cong dead were solemnly credited to 6RAR rather than to 1st Field Regiment who had indisputably done most of the killing . . . admittedly it was hard to sort them out anyway—who is to say a deady [*sic*] was killed by a rifle bullet or by a shell fragment. Incidentally, the relations between the battalions following this deteriorated badly.[137]

The officers of 6RAR conveniently listed the dead as 50 per cent by artillery fire and 50 per cent small arms, which was nonsense.

Subsequently, in the November 1966 Task Force diary, Brigadier Jackson wrote that he had relieved Lieutenant Colonel Cubis of his command for a matter not connected with the Long Tan battle. In 1968, Cubis requested that a personal letter be attached to the 1 Field Regiment Commander's Diary in which he said that he had requested to be relieved of his command. He disagreed with Jackson's entry in the 1ATF diary for November 1966, saying that it was misleading and could be regarded as derogatory to him. The Cubis addendum claimed that Jackson had attempted to countermand an order affecting the engagement of a target by one of his artillery batteries without good reason and in doing so had bypassed him.[138]

New lessons or old ones resurrected?

Lessons and more lessons, some handed down over the years and others just recently learnt by the first Australian battalion to fight in Vietnam had re-emerged. The recent lessons learnt were distributed in a *Training Information Bulletin* in May 1966.[139] However, the newly raised Australian battalions had only begun serious training in the months before their deployment to Vietnam. They had to do some fast running to catch up on the basic infantry skills. For example, 5RAR conducted its first battalion field exercise in March 1966, just three months before the real thing. Companies in 6RAR went through sub-unit training at the Jungle Training Centre at Canungra, also in March. The Anti-Tank platoon fired the Carl Gustav 84 mm recoilless rifle for the first time on 18 March. And, of course, staff from Canberra and the Northern Command came to brief the commanding officer and quartermaster on the proper care, maintenance and accounting methods for loss of stores and equipment. In the early months of deployment, the system just could not keep up and it is surprising this lag time did not have a more serious consequence for the force. In war, sometimes luck overtakes planning and procrastination. Experience now replaced the textbook and some previously forgotten know-how was resurrected.

The 60 rounds of ammunition carried by riflemen was woefully inadequate. Crated ammunition was not the best method of resupply to troops in the thick of battle. Pre-loaded magazines were an absolute necessity, as was the increase of the load to 140 rounds per man.[140] Some weapons could not handle the adverse weather conditions, for example mud and water affected the firing of the General Purpose Machine Gun-M60. The Self Loading Rifle

(SLR) was judged the outstanding weapon of the action, but two firing pins broke during the battle. Owen guns were useless beyond 25 metres. Major Smith, a soldier from the days when rifle companies had a bit more firepower, advocated the revival of some heavier weapons at company level. Most of the suggestions had merit; some could be implemented by battalion, while others needed approval elsewhere. For example, putting a Carl Gustav 84 mm at company would require favourable reception higher up the chain and that would not happen because Sweden refused to supply the ammunition. It was also a cumbersome weapon to carry. The young Australian soldiers were now a bit older and much wiser.[141]

Command and control

When the seriousness of the Delta Company clash became apparent, command went beyond the battalion commander's realm. Although Lieutenant Colonel Townsend was calling the shots with his company commander out in the Long Tan rubber, Brigadier Jackson and his staff had to peer over his shoulder because the safety of the base was at risk. Fortuitously Lieutenant Colonel John Warr discussed with Jackson the return of 5RAR to Nui Dat from Operation Holsworthy, the dates of which overlapped the mortaring of the base on the 17th. The battalion, minus a company, started its move back to the base at 0815 hours on 18 August. Whether Jackson initiated that call is a moot point, but at least the base had some half-respectable defence in case there was more to the enemy's bombardment. From the commander down, everyone at Nui Dat now needed eyes in the back of their head. Townsend fought the 6RAR battle, but there were Task Force strings attached because the *274th Viet Cong Regiment* was also out there somewhere.

One of the most contentious moments during the battle occurred when Delta Company requested an urgent ammunition resupply. Did the RAAF baulk at flying? The charge that they did so is a never-ending story. Brigadier Jackson remained critical of the RAAF's method of operations in his August 1966 report, although he admitted that 'a marked improvement was evident when Group Captain Peter Raw moved forward to the Task Force area'.[142] Two reputable accounts tell of the RAAF's reluctance to commit two of the eight available Australian helicopters for a task that had a very good chance of them being lost. Bob Grandin, a co-pilot of one of the 9 Squadron heli-copters, remembered when commander of D Company Harry Smith called urgently for a resupply:

Group Captain Raw recognised the difficulty of tasking . . . helicopters into an unsafe area in contravention of the Air Staff directives. It was suggested that Canberra would need to be contacted to give approval. This made Brigadier Jackson furious. He turned to the US liaison . . . [and] was told US Army helicop-ters could be up from Vung Tau in about 20 minutes.[143]

Ian McNeill told a similar story in *To Long Tan*. The US response must have been like a red rag to a bull. 'In the face of the US response he [Peter Raw] saw no real alternative but to offer the RAAF aircraft.'[144] There is more to Raw's reluctant cave-in than just the US willingness to assist. Grandin wrote that Frank Riley, one of the Huey pilots, 'stepped forward and said he would go in with his helicopter. He argued that he was commander of the aircraft in the field and had the right to make tactical decisions about what he could and couldn't do'.[145] This was the watershed. After that it was a matter of the pilots and crew figuring out how to get the ammunition to the men on the ground, which they did in superb fashion.

The episode left an objectionable taste in the mouths of many. That a senior Australian officer did not have the moral courage to override a Canberra direc-tive at a time when Australian soldiers were on the verge of being overrun and mowed down was appalling. What did the group captain expect in turn-around times for his message to Canberra? It was after normal work hours back in Australia and into a Thursday night. If Raw were reluctant to make the decision it would be a good guess that a Canberra duty officer would not make it for him. Assuming that an immediate link could be patched through to Air Force Headquarters at Russell Offices, it would have made for an interesting fly-on-the-wall witness to see who flick-passed the conundrum to whom. The Air Force can make many arguments about the restrictive directives in their favour and they sound very convincing, but the unwillingness to go immedi-ately to assist the infantry was wrong. To everyone's credit, however, after that, cooperation improved and the force was the better for it. This altercation even-tually cost the RAAF its control of the helicopters after the war.

Another challenge emerged as Alpha Company was being carried in to counterattack and strengthen Delta Company. This time it was an all-Army affair and there was conflict over who commanded the APCs. Lieutenant Adrian Roberts, the troop commander, was adamant that 'the Infantry must realise that they are under command for movement till I could get them no further'. In the midst of the initial clashes with an enemy group of about 100, a 57 mm recoilless rifle fired upon one APC, and a crew commander was mortally wounded in another. Roberts replaced the wounded soldier and sent a carrier back to Nui Dat with the wounded man. It is doubtful that returning the vehicle was against the expressed wishes of the infantry commander because by this stage Roberts had told Captain Charles Mollison, commanding Alpha Company at the time, 'to get fucked, I ran my troop'.[146] Unfortunately, the APC that went back to Nui Dat also took a platoon headquarters away from the battle.

It was bad enough that the carriers were now among the flanking enemy without having to contend with a jumble of requests, demands, orders and counter-orders along the way. A small group of infantry jumped off one of the carriers in an impulsively brave but dangerous move. Some others got out through the rear ramp, against Roberts' desire to fight his vehicles through mounted. Mollison made it very clear in a report that 'APC's [sic] are a vehicle or a fire support unit and should be under command of the Infantry Commander'.[147] The troop commander's decision also attracted severe criticism from the commanding officer of 6RAR. Townsend judged the return of the vehicle as an 'irresponsible action'. 'The APC Commander must realize that the infantry is in overall command of the force and whilst the APC Commander manoeuvres the vehicles he does so in accordance with the plan given by the Infantry Commander', Townsend wrote.[148]

While he admonished Roberts for his decision, Captain Mollison and Lieutenant Peter Dinham (2 Platoon) escaped a rap over the knuckles for the command mix-up that allowed a few of A Company's soldiers to dismount. These soldiers masked the fire from the armoured vehicles and the command disagreement had the potential to turn the relief into disarray. Both actions were understandable, the junior officers lacked experience, and training in infantry–armour cooperation. The more senior officers should have made it very clear who was in command and given themselves a slap over the wrist for not doing so.

During training, the infantry prepared the plan and gave the orders. The troops got aboard and roared off to a disembarkation point where the APC would face the enemy with guns blazing while the infantry scrambled out the back and shook out into assault formations. It was wonderfully successful at Holsworthy or Puckapunyal bases. No one argued about where to stop, or when to get out, except if the infantry had to walk too far afterwards. The first rule for the APC troops after they got rid of their infantry load, was to make sure that they didn't run over them when they roared off. This was the first rule for the infantry also. But, as in Field Marshal Helmuth von Moltke's maxim, no plan survives contact with the enemy. And so it was in this major battle. Although a mistake was made, 'the surprise achieved by the APC . . . which broke up the movement of an estimated two companies of Viet Cong to the rear of D Coy, undoubtedly saved the day'. Furthermore, Lieutenant Colonel Townsend wrote, 'notwithstanding the criticism [about the return of the vehicle to Nui Dat] 3 Tp deserves the highest praise for gallantry'. One other decision by Roberts was a wise one, although not recognised by the infantry commanders. Roberts recorded:

I did not dismount or request infantry dismount on the move to D Coy because I considered that I could shock assault and control my troop better and quicker than the infantry can when dismounted especially in the terrain we assaulted over.[149]

This was the very lesson that came out of the battle at Ap Bac in 1963 when the US infantry adviser convinced the ARVN commander of the APCs to unwisely dismount his men, with the result that the South Vietnamese lost the tactical advantage. Those who fought in the 1944 battle of Leyte Island in the Philippines during World War II wrote on the close coordination and teamwork necessary between infantry and attached armour. American Lieutenant General John R. Hodge reminded all to keep in mind future battles:

In future battles close coordination and teamwork of infantry with its organic or attached armor will play a great part in attaining decisive results. Progressive development of doctrine and ways and means further to weld the tank-infantry team, including practical means of intercommunication are a must. No infantry division can be considered trained unless it has fully developed this know-how for its infantry and its organic and attached armored units to the point where fumbling is eliminated.[150]

Victory and consolidation

The battle was won. Great courage and resilience had been shown. Each man—rifleman, trooper and gunner—had done what his mind and training would permit. They had been pushed to the limit and some had been pushed beyond their limit, although that would not surface for a few years. The determination and bravery of the Viet Cong also won grudging respect. No Australian battalions experienced enemy artillery fire during their time in Vietnam. A few Australian advisers who fought in battles in the central and northern provinces of the South can certify that it tested their battle spirit to the limits. For example, over eight days in September 1967, 3000 incoming shells from NVA artillery hit Gio Linh, a post close to the DMZ, the border between North and South. Australian advisers frequently manned this base. To the soldiers of *275 Viet Cong Regiment* and *D445 Battalion*, who maintained their assault and pushed on in their efforts to surround and destroy Delta Company through a devastating barrage of shells that fell among and around them, a salute of recognition would not be amiss.

At Long Tan there was a tactical victory by the Australian combined arms team, not just Delta Company, 6RAR, and the presses rattled out headlines about the magnificent Australians. The People's Liberation Armed Forces also claimed a success and quickly spread the word through the local hamlets and villages that an Australian force had been destroyed. Their message of victory was strung in banners across pathways and in village markets. Broadcasts from Hanoi added zeal to the claims. It did not matter that it was pure hyperbole; the allied force in Phuoc Tuy Province had to win the propaganda battle to make sure that the people did not lose faith and turn to the Viet Cong as their protectors.

The Australians had had their wake-up call, which provided the adrenalin that kept everyone alert over the next series of patrols, search-and-destroy operations and cordon-and-search efforts. From August till the end of 1966, the Task Force units conducted thirteen major operations that included joining the second phase of Operation Toledo. With titles such as Vaucluse, Casula, Bathurst, Canberra, Bundaberg and Ingham there was no mistaking their Australian connections. The areas of the operations also covered the diverse range of topography within Phuoc Tuy Province, from the steep and hilly terrain of the Nui Dinh to rubber plantations, through jungle, to road clearances and security, across to the island of Long Son and east over the Song Rai River on the way to Xuyen Moc village. Importantly, the base defences of Nui Dat were also improved during this period. Clashes with the enemy were generally light, with limited casualties to both sides, although good quantities of enemy materiel and documents were captured.

Imperial honours and awards

At any post-war gathering, the quota system for acts of gallantry is guaranteed to raise the ire of many veterans. Very few know about the policy's history, but the battle at Long Tan was a tipping point that raised awareness among soldiers that something wasn't right with the system.

Behind the scenes, among the politicians, bureaucrats and officers at Defence, an argument about awards had been brewing for several years after the Australians first went to Vietnam. The Imperial table of honours and awards prevailed. Citations were written and a formal sifting process took place to make sure that the sanctity of recognition was kept at a high standard. It was a fairly straightforward procedure; acts of gallantry and/ or outstanding service were witnessed, signed off and sent off through the chain of command. Vetting of citations was subjective and the downgrading of some of the initial recommendations was not unusual—not everyone in the combat zone served gallantly or with distinguished behaviour. An old-fashioned sense of what constituted bravery under fire and outstanding duty also prevailed among some of the older generals, in particular among those who had served in World War II. They were adamant that a strong protocol should apply to the honours and awards list.

Before the arrival of 1RAR in June 1965 an agreement was struck between the Deputy Secretary (A) at Army and the Adjutant General that there were insufficient numbers serving in Vietnam to justify an operational scale of awards. After the arrival of the battalion, the Chiefs of Staff Committee advised the Acting Minister for Defence of a proposed scale of gallantry that was one award for each 250 personnel engaged in qualifying service. This reflected an operational awards scale promulgated in a UK War Office pamphlet (1960 edition), which Australia used as a reference.[151] A scale published in the *London Gazette* on 30 September 1966 showed Mention-in-Despatches as one for each 150 personnel.[152] The information in the publications and the correspondence between ministers and Defence was *advice*, but not a formal scale of awards for Australia because the Queen had not approved one yet.

In June 1966, the Minister for Defence, Allen Fairhall, challenged Malcolm Fraser's recent recommendations for awards when he wrote that more selectivity was needed because the number of recommendations processed had exceeded the Chiefs of Staff Committee recommendations. Fraser, Minister for the Army, fired back that each individual recommendation had been carefully scrutinised, but no quota existed at this stage and he understood that the total number to that date did not coincide with the *notional* quota. Fraser added that the citations 'were very deserving examples of courage and devotion to duty' and recommended their acceptance. Fraser also advised Fairhall that he had informed the Commander Australian Force Vietnam that as from 1 July 1966 he must conform to the proposed scale—which followed the *London Gazette* figures—as though it had been approved. In effect, Fraser then set the Operational Scale at zero from 1 July 1966 so that any previous surplus to the anticipated quota level would not be absorbed and impair the scale's future allocation.[153]

The immediate test of Fraser's de facto limitations came on 18 August with the battle at Long Tan. What was awarded to the Diggers has been argued about ever since. The first ripple of discontent appeared to come from scuttlebutt that said Major Smith's Distinguished Service Order (DSO) was downgraded in order to accommodate senior awards for the commanding officer of 6RAR and Brigadier Jackson at Task Force headquarters. Two comprehensive studies conducted many years later in 2008 and 2009 lay out the detail of the awards. Retired Major General Peter Abigail repudiated the DSO claim in his 2008 *Review of Recognition for the Battle of Long Tan*. For the disbelievers, the power of Jackson's citation appeared to depend too closely on the phrase 'he personally directed the engagement which accounted for 254 [*sic*] enemy dead'.[154] Jackson's award of a DSO in the same list as Major

Smith's MC (Military Cross) did not help extinguish the theory of a medal plot among senior officers. Nor did the suggestion that Jackson should have received a CBE (Commander of the British Empire), but that would have left nothing for Major General Ken Mackay at Headquarters, Australian Force Vietnam.

The quota directed by Fraser meant that a limited number of gallantry awards—one per 250—were available to the total force from 1 July to 31 December 1966. The Long Tan heroes had to compete with all other valorous acts by Australians in Vietnam, and for the Mention-in-Despatches that also included distinguished service. The vetting process implemented within 6RAR from platoon to battalion saw disagreements over who was worthy of what. Subsequently, some acts were never rewarded because citations were not written and/or kept on file, irrespective of whether they were approved or not. To grant recognition many years later on the say-so of some personal recollections would undermine the integrity of the awards system and the 2008 and 2009 studies agreed that such awards should not be made.

General Abigail's study also analysed the non-approval of an MC for the two surviving platoon commanders, David Sabben and Geoff Kendall. The citations allegedly were returned from Australian Force Vietnam to be resigned for the lesser award of a Mention-in-Despatches (MID). Why? The Commander Australian Force Vietnam downgraded Major Smith's DSO to an MC in his portion of the recommendation column in the army form without sending it back for resubmission. Such a decision by a commander was just the stroke of a pen. What happened is pure speculation because the only forms retained on file for Sabben and Kendall are for Mention-in-Despatches.

The 2009 Professor Pearce Tribunal studied the unresolved recognition issues for the battle of Long Tan and released its findings in a paper of the same name.[155] In the main, the two studies followed similar processes, but did not agree with regard to an Australian Unit Citation for Gallantry for Delta Company, 6RAR—a citation that was not in existence at the time of the battle—or that a more senior award of the DSM should be approved for Flight Lieutenant Cliff Dohle. Both awards were recommended by the Pearce study but not by the Abigail review. Unfortunately, the Pearce Tribunal got lost with its understanding of the Operational Scale's active dates. By stating that the quota system applied for the whole of the Vietnam War, the tribunal aggravated the continuing arguments that Delta Company and other units in the battle lost out simply because too many awards had been allocated already, or, in a bizarre twist to the arguments, that the Department of External Affairs approved some awards and there were no awards left in the Army barrel. Although such nonsense is easily rebutted, facts often lose out to silliness.

In all battles there are heroes who are not given formal recognition. This is true of Long Tan. Even more damning was the lack of respect given to the other units who were essential elements in the Australian victory. For example, 3 Troop 1APC Squadron's gallantry and their effect upon the enemy's encircling movement 'saved the day', according to Colonel Townsend, but no unit citation was authorised for them. President Lyndon Johnson approved the award of a Presidential Unit Citation (PUC) to D Company, 6RAR, on 28 May 1968 for extraordinary heroism when surrounded and attacked by an estimated reinforced enemy battalion.[156] The details for the citation are obviously taken from the US MACV files, which refer to a VC battalion being annihilated after attempting an ambush.[157] President Johnson presented the citation to Prime Minister John Gorton at the LBJ Ranch on 30 May 1968. Further insult was made against 3 Troop and the other soldiers on the battle-field when every man on the nominal roll of D Company, 6RAR, was approved to wear the US Presidential Unit Citation, whether they were at the battle or not. There was nothing for the artillery or the other infantrymen involved in saving Delta Company. The issues of recognition remain unresolved.

Perhaps the military hierarchy—the generals, the bureaucrats and the politicians—should have abided by Napoleon Bonaparte's adage: 'Give me enough medals, and I'll win any war'. Australia could not bring itself to accept medals from South Vietnam, the country for whose freedom it supposedly fought.

Foreign awards

The potential for foreign medals to be awarded to Australians who served in South Vietnam attracted a cursory note in the 1962 commander's directive to Colonel Serong of the AATTV. 'Your attention is directed to Australian Military Regulations and Orders, Appendix 9.' That appendix referred to

(UK) Foreign Office regulations, which detailed in adamant format the non-acceptance of orders and medals without having previously obtained Her Majesty's permission to do so.[158] It is doubtful that Serong or any of his staff paid much attention to this directive for the first deployment. When WO2 Kevin Conway was killed on 6 July 1964, Vietnamese General Pham Van Dong awarded him the Knight of the National Order and Cross of Gallantry with Palm. The presentation took place at Conway's funeral without consultation with the Australian Ambassador, who said he would have recommended acceptance anyway.

Army Headquarters then directed Serong to refer all Vietnamese and US awards that were also to be adapted to appropriate Australian awards. Before this, Serong had given his verbal decision to the US Awards Board at MACV for any medals to be presented to Australians. This was done much to the disquiet of an American staff officer who complained that nothing was ever given in writing.[159] It is possible that a more dynamic piece of staff work at this stage of the war would have prevented the subsequent embarrassment of rejected awards and also salved a lot of the personal distress that has come to the fore since.

An inordinate amount of administrative time and, what appeared to be occasional pure bloody-mindedness, spelt out Her Majesty's rules on foreign awards. The rules were not always applied with the slavish zeal seen after Long Tan. Previously, Serong had told some of his men to accept any awards but not to wear them. In June 1965, Lieutenant Colonel William Murphy, HQ AAFV, and the Second Secretary of the Embassy were given and sensibly accepted Vietnamese decorations at an International Aid Day Ceremony. It would have been churlish in the extreme to parade with the representatives of 29 countries only to withdraw Australia's hand when Vietnamese recognition was offered. The receipt of the medals warmed the teleprinter lines between External Affairs and the Saigon Embassy in October with further advice that the awards could not be accepted (a cable, no doubt, deftly filed).

After the battle at Long Tan, the Vietnamese High Command wanted to present some of the Australians with awards to recognise their fighting prowess and also to show South Vietnam's appreciation. Their request was rejected and cigar boxes and dolls were handed out instead. What an absurdity. This was one of those times of pure bloody-mindedness. The lack of flexibility imposed on the military commander, the ambassador and every other person involved with this decision was incredibly rude. There was a single simple way out in Foreign Office Order 1, which said: 'No Person in the service of the Crown *may accept and wear* [emphasised] the insignia of a foreign Order without ... permission'.[160] On such a significant occasion, the turning of a blind eye to the order on the basis the awards would not be worn would have been a fitting action of command and diplomacy. To paraphrase a famous sports label, 'Just do it!' It might have been that the obstructionists were protecting their opportunities to obtain orders of the Most Excellent Order of the British Empire and it would not do to displease Her Majesty or her servants.

Amid all the discussions about the non-acceptance of foreign awards—especially South Vietnamese medals, disdain for US awards was not so strong. Much is made of the difference between unit awards and individual medals. The Abigail report, for example, said 'There was an inclination to accept foreign unit awards ... but individual awards by and large were not accepted'.[161] The entire Honours and Awards system has either overlooked or forgotten that the Vietnamese Campaign Medal, approved to be worn in 1966, was an individual medal for service awarded by South Vietnam. The terms of its acceptance and eligibility were under formal discussion before Long Tan.[162] By 1971, recommendations for Vietnamese awards were advertised by 1ATF as acceptable. Although they were not to be worn in Australia, Central Army Records and Army Headquarters would record the medals presented.[163]

All the way with 'LBJ'

Harold Holt had come under heavy diplomatic pressure over Vietnam from the United States from the day he assumed the responsibilities of prime minister. After the visits of Averell Harriman and Vice-President Hubert Humphrey in January and February, Australia hosted the 11th SEATO conference in June 1966. This meeting brought Dean Rusk, the US Secretary of State, to Canberra. Rusk told the press that America appreciated Australia's efforts in Vietnam. When he returned home he pushed the line that Australia was doing its utmost, considering the country's limited resources. Following Rusk's report, President Johnson invited Prime Minister Holt to visit Washington. During a full military honours ceremony at the White House on 29 June 1966 Harold Holt made it clear that Australia was in Vietnam 'all the way':

You have in us not merely an understanding friend, but one staunch in the belief of the need for our presence with you in Vietnam. We are not there because of our friendship; we are there because, like you, we believe it is right to be there, and, like you, we shall stay there as long as seems necessary in order to achieve the purposes of the South Vietnamese Government and the purposes that we join in formulating and progressing together. And so, sir, in the lonelier and perhaps even more disheartening moments which come to any national leader, I hope there will be a corner of your mind and heart which takes cheer from the fact that you have an admiring friend, a staunch friend that will be all the way with LBJ.[164]

Later in the year Johnson commented that an Australian politician dealt with the Labor Party attacks on Holt's phrase 'All the way with LBJ' with another slogan: 'Better all the way with LBJ than half a win with Ho Chi Minh'.

Coincidentally, Senator Mansfield, the Senate Majority Leader, had written to President Johnson on 29 June to report on two meetings held by Democratic members of the Senate. During a discussion of Vietnam by Committee Chairmen or Designees on 28 June, the record showed 'Although the Australians will stand with us, there are indications that they want us to get out'. This was completely at odds with Prime Minister Holt's statement on the 29th.[165] Three months later, Wilfred Burchett, the renegade Australian journalist, was back in the news when he interviewed Nguyen Huu Tho, Chairman of the NLF, who outlined his peace terms in a broadcast by the NLF clandestine radio and Hanoi radio on 13 and 28 September, respectively.[166]

President Johnson visited Australia between 20 and 23 October 1966 on his way to a Summit Conference in Manila—a meeting of the seven nations involved in the Vietnam War—and in doing so became the first US President to visit Australia. Of course the visit was to ensure that Australia would stand firm and display publicly a united front not only to defend South Vietnam, but to end the war without giving in to the North Vietnamese. Johnson's visit was an outstanding success, with the streets lined with hundreds of thousands of people to welcome the president. In Melbourne, the president's diarist recorded:

A group of young girls in maroon skirts were jumping up and down holding their hats on their heads. A sign here read 'Welcome to the 52nd State'. A policeman said, 'Nothing like this since the Beatles were in town a couple of years ago.'

The crowd extended as far as the eye could see down the street from 3–7 deep. Although there was a tremendous crowd . . . it was not altogether friendly . . . at some points considerable boos and 'Go home Yanks' could be heard.[167]

Not even the throwing of paint over his car and his bodyguard, Rufus Young-blood, could take away from the enthusiasm of the crowds elsewhere, with people 30–40 deep along both sides of a street. Johnson was jubilant when he departed Essendon Airport; he was wearing a yellow rose and kidded several staff 'Don't tell me you've been typing again, where were you when I needed help, when they were throwing paint?'[168] In Sydney, the crowds were larger and the president was forced to change his car because ticker-tape confetti had clogged the air-conditioning. Demonstrators with balloons shaped like black bombs attracted attention and a woman threw herself in front of the president's car. Several years later, it was revealed that Bob Askin, the Premier of New South Wales, had said 'Run over the bastards' when more demonstrators blocked the president's car. This comment allegedly influenced future demonstrations when protests took on a more ugly attitude against the government as well as the police.

Even the Americans had speculated that a visit by Johnson might have been seen as an involvement in Australian politics and 'open to sharp criticism from Holt's opponents'. During the Manila Conference, Johnson told South Vietnam's leaders that his reaction to the demonstrators in Australia was that they should talk to Ho Chi Minh, not to him. None of this hurt Holt politically. In September 1966, a Morgan Gallup Poll indicated that 56 per cent of Australians were in favour of Australian involvement in Vietnam, 28 per cent were in favour of withdrawal, and 16 per cent were undecided. The public also supported the government in the November 1966 election in which the Liberal/Country Party Coalition trounced the Australian Labor Party, winning a 40-seat majority in the House of Representatives. The ALP won just 41 seats.

Almost immediately after the election considerations to increase Australia's force in South Vietnam by an additional battalion began, but there was really none ready to send. America had lobbied for this increase well before the Australian election result—Westmoreland did so during the Manila Conference—but understood the political ramifications of letting the troop demands become common knowledge. Australian support did extend beyond the deployment of military units through little-known diplomatic efforts such as providing assistance in repatriating wounded prisoners of war through Cambodia. However, the big newspaper headlines came with the possibility of more troops and Australia obliged with an announcement on 22 December 1966 that an additional 900 would go in 1967. A squadron of eight Canberra bombers would redeploy from Butterworth base in Malaya to Phan Rang on Vietnam's coast, 50 kilometres south of Cam Ranh Bay. With the addition of Clearance Diving Team 3 and HMAS *Hobart*, a tri-service flavour was added to the force while the other reinforcements filled out some of the known deficiencies that existed in the units already deployed. When all the reinforcements were deployed and it was a trickle flow effort through 1967, the Australian force would stand at around 6300 personnel.

5

A YEAR OF MANY QUESTIONS
1967

To be a successful soldier you must know history. Read it objectively.
What you must know is how man reacts. Weapons change but man
who uses them changes not at all. To win battles you do not beat
weapons . . . you beat the man.
General George Patton, 1944

Consolidation

Six months after Long Tan and into 1967, the Australian Task Force had staked out its limited area of operations and a new commander had arrived. Although Phuoc Tuy was regarded as the Australian province, the Australian commander's power within the province was curtailed. Operationally, he did not have the authority to conduct manoeuvres against the enemy beyond the immediate 1ATF tactical area of responsibility without Vietnamese and/or American approval. The American limitations were easier to understand. As operational controllers of the Task Force, they decided the tactical routine to match the bigger picture required within II Field Force Vietnam's (IIFFV) segment of South Vietnam, the III Corps Tactical Zone (CTZ). The Australians were allowed a fairly free hand to do things their way, but any serious effort to threaten the enemy's main base areas needed an injection of American military might to provide the Task Force with additional firepower and manpower. The Australian commander's report for January 1967 shows how the relationship influenced operations.

Since our ability to conduct offensive operations against the Viet Cong in Dec was severely limited by road security operations, a number of fairly ambitious operations in conjunction with Allied forces were planned for Jan. Due to operations elsewhere in III Corps area US forces were NOT available and the operations did NOT eventuate.[1]

During January, Australian operations were limited to company-sized patrols out to the range of 105 mm artillery, not only from Nui Dat, but also from a fire support base west of Nui Dinh, a group of hills 10 kilometres west of Nui Dat. This fire support base supported a patrol program that searched areas that had not been patrolled for several months, with the aim of clearing old known enemy bases and making sure new ones had not been built. Although a number of camps were found, none had been used or built recently. There was no contact with the Viet Cong until 26 and 27 January when Alpha Company, 5RAR, and Delta Company, 6RAR, clashed with groups of between 15 and 25 enemy soldiers.

While the main efforts of the Task Force now were to consolidate its defensive position and keep the enemy forces under combat pressure, beneath the surface there were a few disconcerting niggles. Australia's previous experience in anti-guerrilla operations or its later title 'counter-revolutionary warfare' recognised that while the 'main part of the struggle is political, counter-insurgency operations are simultaneously political and military in their nature'.[2] The doctrine of counter-revolutionary warfare correctly recognised that a deployed Australian force would not have 'any significant role in the political affairs of the country concerned', in this case South Vietnam. The Australian guidelines also explained that, politically, the solution to an insurgency was the removal 'of the causes of unrest and dissatisfaction on which the movement is based'. This was an ambitious challenge in Vietnam, and one that was emphasised in various civil and military programs. The Australian pamphlet continued: 'While the defeat of insurgents is an essential component of success, the campaign from the start must be seen as a joint political-military operation with the closest cooperation between the civil power, the police and the armed forces—both indigenous and external'.[3]

General Westmoreland determined in 1966 that the enemy's political and command infrastructure had to be destroyed or made ineffectual so that they 'could not control the populace through intimidation and terrorist campaigns'. He wanted this objective to receive maximum attention through combined military planning and government participation in both military and the newly named Revolutionary Development program (pacification). In Phuoc Tuy that would require close cooperation between the Australians, the province chief, and his American advisers. A delicate military balancing act between the Australian soldiers, the ARVN and the Regional and Popular Forces would be necessary as well. Notwithstanding some instances of combined training and operations, the Australian Task Force never really took this task to heart. The later increase in AATTV teams in 1967 and their deployment with Regional and Popular Forces went some way towards redressing this deficiency. Among the Australians there was a general attitude of disrespect towards the South Vietnamese forces, as this message recorded in a 5RAR log indicated: 'My sunray [commander] has just informed me that the slopes in this area yesterday found booby traps'.[4] 'Slopes', an abbreviation of 'Slope-heads', was a derogatory term for Vietnamese. The claimed uselessness of the local troops was reinforced by reports in January 1967 that indicated the Viet Cong were back and active again in the villages of Binh Ba and Hoa Long. This information highlighted the imbroglio facing Brigadier Graham: Phuoc Tuy Province was a mixed bag of military and civil agencies that Graham did not control. The province's senior military adviser was an American outside the Australian chain of command; the Vietnamese province chief answered to several masters too. Each province was administered through the government bureaucracy to Saigon, while the same area was also a military sector. In Phuoc Tuy, the province chief Lieutenant Colonel Le Duc Dat was also the military commander. Militarily, he commanded Regional Force companies and Popular Force platoons, answering to the Vietnamese commander of III CTZ for their performance. From time to time Colonel Dat also had troops from the ARVN 18th Division under his operational control, which meant he was also responsible to the commanding general of that division for their wellbeing. As Brigadier Graham said of the Regional Force Company located at Binh Ba in January 1967:

Although a Regional Force company has been established at Binh Ba after operation Holsworthy, their value is doubtful and their patrols in the Binh Ba area

have failed to encounter any Viet Cong that, according to the reports, have been visiting Binh Ba frequently.[5]

Ruff-Puffs: The forgotten men

Captain George Mansford of the AATTV came from the Duc My Training Centre near Nha Trang to the Binh Ba Regional Force Company in mid-January 1967. His comments on the challenges were down to earth.

> In the final phase of my tour of duty I was located with a very much under-strength, poorly trained, and ill-equipped South Vietnamese infantry company at an outpost adjacent to the village of Binh Ba in Phuoc Tuy. The unit's indifference towards the war and the accepted establishment was clearly evident by the abundant dirty and rusty weapons scattered carelessly throughout the area. The company was Regional Force, which in simple terms meant it was at the bottom of the barrel when it came to resources, priorities, and some would argue . . . that such rag tag units had been totally neglected by higher authorities. On arrival it was clear that the outpost was under significant threat and lacked adequate defences.[6]

Mansford's small team consisted of three Australian warrant officers, himself and an interpreter from Task Force, Corporal Mick Henry. They got stuck into the task and built up a respectable defensive position and injected some battle spirit into the ragtag company. Mansford gave credit to the warrant officers and Henry as a loyal and dedicated group. 'More often than not, we begged or stole what we needed including 50 calibre machine guns and a jeep (courtesy of Warrant Officer [Terence Ross] "Sooty" Smith).' The Regional Force Company's previous condition indicated the weakness of having the Regional and Popular Forces—the Ruff-Puffs—as crucial elements of defence at the very forefront of the fight for pacification in the hamlets and villages. Ghost soldiers, men who were on the roll book and being paid, but were not present, added further danger to a Regional or Popular Force unit's capabilities. Corrupt officials siphoned off the salaries of these ghost soldiers, as George Mansford found out when he complained about his company.

It was supposed to be of company strength and yet was perhaps as low as fifty percent. My protests were finally listened to but lo and behold, it was the Vietnamese Colonel himself operating the purse strings who arrived for a very brief few minutes to investigate the shortages. It was never addressed.[7]

Although the Mansford team was responsive to the Australian Task Force and communication with the battalions was good, there were times when coordination was very poor. For example, when a helicopter attempted to land in a newly laid minefield, the aircraft was damaged and two personnel were wounded. (The minefield was marked and recorded.) Mansford's command challenges mirrored those of Brigadier Graham. As Binh Ba village was in Duc Thanh District, Mansford was responsible to an American major at Duc Thanh headquarters for operational matters. The major reported to an American colonel who advised the Vietnamese colonel who had overall command of the Binh Ba ghost soldiers. Mansford's commanding officer in Saigon did not interfere in operational matters and appeared only infrequently.

One of these visits was prompted by the 'two chains of command' that existed for the advisory team and caused relationships to range from tolerable to difficult.

Task Force warned me that a medical team would visit the village and tasked us to assist with security in the general area. No problem. Then the day before, we were directed by Duc Thanh to search for an underground hospital on the same day. Although both tasks were done, it left no one at home looking after the base, an unsatisfactory arrangement. After this, there were some Australian casualties in my area of operations. We cleared the Dustoff [medical evacuation] and 1ATF was advised. The American major publicly rebuked me because he had not been advised as the senior adviser in our area. The bottom line, there was a meeting of all the heavies in Baria: CO AATTV, the Yank major and the Vietnamese colonel who orchestrated the ghost soldiers. I lost![8]

Further north, in Thua Thien Province near Hue, Major 'Vin' Musgrave of the AATTV also recalled the duties of the men who served with Regional Force or Popular Force units in sometimes remote, difficult and dangerous locations with minimal support.

After wasting six months of my tour [at a training centre], I escaped to lead a small advisory team at Nam Hoa and Huong Thuy, two adjacent sub-sectors in Thua Thien. We controlled less than one per cent of this vast area. We also shared part of our boundary with the United States Marine Corps who were a godsend. I don't think that we would have survived without them. As the people were Central Vietnamese they had no great regard for either Saigon or Hanoi. The relationship between the Sector Chief, a local, and the sub-sector Chief of Nam Hoa Captain Dat, a northerner, was an example of this dislike. They hated each other.[9]

A Vietnamese major at the headquarters of the 1st ARVN Division attempted to explain the difference in attitudes to Musgrave. 'You must understand in the North we have the philosophers, in the South we have business men, and in the centre we have the shit.' Although Musgrave did not agree with this opinion, it was a good example of how the tasks of defeating the enemy were complicated by many issues. Musgrave recalled some of the challenges of pacification at the coalface:

Our role in the sub-sectors was to fight the civil war component of the conflict. This was an unpublicised struggle that went on every day and every night throughout the length and breadth of South Vietnam. The protagonists were the paramilitary Regional Force/Popular Force and their Viet Cong equivalents. Although the Regional Force company strength was supposed to be about 120, one company was down to 23 and the other about 50 or so. We could handle the local Viet Cong force . . . our Regional Force/Popular Force could fight their weight in bull ants . . . but the enemy also had Main Force battalions and sometimes two or more managed to concentrate and when they got together we were not in the same league. The Vietnamese I advised were worthy allies and some were exceptional men. I will never forgive the ignorant western media . . . for lumping them into a simplistic denigrated mass.[10]

The tactical jigsaw

At this stage in the deployment of Australians into Phuoc Tuy, the Task Force did not have a civil affairs unit. This meant that although the Australian approach to counter-revolutionary warfare stressed civic action as an important aspect of strengthening the country's political stability, Brigadier

Graham's best efforts boiled down to achieving rapport. He had to establish a bond of mutual trust and agreement with the Vietnamese and the Americans who controlled the Revolutionary Development (pacification) programs in the province. However, mistrust of Vietnamese reliability continued to bubble away beneath the surface.

Nor were relations with the MACV advisers smooth sailing. As Clarry Rule, an Australian adviser deployed with US Advisory Team 89 at Baria, remembered:

> This just might be my faulty perception of what happened nearly 45 years ago, but I felt that there were times when both sides were not telling each other everything that they knew. The Australians didn't trust the Vietnamese; they wouldn't let them into the camp. They did have some interpreters there, but that was it. It was understandable that they would not allow maids and cooks and all to come in because of the security problem. However, they did not operate closely with the ARVN either.[11]

Captain Mike Wells, who had held the position before Rule, found balancing the duties of a sector operations adviser in an American team against the demands of an Australian brigadier difficult.

> After my familiarisation visits around I Corps, I arrived at Sector Headquarters and met the senior US advisor and LTCOL Dat and his Chief of Staff CAPT Quang, my counterpart, along with their key officers. LTCOL Jack K. Gilham replaced the senior advisor about two weeks after my arrival and he made it quite clear to me that 'as I was replacing a US position in US Advisory Team 89, I was there to do that job and not to expect to be running around on Australian Task Force jobs.'[12]

Team 89 covered all the operations conducted by the ARVN and the Regional Force or Popular Force in the province. Team 89 personnel were also required to coordinate 1ATF operations with the Vietnamese to make sure that the villages on the periphery of the Task Force area of operations were not fired upon without Colonel Dat's approval. As Wells recalled:

> 1ATF operations were within their TAOR, however there were nominated 'friendly' villages in the area. They [1ATF] were required by the province Chief

to come back through me should they come under fire and wish to engage. This was usually managed within 10 minutes, as I was pretty much always with him. Any 1ATF activity planned outside the TAOR had to come through me, Senior US Advisor, then Vietnamese counterparts before proceeding.[13]

Although the advisers had convinced Colonel Dat to maintain the confidentiality of operational plans, it is doubtful that complete secrecy was maintained. Operating under such a fragmented system created enormous challenges for the Australian force.

An ambiguous role

The role of the Task Force also remained ambiguous, as some of the commanders grumbled in interviews they later gave for the Australian Army History Unit. Their contention that the Australian government did not provide clear guidance and an unequivocal function for the Task Force is puzzling. Various authors and reporters highlighted the criticisms of the Australian concept of operations. Peter Samuel, for example, wrote in a 1969 *Vietnam Digest*: 'The Australian Government would appear never to have thought in depth about the role of the Australian forces or formulated a strategy for the Task Force in particular'.[14]

Contrary evidence is available in the archival files at the National Archives of Australia and in America. These files reveal the many discussions that took place on where Australians could be deployed and why. Analyses and concepts were produced that included a proposal for an Australian force to be sent to a location near the DMZ with US Marines, or to join KANZUS, or even to operate independently. These proposals were rejected in the main by the spectre of casualties, which spooked the government. The Australian military also reinforced their claim in studies that their tactics were better than the efforts of the Americans and Australians would be better off operating in their own patch. This matched some judicious counsel offered by Colonel P. Roy, an American officer, in Italy in June 1944:

It will be found best to keep each national group separate in its own national sector of the battle line. This was proven sound in . . . Italy in the drive to Rome.

It will prevent one group of nationals within a formation from blaming another group for causing the failure of an operation, or a portion thereof. Wholesome rivalry in battle may be encouraged, but every effort must be made to avoid any situation that would reduce the highest cooperative spirit between the troops of different allied nations.[15]

The proposed mixing and matching of Australian infantry with US Marines was not feasible. The Marines were not established to operate ashore for extended periods and their logistics were stretched to the limit, which meant an Australian force would have difficulty tapping into their resupply system. In addition, there was no space available in the Danang–Hue base area. Furthermore no matter how good the soldiers were, to operate in I Corps was a guarantee to increase the killed-in-action ratio, and the Marines' perceived pile on approach was tactically scary. In fact, the US Marine Corps' concept of operations at that time was similar to the tactics that the Australians planned to use.[16]

The idea of a multinational force along the DMZ continued into mid-1967, when it then 'appeared to have been overwhelmed by the magnitude of the threat in I CTZ'.[17] Both Australia and New Zealand were still being considered as likely providers of troops for the DMZ concept in Quang Tri Province, which was known colloquially as the 'McNamara Line'.[18] The idea eventually fizzled out but not before considerable effort had been expended on the project.[19] The Australians also looked at the Central Highlands. To the enemy, this area was operationally important because of its direct connection to the support in the North as well as being a gateway to provinces in the south and southeast. The NVA also classified the highlands as a main killing ground. To survive in that region, an Australian Task Force would have to attach to a larger American formation. The Mekong Delta to the south was a swamp. These factors made the decision about where to base the Task Force a foregone conclusion for two reasons. The Australian government had embargoed the western provinces of III Corps because they bordered Cambodia. Obviously, no one had looked at a map before this and followed the 1RAR/173rd Airborne Brigade operations conducted in areas contiguous with Cambodia during 1965–66. Furthermore there was very limited other operational space available that matched General Wilton's desire to have the

Australian force in an area in which he could keep a good watch over them, and which had the means of a sea extraction point at its back door.

It is evident why the government made a strategic decision to go to Vietnam. Political directives on the principal points of deployment from the date of the AATTV's arrival in Vietnam in 1962 are clear. The military fundamentals discussed by various committees, such as the Chiefs of Staff, gave their ministers advice that formed the main framework for future government decisions on increased incremental deployments and their tactical duties over the years. Expressed in simple terms, these were the government-approved directives: this is the size of the approved military force; this is where you want to go—Phuoc Tuy; how you fight when you get there is for you to decide. The size of the Task Force dictated whether it could fight to destroy and isolate, or to protect and pacify; clearly it could not do both. It was up to the generals to decide how they fought.

With a fairly free tactical hand permitted by the Commanding General of IIFFV, the Australian brigadiers were in an *enviable* position. Commander Australian Force Vietnam in Saigon had all the attendant administrative headaches that came with the job, but he had no direct command line into tactical operational control over the Task Force. He could influence what the Task Force did and say 'No' if an operation was evidently too dangerous, or crossed the prohibited line set by the Australian government. The Task Force commander decided how to take the battle to the enemy within the Australian area of operations, as long as it fell within the operational guidelines of IIFFV. However, it would be unwise for a brigadier not to keep his Australian boss informed about his proposed activities. The Commander Australian Force Vietnam was ultimately 'responsible for the safety and well-being of [the] force'.[20]

The Combined Campaign Plan

The surprise in the debate over the role for the Australian force and the claimed lack of guidance comes in the form of the 1967 Combined Campaign Plan AB142 released on 7 November 1966. In brief, the plan stated that:

ARVN would be given the primary mission of providing security for RD [Revolutionary Development] while US and FWMAF [Free World Military Assistance

Forces] would continue efforts to destroy NVA/VC main forces and base areas. In the three northern CTZs [Saigon to the DMZ], ARVN would devote at least half of its effort to support RD, but in IV CTZ it might have to devote up to 75 per cent of its effort to offensive operations.[21]

The plan identified Vietnamese national priority areas (provinces) and in the III CTZ this included Phuoc Tuy Province as one of an inner line of provinces that immediately abutted Saigon's northern and eastern boundaries. In the priority areas, the Vietnamese armed forces were assigned the primary mission of providing support for Revolutionary Development activities. The Campaign Plan elaborated what these duties were:

RVNAF [Republic of Vietnam Armed Forces] would defend government centres, and protect and control national resources, particularly rice and salt. The ultimate responsibility for population security in the RD plan rested with the RVN [Republic of Vietnam], but US/FWMA forces would provide a shield to permit RVNAF, National Police, and RD cadres to increase their direct support to RD.[22]

There was criticism of the ARVN role. The plan seemed to give the impression that the heavy fighting was to be done by the Free World Military Assistance Forces while the ARVN just guarded the area to provide local security. That annoyed the Vietnamese leaders, Chief of State Nguyen Van Thieu and Premier Nguyen Cao Ky. Both men stated on numerous occasions that 'only ARVN, an indigenous force, was capable of continuous communications with the peasantry and had the area knowledge and skills essential to the success of RD'. The US agreed:

The broadening of ARVN responsibilities in securing the countryside and working with the civil authorities in the villages and hamlets was of the first order of importance. They also recognised that this called for new sacrifices, high motivation, discipline, and skills from the Vietnamese citizen soldier [the Regional Force/Popular Force].[23]

On a visit to Australia in January 1967 Premier Nguyen Cao Ky made an announcement about the plan and its meaning for the Vietnamese and supporting nations. In Canberra, he said:

Greater numbers of our Armed Forces are broadening their roles beyond the mere military to aid in this vital task of Revolutionary Development. We are not deluding ourselves that this will be an easy job for the Vietnamese soldier . . . Our forces recognise the sober fact that we may take more casualties in this combined military-psychological role than we would in a purely military situation. But we also recognise that it is necessary if we are to be successful in this complicated task to entrust the task to Vietnamese men and women who have the special qualities and virtues, which this special situation calls for.[24]

A joint US–Government of South Vietnam team reviewed provincial plans and, where necessary, ARVN corps and division commanders were required to sign off on the plans to 'signify that they understood and concurred with them and that they could provide the necessary military support'. It is difficult to perceive that, with so much high level planning, support and associated directives issued by both the Vietnamese command and General Westmoreland, none of it reached the Australian Task Force. Here was a plan of operations that clearly answered the conundrum facing the Australian commanders. If they didn't know about the implications of this plan, why didn't they know? Had the Australians cocooned themselves too tightly inside Phuoc Tuy Province? Did they carry an attitude that saw the Americans as buffoons who only blew up everything, and the Vietnamese forces as nothing more than corrupt, lazy, inefficient and cowardly soldiers? A clear war-fighting plan had been announced that covered the Australian force, but only if those commanding the force wanted it to. This was part of the gamesmanship played out within the FWMAF. Operational tasks were accepted or politely rejected based upon the perceived military and/or political risk these actions might have. It also posed an important question: did Australia want to assume all of the duties within Phuoc Tuy Province, which meant taking over the advisory and support duties too? The answer was 'No'; it was too expensive and Australia simply could not provide the required additional personnel.[25]

Good intentions: What happened?

Whether the Campaign Plan worked is a different question. There were many challenges that bit into the plan's efficacy. This included the quality of the ARVN and the Regional and Popular Forces to do their bit, which went back to the days of the Diem regime and the initial training programs for the Vietnamese armed forces. Colonel Herbert Schandler, a US Army, two-tour veteran, suggested that the ARVN had been trained for the wrong mission.

> Instead of concentrating its efforts on guerrilla war, the ARVN was prepared to fight a conventional war with enormous firepower. Ultimately [this] forced the Vietnamese to the road making them . . . inappropriate for the people's war in the countryside. Few ARVN officers or enlisted men were trained for the political war, the ARVN was incapable of directing a complex political and military struggle.[26]

This was the very argument that Lansdale had had with General Samuel Williams in the 1950s, but even he was unsure, when pushed, of predicting what the North might do. Williams retracted his assessment in an oral history interview in 1981. 'After say 1958 or 1959, I did not see a North Korean type invasion from North Vietnam, which I had seen in 1956 and 1957', he told the interviewer.[27]

American General William DePuy wrote a cogent paper in 1986 on the campaign challenges of the Vietnam War. He cut through the counterinsurgency arguments to highlight where the real danger was—North Vietnam and possibly China. DePuy acknowledged that we would never know the answer to a possible replay of the Korean War.

> Emphasis on the military dimensions of the war ran counter to the newly conventional wisdom. If you were 'for' counterinsurgency, you were 'against' conventional military thinking.
>
> 'The old generals don't understand the problem,' it was said. Guerrilla war is not susceptible to conventional solutions—ARVN was organized by the US military for the wrong war . . . we should be fighting guerrillas with guerrillas . . . But while these arguments went on, a combination of Vietcong skill and North Vietnamese escalation of effort . . . led to . . . [Vietnam's] . . . near collapse in late 1964 and early 1965.[28]

The methods of training and deployment for the Revolutionary Development teams also created problems. These cadres had evolved from the People's

Action Teams (PATs) seen in 1964 in Quang Ngai Province with Captain Ian Teague from the AATTV. The organisation and duties of the Revolutionary Cadre teams were also spelled out in the Campaign Plan. The teams were to be:

> A specially trained 59-man Vietnamese group composed predominantly of civilian technicians who would be injected into hamlets and villages as soon as the requisite security was established. These personnel were, and would continue to be, trained at a National Training Centre at Vung Tau. The teams would operate under the control of the district chiefs, principally within hamlets, to establish initial government administration, organize the people for self-defence . . . and initiate simple economic and social development projects to win the confidence and loyalty of the people.[29]

The Vung Tau Training Centre was first built at Cat Lo to expand the PAT concept and by late 1965 it was training 40 teams at a time. Teague advised the American Combined Studies Division (CIA) that he:

> Objected to the mass production of PAT with the removal of recruits from their home districts, and more importantly, not returning the teams to their home districts. When this happened the teams were not familiar with a new area, or the people in it and the issues involved, also the villagers were very wary of strangers.[30]

When he returned to Australia in 1965 he was uneasy about the possible rapid increase in a program that had great potential to provide security and basic government services to a diverse rural community. The difficulties associated with providing teams of cadres were much more complex than even Teague envisaged. Blatant fraud threatened the integrity of the program when, once again, ghosts appeared on the payroll in some provinces. Rapid expansion drained the system of qualified potential recruits and effective instructors. Secular and religious clashes also took energy away from the program. John Vann, a senior US Army adviser during the battle at Ap Bac in 1964, and subsequently 'MACV's only civilian senior corps adviser', complained about the Revolutionary Development training program, especially its sponsorship by the CIA, and 'wanted more respect for Vietnamese sensitivities'. Bill Colby, a former CIA Station Chief in Saigon, headed the Agency's Civil Operations and Redevelopment activities. He said that 'despite the bitterness of his complaints, Vann's prescription seemed at most to call for preserving the essentials and eliminating the imperfections, exactly what everyone wanted to do'.[31]

Combined Action Program

A new local armed force called the People's Self Defence Force emerged out of power struggles among some of the Vietnamese ministers, and was given a role of rudimentary defence in hamlets. 'The effectiveness of this type of force was questionable, and it added one more uncoordinated security force to the many already in Vietnam.'[32] The Australians were reluctant to get close to the Vietnamese and the Regional Force/Popular Force soldiers through programs such as the Combined Action Program (CAP), used by the US Marines in I Corps. The CAP, said to have evolved from the experiences of the Marines in the Banana Wars fought in Haiti, the Dominican Republic and Nicaragua from 1915 to 1934, was a program in which Marines advised, trained and fought in clashes alongside the native police forces. From its experiences in these conflicts, the US Marine Corps produced a *Small Wars Manual 1940*; it is a very informative document.[33]

In Vietnam, the CAP provided security to hamlets and villages by integrating a squad of Marines with a Popular Force platoon to form a Combined Action Platoon, which was placed under the operational control of the local district chief. This gave them firepower, and when added to the local knowledge of the Popular Force troops, provided a vital asset in protecting the people. It also improved the flow of information on enemy activities to the Marines. Lieutenant General Victor Krulak, who assumed command of the Fleet Marine Force Pacific in 1964, was a driving force behind this concept. Krulak had clashed with Colonel Serong back in May 1963 at the meeting of the Special Group for Counterinsurgency in Washington. He admitted that he was influenced by the British success in Malaya, especially by Robert Thompson's principles.

> Sir Robert Thompson . . . established a set of basic counterinsurgency principles in my mind. Thompson said, 'The people's trust is primary. Protection is the most important thing that you can bring them. After that comes health. And, after that, many things—land, prosperity, education, and privacy to name a few.'[34]

Although the National Police Field Force was also seen as an important element in the security aspect of Revolutionary Development, Colonel Serong (later honorary brigadier) who had been the Australian link with that project had gone. He apparently disappeared into the whirlpool of advisers, military consultants and report writers, until he resigned in 1968, when he did some work for organisations like the RAND Corporation, although the people at RAND's Saigon office were not sure what he did.

> In Saigon, he would appear occasionally at the RAND office, and the staff used to wonder what he was really doing and for whom he was really working, and some would speculate . . . that he was in the pay of the CIA. George Tanham, who met Serong in Saigon, . . . would recall that Serong was always very busy, but it was not clear what he was up to.[35]

Following his time as special adviser to General Harkins, Serong's name now came up only occasionally but not in any senior capacity either with the US military or the CIA. There is no recorded contact between Serong and President Johnson in the president's daily diary, or in President Nixon's diary. This is contrary to several claims that Serong had 'sat down with presidents' and briefed them on plans and operations in Vietnam.[36] Some CIA operatives remembered him as an occasional figure lobbying for one plan or another but he was always on the fringe of activities. To be a powerful figure within the Agency, they added, one had to be in control of a program; Serong was not a controller.

ARVN Lieutenant General Ngo Quang Truong was praised as one of the most capable of the Vietnamese generals; he commanded the 1st ARVN Division and subsequently IV and I CTZs. Truong's words on combined action and its influence in winning the *hearts and minds* of the Vietnamese people are instructive.

> Only rarely did they [US forces] suggest combined action. The reason for this reluctance was simple enough: US commanders had varying degrees of scepticism as to the effectiveness of ARVN units as combat companions. They apparently did not always think it worthwhile to cooperate with ARVN units although any ARVN unit, regardless of its size, could in fact make useful contributions to the fulfilment of their common tasks.[37]

Truong was not reluctant to criticise the South Vietnamese Army. In particular, he understood the conditions that 'reduced their combat spirit'. After long periods of 'operating from fixed positions troops tended to become careless and soft, and more disposed toward personal comfort and their combat aggressiveness either decreased or was completely gone'. Although cooperation improved after the Tet 1968 offensive, Truong saw certain psychological 'conditioning and habits among ARVN unit troops and commanders' when they were associated with American units and their abundant resources, which proved adverse in the long run.[38] The wisdom in this observation was relevant to all the nationalities involved in Vietnam.

The limited number of Australian troops available to cover the tactical tasks in their area of responsibility was one factor that restricted deployment of a full-scale CAP program in Phuoc Tuy Province. A good indicator of the manpower needed came from I Corps where a region of 350 hamlets and about 135,000 villagers involved around 2000 Marines and approximately 3000 Popular Force troops. There were 115 hamlets in Phuoc Tuy and 104,000 people, with most of the population located in the major villages in the south of the province. The numbers of Australians needed to run a CAP would have been less than for the I Corps region but still a considerable burden and one that Australia could neither provide, nor afford.

The dubious quality of the Regional Force/Popular Force in Phuoc Tuy Province probably justified the unwillingness of the Australians to enter into a combined arrangement in 1967. As Captain Clarry Rule remembered, 'There was only one group that we would go out with at night and that was 571 Company [Regional Force]. All of the others would leave you out there in the middle of the night'.[39] Without trust, support and mentoring, and protection for the 'poor bastards' at the bottom of the military food chain, they were never going to improve. It would need some risk-taking by the Australians to make it work. This was a lesson from an earlier conflict, recorded by US Colonel Roy in Italy in 1944:

> Situations when troops must be mixed include: a lack of adequate supporting units or troops within a national sector to produce a balanced force, use of combined, composite unit for political reasons. [Some of] the advantages in mixing nationals are: increases strength or support where no other increase is

possible; promotes exchanges of ideas ... thus providing advancement in tactics and technique and promotes closer mutual understanding and cooperation. Cooperation requires willing effort.[40]

Roy wrote that 'willing effort' might also detract from a force's capabilities if the internal effort required could be expended better externally or against the common foe. He listed obstacles such as dissimilarity in weapons, spare parts and equipment; difference in the tactical organisation and operating headquarters; differences in signal equipment and codes; uncommon command and discipline procedures; and an increase in manpower requirements. The need for more manpower was a common and constant theme with the war in Vietnam where more liaison personnel and many more interpreters were needed during combined operations.

Roy's obstacles would have been apparent to the Australians when the Army Reinforcement Unit conducted Operation Vanimo in October 1967. This was a refresher training course for the ARVN's 3/48 Battalion (located at Dat Do) that included two weapons—the M1 carbine and the Browning automatic rifle—that the Australians did not use. Language and the lack of interpreters were also continuing major challenges.

General Truong believed willing cooperation was the vanguard of successful combined action in Vietnam:

Perhaps the foremost requirement for adaptability to the problem was the willingness to undergo hardship and above all affection for the Vietnamese people. In all frankness, we had to admit the cold fact that not all Marines—and US troops by extension—understood and warmed to the local Vietnamese people. While it appears doubtful that as many as 40 per cent of the Marines disliked the Vietnamese, as claimed by a knowledgeable author, the fact was a Marine could not live and work with them unless he sympathised with and came to like them. After all, this was a volunteer, not an assigned job.[41]

The CAP Marines had the additional advantage of a powerful force nearby which could provide quick reaction forces in an emergency. By contrast, the immediate reaction capabilities available to the Task Force were slim. But, again, in the words of Colonel Roy, 'none of the disadvantages was insurmountable. Some of them may disappear, the longer the troops . . . work together'.[42]

Aussies pussyfooting, again

Unfortunately, another factor that lay hidden just below the surface was a feeling of unsureness about the Australians. The Diggers had learnt quickly and their operational techniques were solid and improved with each new tactical challenge. Notwithstanding their good tactical actions, there was an unease about the Australian efforts, almost an air of suspicion that the Aussies were not pulling their weight, that they were scared of casualties. The pussyfooting charge from the 173rd Airborne Brigade days in 1965–66 was whispered again. Disturbingly, a little later in the year two influential visitors to Vietnam confided similar thoughts in writing to their respective countries. Harry McPherson, Special Counsel to President Lyndon Johnson, visited Vietnam in June 1967. His memorandum is noteworthy for its frankness on almost any major question then asked about Vietnam. His views ranged from issues about corruption to expressions of contempt for the Popular and Regional Forces made by the American military in Saigon, which were countered by their officers in the field. McPherson visited Filipino, Korean and Australian locations.

> I visited both the ROK Marines and the ROK [Republic of Korea] Tiger division, God they are a tough bunch. They have a method . . . some of our civilians say . . . that they are too brutal and careless of civilian life. I can't judge the merits of this. I only hope that I never meet one in a rice paddy some night without the right set of credentials. I paid a brief visit to an Australian unit. The CO, a colonel of supply, said he thought the Australians were too cautious; they did not patrol widely, or invite attacks; he thought their effectiveness was being diminished by their conservatism. He suggested that this had political causes, as the home government didn't want to see a big casualty list.[43]

Sir Arthur Tange, Australia's High Commissioner to India, travelled though Vietnam for a few days in August 1967. He sent his impressions in a personal note to Sir James Plimsoll, Head of External (Foreign) Affairs. His report began by expressing admiration for the American efforts.

My first impression was that the Americans have an admirable grasp of the political nature of the contest, for the loyalty of the people of South Vietnam and of the necessity to fight the battle with political as well as military means. They acknowledged that military means have to pay attention to . . . try to avoid unnecessary loss of life and destruction. In making this comment on the American generals, I should also add that I formed a considerable admiration for their ability to express themselves and to conceive ideas and discuss issues: they are educated men as well as fighting men.[44]

The American achievements also astonished Tange. He was not aware of the size of it all from the docks to the roads and bridges through to the vast airfields and ammunition dumps that he said must have been built on bare sandhills or in sleepy towns. The resources were enormous, he said. Tange also commented upon the very high casualties the Americans had taken, which he said were running at about 7000 a month. 'By contrast, the Australians at present are scarcely being scratched.'[45] He went on to discuss the enemy and touched in particular on the increased numbers of North Vietnamese Army soldiers on the battlefield. In the final pages of his note, he discussed his impressions of the Australians:

> There is every reason to believe that Australian soldiers are brave and competent. The fact is that they are maintaining security in an area containing nothing more than a population of 105,000 out of . . . 16,000,000 and have at present no contact with main force elements of the North Vietnamese. We do from time to time make search-and-destroy operations (such as Operation Paddington) in the hope of finding the Viet Cong battalion operating in the east of the province but have so far not had much luck. Otherwise operations seem to be the fairly routine ones. At Vung Tau I was shown over the Logistics camp where the Colonel in command is finally getting the warehouses, dumps, hospital etc into reasonable shape—moving things from side to side while the bulldozer is at work, rather like mending the kitchen floor while the dinner is cooking. It seems to have been a rather odd bit of planning. There must surely have been a lot of leisureliness about the process of getting equipment from Australia and on to the shore at Vung Tau.[46]

Although he resisted the temptation to make a comparison between the American and Australian efforts, he felt it had taken the Australians a very long time to get into the field and back up what was a tiny force. Tange thought it alarming that this was the best Australia could do.

Lieutenant General Weyand [Commanding General IIFFV] stood in front of a full wall map for about an hour and gave us a magnificent personal briefing of his handling of the campaign throughout III Corps, which . . . includes, incidentally, the Australian Task Force. General Weyand, touched on the fact that 'some people' would like to put the Australians into a more offensive role against main force elements; but he went on at once to say that he personally was satisfied with the way they were doing, performing a role that has to be performed throughout the country. *It is a role which is mainly performed by the South Vietnamese army elsewhere, while the Americans take the shock of the main assaults on enemy positions in the hills and close to their sanctuaries in Cambodia and Laos* [emphasised].[47]

Sir Arthur Tange was a distinguished public servant who had headed the Department of External Affairs, but reportedly he was frozen out of the Vietnam commitment process in 1964–65. On his own admission, 'measures in South Vietnam . . . were not my first priority because I could see no initiatives that Australia could effectively take. My newly appointed Minister (Hasluck) thought otherwise'.[48] After five years as High Commissioner to India he was offered three positions, according to historian Peter Edwards:

In late 1969 he [Tange] was successively offered . . . the three most important positions . . . ambassador in Washington, Secretary of the Defence Department, and his former post as Secretary of External Affairs. Although he had started to prepare for Washington, he became Secretary of Defence in 1970. These were years of major, often controversial, reform in the administration of Defence. 'The Tange report' charted the way for the Departments of Navy, Army, Air and Supply to be merged into the Department of Defence.[49]

The tone of Tange's 1967 letter indicated that he disapproved of an organisation that did so poorly and the visit possibly had an influence on his subsequent reforms when he became Secretary at the Department of Defence.

Bubblies, destroyers and emus

Clearance Diving Team 3 (CDT3), RAN, was one of the smallest, least known, and highly decorated Australian units to serve in Vietnam. They were

Diggers' humour in dire times. One of the modified APC used in attempts to clear the infamous Dat Do minefield. Flint was Colonel Charles Flint, the Director of the Royal Australian Engineers. Bukoo Boom Boom is a wry play on words. Mines and a mine-clearer equals Boom Boom, however Boom Boom was colloquial for intercourse that was coupled with Bukoo (beaucoup). *Courtesy NVV Museum*

A dangerous-looking group of 1RAR (1968–69) on their way to the rifle range at Nui Dat. Standing, left to right: Robert Petri, Brian Payne, Robert Rose, Alan Sisley and Edward Houlihan. *Courtesy NVV Museum; photograph by Lynton Malley*

A Centurion from A Squadron 1 Armoured Regiment travelling through rough country, 1970. Chris Prickett is directing proceedings. *Courtesy NVV Museum*

With rifles at the ready, members of 8RAR head to Nui Dat in November 1969 to replace 9RAR. *Bettmann/Corbis/AP Images*

Section Strength, Taor Patrol, Long Binh, Operation Federal, 14 March 1969. 7 Platoon, C Company, 4RAR, guards a captured Viet Cong sapper waiting to be picked up by helicopter and taken to 'Fire Base Peggy'. *Courtesy Dennis Gibbons Collection, NVV Museum*

Brigadier M.I. 'Sandy' Pearson MC, 1ATF, Nui Dat, is shown over the 1966 Long Tan battlefield in August 1969 by Sergeant Neil Rankin, one of the diggers who fought at Long Tan. *Courtesy Dennis Gibbons Collection, NVV Museum*

Australian gunners construct ammunition and protection bunkers within their gun bay at a fire support base in Phuoc Tuy Province in March 1969. *Courtesy Dennis Gibbons Collection, NVV Museum*

Right and opposite page: Diggers from 1 Platoon, A Company, 8RAR, on Operation Atherton, 11 miles northwest of the ATF base at Nui Dat, fix a wounded soldier to a penetrator so he can be winched out of thick jungle by helicopter. One was killed and fourteen were wounded in the operation. *Courtesy Dennis Gibbons Collection, NVV Museum*

Private G.C. Piltz goes to ground when 1ATF comes under heavy fire in Operation Atherton, 10 December 1969. *Courtesy Dennis Gibbons Collection, NVV Museum*

An Australian 105 mm artillery piece fires flechette and canister rounds at Viet Cong 'wave attacks' against FSPB Anderson in Phuoc Tuy Province, 1969. The enemy thought they must be a US mechanised unit. *Courtesy Dennis Gibbons Collection, NVV Museum*

The day after an ambush at Hoa Long on 12 August 1970, 8RAR inspect the dead. Seventeen Viet Cong were killed after Sergeant C.J. Sherrin observed a group of over fifty enemy heading towards Hoa Long; they were engaged on their return in the early hours of the morning. *Courtesy Dennis Gibbons Collection, NVV Museum*

Diggers from 1RAR come under concentrated sniper fire during Operation Goodwood, January 1969. *Courtesy Dennis Gibbons Collection, NVV Museum*

```
URGENT
FOR DELIVERY BETWEEN 6AM AND 6PM
ACKNOWLEDGEMENT DELIVERY


MR J G ████    35
████CHER ST
████ VIC


IT IS LEARNED WITH REGRET THAT YOUR SON 3792██ PRIVATE GERARD
FRANCIS ████ SUSTAINED MINOR FRAGMENT WOUND TO RIGHT ARMPIT
ON 8TH FEBRUARY 1969 IN BIEN HOA PROVINCE VIETNAM AND
WAS ADDMITTED TO 1 AUSTRALIAN FIELD HOSPITAL VUNG TAU VIETNAM
STOP AS LONG AS HIS CONDITION REMAINS UNCHANGED NO PROGRESS
REPORTS WILL BE FORWARDED


TO YOU STOP
          ARMY HEADQUARTERS
   (MR J G 1 379████ 8 1969 1)   38
```

A standard telegram used to notify a next-of-kin about the details of a wounded-in-action. These telegrams were known as a Notification of Casualty (NOTICAS) and were initiated by the Central Army Records Office (Melbourne); they relied upon information sent from the headquarters in South Vietnam. *Courtesy NVV Museum*

Welcome home to the Diggers of 2RAR as they marched through Queen Street, Brisbane, after their return from Vietnam, 13 June 1968. *Courtesy NVV Museum*

jokingly referred to as 'bubblies' because of the bubbles that came from their diving efforts. The first CDT3 contingent of six personnel arrived in country on 6 February 1967. The diving teams served until May 1971, with 49 men serving in the eight teams deployed.

The first CDT3 group was initially attached to a US Navy Explosive Ordnance Disposal Team in Saigon before moving to Vung Tau, where they participated in Operation Stable Door. Naval operations in Vietnam records show:

> The team assumed responsibility for the defence of shipping against enemy attack [and] was responsible for searching the hulls and anchor cables of shipping in Vung Tau anchorages or alongside, mines. In one incident, Viet Cong sappers penetrated the Vung Tau port and placed home made and a Russian limpet mine on the hull of MV *Heredia* and a nearby wharf. The homemade device partially exploded during search operations, and team members removed the Russian mine.[50]

Walter Rice, the US Ambassador to Australia, subsequently presented the US Navy Meritorious Unit Commendation to the 1st Contingent of CDT3. The citation reads in part: 'For meritorious achievement while conducting defence and surveillance operations in the harbours of Vung Tau, Cam Ranh Bay, Qui Nhon and Nha Trang during the period 19 February through 30 June 1967'. The Diving Team moved to Danang in 1970 after three and a half years on Operation Stable Door during which they searched 7441 ships.

Not to be outdone by the mostly invisible diving teams, the warships wanted to get into the war and the Australian Navy committed a destroyer to the US Navy's 7th Fleet gun line on 15 March 1967. HMAS *Hobart* relieved a USN destroyer off Chu Lai, Quang Tin Province, on 31 March and began operations in Vietnamese waters. The ship was armed with two 5 inch (125 mm) calibre guns capable of accurate gunfire at ranges beyond 14 nautical miles (26 kilometres). Before the deployment of *Hobart*, General Westmoreland noted:

> The Australian Government wanted general confirmation that HMAS *Hobart* would be deployed in conjunction with US forces. It was expected that *Hobart* would remain under national command, but under operational control of the US Navy,

and would be on station for at least six months, when she would be relieved by HMAS *Perth* or a British type escort [the Daring class destroyer *Vendetta*].[51]

The ships would be available in all respects as 'an additional ship of the US Navy force, without operational restrictions, for use in shore bombardment of RVN [South Vietnam] and of NVN [North Vietnam], interdiction of coastal traffic, picket duties for carrier operations, and general operations in support of naval forces at sea'.[52] Although these general discussions were held at MACV, naval matters were deferred to a conference at Subic Bay in the Philippines where the Commander in Chief Pacific Fleet drafted the working documents between the two navies. MACV was relieved of any involvement in this agreement.

Guided missile destroyers *Hobart* and *Perth* subsequently deployed three times, *Brisbane* twice, and *Vendetta* once. The warships fired 102,546 rounds at targets throughout South Vietnam and two of them ventured into northern waters to bombard areas between the DMZ and the Red River Delta. Both *Hobart* and *Perth* came under fire from North Vietnamese shore batteries and HMAS *Perth* was hit once. Even the friendlies were unfriendly; on 17 June 1968 an American F4 Phantom off Cape Lay, just north of the DMZ, accidentally attacked HMAS *Hobart*. The fighter fired three missiles, which all hit the ship. Ordinary Seaman Raymond Butterworth and Chief Petty Officer Raymond Hunt were killed and seven others were wounded. Word had spread that the North Vietnamese were using helicopters in the area and the pilot of the aircraft later revealed in an inquiry that he mistook the 'radar paint' of the ship as a helicopter. *Hobart* was not the only ship hit by fighters over 16 and 17 June 1968—a US patrol boat was sunk and several other ships were also attacked.

Following preliminary discussions in January, more Navy personnel were offered formally for service with US aviation units in April 1967, although they did not arrive until October. This was a quaint arrangement whereby the Australian Navy sent off helicopter pilots and maintenance personnel for attachment to a US Army helicopter unit. The offer was contingent upon the pilots serving in a unit that supported the Australian Task Force. General Westmoreland reminded the Australians that 'army helicopters were not assigned to support specific organisations or task forces'. He added that the personnel could be used advantageously, but their use would be dictated by the tactical situation. It was finally resolved that the Navy personnel would be assigned to the 12th Combat Aviation Group, which provided support to units in the III CTZ. That meant attachment to the 135th Aviation Company (Air Mobile Light) that became operational at Vung Tau in November 1967. The unit was to support the Australian Task Force, although it would also be available for American and ARVN units.

Neil Ralph, who later became a rear admiral and Deputy Chief of Naval Staff, joined the newly designated 135th Assault Helicopter Company as its executive officer and head of the RAN Helicopter Flight Vietnam. The unit's designation was 'Emu', which amused the Australians because they knew that bird could not fly. (The name had nothing to do with birds, however, but was an acronym for 'Experimental Military Unit'.) Ralph recalled:

> The type of mission we flew were almost air assault with the 9th Infantry Division. We did work with the 199 Light Infantry Brigade around Bien Hoa area. When the RAAF got on line we became less and less involved with the 1ATF. But almost daily our gunship platoon was involved with the provision of light fire teams [two gunships] to the 1ATF. We had 33 aircraft, 23 of which were . . . 'slicks'—the UH-1H model, we were the first company to be equipped with these—and ten gunships, UH-1Cs [the Taipans]. We got a very good rate of serviceability, always over 80 per cent, which gave us a high capacity for workload. For example, in December 1967 the company flew 3039 hours and we went up . . . that meant each of our aircrew flew between 120 and 130 hours a month.[53]

Bombers

With the proposed deployment of the eight Canberra bombers from Butterworth in Malaysia, the RAAF wanted to operate in a similar vein to the Navy's agreement. The bombers, while under national command, would be under operational control of the US Air Force and placed in an area where the squadron could support Australian forces as part of its operations. Planning arrangements were agreed at MACV in January 1967:

> The squadron would provide its own maintenance in RVN and would rely on major maintenance from Australia, although local logistic support in the form of

POL [petrol, oil, lubricant], rations, accommodations, engineer stores, and other common usage items could be expected [to be supplied by the Americans].[54]

During the MACV discussions, crowded airfield conditions around the country caused some consternation, but the Australians were assured that their squadron was both wanted and needed. The Chief of the Australian team [unnamed] said: 'Deployment of the Canberra squadron was thought ideal for the RAAF because the aircraft were obsolete and had been scheduled for replacement by F-111 aircraft'.[55] Perhaps the comment meant that it would not matter if the planes were lost in action. Alternatively, it might have meant we are sending you planes that will not be very good because they are old. On 19 April, the bombers landed at an air base near the sleepy seaside village of Phan Rang, about 40 kilometres south of Cam Ranh Bay. Ironically, the airstrip was overlooked from the northern side by some high ground called Nui Dat. Wing Commander David Evans—later Air Marshal and Chief of the Air Staff—commanded 2 Squadron from November 1967 to November 1968, and recalled the bombing accuracy of the old aircraft:

No. 2 Squadron had been mostly doing night bombing ... where they were controlled by radar and dropped bombs from 30,000 feet. The squadron had a pretty good name for accuracy ... but we never saw any results. From 30,000 feet you just dropped ... and went home. From my knowledge ... in Malaysia, Canberra bombing was incredibly inaccurate. When I took over ... in Vietnam, the squadron was being tasked for daylight attacks. We then used a technique of bombing from 3000 feet or below. In this way we got bombing accuracy of the squadron down to twenty yards. This was the best ever achieved by Canberra aircraft and probably the most accurate bombing in Vietnam. Later the USAF used ... laser-guided bombs.[56]

He was proud of the high standard to which the small force maintained its aircraft:

Our maintenance was very, very good and indeed the envy of the Americans. One USAF engineer officer remarked that he would only have one in ten of his personnel with the skill and experience of my average flight line mechanic.[57]

The January 1967 MACV meeting concluded with the advice that of the 900 Australian Army reinforcements due to arrive during 1967, approximately half were requested additions to already established units and the remainder were combat reinforcements. Only one additional Australian Army unit, an 80-man civil affairs unit would be deployed.

Builders

Lieutenant Colonel John McDonagh, Royal Australian Engineers, commanded 1 Civil Affairs Unit and, from 14 to 25 April 1967, conducted a reconnaissance of the 'civil affairs problem' in Phuoc Tuy Province and the Vung Tau Special Zone (municipality). During his travels he met with the main American and Vietnamese agencies that had direct responsibility for Revolutionary Development or a close connection with the program. As a result of his study McDonagh and his staff reviewed their personnel establishment and equipment requirements, and just as importantly placed bids for accommodation and storage at Nui Dat and Vung Tau. Space was at a premium and played a significant part in how and where some units were deployed. The approved establishment for the Civil Affairs Unit revealed that its emphasis would be building, not destruction. The unit had personnel for construction, hygiene, electrical, mechanical, medical, bricklaying, carpentry, plumbing and draughtsmen, a total of 49 all ranks, 31 fewer than first forecast.

McDonagh submitted his draft General Service Instruction for Civil Affairs on 17 June 1967, and Brigadier Graham approved it on the 19th. The instruction provided a definition of civil affairs: 'Civil Affairs consists of all relations between the Military Forces, the civil authorities and the people in a friendly country'. There was an obvious disparity between a friendly country and most of Phuoc Tuy Province. Nevertheless, the intention of the instruction was gracious.

Through a variety of carefully considered civic action projects, it is intended to provide the local population with tangible evidence that the Task Force and other Allied Forces seek to offer them genuine help. Every effort will be made to safeguard the lives and property of the local population during the conduct of operations.[58]

Every unit was required to appoint one officer as a unit Civil Affairs representative, and to ensure that the unit actively participated in the Civil Affairs program. Civil affairs consisted of three phases that emphasised gaining the respect and trust of the local people.

> Phase 1: Initial contact with sufficient security to afford protection. The villages are assured that the Task Force is there to help them. Phase 2: Winning the confidence and acceptance of the population. This is done through overt acts of help eg, school rooms, hospital wards, wells, roads and bridge repairs. Phase 3: Complete community rehabilitation. Emphasis is placed on those projects, which will further develop and educate the local population to lead them to a better way of life.[59]

Each Task Force unit was allocated villages in which they were to undertake projects—with limitations imposed by security. A warning was added: 'Care must be taken to avoid exposing friendly people to subsequent VC reprisals'.[60] That was more easily written than done. A plan was in place and projects could begin when the men, machinery, materials and money were approved— a mix and match that probably never got the resources it needed.

In July, the unit received an interesting visitor, Lieutenant Colonel Chang, a Chinese Nationalist and Political Warfare Adviser to the ARVN. A few days later, a brick building at the Baria Orphanage opened, with the 2RAR band providing musical entertainment.

Combat

Although many went to Vietnam, fewer went into battle, so it is probably unfair to write about the war through selected combat operations based upon either the casualty count or some well-known incident. Nevertheless, those actions have left an indelible imprint upon the veterans and the country that sent them on their behalf. Notable acts of heroism, major battles, political chicanery, strategic insights, and the decisions made by commanders can be examined by asking questions such as: Why did they do what they did? Was it in the hope that some good would emerge as a result?

For the Australian campaign, 1967 was a pivotal year. Brigadier Graham wrote that he believed that the Task Force did not have the information on the enemy or the military strength to attempt to destroy main force elements of the enemy. As a result of his analysis, he set the Task Force's operational objective to be one that denied the Viet Cong access to the main area of population and resources.[61] From his comments, it would appear that Graham was well aware of the Combined Campaign Plan but he did not agree with the duties allocated to the Free World Military Assistance Forces. His operational objectives for 1967, which were apparent to Sir Arthur Tange during his visit, reflected a general concentration upon keeping the area within Line Alpha— and occasionally a little beyond—cleared, as well as trying to establish some semblance of control over the enemy's infrastructure through cordons and searches of nearby villages.

One operation named Tamborine (1–8 February 1967) covered an area to the east along Route 23 out from Dat Do village, which was a constant thorn in the side for the Australians. Contact with the enemy was minimal, but a dreadful accident of war happened when the headquarters of Delta Company, 6RAR, was hit by artillery fired by the New Zealand 161 Battery. Any death caused by a fault, whatever the reason, devastates the people involved. In this case, there was added distress because one of the heroes of Long Tan, WO2 Jack Kirby, the Company Sergeant Major, was killed instantly. Private Barry Kelly was also killed and sixteen others were wounded. Two of the wounded died later: Gunner Richard Cliff on 6 February and Private Douglas Powter passed away at the US 36 Evacuation Hospital at Vung Tau the next day.

A major clash between 6RAR and an enemy battalion took place during Operation Bribie (17–18 February). The Australian battalion was sent as a reaction force to block and destroy an enemy group that had attacked South Vietnamese troops north of Lo Gom on a track that led off Route 44 towards My An hamlet. The track was mid-way between Hoi My and Lo Gom, south of Dat Do. Some Regional Force soldiers stationed there had fought strongly against a powerful VC unit and joined up with the South Vietnamese 3/43 Battalion on Route 44 to block any enemy movement towards that road.

Alpha Company was inserted by helicopter to the east of My An and at 1335 hours made contact with the enemy in a blaze of heavy small-arms fire. The lead platoon suffered badly during this firefight and Major Owen O'Brien was forced to break contact and withdraw his company. Townsend, the battalion commanding officer, then ordered Bravo Company, who had also flown in, to attack the enemy position. Alpha Company was to provide fire support for the assault while Charlie Company—lifted in by APCs—established a blocking position on the western flank. A Squadron, 3 Cavalry Regiment, had carried the group into the battle area in a cross-country move that had fortuitously avoided an ambush on Route 44. The carriers then deployed to provide heavy support with their machine guns. Delta Company was reserve.

The attack started at 1555 hours, but the enemy soldiers stood their ground and 6RAR reported that 'The leading platoons came under sniper and small arms fire from both flanks, the front and the rear. This fire continued in intensity and HMG [heavy machine gun] fire, claymores and light mortars were used by the enemy'.[62] The infantry—who now carried 180 rounds per rifleman, the APC, air strikes and artillery barrages battered away at the Viet Cong, but they held out and stopped the Australians from penetrating their well-defended position. Although Major Gordon Murphy attempted to add more weight to the assault with his APCs they were severely hampered by the terrain and they were not tanks. One carrier from 2 Troop was lost to enemy recoilless rifle fire when they supported Bravo Company to recover their casualties and withdraw. It was a close-quarter battle that included a bayonet charge by 5 Platoon, Bravo Company. That assault was reportedly the last bayonet charge by Australian forces in combat, a fact mentioned when the US Army declared the bayonet obsolete in 2010.[63]

Five hours later, as night fell, Townsend ordered the assault to stop and the companies to break contact, which they did at 1915 hours. The enemy then disappeared, but left eight dead on the battlefield. Although the estimated killed in action numbers (including air strikes) were between 50 and 75, only one weapon was found. Eight Australians were killed, 28 were wounded, and 1 APC was lost to enemy fire. Both the infantry and the cavalry lamented the lack of tanks in the force.

Seven awards—five Mention-in-Despatches and two Military Medals—were awarded for gallantry during this battle. The citation for Private Richard Odendahl's Military Medal highlighted the battle's ferocity:

During the assault 5 Platoon suffered fourteen casualties, all of whom were lying in an area swept by machine gun fire, and into which snipers were directing well aimed fire. Showing complete disregard for his own safety Private Odendahl moved forward into the area and carried or dragged a number of the wounded back to an area out of the direct fire of the machine guns. Although under continuous fire from the enemy he assisted and treated the wounded for over three hours until their evacuation was completed.[64]

The Task Force commander was surprised by the tenacity of the VC force and wrote in his monthly narrative:

A and B Companies were soon involved in a fierce fight with a Viet Cong force of battalion size equipped with support weapons. Surprisingly the Viet Cong showed no sign of giving ground and displayed excellent fire discipline and control [although their marksmanship was poor].[65]

The Viet Cong had previously demonstrated that they could stand and fight until the weight of firepower from either artillery and/or air strikes forced them out of the battle. The lessons of the August 1966 battle at Long Tan would not have faded from the memories of 6RAR. It should not have been a surprise that the enemy had a tactical doctrine. Their battle lessons were clearly based on extensive experience gained from the days of the French war through to their current enemies. They practised their battle procedures and it was not always 'shoot and scoot'. As the Bribie battle developed, the Australian commander had to call upon assistance from the Americans to bolster his understrength command. Brigadier Graham explained:

In an endeavour to cut off the Viet Cong force, which undoubtedly suffered a number of casualties, I requested assistance from HQ II Field Force Vietnam. The 2/47 Mechanised Battalion and Battery C1/11 Artillery from the US 9th Infantry Division arrived early on the 18th February. No further contacts were made.[66]

Lieutenant Colonel Townsend believed that more could have been achieved and complained in his after action report that his desire to conduct a battalion attack was inhibited by a Task Force restriction:

placed on the Battalion not to get deeply involved with the enemy to the extent that disengagement and extraction could not be effected that afternoon [17 Feb].

This was brought about by the concern of the Task Force of a major attack on 1ATF by 5 Viet Cong Div which was believed to be planned to be launched that night.[67]

Although Brigadier Graham admitted that the final result of Bribie 'will probably never be known', he was convinced that 6RAR had 'inflicted severe casualties upon elements of *D445 Battalion* and probably rendered them inoperable for some time to come'.[68] Historian Chris Clark saw it differently:

The action had clearly been no Australian victory. Instead, it was perhaps the closest Australian troops came to defeat in a major battle. Despite showing courage and determination, the Australians had been matched by an enemy equally tenacious and disciplined.[69]

Information about the enemy's possible force structure during Bribie was released in the 1ATF Operation Instruction 5/67 of 15 February, which recorded that the *D445 Battalion* now operated as independent companies. That was just two days before the Lo Gom battle. Townsend thought it was a VC battalion, which explained why they had fought so doggedly. He believed they were protecting a command organisation of at least regimental size; 'It could even have been a command element of *HQ 5 Div*', he wrote.[70] The Australian Task Force reported to II Field Force Vietnam the next day that the enemy position was a 'hastily, but well prepared and well sited position of at least company size'.[71] In addition, but unknown to the Australians, *D445 Battalion* had probably been re-equipped before this battle with advanced weapons that included AK47, RPD machine guns and RPG7 rocket-propelled grenades.[72]

According to the *Viet Cong 5th Division*'s history, its two regiments had conducted operations well away from the Lo Gom area in the months preceding this battle. For example, *274 Viet Cong Regiment* was active in the Hat Dich and the northern area of Route 2 while *275 Viet Cong Regiment* was based around the Ray River, just south of Highway 1 in Long Khanh Province. The divisional headquarters was somewhere around May Tao Mountain.

A month later, two enemy soldiers were captured at Lo Gom on 21 March and they revealed that the *2nd Battalion* of *275 Viet Cong Regiment* had attacked the outpost at 2300 hours on the same day.[73] According to a medical report the enemy battalion suffered 'heavy casualties'—dead unknown (Australians reported 36 dead), 40 wounded—'as a result, it was only able to raise two understrength companies'.[74] The Americans and the Australians believed that more than one enemy battalion was involved in the attack and that the enemy had 'probably lost up to 150 killed in the battle and aftermath'.[75]

Another report by the Australian Task Force, dated 22 February 1967, mentioned the *275 Viet Cong Regiment*'s unsuccessful ambush on Highway 1 in December 1966 in which the enemy formation had allegedly lost 100 killed in action.[76] This unit supposedly was devastated—with up to 500 claimed dead—at Long Tan, just four months before.[77] With such reported very high losses the organisations could be regiments and battalions in name only, or the body counts and the estimates were extremely faulty.

A more pertinent consideration might have been why did 6RAR attack a very strong and well-dug-in enemy position during Operation Bribie? 'It was sited for good all-round defence and the individual pits were sited very skilfully with very good fields of fire', Townsend reported.[78] Taking into account the confused battle information, the answer appears to be because they were there. Attacks against defended localities like Lo Gom were nearly always expensive in terms of casualties, a fact later highlighted by a Scientific Adviser's Study in 1969. In statistical terms, bunker assaults were the deadliest form of battle for the Australians, according to that report.[79]

Major Đu, a Vietnamese battalion commander, agreed. He commanded the 1st Battalion, 5th ARVN Regiment, during a 1967 battle that had caught that ARVN battalion on the move. He told his adviser:

> I will not attack. They have a good position from which they can shoot all around. We will stay here and shoot at each other, but my men will find where they will move and then we will ambush or attack or harass when they move. They will move because there is no water. Some might get away, but we will kill more if we wait. If I attack, I fight where the VC can kill me and they will get away and I will have many dead.[80]

Major Đu and his men were not cowards, as they proved during the battles that followed. Đu was a pragmatic officer who had learnt his tactical lessons from too many battles. To assault prepared enemy positions like this one was a dangerous tactical concept that many western allied commanders did not grasp very well. Was the fixation on body count too strong to allow a more flexible approach to beat the enemy? To not attack was probably to invite a stigma that would border on a charge of cowardice. Although there was no clear-cut tactical solution to enemy and bunkers, one point was certain: a successful attack needed plenty of powerful firepower in support.

Despite the closeness of the outcome during Bribie, the Viet Cong were being hurt in Phuoc Tuy Province by the sharp attacks into their base areas with the assistance of the more powerful American forces. The loss of food in particular was a great concern to the *5th Viet Cong Division*. Soldiers in *275 Regiment* 'lived in situations lacking rice, vegetables and medicines to cure their ailments'. A soldier wrote in his diary: 'I would greatly regret it if I were to die of malaria before I fought the Americans'.[81]

Controlling the enemy

Earlier in 1967, the Australians suffered a crushing blow during Operation Beaumaris (13–14 February) when three officers were killed and five soldiers were wounded. The Charlie Company, 5RAR, headquarters group was decimated by a booby trap laid by a friendly force to protect the An Nhut village, south of Route 23 between Long Dien and Dat Do. More were killed during Operation Renmark when 5RAR was tasked to clear the Long Hai hills so that the ARU could train there, which in itself was an interesting concept. The battalion started their search on 19 February without incident in an area only a few kilometres southwest of Lo Gom. Although there was no contact, there were signs that up to 80 enemy soldiers or more, possibly some of those involved in the Bribie battle, had moved that way recently. On 21 February, infantrymen triggered two mines and then an APC struck a mine, which blew it over, and another explosion ripped through the troops when they got out of the following carrier. In all, 7 men were killed and 26 more wounded. Brigadier Graham terminated the operation. In his monthly narrative, he explained what had happened: 'The mine incident . . . virtually annihilated Company HQ and a platoon of B company 5RAR [it] was a sharp blow to the morale of 5RAR'. He then wrote:

I decided to terminate the operation as reports from intelligence sources reported sightings of Viet Cong artillery suggested that the HQ of the Viet Cong 5th Division, 275 Regt and supporting elements were moving much closer to the Task Force base than they had previously.[82]

The Task Force reports for this period are jumbled and do not portray any anxiety that a large enemy force with artillery was closing on the base. On 20 February, air support reported that a 105 mm howitzer had been located and attacked, although not hit. The Task Force Intelligence Summary 52-67 that covered 21 February is almost blasé in its explanation that two aircraft had spotted artillery firing into a grid square that the friendlies knew nothing about. No one warned that the *5th Viet Cong Division* was manoeuvring in preparation to attack the Australians.

Lieutenant Colonel Townsend at 6RAR had reported on the 18 February battle that it was possible the main elements of the division were near Lo Gom, 30 kilometres away from the artillery sightings. This was not correct, but it appeared as if the two headquarters were operating on contradictory information about the enemy. Did Brigadier Graham use the reported—assumed to be enemy—artillery firing into an area northeast of Binh Ba as an excuse to extricate himself from a nasty situation? In the short time he had been commander, the Task Force casualty figure had shot up markedly. This did not mean he was to blame, but as commander the dead and wounded were listed against his watch. The mines and booby traps that caused the deaths were a sobering reminder and an omen that these were a two-edged weapon that had to be handled with caution. Graham had a plan to keep the enemy away from the people and it included mines, lots of them.

Who to keep away from whom

Brigadier Graham had set his operational objective: the Task Force was to deny the Viet Cong access to the main area of population and resources.[83] He was not going to search out and do battle with the main force regiments of the *5th Viet Cong Division* unless he was supported by American power. Chasing *D445* or any other local force or guerrilla group was okay because that was within the capability of the Australians, with a little bit of help if things got too messy. It was possible for the Australian force to attack the VC infrastructure in conjunction with the South Vietnamese who would provide the police force–type assistance needed in these operations. The problem was working out who was who. A variety of acronyms referred to enemy groups that brought either a shiver of apprehension or a 'She'll be right, mate' approach to any potential armed clash. At the top of the danger list were units of the North Vietnamese Army (NVA).

The NVA/VC military organisations were known as main force troops, local force troops, and militia or guerrilla groups, as well as the behind-the-scenes infrastructure personnel. MACV defined the units:

> NVA formations were units formed, trained and composed completely or primarily of North Vietnamese personnel. Viet Cong units were formed and trained in South Vietnam (or sometimes in Laos and Cambodia) whose original composition consisted primarily of people who lived in South Vietnam.[84]

The qualification that VC units consisted of South Vietnamese people is interesting because North Vietnamese were assigned to VC units, but the units retained their VC tags, sometimes even when the unit had more northerners than southerners.

Whether a unit was main force or local force depended upon its superior command. Main force units were either under the command of *COSVN* or a military region, and manoeuvred over a wide area of provinces. A province controlled local force units and they remained within that provincial boundary, for example *D445* belonged to Phuoc Tuy Province. The village and hamlet troops, the guerrillas, were generally part-time soldiers who undertook limited operations such as the collection of taxes, harassment, and sabotage and propaganda duties. More bothersome, in a pacification sense, were the members of what could be described as a shadow government, the VC infrastructure which provided the political and administrative framework to support the goal of liberating the South.

The challenges for Brigadier Graham and his Australian Task Force were manifold but he had set his priority: to keep the dangerous Vietnamese away from the ones deemed to be pacified. Brigadier Graham decided that a minefield was one part of the solution.

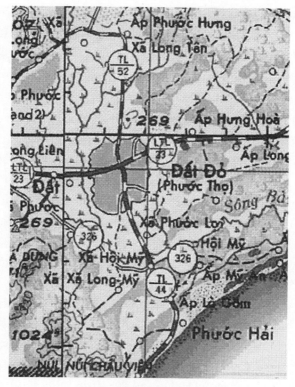

Map 8: Dat Do minefield area
The 11-kilometre barrier fence and minefield started at the 269 hill, on the northern side of Dat Do. The field then skirted the eastern edge of Dat Do before continuing along the eastern side of Route 44 to the sea, east of Phuoc Hai. The Long Hai hills are to the west of Route 44 and 1ATF was to the northwest of Dat Do astride Route 2.

The Dat Do minefield

The Australian commander had the problem of too few soldiers and an apparently hostile populace nearby who were providing assistance to the enemy. The idea of a barrier to separate people or people from resources is an ancient one. Brigadier Graham ordered that an 11-kilometre-long fence and minefield be constructed from Dat Do to the coast. The Australian engineers were to lay 20,292 US M16 'jumping jack' mines in the barrier field. It was an enormous undertaking not only physically and logistically, but the laying and arming of the mines was extremely dangerous. Greg Lockhart's book *The Minefield: An Australian Tragedy in Vietnam* is a detailed and powerful explanation of what happened. It truly was an Australian tragedy.

Lockhart was blunt in his description of the proposed minefield. He saw the Australian barrier mentality as a military version of a racist barrier placed between Australia and the Asian hordes. It is an extreme charge against the generals of the day. He claimed that their incompetence was fuelled by a flawed premise.

It can be argued that the generals fought the Vietnam War through the memories of their past battles. Who could plead not guilty to that? Books such as Bernard Fall's *Street Without Joy* and *Hell in a Very Small Place* were among the military bibles studied by some going to Vietnam. The books provided pearls of wisdom that many would have liked to apply. However, knowing which lessons to use, as well as where and when, was also a lesson. Scrambling into bunkers under an artillery barrage on the edge of the DMZ might have encouraged thoughts of a Korean-style conflict. Patrolling in Phuoc Tuy Province might have reminded others of the Malayan Emergency. Clearly, each experience highlighted different lessons and their application. If establishing an Australian base at Nui Dat was foolish—and that statement had its advocates—then South Vietnam was dotted with folly. However, it was too late to change the horse now; the new Nui Dat village was there to stay. One of Nui Dat's accompanying problems was the southeastern corridor between Dat Do and the ocean at Phuoc Hai. The Dat Do gap was an enemy resupply route that needed to be blocked, and that is where the idea of the fence and the 20,292 mines was born.

Lockhart assumed that Brigadier Graham carried the concept of a barrier minefield from his days as a junior armoured corps officer in North Africa. On that battlefield, large areas were mined principally to prevent an opposing force outflanking or breaking through a defended line. As he had not served in Korea, Graham was not experienced with the infantryman's distaste for minefields, whether friendly or enemy. To the Korean veterans they were neither; they were a constant menace to both sides. No matter, Graham wanted a barrier and examples of barriers abound in Lockhart's book, but noticeably the fortifications erected near Dong Hoi that kept the Trinh and Nguyen apart—Asian repelling Asian—for 100 years were not mentioned. Less than one degree of latitude south and many years later in 1967, Robert McNamara pushed for an anti-infiltration barrier to be built along the southern edge of the DMZ.

During the 1954–62 French–Algerian conflict there were two mined-lines known as Morice and Challe, but the Morice Line allegedly had a strong influence over Graham's tactical decision to build a barrier in Phuoc Tuy. If so, it was the concept rather than an attempt to replicate what were enormous eastern and western border fences in Algeria. The Morice Line was more than 300 kilometres in length, it held more than one million mines in an area that contained a deadly electrified fence, sensors, searchlights and radar-guided artillery and the fence was constantly patrolled by ground and air groups. An 80,000 multi-corps force protected the barrier. It is difficult to perceive how an intelligent officer of Graham's calibre could translate the success of Morice into something that became an 11-kilometre, piecemeal and unpatrolled hindrance at best. At least the McNamara concept was similar to the Morice plan, but its challenges were immense as will be shown later.

Despite strong advice against the idea from Major Brian Florence, his senior engineer officer, and his battalion commanders—especially John Warr who had been wounded by a mine in Korea—the commander ordered the building of the barrier. The fence came first. Bravo Company, 5RAR, flew out to an obvious feature named the Horseshoe, just north of Dat Do. This was to be the anchor point for the minefield. Now a 'shit of a job' started and it was not long before the enemy had figured out where the mines had been laid each day. Two weeks after the 5RAR started to build the fence, exploding mines began to shred the working parties:

> On 6 April, Private Richard Lloyd was killed and two others were wounded. Lloyd had just been released from hospital after having been wounded in the . . . Long Hai Mountains. Private Lloyd had been blown to bits and [Second] Lieutenant [Kerry] Rinkin . . . was organising the troops to collect the body parts.[85]

Later that night, the enemy probed the position and clashed with the Australians in an action that wounded one of the 5 Platoon soldiers. The next day, 7 April, Kerry Rinkin was killed when he stepped onto a mine. He died a terrible death, one which made clear again—if a warning was really needed—the dangers of mines to friend and foe alike. Ross Wood, the medic from Bravo Company, treated the shattered Rinkin who had come to the battalion to replace a platoon commander killed in the 21 February Long Hai mine explosions.

The men of 5RAR now probably thanked their lucky stars when the battalion was relieved by 7RAR. Brigadier Graham's demands to get the minefield finished had also increased, but the complications of doing so appeared not to be recognised by the Australian commander. Not only had the Australian engineers not seen an M16 before March 1967, they were now required to lay an unrealistic 1000 mines a day, according to Greg Lockhart. Mine laying training was another weakness; some sappers said they had barely any familiarisation and rehearsal on laying and setting the powerful mines. Although the 1000 mines a day figure was achieved, the stress was immense. First the physical demand, in the unrelenting heat of the day was followed by mental stress when the mines were armed. Then the tricks of the Viet Cong made life more interesting. Water buffalo were pushed into the field, which was a piece of cunning the enemy also used to set off false alarms at remote electronic sensor locations. Dogs, pigs and other unsuspecting animal foragers blew themselves up and created havoc in mined sections, which in some cases were not re-laid. And the accidents—or as Lockhart said the inevitable—continued. John Thompson related years later after his physical wounds had healed, 'my dick is longer than my left leg and I'm not boasting', a great piece of wry humour from a Digger who had suffered badly in a mine explosion. The end to the laying came when Sapper Terry Renshaw was killed and two other engineers, Bruce Bevan and Lothar Sempel, were wounded at the end of May 1967.

That was not the end of the story, however. Not only was there a large gap of some 4000 or 5000 metres in the minefield, it was obvious that 'the enemy was lifting the mines while the laying was in progress'. Worse was to follow. There is no better explanation of what happened than this excerpt from *The Minefield*:

By late 1967, thousands of M16 mines from the Australian minefield were replanted—they were often laid, lifted and replanted many times in attempts to catch moving targets—across Long Dat. The local historians say that: 'From Mount Da Che running past Gieng Gach temple to the fields at Bong we re-laid over 200 mines. In the Villages the guerrillas also used the Australian mines to create suicide zones for the enemy and to protect the base'. Graham had unintentionally armed the Long Dat guerrillas . . . and turned the vital Long Dat/Minh Dam area into a vast explosive trap.[86]

Brigadier Graham went home in October 1967 and the anger against the minefield followed; it has never stopped. Brigadier Graham was convinced that the barrier was a 'serious blow to the VC supply system in the South East of the province'.[87] The Vietnamese histories of the Dong Nai Province and Long Dat District quoted by Lockhart admit that the 'barrier fence and minefield' had some effect:

> Those accounts may be read partly as literary clichés designed to dramatise the ethos of a struggle able to overcome great odds. The overall purpose of the Vietnamese accounts . . . [was] . . . to explain the measures that defeated the minefield strategy.[88]

It is hard to believe that the incomplete barrier, which later showed foot and cart track marks through the unmined areas, had seriously affected the operations of the Viet Cong. The Minh Dam base, which was centred on the Long Hai hills, held some significance for the main force Viet Cong in the early days of the war in the Baria/Phuoc Tuy Province. A force from the *Viet Cong 5th Division* moved through the base in March 1966 to cross over the Lap River to the west of Long Hai and mortar the Vung Tau airfield. Its importance to them apparently paled, however, with the arrival of the Australian and American forces in the region. The Minh Dam retained a strong connection with the local force VC units and, although the minefield disrupted their activities, it did not stop them. The main force bases were set up in the northwest, north and eastern sectors in such zones as Hat Dich and Slope 30 and southeast of Xuyen Loc around to the sea docking points near Cape Ho Tram. The Minh Dam base is not mentioned in the *5th Division's* history after the March 1966 Vung Tau attack.[89]

In the game of maths tactics, the VC leaders probably knew to the metre where the Australian Task Force artillery could hit. That meant if they wanted to avoid an armed clash against Australian troops, they could simply stay out of the way by walking a few extra metres. A similar approach might have been used to overcome the barrier fence. First, they would have stolen the mines and then walked through the fence, or they could have avoided it altogether.

The Dat Do minefield story would haunt new faces and taunt new Australian commanders who had to grapple with what had become an unwanted and deadly legacy. Brigadier Graham may have taken some solace from the fact that a grander minefield plan had started in Quang Tri Province by the direction of Robert McNamara, the US Secretary of Defense. That, too, would turn into a nightmare, but for entirely different reasons.

The McNamara Line

The American commanders were annoyed by the hide-and-seek fighting of guerrilla warfare and the seemingly never-ending materiel resupply and stream of reinforcements that made their way to the South from North Vietnam—the 'Great Rear Area'. McNamara believed they could be blocked. The US Strong Point Obstacle System was underway in the February–March 1967 time frame, which coincided with the 1ATF plan, even though they were hundreds of kilometres apart. Although McNamara's anti-infiltration barrier also took heed of the French's Algerian fences, it was not planned as an invasion blockade. If Brigadier Graham were aware that an idea copying Morice was on the American drawing board, it would have reinforced his belief in the Dat Do–Phuoc Hai minefield.

The initial size of the force being considered to protect the American barrier was a division with aerial support. There was also a plan for an international force to patrol the barrier which might have included Australians, but Admiral Ulysses Sharp, CINCPAC, thought that additional force contributions from Australia would be desirable but doubtful. A protection force was required to watch over a conventional fence of barbed wire, mines and flares. Multiple types of sensors, and other alarms, infrared detectors, combat surveillance radars and night observation devices were also to be installed within the line. An anti-vehicular air operation was also planned for the Laotian segment of the Ho Chi Minh Trail.

However, the enemy was not deterred and activity in the area increased to the point where a four-battalion combat force, with support provided by continuous artillery and extensive use of air power, including B-52s, could not fight and build the barrier at the same time. The enemy hammered the area with powerful artillery and construction dates slipped as weather also hampered the work, but by November 1967 some sites were operational. In spite of the enormous efforts, enemy infiltration continued and the Americans considered building a barrier all the way to Laos. But, as one US officer said: 'With these bastards, you'd have to build the zone all the way to India and it would take the whole Marine Corps and Half the Army to guard it; even then they'd probably burrow under it'.[90]

McNamara's line just seemed to fade away in early 1968; it was all too much and the official order to stop came from General Creighton Abrams on 22 October. Abrams had taken over from Westmoreland on 3 July 1968. The obvious lesson from this attempt to blockade troop and resupply movement was the absolute requirement for observation over and protection of the barrier. The officers and the men around Brigadier Graham at the Australian Task Force understood that, and they also believed that the Vietnamese Regional/Popular Forces were not reliable enough to be entrusted with the Dat Do task. The spirited defence of the Regional Force Lo Gom post in March 1967 apparently buoyed Brigadier Graham and boosted his confidence that the South Vietnamese militia were worthy of the role he envisaged for them.

Detailed information on how the South Vietnamese operated was also available to the Australian commander from Australian advisers who were dotted around the countryside in every type of army unit. Their experiences would have been invaluable to a new commander who wished to win an infiltration challenge. Most advisers would have replied that too many Vietnamese minefields were rarely maintained and were allowed to degrade through natural growth of flora or detonation of mines caused by weather or age. At older outposts, the minefields were crisscrossed by various tracks used by the soldiers as shortcuts and all sorts of rubbish tossed over the inner fence as a convenient disposal point. The advisers would have also warned of the enemy's sapper capabilities to get through minefields and to take mines. It was a pity that he did not ask, but Brigadier Graham would not be the only commander to disregard this asset.

The often-inscrutable South Vietnamese might have nodded in agreement with the Australian commander's plan even though its disadvantages might have been apparent to them. They may have also thought that having established the minefield, it was the Australians' responsibility to look after it.

Operation Paddington

Beyond the minefield and the sufferings it caused, the war went on. American Marines fought some battles called the Hill Fights around an isolated outpost known as Khe Sanh that started on 24 April 1967. On 25 April, three Australian battalions paraded on Luscombe Field at Nui Dat to commemorate Anzac Day and two days later the bombers of the RAAF's 2 Squadron flew their first mission in support of 7RAR during Operation Puckapunyal.[91] HMAS *Hobart* was dodging North Vietnamese gunfire in northern waters and a task force of Australians, Americans and Vietnamese swamped the Xuyen Moc area during Operation Paddington in the first half of July.

The origins of Operation Paddington are a confusing story. Major General Douglas Vincent, COMAFV, recalled a discussion that he had with General Westmoreland:

'Look [said Westmoreland] I don't think your Task Force Commander is aggressive enough . . .'

'Well you're so wrong' [replied Vincent] . . . 'We've freed Xuyen Moc' . . . 'If you're expecting me to go barging off into the far mountains with only two battalions; well I'm not going to do it.' 'Well Vince [said Westmoreland] why don't you generate an operation and I'll give you the troops?'[92]

Brigadier Graham believed that his idea of pacification had worked and that the Viet Cong would attack the Australians because of this success. General Westmoreland wanted to have Americans and Australians out hunting for the enemy's main forces, not sitting around on pacification tasks, but Brigadier Graham was not enthusiastic:

Graham's reaction was cautious. The jungle-clad, dark and forbidding May Tao Mountains sheltered the headquarters of 5 *Viet Cong Division*. Intelligence had a vague awareness that the area also contained [a variety of enemy headquarters and service units]. Beyond that, little was known of its significance, its defences . . . it was 'almost a mythical area to us'. Graham recognised the importance of penetrating the May Tao but to him such an operation was premature at this stage.[93]

The push by Westmoreland and the reluctance of the Australian commanders epitomised the lack of combat power available within the Australian Task Force. For them to venture far from the Nui Dat base and into a known enemy main force lair required the addition of some real firepower. This was something General Westmoreland had promised and, according to General Vincent, he gave Graham the 'task of planning and execution' of an operation. Major General George G. O'Connor, Commanding General of the US 9th Infantry Division, was the overall operational commander.

Information on the enemy was now critical and Graham said that he 'flogged' the SAS through the area to 'almost a standstill'. When everything was analysed, he believed that elements of the *5th Viet Cong Division*, its support units and *274 Regiment* were somewhere northeast of Xuyen Moc, probably mid-way between that village and Nui May Tao, not far from the area that the 173rd Airborne Brigade had pounded during Operation Toledo in August 1966, just before the battle at Long Tan. According to Brigadier Graham, the May Tao operation was selected because:

At the beginning of June our intelligence reported the presence of Viet Cong main force units in the area north and north east of Xuyen Moc. These units were identified as *274 Regiment* and HQ 5 Div. It took us some time to convince the Americans that these units were in this location. Eventually Operation Paddington was planned.[94]

There was a clutter of reports on enemy activities around May, June and July 1967 that tracked some of the *5th Viet Cong Division*'s movements. Apparently *275 Regiment* had moved during May into Binh Tuy Province and attacked several outposts about 40 kilometres north of the May Tao region. They were then ordered to move west to cross the Dong Nai River, 70 kilometres away and regroup. In June 1967, *274 Regiment* fought a strong battle against a squadron of the US 11th Armored Cavalry Regiment (11ACR) in the area of the Hat Dich–Slope 30, to the west of Route 2. During Operation Akron I, the 3rd Squadron, 11ACR, was hit hard by anti-tank fire and attacked by two battalions of *274 Viet Cong Regiment* that were supported by the *5th Viet Cong Division*'s anti-aircraft—12.7 mm machine gun—company.[95] The battle raged for 45 minutes and cost the Viet Cong dearly, which they admitted. They reported losses of 47 killed and 69 wounded, but the Americans claimed 56 dead and two prisoners. This was a known battle against *274 Regiment* on 19 June in a location north of Duc Thanh, approximately

30 kilometres northwest of Xuyen Moc.[96] Graham had also recorded in his
June commander's narrative that the purpose of Operation Akron that started
on 9 June was to destroy *274 Regiment* located in the Hat Dich area. Did
anyone read these reports and ask the obvious question before the start of
Paddington, or was the VC regiment a truly Hydra-headed organisation?[97]

There was little doubt that a lot of enemy were moving in and through
their traditional base areas to the east of Route 2 and out northeast of Xuyen
Moc towards the May Tao during June. SAS patrols clashed with some of
them, but they were not identified as soldiers from *274 Viet Cong Regiment*.
During the period 1–25 June 1967, twenty SAS patrols were inserted inside
an area of approximately 200 square kilometres that covered suspected base
areas between Route 2 and Route 329. Most of the major sightings and
contacts were in a segment northwest of Route 329 that headed out of Xuyen
Moc in a northeasterly direction towards the May Tao Mountain.

On 10 July Brigadier Graham ordered his force to attack and destroy *274
Viet Cong Regiment* in the Xuyen Moc area, a very large and general objective.

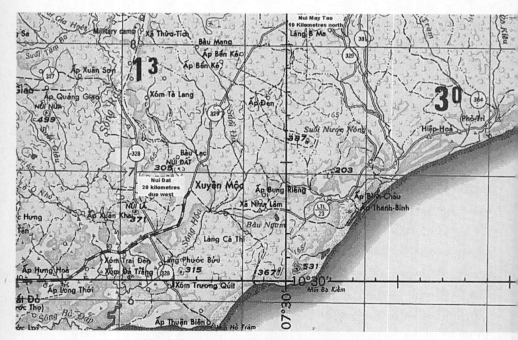

Map 9: Operation Paddington—area of operations
Operation Paddington was conducted in cooperation with the US 9th Infantry Division
in the general area of Xuyen Moc. The results were disappointing.

This was to be achieved in close cooperation with the American 9th Infantry Division and Vietnamese marines. Route 329 was the main road into the area of operations and marked the boundary between the Australian troops and some of the American/South Vietnamese forces on the operation. Brigadier Graham ordered the US 1st Squadron, 11ACR, to attack north astride Route 329 to rupture the enemy's defence and seize Objective Jack, about 15 kilometres north of Xuyen Moc. The powerful language of this directive really meant to drive along Route 329 tactically alert and to destroy any enemy who might be caught in the area or sufficiently foolish to engage the armoured vehicles.

Following an inauspicious delay when a bulldozer on a low loader blocked the main road, some Viet Cong took up the challenge and destroyed an 11ACR armoured personnel carrier with rocket-propelled grenade fire. When 11ACR got to Jack, the tactical plan then required 2RAR—who had replaced 6RAR in May—to airmobile assault into a landing zone (Bob) on the southeastern side of Route 329. 7RAR would then walk into an area known as Bert, which was also on the southeastern side of the road. The Kiwis' Victor Company was also involved under the operational control of 2RAR. No enemy activity had been reported around objectives Jack and Bert.

The next two significant phases of the operation required South Vietnamese forces to block areas to the north and the west, while the American 3rd Battalion, 5th Cavalry, pushed downwards from the northwestern sector off Route 330. This was to be the main thrust towards Route 329, through the area shown to contain *274 Viet Cong Regiment*. That projected movement was drawn on the map annex attached to the written orders but there were no specific tasks listed for the US battalion in the orders, that is, there were no instructions such as date and timings to tell the commander what he was to do and when he was to do it.

All of this action was to be in an arc 10–15 kilometres to the south and southwest of the May Tao Mountain, but the enemy had gone. Once they detected a swarm of vehicles heading east in a logjam of convoys from Nui Dat to Xuyen Moc, the enemy moved out. A copy of a written message of warning that had been sent to VC units in the operational area was found on 13 July. The note said: 'US and Allied troops had begun an operation on 9 July and all VC units must immediately prepare to move'. As the commander of the US 9th Division observed:

On 10 July 1967, elements of the 9th US Infantry Division . . . launched Operation Paddington against elements of the *274th Viet Cong Regiment*. The Viet Cong moved with their women and children at night and they were able to avoid major contact with allied forces. During the operation a [captured] NVA 2d Lt [*50th Training Group*] . . . reported that the *5th Viet Cong Division* had received approximately 105 replacements from the *325B NVA Division*.[98]

Brigadier Graham wrote in his July narrative that his aim was to destroy *274 Viet Cong Regiment* along with *HQ 5 Viet Cong Division* and elements of *Group 84*, the logistical support units of the division. This did not happen and, despite considerable effort over ten days, the Task Force did not achieve very much. The Task Force headquarters deployed into the field for the first time during this operation, and that was an achievement in itself. Graham's post-operation commentary claimed success although the enemy units were not destroyed. The report also delivered a backhanded swipe at some of the American troops and the South Vietnamese, who supposedly got into their blocking positions 24 hours late, thus allowing the enemy to escape. If all the Task Force log entries are correct, then that claim was an incorrect assertion.

The results of the operation were mixed, with the number of enemy killed listed at 92, the entire number for all the forces involved. The US 9th Division claimed 45 of those and the Australians, 31. One Australian was killed accidentally. The main clash involving an Australian occurred when the pilot of a Possum aircraft detected what he believed were two enemy battalions on the lower slopes of the May Tao. Two air strikes then hit them and the reconnaissance aircraft directed 175 mm artillery fire against them as well. This attack had started on 14 July when a reconnaissance pilot reported a mass exodus from a base camp with people carrying bodies. Afterwards, he called in that possibly two VC battalions were moving out.[99]

Brigadier Graham reported the strikes to General O'Connor and wanted him to use his influence to get 'immediate combat proofs [photographs?]' as he was sure that they had a good chance of getting two battalions. In his subsequent report, Graham claimed the air strikes had killed 29 and the target area had been an estimated battalion.[100] It was almost as if the Australian commander had bamboozled himself. Because he wanted to 'destroy *274 Regiment* along with *HQ 5 Div* and elements of *Group 84*', any large group of people in the enemy's area must have been at least battalions of *274 Regiment*. It was a naïve assumption. A large area around the May Tao Mountain was a well-known base for resupply, training and rest. The *5th Division*'s *50th Training Group* had been reported by the US 9th Division to be in the Paddington area of operations. Their report of women and children moving out with the Viet Cong also suggested that this was probably not an infantry base location.

If the goal of destroying *274 Regiment* was so strong, and if Brigadier Graham was given the authority to plan and execute Operation Paddington, albeit under the operational control of Major General O'Connor, then the time to react was immediately after the air strikes on the enemy battalions. They did not because the troops in the Paddington area of operations would need to leapfrog across the May Tao Mountain and block the enemy's possible movement northwards into Long Khanh or east into Binh Tuy. This was beyond the capabilities of what was now a road-bound force. Instead, success was claimed in a report that stated: 'The major effect of the operation was the denial of this area to the enemy as a safe base area'.[101] This was effective for a few days only because no allied troops went into the foothills of the May Tao to confirm the battle damage caused by the air strikes. That would have been a mountain too far. Even though some camps were destroyed, the damage caused by all the other sorties, artillery fire and naval guns was an unreliable guess. Action-wise, everything had fizzled out. It was time to go home, and this needed calmness and patience, as the main road had deteriorated because the streams had flooded and the bridges were suspect.

After the operation, a blame game began. Clearly some of the scuttlebutt circulating among the troops stung the headquarters, and the commander responded with an information sheet on the operation:

Now that Operation PADDINGTON is over and while each 'expert' tells his mate what it was all about and what it did or did not achieve, it might be as well to review what actually did happen. The operation was planned to catch 274th Regiment and destroy him and his base areas around the general area of Ben Ke Villages [hamlets] (YS6979).[102]

This explanation tightened the target from the general Xuyen Moc area in the commander's mission statement to a more specific location 10 kilometres north of the original objective. The commander's complaint that the northern blocking forces—South Vietnamese Marines—had been delayed by 24 hours was watered down to a more subtle 'there was some delay'. To place the fault for the escape of the Viet Cong upon the South Vietnamese forces was a lame excuse. They had landed within tolerable times for an airmobile insertion. The Vietnamese were easy scapegoats because people believed they were useless. Despite that disapproval, the South Vietnamese Marines had one of the major contacts of the operation and reportedly killed 30 of an enemy force on 12 July.

Remarkably, the Task Force explained why the operation had not destroyed *274 Viet Cong Regiment* by saying: 'Again the Viet Cong slipped away from a decisive battle and was forced back into the depth and isolation of the May Tao'.[103] For all the studying of Bernard Fall's books and Mao Zedong's theory of guerrilla warfare, the numerous lessons learnt, and advice from a variety of experts, that an Australian commander could make such a justification for an operation's weakness is difficult to understand.

The main battle had been about coordination and logistics for a tri-nation nine-battalion mixed force. General O'Connor acknowledged this when he reported on some of the statistics:

> The 9th Aviation Battalion lifted 2500 troops during the first day and forty-two refuelling points were needed during the initial phases of the operation. Two logistical bases were established with one at Xuyen Moc, which was supplied out of Vung Tau. It should be noted that an operation involving other FWMAF, where a US division is the controlling headquarters, detailed planning and coordination . . . must be affected.[104]

Brigadier Graham might have been handed the task of planning and execution, but the real burden fell upon the US 9th Infantry Division. O'Connor's report held a subtle hint that the planning and coordination might not have been up to scratch. The lack of orders for the US 3rd Battalion, 5th Cavalry, was also puzzling. They were the principal 'hammer group' that was to push the enemy against the Australian 'anvil'. Which commander was responsible for fitting that piece into the jigsaw? No matter how smart the Australian commander, planning and coordinating a nine-battalion operation with all its accompanying support was a demand beyond an Australian Task Force headquarters. The operation involved a larger force than the entire Australian Army could put into the field in 1967.

More war

Operations for the Australians during the remainder of July were quiet, with little or no contact with the enemy. Away from Phuoc Tuy and out at sea, a catastrophic fire engulfed the aft flight deck of USS *Forrestal* on 29 July 1967. The accidental firing of a Zuni rocket that ruptured a fuel tank on a parked aircraft created a holocaust that destroyed 21 aircraft and damaged another 40. One hundred and thirty-four sailors were killed, 161 were injured and four were lost overboard. The damage bill as at 15 September 1967 was US$72,203,000.[105]

August 1967 started fairly quietly for the Australians but soon saw a major combat clash. During Operation Ballarat in the Hat Dich zone, the Task Force commander reported that Alpha Company, 7RAR, had a four-hour firefight on 6 August with *C12 Company* of *274 Regiment*, in which the Australian company, led by Major Ewart O'Donnell, and the Viet Cong attacked each other with machine guns and flanking attacks. The Task Force operations log serialised the frenetic activity with staccato entries about the battle that lasted for just over an hour. The Australians lost five killed and fifteen wounded. They found four enemy bodies. During the firefight, the Australians experienced the enemy's tactic of 'hugging', which saw the Viet Cong close upon them in an attempt to neutralise artillery and air support—a previous lesson learnt distributed in information letters from MACV. During the action, the close support provided by the RAAF to get the casualties out of a very hot zone was notable and greatly appreciated by 7RAR. It was very different from the quarrelsome days of Long Tan.

This had been a hard firefight. These elements of an enemy formation were allegedly harassed and battered to leave the May Tao region, 30 kilometres away from the Hat Dich across highly contested territory, in mid-July. For the enemy to have moved this distance without detection would be remarkable. Of course, they might not have left the Hat Dich—or a base not far away—at all. A block of territory that stretched from the Suoi Tam Bo, which was east of Route 2 and extended north to the east of Xuyen Loc across Route 1, was an old and frequently used hiding place for the enemy. The regiment might have been located there all along.

Between August and December 1967, there were another seventeen named operations conducted by units of 1ATF, and on 20 October Brigadier Ronald Hughes—Regimental Number 72—assumed command of the Task Force. Some operations went for a day while others continued over an extended period and included subsidiary operations within the main deployment. This workload did not include the standard everyday clearance around the Nui Dat base, or other security tasks that could be just as dangerous as a main operation. Some soldiers spent the greater part of a month wandering the paddy fields and jungle tracks, wondering what was around the next bush.

Further north, in I Corps, the US Marines at Con Thien didn't have to wonder. In mid-1967, the NVA had gathered approximately 130 pieces of artillery and hidden them in firing positions just north of the Ben Hai River, which was the visible border between the North and the South. The guns ranged in calibre up to 152 mm and could hit any of the US–South Vietnamese bases near the southern edge of the DMZ. Con Thien and Gio Linh were two of their favourite targets and there were periods when these bases were bombarded with an average 100 shells a day.

Australians were in the thick of an attack on Con Thien in May 1967. Captain Karl Baudistel and six other men from the AATTV went into action with a Mobile Strike Force company to reinforce the position following a two-battalion NVA attack that had been preceded by a barrage of 300 rounds of mortar and artillery fire. The North Vietnamese were armed with flame-throwers and rocket-propelled grenades as well as automatic weapons. The NVA assault force got through a breach in the wire before they were repelled. Casualties on both sides were high: 44 Marines were killed and 110 wounded while the North Vietnamese lost almost 200 dead.

Activity continued to centre on the McNamara Line, which the NVA attacked and bombarded furiously. In one day, 700 shells fell on the 1st Battalion, 9th Marines, while the American artillery fired 453 missions in reply. During this action, the 9th Marines lost 84 killed, 190 wounded and 9 missing. The North Vietnamese pressure was relentless and in the week 19–27 September 1967 they bombarded Con Thien with just over 3000 rounds of mortar, artillery and rockets. Con Thien was known as the Hill of Angels, but its name came from its shape that looked like wings and not because of the numerous combatants killed in its vicinity. General Krulak counted the Marine Corps losses for September and noted that they had 956 casualties, and for 1967 their dead and wounded numbered nearly 5000 along the DMZ alone. In a classic military understatement Krulak said 'the operational benefits now being achieved in the area . . . are not consistent with the losses incurred'.[106] The Australian Diggers might have muttered some prayers of thanks if they had been aware that their generals had prevented Australia from putting its battalions into the DMZ region during the initial deployment planning talks back in 1965. It also reinforces the big difference in operations between Phuoc Tuy and the northern provinces, and the fact that this was an area that had been considered for Australian deployment. Imagine if Australian casualties were anywhere near as severe as those suffered by the Marines.

In Phuoc Tuy Province, the Diggers slipped, cursed and patrolled in miserable conditions back around Xuyen Moc on two operations during October and November 1967. The first was Operation Kenmore that saw the Australians search an important VC supply region, of which Brigadier Stuart Graham said erroneously that 'there had never been a ground operation in the area previously'. In fact, in September 1966 the 1st Battalion, 26th Marines, had landed along the coast near Cape Ho Tram and Thanh Binh and operated in a similar area of operations to that used during Operation Kenmore. The Marines didn't find very much and contact with the enemy was minimal, resembling the Kenmore pattern of activity. If nothing else, the operation was a good muscle-flexing exercise for the Task Force headquarters, using a purely Australian operation of a couple of battalions, artillery, APCs and heli-copters. A landing ship medium also landed some Diggers at Cape Ho Tram, from where they patrolled in the footsteps of the US Marines.

Operation Santa Fe followed during November 1967. The Task Force, in cooperation with the American 9th Division and the 18th ARVN Division, was directed to attack and destroy elements of the *5th VC Division* in the May Tao Secret Zone.

The intelligence report attached to the Santa Fe order referred to all the possible enemy computations from guerrillas to main force battalions. It also

warned that the *5th Viet Cong Division* might have a third regiment and that
was correct. The *88th Regiment* of the *308th NVA Division* joined the *5th Viet
Cong Division* in September 1967. The bad news, or rather the good news,
was that the division was nowhere near the May Tao. Although it is not clear
exactly where the division went, the base area was the Kho Xanh–Phuoc Long
provincial area and it probably backed on to Cambodia. The VC regiments
had redeployed during August and September 1967, with *275 Regiment* being
the first to arrive, probably at old bases in the Song Be/Dong Xoai area in
Phuoc Long Province. In the words of the division's history:

> At Kho Xanh [from August], the units of the 5th Division re-organised, conducted
> a series of study groups, and grasping thoroughly the resolution of the Executive
> Committee of the Party's Central Committee, increased their training activities.
> This was a time when the unit's capabilities were very high. At the beginning of
> November 1967, the Division had brought to full strength three infantry regi-
> ments: 4th, 5th and 88th—and their nine subordinate battalions [the paper does
> say what full strength meant], but 500 recruits were added.[107]

The *88th NVA Regiment* went back to *COSVN* at the end of November 1967.
Perhaps the regiment had been attached to the division to strengthen the
resolve of the VC formation during their retraining period.

Operation Santa Fe proved to be a frustrated effort. Conditions were physically demanding, the area was flooded, and the terrain sucked the energy out
of the soldiers. They struggled through the dense scrub and fought leeches
and other crawly things more than they did the Viet Cong. Enemy camps
and tracks were found, but contacts were infrequent. In one sad incident, a
platoon commanded by David Webster contacted what they thought was an
enemy group. They were fired upon and figures in black were seen through
the bushes. Webster quickly got his men into action and conducted a classic
infantry drill, with one section that protected the movement of the others.
Unfortunately, they killed two children and wounded two adults, one of
whom later died.[108] It was a justifiable immediate action drill, but a devastating blow to the soldiers involved nonetheless.

On 17 November, the Task Force ended its part in the operation and returned
to Nui Dat. A lot of bunkers and camp facilities were destroyed and that proved

to the Task Force that the Thua Tich area was an important logistics base. The Australian commander concluded: 'The lack of contact with Viet Cong Main Force elements tends to support the theory that the May Tao is primarily a HQ and depot area not often occupied by combat units'.[109] This was quite a remarkable turnaround from the heady days of Operation Paddington in July.

Although the Santa Fe mission had been to fight in 'close cooperation' with the 9th US and 18th ARVN divisions the US summary did not even mention the Australian Task Force. However, the 9th Division paper did define the area of the May Tao zone. They placed the boundaries at south of YT06, north of YS67, east of YS67 and west of ZS19, a box of land measuring about 1500 square kilometres. The allied forces covered only a small segment of that vast area with the US/ARVN to the north and east along Highway 1 and Route 331, and the Australians centred on Thua Tich village in the western portion of the operational area along Route 330.

To illustrate the size of the American contribution, they fired 33,615 shells of artillery, flew 1610 sorties of divisional aviation, conducted 62 air strikes and killed only 18 Viet Cong. The division concluded:

The results of the operation did not substantiate previous intelligence information regarding the 5th Viet Cong Division. There was insignificant sporadic contact during phase 1. The lack of booby traps along trails and base camp areas indicated the Viet Cong attached little importance to the area. Equipment and documents captured . . . were deteriorated . . . the base camps were vacated before Operation Santa Fe was initiated.[110]

The US 9th Division summary displayed a great difference in tactical thought between the Australians and the Americans. Brigadier Graham believed— albeit several years later—that the reason for the lack of booby traps or mines and an unprepared defensive layout was due to the enemy's belief that he was safe 'in the middle of the wet season and in the middle of the jungle'.[111]

Protesters in Australia

Although there had been some early protests in Australia against the war in Vietnam, they were mild affairs. The initial objectors disagreed with war in general and in the mid-1960s small, well-behaved groups appeared in the streets of the main cities with placards demanding 'Get out of Vietnam', or brandished signs plastered with biblical verse. These protests were the domain of organisations like the Women's International League for Peace and Freedom and Save our Sons (SOS). Members of the latter group were mainly middle-aged women, some younger women and some men. Joyce Golgerth first formed the group in Sydney in 1965, based upon her belief that conscription for overseas service was morally wrong. One of their first advertisements called for people to resist conscription:

> Mothers resist ... pressures to bring up their children as useful citizens ... then suddenly their lives are disrupted. After six months training these boys could be sent overseas for 4½ years war service. They could come home maimed or blind, or die in a war that has been described as a bottomless pit of violence and horror.[112]

In general, the protests were peaceful handouts of petitions, or silent vigils held at war memorials or military headquarters like Victoria Barracks in Melbourne, which attracted abuse that included a label of communism. President Lyndon Johnson's visit in October 1966 was successful even though there had been a few clashes with some demonstrators that indicated there was potential for a more militant approach to an anti–Vietnam War and anti-conscription message. Nevertheless, the Australian federal election of 26 November 1966 provided the government with a moral victory to forge ahead with its support for the conflict in South Vietnam. The Liberal/Country Party Coalition thrashed their political opponents in the House of Representatives, but did not fare well in the Half Senate election a year later when their share of the vote dropped by 2.9 per cent. The Democratic Labor Party won two more Senate seats, which meant that the Coalition government did not control the Senate (they had not done that since 1962).

The public supported the government's policy on Vietnam and when 5RAR marched through Sydney in May 1967, a huge crowd applauded them. There was no woman with red paint at that march, although the voices of the Save our Sons group got a little louder with the William White case that had begun in 1966. White was a teacher and a conscientious objector who refused to serve in the national service. Even though legal rulings ordered that he perform non-combatant duties only, White refused. As a result, White was sacked from the NSW Public Service and just before the November 1966 election, he was arrested. At a public gathering in Rockdale, a Sydney suburb, demonstrators spat at Harold Holt, an action that warned that the political road ahead was going to be rocky. An opinion poll taken in February 1967 showed that 72 per cent thought that White should have served; the remainder said that he should have been given an exemption.[113]

US polls and visitors

In America, public support for the war had started to tumble and by mid-1967 just over half of those polled disapproved of President Johnson's handling of the war and more than half answered a question on who was winning the war by saying they thought the US was losing or it was stuck in a stalemate. Australia's participation alongside America was an important boost for the American President and his senior officials, a support that President Eisenhower had pursued in the dark days of Dien Bien Phu in 1954. The pressure was on Australia to do more, to show more support for the policy that America was pursuing in Vietnam.

Secretary McNamara had been back to Vietnam and briefed Johnson on 12 July 1967 about his recent trip. Among a long list of observations, the Secretary reported that 'senior officers complained because they want their families with them'. He also advised that 'Australians [and other nations] should be asked to carry more of their share of the burden . . . he was referring to combat troops'. The president replied that he might ask Clark Clifford—an adviser and later Secretary of Defense—and General Maxwell Taylor to go on a mission to speak with regional leaders, including the Australian Prime Minister, Harold Holt. General Taylor was now a Special Consultant to the President.[114] On 20 July, he told McNamara that:

> Australia might be able to provide one additional battalion. He said that he had military reports that the Australians are ready and willing and that the Australian government would be receptive to a request for additional troops. McNamara said . . . 'that more Australians and Koreans would be a valuable asset to the total effort'.[115]

All the president's advisers agreed that Australia was ready to be asked to provide more troops. With only two battalions, the Australian Task Force lacked balance; its firepower was weak, as was its mobility. Obviously more troops were needed. Militarily, the Australian government would not get an argument against an increased force from its military leaders, if the Australian political plan were to stay the course.

After their travels through the region, the two advisers reported to the president in August 1967 that every country 'has very enthusiastic ideas about new ways to end the war'. Clifford believed that 'it would be difficult for the Australians to turn us down when they are in touch with the president directly'. He also added that 'each head of government had to say publicly something that would show that they were not on the tail of the kite of the United States'. Clifford's bullet-point notes of the discussions in Australia indicated a slightly different point of view on Prime Minister Holt's reaction during private discussions from the hard-nosed attitude shown at the general meeting.

Met all day Sunday [30 July 1967]. They were hard nuts. They had a long list of their contributions to Vietnam already. Real progress was made with Holt when went upstairs alone and told of the seriousness of the matter. Holt told Taylor that he was such a good salesman that he was glad he had not brought his wife to the meeting. The Australian commander in Vietnam is interested in filling out his contingent from current strength of 6500 to about 9000.[116]

Several years later, Clark Clifford recorded his recollections of the visit, expressing disappointment with the unwillingness of Australia and Vietnam's near Asian neighbours to increase their troop commitments. 'In the main our plea fell on deaf ears.'[117] He pondered why Australia, 'then with a much smaller population had . . . well over 300,000 troops overseas in World War II [but] only 7,000 to Vietnam'. The reluctance to commit puzzled Clifford:

Was it possible that our assessment of the danger to the stability of Southeast Asia . . . was exaggerated? Was it possible that those nations, which were neighbours of Viet-Nam had a clearer perception of the tides of world events in 1967 than we? Was it possible that we were continuing to be guided by judgements . . . now obsolete?[118]

Korea's reluctance stemmed from a 'higher level of activity by North Koreans' that meant they had to look towards the Korean 38th parallel as well as the Vietnamese border, a strategic lesson not often raised in Australian conversations about Vietnam. America had to keep its eyes on many parts of the world, for example in the early days there was a lot of concern about what would happen in the European theatre if the United States were to overcommit in Southeast Asia.[119] Later, when he was Secretary of Defense, Clifford said: 'The more we continued to do in South Vietnam, the less likely the South Vietnamese were to shoulder their own burden'.[120] Ironically, this was a point made by Maxwell Taylor when he was Ambassador to Vietnam in 1964 and had opposed the introduction of US combat troops into Vietnam.

Australians in Washington

Prime Minister Holt had told McNamara that he wanted to wait until after the Senate elections—November 1967—before he sent more troops. McNamara reported that conversation to the president who reflected: 'I think I could tell Clark [Clifford] that it's hard to fight a war if we have to wait on the elections'.[121] Clifford got a taste of politics and the Asian war when he asked Singapore's Prime Minister Lee Kuan Yew when he thought troops might be sent. Lee replied that 'he saw no possibility of that taking place because of the adverse political effect in Singapore'.[122] That answer greatly influenced Clifford's thinking. Singapore who 'knew the bitterness of defeat and occupation had declined to send any men at all to Vietnam'. What Clifford didn't mention was the dislike between Asian neighbours: Vietnamese against Cambodian against Thai, with a close-run race between the Chinese and the Koreans for last place. Nevertheless, they were pragmatic bedfellows, even if each had a shotgun under their pillow.

On 25 September 1967, former Prime Minister Sir Robert Menzies had lunch with President Johnson during which Menzies discussed the war in Vietnam:

> He [Menzies] did not see how we could win the war without more public statements. He said there is a need to repeat statements over and over. He thinks that we should repeat again how we got into Vietnam, why we are there, and what our purpose is [Johnson told his advisers].[123]

Johnson then met with William McMahon, the Australian Treasurer, on 2 October, telling McNamara after the meeting that he wanted 'Prime Minister Holt [to] put in 5000 more men'. McNamara replied: 'I told him the same thing . . . It is important for us to get extra Free World troops into Vietnam. We need them'.[124] The need was not tactical although the numbers were helpful; it was a need to show the world that America was not acting alone. Secretary McNamara admitted as much when he told the president that the extra forces from Australia and others would have a 'very beneficial impact in the US'. The president repeated what he had told McMahon. 'I told him we need some more troops. He told me how he [Holt had] lost some elections and they were not in a good position at the moment.' This was a misunderstanding because there had not been a federal election since November 1966. Paul Hasluck, the Minister for External Affairs, had followed McMahon through Washington. Hasluck broached the same subject when he met with the president on 10 October, but the gist of that conversation acknowledged 'the forthcoming Senate elections . . . and their possible implications . . . to pursue present policies'.[125]

Hasluck met with Dean Rusk and Robert McNamara on 9 and 10 October 1967 and at both meetings raised the sensitive matter of the withdrawal of British forces from Malaysia and Singapore. Australia wished to know whether, if its forces remained after the British withdrawal, they would be covered by ANZUS if they got into trouble. Another issue, of course, was whether the two Southeast Asian governments would permit the Australian troops to remain. If they did, 'could they be used in support of SEATO commitments, such as Vietnam?'[126] Hasluck raised an interesting point during the conversation with McNamara: he assumed that America would maintain a military capability in Thailand after the Vietnam War ended. 'He did not, therefore, anticipate a threat of attack from the North.'[127] America could not answer what Secretary McNamara saw as complicated questions and he asked Australia to obtain further information on the feelings of the other governments involved. Hasluck asked the Australian Ambassador Keith Waller to follow up, hoping that would allow the United States to provide some guidance on the Malaysia/Singapore issue.

McNamara then turned to Australia's advice that they would increase their commitment to Vietnam by sending more ground forces. The Secretary of Defense said that he was delighted by the information in a letter sent by Harold Holt to the president and asked when the decision would be made public. Hasluck thought that a statement would be made in Parliament on 17 October. Later that day, Hasluck met with Johnson, who was not so delighted by Australia's offer, and told Hasluck that 'what Canberra envisaged was not enough'. In his 6 October letter to the president, Prime Minister Holt had indicated that Australia 'would augment its forces by 1700 men before the end of the year [1967]'. This would be 'an extra infantry battalion with helicopter support, a tank squadron, extra helicopters and pilots, extra engineer capacity, ten Skyhawk pilots and Skyhawk maintenance personnel'. The president grumbled:

> The US was three times as far from the Viet-Nam battlefront as was Australia and was only fifteen times its size. If effort . . . was proportional to the present Australian commitment, we would have no more that 100,000 men there. In the Senate . . . there is an increasingly strong insistence that threatened countries, including Australia, must do much more, if we . . . consider justifiable situation . . . 600,000 [sic] of our boys are in the battle . . . and we are devoting $30 billion to their support.[128]

Hasluck answered with an ingratiating piece of diplomacy that the US commitment to Vietnam 'could only be understood if it was acknowledged that great people were obliged to bear great responsibilities'.[129] The problems for Australia were twofold: first, the perceived potential for a coming political loss in November and second, the money, which had been discussed during McMahon's visit. Secretary McNamara had signed off on an agreement to supply credit up to US$90 million to Australia without provisos, but the US Congress had recently denied him that authority and that was a problem. He had told McMahon, 'We will stand behind this somehow'.[130]

More combat troops

Before the visits to Washington, the question about what additional troops Australia could or should deploy was discussed in Canberra. The proposal to send a squadron of tanks was thrown into disarray when Brigadier Graham, the Task Force Commander and a past Director of the Armoured Corps, advised against sending them. He felt that the tanks were 'too old to be mechanically reliable' and that logistics and maintenance would be difficult for the Task Force to achieve. He was apparently not aware that the tanks had undergone a complete refurbishment at Bandiana workshops near Wodonga in Victoria; nonetheless, they were still very old tanks.

Another argument that armoured vehicles could move across 46 per cent of the Vietnamese countryside throughout the year was used to quash the no-tanks argument. This was based upon a US study that discussed armour operations, and included 'trafficability analyses' for APCs as well as tanks. In the Mekong Delta tanks were able to operate in 61 per cent of the area in the dry season, but that figure fell to zero in the wet, while APCs were able to operate in 87 per cent of the area throughout the year. Phuoc Tuy Province had good going all year round, with about 80 per cent of the countryside suitable for tanks, but when a tank got bogged, it was bogged, whether it was the wet season or the dry. The enemy's lack of a sophisticated anti-armour weapon also allowed for a role reversal between tanks and infantry, in which the armoured unit could absorb the smaller mine blasts and smash pathways through the jungle to clear the way for the infantry.[131]

Armour remained vulnerable to mines, however. From June 1969 to June 1970 in III CTZ, the 11th US Cavalry 'encountered over 1100 mines for the loss of 352 combat vehicles [not defined]'.[132] How much of the going would have remained 'armour country' if the enemy forces had possessed an effective anti-armour weapon was not clear. The enemy's shortcomings in anti-tank weapons and heavy artillery were discussed in the US study and it was because the enemy lacked those weapons that it was considered acceptable to deviate from tactical doctrine in battles against the Viet Cong.[133] In the Australian discussions, the suitability of the Centurion tanks for action with the Task Force seemed to be based upon possible mechanical limitations and topography, without mention of the enemy's very limited tank killing capabilities.[134]

Although the tanks later proved their worth—as some said, they saved lives—the maintenance effort to keep them in the field was hugely demanding. Australia could not afford the immense tail that came with large armoured forces in not only equipment and space but also manpower. For example, a

US tank battalion (54 tanks) had 570 personnel, but only 220 of those were fighters; the rest were support troops. The cobbling together of personnel to get the Australian squadron—tantamount to a US tank company (17 tanks)—into service in Vietnam was another dreadful piece of Australian Army administration. It was hampered by 'secrecy' and the need for tank crews to go through infantry training at Canungra instead of tank training and preparation at Puckapunyal, the Armoured Corps Centre. A two-troop squadron of 10 gun tanks and 103 personnel deployed first, but the squadron (not at full strength) was not fully prepared for war when it arrived in Vietnam in February 1968.[135]

There were also arguments about the provision of a third infantry battalion, and Graham thought that emphasising the need for tanks would prejudice the getting of a third battalion. It all came down to what Australia could afford, not only financially but also in manpower. To deploy an extra battalion to the battlefield meant that another would need to be raised back home to ensure that a fair rotation of units could be maintained. This meant many more dollars out of the Defence budget. In the words of the Secretary to the Prime Minister's Department, the third battalion had become 'the test of our adherence to the Vietnam issue and to the United States'. Historians Ian McNeill and Ashley Ekins summed up: 'The original basis of the request for the third battalion—the operational effectiveness and safety of the Task Force—was an incidental consideration'.[136] Lieutenant General Thomas Daly, then the CGS, said later that he thought it was more important for the Task Force to have three battalions, rather than two battalions and some tanks.[137] The prime minister made the announcement to Parliament on 17 October and 3RAR arrived at Nui Dat in December 1967, followed by some tanks and more personnel into 1968.

A war report: December 1967

The change of command at 1ATF in October when Brigadier Hughes took up the post brought a change of attitude to the tactical expectations on how the force was to operate. As Brigadier Graham departed with an autographed photograph of General Westmoreland presented by Westmoreland and a Certificate of Achievement, some of the comments on his efforts as commander were not complimentary. There were many who thought that he had been too cautious. General Westmoreland was one of them. Graham was labelled by a few as that fool who put in the minefield, regardless of any damage the mines may have inflicted on the efforts of the local Viet Cong. However, his promotion to major general and to the position of Deputy Chief of the General Staff said that not everyone agreed with that assessment. The commanding officer of 7RAR, Lieutenant Colonel Eric Smith, said that Graham would not permit companies to put out listening posts or standing patrols, even around Nui Dat. When Brigadier Hughes arrived that changed. 'We were able to get back to standard infantry patrolling at night time . . . to listening posts, standing patrols and company, or platoon harbours. In other words, we were given back our flexibility and that worked.'[138]

On the bigger war front, General Westmoreland and his senior commanders reported with confidence that the enemy had suffered badly during 1967; and the trend may have been at the point where enemy losses were greater than replacements. They claimed that the enemy did not win a major battle in Vietnam during 1967. In addition, enemy base areas were under constant threat with large quantities of food and medicines captured and/or destroyed. Local recruitment had declined and the areas of population that the Viet Cong controlled had reduced. It was apparent that the North Vietnamese had to pick up more and more of the burden. The war had become increasingly an NVA war, which meant that Laos and Cambodia were extremely important sanctuaries for their operations. Somewhat ominously, the Commander of MACV outlined the enemy's current strategy:

> The enemy's strategy continues to reflect an effort to draw allied forces into remote areas of his choosing, especially those areas adjacent to border sanctuaries, thereby, enabling his local and guerrilla forces to harass [and] attack. He has shown a recent willingness to engage our forces in sustained combat. Recent large unit deployments from North Vietnam indicate that the enemy may be seeking a spectacular win in RVN [South Vietnam] in the near future.[139]

The death of a prime minister

On 17 December 1967, Harold Holt vanished at Cheviot Beach near Portsea in Victoria. The coroner declared Holt was 'presumed drowned' on

19 December. Holt's body was never recovered and for this reason a coroner could not examine the circumstances of a presumed death. For nearly 40 years after his disappearance, fact, fiction and alleged conspiracies ran riot. His death was linked to countless theories: Australia's Vietnam commitment, spying for the Chinese, and even a Satanic agenda. His wife Zara ridiculed the assertion that he was a Chinese spy when she said: 'Harry? Chinese submarine? He didn't even like Chinese cooking'.[140] His death was not formally investigated until September 2005 when the Victorian State Coroner found that the prime minister had simply drowned; he said that everything else was unsubstantiated rumour and unusual theories.

Holt's death caused turmoil inside the Liberal/Country Party Coalition. John McEwen, the leader of the Country Party, refused to serve under William McMahon, the deputy leader of the Liberal Party, if elected to the leader's position. Under those conditions, McMahon had to stand aside from the Liberal ballot. McEwen was sworn in as 'caretaker prime minister' until the Liberal leadership was decided. Senator John Gorton, a former fighter pilot, won the tussle against Paul Hasluck, becoming the 19th Prime Minister of Australia on 10 January 1968. He immediately resigned from the Senate and stood for the House of Representatives electorate of Higgins—Holt's seat— which he won easily. Gorton proved a popular man and a bit of a larrikin. He wanted to change Australia's policies so that the nation became more independent, but continued to support Australia's commitment to Vietnam. The coming year would test his and his party's resolve on this policy.

6

THE DEADLIEST YEAR
1968

All men can see these tactics whereby I conquer, but what none can see is
the strategy out of which victory is evolved.

Sun Tzu

A balanced force, but not combat-ready yet

With the arrival of 3RAR on 27 December 1967 under the command of
Lieutenant Colonel Jeffrey J. 'Jim' Shelton, a Korean War veteran, the Task
Force started to get some combat balance. Having sufficient troops to ensure
the base was protected when a major operation was underway must have
been a relief. No doubt there were times when a commander would have
been uneasy with his main fighting force out of Nui Dat. During Operation
Kenmore, for example, when the strength of the Task Force was away from
the hill, a busload of enemy could have conducted a local tour of Nui Dat
with little effort. The newly arrived 3RAR needed to find its combat feet
quickly, as its final field exercise in Australia had not gone well. Following
the battalion's combat defeats during Exercise Piping Shrike at Shoalwater
Bay in Queensland in September 1967, some officers thought that the 'battalion needed more time to fully prepare for Vietnam'. Brigadier Hughes
was warned by the CGS that 'the battalion would have to be handled fairly
gently for the first few weeks'.[1] Their first two operations—Balaklava and
Bordertown—were good shakedown manoeuvres with little contact with

the enemy but with sufficient shooting activity to settle the men into active service.

Before the arrival of the battalion's main body, the advance party had taken responsibility for an area of operations to the southeast of Nui Dat. Lieutenant Henry 'Harry' Clarsen led out their first patrol on 17 December 1967 in conjunction with a patrol from 1ARU. The use of the Reinforcement Unit as a fill-in small rifle company went against the directive from the Task Force commander that all reinforcements were to complete fourteen days of acclimatisation training before being deployed on operations. In practice, the directive was repeatedly ignored. When 60 national servicemen rein- forcements arrived from Australia in February 1968 they were immediately formed into two platoons and placed under command of 7RAR for a cordon- and-search of Hoa Long village. Training was postponed. On 19 February, the training program was suspended again for Operation Clayton.

Constant demands for the troops left the commander of 1ARU in a bind between 1ATF, HQAFV and directives from Australia. Demands for work parties and arguments for 1ARU to hold sufficient men to accept responsibil- ity for the defence of a portion of the 1ATF base area flew back and forth. In the early times, the duties of 1ARU would be best described as inconsistent. In one plan, the unit was to be redesignated 1ATF Logistics Company, with reinforcements to be handled by headquarters Australian Force Vietnam. Major Robert Sinclair commanded 1ARU when he received three direc- tives from three commanders—AFV, 1ALSG and 1ATF—to perform three separate and conflicting tasks. The command issues were eventually resolved but the interruptions to training and the arguments over a training area and the location for the unit continued.[2]

In what was a hangover from the 1966 days of being the Logistics Company, 1ARU retained responsibility for sub-units such as the 1 Division Postal Unit and the Cash Office until April 1967 when 1ARU's duty was solely to train infantry in local conditions and make them ready for combat. The New Zea- landers also put their new arrivals through the 1ARU course, but the Australian armour and artillery reinforcements moved directly to their units. Captain Karl Jackson, who commanded 1ARU in early 1967, also looked at moving the unit to an area near the Long Hai hills, to the south of Nui Dat, in what appeared to be an attempt to escape from stifling bureaucracy and interruptions to acclimatisation training. All of these odd jobs and operational demands placed unnecessary pressures upon what was essentially a preparatory unit. Maybe luck played a part in their survival. One can imagine how messy it might have been should a group in training—who were not really in training—be lost to enemy action, especially if they were national servicemen.[3]

Tanks, Thailand and more training

Before the arrival of the tanks, which were on their way aboard HMAS *Jeparit*, the C Squadron headquarters waiting at Nui Dat was required 'to provide movement data tables for a contingency plan for the move of 1ATF to Thailand'.[4] Half a squadron of tanks arrived at the end of February 1968, which meant that there were only ten gun-tanks at Nui Dat.[5] The squadron also needed time to get up to an acceptable level of operational skills.

The ongoing argument over the usefulness of tanks had been won, but as Major General Ronald Hopkins lamented in his history of the Armoured Corps:

> The secrecy which prevented even the commanding officer of the unit being warned [of the deployment to Vietnam] . . . added to the difficulties; the squadron arrived in Vietnam with a training problem. Early operations were hampered, in addition, by an unforgivable shortage of spare parts. Within a month of arrival it had been necessary to cannibalise three tanks to keep the remainder running.[6]

These difficulties posed a question: how many tanks would be required to keep the squadron in the field for the total period of deployment from February 1968 to September 1971? Apparently 58 tanks were cycled through Vietnam in just over three years of operations. Age and operating conditions certainly wearied them.[7] Nonetheless, they were a deadly machine and certainly frightened the daylights out of friend and foe alike. Its guns aside, there was nothing quite like listening to the noise of an armoured monster smashing its way through heavy undergrowth while not knowing if it headed towards or backwards at you.

A squadron program of training was started on 2 March 1968 with a gunnery practice. An immediate problem was the .50 calibre machine gun, a new weapon for which the squadron gunners had not received training. Further problems were found with the 20-pounder (84 mm) main gun control, as the squadron diary noted:

Further zeroing was carried out in some cases as inexperienced commanders continually made mistakes with the FCE [Fire Control Equipment] checks and pre-firing sequence. The squadron contains many people with gunnery instructor backgrounds but the problems we faced were many. It appears at this stage that experience will be the best teacher.[8]

A learn or die technique! This method of training accorded with the previously mentioned Australian and US assessment that the tanks' main challenges were topography, logistics and age, not strong anti-tank weapons.[9] The point was highlighted in the American study *Mechanized and Armor Combat Operations in Vietnam*, which concluded: 'Although numerous AT mines and some recoilless rifles are encountered, no significant enemy antitank capability exists'.[10]

For all of the enthusiastic support given by some infantry and armoured corps officers for the deployment of tanks—especially after Operation Bribie— the planners were nevertheless worried more by the jungle terrain than the enemy's anti-tank capability. Contrary to popular belief, though, the jungle was a natural barrier against anti-tank weapons even while it impeded the free movement of armoured vehicles. The more dangerous areas for armour were the open spaces such as roads, bridges and clearings that were inevitably encountered on operations. These places either channelled the movement so that mines could be laid in likely approaches, or they provided the attacker with space for observation and the distance for the anti-tank weapons to arm.

Operational disagreement

Disagreement over the use of Australian ground forces had started soon after the arrival of the first combat battalion back in 1965 and the differences continued throughout the years of the war. General William Westmoreland was well known to have preferred the search-and-destroy mission and the big battle strike, but it is too harsh to judge that Westmoreland did not understand the need for pacification. His first priority was the destruction of the enemy's main force power and he was not alone in that objective. It is also worth recalling that the Australians were willing to call upon American battle tactics to blast the enemy when the situation required more than their limited combat power.

The Australians also wanted to conduct the more traditional counter-revolutionary operation to separate the people from the insurgents, which they believed would destroy the enemy's capability to fight. At the same time, they recognised that the greater danger was the power of the enemy's main force units. Whenever they cast their shadow the Australians jumped, but the advantage that the Australian Task Force had was location. Phuoc Tuy Province was at the end of the main supply chain by 1968 and the *5th Viet Cong Division* had been redeployed northeast of Saigon. In spite of the fact that Phuoc Tuy Province was not a priority enemy operational region, the *274th Viet Cong Regiment* remained in the area 'on independent operations around the Baria–Long Khanh–Bien Hoa battlefield'.[11] Although the *5th Viet Cong Division* had been strengthened with additional troops from the North it was still known as a Viet Cong division simply because of computerised records. As Major General Phillip Davidson—the MACV senior intelligence officer (J-2)—later told General Abrams, Westmoreland's successor:

> Automated intelligence [*5th Viet Cong Division*] data is under this term ... at one stage there was a *5th NVA Division* that got us all lashed up. The question has arisen ... for the last 22 months. We've tried ... I believe it's three times, to get this thing straightened out. We're confused enough ... without confusing ourselves by designations.[12]

The relentless Australian program of patrolling and cordon-and-search disrupted the food supply and interfered with the Viet Cong infrastructure around Nui Dat. This bothered the Viet Cong and made their operations much more difficult to mount. As Trinh Duc, a Viet Minh stay-behind and subsequent Viet Cong village chief recounted:

> Worse than the Americans were the Australians. The Americans' style was to hit us, then call for planes and artillery. Our response was to break contact and disappear if we could, but if we couldn't we'd move up right next to them so the planes

couldn't get at us. The Australians were more patient than the Americans, better guerrilla fighters, better at ambushes. They liked to stay with us instead of calling in the planes. We were more afraid of their style.[13]

Additionally, the pacification-cum-Revolutionary Development programs had a hitherto unrecognised influence over NVA operations in the South. In well-run pacified areas it created friction between northerners and southerners, which had attracted censure from *COSVN*. Viet Cong political officers reminded the locals of their duty to assist their northern kin in the reunification battle. The other effect, more damaging to the NVA main force, was the loss of local knowledge when the Viet Cong infrastructure was destroyed. Lieutenant General William Peers, the Commanding General of I Field Force Vietnam, sent a note on the matter to General Abrams, who told a weekly intelligence update meeting:

This [NVA] lieutenant . . . says that the NVA can't do a thing down here without the cadre and the guerrillas. It's nothing new, and people out here have been saying it all along—forever. I guess—but we ought to get so serious about it that we really get after it [the infrastructure] [underlining in original to highlight spoken emphasis].[14]

General Abrams repeated the importance of the local infrastructure to the NVA a year later when he said:

The NVA are screwed if you can get in there, get the guerrillas, and get the local people out. The NVA then are lost, really. They don't know the country that well. This is really the name of the game here for the next few months [underlining in original].[15]

The operational enigma continued, however. From the commanders down the ranks, suggestions ranged from the apocalyptic—bombing North Vietnam into oblivion, to the facetious—turning the countryside into a concreted car park for a supermarket. Within the Australian camp there appeared to be more support for a program of operations that 'placed greater value on low-level operations than on conventional infantry operations directed

against enemy regular units'.[16] But in intelligence summaries and operational plans the words 'main force threat' or *5th Viet Cong Division* and its
subordinate formations seemed to overshadow everything else. As McNeill
and Ekins point out in *On the Offensive*, Major General Vincent apparently
accepted the Westmoreland approach while espousing the tactics of Revolutionary Development. Vincent said:

> To deal effectively with sporadic enemy contacts and to impose a conclusive
> outcome on larger encounters . . . the Task Force needed to locate the enemy, pin
> him down and then bring overwhelming firepower to bear before he can disperse.
> This was the only proven formula for killing Viet Cong at an economic and accept-
> able rate [the American approach] that was equally applicable to the Task Force.[17]

A similar argument had been going on among the senior NVA generals.
Vo Nguyen Giap, the Minister for Defence, had advocated a return to guerrilla
warfare style operations following the successes of the more aggressive and
powerful American forces. General Nguyen Chi Thanh at *COSVN* believed
in a big battle strategy. He also saw the Viet Cong troops as nothing more
than fillers for his main force units. General Thanh's battle concept was one
of momentum; 'to pause when the troops were flushed with many recent
victories would deprive them of the psychological momentum necessary to
counter the influx of American troops'.[18] General Thanh's plan to go on the
attack was approved, but the Free World Forces seriously damaged his battle
efforts and a series of debates between the northern classic guerrilla warfare
advocates and the southern revolutionaries in the Politburo followed. A paper
by Cuu Long—an alias for General Tran Do—that criticised part of General
Thanh's tactics was broadcast on Liberation Radio in 1967. In it, Cuu Long
disagreed with Thanh for:

> emphasising main-force attacks and neglecting guerrilla force operations. Fur-
> thermore, Thanh's policies had demoralised rank-and-file Viet Cong and had left
> the Viet Cong leadership confused about their role in the war.[19]

General Thanh relented and in an article written under one of his aliases—
Truong Son—he virtually admitted that the allied forces had stymied his

main force efforts. Thanh went on to say that guerrilla warfare in conjunction with main force efforts was necessary for their success in battle.

General Thanh died in early 1967 at Hanoi, but the cause of his death is wrapped in intrigue. Some report that he died from wounds inflicted in a B-52 strike at *COSVN*, while others say he had a heart attack at Hanoi. Recently his widow wrote that he 'became ill for inexplicable reasons', which might support the theory he was assassinated (poisoned) by Le Duan, the Party Secretary, who then held real power in the North.[20]

As the NVA/Viet Cong push had stalled by 1967 because of the strong allied military operations, the northern leadership was beset by the strategic challenge of three possible main methods of warfare. The choices were: Thanh's new attack plan, an all-out confrontation that used every manpower resource to achieve victory; Giap's protracted grinding away at the enemy to a point where war-weariness would cause the Americans to leave; or, as others wished, not to fight a war in the South at all. Each plan had its supporters and detractors that included differences of opinion and advice from Russia and China. Russia, then a major supplier of military equipment to the North Vietnamese, recommended a diplomatic solution to the fighting. China's advice was more along the lines of continuing the war to the last bullet, but preferably to the last Vietnamese. However, the Chinese deployed 320,000 troops to North Vietnam during 1965–1968, and some of them went into the South. Reportedly, the Chinese suffered 20,000 dead and wounded. As well as the troops, China supplied North Vietnam 'over US$20 billion worth of materiel' including weapons and vital infrastructure support. China also claimed to have shot down nine US aircraft in aerial combat.[21]

The Australians make an aggressive change

At Nui Dat, the changes that came with Brigadier Ron Hughes in October 1967 may have been subtle at first. In military terminology, 'search-and-destroy' became 'search-and-kill' and the SAS were questioned as to why they watched some enemy but did not kill them. Altered operational techniques soon became more noticeable when Hughes permitted the battalions to move at night and to be more flexible with their tactics. At the higher command level, the advice and guidance to 1ATF not only from Commander AFV but also from Army

Headquarters and Australian politicians now went close to interfering in the operational chain of command, especially when military tactical decisions attracted comment by both Australian and American politicians.

At first Brigadier Hughes said that he 'was doing exactly what Graham was doing and that was ... pacification ... to keep the Viet Cong in the jungle off the peasants'.[22] His interest in cordon-and-search style operations soon waned and Hughes 'came to believe that the role of the Task Force was not pacification of Phuoc Tuy, which he saw as the responsibility of the South Vietnamese forces'.[23] Déjà vu or back to the Combined Campaign Plan AB 142 of 1967. As a result, he was more willing to expand his area of operations and commit Australian troops to operations outside of Phuoc Tuy Province.

Major General Arthur L. 'A. L.' MacDonald, who had taken over as COMAFV at midnight on 30 January 1968, also supported the use of 1ATF against the enemy's main forces rather than on pacification duties. He believed that it was not justified to tie up the Australian Task Force in Phuoc Tuy Province. In a post-war interview, he said:

> Where the only possible threat [in Phuoc Tuy] ... was posed by parts of *D445* or even less than that. There were much bigger threats ... vital to the Americans, and therefore, our effort there [in Phuoc Tuy], could not be justified.[24]

Major General Vincent, his predecessor, had permitted the Task Force to deploy beyond Phuoc Tuy's borders to assist with the defence of Bien Hoa earlier in January 1968. His decision had attracted considerable criticism, but the field commanders were quite within their command rights: the May 1966 Directive to the Commander Australian Force Vietnam had approved an expanded area of operations for the Task Force that included all of the provinces within the III Corps Tactical Zone.[25] The commanders had felt the sting of a critical press, and political pressures inevitably followed.

A New Year truce

Nineteen sixty-eight began with a customary truce for the Gregorian New Year that saw allied troops stand down for two days from 31 December 1967. As expected, there were a number of infringements and the cease-fire ended at 0600 hours on 2 January 1968. More importantly, the people and many of the South Vietnamese armed forces began to prepare for the Chinese Lunar New Year that would fall at the end of the month. Traditionally this was a time for family and enjoyment and a rest from the arduous war, at least for a few days, for both sides. The coming new year was the Year of the Monkey.[26]

When the fury of the Tet Offensive burst upon South Vietnam at the end of January 1968, many commentators declared that the North Vietnamese had made monkeys out of those who controlled the allied effort. The effects of these battles would reverberate around the world, but the most telling victory was not on the battlefield. To understand what happened during this most sacred time of the year for the Vietnamese of both the North and the South, we need to go back in time into the earlier months of 1967.

The intelligence debate

One of the oldest cutting remarks about military intelligence is that it is an oxymoron, but that unflattering joke belies the crucial worth of information-gathering for analysis and prediction. Saigon housed four combined intelligence centres that serviced the allied forces' needs for the exploitation of information on the enemy and their possible intentions during the Vietnam War. Major Peter Young, a former member of the AATTV and in 1967 the Assistant Military Attaché, said that he had access to the innermost secrets of one of these centres. Peter Young's tale will be told as one part of the story in the lead-up to the Tet Offensive.

Intelligence analysts in Vietnam were confronted with vast amounts of material from which they had to produce sound information and then build a comprehensive intelligence picture, which was in reality their best assumption. In March 1967, the Combined Document Exploitation Centre 'received 495,184 pages of captured documents . . . 58,667 pages were of intelligence value'.[27] Unfortunately, despite best intentions the results of such intelligence-gathering were not ideal. Each of the allied nations that had combat troops in South Vietnam was known to hold some of the valuable information within their own bailiwick. The Koreans didn't share anything. Within the giant US commitment, fragmentation of effort caused inefficiencies not necessarily by intent but because there was too much detail to handle. Command jealousies also weakened the efficacy of the so-called combined effort. One example that could have affected the Australians in Phuoc Tuy was the reported retention of the *275th Viet Cong Regiment* commander's diary by the 18th ARVN Division in October 1967. Brigadier Stuart Graham said that he had seen pages but he was not permitted to see the diary's entire contents, and the diary never surfaced subsequently.

Further north in I Corps, the United States Marines held sway but there were Army units there too. Sometimes the reports submitted by the two US forces were contradictory and the lack of comment by a superior headquarters about a disagreement on information, such as the numbers of enemy killed, is a mystery. Beyond an executive summary, it was almost as if the pages of detail were only relevant to the clerk who ticked off that the month's report had been received and filed. In one 1968 example, the 1st Marine Division and the Army's 23rd (American) Division each submitted their commander's report for January. One commander boasted that the enemy's *2nd NVA Division* had suffered losses that impaired its future effectiveness. The other warned that the strength of the ARVN and the US Marine battalions had been drawn down while the *2nd NVA Division* still had uncommitted units. Even more startling was the claim that more than 4500 of the enemy had been killed in this area of operation over several months, but the enemy's division was still held as a major threat. That division had no more than 6500 personnel.[28] Looking back now, this was an unbelievable body count and it was an absurdity that should have been picked up at the time. A simple addition of the standard ratio of killed to wounded would have concluded that some of the enemy units had been wiped out. The disparity may have been seen but not questioned; careers rode on those figures.

Good information was also locked away in 'need-to-know' boxes that meant those who really needed to know, didn't, creating further stumbling blocks and restrictions to distribution of beneficial intelligence reports. The NVA Lieutenant Colonel Le Xuan Chuyen's defection to the Americans in August 1966 is one example of this. At the time that he was under interrogation, the 173rd Airborne Brigade was out on the hunt for his headquarters. They missed getting it because Chuyen's information was not passed to the combat unit. The 173rd's search continued 20 kilometres to the south of the location revealed by Chuyen, where they found nothing.

Signals intelligence was another closely guarded secret. The withholding of hot information from that source is something that has been argued about for years. For the Australians, the tight restrictions on release of intelligence information gathered before the battle at Long Tan is a prime illustration of over-the-top secrecy applied to signals intelligence. In some locations like the Studies and Observation Group command centres for their cross-border operations, physical barriers were erected between them and allied contingents in the same camp. To get too close to the SOG bunker was an invitation to be shot, whether the offender was American, Australian, or any other nationality.

The intelligence jigsaw

National archives and the shelves of bookshops are replete with words on the North Vietnamese 1968 Tet Offensive. Who knew what? When did they know it and what did they do with the information? The answers to those questions might stir thoughts of incompetence or, conversely, understanding for the challenges faced by the intelligence analysts who had to piece together a picture of the enemy from diverse sources.

Some of the strongest claims about the Tet Offensive assert that an intelligence failure permitted the North Vietnamese to achieve a strategic victory through its demoralising impact upon the American people. As North Vietnamese General Tran Do observed:

> In all honesty, we didn't achieve our main objective, which was to spur uprisings throughout the South. As for making an impact in the United States, it had not been our intention—but it turned out to be a fortunate result.[29]

James Wirtz at Cornell University wrote a cogent argument about the weaknesses of allied intelligence in his 1991 book *The Tet Offensive*.[30] In his account, the intelligence failure was threefold. First, the analysis of information failed. This was followed by a 'mundane response to predictions of an attack' and finally, 'the dissemination of information directly contributed to the failure of intelligence suffered by the allies during Tet'.[31] These were severe charges to be laid at the feet of the generals and all of the intelligence agencies.

Wirtz attempted to soften the blow in his introduction, in which he wrote, 'it would be wrong not to state . . . that US intelligence . . . missed avoiding the operational consequences of surprise by just a few hours. They almost got it right'.[32]

Arguments erupted among commanders, intelligence agencies, politicians and the press almost as quickly as the battles rolled through the Vietnamese countryside. How could this have happened? A definitive answer still eludes us. Like the 1967 analysts, we must assemble a jigsaw puzzle to decide what happened, but with one distinct advantage: the battle picture is now obvious. Many of the details of the North Vietnamese campaign plan, however, such as when it was agreed upon and some of its objectives, remain hidden.

The Tet campaign plan

The NVA plan for Tet has never been divulged by its architects. As a consequence, an attempt to examine the battle plan is dependent upon the memories of a select few and, as expected, opinions variously support the conclusions of the Americans, the North Vietnamese or the NLF (Viet Cong). In general, there is agreement that by the end of 1965 General Westmoreland's operations had bitten into the enemy's capabilities and reversed the trend of the losses suffered by the South Vietnamese forces. This was followed by a period of stabilisation in 1966.[33] Then the war reached a point of stalemate in 1967 when allied successes in search-and-destroy battles hurt the NVA/Viet Cong efforts badly. American operations Cedar Falls and Junction City conducted from January through May 1967 claimed impressive victories against the NVA/VC forces. Not only did the American units kill a lot of the opposing soldiers, they also captured damaging amounts of weapons, ammunition, foodstuffs and documents that included cryptographic equipment. COSVN was also forced to move into Cambodia.[34] The much maligned search-and-destroy missions achieved more through the destruction of the enemy's supply caches than the killing of their soldiers.[35]

It was now apparent, however, that neither side was winning the war. The losses by the North, which were followed soon after by the death of General Nguyen Chi Thanh, rocked the North Vietnamese leadership. They realised that America had the potential to bring more force to the battlefield and they

were also concerned by the possibility of an invasion of the North. It was at
the time of the funeral for General Thanh on 7 July 1967, many commentators believe, that the plan for Tet 1968 was approved, with General Giap a
strong supporter. General Phillip Davidson—the MACV J-2—disagreed. He
wrote the following in 1988:

> It is now known, from an unimpeachable and still-secret source, that Giap argued
> at length that the all-out offensive would fail, and that it would entail heavy casu-
> alties. Giap held obstinately to his theory of the protracted war. Giap fought
> adamantly during July, August, and September to get the concept abandoned, or
> somehow modified. On 14 September he published . . . The Big Victory, the Great
> Task, a plea for return to the protracted war of guerrilla-type actions.[36]

James Wirtz interpreted the Giap article as a 'general description of the Tet
Offensive', although several of his referenced authors did not agree.[37] Stanley
Karnow wrote in *Vietnam*, 'Giap . . . conspicuously avoided any mention of
the imminent Tet campaign, then being planned in secret. But his assessment furnished clues to the . . . motives'.[38] Richard Betts in his contribution
to *Strategic Military Surprise* spelt out his contention that the Giap article
was a piece of deception. In a paragraph headed 'Uncertain Warnings, Partial
Preparedness', Betts said:

> Giap affirmed . . . the DRV [North Vietnam] and Viet Cong intended to conserve
> forces and wage a protracted war of attrition. In retrospect this appears to have
> been a deception. At least one captured document said the decision for a general
> offensive was made in Hanoi two months earlier [July 1967].[39]

Richard Betts also noted the puzzling 'Viet Cong attacks in the months
before Tet against objectives they could not hope to hold and [which] yielded
high losses to little apparent purpose'.[40] Later, captured documents suggested
that the tactics were designed to lure American forces away from the populated regions and also to practise large attacks against their more powerful
troops; tactics that according to some critics also worked against the Australian commanders when they approved the deployment of the main elements
of the Task Force away from Phuoc Tuy in January 1968.

According to Merle Pribbenow's translation of *Victory in Vietnam*, the Politburo decided in October 1967 when to attack. The decision had an interesting notation, which suggested that Tet 1968 was not the first date selected for the offensive.

> *The Politburo realised it was possible to carry out the plan earlier than we had initially planned* [emphasised]. To achieve the element of surprise, the Politburo decided to launch the General offensive during Tet 1968.[41]

These differing opinions suggest that there was no single decision taken on the attack plan. Permission to proceed came in a series of conferences and approvals-in-principle until a Politburo directive was issued in December 1967 that was formalised by the 14th plenary session of the Party's Central Committee in January 1968.[42] How the plan was approved is of interest, but the greater curiosity is hidden within the plan itself. If Nguyen Chi Thanh delivered his battle concept to the leadership at Hanoi before he died, did Vo Nguyen Giap follow the plan that he allegedly disagreed with or did he devise a new scheme? Was General Giap just a military figurehead who supervised a plan of action decided elsewhere, perhaps by Le Duan? Without the release of the details by Hanoi, any answer is a guess. If Davidson's unimpeachable source was accurate, Giap was correct in one aspect: the offensive would fail with heavy casualties.

Remarkably, General Davidson, a career intelligence officer, was the chief of Plans and Estimates Branch on General Douglas MacArthur's GHQ the Far Eastern Commission when North Korea invaded the South in June 1950. Critics also called this a severe intelligence failure because the invasion and the subsequent involvement of the Chinese caught the US off guard.[43]

Major Peter Young: a brilliant analysis or a good hypothetical?

Peter Young transferred into the Australian Army from the United Kingdom in 1959 as an infantry lieutenant and then a little over a year later he moved to the Intelligence Corps. He was no stranger to Southeast Asia, having served in Malaya for two years between 1955 and 1957. In February 1962 he attended an advanced training course in air photo interpretation at Far East Land Force, then based at Changi on Singapore Island, and in July 1962 he was deployed to South Vietnam as a member of the first group of the AATTV. Major Peter Young returned to South Vietnam in 1965 as the Assistant Military Attaché and served in that position for two years.

Young was a thinker, just a little too smart for some, and his self-assuredness perhaps tended towards arrogance. He didn't like the Australian Military Attaché in 1967—Colonel Alan Swinbourne—and the MA didn't like him. Peter Young wanted to get into the real world of intelligence, away from the artificial world of the embassy. Young got his chance when he was approved entry into the Current Intelligence and Indications Branch (CIIB) at MACV. In here, the analysts could give their intelligence prowess free rein to provide the US commanders with their best calculations on the enemy's strength and intentions. Today he makes no secret of his belief that he accurately predicted the 1968 Tet Offensive.[44]

The internationally renowned Australian journalist—and some think part-time intelligence agent—Denis Warner wrote of Peter Young's analysis in 1977:

He not only tipped the Tet offensive, he tipped the time! It was, without doubt, one of the most brilliant pieces of intelligence assessment of the war.[45]

Warner followed with a more subdued observation in 1997:

Young set out his views in a report for the Australian Embassy, in which he outlined a course of enemy action involving major attacks in the two northern corps areas and a possible special attack against Saigon. The period when the attack could be expected ranged from September through January 1968.[46]

Warner's summary of Peter Young's prediction came about as a result of a dinner party at Young's house in Saigon early in 1967. Young had invited a small group of intelligence men to discuss a controversial subject, 'We are losing the war'.[47] Colonel Ted Serong was included, as were the US intelligence analysts who looked over the areas of I, II and III Corps Tactical Zones. Major John 'Jack' Fitzgerald, the I Corps analyst, and Peter Young had struck up a personal friendship during the time they waited for their clearances into the rooms of the CIIB. They were similar thinkers. Added to the mix was the British MI6 man and the CIA deputy chief of station. What was said at the dinner is difficult to ascertain but Denis Warner wrote, 'If there was a certain unwillingness at the dinner to accept that the war was being lost, there was general agreement that a major push was coming'.[48] The pessimistic subject of losing the war was worthy of strong debate, especially as to whether the war was at a stalemate with the enemy forces damaged and pushed back to the borders. Wary eyes nonetheless were being kept on the NVA main force divisions, especially around the bases such as Con Thien and Khe Sanh near the DMZ. There was almost a sixth sense that something was going to happen. What that something might be exercised the minds of the intelligence forecasters to the limit.

Each man at the dinner put his point of view except the MI6 official who did 'not want to be involved in such a defeatist discussion'.[49] Paul Ham wrote that Young and Fitzgerald persisted with their belief that 'Hanoi had one choice: a single massive uprising—a short sharp nationwide attack aimed at the cities'. Serong supposedly 'accepted the major offensive theory, but insisted, with great prescience, the South would fight back and fight well'.[50] But, in his 1994 interview with Anne Blair, his biographer, Serong said:

Several weeks before the Tet Offensive happened, it was obvious that something was going to happen. Those of us whose job it was to make estimates, we made our estimates. I made mine and my estimate was that there would be no attack because if they attacked they would be certainly destroyed. These people are not idiots. So therefore there won't be an attack.[51]

Paul Ham added that Young and Fitzgerald 'timed the conflagration for the Buddhist lunar holiday of Tet 1968, in the first week of February'.[52] That statement disagreed with Denis Warner's report, which said that Peter Young had tipped the time. Warner may have meant time frame. In any case, no one tipped the time, not even the NVA commanders who attacked a day early in the Central Highland provinces in the early hours of 30 January 1968. The subsequent attacks that included Saigon started on 31 January.

Why there was a difference in the dates is open to a lot of speculation. Some commentators say it was just a simple hiccup, others believe that some of the enemy commanders thought that their plans had been discovered so they ordered an immediate attack. The idea that the commander of the enemy's *Military Region 5* (Central Highlands) used a different calendar to that used by *COSVN* is a better story. Bearing in mind that the attacks were to be launched during the first night of Tet, Hanoi had changed to the seventh time zone in August 1967 while Saigon remained on the eighth time zone, which was the traditional calendar for celebrations. Although there was only one hour's difference between the calendars, the lunar months change each solar year by about twelve days. This put the first day of Tet on the 1968 southern calendar at 30 January but in the North it fell on 29 January; hence, the misinterpretation of the attack timetable by the commanders.[53] Even the mythical invincible had their fallibilities.

Senior Lieutenant General Nguyen Huu confirmed the confused attack timetable years later. He wrote:

> On December 29, a telegram from the Command of Front B3 to the Command of the 1st Division said, "Our superiors' opinion is to defer the N [attack] day for one more day. Can we pull back our military formation?" It was said that trouble might result from the differences in calendars between the North and Saigon at that time.[54]

Peter Young had written a ten-page assessment on the military situation for the Australian Embassy. The paper was dated 9 July 1967 with a covering letter dated 27 July, which did not note any particular urgency in relation to what he had deduced about the enemy's activities. A single paragraph read, 'Attached is the paper on the military situation for your retention [addressee not shown]. Perhaps you could passit [sic] up if you feel it worth it'.[55] While the paper was an easy-to-read analysis on the recent years of war and the future possibilities, it was also just another hypothetical that could be lined up against several others then emerging in Saigon. One of Peter Young's conclusions matched Denis Warner's tag of brilliance, and that was:

> He [the enemy] will wait until he has maximum potential for a coordinated effort throughout the country. In assessing his potential . . .[the enemy] will wait until he has completed a major reinforcement . . . [that would allow] . . . a major effort across the DMZ with a coordinated effort throughout Two Corps and a

secondary harassment throughout the remainder of the country, with a possible special effort against Saigon. If [this] course is accepted, then the period is given as September to January with December as the most likely time.[56]

Even though the Australian Ambassador saw the paper, it apparently was not sent further through the External Affairs network. Young explained that a specific date was not provided at that time because he could not identify his source material to people who were not security cleared to the highest level. The claim by Paul Ham that Australian generals Wilton and Daly ignored or downgraded the report is made without foundation.[57] That allegation does not recognise that Peter Young's paper was a military appreciation, not an intelligence analysis. Young's conclusions were based upon some generally known facts plus selected assumptions about the enemy's behaviour and possible intentions.

At this stage in the planning process the leadership in the North was severely divided and several purges of officials took place before approvals for an offensive were released later in the year. Ironically, the first of these purges took place in Hanoi on the same day that Peter Young submitted his paper, 27 July. With the differences between the northern leadership's strategic concepts being so significant, one of Peter Young's options had guessed at a possible course of action that even the northern command had not yet decided to follow.[58]

In any case, the Peter Young paper would be overtaken by a rapidly changing sequence of events and an increasing flow of information that brought with it more arguments on what the enemy's possible intentions might be. As Major General Phillip Davidson, the MACV J-2 (Intelligence), said:

Even if I had known exactly what was to take place, it was so preposterous that I probably would have been unable to sell it to anybody. Why would the enemy give away his major advantage, which was his ability to be elusive and avoid heavy casualties?[59]

General Davidson's statement is a direct challenge to the notion also mentioned in Paul Ham's book that Major Fitzgerald dressed as a People's Army colonel to brief General Westmoreland in September 1967. If Davidson didn't believe that a nationwide attack against the cities was planned, then it would be unheard of for one of his junior officers to dress up and deliver an unapproved hypothesis to COMUSMACV.[60]

When the intelligence heated to the point that it was now a foregone conclusion that something big was definitely going to happen, a CIA analyst based in Saigon could not believe his own findings. A CIA team that included Joseph Hovey resolved that an attack against the cities was pending and 'the message was passed to General Westmoreland [on 23 November] and eventually to President Johnson on 15 December 1967'.[61] It appeared that some people within the intelligence agencies had drawn the right conclusions about what the enemy was going to do, but the majority of the fragmented intelligence community kept looking for other objectives. There is no doubt that an attack was anticipated, as President Johnson told the Australian Cabinet on 21 December 1967 that he expected 'kamikaze attacks in Vietnam'.[62]

Battle preparations

Tactical uncertainties had beset some of the allied generals in the second half of 1967. There was a decrease in activity along the DMZ, but an increase along the western edge of the Highlands. Then back near the DMZ, battles erupted around Con Thien, but in III and IV Corps areas things went quiet after the September South Vietnamese presidential elections. Heavy fighting in the Western Highlands near Dak To followed in November. Westmoreland was pleased with this because it 'would allow his forces to make maximum use of [their] superior mobility and firepower in inflicting severe losses on the NVA/VC forces'.[63] With one eye fixed upon the tri-border area—Laos–Cambodia–Vietnam—most attention was now focused on the northern I Corps and Khe Sanh, in particular.

A predicted offensive was studied in terms of a Dien Bien Phu style battle that would culminate in some form of negotiation. A Battle of the Bulge analogy from World War II was also discussed; it was a battle that both generals Westmoreland and Abrams had experienced. Then there were considerations on the possibility of attacks at Christmas time and the impact that might have on the American public. Tet was seen as sacrosanct. (There were some who knew of the 1789 Tet attack against the Chinese, a bit far back in history for the current planners, but old hands in this war might have recalled the 26 January 1960 attack in Tay Ninh. It had been the start of a new phase of warfare and the attack 'gained additional symbolic importance ... by occurring on the eve of Tet', the US Joint Chiefs of Staff had said back then.)[64]

By the end of 1967, both sides had moved to prepare themselves for battle. The northern leaders had sent new commanders to the Central Highlands and to *COSVN*. Training cadres strengthened the resolve of the fighters in the South and detailed training pamphlets had been distributed, some cunningly disguised as the teachings of Buddha. Ho Chi Minh read a four-line poem over Radio Hanoi in December in which he wished the Vietnamese people success in the coming Year of the Monkey. Many historians now believe that the poem signalled Hanoi's approval for the *general offensive – general uprising* that followed.[65]

Inside the tactically critical III Corps, Lieutenant General Frederick Weyand reported that his troops had pushed the enemy out from the more heavily populated areas and into the border regions. As a result, conditions around Saigon had improved so much that the US 199th Light Infantry Brigade (LIB) could leave the primary security responsibility of the Capital Military District to the 5th ARVN Ranger Group. Three of Weyand's American divisions—the 1st, 9th and 25th—continued to conduct successful operations in an arc around Saigon that damaged enemy operations in *War Zones C* and *D*, and as a result more responsibilities were transferred to ARVN formations. 'The Viet Cong were also in serious straits in Phuoc Tuy and Long Khanh Provinces where allied pressure had broken down their supply system.' New clashes out in the western border regions suggested that a major dry-season effort would launch out of the Cambodian border zone and Weyand thought that an attack was probably coming after a Tet truce.[66]

On 10 December 1967, General Westmoreland issued a directive which obliged Lieutenant General Weyand to adopt 'a border strategy and deployment posture ... both to destroy his [enemy] main force units ... and to frustrate any large scale Tet truce violation'. This plan would have placed 39 of Weyand's available 53 battalions outside the allied base area and up to 150 kilometres from Saigon.[67] Following a series of enemy attacks against several district and provincial capitals, some information was found that warned of more enemy action. The details obtained from those documents indicated that the enemy would conduct a major offensive against the cities. The Tet period remained an inviolable time in the minds of the allied commanders and their staff, however.

While each side was manoeuvring to obtain some form of tactical advantage, the Viet Cong played out an interesting radio game during a battle on 5 January 1968. A MACV report commented upon the misconception in previous years that the enemy were unsophisticated in technical communications and as an example the report highlighted this attempt by the enemy to stop artillery fire:

A voice, with an Australian accent radioed a request that the commander of the 4th Battalion of the 49th ARVN Regiment refrain from further artillery firing in the area. The requester claimed to be a member of an Australian team, which had been inserted by the '173'. A check . . . confirmed that no personnel were out of their area of operations and the fake request was not honored.[68]

Australian Major William E. Hughes, OC 547 Signals Troop also noted, years later:

The lack of enemy transmissions, from around 10 January 1968, across the frequency bands most commonly used by the Viet Cong, failed to detect any transmissions by *274* and *275 Regiments* or their sub-units. It appeared . . . that *5 Viet Cong Division* had disappeared completely from the airwaves.[69]

According to the *5th Viet Cong Division*'s history, the division had moved well away from Phuoc Tuy Province in September 1967. During the period before Tet 1968 they were retraining and, in accord with their usual routine, radio silence would have prevailed. If their radio silence only became apparent on 10 January 1968 then they were much smarter with their signals behaviour than 547 Troop gave them credit. No one had picked that they had gone far away from Phuoc Tuy Province[70]

When the information on the enemy's probable attack intentions had reached fever pitch in January 1968, General Westmoreland changed his directive on the deployment of allied forces. One of the saving graces for South Vietnam during the Tet Offensive came about because General

Frederick Weyand had turned, or had requested permission to turn, his force inwards to protect the main basin of population around Saigon. As General Davidson said in a later interview:

> Fred really opposed Westmoreland's ... big-unit war. His senior pacification adviser [John Paul Vann] had decided that we were fighting the war the wrong way. So he [Weyand] began to pull his forces back in toward Saigon. This coincided with Fred's natural bent ... I don't think he really foresaw it; if he did, he was careful not to tell anybody. He told General Westmoreland ... and Westmoreland says, well, you go ahead and do it, because we're seeing the same thing.[71]

General Westmoreland did not acknowledge that Weyand had influenced his decision to change his December directive. In his 1968 *Report on the War in Vietnam*, he wrote:

> In January I modified previous plans to conduct major offensive operations into the enemy's well-established base areas in *War Zones C* and *D* ... and directed Lt. Gen. Frederick C. Weyand ... to strengthen US forces in the areas around Saigon by redeploying forces which had been targeted on the bases of the Viet Cong main forces and the North Vietnamese Army.[72]

Weyand did meet with Westmoreland on 9 January 1968, which would indicate that the change of directive on this occasion was probably a decision by mutual agreement. In any case, the new directive included the Australian Task Force and General Weyand reported:

> The 1st Australian Task Force (1 ATF) commenced its first operation outside Phuoc Tuy Province when two of its three battalions conducted Operation *Coburg* in AO *Columbus* against the suspected locations of the *274, 275 Viet Cong Regiments* and the *5th Viet Cong Division*.[73]

The battle for Bien Hoa and Long Binh

Operation Coburg eventually ran for five weeks (24 January – 1 March) in the northeastern sector of Bien Hoa Province. The three Australian battalions—2RAR/NZ (ANZAC), 3 and 7RAR—as well as supporting arms were involved. The value of having a three-battalion Task Force proved itself in several ways during this deployment. One battalion would remain at Nui Dat for local protection—initially this was 3RAR—and that fortuitously placated some of the military and political criticisms that followed this operation. The initial plan for Operation Coburg was to conduct reconnaissance in force from two fire support bases—Harrison and Anderson—and to prevent enemy ground and rocket attacks against the vast Long Binh–Bien Hoa base area. Subsequently, the Task Force mission was altered to block and destroy the NVA/Viet Cong elements within an expanded area of operations named Columbus.

The Australian Operation Order 4/68 (Coburg) badly underestimated the enemy forces that were possibly in the area of Columbus. Admittedly they just repeated the American summary, which said that elements of *273 Regiment (9th Viet Cong Division)*, up to a battalion group of *274 Regiment* and small elements of the *Dong Nai Regiment* might be in the area. Although the allies carried the *Dong Nai Regiment* as an independent formation, in Pribbenow's book that title belonged to the *274 Regiment*. It is apparent from other reports that two separate formations had that title although the allies rarely referred to the *274th Viet Cong Regiment* as *Dong Nai*. The Australian orders estimated that the identified units would be supported by up to a battalion of *84A Rocket Regiment* and an assortment of local force VC units.

It wasn't long before the fighting began and during the week of 25–31 January, the Australians had 41 contacts, during which 45 of the enemy were killed. As a result, an interesting mix of weapons was also captured that suggested the dead enemy soldiers were mainly local force who had been committed to prepare the battlefield and guide the main force units to their assembly areas. Despite the increasing tempo of clashes the enemy's true order of battle had not yet been identified. One point was clear, there were a lot of them—so many that SAS patrols could not operate—and the enemy were on the move.[74]

Then in the early hours of 31 January, the 1968 Tet Mau Than battles— *New Year of the Monkey*—merged into one rolling series of explosive firefights across the fields, districts, provinces and cities of South Vietnam. The NVA/ Viet Cong preparation for the attack on Saigon had started in December when *COSVN* disbanded its military region command structure that surrounded Saigon and Gia Dinh Province. In its place, six sub-regions were established for a multi-pronged assault upon the capital. In the northeast—*Sub-Region 5*—the main attack force was to be the *5th Viet Cong Division* supported by the *724th Artillery Regiment*. They were to coordinate their efforts with a sapper battalion and the *Bien Hoa Special Forces Company*. Their objective was to attack and seize the Bien Hoa airfield and the prisoner-of-war compound, the ARVN III Corps Headquarters, the US II Field Force Vietnam Headquarters at Long Binh, the Officer Training School at Thu Duc and join with the masses in the expected uprising to seize Bien Hoa City. From around 20 January, the *5th Viet Cong Division* command group conducted a reconnaissance of the main targets and the Viet Cong regiments were ordered to begin their approach marches.

According to the *5th Viet Cong Division*'s history, the *275 Regiment* crossed the Dong Nai River from the north and got to its assembly area at Hamlet 3 of Tan Dinh village, approximately 15 kilometres northeast of Bien Hoa airfield during the night of 29–30 January 1968. Deputy commander Nguyen Minh Thang marched *274 Regiment* from the vicinity of Suoi Quyt—west of Blackhorse—to the west of Trang Bom on Route 1, 20 kilometres east of Bien Hoa. One of its battalions was designated a deep strike unit and it plus Nguyen Nam Hung, the regimental commander, moved on to Thu Duc village, between Bien Hoa and Saigon. The battalion's task was to prepare for an attack upon the Dong Nai Bridge and the Thu Duc electrical generators. The *273 Viet Cong Regiment* was on the western side of the Dong Nai River, 30 kilometres away and well outside the Australians' area of responsibility.

The *5th Viet Cong Division* tactical headquarters and *275 Viet Cong Regiment* had slipped around the western edge of 7RAR, probably through river crossings as far out as the Cay Gao rubber plantation. The *84th Rear Services Group* had stocked food, equipment, weapons and tools in this area, which was 35 kilometres northeast of Bien Hoa. When the enemy evaded the Australians they moved into an operational area controlled by the American 199th Light Infantry Brigade that previously had the responsibility for AO Columbus. The 199th Brigade handed over to the Australians on 24 January and then moved back to strengthen the security around the Bien Hoa airfield and the two main headquarters—IIFFV and III Corps—and the prisoner-of-war compound that were located nearby. By pure chance, when the tactical division between the American and Australian forces was redrawn the enemy's forward headquarters and assembly areas were almost astride the new boundary. Fire Support Patrol Base (FSPB) Harrison—4 Field Regiment and 7RAR—for example, was just 2 kilometres north of the *5th Viet Cong Division*'s forward command post.

General Weyand forewarned the units of II Field Force Vietnam in a flash signal on 29 January about possible attacks and he directed units to a 'maximum alert posture through the TET period'.[75] The next day, a secondary explosion caused by artillery fire warned a patrol from the 199th Brigade that a large number of enemy soldiers were north of the Dong Nai River. This was just before midnight on 30 January and the brigade was placed on 'Red Alert'. Then, at 0105 hours on 31 January, a group of about 80 enemy soldiers with small arms and automatic weapons was reported 'double-timing' past Reconnaissance Team 37 near Ho Nai village just 4 kilometres to the east of II Field Force Vietnam's headquarters. As a result, helicopter gunships were aloft, a ready reaction force with armoured vehicles was on the move and artillery was ready to respond immediately with counter-bombardment fire.

Although the battalions of the *5th Viet Cong Division* had got around the outer screen of Australians, some elements were lost and they arrived at the area of their objectives in fragmented groups. In particular, *275 Viet Cong Regiment* had marched over 80 kilometres from Phuoc Long Province or northern *War Zone D* to their positions near Bien Hoa in four days. Tran Minh Tam, the *Bien Hoa Front* commander, ordered that the assaults would go ahead regardless.[76] The enemy began their offensive upon Bien Hoa–Long Binh with a widespread rocket and mortar barrage that started at 0300 hours on 31 January. *275 Regiment*—supported by local force *U-1 Battalion*—then attacked south across Route 1 through Ho Nai village and struck the perimeter of Long Binh at the Widows' Village, while *274 Regiment* hit Bien Hoa from the east.

The 199th Brigade, the US 2/47 Mechanised Battalion that had redeployed from Camp Bearcat, 15 kilometres southeast of Bien Hoa, and 3/17 Air Cavalry Squadron stopped the assault elements of *275 Regiment* and by 0600 hours they were 'killing them at the sustained rate'. Alpha Troop of 3/5 Cavalry caught two battalions of *274 Viet Cong Regiment* who had attacked from the east. The cavalry troop had advanced along Highway 1 from Blackhorse and they ploughed into the flank of the Viet Cong regiment and inflicted heavy casualties upon them. The 3rd Brigade, 101st Airborne Division was also directed to fly its 2/506 Battalion into Bien Hoa and attack south out through the east gate and link up with Alpha Troop.[77]

Although the Viet Cong ground forces got into and around some of their intended targets and their rockets destroyed two aircraft and damaged 23 others at the Bien Hoa airfield, they suffered badly. The powerful and very mobile American Army units all but destroyed the *5th Viet Cong Division*'s attack formations on 31 January. On that day the 199th Brigade reported that they had killed 527, captured 30 prisoners as well as 78 small arms and 68 crew-served weapons.[78] The 11th Armored Cavalry Regiment in one daring and notable move applied the final crushing blow. The cavalry pulled out of operations around the Michelin rubber plantation in northern Binh Duong Province on 31 January and moved over 100 kilometres in ten hours to reinforce the Bien Hoa–Long Binh bases by the end of the day.

A concerted allied fighting effort continued over the next three days before the threat was fully extinguished and the enemy force was dispersed and in retreat. In two days of fighting according to the *5th Viet Cong Division* they had lost 728 comrades, had more than 1000 wounded and suffered heavy losses to equipment and weapons.[79]

The Australians were deadly during this period, which was the second week of their deployment into Bien Hoa Province, when they had 55 contacts and killed 90 Viet Cong. Their task now was to block elements of the *5th Viet Cong Division* who were fleeing in disarray from the slaughter of the Bien Hoa battlefield. The Australian efforts attracted a commendable comment by General Weyand, which was noted in the *MACV Command History*:

ATF commenced its first operation outside Phuoc Tuy on 24 January . . . to the east of Bien Hoa city. Up until 31 January the 1ATF had been operating offensively to the northeast of AO *Columbus*. Once the attacks on Long Binh demonstrated that the bulk of the Viet Cong were between Long Binh and *Columbus*, the ATF did a tactical about face, and deployed a series of company and platoon sized day and night ambushes between the Dong Nai River and Highway 1. It was during this period, roughly 4–8 February that the two battalions began to exact their toll from the Viet Cong.[80]

Apparently expecting success, the enemy units had not planned a withdrawal. Although it is not absolutely clear which routes the enemy regiments used to get away from Bien Hoa, the IIFFV report said that both Viet Cong regiments moved towards *War Zone D*, although more clashes indicated that *274 Regiment* continued operations to the east of Bien Hoa in February and then moved back towards the general vicinity of its old base area in the block of territory on the edge of Phuoc Tuy Province formed by highways 15, 1 and 2. The enemy wounded, according to the *5th Viet Cong Division*'s history, were taken to the Bau Tien surgical station. This was about 20 kilometres north of the Dong Nai River. The *275 Viet Cong Regiment* probably retreated back along the Dong Nai River through the Cay Gao base area and hid out somewhere west of Route 20, or headed towards *War Zone D*. Xuan Thanh, the regimental commander, was killed at some point in the operation. In the second phase of Tet that started in April 1968, *275 Viet Cong Regiment* was ordered to strike and seize Trang Bang, a town 40 kilometres northwest of Saigon on the road to Tay Ninh. This information supported the IIFFV report that the regiment had retreated back to *War Zone D* after the Bien Hoa battles.

In a subsequent phase of Operation Coburg, FSPB Anderson—3RAR— was assaulted on 18 February by a well-coordinated infantry attack that was supported by mortars, rocket-propelled grenades and machine guns. Seven Australians were killed and 22 were wounded, of which 13 needed to be evacuated. The number of casualties suffered by the Viet Cong was unknown. FSPB Anderson was attacked again the next day, 19 February, and four Viet Cong were killed. The members of 3RAR who fought and repelled the attack on Anderson might have been amused to learn that the enemy thought they were a US mechanised unit. The elements of *274 Viet Cong Regiment* involved in the attack reported:

> After a two-hour battle, the *3rd Battalion* and two companies of the *1st Battalion* had completely destroyed the enemy post [FSPB *Anderson*], driven more than 100 enemy from the battlefield, and destroyed seven military vehicles by fire.[81]

The Australian toll for the entire period of the Bien Hoa deployment was 17 killed and approximately 65 wounded. A mine also killed one New Zealander. It was a shock to the Australian system to have so many casualties over such a short period and the figures prompted questions from Australia. The casualties also brought home to the Australians that there were several types of warfare underway in this conflict. Nonetheless, in the eyes of General Weyand the Australians had played a key part in the disruption and defeat of the enemy's activities.

General A. L. MacDonald was not so happy. As noted by Ian McNeill and Ashley Ekins in *On the Offensive*, after he had seen some reports that Australians had fired upon Australians he concluded that:

> They were mostly due to a combination of poor (or even lack of orders), failure to observe such orders . . . and trigger-happy soldiers. He commented that despite the frequent praise he received from American commanders regarding the professionalism of the task force, these incidents highlighted the sheer lack of basic knowledge of many junior NCOs and officers. The army was paying the price . . . for its rapid expansion and transition.[82]

Command and control and controversy

Gough Whitlam, then the Leader of the Opposition in the House of Representatives, said in an interview with *The Australian* that the absence of the battalions from Phuoc Tuy had allowed the enemy to attack and occupy Baria. He followed that up with a statement to the House in March 1968 in which he said, 'for the first time in two years, areas which had seemed secure were proven not to be secure'.[83]

The *D445* attacks around Phuoc Tuy, along with other local force units, were reliant upon the bad assumption that the people would revolt against the government in support of the Viet Cong. *D445* was now commanded by Nguyen Van Kiem and consisted of 'four companies and 608 soldiers', its highest strength since it had been formed. *C610 Baria Town Company* supported the battalion and their attack objectives during the Tet Offensive were:

> The reconnaissance element attacked the administrative headquarters and the province Chief's official residence. The 1st Company attacked the self-propelled artillery base. The 2nd Company attacked the Police Field Force and the compound of the public security service. The 3rd Company attacked the

provincial Regional Force Group. By 3pm, all of the Battalion's attacking columns had still not been able to take all of the objectives.[84]

Initially the South Vietnamese Regional Forces took the brunt of these attacks, but 3 Battalion 52 Regiment from the 18th ARVN Division at Xuan Loc quickly reinforced them. The 52nd Ranger Battalion then landed at Van Kiep and soon after another South Vietnamese battalion, 4/48 ARVN, moved west from Dat Do. These were not easy battles, however, and a reaction force from 3RAR and the 3rd Cavalry Regiment were also sent from Nui Dat to strike at the enemy lodged in Baria.

The Viet Cong attack faltered when the defenders got over their initial shock of the assaults and the allied reinforcements trapped them in the pincers of multiple counterattacks. The Viet Cong losses were heavy: they admitted 35 were killed and 108 wounded and an even greater number seriously wounded—probably killed—that were unable to be evacuated. On the fourth day of Tet, *D445* withdrew two companies to Long Dien and another to the Rach Vang Bridge on Route 15 and admitted: 'The attack on Ba Ria Town was not the final battle. The victory at Tet Mau Than was not yet the final victory'. In other words, they had been defeated.[85]

Lieutenant General Weyand at IIFFV recognised the important role that the Australian force had played in the defeat of *D445* at Baria:

It was this small armored-infantry force which broke the Viet Cong grip on all of the key centers in and around Ba Ria. The Australian force swept to the center of the town and cleared the Viet Cong from the church, JUSPAO, the hospital, PRU Hq and theater. Later it relieved the district headquarters and the Van Kiep Training Center, where elements of 11 Abn Bn were in contact.[86]

Major Brian 'Horrie' Howard commanded Alpha Company, the 3RAR reaction force that included 3 Troop, A Squadron, 3 Cavalry Regiment. Second Lieutenant Roger Tingley commanded the APC troop. Howard's mission was to assist with the defence of Baria Sector Headquarters. Soon after their arrival, the fighting within Baria fragmented into separate smaller battles around the sector headquarters, a house in which the Provincial Reconnaissance Unit was based, as well as other allied compounds. The Australian soldiers were challenged not only by the ferocity of the enemy's actions but also by the confined urban spaces and a very confused overall battle picture.

To add to the battle conundrum, Major Howard was requested to rescue a Mr Johnson, an American who held important intelligence documents in his house. Although Johnson was rescued and the classified maps and documents were destroyed, he was killed on the way out of the compound when rocket-propelled grenades hit the rescue team's two armoured personnel carriers. AATTV Warrant Officer Tony Parrello was also killed. The carriers were initially abandoned until a company from the 52nd ARVN Ranger Battalion was requested to assist in their recovery, but their efforts failed. The enemy's positions were subsequently hit by air strikes that allowed for the withdrawal of the damaged vehicles. Howard's company then moved to the west of Baria, where in a brief, confused clash the South Vietnamese soldiers fired upon the leading Australian platoon. Fortunately there were no casualties.

Thereafter, the battle quietened to sporadic contact and sniper fire and on 2 February the Australians returned to Nui Dat. The fight in the built-up area was very different to the Australians' experiences in the jungle and Major Howard listed some of the lessons learnt from the battle for Baria:

> The APC and troops were very vulnerable inside the built up area. It was found better to move mounted at speed ... than to move with infantry deployed on foot. The RPG2 was used extensively by the Viet Cong ... [as was] the use of snipers. Stonewalls around the houses were a problem. Casualty evacuation was difficult because of the lack of safe areas ... and landing points. An increased scale of ammunition would have been valuable. Casualties claimed by the Australians were: A Company 30 Viet Cong killed and 14 possible; 3 Troop 10 Viet Cong killed. Alpha Company and 3 Troop suffered 19 wounded (12 evacuated) and three friendly were killed: Mr Johnson, Parrello and a Nung guard.[87]

The Australian efforts to secure and protect the area were also recognised by the people of Baria, who assisted them with information about the enemy and in the main rallied behind their protective shield.[88] The people of Long Dien were not so supportive.

The South Vietnamese saw the battles around Phuoc Tuy Province as 'harassment on the outskirts', even with the firefights through the built-up areas such as Baria and Long Dien. They also said that the Phuoc Tuy fighting and clashes in nineteen other provinces—there were 44 provinces in total—were 'relatively unimportant'. The South Vietnamese analysts believed that the enemy's plan was to achieve major successes in the prominent cities and such successes would automatically yield victory in these minor localities.[89] That analysis supported the decision by Brigadier Ron Hughes and Major General Douglas Vincent for the Australian Task Force to go out of Phuoc Tuy Province and help to defeat the NVA/Viet Cong major push, which would more effectively protect the minor areas than by staying in them.

General A. L. MacDonald told General Daly on 10 March 1968 that Phuoc Tuy had suffered relatively little damage, which may have been a little blasé if the IIFFV report was correct that 755 homes had been more than 50 per cent destroyed in the province, with 1000 people listed as refugees.[90] The cost to Phuoc Tuy in loss of civilian lives, houses destroyed and refugees taken in for care varied greatly between reports produced by Australian and American agencies. In an overall summary, the cost to Phuoc Tuy Province was substantially less than most other provinces.

General MacDonald and other senior Australian commanders, in Vietnam and Australia, expressed their belief that the Task Force could not isolate itself within Phuoc Tuy while more serious dangers lay nearby. Such thoughts opened again what now seemed to be the perennial debate about pacification versus search-and-destroy, which General Westmoreland believed was a much misunderstood term for the 'infantry's traditional attack mission'. In April 1968, he directed that search-and-destroy be replaced by 'basic military terminology such as, ambush, raid and reconnaissance in force'.[91] There were also suggestions that the Americans continued to try and pry the Australians out of the province and move them to more hectic locations. Although there were several informal discussions along these lines in 1967, and maybe into 1968, they fizzled out when there was a clear Australian political message that such a move would not be countenanced. Some generals did not support such a move either. There were certain zones within South Vietnam where the battles were fierce and no matter how good a force, the inevitable would be more dead and wounded. For example, 879 Americans were killed within the III Marine Amphibious Force area of operations in I Corps during the *month* of February 1968.

The Australian deployment question continued to baffle the American President, nevertheless. At a meeting with the US Joint Chiefs of Staff in Washington on 9 February 1968, the president asked:

> What mobile reserve forces does Westmoreland have between now and the time he gets more men? General Wheeler replied we are not getting much mileage out of the Australian or South Korean troops. They must go back to their home country for their orders. The president questioned, do you mean that the Australian and Korean commanders have to go back to their capital before they can be deployed? Wheeler, yes sir, they remain under the operational control of their government.[92]

One wonders what influence a trip to Australia had on the president's thinking about the Australian deployment in Vietnam during the 1960s. According to *The Australian*:

> Johnson's diary shows that he had dinner on June 17, 1942 with US journalist Bob Sherrod, who wrote for the magazines *Time* and *Life*, and was scathing about Australia's commitment to fight. After a briefing requested by Johnson, Sherrod wrote: 'The country in which we are building our last ditch in the Pacific is disappointing. It lacks resources. It lacks leaders and it lacks intelligence.' Johnson went on to paraphrase the journalist in his typed notes. 'The unified command in Hawaii and Australia is purely a myth', LBJ [Lyndon Baines Johnson] wrote. In a handwritten entry . . . 'too much jealousy among the brass hats'.[93]

At the February 1968 US Joint Chiefs of Staff meeting, Secretary of Defense Robert McNamara joined in:

> I am under the very clear impression that they have been told by their home governments to do everything possible to hold down their own casualties. Our losses are running six times the level of Korean losses on a percentage basis. The president replied we ought to try and bring all of the allied forces under Westmoreland's command. To which General Wheeler replied, in all fairness, the allies have operated well in areas where they have been located.[94]

But General Wheeler had not been happy with the efforts of Australia and at one point he had asked General Westmoreland directly whether Australia was pulling its weight. Wheeler's reply to the president's statement was an echo of Westmoreland's reply to him. The theme of the military discussions was one of respect for the Australian soldiers and exasperation at the restriction that kept them in a backwater province. Their combat skill was wanted elsewhere.

Perversely, the Americans who protected their commands with a passion and rejected command of their troops by other nationalities wanted to hold a tighter rein over the troops of their allies, except for the South Vietnamese. Westmoreland always argued against taking the ARVN under command as he believed an accusation of neo-colonialism would be levelled against him in propaganda if he did so. General Abrams was quite happy to allow Australians command over American units as he told the American Ambassador in 1969:

> The Australians and New Zealanders are <u>really</u> first-class people. We put American units under [? operational] command of the Australians . . . you just do, where the Australians are, what needs to be done, and nobody cares—either way.[95]

Unbeknown to many, Captain Ivan Cahill, an Australian infantry officer commanded Company E, 2nd Battalion, 3rd Marines from 6 November 1967 until 1 March 1968. He had slipped under the command radar rather neatly by being attached for training with the 2nd Battalion, 3rd Marines, Battalion Landing Team, which was a reserve unit afloat and which landed to support the 1st Marine Division operations in the districts to the south of Danang. Cahill remained with the battalion until his presence caught the eagle eye of Lieutenant General Victor Krulak, who directed that he be removed from command immediately, for the following reason:

> I realise that there is a precedent for such an assignment in peacetime. However, the combat environment is quite different, basically because the foreign officer has no disciplinary or administrative authority, and he cannot be brought to account under the UCMJ [Uniform Code of Military Justice] for derelictions in combat, which might affect US lives. This removal must be accomplished in a manner, which will cause no adverse reaction on his part, on the part of the troops involved or on the part of his government.[96]

The president had summoned his senior officers and advisers to come to his meeting in February 1968 on the basis that they would hope for the best and expect the worst. He wanted to see what the US should do in Vietnam, he told them. The Tet Offensive had clearly rattled them all and the battles that now raged at Khe Sanh and Hue were discussed in terms of an emergency situation. As the Australians had discovered during their out-of-province deployment for Operation Coburg, logistics was a key to success, now battles were raging further north and the logistics for the Americans equalled immense strategic lift proportions.

The battle at Khe Sanh

Following a trip to Khe Sanh in January 1968, Lieutenant General Phillip Davidson reported to General Westmoreland that the Marines were ill prepared for an attack on the combat base. Westmoreland was angered by the report and he sent his deputy General Creighton Abrams up to I Corps to take over.[97] The Westmoreland anger went deeper than just fixing up a command family tree, as General Abrams told General Earle Wheeler, Chairman of the Joint Chiefs of Staff:

> While the Marines are second to none in bravery, esprit and the intrinsic quality of their men, I consider them to be less qualified in the techniques and tactics of fighting than the US Army, the Korean Army and the Australians.[98]

The US Marine head of the MACV Combat Operations Centre, Brigadier General John Chaisson, said that he had warned Westmoreland if 'he took tactical command away [from Cushman, the CG III MAF and senior American in I Corps] that he could never again expect the real loyalty of any Marine commanders in the country'.[99] The NVA manoeuvring to surround and attack Khe Sanh had unwittingly created psychological distress at the highest level of the American operational command that rippled out from MACV across the Pacific and into the bowels of the Pentagon.

The US combat base at Khe Sanh was wrapped around a 1200 metre long airstrip on the Xom Cham Plateau where the French had built a small light aircraft strip in 1949. A ring of hills dominated by the 1000 metre high

Tiger Tooth Mountain surrounded the base, which was 2 kilometres north of Route 9 and 25 kilometres south of the DMZ in the remote northwestern segment of South Vietnam. Route 9 started inside South Vietnam at Dong Ha, 15 kilometres north of Quang Tri, and wound its way through some very dangerous countryside to the border town of Lao Bao, 10 kilometres beyond Khe Sanh. The road was impassable owing to enemy action, which made Khe Sanh dependent upon air resupply. This included materials for all of the fortifications. Water for the base was pumped up from the Rao Quan River, which flowed south from the hills controlled by the NVA. Surprisingly they didn't interfere with the stream, which would have caused serious problems for the Marine defenders.

Although no Australians fought in what became known as the Siege of Khe Sanh, the AATTV had a connection to the district in earlier years when men like Ray Simpson, VC, DCM were deployed there to assist the Special Forces team then at Lao Bao and later at the village of Khe Sanh. For three weeks in April 1967, WO2 Bert Gruetzner was part of a recently installed MACV advisory team put into the village after a dreadful bombing accident at Lang Vei. On 2 March 1967, two USAF aircraft struck the village by mistake, killing 112 civilians, wounding 213 and destroying 140 buildings. The bombing prompted MACV to rush a newly formed team led by Major James Whitenack out to the village. Whitenack had not long arrived from Germany and he was established in an administrative position when he was literally given some rations and a radio and told to go to the village of Khe Sanh.

The Khe Sanh threat raised a tactical conundrum for Westmoreland. Was this a deliberate plan to pull the American strength away from not only the northern cities, but also from southern regions as well? The potential battleground also had an ominous similarity to the fields of Dien Bien Phu that worried the commanders and the politicians to the point of distraction. The American President was so absorbed by the fight that a model of Khe Sanh was built in the White House situation room where 'at critical periods during the siege the president received reports at 50-minute intervals'. President Johnson also 'demanded repeated assurance from the Joint Chiefs that Westmoreland would be able to hold the firebase'.[100]

During the first week of the main battle, 22–29 January 1968, 3000 tactical fighter strikes and over 200 B-52 sorties bombed around Khe Sanh with the rules of engagement relaxed to permit the B-52s to drop within 1 kilometre of the base. One NVA soldier, a veteran of Dien Bien Phu, wrote in his notebook:

> From the beginning until the 60th day, the B-52 bombers continually dropped their bombs . . . at any moment of the day. If someone came to visit this place, he might say that this was a storm of bombs and ammunition, which eradicated all living creatures and vegetation, even those located in caves or in deep underground shelters.[101]

Khe Sanh was relieved in April, but the arguments over its purpose raged on. NVA General Tran Van Tra said in a post-war interview that Khe Sanh was a diversion, nothing more than a feint to get the Americans to move their forces away from the main cities.[102] General Davidson, MACV J-2, said that the siege made no discernible sense. The claim that Giap besieged Khe Sanh to divert US forces from his attacks on the cities was obvious nonsense, he thought. There was a greater need for the NVA forces at Quang Tri City and Hue. This was a corps-sized force and Giap must have had some important purpose in mind for it other than tying down a few Marine battalions at Khe Sanh, Davidson wrote.[103] General Abrams called him 'poor old Giap'. He said:

> Look at Khe Sanh. . . [he] chewed those divisions up so there wasn't a damn thing left . . . if he'd been the brilliant tactical commander . . . [and] moved one or both of those divisions down on the coastal plain. I don't know how the hell we'd ever gotten them out of there.
>
> I don't think Giap is very smart [underlining in original].[104]

Westmoreland was in no doubt that Khe Sanh was important to the security of the western flank of the top two provinces of South Vietnam. The Marines had differences of opinion, but it was Westmoreland's call that counted—and his decision was to defend the base. He also argued that it was better to fight the enemy in the remote and relatively deserted mountain area rather than in villages along the coast. And, of course, a withdrawal from Khe Sanh would be seen as a major psychological blow that General Giap could use to his distinct advantage.

The American fear, from the top down, was a Dien Bien Phu style defeat. In a January 1968 top-secret message that was repeated in a Marine Corps back channel signal, General Westmoreland spelt out how Khe Sanh was different to Dien Bien Phu. In the final paragraph of that message, Westmoreland replied to a question from General Earle Wheeler:

> The use of *tactical nuclear weapons should not be required* in the present situation. However, *should the situation in the DMZ area change dramatically we should be prepared to introduce weapons of greater effectiveness against massed forces* [emphasised]. Under such circumstances I visualise that either tactical nuclear weapons or chemical agents would be active candidates for employment.[105]

A summary of notes taken of a meeting at Washington on 26 March 1968, which the president attended, recorded that 'the use of atomic weapons is unthinkable'.[106]

In the end, the battle became a siege whereby the Marines maintained an impenetrable barrier around Khe Sanh and a deadly curtain of air power shattered the NVA divisions beyond the wire. The North Vietnamese losses were dreadful. If there was the slightest hint in the NVA commander's plan that Khe Sanh could be another Dien Bien Phu, rather than a feint, then not knowing the true capabilities of US air power was an unforgivable error that presented the northern leaders with a butcher's bill, a death list that they did not admit to their people.[107] Although the information is disputed, General Vo Nguyen Giap was allegedly based nearby to control the battle.[108]

The battle statistics are staggering. The artillery at the camp fired 158,891 rounds in direct support. Fighter-bombers from the three services dropped 38,789 tons of bombs and B-52s unleashed a further astounding 59,542 tons. MACV staff estimated that between 10,000 and 15,000 NVA soldiers were lost, but based upon latter-day information these figures are considered to be dubious. The official casualty figure for American forces—these numbers exclude ARVN casualties—was 205 killed, 1668 wounded and one missing. An unofficial, but probably more accurate figure is 353 Marines killed between 20 January and 31 March 1968.[109]

After the allies withdrew from the base and deliberately destroyed it, the North claimed: 'We had liberated an important strategic area in the western part of Route 9 in Quang Tri province and expanded our strategic North–South transportation corridor',[110] a strategy for Khe Sanh that was more important than a feint, it would seem.

The battle for Hue

Hue was the third-largest city in South Vietnam, with a population of approximately 120,000 in 1968. A magnificent citadel of 6.5 square kilometres abutting the northern bank of the Song Huong—Perfume River—dominated the city.[111] This immense fortification encompassed and protected an imperial palace of approximately 1 square kilometre, which was immediately inside the southern wall. Stone walls that were up to 6 metres thick and 9 metres in height, as well as a moat, surrounded a maze of narrow streets and houses in which most of the city's civilians lived. A small airstrip—Tay Loc—of around 800 metres cut an asphalt pathway through the western sector of the stronghold. This strip permitted light aircraft to operate in support of the ARVN's 1st Division Headquarters adjoining the Mang Ca compound, which was in the north corner of the citadel. Brigadier General Ngo Quang Truong commanded the division and he was renowned throughout Vietnam as one of the best, if not the best of the ARVN generals.

A lightly guarded MACV advisers' compound that included some Australians from the AATTV was located across the river to the south, just over the Nguyen Hoang Bridge and to the east of Highway 1. There were a few other small detachments nearby, such as a radar station to the east of the compound, and some US Navy personnel at the boat ramp near the southern pylon of the Nguyen Hoang Bridge. Many of the ARVN officers and men lived on the southern side of the river, too. The main buildings housing the Thua Thien provincial administration and the jail, a hospital complex, Hue University, the main power station and the police compound were all located to the south of the river.

Hue carried an air of royal approval from the days of the emperor, which permeated the local society who treated both the North and the South with disdain. The war flowed around the city, perhaps because of its regal standing among all Vietnamese. No American units were stationed at Hue and only two ARVN companies were in the immediate vicinity of the citadel at the end of January. These were the division's understrength Reconnaissance Company and the famed Hac Bao—Black Panthers—the Ready Reaction Company. Lieutenant Nguyen Tri Tan commanded the Reconnaissance Company and his adviser was Terry Egan, an AATTV warrant officer.[112] Lieutenant Tran Ngoc Hue, known as 'Harry', commanded the Hac Bao and his adviser was American Marine Captain James Coolican.

Although the 1st ARVN Division had three regiments they were dispersed across the two top provinces with the 1st Regiment 50 kilometres away in Quang Tri and the 2nd Regiment further north at Dong Ha. The 3rd Regiment was sprinkled around the districts that surrounded Hue. Two troops of the ARVN 7th Cavalry were stationed in the province; the 3rd Troop was north of Hue at Post Kilometre-17 (PK-17) and the 1st Troop was south of the citadel. The South Vietnamese 1st Airborne Task Force, part of the country's strategic reserve, also had two battalions at PK-17, which was 17 kilometres north of Hue.

When the first attacks of the Tet Offensive further south were reported no one expected a major attack on the city, but Brigadier General Truong felt uneasy. When Saigon cancelled the Tet truce on 30 January he ordered his troops back to duty, but many of the men had gone on leave. The available numbers were well down, with some units significantly understrength. Fortuitously, his headquarters remained manned inside the citadel.

General Truong also sent his Reconnaissance Company to patrol out to the west, which was a likely avenue of approach for the enemy. Lieutenant Tan's company was down to only 36 men and he moved them cautiously along the edge of the river to a small hill that overlooked Route 549. This road skirted the royal tombs and then linked with several other avenues of approach into Hue, which made his position a good point for an observation post. The patrol was about 7 kilometres north of Nam Hoa when it settled down to watch over the area. Lieutenant Tan recalled his experience of that night:

1st Recon Company was not full of soldiers, because some of them have been taking leave. We must go to field in urgent, so we couldn't call them back [to the] company. At the overnight position, I discovered [an] enemy artillery position from the mountain area of Nam Hoa district. I immediately reported to the Division Headquarters, and also requested friendly artillery counter-fire.[113]

The rocket-artillery that fired from the hills to the west of Tan's position was the major blast of activity that heralded a main attack and ended any attempt at a silent penetration of the city. Not long after this barrage, Lieutenant Tan said:

> In [the] morning [31 January], it is very early, we saw some big enemy element moving direction to the Hue city [units of the *5th NVA Regiment*], and they shot some recoilless rifle shell into our position, but did not attack my company position. Then 1st Division headquarters ask us to move to a location on the road connecting [Route 550] Long Tho Training Centre with 101st Combat Engineer Battalion (near railway bridge) [southwestern corner of the citadel, but on the south side of the river] about two hours later we continue to move up to the 101st battalion compound to reinforce this battalion.[114]

The attack had now burst into a ferocious assault that was aided by the bad weather. During the immediate reaction, a helicopter flown by Lieutenant Colonel Jackson, the Commanding Officer of the US 227th Aviation Battalion, was shot down. ARVN soldiers from the 127th Ferry Company located on the southern side of the Perfume River and immediately adjacent to the 101st ARVN Engineer Battalion rescued the wounded crew. Lieutenant Tan remembered that another helicopter came soon after:

> After the Engineer soldiers come out to rescue the crew, one helicopter has been sent to pick them up and at the same time the senior advisor (Australian) [WO2 Egan] helped the crews (pilots and gunners) and accompany them. The advisers had to fire to get to the compound because the situation was very serious. In about two weeks later, our company left the 101st Engineer Battalion to link up with 1/5th USMC Battalion, after that the advisers continued to work with us. We combine operated with USMC until Hue city liberated.[115]

Chief Warrant Officer Fred Ferguson flew the helicopter rescue mission. His crew chief was Jack Etzle, who remembered the pick-up:

> The compound was real tight; we just made it in. It was very foggy; we broke through at about 300 feet and started to receive automatic fire right then. As I

remember there were eight soldiers picked up from that compound. We were under heavy fire the whole time; I was busy trying to return fire and help get everybody on board. When we finally got out we took a lot of hits, but we did make it to a medical unit that was at Phu Bai. We were escorted by two gunships. After we got to Phu Bai, we did a check of the helicopter and counted 209 hits.[116]

Ferguson was awarded the Congressional Medal of Honor, the co-pilot Captain Buck Anderson received a Silver Star and Jack Etzle was honoured with a Distinguished Flying Cross. Warrant Officer Terry Egan received the Distinguished Conduct Medal for his outstanding conduct under fire.

The attack on Hue became a multi-pronged assault by at least eight battalions plus supporting units that included sappers. These troops were adept at getting through minefields or any other obstacles that appeared to be impenetrable. Grappling hooks were used in attempts to climb over the citadel's walls and some men crawled through a drain in the southeastern wall to get inside the defences. Their principal target was the 1st ARVN Division's headquarters. If that fell, the division's morale and battle resolve would have crumbled.

On the southern side of the river, the MACV compound also came under attack. Captain Jim Coolican, the Hac Bao adviser, had just got back to the compound following an operation up in the Quang Tri area. He remembered:

When we arrived in Hue, instead of allowing the soldiers to go home we went into a defensive position; this probably saved the Division HQ from being overrun. When the first salvo of rockets hit around 0330 hours, I was back at the MACV compound. It was obvious that this was a major attack. The compound was not organised or prepared for the attack, resulting in confusion and lack of leadership.[117]

Even though a major battle had exploded around the allied troops, information about what had happened was not clear—the enemy had cut the telephone lines—and at one point it was thought that General Truong's headquarters had fallen and that he was captured. The initial saviours inside the citadel were the 50 Hac Bao soldiers, commanded befittingly by Lieutenant Tran Ngoc 'Harry' Hue, born at Hue and named for the city. They, and some ARVN administrative personnel, held back the NVA *800th Battalion* that had tried to capture the Tay Loc airfield. Two enemy battalions had got into the citadel from the west; the other battalion, the *802nd*, went for the 1st Division headquarters.

Lieutenant Hue had been at home when the attack began and as he raced to get to his company's position he virtually pushed his way through disoriented enemy soldiers. He remembered:

> My home was near An Hoa gate [the northwest corner]. When the Tet fireworks came, I am thinking it was too intense. I got up and got dressed in my gear. I saw the North Vietnamese sappers on the road. But, I hesitated, not knowing whether to go or stay at home with my wife and daughter – she is my first born only one month ago. But, I rethink the responsibilities of a soldier and commander. So I've got to do my duty. So I see them [the enemy] move to the other side, I ride a bicycle slowly behind them. I waited until they turned left at the airstrip area and I went very fast to my headquarters and put everything on the front line.[118]

The Hac Bao held off the first of the assaults against the airfield and during the battle they caught two enemy soldiers, which Harry Hue recalled:

> We capture two NVA and I asked where were they from and how long they wished to stay here? One week or two weeks, they said and they also said they came from North Vietnam. They are frightened and think that we will shoot them. I tell them, you are prisoner without gun we do not kill you. If you have a gun and shoot, we will shoot you. I then put them in the rear and one or two of my fellows take care of them. We then counter attack and fortify the airstrip. We also help the transportation people there.[119]

At about five or six o'clock, Lieutenant Hue got in contact with the headquarters by radio. He recalled what happened then:

> I hear on the communication channel Colonel Chung call the cavalry squadron at An Cuu [Nui Tam Thai] to the south of the city. Colonel Chung tells the squadron commander to take the M-41 tanks to Division Headquarters right away. The commander replied that they are surrounded; it's hard to get out. Chung then threatened to court martial the cavalry commander. But 15 minutes later, the cavalry headquarters is destroyed [commander was killed]. Some tanks later meet with Marines from Phu Bai.[120]

That was when Lieutenant Colonel Ngo Van Chung, the division's senior operations officer, ordered the Black Panthers to consolidate the defence at the 1st Division's headquarters. Harry Hue led his men back along the internal canal to the bridge that entered the southern side of the division's compound. To get into the compound they had to fight their way across the bridge, which cost the Hac Bao a section of men but they made it in time to stop another enemy assault on the headquarters. The defenders didn't have the power of heavy fire support because no artillery or air attack was permitted against the citadel. For the first day and night, Harry Hue built a defensive phalanx centred on his few battle-experienced warriors who remained. The men he had posted across the river to protect some of the facilities on the south bank had been destroyed as a fighting force. The remainder of his group consisted of a mixed bunch of clerks, cooks and administrative personnel that included the division's band. One real concern for Harry and his men was the loss of contact with Jim Coolican, their adviser. They also thought that the Americans might have left them behind. Harry recalled a pact sworn among them at the time:

Ok, we said if you leave us behind we will fight until the last bullet and save one for each of us. We swear, me and my officers and my children [his soldiers]. If our allies leave us behind, it is no way to survive.[121]

In an untimely coincidence, Marine formations in I Corps were being shuffled as a result of a recent change to operational areas that had moved the 3rd Division further north into Quang Tri. Ironically, this placed Brigadier General Foster C. La Hue in command of Task Force X-Ray based at Phu Bai just south of Hue City. When the battles burst across the region, La Hue was directed to provide a reaction force to go to Hue but he didn't know what had happened. Initially it seemed to be one of many clashes, so La Hue only sent a company of Marines that drove up Highway 1 and fought their way through to the MACV Compound on 31 January. Soon after their arrival at around 1425 hours, the Marines were ordered to get into the citadel and to get General Truong safely away. That directive turned into a bloody task. Several platoons attempted to get across the Nguyen Hoang Bridge without major fire support. Despite their gallant efforts they could not and they were forced back with heavy casualties. American (M-48) and Vietnamese (M-41) tanks provided fire support, but the Americans did not employ heavy weapons against the citadel at this stage. The American commanders had sensibly decided that any fighting damage to be caused in the clearing of the imperial grounds was to be done by the South Vietnamese, or on their explicit orders. These came later.

At first, it was anticipated that the fighting in the Hue area would be over in a few days at the maximum. The operation officially ended on 2 March 1968. At the end, the Marines and the South Vietnamese had fought bitter battles around the city walls and through the houses and the rubble of the streets on both sides of the river to destroy the enemy. This was the equivalent of the classic World War II battle for Berlin and the Marines had to learn old tricks, quickly. All of their training and previous experience had been in the paddy fields and jungle. Blasting entrenched enemy out of solid stoneworks was a whole new ball game. The final death knell for the enemy came when elements of the 1st Cavalry Division (Airmobile) blocked the western approaches to the city and strangled enemy resupply and escape routes. It was a bloody month during which a lot of good men died. The NVA/Viet Cong count was imprecise, but guessed to be somewhere between 2500 and 5000. The allied losses were:

> USMC had 142 killed and more than 1100 wounded. The 1st Air Cavalry Division and the 1st Brigade, 101st Airborne Division had 74 killed and 510 wounded. The ARVN lost 333 and a further 1775 wounded. A total of 549 killed and probably more than 3400 wounded.[122]

A fact not so well known is that eight Australian AATTV soldiers fought with their ARVN units or were actively involved in the Hue Tet Offensive. Their battles began with Terry Egan's first observations on 31 January and went through to the final retaking of the citadel and the raising of the South Vietnamese flag on 24 February at 1515 hours. Captain Don Campbell was at the 1st Division's headquarters and later in February Captain Neville Wilson made it back to Nam Hoa village from Saigon where he had been trapped when that city was attacked. WO2 Graham Snook was with 3 Troop, 7th Armoured Cavalry who were ordered, along with the 7th Airborne Battalion, to break through an enemy cordon about 400 metres north of the citadel, but had their first two carriers knocked out by anti-tank fire. Graham Snook was awarded a Mention-in-Despatches for his exceptional gallantry. WO1 Max Evans, WO2 Tony Egan (not related to Terry), WO2 Donald MacDonald, and WO2 Barry Silk were also in the front line with their ARVN battalions as they fought a deadly struggle firstly to get into the walled fortress and then to defeat the enemy lodged within.

In one final act of perverse bastardry, the NVA rounded up several thousand southerners from Hue and surrounding districts and executed them. The exact number has never been determined but it has been put at between 3000 and 6000 people. North Vietnamese officials denied that atrocities took place, but Truong Nhu Tang admitted in his *A Viet Cong Memoir*:

> This initial victory [at Hue], however, had not turned out to be one of the revolution's prouder moments. Large numbers of people had been executed, most of them either associated with the government or opponents of the revolution. Others had been killed as well . . . captured American soldiers and several other foreigners who were not combatants.[123]

The killings emotionally devastated one Australian soldier, WO2 Donald Killion, an AATTV medical adviser at Hue. A little over a year later, he wrote:

> I was instructed to visit Nam Hoa District Village to ascertain whether it was a fact that the remains of some of the victims of the massacre (Tet, 1968) had been found. Approximately one thousand bodies had been retrieved and placed in Nam Hoa Village. I cannot, in words, describe the scene that confronted me when I arrived at this place. A shrine had been erected and the skeletons separated, i.e. skulls together, femur bones together, etc. In front of the shrine was a large open space where skeletons were laid on plastic for identification. The skeletons were with clothes and jewellery intact. Relatives were identifying bodies. It was a devastating sight, but being a professional soldier, my outward appearance was one of calmness, hiding emotional devastation.[124]

One of the most inaccurate latter-day efforts to describe the battle for Hue can be found in Paul Ham's *Vietnam*. This is part of what he wrote about the first day, 31 January 1968:

The South Vietnamese Regiments—notably the Black Panthers [the Hac Bao *Company*][emphasised], notorious for their cruelty—mutilated enemy corpses and hung them like bleeding harlequins on the city walls. Yet by dawn . . . the blue-and-red flag of the Viet Cong flew over the citadel. Hue had fallen in a single night.[125]

This uncorroborated claim also impugns the integrity of the advisers who served with those ARVN regiments during the Tet Offensive. Immediately after the battle and over the intervening years that have included numerous interviews with American and Australian advisers and Vietnamese soldiers—including 'Harry' Hue, the Hac Bao commander—not one of them provided even the slightest piece of a suggestion that such a barbaric act happened.[126] Furthermore, on 31 January, the first day of the battle, there were no ARVN regiments within the citadel; they were fighting to get in from the east and southwest. Three platoons of the Hac Bao were deployed away from the citadel, protecting vital installations south of the river. The remaining 50 Hac Bao and some ordnance soldiers fought to stop an attack on the Tay Loc airfield. Then the Hac Bao were ordered to the 1st Division's compound, where they and divisional headquarters personnel fought for their lives to defend the headquarters. Under those battle conditions no one had the opportunity to mutilate and hang bodies on the walls of the city.

In addition, the exceptional battlefield behaviour of both Australian and American advisers and the Vietnamese was recognised with awards that would not have been allowed if the alleged despicable behaviour had happened. For example, Captain Jim Coolican, USMC who served with the Hac Bao was awarded a Navy Cross for his exceptional heroism during the Hue siege. General Creighton Abrams decorated the battlefield-promoted Captain Tran Ngoc Hue with the US Silver Star for his gallant behaviour during the battle. He was one of the few Vietnamese to receive that award during the war. Abrams also commended Captain Hue's leadership to President Johnson at a National Security Council meeting on 27 March 1968.[127]

Ripples of discontent

Tactical arguments and politics aside, some worrying aspects of poor discipline and/or the stresses of fighting a war that was losing its support back home also bubbled to the surface in the Australian force. The alleged killing of an officer in 106 Field Battery in December 1967 by 'fragging'—a grenade thrown into a tent—saw an Australian soldier convicted of manslaughter and sent to jail for five years. He was released on 28 September 1968, following an appeal. One of the disturbing claims presented by the defence lawyer included a statement that the soldiers of the artillery battery wandered outside the perimeter of their fire support base to buy beer from local Vietnamese vendors and returned to drink at their gun positions.[128] Lieutenant General Daly was rightly annoyed by the information and Major General A. L. MacDonald was disturbed by the amount of beer being consumed by the Australians overall.

Brigadier Hughes discussed several associated issues at his Task Force commander's conference on 21 December 1967. One of the points raised by the commander was the impression among troops that they were 'immune from operations one month before RTA [Return to Australia]'. General Westmoreland had discussed this matter previously with Australian generals. He thought that the Australian method of changeover was inefficient because of lost combat time when units rotated. The American system cycled personnel through a permanently stationed unit, which allowed for continuous operations.[129] The Australians didn't like this system because it fragmented a unit into cohorts based upon arrival and departure dates. Brigadier Hughes also highlighted the six-months mark as the point at which 'a rise in crime' occurred.[130]

Further suggestions that the Australian fighting elements were under constant stress brought a thought from Lieutenant Neville Clark, an artillery officer who wrote that 'infantry battalions should serve nine-month tours of Vietnam . . . 12 months . . . is just a little too much'.[131] This was a rather interesting observation when compared against the operations conducted by the poorly regarded ARVN units, and of course the enemy that they chased were in a constant operational area, albeit not always on operations. On the other hand, maybe Clark had a point. Some of the Task Force commanders only served nine months and General Cao Van Vien, Chief of the Vietnamese Joint General Staff wrote about exhaustion among Vietnamese troops. He said, 'Rotation was perhaps the only way to avoid physical and mental exhaustion . . . rotation time could be from six months to one year in mobile combat duties'.[132] The normal tour of duty for the French in their Indochina war was 26 months.

The aftermath of the Tet battles also brought a flow of dissatisfaction that, in the main, overlooked what had happened to the enemy's *general offensive – general uprising*. The war not only exploded around the South Vietnamese countryside, it also burst into the living rooms of a worldwide television audience. How could the allied effort be winning the war when enemy sappers were inside the American Embassy compound in Saigon? Walter Cronkite's personal editorial at the end of the CBS evening news on 27 February 1968 probably affected the American psyche more than any other image. No matter that the US and ARVN commanders told their interviewers that the enemy had been badly beaten in their fruitless attacks and that many of the northern troops were nothing more than untrained and confused teenagers. Cronkite, later labelled the *most trusted man in America* in a 1972 Quayle Poll, told his audience of millions that the United States was mired in a stalemate which it could not win.[133]

Walter Cronkite's World War II assignments show that he did not shirk dangerous duty as a reporter. But George McArthur, the Associated Press bureau chief in Saigon and a veteran reporter from Korean days, had little time for Cronkite. McArthur said that Cronkite had arranged for artillery to be fired in the background while he did a stand-up to camera in Hue on 10 February 1968 and then he flew out soon after.

> He arranged to have a shelling of the ridgeline behind him. This was his famous trip when he supposedly changed his mind. Baloney. He'd made up his mind before he ever came there. He was up on top of our mission building in Hue doing his stand-upper, wearing a bullet-proof vest and a tin pot [helmet]. And I was up there [on the same roof] doing my laundry. Crap.[134]

Back in Australia, Malcolm Fraser explained that the Australian Task Force's operations out of Phuoc Tuy had helped bring about the better security that now prevailed in that province. Also, the arrival of the third battalion at Nui Dat allowed one of the battalions to protect the base while the others were away, he told a press conference in February. Many in defence circles and the general public had become comfortable with Australian operations in Phuoc Tuy, whereas the severity of the fighting outside of the province during Tet unnerved people.

Not only did the tactical picture appear to change dramatically with an out-of-province deployment, but there was a significant clash with a major thrust by the enemy at the same time. The two factors combined to form a fiery image of Americanisation. Suddenly it looked like the Australians had succumbed to the US perceived overly aggressive method of fighting at the expense of a slow and methodical counterinsurgency plan. Political oil needed to be poured onto troubled waters and Allen Fairhall, Minister for Defence, followed Malcolm Fraser with an explanation that movement out of the province had been permitted from day one for the Australian Task Force, which was correct.[135]

The arguments continued. Peter Samuel at *The Bulletin* emphasised what he saw as the difference between the methods adopted by brigadiers Graham and Hughes. Samuel wrote that 'Hughes was far more willing to fit in with American-style operations'. Brigadier Graham, on the other hand, had 'developed the emphasis on pacification and the policy which laid emphasis on the "fence" [minefield] and police type activities'. Hughes was annoyed by the comparison and he later replied, 'the article is based on rubbish'.[136]

Defeat into victory

The Tet Offensive has been labelled as the tipping point on a downhill slide towards an ignominious end for the efforts of the American-led Free World Forces. The fact that the offensive was a severe loss for the enemy somehow became irrelevant. The images of the Tet battles continued to disturb people and many commentators and military experts misread the absolute misery caused by the communist offensive as an allied military defeat. Almost every televised scene of destruction and loss of life among the South Vietnamese communities tended to emphasise the so-called failures of the allied forces. Although no accurate figures are available, it was estimated that 14,300 civilians were killed and 24,000 were wounded with 72,000 houses destroyed and 627,000 people classified as refugees. In Saigon alone, 6300 civilians were killed, 11,000 were wounded and 19,000 houses were destroyed.[137] When added to the destruction at Hue, no explanation other than a humiliating defeat of the American war effort appeared to be plausible.

Statistics on the enemy dead, weapons captured, prisoners taken and tales of woe by enemy turncoats were either ignored, or treated with disdain. There were no burning enemy cities, or withdrawing columns of broken and defeated battalions to film. The enemy just disappeared—albeit under harrowing circumstances—back into their jungle redoubts to lick their wounds and bury their numerous dead, of which there were tens of thousands. Some said that more than 45,000 were killed. *K2 Battalion* of the *9th Viet Cong Regiment* reported on the difficulties that it had experienced during Tet:

On 1 February, the battalion was detected before reaching its objective, however, and for the next 21 hours or longer engaged in fighting with ARVN and American forces in the vicinity of Phu Loi base [20km north of Saigon]. K2 left the battle-field at 11 pm, February 2. Le Van Chien wrote that desertions under fire were a problem for his battalion. Some comrades became 'confused' and fled to the enemy. The men were worried about the losses of weapons, decreasing strength and lack of replacements. They feared also that they lacked 'the strength for con-tinued combat'. Their losses were 22 killed, 48 wounded and eight missing.[138]

The forces of the Viet Cong—the NLF—bore the brunt in many of the battles. Their losses were extremely heavy and rather ironically, the Northern Command had done what the allied pacification programs and military oper-ations had failed to achieve; they had all but destroyed the Viet Cong. There are many suggestions that this was a deliberate ploy by the northern leaders. If that were so, the losses placed burdensome demands upon the North for replacements that could not be filled through southern recruitment and the number of teenagers found on the battlefield increased as a result. The war now became a truly North versus South conflagration.

In early 1968, President Johnson's approval ratings for handling the job as president fell to just 36 per cent and barely 26 per cent approved of his handling of Vietnam. Increasing the president's strategic worries, the USS *Pueblo* was shot up and captured by the North Koreans on 23 January 1968. At the National Security lunch on that day, Defense Secretary Robert McNamara told his replacement, Clark Clifford:

This is what it is like on a typical day. We had an inadvertent intrusion into Cambodia. We lost a B-52 with four H-bombs aboard [a crash in Greenland]. We had an intelligence ship captured by the North Koreans. Clifford replied: May I leave now?[139]

On the same day, Senator Edward Kennedy discussed his recent visit to Vietnam with the president, emphasising the state of corruption in Vietnam and the poor quality of the Vietnamese government. Fortuitously for the administration, Kennedy's comments about the disagreement among the US generals in Vietnam on the tactics being followed were not made public.[140]

The Cronkite broadcast in February also supposedly affected President Johnson, who is said to have told an aide, 'if I've lost Cronkite, I've lost America'. That comment may have been apocryphal; nevertheless, an air of exasperation was now evident in Johnson's discussions on Vietnam. And on 25 March, Johnson gathered a group of 'wise men' to review and discuss his war options.[141] They were briefed at the Operations Centre, where the most pessimistic of the three assessments portrayed military victory as being unachievable. The next day he met with generals Wheeler and Abrams for what was a real heart-to-heart on Vietnam, during which the president acknowledged that 'the country [America] is demoralised'.[142]

He went back to his 'wise men' on the same day, but they were also divided over what should, or could be done. The president was now in the process of having a draft speech prepared for his 31 March televised address to the nation. Clark Clifford told a meeting that included some of the secretaries of the administration and special counsels who had met to discuss the drafting of the speech that American business leaders just wanted the US to halt the bombing and get out of the war. Surprisingly, after all the policy disagreement, no one argued against him. There were two draft speeches written for the president, a hardline and a winding-it-down version. Johnson made his personal notes on the latter.

His announcement on 31 March 1968 that he would not seek re-election was a tremendous shock to the nation. Although there was a suggestion that the Democrats would draft him anyway, Johnson was adamant that he would not stand again. He reasoned, 'I have 525,000 men whose very lives depend upon what I do, and I can't worry about the primaries. Now I will be working full time for those men out there'.[143]

A further jolt to his administration came with the release of a Harris Poll on 31 March that showed 60 per cent of those questioned thought the Tet Offensive was a defeat for America.

President Johnson's plan to curtail US bombing to targets below 20 degrees north—Hanoi is at 21 Degrees—and his willingness to open negotiations caught Australia on the hop. Only a few days earlier, Paul Hasluck at External Affairs had reinforced Australia's support for a continuation of the hardline approach including a continuation of the bombing campaign. Although Australian polls had indicated that opposition to the war had increased following the deployment of the third Australian battalion to Vietnam, anti-war sentiment had not got to a point where a majority was against the conflict, yet. However, opposition to conscription still rallied strong support.

The Long Hai

Although most of the Australians had now returned to Nui Dat following the heavier than normal clashes of Tet, the Viet Cong of Phuoc Tuy would not let them rest. Once more, it was the question of how to keep the people and the enemy apart. Brigadier Hughes's ideas were a combination of the village cordon-and-search and the harder option of base destruction. One of the region's most daunting of enemy bases, the Long Hai hills, sat with a daring arrogance just 15 kilometres to the south of Nui Dat. The hills were like an impregnable castle of old; but an ogre who had sprinkled mines in almost every nook and cranny had designed its ramparts. And to add insult to any death or injury that the mines might cause, most of them had been taken from the Australian minefield at Dat Do.

Although the allies saw the *Minh Dam base*—the Long Hai hills—as a significant Viet Cong bastion, it was more a symbolic area rather than a tactically practical base. Generally that meant some of the Viet Cong political cadre supported by local forces occupied the base. Local legend said that the hills protected an historical centre of resistance in the province and this supported its psychological influence upon the allied commanders. In a tactical sense the base did not develop much beyond what was experienced by the American 173rd Airborne Brigade during Operation Hollandia in June 1966. Brigadier General Paul Smith, the 173rd Airborne Brigade commander, reported:

The lack of major installations or defensive works is significant in that the area appears to be used only by small local force elements under the most austere conditions. VC forces encountered were platoon-size or smaller . . . who apparently were intimately familiar with the terrain. The Long Hai Peninsula area should not be considered a major Viet Cong stronghold but rather a lightly defended, difficult area, from a terrain standpoint, from which small Viet Cong elements can conduct harassment and interdiction missions. It is unlikely that the elements constitute a single force of greater than company strength.[144]

On 27 February 1968, Phuoc Tuy Sector requested assistance to re-establish government control of Long Dien, a village at the northern edge of the Long Hai. As a consequence after an initial sweep by 2RAR, Operation Pinnaroo began; its aim was to clear the mountain stronghold. The other battalions were engaged elsewhere: 3RAR was still over in Bien Hoa Province until 1 March, and 7RAR was winding down and preparing to go home in early April. 1RAR came back for its second tour to replace 7RAR.

The advance on the Long Hai hills was conducted with trepidation. The heights glared down upon those who might have the effrontery to approach. Not only was the area an enemy haven laced with mines and other traps, which 5RAR had experienced in February 1967, but it was also a great training place for mountain goats with its southern peak at 327 backbreaking metres. During the first two days of March, 2RAR suffered multiple casualties caused by mines; in all they lost one killed and 23 wounded. And this was in the foothills known as Dinh Co, just a bit over a kilometre away from Long Dien. Gordon Hurford, the reluctant conscript of 1965, was now in command of 12 Platoon, 2RAR and the citation for his skilful leadership praised his 'control and coolness to have the wounded collected and treated, then evacuated . . . without any further casualties occurring'.[145] Major Ian Hands, Sergeant Ray Ewell, Sapper Murray Walker and Corporal Phillip Williams were also decorated for their gallant and outstanding efforts during the operation.

Brigadier Hughes had 3RAR join the operation on 8 March and the plan now was to seal off the hills on both the western and eastern sides and to blast the area with artillery and air strikes including by B-52s. The enemy were soon gone again, or hidden deeper underground; the hills were a fortress of 32 square kilometres, with numerous routes by which they could scurry away.

Although the Australian force dared and conquered the heights of the Long Hai, enemy mines—or more correctly, stolen Australian mines—did most of the killing and the wounding.

One significant advantage that the Australians had taken into this operation was the service of Huynh Phien Kiet, a Viet Cong defector. He had lived in the hills and had knowledge about the caves and the signals that indicated mined and booby-trapped areas. Some of the hides were multi-level rooms that had been expanded and connected so that hundreds of personnel could live there. Water flowed through many of the underground rooms and supplies were stocked for extended periods of accommodation. Despite the pounding by the bombers, many of the caves needed to be demolished by the engineers but even this task, which took many tonnes of explosives, could not destroy the total base area.

Apparently *D445 Battalion* was not based in the *Minh Dam* during this period. According to the battalion's records, just before 1968 they had established a headquarters in the Nui Dinh area, 15 kilometres northwest of the Long Hai. The battalion then operated north along Route 2 and east to Xuyen Moc before they returned to assist the local force that had suffered badly during the bombing and the restrictions applied by the Australians around the *Minh Dam* during Operation Pinnaroo.

After six weeks of nerve-racking hide-and-seek, on 15 April the operation was over. The Australian commander claimed a victory in his report to II Field Force Vietnam. The clashes with the Viet Cong had been few, although 21 enemy soldiers were killed and 14 wounded against 10 Australians killed and 36 wounded. Many of the caves and other hiding places in the hills had been destroyed. Brigadier Hughes conveyed his approval on 20 April:

> I want to commend all who participated in operation Pinnaroo . . . an operation which I believe has been the most difficult and the most dangerous yet undertaken by 1ATF.[146]

The enemy also admitted that the Australians had hurt their local forces and caused a critical shortage with their resupply into the hills, but the core elements of the base remained intact.[147] In spite of the well-deserved accolades, the Australians were all glad to be out of there. This was a type of warfare that burnt soldiers mentally. Every step was a nightmare as soldiers searched for any telltale sign of a mine, often overlooking other potential dangers.

Brigadier General Paul Smith had said of Operation Hollandia in 1966:

In this type of operation the advantage is decidedly with the enemy. Consideration should be given to sealing off such area and keeping friendly forces in the area long enough for them to gain familiarity with the area. Additionally, friendly forces remaining in the area will force Viet Cong elements into movement for food and water. Once he is forced into movement, friendly forces would enjoy equal or better advantages.[148]

Operation Hollandia had a similar objective to Operation Pinnaroo, but the American force had been larger with two infantry battalions, tanks, cavalry as well as artillery and aviation units. The periods of deployment were also very different, with the Australians staying in the area for six weeks. The US brigade suffered nine killed and 68 wounded against four confirmed Viet Cong killed during their eight-day operation. In general, trip-wired grenades and rifle grenades caused most of the US casualties, a significant difference to the mines encountered in the later Australian operation and further proof that the enemy had utilised the mines from the Australian minefield.

Operation Pinnaroo also played upon the minds of the commanders. Lieutenant General Daly, the Chief of the General Staff at the time, said, 'it was the last place in the world that I would want to operate'. He also recalled that the operations were 'dangerous, difficult and costly'.[149] Although the Task Force commander claimed that the hills had been cleared, the enemy soon came back simply because the Task Force could not provide a permanent deterrent force to be located there. Any wishful thinking that the Vietnamese would keep an outpost on a Long Hai hilltop proved to be fruitless. The massif might have been controlled if the Task Force had built its base upon it, but that was never an option. Also, the operation raised questions on the efficacy of attempting to oust an enemy from natural bastions that provided them with distinct tactical advantages, often at little cost and with a basic weapon of fear: the mine.

Such questions brought the Dat Do minefield back into focus. It was obvious that the field was not being protected. There were tracks through it in numerous places, the fence required repair, mines were missing and some had been re-laid within the field so that the pattern was disrupted to create even more danger for the Australian engineers. The claim that the Viet Cong had lifted thousands of mines was rejected outright or countered with another set of figures by those who disbelieved the reported efforts of the Viet Cong. Brigadier Hughes now wanted the minefield gone, but that was easier said than done. The first attempts during April and May 1968, using tanks, failed. Nothing more would be done about clearing the minefield until 1969.

Strategic wobbles

An air of wariness followed the battles of Tet, along with some soul-searching and prevarication by those with an Intelligence function. A new question rolled through the military headquarters: will there be another big effort? The American President again asked how the Australians had done. This time he questioned General Abrams who replied 'that the Australians had performed very well'. The Australians also wanted some answers and Paul Hasluck questioned Dean Rusk at the 17th ANZUS council meeting at Wellington, NZ, in April 1968. Hasluck enquired:

> In light of the Tet offensive is there perhaps some need for improvement of allied intelligence techniques? How long can the North Vietnamese sustain their present level of military effort? Hasluck also asked about the effectiveness of additional South Vietnamese troops and how soon would it be achieved.[150]

Dean Rusk answered positively, although he included several options in his reply just to cover all of the possibilities. He did not mention that two American private individuals were in North Vietnam at the time Johnson had announced the bombing halt on 31 March.[151] A possible meeting between American and North Vietnamese officials might have been initiated by 'two blind hogs who have found an acorn', noted Walt Rostow, a special assistant to Johnson.[152] The president and his advisers understood that battlefield manoeuvring would influence how the North Vietnamese might enter into any possible negotiation. More battles, more bodies, more insecurity equalled more power during any discussions. General Westmoreland was pulled back to Washington for discussions with Johnson and his senior national security advisers on 6 April in a meeting that wanted some difficult answers to some equally difficult questions, including who would replace Westmoreland. General Abrams, his current deputy, assumed the duties of acting commander on 9 June until he was formally appointed on 3 July 1968. Westmoreland also told the president that Averell Harriman—the designate US lead at any talks with the North Vietnamese—would be negotiating from a position of strength, as the enemy had suffered a 'colossal military defeat' at Tet and after. 'Harriman will have four aces and the enemy two deuces', Westmoreland added. Harry McPherson, a special counsel to Johnson, asked:

> Have you noticed any change in the enemy since the peace initiative? Is the enemy in a position to capture a city, score tactical victory, or attack Saigon? Westmoreland replied he will have some initiatives.[153]

The Tet Offensive deeply divided the American administration. General Westmoreland's subsequent request for a 206,000-man augmentation of troops fuelled a perception of defeat that sent shock waves of despair through the home front. The large number of reinforcements was supposedly needed to bolster the *winning* side. Westmoreland was confident that the enemy was in difficulty following his recent bad losses, but some other advisers were not so positive. Arthur Goldberg, one of the wise men, challenged the casualty figures that had been presented by the military to prove their positive outlook on the battles:

> How many effective regular soldiers do you think that they now have, Goldberg asked. Perhaps 230,000 maybe 240,000, said DePuy [the briefing officer]. With 80,000 killed and a wounded ratio of three to one, that makes 320,000 men killed or wounded, *who the hell is there left for us to be fighting, Goldberg asked* [emphasised].[154]

Although more enemy reinforcements were in the pipeline from the North, a good watch was being kept over the movement of their divisions. The North Vietnamese are not ten feet tall and Khe Sanh was a Dien Bien Phu in reverse, Westmoreland reported. The ARVN had fought well, new weapons and equipment would flow down to the troops in the Regional Force/Popular Force and a protective force had circled Saigon. President Johnson told a gathering of close advisers on 8 April:

> He did not accept Westmoreland's view that North Vietnam was crying for peace because of battle wounds. He said he saw some bitterness in the General, who feels he has been made the goat and has been pulled out because he didn't get support in Washington.[155]

Back in Vietnam, several large-scale operations that were designed to deny enemy access to food resources and to destroy their base areas continued around Saigon and the western provinces. In the Australian area of operations, a slower tempo of recent operations had concerned Brigadier Hughes at 1ATF. The pace of Operation Pinnaroo had been sluggish because of the dangers of mines and the wait for B-52 strikes and Hughes warned his commanders:

> Future operations are not likely to be inhibited . . . to the same degree. A warning is now issued regarding officers and men reducing their own tempo of operations. Members about to go home sometimes get the idea that it is their right to avoid contact. The soldier in the field who avoids contact is guilty of cowardice and if caught will be court-martialled.[156]

Brigadier Hughes was somewhat prescient when he warned that future operations would not be subdued. America and North Vietnam had agreed to meet at Paris on 10 May 1968 to start to talk about the Vietnam War, and as the *MACV Command History* noted, the enemy having been defeated on every battlefield would come to the conference table with the philosophy that 'politics is an extension of war'. Accordingly, the North Vietnamese launched another offensive in May 1968 to support their official conversations at Paris with the Americans.

The Guardian newspaper recorded on 4 May:

> Finding a place for a parley is the first shy step towards an armistice. America and Vietnam have a long way to go yet before they come to terms. But by their agreement to meet in Paris next Friday they each confessed to a mutual interest

in limiting, moderating, or even ending the Vietnam War. Yesterday's agreement means that each side has swallowed a tiny morsel of pride. It means that they were in earnest after all about wanting to talk. But beyond this there are no solid grounds for rejoicing yet.[157]

Why did the NVA/Viet Cong attack again after their savage mauling during Tet? Although their losses were terrible, CIA analyst Patrick McGarvey defined Giap's thinking when he said that General Giap did not measure failure by counting his own casualties, but he saw success with 'the traffic in homeward-bound American coffins'. The Americans were confident that winning every battle must eventually bring victory. But it was a false premise, as they would eventually discover.[158] The NVA attacked again after the Tet Offensive to obtain strategic influence through more homeward-bound American coffins and to maintain the image of an unvanquished enemy in the eye of the media and in the fractured minds of the western politicians. The NVA could also show that although damaged they were not a spent force. They could continue the fight while negotiating, which was a natural stage of warfare for the northern leaders. General Giap was also considered by some to be nothing more than a butcher's logistician who believed if force failed, use more force.

The forgotten battles at Coral and Balmoral

On 5 May 1968, an anticipated mini-offensive struck throughout Vietnam. It was an attack mainly by rocket and mortar fire followed by limited ground assaults. Defectors had warned of the coming attacks and American and Vietnamese units had been deployed to intercept and destroy the North Vietnamese controlled troops. Nonetheless small teams of enemy got into Saigon and the fighting was very messy, especially in the Chinese suburb of Cholon.

It was during this fighting that a group of Australian journalists and a British correspondent pushed their luck too far. In an act of extreme foolishness, the men travelled by Jeep into Cholon because of the reports that the Viet Cong were fighting in its streets. As they followed the action of a helicopter gunship overhead, John Cantwell drove them down a small side road. Frank Palmos reportedly said, 'Stop, John, don't take a small street, let's take a big street—the Viet Cong are not going to be piddling around in a big street'.

Palmos said he was outvoted, four to one. When he demanded that they stop, two Viet Cong appeared suddenly in front of the Jeep.[159] The journalists found that shouting 'Bao Chi' (Press) did not afford them any protection and four of the men were killed. Frank Palmos escaped after a hair-raising chase through the streets by his intended executioner.

Australian battalions were also moved out of Phuoc Tuy as part of the screen put in place to protect Saigon. On 5 May, 1RAR and 2RAR/NZ went over into an area known as Columbus in Bien Hoa Province with a mission to block any NVA/VC forces from moving south towards Saigon. On this occasion, 3RAR remained at home until 10 May when it relieved 2RAR. Operation Toan Thang (Complete Victory) began relatively slowly for the Australians with minor contacts and no friendly casualties, but that would soon change. A new plan of action for the Australians directed that they close down the enemy's withdrawal routes and destroy the forces that had created the mayhem in and around Saigon.

The battalions moved out of Columbus on 12 May and headed west to an area of operations known as Surfers and a fire support base called Coral, which was 6 kilometres northwest of Tan Uyen along Route 16. This area was an old stomping ground from 1RAR's first tour. The Australian area was linked in with the 3rd Brigade, 1st (US) Division that operated to their west and the 2/506th (US) Battalion who were to the east of Surfers. ARVN units were to the south and the southwest, around Tan Uyen. The Australian artillery, defence stores and personnel were lifted into Coral in an extremely disorderly manner. 3RAR had arrived first, but they were gone from the vicinity of Coral when some of the artillery arrived. Then 1RAR flew in and the guns from 102 Battery followed, but the 1RAR mortars did not arrive until the end of the day.

Neil Weekes, a national serviceman and graduate of Scheyville OTU, was a second lieutenant platoon commander in 1RAR at the time. Weekes distinctly remembered they were there to cut off the retreating enemy who supposedly would be demoralised, out of ammunition and food and carrying wounded. It all gave the impression that they were there for a great turkey shoot and to really get these fellows as they tried to get away from Saigon. He recalled:

> The fly-in to Coral was a shambles—we flew into the wrong LZ, our aircraft were taken away from us because the Yanks were in contact in the same area. There was

a lot of evidence of a large number of enemy in the area. Delta Company had a contact that night and Bravo Company was also engaged. The night seemed to settle down and about 2.00am all hell broke loose at FSB *Coral*. Mortar fire, rockets and a lot of small-arms fire. Then 'Spooky' arrived with mini-guns. All of the companies had dispersed and we were at least 1000–2000 metres away. I wondered what the hell was going on, so I flicked my radio to the battalion net and listened.[160]

At the witching hour, close to 2.00 a.m., an estimated enemy battalion of the *141st Regiment* from the *7th NVA Division* attacked the fire support base. As a result of the last-minute and rather jumbled arrivals the defensive layout of the position was only at a basic level, but as luck would have it the 105 mm howitzers were aimed east. Vince Dunn, a gunner with 102 Battery, recalled the fear of it all 40 years later:

It was very early morning when they mortared us or hit us with RPG. Then once they'd done that, they all stood up from about 100 metres out and came at us. There were hundreds of them. It was only luck those three guns were facing the direction of their attack. They walked straight into the mouths of the guns.[161]

At first the 105 mm guns could not fire their Splintex—a shotgun type shell that contained flechette darts—because the Mortar Platoon was between the guns and the enemy. But the enemy overran parts of the mortar area and headed straight for 102 Battery. Dunn continued:

They swung away from the mouths of the guns to our left flank to find a way into us. That's where 1RAR Mortar Platoon and the boys from Headquarter Battery were. But they just went straight over the top of them. One of the howitzers was overrun, but the gun crew fighting for their lives retook it.[162]

The New Zealand 161 Battery and the 3RAR Mortar Platoon fired across the front of their 1RAR mates. Then the 1RAR Anti-Tank Platoon hit the charging enemy with flechette rounds from their recoilless rifles. 'It was the best gunnery I've ever seen', Dunn said.[163]

American gunships and a Spooky then sprayed the enemy with blasts of fire from their mini-guns and they also kept the area lit up with flares, forcing the enemy's main group to fall back to the northeast. Any enemy that remained were engaged by 102 Battery with Splintex rounds and high explosive shells fired over open sights. But the NVA had not finished yet and they made another effort to take the Australian position. This time the combined fire from 102 Battery and the Anti-Tank Platoon knocked the stuffing out of the attack and at 0610 hours the last enemy on the Australian position was killed by 102 Battery.

It had been a deadly clash for both sides, which a report from 1ATF confirmed the next day. A quantity of assorted enemy weapons that included rocket-propelled grenades had been captured. Task Force reported that 51 enemy soldiers had been killed—1RAR said 56—and two men were taken prisoner. One of the howitzers and two 81 mm mortars were damaged and the Australians suffered 9 killed and 28 wounded, although the reported figures varied. Lieutenant George Hulse, an engineer who arrived at Coral after the battle told *The Australian:*

> The first thing we saw was several dead Australians lying by the roadside. That was our welcome to Coral. We spent much of the day digging a mass grave for the North Vietnamese dead and burying them. The official estimate of enemy dead was about 50, but I believe there were a lot more than that.[164]

These attacks were just the preliminary round of what would turn out to be a rolling series of clashes over three weeks. A reported enemy battalion group attacked FSB Coral again in the early hours of 16 May when five Australians were killed, and 19 wounded. Once more, the enemy casualties were heavy with 34 killed. The Coral base was hit again by mortar and recoilless rifle fire on 22 and 26 May. That was when George Hulse thought he was about to die. He recalled that he was a man of two parts:

> One was saying, think of your flag, think of Australia, think of the Anzac tradition, and think of yourself as a Portsea graduate. You can't possibly be weak in front of your soldiers. Another part is starting to sneak up on you and it comes from the pit of your stomach . . . and this thing is called fear.[165]

The fighting was intense and at close quarters. The Australians had not developed their defensive position because of their piecemeal arrival and as a consequence there was a lack of barbed wire on their perimeter. What was erected was called 'laughing wire' by one Digger because he figured the NVA would stop, see the wire, and laugh at the puny obstacle. On 22 May, Colonel Donald Dunstan ordered the tanks of C Squadron that were back at Nui Dat to come forward to Coral. Dunstan, the Deputy Commander of the Task Force and in later years the Chief of the General Staff, commanded during this phase of the operation because Brigadier Ron Hughes was on leave. The battalions welcomed the additional combat power but the first challenge for the tanks was the drive over a distance of approximately 100 kilometres from Nui Dat to the fire support base. Friendly American support saved the day once again with repairs and refuelling permitted at the 11th Armored Cavalry Regiment's staging area at Long Binh. All of the gun-tanks made the distance, much to the squadron's surprise. The two dozer-tanks did not fare as well; one hit a mine back on Route 2 near Blackhorse, (the damage was minor) and the second died mechanically. Soon after their arrival at 1430 hours on 23 May, the tanks were on the perimeter of Coral and 2 Troop was warned for a move to FSB Balmoral to support 3RAR.

Two days later, on 25 May, Bravo Company, 1RAR escorted the tanks of 2 Troop across to Balmoral, which was about 5 kilometres north of Coral. On the way, they had a firefight with an enemy platoon that fired on them with machine guns and rocket-propelled grenades from bunkers, which were hit by an air strike but the results were not checked immediately. Delta Company and the tanks of 1 Troop went out to check the area on 26 May and the enemy fired at them with rocket-propelled grenades that missed. The Centurions replied with their signature response of shock and awe, destroying fourteen bunkers with their main armament. Even more terrifying for the enemy, a few occupied bunkers were collapsed by the weight of the tanks. No one counted how many enemy soldiers died as a result.

In spite of the deadly risks before them, the enemy persisted and on 26 May a suspected company-sized attack hit 3RAR at Balmoral. Although the enemy withdrew at about 0500 hours, all of the indicators pointed to the nearby presence of an enemy battalion. During this fighting, two Australians were killed and fifteen were wounded; one of the wounded died later. Subsequently six enemy bodies were also found during a search of the area.

Both of the Australian battalions continued to make contact with the enemy and Coral was hit by indirect enemy fire again on 26 and 28 May. Then the enemy turned their attention to Balmoral and attacked the base in the early hours of 28 May. National serviceman Private Brian Cleaver, a newly arrived reinforcement for 3RAR, remembered the attacks:

> I had just woken my relief after an eerie two-hour stint on picket duty ... when I heard the mortars. RPG fire, small arms and an infantry assault, followed the mortars. The old saying about being so scared that you shit yourself rang true that day.[166]

The main attack from the south stopped at about 0300 hours, but this was followed by several attempts to come through the wire to the north-east of the position. Australian tanks and American firepower from Spooky and helicopter gunships made the enemy pay a heavy price for their efforts. Daylight revealed that the body count for the enemy was 42 with another possible twelve dead. The Australians had one killed and six wounded. Brian Cleaver said that he and his mates were ordered to search the area for enemy wounded and to help with the burying of enemy dead. Cleaver recalled:

> As they were tending the enemy wounded, an NVA soldier produced a grenade and detonated it, which wounded an Australian doctor. An immediate disgust and rage sets in when something like that happens. You just want to kill someone. The wounded weren't treated too gently after that.[167]

Was this what was meant by the sentence in Lieutenant Michael Butler's C Squadron report that had been inked over, 'ten en [enemy] were shot for either resisting or making a dangerous move'?[168] The Australians were well aware of the furore caused by any suggestion of atrocious behaviour in battle. In March 1968, Mr Phillip Lynch, the Minister for the Army, had been required to answer questions on the much-publicised alleged water torture of a female during interrogation in 1966. Another claim in 1968, strongly rejected at the time, said that wounded soldiers had been shot after the battle at Long Tan. Although the battle veterans rebuffed the allegation at the time, former platoon sergeant Bob Buick admitted in 2000 that he shot a severely wounded enemy soldier twice through the heart when the battle was over.[169] Michael Butler's comment about what happened at Balmoral may have been nothing worse than a badly written sentence, which could have been mis-interpreted and that was the cause of its attempted erasure.

The next task was to find and bury the dead. 'We disposed of them in a bomb crater that was used as a mass grave', Cleaver remembered. More than 40 years later Cleaver had gone back to the old battleground searching for the crater and the remains of those who tried to kill him all those years ago. Brian Cleaver made four visits to the old battleground and he dearly wanted to find the grave. He said that there was no mention in the Vietnamese war records of a mass burial; however, an article dated 18 November 2007 in a Vietnamese publication, *Viet Bao*, mentioned the following:

A battle lasting 25 days and nights in May and June 1968 involving 141 Viet Cong [NVA] Regiment against an Australian fire support base. Colonel Tran Xuan Ban, the former operations officer of 141 Regiment said that this was the only battle the regiment had with Australians. As there were few of us, we attacked quickly and then withdrew before you could respond.[170]

The article was supported with a photograph of a monument at the apparent battle site that commemorated 35 Vietnamese bodies that had been recovered from a mass grave used by the Australians.

There were no further major attacks in the Australian area of operations after 27–28 May and the Task Force ended its operation on 6 June and returned to Nui Dat. After a month of hunting in these dangerous grounds nearer to Cambodia, the Australians had fought hard and repelled solid attacks against their bases. The results were:

Twenty-seven Australian soldiers were killed and 113 were wounded. Materiel damaged or lost included: 1 Centurion tank, two 81 mm mortars, two M113 and one 105 mm howitzer were damaged. One Cessna aircraft was destroyed in an accident. One M-16 rifle and a Claymore mine were lost. The NVA had 276 killed. Materiel captured: 36 crew served weapons and 124 small arms.[171]

The Operation Toan Thang clashes are generally acknowledged as the most intense operational period that the Australian Task Force soldiers experienced during the war. The action also reinforced the knowledge that the Australian force in Vietnam lacked the combat power to operate completely independently, especially in regions where the enemy's main force had established base areas that backed on to a sanctuary and a major resupply route.[172]

NVA 141 Regiment's combat achievement medal

For their successful battle at So Hoi—FSB Coral—the *141st NVA Regiment* of the *7th NVA Division* was awarded the Liberation Combat Achievement Medal 3rd Class, which was announced by the divisional commander in May 1968. The following piece of hyperbole by the NVA will bring a wry smile to the faces of the Australians who fought the battles of Coral–Balmoral.

On 12 May, the reconnaissance element of 141 Regiment discovered an enemy battalion at So Hoi [FSB Coral]. Following an engagement, they realized it was the 4th Battalion of the Royal Australian Regiment [*sic* 1RAR]. The Divisional Commander, The Bon, conferred with Political Commissar Hiep and ordered that the enemy be attacked immediately on the night of 12 May. Regimental Commander Doan Khiet and the battalion commanders did a reconnaissance, and the orders for the attack were given. Meanwhile Political Commissar Nguyen Van Nhat and Chief of Staff Ha Xuan Truong organized the troops moving forward. The enemy had not yet prepared defensive works, could not respond in time. They were attacked fiercely and by surprise. The enemy was in panic, unable to resist, and were completely wiped out. We seized 40 weapons (including two HMGs, an 81 mm mortar and two 60 mm mortars) and swiftly withdrew before the enemy could employ their artillery. The battle was truly successful. With the Australians defeated, they were immediately replaced by American troops. The Americans entered So Hoi with artillery and tanks, and more armoured vehicles. Regimental Commander Doan Khiet did a reconnaissance, and the enemy was attacked immediately. Reinforced by the Tan Uyen District Company and H12s (Type 63, 107 mm MRL, 12 tubes) on the night of 15/16 May, 141 Regiment inflicted heavy casualties on a US infantry battalion, two artillery batteries and an armoured troop.[173]

The battles at Ngok Tavak and Kham Duc

Much further north, three Australian AATTV soldiers fought their way out of a remote Special Forces camp close to the Laos border on 10 May 1968. They led a group of Nungs (Chinese mercenaries) and US Marines that had been routed by the *40th Battalion, 1st Viet Cong Regiment* of the *2nd NVA Division* as a prelude to its attack upon a larger camp at Kham Duc, just 7 kilometres away. A company from the US Special Forces Mobile Strike Force—known as Mike Force—that was commanded by Australian Captain John White, had been directed to conduct reconnaissance patrols along Route 14 in western Quang Tin Province to determine what enemy might be in the area. An American Marine two-gun artillery detachment commanded by Lieutenant Bob Adams supported them.

Major Dang Ngoc Mai's *40th Battalion* struck the Ngok Tavak hilltop fifteen minutes after the Kham Duc base was also hit with mortar and recoilless rifle fire at 0245 hours on 10 May. A fierce battle at Ngok Tavak followed as the enemy poured onto the position and sprayed the 105 mm howitzers with their flamethrowers. This assault broke the defensive lines on top of the hill, but some of the Marines and Special Forces troops stopped the enemy's attack. The enemy withdrew when a mini-gun equipped Spooky aircraft arrived and blasted the surrounds with 21,000 rounds of 7.62 mm, which was followed by a counterattack led by AATTV Warrant Officer Don Cameron. Although the enemy moved off towards Kham Duc, they kept Ngok Tavak under sporadic fire, hoping to hold the defenders there so that they could kill them and destroy the position later.

Captain White's company suffered 16 Nungs killed and 33 wounded. Sergeant Glenn Miller, an American Special Forces soldier, was also killed in the action. The Marine detachment of 46 had 14 killed and 20 wounded. Although some reinforcements were lifted in by helicopter, two Marine CH-46 Sea Knight helicopters were shot down and they lay smashed on the hilltop's pad, making it unusable. When the enemy withdrew, they left 31 bodies and 50 weapons inside the camp's perimeter. Captain White then disobeyed his US commander's radio messages and withdrew what was left of his force. White also had to make an agonising decision on what to do with the bodies of those killed. He decided to protect the living, which meant that twelve American bodies were left behind. The two 105 mm howitzers were spiked and abandoned, but were noticeably missing from the hill the next day. An attempt was made to destroy 150 weapons abandoned by White's force, but in reality they could be classified as lost to the enemy.

Captain White led the survivors off the hill and headed into the jungle to hack out a landing zone from where several courageous Marine Corps helicopter crews lifted them to safety.[174] 'To safety' meant a stop at Kham Duc to refuel, but the base was under siege and fast becoming a cauldron. It was an isolated camp built near an airstrip in a valley surrounded by mountains and it was known that Lieutenant General Cushman at III Marine Amphibious Force was not a supporter of isolated Special Forces camps. With the glare of the media spotlight not yet fully extinguished from the battles around Khe Sanh, no one dare mention the similarity between Khe Sanh, Kham Duc and Dien Bien Phu.

The battle at Kham Duc turned into a debacle. There was tactical disagreement between the senior Army and Marine commanders at MACV and III MAF and the camp was abandoned at 1625 hours on 12 May. Some of the allied losses were listed:

Ten aircraft were destroyed, which included two C-130 Hercules. Seven 105 mm howitzers, fifteen 81 mm mortars, four 106 mm recoilless rifles, more than 100 small arms and an undetermined amount of ammunition were lost. Fifteen trucks, two bulldozers, two front loaders, one road grader, 28 radios, 675 gas masks and 475 sets of protective body armour were captured. Twenty-four Americans had been killed, 133 were wounded and 26 were missing in action. Up to 150 villagers had been killed aboard a C-130 that was shot down immediately after take off. Five hundred and eight Vietnamese and Montagnard troops were missing. Three hundred and forty-five enemy soldiers were recorded as killed.[175]

In a subsequent press conference, an American officer claimed that the forces had been withdrawn to allow air power to decimate the enemy, which was a disingenuous explanation of what really happened. General Creighton Abrams said it was a minor disaster and Brigadier General Chaisson, who headed the MACV Combat Operations Centre, told his wife that the battle was an ugly one and he expected some repercussions. But nothing happened.[176]

Peace talks and time to refit

In the Australian camp, 4RAR/NZ (ANZAC) replaced 2RAR/NZ (ANZAC) on 1 June 1968 and Prime Minister John Gorton visited the Australian forces at Nui Dat, Vung Tau and Phan Rang between 7 and 9 June. The former RAAF pilot and reputed larrikin looked to be at ease with the troops, despite the presence of a press contingent of 26 who were covering the visit. There were further flurries of military activity through to the end of 1968, but overall the clashes were at a lower level of intensity and there was some hope that progress would come from the Paris talks. Although there was a slight surge of enemy activity during July and August, the main enemy units appeared to have withdrawn across the borders of Cambodia and Laos or into other sanctuaries to refit, rest and retrain.

One of the major attacks in August was against the isolated Duc Lap Sub-Sector camp on 23 August. Duc Lap was just 12 kilometres from the Cambodia border in the lower Central Highlands and 120 kilometres west of Nha Trang. The first assault followed the normal pattern of NVA attacks. A large number of rocket-propelled grenades, 60 mm, 82 mm and 120 mm mortars were fired into the compound, and sappers who threw satchel charges in or around the buildings followed immediately behind the barrage. A reaction force located at the Special Forces camp, 8 kilometres to the east, was fired upon when they attempted to reinforce the sub-sector and they turned back into the safety of their compound. A relief force under the command of Australian AATTV Captain David Savage was committed from Pleiku, 150 kilometres north. Savage and three Australian warrant officers: Barry Tolley, George Smith and Laurie Jackson, led a company of 130 Montagnards, two Vietnamese Special Forces personnel and American Sergeant John Wast into the fray. David Savage's name delighted the Montagnards because it translated into 'Moi', which was the derogatory term for 'savage' used by the Vietnamese for Montagnards.

Two more Mike Force companies out of Pleiku followed Dave Savage's company into Duc Lap. Although Savage's company made it into the Special Forces camp, it was surrounded and only two of the fifteen American advisers had not been wounded. David Savage was also wounded on his way into the camp. The enemy continued their attacks and broke through the camp's perimeter and occupied some of the outer ring of trenches that provided ready-made protection and an avenue of approach to the command centre. They also shot down several helicopters and an F-100 Super Sabre that had provided air support. The position was on the verge of being overrun when American Lieutenant William Harp called his commander and told him that without more reinforcements the camp would fall. The Australian warrant officers now manned mortars in an effort to keep the enemy at bay. Air strikes pounded the enemy as they advanced through the protection of the camp's trench lines and by midday on 25 August, matters were extremely grim:

> There was no water and the wounded added to the torment by crying out for water. Water had been airdropped but it had drifted outside the camp's perimeter. The temperature and humidity had reached their highest at midday and the sickening stench of the dead hung over the trenches and the bunkers. Not even the acrid smell of burnt explosives provided any relief from the [smell of] bodies which had been lying for up to three days around the camp. Almost when all seemed to be lost, more relief companies arrived and the NVA's assault on the camp was defeated.[177]

The Duc Lap battle was a series of major area assaults on both the sub-sector headquarters and the Special Forces camp by an estimated 4000 North Vietnamese soldiers from the *1st NVA Division*. Although the clash continued into September, the heaviest fighting had been in August and those clashes claimed the lives of 114 allied and 715 enemy soldiers. The enemy also lost 67 crew-served weapons and 184 small arms. As Warrant Officer Barry Tolley said:

> There is no doubt that if the relief had not come, the enemy would have taken the camp. His attacks had gained an intensity and ferocity that must have eventually swept over us. Our Montagnards did a magnificent job.[178]

There was a method in the madness of this costly attack by the NVA/Viet Cong command. The Duc Lap area was astride a major infiltration route that came into South Vietnam from Cambodia and linked with Route 14, the main road that snaked along the spine of the Central Highlands and the western border region of the III Corps Tactical Zone. It was also another reminder from the battlefield for the negotiators at Paris: no matter how many of us you have killed, we are still dangerous.

Political and diplomatic turmoil

Martin Luther King and Robert Kennedy, a presidential hopeful, were assassinated in April and June 1968. Soviet Union–led Warsaw Pact forces invaded

Czechoslovakia in August and serious civil unrest appeared to be the order of the day in countries like Britain and Japan. Although Australia appeared to weather the turmoil, dissatisfaction against conscription for the Vietnam War was growing, fuelled by university students, or so it seemed. The manner of warfare being used in Vietnam by the southern allies was also subjected to increased criticism; especially the use of defoliants (Agents Orange, White & Blue). Demonstrators in the bigger cities became more confrontational and abusive, not only towards the police but also towards anyone showing disagreement with the protest of the day. Some returned Vietnam veterans were abused and even spat upon.

The discussion among political and diplomatic circles now appeared to be how to end the war honourably. Could the dominoes of Southeast Asia now stand unaided without American involvement in Vietnam? Was the theory valid to begin with? These questions and many more had troubled policy makers over the years, but now the reality of fighting a war in support of a contested theory generated more open public dissatisfaction. Clark Clifford, President Johnson's Defense Secretary, had expressed his deep concerns on the matter before the president's announcement of his resignation on 31 March 1968. Although not yet generally apparent, there was a strengthening desire to get out of Vietnam via some sort of face-saving agreement. The costs were too high in dollars and lives and the world was war-weary. Australia now also had another worry: the British withdrawal from east of Suez. Should both America and Britain withdraw militarily from Southeast Asia, Australia would be vulnerable. Prime Minister John Gorton had already announced that Australia's commitment to Vietnam was at its peak; there would be no increase in the size of the force. It would seem that matters in Malaysia and Singapore were far more important than Vietnam in the minds of some senior members of Cabinet who had fought in World War II.

President Johnson's previous questions about the performance of Australian troops are better understood when they are combined with his new desire to achieve a peaceful solution to the war. Because of a lack of early warning, Australia had been embarrassed by Johnson's announcement on the bombing restrictions in March 1968. But Johnson now wanted to ensure that the American negotiators in Paris did 'not say anything which might divide us from our South Vietnamese [and] Australian ... allies'. Cyrus Vance, at

Paris with Harriman, had told the president that 'Australians are good allies in Paris'.[179]

At home, in Australia, political problems on matters Vietnam resounded through both Labor and the Coalition parties. Gough Whitlam, now the leader of the Labor Opposition, had been to Vietnam on a long trip in early 1968 that gave the impression he was not so anti-Vietnam as many on the left of the Labor Party wished. His visit to Danang was not an affair to remember either, as Major Harry Lovelock recalled:

> One of the real chores of my job was looking after Australian visitors probably looking for some excitement. Mr Gough Whitlam who performed well as the barman in Uc House [Australia House, the AATTV HQ in I Corps] but very poorly when a guest of the mayor of Danang. A bottle of whisky and damage to furniture was cause enough for me to say I had more important things to do the following day. Years of good public relations by AATTV members took a setback with this opinionated bully.[180]

Both the recently appointed prime minister and the young Minister for the Army, Phillip Lynch, were put to the test when the previously mentioned 'water torture case', the alleged torture of a female during interrogation, was raised in Parliament. The press virtually licked its lips with the potential for a headline to match the American shame of the My Lai massacre. There wasn't one. Nevertheless, the water torture case and the arrest of Clarry Rule, an AATTV officer, at Melbourne airport for allegedly sending classified material and weapons through the post tested the government's openness on information about the war with both the Parliament and the press.

The issue of conscription continued to bedevil the government, too, as public dissatisfaction gathered vociferous momentum. There were some good news stories associated with the call-up: Normie Rowe, a pop star of the day, accepted his call-up and served without fuss; a point not lost on many veterans. It was a military offence to refuse to obey a conscription notice and the images of military police and officers when they attempted to arrest offenders added to the anti-conscription angst. Following considerable debate, the law was changed in 1968 to make disobeying the call-up a civil offence. This shunted the public relations problems of arrest across to the civil police, which supposedly reinforced the public image of keeping law and order. Anti-conscription protests also turned violent during the year. In one example that did their cause more harm than good, protesters attempted to disrupt World War II veteran Sir Roden Cutler during his inspection of the Sydney University's guard of honour. Cutler was a recipient of the Victoria Cross for valour and when he was hit with a tomato during the scuffles, public feeling against the protesters ran high. The main element of complaint in the increasing number of more violent demonstrations remained conscription for war rather than the war in Vietnam. That would come to the fore later.

A new method of warfare, or was it?

At a regular Tuesday lunch meeting at the White House on 4 September 1968, President Johnson as usual turned the talk to the situation in Vietnam. Defense Secretary Clifford said:

> There is more activity, but we don't know whether this is the third offensive. The attacks are not coming off very well. It may be Abrams spoiling the operations. I heard about a plan to assassinate General Abrams because he has been so successful.[181]

The comment did not attract a reply other than General Wheeler's advice that he had asked Abrams to increase his security detail. On 14 October when Clifford told the president that 'Abrams has shown more flexibility and mobility than Westmoreland', Johnson differed. 'I do not agree ... I think Abrams has inherited most of this from Westmoreland.'[182]

The arguments on how to conduct the war had resumed. As Andrew Birtle's paper 'PROVN, Westmoreland and the Historians' contends, Abrams' campaign efforts were 'firmly rooted in policies and procedures of his predecessor [Westmoreland]'.[183] Westmoreland had rejected the 1966 pacification study principally on the grounds that it told him nothing more than what he was doing anyway. The desk jockeys were interfering with a soldier in the field, he intimated. A similar argument had happened between the NVA/Viet Cong commander in the South (Thanh) and the general behind his desk in Hanoi (Giap).

When General Creighton Abrams first took over from Westmoreland, he emphasised looking after the villagers, but always with an eagle eye on a link to the destruction of the enemy's main forces. At a special briefing for commanders on 4 July 1968, Abrams said: 'is there any way to get at him [the enemy], get a <u>hold</u> of him? Because that's—the <u>payoff</u> is getting a hold of this fellow and killing as many as we can [underline in original]'.[184] Abrams reinforced his concern about the enemy's main force troops at a weekly intelligence update on 6 July: 'the pacification effort is the ultimate effort, which has to be made. But right now I think we have to focus on what he's [NVA/ Viet Cong] going to do with his major formations'.[185]

Australians also changed their commander in October 1968 when Brigadier C. M. 'Sandy' Pearson arrived to take over at 1ATF, prompting renewed speculation about the role of Australian troops in Phuoc Tuy. If pacification was to prevail and if Phuoc Tuy was to be the core area of Australian effort again, a closer operational link needed to be established between 1ATF and the South Vietnamese provincial forces. Pearson thought that the Regional and Popular Forces were 'bloody terrible' and he set about trying to improve their skills, in what seemed a full-circle return to earlier tactics. Ian McNeill described in *The Team* how bad the local forces were: poor leadership, corruption, live-and-let-live understandings with the Viet Cong, lack of aggression and flimsy defences were just a few of the recognised weaknesses that he noted.[186]

The AATTV provided some support to establish a training camp at Heavyweight, near Hoa Long, in the hope that improvements could be achieved in conjunction with Mobile Advisory Teams provided by the Australian battalions. Once again the concept was to get the Vietnamese up to a standard whereby they looked after the locals and the Australians would hunt the enemy's main units. Surely it could be done because the enemy had suffered so badly in all of their 1968 offensives. The enemy's win in the public relations stakes via the images of Tet had been a pyrrhic victory. The Viet Cong infrastructure in the South was under severe strain and the struggle now was a real hearts and minds battle. It was back to guerrilla warfare once more and to fight in line with General Abrams' concept, which emphasised 'One War'. This plan combined tactical operations and improvement of the South Vietnamese forces and a vigorous pacification program into one overarching effort. One War resurfaced again in Afghanistan in 2010, but then the basics of warfare always continued to roll around into fresh ideas relearnt from the lessons of the past.

Australia's total force in Vietnam at the end of 1968 numbered 7596, of which 6840 were Army. Since June 1965, the Australian Army had suffered 239 soldiers killed in action, 28 had died from other causes and 1102 had been wounded. America's military strength in Vietnam at 31 December 1968 was 536,040.[187]

7

THE BEGINNING OF THE END: VIETNAMISATION
1969–1970

Better the Arabs do it tolerably than that you do it perfectly. It is their war, and you are here to help them, not win it for them. Also, under the very odd conditions of Arabia, your practical work will not be as good as, perhaps, you think it is.

T. E. Lawrence
Arab Bulletin, 20 August 1917

New troops, new ideas, same questions

With combat tours of around twelve months, it is possible that both the Australian and American units rotated through Vietnam too quickly to achieve their best combat capability. General Westmoreland thought the Australian unit changeover system was inefficient, but others disagreed with the American system which replaced individuals while the unit remained permanently deployed. Arguments against longer tours of duty generally revolved around the mental and physical demands upon the combat soldier but perhaps those arguments were no more than a reflection of a softer western culture when it came to fighting in Southeast Asia, a cultural and physical environment in which many westerners felt uncomfortable. American Admiral Arthur Radford, a future Chairman of the Joint Chiefs of Staff, told an ANZUS conference in 1952, 'what we have there now is pretty much what can be absorbed, as *Europeans could hardly live and fight successfully there* [emphasised]'.[1] The 1964 words of US Ambassador Maxwell Taylor, a previous Chairman of the Joint Chiefs of Staff and a four-star general, again come to mind: 'White-faced soldier armed, equipped and trained as he is, is not [a] suitable guerrilla fighter for Asian forests and jungles'.[2] Whatever the most effective use of western soldiers might have been, new troops brought with them new tactical ideas—or old ones rehashed—but the operational questions generally remained unchanged.

Isolated from the more dangerous and heavy fighting provinces, the Australians in Phuoc Tuy had the luxury of an area in which they could operate with some tactical planning trial and error.[3] Those senior officers who believed that the war would be won through the efforts of pacification-cum-Revolutionary Development could ply their theories and be successful. On the other hand, generals such as A. L. MacDonald, who believed that the Task Force's main effort should have been against the enemy's main force, were also correct. Even the enemy agreed that there was a need for both types of operations.

Before his death in 1967 General Nguyen Chi Thanh, the *COSVN* commander, wrote articles that were broadcast on Radio Hanoi to rally the troops. Not only did he speak of defeating the South's political offensive, but the destruction of the rural pacification construction was also a priority. General Thanh outlined the varied and versatile tactical methods used by his forces in the South. Following his arguments with Hanoi's guerrilla warfare advocates he moderated his stance, highlighting the value of guerrillas to wear down and annihilate the opposition piecemeal. He said:

According to the enemy himself, the American mobile forces fight for one week; then they have to take a rest . . . to make preparations and reorganise. The attacks on communication routes and at his bases . . . forced him to defend everywhere. This battle alignment has obliged the enemy to tie down his troops . . . and to scatter his forces so that he sinks deeper into the defensive abyss. In the meantime, our main forces are free to operate anywhere and possess the conditions to concentrate and launch big offensives to annihilate the enemy. The longer he fights, the more men he loses. Confronting such a battle alignment is like beating one's head against a stone wall. The enemy naturally must reap bitter defeats.[4]

General Thanh added that fighting methods were different in Vietnam's many areas:

> Fighting methods at Ben Cat were different from those at Danang and Chu Lai. Combat hamlets in Cu Chi resorted to fighting methods different from those of Phu Yen and Binh Dinh. There were differences between the attacking methods in central Trung Bo and those in Nam Bo, between those in the delta and those in the mountainous areas, between attacks against Americans and those against the puppets [South Vietnamese; Australians were satellite troops].[5]

The advantage for the Australian occupants of Nui Dat was that the opposing forces in Phuoc Tuy Province were depleted—not only by battle losses—to the point where the threat of a major attack against the base facility was negligible. The Australians also had a disadvantage; each new senior Australian commander brought with him his own tactical solution to the fighting. The lack of a constant Australian tactical plan for the Task Force is evident among the reports and subsequent post-war interviews with commanders. In other words, the Australian force did not have a campaign plan other than to place themselves under the operational control of the Americans and display their independent national command card should an operation be not to their liking. According to many sources that card was never used, although polite questions on operational objectives were supposedly raised on several occasions. Back in 1965–1966 Australia adamantly rejected the use of its battalion on operations in non-approved locations; for example, in the Central Highlands.

Concern over Australian casualties was also now more evident. A. L. MacDonald knew that the Americans wanted to move the Task Force out of Phuoc Tuy, 'out into the big league', as he told General Daly, the CGS.[6] General Wilton, the Chairman of the Joint Chiefs of Staff, never agreed with the idea because Wilton understood a move meant going further north inside South Vietnam or into provinces contiguous to Cambodia, or Laos. That would have meant a loss of independence because the Task Force was not capable of separate operations in these more hectic locations. More casualties would also be an unbearable price. In 1969 when the Australian Defence Secretary, Sir Henry Bland, met with General Creighton Abrams, he concluded that the best approach was to minimise casualties; a view supposedly shared by Defence Minister Allen Fairhall and Prime Minister John Gorton.[7] When 8RAR suffered badly during another foray into the Long Hai hills in 1970, General Daly was most distressed by the casualties. Each of these examples counters the later claims by commanders that they were not under any restrictions regarding casualties. There may not have been a written directive but there is little doubt that the word was to keep the casualties to a minimum, and it was clearly factored into the questions asked about Australian operations by senior American commanders, all the way to the president of the United States.

Now, with a newly inaugurated American President—Richard Nixon—the course of the war was to change. Costs, both social and economic, combined with an increasing disbelief that success on the battlefield was within reach, started the inexorable decline in support for the South Vietnamese. Criticism of the government in the South as being a corrupt and incapable administration also continued unabated into 1969.

An updated Combined Campaign Plan saw the South Vietnamese government introduce a Pacification and Development Plan, released on 15 December 1968, which directed the strategy, concepts, priorities and objectives of the total pacification effort. There were eight primary objectives to be achieved in 1969, with area security listed as the principal aim. Security was to be provided by the regular forces while the local units such as Regional Force/Popular Force and police could be deployed so that hamlets and villages would be safer. The aim was to extend national sovereignty throughout South Vietnam.

The other objectives of the plan were to be implemented in concert: to eliminate the Viet Cong infrastructure, to establish local governments in all villages and to elect officials to manage hamlets and villages, to get more people involved in the People's Self Defence Force, rally returnees, decrease the number of refugees, increase information and propaganda by training, and to encourage the rural economy. All of this was to be accomplished behind the bulwark provided by the military operations of the ARVN-US and other Free World Military Forces. In a major change in procedure, the Vietnamese Joint General Staff assisted by MACV prepared the military plan. Previous plans had been prepared by MACV in *cooperation* with the

Vietnamese staff. In addition, and 'most significantly', the 'plan was signed by *each of the national commanders of Allied armed forces in RVN* [emphasised]'.[8] The priority of military tasks, therefore—and there were only two military objectives—must have been clearly understood by the Australians. The two military objectives were: to defeat NVA/VC forces and to extend government control in the Republic of Vietnam. The second military objective highlighted the need for more active operations to stop enemy infiltration into 'the fringes of towns, cities and areas adjacent to population centres'. Phuoc Tuy Province was listed as one of approximately 28 priority zones for military offensive operations. It was not a priority province for the allocation of pacification resources.

Here were clear guidelines on what was expected of the combat forces, Australians included, but again, how to achieve the agreed objectives was the decision of the current Australian commanders. The tactical burden was intensified because the Australians thought that the South Vietnamese forces weren't up to the task. General A. L. MacDonald and Brigadier Sandy Pearson were also of a similar mindset because they thought that it was the 'proper function of the Task Force . . . to get out after the regular Viet Cong and knock them out, eliminate them and separate them from the population'.[9]

Although the senior Australian commander had an obligation to watch over the Task Force, he had no operational planning authority. David Horner quoted an amusing observation by Colonel Donald Dunstan, the 1ATF Deputy Commander (January 1968 – January 1969), 'I don't think that even A.L. MacDonald, a professional interferer, ever interfered [in the operational command of the 1ATF]'. For those who served at any stage during MacDonald's tenure as a senior officer, that would be a difficult observation to swallow. Brigadier Ron Hughes had 'at least one occasion to resist strong advice from MacDonald about where to conduct one of his operations'. Also, allegedly during the enemy offensive of February 1969 MacDonald refused to allow the deployment of the Task Force out of Phuoc Tuy because Lieutenant General Walter Kerwin, the commander of IIFFV, had not asked him personally for permission! He gave way after Brigadier Pearson told him the Americans were 'strapped'.

MacDonald also thought 'Kerwin to be a bit bristly—a bit of an RSM of a commander who issued orders without prior consultation'.[10] This was the pot that called the kettle black considering MacDonald's disapproval of soldiers who did not salute smartly. A Land Rover–load of engineers who had not saluted General Wilton's party during a visit to the Task Force prompted the very strong rebuke from COMAFV that, 'If necessary he would remove the CO or OC of any unit who did not comply [to salute]'.[11]

This was also a time of changeover within the Australian Force Vietnam. Two of the infantry battalions rotated at the end of 1968 and early 1969 when 9RAR replaced 3RAR (November 1968) and 5RAR took over from 1RAR (February 1969). Tank squadron commanders also handed over, which meant that squadron titles changed with the new commander; C Squadron became B Squadron in February 1969.[12] Brigadier Pearson had assumed command of 1ATF in October 1968 and Major General Robert Hay was appointed Commander Australian Force Vietnam on 1 March 1969.

As the war rolled on and the Australian commitment reached its peak, the creep of military bureaucracy also became more obvious. During December 1968, an interesting administrative decision about standard of dress on leaving South Vietnam was promulgated in Task Force Routine Orders. It read:

All members . . . leaving the theatre on RTA [Return to Australia] or R and R are to be inspected by an *Officer of HQ 1ATF* [emphasised] at Luscombe airfield before departure. Any member who is improperly dressed or whose dress is not up to standard will be returned to his unit.[13]

A little earlier in the month the Task Force had provided a list of targets considered suitable for engagement by the USS *New Jersey*, a battleship armed with nine 16 inch (405 mm) and twenty 5 inch (125 mm) guns. The Australians identified 116 targets, with some as innocuous as a hut and suspected trenches. A wag might have considered adding target 117, the officer who turned back a soldier on his way home after twelve months of active service because of crumpled greens and dirty boots. The suggestion that an officer might be targeted is a bad joke, but the threat of a breakdown in discipline that might result in a physical altercation was not an American problem alone.

Fragging, the murder of officers, non-commissioned officers and enlisted men in the American forces was raised frequently in discussions and publications as an indicator of the command and training problems experienced by the Americans during the war. The Australians were praised for their close-knit military society and soundness of training as an illustration of a supposedly higher quality combat force. Both defence forces experienced similar difficulties with discipline, but the quantity and severity of offences were obviously reflected by the size of each nation's military deployments. At the height of these commitments, America fielded more than half a million troops in one year, in contrast to around 8000 Australians.

The American population was 200 million in 1968 and it was a nation in the midst of major sociological changes, which were frequently linked to some of the bad military discipline experienced in Vietnam. These changes caused severe cultural divisions and differing attitudes towards the war, according to investigative journalist Eugene Linden, who also wrote in the *Saturday Review* that the 'roots of these murder attempts [within units in Vietnam] lie outside the military and even the war'.[14] By comparison, the Australian population in 1968 was 12 million with an anti-war voice that had increased in volume, but the growing unrest within Australian society was less severe than America's troubles. Although the anti-war dissent did disturb some soldiers while on tour in Vietnam and after their return to Australia, their anger was mainly directed at the protesters, not the military command structure.

Even though Australians were proud—even boastful—of their military standards, as most armies are, excellent performance in combat was not the sole preserve of any one particular nationality in Vietnam. Major General Douglas Vincent, who had commanded Australian Force Vietnam in 1967, said when he wanted to strengthen the Task Force:

> The fleeting enemy and our rifle are too evenly matched . . . dispersing Viet Cong can nearly always elude our foot infantry who have insufficient immediate contact firepower . . . the ground mobility of our infantry is no better and usually inferior to that of the Viet Cong. As a killing machine . . . the infantry were achieving a kill ratio of less than three enemy killed for each Australian soldier killed.[15]

Australia also suffered weaknesses within its training systems that had a direct impact upon combat operations. Lieutenant Colonel Colin Khan, who commanded 5RAR during its second tour (1969–1970), observed following his visit in 1968 that Vietnam was 'a completely different war to the one he was training his unit for back in Australia'.[16] The number of Australian accidents on operations that had resulted in death or injury also raised serious concerns not only about training but also the level of combat knowledge of junior commanders. Exercise Lifesaver was implemented in February 1969 when the Commander 1ATF directed that every soldier be exercised in precautions to avoid accidental injury and death. Brigadier Pearson recommended the units look at the training program conducted successfully by the Army Reinforcement Unit. The aims of the retraining were:

> To exercise soldiers: in the correct procedures for handling weapons, and in the implementation of the rules of engagement, to practise states of weapon readiness, and to exercise junior commanders in the correct briefing of patrols, sentries etc.[17]

Major General A. L. MacDonald had mentioned his dissatisfaction with standards early in his tour of duty when he noted incidents that highlighted the sheer lack of basic knowledge of many junior non-commissioned officers and officers. When he had first arrived, MacDonald told Lieutenant General Daly, 'I did light a fire under the mess and I'm keeping it burning too'.[18] MacDonald was also unimpressed by the large amounts of alcohol consumed by Australians, a habit nevertheless considered less detrimental than the often-mentioned drug-taking by other allies. He acknowledged later that the Australian battalions fought well when up against the enemy's main force units and he was a staunch supporter of the infantry–tank combination, especially after the battles at Coral and Balmoral. MacDonald's personal convictions about the war also underwent a complete change at the end of his tour. According to David Horner, MacDonald believed the war was being won when he visited in 1967, but when he relinquished command of AFV in 1969 he had 'lost confidence in American intelligence assessments and had begun to doubt the outcome'. Furthermore, 'he believed that the Department of Defence and the government were trying to work out how to get out'.[19]

Change in the war effort was definitely underway in 1969. General Creighton Abrams, the Commander of MACV, championed his One War concept with an objective that everything—military, Revolutionary Development and all government agencies—must work in coordination to achieve success. The US Army's subsequent analysis on controlling the war also made mention of the Malaysian technique and its impact upon the Australian Task Force's successes in Vietnam. Lieutenant General Julian Ewell, US Army, who commanded IIFFV in 1969–1970, wrote this contentious observation on the Australian methods:

> The Malaysian experience tended to support the soft approach as it was quite successful in that case. What the casual observer missed was that the Malaya insurrection was a relatively weak and soft Communist effort, whereas the Vietnamese effort was a real war made possible by massive external support and intervention. As a result the rules in Vietnam were almost opposite from Malaya. This was graphically illustrated by the experience of the Australian Task Force. It has Malaysian experience in the jungle, stabilized units, extensive training and so on. Yet its successes were based on innovation and its least productive efforts were based on Malaysian type operations.[20]

In line with past complaints of pussyfooting and the known anger by several senior American generals that Australians were not pulling their weight, perhaps Ewell's mention of 'innovation' meant an operational willingness to be involved in the application of maximum force. Ewell and Hunt explained the concept:

> Once one decided to apply maximum force, the problem became a technical one of doing it efficiently with the resources available. However, the constant pressure concept, well applied did not lead to a brutalizing of the conflict. In fact, the reverse was true. It was a provable fact that it led to more prisoners of war and Hoi Chanhs than a soft approach. It also led to less civilian casualties and damage. It resulted in fewer friendly casualties ... more importantly pacification progressed more rapidly. The avoidance of civilian casualties and *body count padding* [emphasised] was more a matter of training and standards regardless of the approach involved.[21]

The explanation does not appear to offer anything different to General Westmoreland's plan to hunt down and destroy the enemy's main force

A day at the beach Vietnam War-style. A group of Australian soldiers takes a break watched over by two Centurion gun-tanks while a bridge-layer provides the shade. *Courtesy NVV Museum*

Trooper Normie Rowe, in from the field, entertains 4RAR/NZ (ANZAC) as a special guest artist at their farewell concert. *Courtesy Dennis Gibbons Collection, NVV Museum*

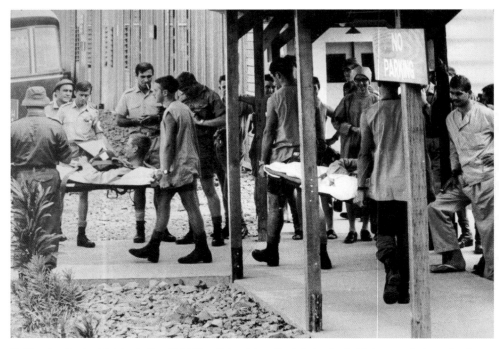

Staff and patients at 1st Australian Field Hospital watch patients being loaded into an ambulance for the journey to Vung Tau military airfield on their way to Australia for treatment. *Courtesy Dennis Gibbons Collection, NVV Museum*

Occasionally, recovering patients were taken to the beach near the 1st Australian Field Hospital, Vung Tau, by Red Cross staff. *Courtesy Dennis Gibbons Collection, NVV Museum*

An Australian military supply convoy on their way from Vung Tau to Nui Dat passes a Vietnamese wedding in Baria, the capital of Phuoc Tuy Province. *Courtesy Dennis Gibbons Collection, NVV Museum*

During a visit to the 1ATF Base at Nui Dat, Captain Amy Pittendreigh, and lieutenants Terrie Roche, Margaret Ahern and Colleen Mealey, watch the diggers from 2RAR leave on a mission. *Courtesy Dennis Gibbons Collection, NVV Museum*

An O-2 Super Skymaster—with leaflets streaming behind—as it completes a 'psychological warfare' mission. This aircraft was flown by the 9th Air Commando Squadron based at Danang. *Courtesy Photograph Department of the Air Force, Headquarters Seventh Air Force (PACAF)*

A novel use of steel helmets to collect and distribute water in the field, ARVN-style. ARVN units often lacked the basics in their logistics system; in this case, the unit did not have the plastic water cans that were a common item in the Australian Army. *Author's collection (BD)*

ARVN airborne troopers about to 'pop' smoke into an enemy bunker. The smoke was used to make it more difficult for anyone in the bunker to see and breathe. Note how well the bunker is camouflaged within its surrounds. Fighting through bunkers was the most deadly form of contact for the Australians during the war. *Author's collection (BD)*

ARVN in action (unknown date). Troops jump from their helicopters and head for the relative safety of the jungle.

Heavy fighting in the Highlands near Dak To, November 1967. General Westmoreland was pleased with clashes like this because it allowed American forces to utilise their superior firepower. Losses during this 21-day battle were heavy on both sides. *AP Photo*

Captain Tran Ngoc Hue receives the US Silver Star from General Creighton Abrams after the battle for Hue in 1968. Pham Van Dinh (right) awaits an award of the Bronze Star. Captain Joe Bolt (sunglasses) served as Dinh and Hue's adviser. *Courtesy Joe Bolt*

Prisoners captured during the early days of the war in the Mekong Delta, watched over by a South Vietnamese soldier holding a cocked pistol, August 1962. The prisoners were taken to a prisoner compound. *AP Photo/Horst Faas*

An exhausted South Vietnamese soldier among the debris of the NVA attempted invasion of the South, September 1972. The North Vietnamese admitted losing 140,000 regular forces during these battles. *AFP Photo*

Deadly souvenir. Sergeant John Shay, 1RAR, looks over an enemy heavy anti-aircraft machine gun (12.7 mm) captured during Operation Platypus, July–August 1968. *Courtesy NVV Museum*

A different type of warfare. Just to the south of the Demilitarised Zone, a US Marine CH-46 Sea Knight helicopter is shot down in flames, 15 July 1966. The helicopter crashed and exploded on a hill, killing one crewman and twelve Marines. *AP Photo/Horst Faas*

beyond their capacity to reinforce and continue the war. Westmoreland had also made quite clear in his directives to subordinate commanders that the killing of civilians through the use of indiscriminate force was an unacceptable tactic. Hounding, hammering and killing the enemy and the destruction of their safe bases was considered by many commanders— Australian, American and South Vietnamese—to be the winning formula. This was the shield behind which the South Vietnamese nation could stand firm and develop. The Australian Task Force would continue to follow this tactical plan into 1969 with some operations outside of Phuoc Tuy, but new orders were also on the way.

The Nixon plan—Vietnamisation

President Richard Nixon was sworn in as the 37th president of the United States on 20 January 1969. His Secretary of Defense was Melvin Laird, who had served as a politician in both the Senate and the House of Representatives. Laird had two advantages over the better-known Robert McNamara, a man many saw as arrogant and abrasive in his dealings with the military and with Congress. Laird had served on the Defense Subcommittee of the House Appropriations Committee, which provided him with strong connections within the bureaucracy. He had also worked more closely with the defence chiefs; in effect he trusted them more than McNamara did.

Laird travelled to Vietnam for five days in early March 1969 to review the progress of the war. From his subsequent report to the president, Laird reviewed five major topics:

> The current military assessment. The status of our [US] forces, specifically whether Abrams has everything . . . to insure the maximum safety and security of our personnel. The present readiness and progress of the Republic of Vietnam Armed Forces (RVNAF). The plans for withdrawal of American Forces. Termination Day ('T' Day) [end of hostilities] planning.[22]

All of these issues would have a profound impact upon the Australian commitment, too. When II Field Force Vietnam issued operational directives to the Australian Task Force, Major General Robert Hay, the overall commander of the Australian Force Vietnam, told the Australian Ambassador:

> The Australian military effort is under the operational control of MACV, and AFV quite rightly, is obliged to follow US priorities. It would be unthinkable for Australia to contemplate developing independent operations on national lines.[23]

At this stage, the so-called peace talks in Paris that began in 1968 were grinding on in an unproductive diplomatic effort to achieve an end to the war. The Americans and the South Vietnamese believed that they had sufficient military strength deployed to deny the enemy a military victory. At the same time, they also recognised that such a victory also eluded them. Laird understood that the American people were fed up with the war and wanted out of Vietnam. He effectively offered Richard Nixon a clean slate when he told him, 'your administration is not being held responsible for past decisions . . . which committed more than half-a-million troops, nearly 100 billion [100 thousand million dollars] . . . and more than 33,000 lives. They represent sunk costs'.[24]

Laird emphasised that in order to maintain the support of the American people for the war, the burden of combat should be promptly and methodically shifted to the South Vietnamese. The South Vietnamese already carried that burden of combat, if killed-in-action statistics meant anything. Turning the vast ship of military action around now would demand a new policy, one that became known as 'Vietnamisation'.

The fighting problems persisted. The enemy had launched another round of offensive strikes around the country, some of which would take the Australians back into Bien Hoa Province. No one believed that the enemy would achieve any form of battlefield success and the attacks were recognised as a means by which the northern leadership might influence the Paris negotiations. The sanctuaries enjoyed by the enemy in Laos and Cambodia as well as their refuge of North Vietnam allowed them to escape the overwhelming firepower available to the allied forces, and to conduct intermittent attacks in the hope that a disaffected American public would demand an early but disorderly withdrawal.

Laird went on to tell the president that:

General Abrams had made remarkable progress in achieving a measure of military superiority throughout South Vietnam. The pacification program, which must depend primarily and increasingly on South Vietnamese efforts, is also proceeding, though at a slower rate.[25]

The first part of that piece of advice is debatable. Even President Johnson had said that the military success had built upon a base laid by General Westmoreland, Abrams' predecessor. The comments about pacification merely reinforced what had previously been issued in campaign plans, even though the results were less than promised. Laird also gave a hint that some form of military operation in the border areas might create a diplomatic advantage for the US at Paris. This was a suggestion that he would discuss with the president in private.

He then provided what he said was an illustration of the complete adequacy of US military support, based on a comparison of expended tonnages of air ordnance!

In World War II, air ordnance utilized by the US in the European and Mediterranean theaters amounted to 1.5 million tons. The Pacific was . . . 0.5 million tons. The Korean War was . . . 0.6 million. World War II and Korea . . . accounted for 2.6 million tons. During the years 1966 through 1968, 2.8 million tons have already been expended in Southeast Asia.[26]

Laird was not impressed by the low rate of progress made by the South Vietnamese 'to assume more of the burden of the war'. He also noted that the South Vietnamese modernisation program was designed to cope with the Viet Cong, not the North Vietnamese Army. Military Assistance Command Vietnam had briefed the secretary that it would not be possible to reduce American forces without the withdrawal of the North Vietnamese. Laird did not accept that premise and he felt that true pacification could not be achieved 'while our own forces continue such a pervasive presence in South Vietnam'.[27] American orientation, he added, seemed to be more on operations than on assisting the South Vietnamese to acquire the means to defend themselves.

The question now posed by Laird was not whether they should do more, but less. With an improvement in South Vietnamese performance, America should be able to contain the enemy and at the same time reduce their military effort, he concluded. He believed by the end of 1969, 50,000 to 70,000 troops could be redeployed. American Embassy officials suggested that a reduction would trigger a proportionate reduction in other allied forces and Secretary Laird advised the president:

> Given the *highly disproportionate contributions* [emphasised] ... as compared with our own, such a withdrawal of Korean, Thai, Australian and New Zealand troops in an equal percentage would not significantly affect the total military strength confronting the enemy.[28]

Secretary Laird's example of the tough challenges America faced in trying to get out of the war touched the fringe of the Australian area of operations. 'We [US] have continued to tolerate notoriously incompetent commanders in the Fifth and Eighteenth Divisions', he told President Nixon.[29] Major General Pham Quoc Thuan commanded the 18th Division and it was headquartered at Xuan Loc, 45 kilometres north of Nui Dat. It was the main ARVN unit located in the eastern approach corridor to Saigon. Occasionally, the division deployed some troops into Phuoc Tuy Province but the principal Vietnamese security forces in the province were the poorly rated Regional and Popular Force soldiers.

Their standards were not helped by the Australians' reluctance to operate with Vietnamese forces. Although they made the effort to train and conduct some combined operations with the Vietnamese, in the main the Australians didn't trust them. It was not unusual to hear Australians describe the Vietnamese as lazy, corrupt, cowardly and inefficient, amongst less polite epithets. Their judgements were probably harsh but there is nothing new about criticisms levelled by one nation's armed forces against others in a multinational contingent, in both war and peace. In Vietnam, the Australians were not overly fond of American efforts and sometimes vice versa, while the Kiwis thought the Australians were amateurs. No one argued with the South Koreans.

The South Vietnamese had their veterans, too. There were many Vietnamese who fought overseas during World War II and also with both the Viet Minh and the French in Indochina. For all those times when the South Vietnamese troops in the vicinity of the Australian base appeared to be little better than useless, there were many other examples of the bravery and resourcefulness of ARVN soldiers. Vietnamese soldiers had also trained at Kota Tinggi, the British Jungle Warfare School in Malaya, in French military academies and also in US schools. Two hundred and twenty-two officers graduated from the US Army Command and General Staff College and there was a sprinkling of Vietnamese officers who were multilingual in French, English and Vietnamese. Most Australians struggled to say hello in Vietnamese, which was an embarrassment for a force that sometimes wanted to be involved at the forefront of pacification.

The South Vietnamese armed forces suffered from a rapid expansion through conscription and a shortfall of experienced or well-trained officers and non-commissioned officers to command and lead; a similar weakness to that commented upon by Major General A. L. MacDonald about the Australian Army's recent increase. The American Army had also scrambled to cope with a dramatic increase in its ranks. As an example, the American officer corps increased by 56 per cent from 1964 to 1969, bringing with it the associated problems of selection suitability and the correlated quality of trained graduates.

The ARVN acknowledged some of its weaknesses in articles like the one written by Nguyen Ngoc Linh, an influential editor in Saigon. He wrote the following on Brigadier General Phan Trong Chinh, who commanded the 25th ARVN Division from 1965 to the end of 1967:

> The 25th improved its intelligence network, learning more about enemy dispositions; and it improved its ability to march its troops in the opposite direction. Thus month after month the 25th would find itself on the bottom of the list of divisions rated by the number of enemy contacts per operation.[30]

This was understandable because the South Vietnamese Army was established in the early 1950s out of the native auxiliaries of the French Union Forces. The official language of the Vietnamese defence force until 1955 was French just eleven years prior to 1ATF's deployment and many expert advisers in between. The ARVN had evolved from the disparate training methods of their saviours and that included earlier versions of Vietnamisation.

Disapproval also flowed more easily when the US or Australian critic only had to survive an average deployment of less than twelve months with some rest and recreation and other in-country rest periods thrown in as well. In addition, the ARVN could not call on the plentiful combat support available to the Free World Forces. Getting their wounded evacuated from the battlefield was another morale-busting delay for the Vietnamese. They had limited access to helicopters at the best of times and they lacked decent first-aid medication. Wound treatment in the field was basic but creative; there were times when green coconut milk was used as quasi-plasma. It was not unusual for ARVN soldiers' families to be nearby the military bases, or inside a compound, and sometimes to be involved in battle. Those who fought alongside the Vietnamese noticed that the years of warfare for them tended to tear the energy from the soundest of men.

The doubts about the outcome of the war expressed by several previous Australian senior officers, including two AFV commanders at the end of their tours, were also disturbing and surely should have been expressed in the most emphatic manner at the highest levels at Canberra. According to David Horner, Major General Mackay had an informal discussion with General Wilton but Admiral Alan McNicoll, who at least wrote to Wilton, got a non-committal reply. McNicoll was the Chief of Naval Staff and he was shocked by his visit to Vietnam during Tet 1968. 'When he returned to Australia neither the Chiefs of Staff Committee nor the Department of External Affairs gave him the opportunity to comment on what he had learned. He came to the conclusion that no-one in Australia was really interested in what was going on in Vietnam.'[31]

Colonel Alan Stretton, the Chief of Staff to COMAFV from April 1969 and later a major general, took a disdainful view of the allied effort. He had visited Vietnam several times before his appointment as the Chief of Staff; his last visit before his appointment was for four days in July 1967. He felt that the situation was crumbling, he revealed many years later in his autobiography. This was a view that smacked of wisdom in hindsight, as both sides admit the war had reached a stalemate in 1967 and South Vietnam was certainly in its best position for many years. Stretton's suggestion that the lack of Australian participation in the formulation of the 1968 Campaign Plan 'lost us the opportunity of asserting Australian leadership . . . in which Australian professional advice may well have changed the course of the war' is amusing at best. Some might consider it overly arrogant and nonsensical.[32]

The Australian flag that flew at the Free World Headquarters at 12 Tran Quoc Toan, Saigon, was a diplomatic necessity but its influence in the high-powered military stakes at MACV and the Vietnamese Joint Chiefs of Staff was insignificant. Australia had had its chance with the positioning of Colonel Serong on the MACV Headquarters where he served as a counterinsurgency special adviser to generals Harkins and Westmoreland, as well as being the commander of the AATTV. American command had reluctantly accepted his appointment in the early years, but whatever influence he might have had soon fizzled out and the dual duty of special adviser and commander AATTV was not continued when his tour of duty expired in 1965. The Americans and the South Vietnamese had an overabundance of advisers, consultants, experts and critics on how to fight the war. The RAND Corporation had more influence with their broad range of studies undertaken over the years than any attempt made by the Australian Army at tactical guidance.

The Australians were acknowledged as being worthy soldiers. They fought well and the accolades flowed, but there were also feelings of anger and sometimes hidden contempt for the isolated Australian force that was unwilling to get out into the major battleground. Senior American officers and some Australians also questioned the relevance of Australia's frequently cited Malayan experience. Most of them said that the Malayan conditions did not match the combat conditions throughout Vietnam. In any case, although Australians became very adept at Malayan jungle patrols, by the time the Task Force was deployed into Nui Dat (1966) there were few soldiers left in the ranks with that experience. And even in the almost continuous cycle of troops flowing through Vietnam, the current experience pool soon evaporated. Navy (sea-going) personnel, for example, sailed in Vietnamese waters for 34 days, on average. The most common tour for army personnel was 311 days in Vietnam; the majority (75 per cent) served up to one year. Based on days of service—not to be confused with tours—only about 668 soldiers served more than two years in Vietnam over the ten-year war.[33]

The main reasons for the Task Force's limitations lay in the size of the Australian Army as well as its British influenced counterinsurgency doctrine and training. The Task Force was suited to the conduct of mid-level anti-guerrilla warfare that matched their deployment in Phuoc Tuy Province. To go chasing main force regiments needed a gamut of firepower and support that the Australians did not have. They would need to link into a larger US formation for them to be involved in operations on a scale beyond a light brigade's capabilities and that was not advisable. As General Julian Ewell at II Field Force Vietnam noted, 'the sizeable and widespread enemy pressure here doesn't quite fit the Malaysian [Malayan] experience'.[34]

An ARVN general's point of view

Major General Nguyen Van Hieu replaced the previously ineffectual commander of the 5th ARVN Division in 1969. The division was located north of Saigon and at the time it was rated as one of the three worst of the ARVN's ten infantry divisions. The other wooden-spoon nominees were the 18th and 25th.[35] Hieu previously commanded the 22nd ARVN Division at Qui Nhon where he had worked closely with the US 1st Cavalry Division (Airmobile) on pacification efforts in Binh Dinh Province.[36] He drew an analogy for the problems of pacification when he was told to move his forces away from the pacified areas and leave them to the Regional Force/Popular Force to secure:

> Thrusting one's fist into a fish bowl, the fish move away and stay away as long as the arm is in the fish bowl; however, as soon as the fist is withdrawn, the fish return to that spot. He said the same thing can happen with regard to the Viet Cong in populated areas, that is, when ARVN and US forces move away, the Viet Cong tend to return. In [Hieu's] view the province had sufficient Regional Force/Popular Force forces, but these forces require further improvement in combat effectiveness, and need the reassurance of support from nearby US and ARVN forces in order to keep out the Viet Cong.[37]

The full effect of Vietnamisation also opened the eyes of Tran Van Don, a retired general turned politician when he spoke with General Hieu during a field visit.

> I visited (some units in the field) and tried to understand the program of Vietnamisation of the war . . . it was in the headquarters of 5th Division. I discussed the question with the commander of the division, General Minh [Nguyen] Van Hieu, a most honest general, and capable, too. I was surprised by his answer; it

opened my eyes. I asked him, what do you think of Vietnamisation? He said to me, it's impossible to be implemented. Why? He said, the 5th Division covers an area where there were two other divisions, Americans, and now with the departure of the two American divisions I have only my division to cover the whole area. I have three regiments for this area and must use one regiment to replace one division. How can I face the enemy like this? I have become weaker. He looked very disappointed. I was surprised; he was a quiet man, a polite man, and he tried to do his best. But he said to me that this was impossible. How can I cover a bigger area with fewer units?[38]

General Hieu's soldiers fought against some of the same main force units that the Australians had previously clashed with during their forays into Bien Hoa Province during Tet 1968 and after at the Coral and Balmoral bases.

Slogging on

Renewed possible threats against Saigon by the enemy's *5th* and *7th* divisions had been detected at the end of 1968, but this time the allied forces were well prepared. Although Operation Toan Thang (Complete Victory) is the often-quoted counteroffensive that was launched against the NVA/Viet Cong, it was an umbrella name that covered numerous individual unit operations. Toan Thang I and II continued throughout 1968 and well into 1969 and the Australian Task Force's Operation Goodwood was part of it.

Goodwood started on 3 December when the Task Force headquarters, the tanks of C Squadron, and 3 Cavalry Regiment's A Squadron, neither of which were at full strength, moved to Fire Support Base Julia. This base was to the east of Route 15 on an old airstrip south of Tham Thien hamlet and just across the Phuoc Tuy–Bien Hoa provincial border. The Goodwood plan was to conduct reconnaissance in force operations in the Hat Dich base area to engage and destroy elements of *274 Viet Cong Regiment* and to demolish any of their installations. Brigadier Pearson had somewhat of a mix and match force with Australian, Vietnamese and American units in contiguous areas of operations. Not only did Pearson have 1RAR with him, but he also had a bundle of other allied units in direct support. The ARVN 2nd Airborne Brigade was 15 kilometres to his northeast, in Long Khanh Province. A reduced squadron of the US 11th Armored Cavalry Regiment was due east about 15 kilometres away and the 4th Battalion, 12th Infantry from the US 199th Light Infantry Brigade was also involved.

This meant that the Australian Task Force as the coordinating headquarters had about the equivalent of six battalions under its control, but in the first week only one infantry battalion (1RAR) was Australian. The new boys on the block, 9RAR, were just finding their operational feet on a trial run north of the Nui Dat base, and 4RAR was back at Nui Dat. An American officer created a minor command hiccup when he questioned the legality of placing his force under a foreign commander, but he was told to get on with it. General Abrams approved of such arrangements at a weekly meeting later in the year. Throughout the operation that went through until 17 February 1969, several of the allied units were released from direct support of the Task Force and both 4RAR and 9RAR would join the fray. Protection of Nui Dat was then handed over to 1RAR, allowing them a comparative rest, although patrolling around the home base did not stop. The two older battalions (1RAR and 4RAR) swapped around again two weeks later while 9RAR soldiered on. Although companies from 1RAR then became involved in land clearing operations across Route 15 around Phu My, the battalion was at the end of its tour and handed over to 5RAR on 15 February 1969.

Overall, Operation Goodwood was successful with frequent minor-scale contacts with the enemy. There was one enemy attack upon an ARVN fire support base at Red Hat, which was about 20 kilometres north of Tham Thien and just north of a rubber plantation near Binh Son. The attack was not successful. At the conclusion of the operation, the Australian Task Force produced a list of the results achieved by all of the units involved:

Total number of contacts 274. Enemy killed by body count 245, with another 39 possibly killed. Individual weapons captured 195. Crew served weapons captured 21. Various quantities of mines, grenades, mortar and recoilless rifle ammunition, rocket-propelled grenades and explosives were captured or destroyed. The haul also included 11 tons of rice.[39]

But, as always in hotly contested locations the achievements did not come lightly. Nineteen Australians and one New Zealander were killed or died of their wounds during Goodwood and 105 soldiers were wounded in action. The ARVN forces suffered 25 killed in action and 75 were wounded. The results attracted favourable comment in the *MACV Command History* for February 1969 with an acknowledgement that the Australian-led operation had caused more problems for the enemy and a severe impact upon their morale:

Goodwood, a four-nation Australian-directed operation that included US, Australian, New Zealand and Vietnamese [was conducted] in the Hat Dich area, approximately 43 km southeast of Bien Hoa. The operation disrupted enemy logistic support and kept the enemy on the defensive throughout the area that he had previously regarded as his own. It denied enemy infiltration routes to Saigon, to . . . Hat Dich–Binh Son and other [areas] of importance. The remainder of the year [1969] saw the 1st ATF finding only numerous small contacts.[40]

Although some elements of *274 Viet Cong Regiment* were detected in the Goodwood operational area, they did not mention fighting against the Australians in their historical records. *274 Viet Cong Regiment* was previously listed as a *5th Viet Cong Division* formation, but it was now operating well away from that division and it was probably under operational control of the Viet Cong *T7 Military Region*.[41] At the end of 1968 and into the first quarter of 1969, the *5th Viet Cong Division* had been reorganised. Tran Minh Tam was appointed the divisional commander and the division now had four regiments:

The 88th Regiment rejoined the division near the Cu Chi–Trang Bang area [northwest of Saigon]. The 174th Regiment that had been raised in 1949 in the Cao Bang region of North Vietnam had been ordered to go south in 1967. It fought in the Central Highlands against the 173rd Airborne Brigade and then redeployed to Phuoc Long Province where it joined the 5th Viet Cong Division. The 33rd and the 275th regiments were in an assembly area mid-way between Saigon and Tay Ninh at Chua Mountain [well to the west of Phuoc Tuy].[42]

This structure changed soon after when the *88th Regiment* disappeared from the *5th Viet Cong Division*'s organisation.

During this early part of 1969, the regiments of the *5th Viet Cong Division* were also involved in attacks against Bien Hoa from the opposite side of the base to that of the Australian Operation Goodwood. They did not do well and they failed to complete their main task, which was noted in the *5th Viet Cong Division*'s history:

> Our plan was to lure out the enemy forces northeast of Saigon in order to destroy them in the two main areas of Tay Ninh–Binh Long and Long Khanh. After the first phase, the division's personnel numbers and equipment had declined. Specifically, in February [1969] the number of wounded in the division had reached 597 comrades [estimated 800 killed and wounded]. In the second phase, the division organised a series of political activities . . . to redress any negative thoughts and lessening of fighting resolve among a number of cadre and soldiers.[43]

Obviously the political commissar's activities were successful, as the enemy regiments fought a series of battles against American and ARVN troops in a general arc north of Route 1, west of Highway 20, and across the Dong Nai River. The 18th ARVN Division was also put under considerable combat pressure in the area north and west of Xuan Loc. They needed help and the US 199th Light Infantry Brigade was moved to Long Khanh Province, where it operated in conjunction with the ARVN division in the combined Dong Tien (Progress Together) program.

A strong allied force now circled Saigon. In the eastern area of operations, the Royal Thai Army Volunteer Force of nearly 12,000 personnel—a six-battalion division—now joined the protective ring in Long Khanh and Bien Hoa provinces. The enemy soon put them to the test, but the Thais proved their fighting resilience in several major contacts in which they killed 56, then a further 65 and several months later in May, in two battles over two days, the enemy lost 41 and 87 killed against the Thai force. A few weeks later the Thai Volunteer Force killed another 212 Viet Cong. These battles cost the Thais 9 killed and 72 wounded, which was a notable battle achievement.

New directives

In May 1968, the AATTV had expanded its activities into IV Corps, which encompassed the Mekong Delta. Although the representation was a small group of warrant officers headed by Major Graham 'Curly' Templeton, attached from Headquarters AFV, Major General George Eckhardt appreciated the offer. Eckhardt was the senior American adviser to the region that was commanded by Lieutenant General Nguyen Duc Thang. Lieutenant Colonel Ray Burnard, CO AATTV, was pleased with the change in the method of operations by the Regional Force companies instigated by General Thang. The general had directed that the Regional Force was to be a mobile reserve under the command of the province chief rather than being stuck in a static role as was common in other tactical zones. When Burnard visited Vinh Binh Province, the province chief was out in a tactical command post conducting an ambitious and successful mobile operation. This impressed Burnard and he arranged for four Australians to be attached to two of the Regional Force companies. The Americans would provide a Mobile Advisory Team (MAT) for the third company.[44] They welcomed the more experienced Australians. 'Their professionalism, experience and motivation help to provide a backbone for the inexperienced members of [US] MAT', one glowing US report said.[45]

The method of assisting the inhabitants of the Mekong Delta region developed into a most worthwhile effort with not only the Regional Force/Popular Force teams, but also an old system that regained favour when Village Defence Advisory Teams were also deployed in the provinces of IV Corps. This operation was based on the principle that a strong village would repel the Viet Cong and eventually the villages would band together to take control of their own region. It was known as the tactic of the spreading ink blot or oil stain, and both sides in the conflict used it. This tactic also resurfaced in Afghanistan during 2010.

The AATTV would later expand its involvement in mobile training teams in various locations around South Vietnam with its greatest number of teams eventually being established in Phuoc Tuy.[46] The mobile teams concept was not an Australian idea. It was an American training method and team members were trained at Di An, a base on the northeastern outskirts of Saigon. Australians also attended this course.

With the new deployments came a change of thinking about the type of soldier to be allotted to the AATTV. As the monthly reports recorded:

The men have assisted and advised on village self-help and administration. The Team must be prepared to advise in these and other non-military fields if they are to be accepted at this level. The maturity and down-to-earth approach of the older and more experienced members of AATTV makes them admirably suited to this project.

That was reinforced by a later commanding officer, Lieutenant Colonel Alex Clark (later colonel) when he reported the following:

> In very general terms there are two quite different types of warrant officer in AATTV. One type is a commander at platoon level in SF [Special Forces] and can be young and a dasher. The other type is an adviser and should be a mature, tolerant and knowledgeable man at battalion and company level tactics. With the run down in SF there will be no requirement for the young dasher type. Training in Australia should be directed towards this end. It is becoming more important that advisers arrive in country with at least a smattering of the Vietnamese language.[47]

Australia now had troops with the Task Force at Nui Dat in III Corps Tactical Zone as well as just over 100 advisers spread from the Demilitarized Zone in the north to the southern Mekong Delta. The activities in which Australians were engaged were as diverse as the countryside in which they all operated. They were being bombarded by North Vietnamese artillery, leading Montagnards in the highlands, slogging through waterlogged paddy fields of the Delta and searching out the enemy in their Phuoc Tuy bases as well as providing a helping hand to local villagers. Hunting down the Viet Cong infrastructure in organisations such as the Phoenix Program's Provincial Reconnaissance Units also involved a small number of Australians. Captain Len Opie DCM was the chief of training at their centre near Vung Tau and Warrant Officer 'Ossie' Ostara DCM controlled a very successful PRU at Qui Nhon. Later on, the concept was frowned upon; reportedly, it became a private army that got out of control, and Australian involvement was reduced and restricted wherever possible.

New edicts from Lieutenant General Julian Ewell, who had assumed command of IIFFV on 3 April 1969, changed the priorities for the Australian Task Force. Ewell met first with Major General Robert Hay, COMAFV, to clarify if there were 'any strings' attached to the employment of the Task

Force. He was particularly interested in any restrictions with regard to the acceptance of casualties. General Hay replied:

> I said quite clearly there were no restrictions, and that our national attitude was that our Field Commanders were competent, well trained and capable of producing sound military plans with adequate fire and air support [perhaps in a side whisper, if you will provide it] and that under such circumstances we hoped that our casualties would be kept to a minimum.[48]

Subsequently, General Ewell altered the directive to 1ATF. Pacification was now the Australians' first priority. In order of precedence, the next task was the upgrading of the South Vietnamese forces and the third priority was military operations, or defeating the enemy's main force. This was a reversal of the roles over previous years, although it was argued that a military operation—defeating the main enemy force—was a necessity for a successful pacification effort.[49] The methods and priorities were a never-ending debate, but all of this came with the caveat that Saigon was to be protected at all times.

Peace negotiations and deceit on both sides

The Paris negotiations that had begun in May 1968 eventually brought a halt to all air, naval and artillery bombardment of North Vietnam on 1 November 1968. President Johnson made much of the assurances from the Joint Chiefs of Staff and General Creighton Abrams that the halt would not result in any increase in American casualties. By this date, most of the major main force enemy units were in border sanctuaries that provided them with security and flexibility to attack significant targets such as Saigon—which was what the COSVN forces attempted during their weakened offensives throughout 1969.

Following on from the Johnson efforts, President Nixon and his senior advisers attempted to use the private sessions of the Paris talks to negotiate a settlement in Vietnam in early 1969. When this failed, Henry Kissinger, the Assistant to the President for National Security Affairs, met secretly with Xuan Thuy and Le Duc Tho, the senior negotiators from Hanoi. Saigon was excluded and the South Vietnamese held deep suspicions about America's intentions. As Ambassador Ellsworth Bunker reported to Washington:

Were we ready to turn our backs on them? Was the outgoing [Johnson] administration perhaps so intent on results that it was ready to sacrifice vital interests of
our allies? Unfair questions perhaps, but deeply troubling ones to many of South
Vietnam's leaders.[50]

President Nixon was determined to bring the war to an end in a manner
that got Americans out of the conflict, come what may. He had been elected,
after all, as the peace candidate, but it is doubtful that US adherence to the
concept of a peaceful self-governing South Vietnam was an unviolable principle in the president's mind. President Nixon was determined to use force to
influence a resolution of the Paris negotiations by bombing the enemy's sanctuaries in Cambodia. Unbeknown to all but a handful of civilian and military
personnel, the president had ordered that enemy positions located inside
Cambodia were to be bombed by B-52s and the first missions were flown
during the night of 17–18 March 1969. The bombing was done at a time
when American troop withdrawals had been signalled as a probability and it
continued during the period when the redeployments were in progress.

When the deceit was uncovered, the explanation was that the missions
were conducted against North Vietnamese and Viet Cong logistic and troop
build-ups in Cambodia, especially *COSVN*, the enemy's southern military
region headquarters. All of which—the bombing and the NVA routes—made a
mockery of Cambodia's supposed sovereignty. The missions were also described
as a protective barrier for the withdrawing US forces. Regardless of the later
anger expressed by the American public about the bombing, senior American
military commanders had complained previously about the unbearable situation where more and more enemy supplies were coming in through Port
Sihanoukville in the southwestern region of Cambodia. Although the military
commanders did not obtain approval from the Johnson administration to use
B-52 strikes inside the so-called neutral country, they had used tactical fighter-
bomber strikes across the border, probably from around late 1965.

Australia had retained its sensitivities on Cambodia's neutrality at the
time in 1968 when General Earle Wheeler, the Chairman of the Joint Chiefs
of Staff, lobbied President Johnson with the words, 'We are going to have to
go after Cambodian sanctuaries . . . It is intolerable. We must do something
about it'.[51] Wheeler also expressed a strong censure to Johnson about the

Australian Ambassador at Phnom Penh: 'The Australian Ambassador there isn't worth a damn. He told me there wasn't a single NVN [North Vietnamese] in Cambodia'.[52] Australia's leaders were not told of the B-52 bombing of Cambodia in 1969.

My Lai carnage

Ironically, at around the same time that President Nixon approved the bombing of Cambodia, a heartrending complaint against members of the US 23rd (American) Division was gathering pace. On 29 March 1969, Ron Ridenhour, who had served as a private in the division, wrote a letter addressed to congressional and military officials in which he detailed alleged killings in a Vietnamese hamlet known as My Lai in March 1968. A friend, Private First Class 'Butch' Gruver, had told Ridenhour of the killings. Gruver said that:

> We massacred this whole village. We just lined them up and killed them. Men, women and kids, everybody, we killed them all. Ridenhour asked how many was that? The friend replied, Oh, I don't know, three or four hundred I guess, at least. A lot, everybody we could find.[53]

The final number of civilians slaughtered in the area of Son My village that encompassed My Lai (Number 4) and another hamlet, My Khe (Number 4), will never be known. The Vietnamese District Chief, Lieutenant Tran Ngoc Tan, wrote to the Quang Ngai province chief in April 1968 and said that 'the allies killed near 500 civilians . . . really an atrocious attitude if it cannot be called an act of insane violence. Request that you intervene on behalf of the people'.[54]

Alongside the darkness of hatred there was also a light of humanity. Warrant Officer Hugh Thompson, an American army helicopter pilot, landed his helicopter several times in attempts to assist the villagers and to stop the killings. During this standoff, he told his gunner to fire on American troops if needed to stop them moving towards the villagers. He later reported to his company commander what he and his crew had witnessed. This report was passed up the chain of command, but Lieutenant Colonel Frank Barker— commander of the task force conducting the operation—allegedly stifled the complaint and did nothing.

Subsequently, in November 1969, Lieutenant General William Peers was ordered to review the incident and he recommended that the information he uncovered should be referred to respective general court-martial convening authorities. He also recommended possible disciplinary or administrative action against 28 officers including Major General Samuel Koster, the commander of the division, and two non-commissioned officers. Just thirteen men were charged, but only Lieutenant William Calley was convicted. He served a mere three years of a life sentence, and that was under house arrest.

Hugh Thompson and his crew members were later awarded the Soldier's Medal, the highest award granted by the US Army for valour in a non-combat situation.

Cape Batangan encompassed the hamlets of Son My village. The bulbous headland, sprinkled with rice paddies that merged with coastal sand dunes, was well known to Australian advisers. The whole coastal stretch from Quang Ngai north to Hoi An was dangerous territory. It had many hidden coves and landing places used by the enemy as resupply routes from the South China Sea. It was at the Sa Ky River in 1967 that a North Vietnamese steel-hulled trawler was captured with nearly 90 tons of ammunition and supplies on board. The Sa Ky River was 4 kilometres northeast of My Lai. In a 1967 action that was almost a forerunner to My Lai, an Australian adviser had the unpleasant experience of accompanying troops of the newly arrived American Task Force Oregon on an orientation patrol to the east of Highway 1, north of Quang Ngai. He recalled:

I was an adviser with an ARVN battalion then located on a small hill to the north of Tam Ky when an American force set up nearby. We were asked to assist them get to know the immediate area and my battalion commander agreed to send a few of us on patrols toward the coast. This area is scattered with hamlets from where the people tended the rice and also went fishing. It was flat, almost featureless, sandy and the home to poor peasants, a good number of Viet Cong and occasionally some of the 2nd NVA Division. As we approached one of the hamlets on a daytime patrol, we were shot at. Not a serious engagement, it was almost like go away and leave us alone. Well, the response was a mind-boggling explosion of firepower up to and including tanks and mortars. I grabbed my Vietnamese radio operator and we walked backwards away from what seemed to be an unstoppable inferno. I trembled with anger and probably fear as well, as I thought to try and stop this would be my death.[55]

An argument with the American captain who led the advisory team followed, and harsh words were exchanged along the lines that this was no better than murder. It was not combat. Subsequently, following a few *discussions* up the line, the matter was resolved by moving the Australian adviser to another ARVN battalion.

Task Force Oregon was redesignated the Americal Division on 25 September 1967.

The times they are a-changing

Clinton Heylin, a Dylan biographer, told the story of how Tony Glover, an American singer and author, picked up a page of a song that Dylan had written in 1963. Glover read a line, 'Come senators, congressmen, please heed the call', which prompted him to ask, 'What is this shit, man?' Dylan reportedly shrugged and replied, 'Well, you know, it seems to be what the people want to hear.' Christopher Ricks, a literary critic, suggested the song went beyond the political preoccupations of the time in which it was written; a comment that was borne out when the lyrics stirred the emotions of the strong anti–Vietnam War movements that gathered pace a few years after the song's release. The verse about senators and congressmen not blocking the hall, as there is a battle outside and it is raging, and it will soon shake your windows and rattle your walls, was powerful stuff even though the words were not specifically anti-Vietnam.[56] But the times were about to change markedly for South Vietnam on a small island in the middle of the North Pacific Ocean where presidents Nixon and Thieu met on 8 June 1969.

Midway Island—actually two islands, Sand and Eastern—is halfway around the world from anywhere. It was here that President Richard Nixon announced the first withdrawal of 25,000 American troops, the equivalent of a US division, from South Vietnam. The troop redeployment was to begin within 30 days and be completed by the end of August 1969.

Behind the initial agreement, the Nixon administration was embroiled in a planning process for continued withdrawals—although the term withdrawal was not to be used—that pitted the departments of Defense and State against each other. At the same time, General Abrams wanted to be cautious. The possibility that some of the other nations might also reduce their troop numbers did not overly concern the American Secretary of Defense. He had previously stated that the loss of Australian troops would not significantly affect the force confronting the enemy. Prime Minister Gorton had only been told of the American redeployment decision just hours before it was made public. His reaction, when questioned on Australia's commitment, was to say that the current force in Vietnam was well balanced and to remove part of it would be dangerous. The Chiefs of Staff Committee supported Gorton on this decision.

In Australia, public opinion had now swung away from support for the war when a Morgan Gallup Poll taken in August 1969 showed that 55 per cent of respondents favoured withdrawal. Forty per cent supported staying on, which was a markedly different tone from May 1967 when 24 per cent who answered said to get out but 62 per cent had supported the war.[57] The projections of a rolling communist takeover of Southeast Asia that had troubled the leaders of the late 1950s and early 1960s had been replaced in 1969 by a picture of regional stability; ironically, something not generally attributed to the Vietnam War.[58]

Of course the problems between China and the Soviet Union that had fractured the monolithic structure of communism also helped erase some of the fear held about their capabilities to conquer the region. Prime Minister John Gorton had previously indicated in July and October 1969 that 'the withdrawal of the army component, when it occurred, would be total'.[59] Gorton was also recorded on 8 October as having said that Australia would not pull its troops out of Vietnam because 'to do so would be to abandon an objective, to betray our allies and, I believe, to imperil Australia's future security'.[60] This philosophy was now very much out of step with the American government's actions as well as the changed regional strategic environment.

Pacifying Phuoc Tuy—again

The Australians understood that controlling the enemy's infrastructure was no easy task. Task Force commanders from the earlier days had worried over the enemy's main force threat to the Nui Dat base, but that challenge had been met and defeated in combination with American combat power. A more insidious threat now came in the form of guerrilla squads and a quasi-political grouping that operated against the allied pacification programs. The ever-present *D445 Viet Cong Battalion*—or a lurking main force regiment—provided the heavy muscle if and when it was needed to remind the Australians that they could not treat the Phuoc Tuy battlefield as their own backyard.

The NLF infrastructure had its tentacles wrapped around the main areas of population in the province with hard-core cells in places such as Dat Do, Long Dien, and Phuoc Hai and among the disaffected people of the destroyed Long Phuoc now at Hoa Long. There was an increased countrywide effort by the South Vietnamese and their allies to win over the people and to improve the provision of government services into those areas that previously were badly provided for, or went without. Regional and Popular Forces were re-equipped with M-16 rifles, which was a great relief for the average five-foot tall (1.6 metre) South Vietnamese soldier who had struggled to drag around an M-1 Garand that was nearly as long as he was tall. An old program organised originally by the French as the hamlet militia was revamped as the People's Self Defence Force in the hope that with more training and more weapons the campaign at the grass roots against the Viet Cong infrastructure would gain momentum. In general, the main principles of counterinsurgency—security, food, intelligence and communication—remained unchanged.[61] The ongoing dilemma for the Australians, and other westerners as well, was the challenge of separating the enemy infrastructure from the villagers. Joining the battle out in the fields against an armed enemy was fairly straightforward in that someone generally shot at someone else and a firefight followed. Around the hamlets and villages, identifying friend from foe required a little more finesse.

Obviously the Australians knew where the worst areas were within Phuoc Tuy with regard to enemy influence and sympathisers. Regardless, they didn't necessarily want to go into some places to clear them out; the Long Hai hills, for example. Although a known Viet Cong base area, efforts to clear the area had come with morale-busting psychological scars, ironically caused by Australian mines lifted from the Dat Do minefield. To root out the Viet Cong infrastructure and possibly capture or kill some armed enemy in other hiding places meant going into the villages, or isolating a village while the South Vietnamese did the search. This was a core decision that had waxed and waned in implementation over the years, but now with the change in directive from IIFFV the Australian effort had returned to Phuoc Tuy Province and the problems of keeping the Viet Cong away from the people. In some areas, separating the two was a directive that the people didn't want to obey.

This was obvious in Dat Do and along the more heavily settled strips to Phuoc Hai and Long Dien. Old lessons now resurfaced, not only with the changing structure of the Task Force as the main combat units rotated but also as successive counterinsurgency concepts struggled to take the lead in military operational plans.

The more successful efforts to control the villages around South Vietnam involved continuous security. In heavily contested areas that meant the nearby deployment of an allied or ARVN battalion as a minimum until the threat was either destroyed or the enemy moved off to wait until the strong government force was withdrawn. The latter was inevitable with too many village regions and too few troops to protect them all. The withdrawal of regular battalions then placed the responsibility for security upon the Regional and Popular Forces, which could handle the low level actions provided they were well led, motivated and well equipped.

There was another problem: too often the Regional Force/Popular Force were required to combine the tasks of internal and external security. Arguments among the experts attempted to divide the external protection force from the internal duties, which were seen as the function of a local police type unit like the hamlet militia or People's Self Defence Force. They were close to the community and conducted their activities in a different manner to an army formation and that should have allowed the military arms to be more active outside the village.

The Australian Task Force took on the challenge to assist by training Regional Force platoons. These courses were conducted at the Heavyweight base under the auspices of Captain Robert Guest of the AATTV and some instructors provided by the Australian battalions. But the less powerful local units could not be expected to take on the enemy's main force in a fight to protect their village. This often meant that as soon as the ARVN or allied battalion left the immediate vicinity of a village, cooperation—or sullen obedience—with the government stopped.

To ferret out the NLF's infrastructure from within the villages was beyond the capabilities of the Task Force.[62] The first difficulty was language. With a very limited number of interpreters, it did not require great expertise on the part of a Viet Cong cadre to escape the gaze of a puzzled Australian soldier as he attempted to read a Vietnamese language document or to ask basic questions. Although there were some successful raids conducted against the Viet Cong cadre in conjunction with Vietnamese police, no one really knew what damage had been done to the political infrastructure—and that probably included the Viet Cong. Their methods of hiding the make-up of their establishments also meant that most people did not know who was who within the organisation. No foreign military unit could expect to establish the rapport necessary to identify the enemy within a local Vietnamese community. This would require long-term commitment to a locality and a strong understanding of Vietnamese culture. The short operational deployment of the military personnel who worked on this type of operation where the gathering of information was combined with cultural knowledge also limited its success.

Army units by necessity looked outwards, dug bunkers, patrolled the fields, set up roadblocks, destroyed crops and damaged land—the worst effects of which the Australian Task Force understood had to be minimised if they were to have any chance of managing a productive pacification program. Tanks that manoeuvred through rice paddies to protect advancing infantry, or harassing and interdictory artillery fire that killed a water buffalo because it wandered into an area where someone thought the enemy might be located, were not helpful to a hearts and minds program.

Training and language

Language difficulties were experienced by 5RAR when the battalion deployed mini-Mobile Advisory Teams to train Regional Force soldiers in the siting and conduct of ambushes in 1969. Sergeant Alan McNulty, Alpha Company, told of his problems in getting his message across:

> This was a difficult job as the interpreter I had could not speak good English and he could not explain the action side of it so it took a long time trying to get him to understand and pass the info on. With the corporal I had with me going around also checking and explaining again to every man. This took all day to do.[63]

Sergeant McNulty was later awarded a Distinguished Conduct Medal for his aggressiveness and courage in a number of contacts with the enemy.

McNulty would have fitted Colonel Alex Clark's perfect mould of a platoon commander in Special Forces; he was young and a dasher.

A team from Bravo Company also went out to train 609 Regional Force Company at Hoa Long, where they were troubled to find the soldiers out shooting at birds. During their first night ambush, the Regional Force soldiers got up and left the site at 2300 hours, which did not impress the Australians. The team leader's comments summarised the challenges and highlighted the differences between the Australians and the Regional Force soldiers:

> The time available to prepare for such a task is short. Equipment and stores were insufficient to be able to operate effectively. Interpreters, if he is not interested, are useless without constant reprimand, would have gone AWOL at any time. A period of three weeks as a minimum be set aside to be able to get the maximum effort from them. [This course was six days.] As far as their training goes, they seem to think it is a nine to five effort and that's as far as it goes. The routine into which they are accustomed to working would take extensive training to break them out of it.[64]

To a Regional Force soldier, it was a nine-to-five job at least six days a week for years, or until you were killed. Technically the draft was for four years, but after the 1968 Tet Offensive military service became 'for the duration'. The Regional Force/Popular Force soldiers earned less than US$30 per month, but because they served in the general area of their homes it was an advantage that kept members in this most dangerous of the services. No barracks existed for Popular Force soldiers, so they lived at home. Regional Force companies were rarely at full strength and frequent all-night ambushes soon lost their appeal. The People's Self Defence Force was unpaid and they only had one weapon for every three members.

Another team led by Sergeant Colin Cooper went to hamlet Hoa Long 4. Cooper also endorsed the need for longer periods to be spent on these teams, 'as they don't get to know you in a such a short time', he reported. Cooper observed that 'the troops carried out all they knew with enthusiasm. It is just that they don't know. But with more time spent on these teams, the achievements would be quite rewarding'.[65] It is interesting to note that Sergeant Cooper was 38 years of age at the time and an apparent difference in attitude between him and McNulty about the Regional Force flowed from his report.

Lieutenant General Julian Ewell complimented the officers and men of 1ATF for the success of the Task Force's operations during May 1969 when 62 enemy soldiers had been eliminated, which was 'a noteworthy achievement'. Ewell also wrote, 'I am very much aware of the emphasis you are placing on the pacification effort in Phuoc Tuy Province . . . I am impressed with your handling of these operations. Particularly noteworthy is the good work you are doing in training Regional Force/Popular Force and PSDF as well as ARVN'.[66] Lieutenant Colonel Colin Khan's letter to the Task Force commander on 5RAR's training efforts was not so effusive. Khan reported to Brigadier Pearson:

> The time available was too short to permit adequate training of Regional Force Companies in ambush drills. This was caused by previous lack of training, conflicting training given earlier on ambushing by other groups and the time taken for the teams to be accepted and settle in. Efficient interpreters are essential to the success of the training. Most of the interpreters deployed were unsatisfactory.[67]

The Australian force was not established to conduct this type of activity and as a result there were shortages in equipment and also manpower. To take resources away from operational platoons or other elements within the battalions put the depleted organisation at a disadvantage. This was a juggling act that was not resolved to everyone's satisfaction. A good example of this discontent is seen in the 'Q' Instruction when ARVN battalions were trained at the Horseshoe.[68] In spite of the pacification and training efforts by the Australians, a connection between the enemy's infrastructure and the people who lived in the shadow of the Long Hai hills remained active. Later in 1969, the Australians conducted a concerted effort during Operation Esso to break the link between the Long Hai base and the nearby villages. That effort would come at a cost and it will be discussed later in this chapter.

Dong Ap Bia—Hamburger Hill

Regardless of the big battle losses inflicted upon the enemy forces, the NVA/Viet Cong high command had not lost their desire to fight and there were several significant battles in 1969 that involved Australians away from Phuoc

Tuy. On 10 May 1969, the 101st Airborne Brigade and elements of the 1st ARVN Division started Operation Apache Snow. The purpose of this operation was to prevent enemy movement along routes 548 and 922 at the western edge of Thua Tien Province in I Corps. The two poor quality roads intersected 10 kilometres north of A Luoi, which was an old base mid-way along the notorious A Shau Valley.

General Westmoreland had moved on from Vietnam and was now the Chief of Staff of the US Army, but in his memoirs, *A Soldier Reports*, he sent mixed signals about the importance of these remote hilltops:

> In many cases, a specific hill . . . had no intrinsic value except that the enemy was there. The enemy had almost no artillery, so that the . . . advantage of observation and command of surrounding territory had less long-term meaning. Hamburger Hill—in reality, Apbia Mountain—is a commanding feature near the Laotian border in the rugged A Shau Valley which points like a spear at a throat toward the cities of Hue and Danang. To have left the North Vietnamese undisturbed on the mountain would have been to jeopardize our control of the valley. The commander of the 101st, Major General Melvin Zais, quite properly ordered an attack.[69]

'The enemy long controlled the A Shau valley after March 1966', Westmoreland admitted.[70] A Mobile Strike Force operation that went into A Shau on 22 April 1966 proved this. WO2 Alec Morris, AATTV, commanded the company when they were landed at A Luoi to conduct a reconnaissance in force. They were lucky that any of them got out alive:

> Within two hours of landing they had a heavy contact with an estimated North Vietnamese Army battalion. This action continued until late afternoon when they were forced to break contact with the enemy, split up, and move away on an escape route. At this time 63 of the company had become casualties. During the extraction of the company, under fire, two helicopters were shot down and WO2 Morris, a United States Army NCO and about 40 troops could not be taken out, so they continued withdrawing along the escape route. During this withdrawal they contacted a small enemy force that they attacked, killed 10, and forced the remainder to flee. On the second day, during the withdrawal to the east, they contacted an enemy base that they attacked and destroyed, WO2 Morris personally killed at least

8 enemy. The force remained in this area until 26 April when helicopters lifted them out; during the intervening period WO2 Morris moved his force from defensive position to defensive position, successfully repelling at least five enemy assaults.[71]

Now, in 1969, at least two battalions of the NVA *29th Regiment* supported by heavy anti-aircraft weapons and engineers had established positions on the kilometre long mountaintop. The battle that followed had lasted into its ninth day when Jay Scharbutt filed this report with *The Washington Post*.

Heavy artillery barrages pounded the 3000 ft mountain overlooking the A Shau Valley. American paratroopers were beaten back with 12 men killed and 79 wounded in a tense attempt to seize the North Vietnamese fortress. The US command reported that 125 North Vietnamese soldiers were killed in the 14-hour fight Sunday, but Scharbutt reporting from the mountain said most of the communist losses were estimates by US air observers after massive airstrikes.[72]

The 3rd Battalion of the US 187th Infantry Regiment had made it to the top of the mountain three times, but had been beaten off each time by a shattering stream of NVA rocket-propelled grenades and machine-gun fire. Specialist 4 Anthony Toll, who had been in nine assaults, said:

After all of these air and artillery strikes, those gooks (North Vietnamese) are still in there fighting. All of us are wondering why they just can't pull back and B-52 the hill. Not many guys can take it much longer.[73]

Lieutenant Colonel Weldon Honeycutt, who commanded the 3rd Battalion, was asked why the paratroopers wanted to take the hill. 'Well, for one thing, it overlooks a good deal of the A Shau Valley', he replied. Colonel Joseph Conmy, the brigade commander, said 'the mountain isn't worth much from a strategic standpoint . . . we really don't go out for a piece of terrain. We go out to clobber him . . . that's what we've done'.[74]

Jay Scharbutt filed another story from the battle site that said, in part:

Paratroopers came down from the mountain, their weapons gone, bandages stained brown and red from mud and blood. Many cursed their hard-nosed battalion commander, Honeycutt, who sent three companies to take the mountain. They failed and suffered. That damn Black Jack won't stop until he kills every one of us, said one of 40–50 wounded troopers.[75]

WO2 Max 'Dad' Kelly was an AATTV adviser with the 2nd Battalion, 3rd Regiment of the 1st ARVN Division that was moved in to assault the mountain from the east when the battle appeared to be stalled. The American units had gone up the western side. On 20 May—ten days after the American assaults started—the American commander, call sign Black Jack, ordered the ARVN battalion to move a company up to occupy one of the features that comprised the mountain's top. Kelly later reported to Lieutenant Colonel Russell Lloyd, who commanded the AATTV:

> The company occupied 937 but it was outside of our area of operation. The 1st Battalion US 506th Infantry was proceeding from the west with 937 as their objective. 2/3 Bn was ordered to withdraw. We were ordered to take up a position on the left flank of 3 Bn 187 Infantry and commence an assault on the NE ridge of 937. Our other companies had occupied the SE knoll. The 2nd Coy moved forward to assault the position and came under heavy fire from the NVA. The Coy received fire from our right flank from the US Coy of 3 BN 187 Infantry. As the advisor with the Coy I notified *Black Jack* in a LOH [helicopter] . . . and was told to continue . . . that we were receiving fire from the NVA not friendly forces.[76]

Kelly's battalion was stuck between the rock of a dug-in NVA enemy and the hard place of an assaulting American battalion. Neither side was in the mood to stop shooting. Fortuitously, the enemy decided at this stage to fade away and all of the allied companies were ordered to halt and consolidate. On 21 May, Max Kelly reported that Lieutenant General Richard Stilwell, the Commanding General of the US XXIV Corps, told the ARVN battalion that 'by coming up the way we did took a lot of pressure off the US troops and stopped the NVA from re-enforcing their unit on 937'.[77]

A further news release, filed just after the battle by Les Santorelli, high-lighted the criticism of the 'controversial assault' on what was now known as Hamburger Hill. At a press conference, when Major General Melvin Zais, who commanded the 101st Airborne Division, was pressed on the hill's importance he replied: 'the only significance of the hill was the fact that your North Vietnamese [were] on it . . . the hill itself had no tactical significance'.[78]

American casualties were high with 56 killed and 367 wounded and evacuated during the assault.[79] There were also seven men listed as missing. The total was higher when added to preparatory firefights as the troops moved to the battle location, and a final figure of 72 killed is probably more accurate. Once again, powerful weaponry saved the day for the Americans. Fine weather permitted ground attack aircraft to plaster the hill with over 1000 tons of bombs and the artillery fired more than 19,000 shells in just over ten days.[80] The total number of enemy killed was put at a very doubtful 'more than 600', but the American battle losses and political repercussions would influence the manner in which Americans would fight their battles for the remainder of the war. The hill was quietly abandoned on 5 June 1969.

While this battle was underway, about 150 kilometres due south, in Kontum Province, two Australian warrant officers of the AATTV assigned to the US 5th Special Forces Mobile Strike Force out of Pleiku displayed outstanding courage and valour against the enemy during two separate operations. On 6 and 11 May, WO2 Ray Simpson's repeated acts of personal bravery whilst he commanded 232 Company were recognised by the award of the Victoria Cross. Ray Simpson had also been awarded a DCM in 1964, which made him Australia's most highly decorated soldier of the war.[81] WO2 Keith Payne, who commanded 212 Company, was on an operation in the mountains near Ben Het on 24 May when they struck a strong enemy force. Keith Payne's repeated acts of exceptional personal bravery and unselfish conduct during the battle inspired all of the soldiers who served with him. He was also awarded the Victoria Cross for his conspicuous gallantry. An interesting note to these Special Forces operations was that Australian warrant officers commanded platoons and companies within the Mobile Strike Force.

The elusive *5th Viet Cong Division*

Back down in Phuoc Tuy Province, elements of the old arch-foe of the Australian Task Force were on the move again. The *5th Viet Cong Division*'s political officers preached that their successful counteroffensive had forced the Americans from a 'Limited War' to 'Vietnamisation of the war'. The southern revolution had inflicted 'heavy casualties on the US imperialists in Tet 1968 and the 1969 Spring Campaign', the Viet Cong officers crowed. *COSVN* now directed that all of the effort was to be concentrated on defeating the 'accelerated pacification plan'. This directive supported anecdotal reports that some senior *COSVN* officers believed the most deadly weapon being used against them was a village doctor. The Viet Cong headquarters also directed that the 18th puppet (ARVN) Division be destroyed.

The structure of the *5th Viet Cong Division* had changed markedly over the years, as had its area of operations.[82] Six regiments had been associated with the division's order of battle over the past two years. In May 1969, a newly raised *29th Regiment* and an artillery battalion from *COSVN*—probably equipped with H12 Type 63 (107 mm) rocket launchers—were added to the *33rd*, *174th*, and *275th* regiments.[83] Although the allied information notes mentioned the *95th NVA Regiment* as being part of the *5th Viet Cong Division*, they do not mention the *29th*. In any case it was a question about the identity of one regiment, not two. The standard organisation of three regiments plus supporting units remained as the division's principal operational formation, which was added to as required for specific battles. The odd one out now was the *274th Viet Cong Regiment*; it had been moved to the *Ba Long* (aka *Ba Bien*) *Regional Command*.[84] The *88th NVA Regiment* had also gone from the line-up.[85]

Following *COSVN's* acknowledged heavy losses in the 1968 battles, up to seven regiments were marched south out of North Vietnam to reinforce the divisions deployed around Saigon. This large batch of reinforcements included the *33rd*, *95C*, *174th*, *10th* and *20th* NVA infantry regiments.[86] Two of the regiments, *33* and *174*, were acknowledged in MACV reports as being allocated to the *5th Viet Cong Division* and *95C Regiment* was a *1st NVA Division* unit. Although a *29th NVA Regiment* was identified in 1969, its area of operations was well north in I Corps. Without information to the contrary, maybe the *29th Regiment* of the *5th Viet Cong Division* was an ad hoc establishment with manpower creamed off from various organisations to cause a misleading image of the division's battle establishment.[87] There were also occasions when enemy units were misidentified by allied forces simply on the basis that when captured, some soldiers carried documents that were like a personal record of service, causing confusion about a soldier's current parent unit.

The *5th Viet Cong Division*'s main base was now somewhere in north-western Long Khanh Province to the west of Dinh Quan village on Route 20, 80 kilometres north of Nui Dat. The area of the May Tao Mountain was no longer the principal divisional base, but a hospital or some type of casualty evacuation centre remained in the district. Before May 1969, the division's regiments had been operating independently but the plan now was to con-centrate so that they had the strength to destroy the ARVN 18th Division. As a consequence, the headquarters of the *5th Viet Cong Division* moved into an area around the confluence of the La Nga River and Tam Bung stream about 10 kilometres south of Dinh Quan. Two regiments—*174 NVA* and *275 Viet Cong*—then attacked elements of the 18th ARVN in a wide area of operations along Route 20 and north and east of Xuan Loc during May 1969. Although the Viet Cong claimed great successes they were false victories, but they also admitted that they suffered costly battle losses. ARVN forces that fought in the area reported 221 enemy graves and bodies caused by B-52 strikes and firefights on 8, 9 and 11 May 1969.[88] These figures are supported by the order for the *275th Viet Cong Regiment* to withdraw as 'a high number of casualties had been suffered . . . one company had only 25 riflemen left'.[89] The regiment most likely headed into a rugged area north of Gia Ray, which was 20 kilo-metres to the east of Xuan Loc along the disused trans-Vietnam railway line.

Two regiments continued the battles against the ARVN with the *174th* fighting around Route 20 and the *29th*, which was ordered to move against the Xuyen Loc area. In mid-May, the headquarters of the *5th Viet Cong Division* was seriously threatened by the 11th ARVN Airborne Battalion. The enemy commander directed the *174th NVA Regiment* to protect his headquarters while the *29th Regiment* was told to continue to attack Xuan Loc and menace the ARVN headquarters in an attempt to relieve the pressure on the *5th Viet Cong Division*'s command centre. It was a hard battle, which was acknowl-edged in the division's history:

On 23 May, the 6th Battalion of the 174th Regiment and a defence company of the Division attacked [the allied force] . . . at High Point 152 when they were pre-paring to sweep into the Division's headquarters area. The battle was very fierce and lasted throughout the day. At 2pm, having discovered firepower weaknesses in the defensive positions of our Division's defence company, the enemy launched a strong counterattack. Platoon Commander Tran Ngoc An . . . died bravely while engaging the foe. Following the brave example . . . the whole defence company . . . secured the area of the Divisional Headquarters.[90]

Although the dates and the unit identification do not agree precisely, the 11th ARVN Airborne Battalion's report said that they had engaged an unknown enemy size force on 23 May that resulted in 43 enemy killed from a group identified as the *3rd Battalion* of the *174th Regiment*. They obviously did not realise how close they came to overrunning the head of their military nemesis.

Battles then flared throughout the *5th Viet Cong Division*'s area of operations with ARVN reinforcements pushed north on Route 20. They were supported by elements of a US Airmobile Cavalry battalion. According to the Viet Cong records, they were attacked heavily by aircraft sorties in the area of the La Nga River and the village of Dinh Quan. The divisional headquarters continued to come under heavy attack, which they reported in their inimitable style:

> In extremely difficult circumstances, the cadre and soldiers of the Division remained enthusiastic and brave – despite the bombing, and resolved to achieve our plan for the second phase of the campaign.[91]

The *174th NVA Regiment* was pushed across the Dong Nai River in an attempt to lure the ARVN and US troops away from the *5th Viet Cong Division*'s headquarters area while the *29th Regiment* continued to harass Xuan Loc. The two other regiments, *33* and *275*, were ordered to destroy the ARVN 52nd Regiment in an area north of Gia Ray. In late May, the regiments of the *5th Viet Cong Division* were found and attacked by both ARVN and US forces. The *174th NVA Regiment* had been pounded heavily for their efforts as a decoy and the divisional headquarters recorded that they 'were lost on the march for four days'. They reappeared at the end of the first week in June when they went back into action south of Dinh Quan.

Allied intelligence summaries concluded that enemy activity around Xuan Loc in May was initiated by elements of *174th NVA* and *275th Viet Cong* regiments and that an attack northwest of Gia Ray in which 23 enemy died was conducted by an unidentified unit. The allies also thought that the *33rd NVA Regiment* was probably responsible for an attack on the Xuan Loc area in the middle of May as well as a contact against the US 11th ACR northwest of Blackhorse on 24 May.[92] Whilst the clashes correspond with the information gleaned from the Viet Cong history documents, the identities of the units involved contradict. According to the *5th Viet Cong Division*'s history, the *33rd* with the *275th* were fighting to the north and east of Gia Ray and the regiment near Xuan Loc was the *29th* (possibly aka *95th*). They acknowledged that the *29th* suffered 'difficulties' when an allied force blocked its attempts to attack the Xuan Loc base area. This upset a planned attack by the *33rd NVA Regiment* that was ordered on 2 June:

> To secretly deploy to the northeast of Gia Ray and attack the forces of the [ARVN] 52nd Task Force at Suoi Cao – and afterwards, to ambush the enemy's reinforcements to the west of Route 3 [Route 333].[93]

Suoi Cao was to the west of Gia Huynh along Route 333 which ran north from Gia Ray.

Although the *33rd NVA Regiment* moved swiftly to meet its attack deadline, the blocking of the *29th* (*95th?*) *Regiment* forced a change of plan by the Viet Cong campaign headquarters. The *275th Viet Cong Regiment* was ordered back into the fray. It was to attack an American force at Tra Tan, about 10 kilometres southwest of Vo Dat, while the *33rd NVA* ambushed Route 333. This road was the main link from Gia Ray to Vo Dat and the *33rd NVA* reportedly 'ambushed and destroyed an engineer company patrolling along Route 3 [Route 333] on 6 June'. Later that afternoon, the *33rd NVA* exaggerated the outcome in an after action report:

> The enemy [allied forces] deployed the 2nd Armoured Company and two companies of the 52 Task Force [ARVN] to break through and clear Route 3 [Route 333]. The *33rd Regiment* conducted a blocking operation and attacked, destroying 11 armoured vehicles and inflicting heavy casualties on two enemy companies.[94]

Although all of this activity by the *5th Viet Cong Division* was in the province immediately north of the Australian base, it corroborated that

COSVN's priority of battle was against the ARVN's 18th Division and the country's pacification program. The fighting also had an impact upon the Australians' intelligence-gathering efforts and knowledge on what units they were fighting, which was a continuation of the deliberate obfuscation created by the enemy. A Vietnam Digest that was issued by the Australian Task Force at the time reported a contact by 2/5 ARVN Cavalry and US B/1-11 Armored Cavalry Regiment near the intersection of Route 1 and Route 333 on 7 June 1969. The enemy force was identified as the *3rd Battalion, 95 NVA Regiment* and the allied force claimed 41 enemy soldiers killed.[95] However, a 95th Regiment had also been identified 400 kilometres away to the north of Phuoc Tuy.

Just tear their guts out and pacification follows

The on again, off again pacification drive in Phuoc Tuy had been reignited by the II Field Force Vietnam commander's directive to the Task Force in April, albeit the message was somewhat confused. Lieutenant General Julian Ewell was known not to shy away from a fight with the Viet Cong. He had displayed his fighting colours when he commanded the US 9th Infantry Division in IV Corps. Although he believed that pacification was 'extremely important', Ewell thought that the 'central theme, the cutting edge as it were, of success-ful operations against the communists should be active and effective military operations' because 'pacification . . . progresses more rapidly in an area where the military pressure is high'.[96] Maximum pressure to Ewell was measured in contacts with the enemy and a routine kill ratio of 50 to 1 that could be achieved by relentless pressure on the Viet Cong. That pressure was to be 'so intense that it just tears their guts out', Ewell said.[97] He rated a division that achieved 25 contacts a day as very good, 50 encounters as outstanding and 75 phenomenal.[98] Routine tasks that he labelled ash and trash—guarding a bridge or a signal installation—were necessary but unproductive because they did not 'eliminate a single Viet Cong'.[99] 'Brute force', he said 'was the only way to overcome Viet Cong control and terror in the Delta'.

The Australians and their American operational commander Ewell—who carried the nickname 'Butcher of the Delta'—would have their moments of disagreement, but Ewell was gracious with his praise when he wrote many years later that 'this fine outfit [1ATF], [was] one of the best in the theater'.[100] Although his operational ideas have been read as nothing more than combat thuggery by some commentators, there were Australian commanders who believed in his tactical concept but disagreed with his mathematical ratios for the number of contacts and casualties to be achieved in combat.

Now that the operational guidelines had been rewritten, the Australian Task Force needed to gather its thoughts on what was happening back in its home province. The Task Force deputy commander, Colonel Kenneth McKenzie, told a United Services Institute gathering in Brisbane in June 1970:

> The first requirement was to send liaison teams into the districts to discover where the main problems lay. We had . . . ceased really to have a grip on the situation in Phuoc Tuy. We knew what was going on in our TAOR but we really didn't know what was going on in the centres of population.[101]

All of this meant that the enemy was getting back into the hamlets and villages in spite of the active operational program being conducted by the Australians within the province. The challenges of fighting the enemy and/or aiding the people had not lessened.

Operation Lavarack—no nursery story

At the end of May 1969, 6RAR/NZ moved into an area of operations known as Vincent and set up a fire support patrol base at Virginia, which was 6 kilometres north of Binh Ba and slightly west of Route 2. This operation was to be a basic settling-in task for the battalion, which had recently arrived to replace 4RAR/NZ. Lieutenant Colonel David Butler, a Korean War veteran, commanded the battalion. He had taken note of advice offered by Lieutenant Colonel Phillip Bennett, CO 1RAR, who believed that, 'we could have spent less time thrashing through the undergrowth and more time waiting for the enemy to put himself in a very vulnerable position'.[102]

Butler thought that during a contact 'the odds were with the side that was stationary. I was very keen that my companies should, on our first operation . . . be sitting down . . . so that the enemy could come to us'.[103] As long as the enemy didn't come in overwhelming numbers, it was probably good tactics to begin with. Butler spread his five rifle companies—A, B, D plus the New Zealand Victor and Whisky companies—rather widely around his area of operations. They were beyond mutual support range at more than 5 kilometres apart, which concerned Brigadier Pearson, the Task Force commander.[104]

The enemy situation report that was provided by the Task Force in the May/June 1969 period identified the usual hides for the *274th Viet Cong Regiment* to the west of Route 2, with a new face nearby; the *33rd NVA Regiment* was supposedly around Xuan Loc. The *84th Rear Services Group* was also thought to have moved supplies along resupply routes across northern Phuoc Tuy and southern Long Khanh from the May Tao region. Two local force units were also identified in the area of Vincent: *D440* and *C41*. As discussed earlier, for all of the intelligence assumptions, the allies did not have a complete or accurate picture on where the enemy's main units were deployed. Significant clashes had occurred with other allied forces north of Route 1 during May and into June, but the Task Force summary for 6RAR's Operation Lavarack was a benign assessment that also lacked any comment on how quickly the enemy units could move.

> There are no known enemy Main or Local Force Units in AO Vincent . . . Guerrilla Units from villages and hamlets along Route 2 are believed to be located in base camps adjacent to their home areas but none are likely to be more than section strength.[105]

Operation Lavarack was to be a 'nursery operation' to shake out the cobwebs and to sort out the battalion's operational procedures, hopefully without being bothered too much by the enemy. When the operation got underway the Australians clashed immediately with small groups of enemy, especially around the Courtenay rubber plantation. On 4 June, Alpha Company came across an enemy camp that they attacked without preparatory fire only to encounter a larger force than anticipated, forcing them to withdraw. This was an interesting action. The Australians attacked the enemy's static and prepared position, which was the exact opposite to Lieutenant Colonel Butler's tactical plan. He wanted his men to be static and the enemy to be at the disadvantage of fighting through a prepared position. Through some commendable leadership by Second Lieutenant John Mellington and the fighting skills of his soldiers, the Australian forward platoon managed to withdraw with minimal casualties. Getting out of the contact so lightly went against the trend recorded by an earlier American study on bunker attacks that concluded: 'without intense artillery and/or airstrikes it generally meant the payment of a high price by the attacker . . . or a belated reinforcement and a more prolonged involvement than was anticipated or is judicious'.[106]

More contacts followed the next day when Bravo, Victor and Whisky companies fought against elements thought to be from two regiments, *33 NVA* and *274 Viet Cong* plus *C41*, a local force company. What was the enemy doing? The *COSVN* command directive to defeat the pacification scheme was clear. The order called for concurrent political proselytising to convert the people alongside military efforts to defeat or reduce South Vietnam's regional security, especially that provided by the ARVN puppet army.[107] In *COSVN*'s *Military Region 7*—the area that included Phuoc Tuy—the priority was to defeat the puppet 18th ARVN Division based around Xuan Loc.[108] The Australian force was not the main military target. Enemy regiments who were lucky to field more than 1000 personnel did not have the combat power to attack both the ARVN and the Australians. Even so, the party's political demands could not be ignored. Although the *5th Viet Cong Division* was engaged in a very difficult combat operation to the north of Route 1, outside of Phuoc Tuy Province, a military force was patched together to spread the communist values in the village of Binh Ba, just north of Nui Dat. Its task was to destroy the aura of Australian security and stability.

The battle at Binh Ba

Binh Ba was 8 kilometres north of the 1ATF base on the western side of Route 2. The rectangular shaped village of approximately 600 metres by 300 metres was slightly offset to the northwest and it held a population of around 1300. Village houses had concrete walls and tiled roofs, a better standard than in most rural hamlets, and many dwellings included a simple protective bunker that was used by the family when warring sides clashed nearby. A large rubber plantation owned and operated by the French Gallia

Company surrounded the village and the satellite hamlet of Duc Trung 800 metres further north. The rubber plantation provided the main livelihood of the people here and generally they were apathetic towards both the government agencies of South Vietnam and the efforts of the Viet Cong. The French planters allegedly accommodated Viet Cong demands in order to prevent the destruction of their rubber trees or any disruption to production and sales.

An Australian Centurion tank and an armoured recovery vehicle had been sent north from Nui Dat along Route 2 in the early hours of 6 June 1969 to replace a tank on operations with 6RAR/NZ. The vehicles had no escort, which as events unfolded was probably a saving grace. As the vehicles were about to pass by the edge of Binh Ba, the tank was hit and penetrated by one of two RPG-7, the powerful rocket-propelled grenades, fired from the left (west) of the road. A crewman was wounded and he collapsed into a position that prevented the tank turret from traversing, which meant the tank's 20-pounder (84 mm) gun could not be used. Crewmen in both the tank and the ARV returned fire with machine guns and the tank sped through the contact to the district headquarters at Duc Thanh, 4 kilometres further north. The ARV returned to Nui Dat.

Why did the enemy fire at the Centurion tank? Was it a spur of the moment action against a two-vehicle convoy, even though it was armour, with the hope of drawing them into a firefight inside the village where the close confines would be to the enemy's advantage? The lack of an infantry escort—and the tank's inoperable 20-pounder—probably prevented that option being taken, which possibly saved Australian lives. In any case, the reaction by the Australians was powerful, destructive and deadly.

The first response to the attack came from South Vietnamese troops—probably elements of 39 Popular Force Platoon—controlled by Major Tran Van Ngo, the Duc Thanh district chief. The Popular Force troops struck heavy resistance as they approached from the north and Major Ngo requested Australian assistance. At this stage, the enemy force was thought to be approximately two local force platoons. Delta Company from 5RAR, commanded by Major Murray Blake, was despatched from Nui Dat at 1000 hours with the directive 'to destroy the enemy in village Binh Ba'.[109] Lieutenant Colonel David Butler at 6RAR/NZ commanded the Australian response at first—that included Blake's company—because the 6RAR operational area surrounded

Binh Ba. The South Vietnamese held overall authority for any action to be launched *inside* the Binh Ba village.

When Blake's company got to the southeastern edge of Binh Ba they waited for approval to move in. The mission of this attack was to kill the enemy troops and it had the potential to go horribly wrong because the enemy soldiers had merged with the local population and ensconced themselves in their houses and family bunkers. To have the district chief as well as Regional Force/Popular Force soldiers involved not only matched operational responsibilities, it was also a sound battle technique. As a former high-ranking South Vietnamese officer was reported saying in 1980:

> As long as the Vietnamese had American advisers at all levels, the Americans should have had, and heeded, Vietnamese advisers. Had such a system been practised, he thought, My Lai could not have occurred and there would have been fewer incidents of the type that fuelled resistance to the war in the United States and around the world.[110]

While they were waiting for clearance, the 5RAR combat team that included tanks and armoured personnel carriers were fired upon from the south of the village. Tank main armament and the armoured personnel carriers' machine guns soon silenced the gunfire. The order to move in came at 1120 hours, approximately an hour after Murray Blake's force had arrived on the outskirts of the village. At first, the enemy's defence was light but when the Australians got to the centre of the village they were engaged by heavy fire from both rocket-propelled grenades and small arms. This part of the battle raged for two hours during which rocket-propelled grenades hit four tanks, causing one of them to be put out of action. Five crewmen were wounded. Second Lieutenant Brian Sullivan, a national service officer who had graduated from Scheyville in 1966, commanded the tank troop during the battle. He was awarded a Military Cross and the citation for that award is a good snapshot of the firefight and a testament to Sullivan's leadership and gallantry.

> On arrival at Binh Ba Village ... the company group immediately encountered heavy, sustained anti-tank and small-arms fire from strong elements of a North Vietnamese Regiment. Counter action by the force involved sweeps through the

village with armour leading, followed by a detailed search by infantry supported by armour. House to house fighting developed. Second Lieutenant Sullivan ... and his troop were constantly required to destroy enemy strong points and retaliate to heavy enemy fire. Throughout heavy fighting for more than two hours ... Sullivan's tanks bore the brunt of the action. Countless rockets were fired at Sullivan's tank. One wounded him. Despite this, and penetration by rockets of three other tanks ... he and his Troop continued to fight with aggression.[111]

The buildings within the village could not withstand the power of the Centurions' 20-pounder main armament, but the houses provided excellent concealment from where the enemy soldiers engaged the Australians, and covered the enemy's quick movement to alternate fighting positions. This battle was a different kind of firefight to one conducted in the open paddy fields or the close vegetation of the jungle; infantrymen had to go house to house and kill at point-blank range. The men were well supported by the fire from the Centurions but some of the houses literally collapsed when they were hit.

It was obvious from the resistance by the enemy and the numbers seen moving in the area that this was more than two enemy platoons as had been first reported. Bravo Company of 5RAR was sent to assist when Delta Company entered the village and Lieutenant Colonel Colin Khan, CO 5RAR, was directed at 1242 hours to move to Duc Thanh as soon as possible and assume command of his battalion's two-company action at Binh Ba. The battalion second-in-command was at Duc Thanh by 1603 hours, but the move of a 5RAR tactical headquarters from Nui Dat to Duc Thanh took an extraordinary nine hours to complete.[112] The two Australian companies and probably elements of 655 Regional Force Company and 39 Popular Force Platoon were now involved in the battle. The South Vietnamese blockaded the northern avenues of possible escape and they also cleared the church on the northern edge of the village.[113]

Some of the enemy stood and fought and the fierce fighting that erupted as Delta Company swept through to the west had cost the Australian company one soldier killed and two wounded. The tanks attracted rocket-propelled grenade fire almost as if they were large magnets and to make matters worse they started to run low on ammunition. Some of the RPG strikes penetrated or struck glancing blows that either wounded crewmen or damaged operating systems. With a bit of luck on their side, a high explosive rocket grenade had not hit the infantry-laden armoured personnel carriers. What happened next is jumbled among many reports and memories of individual firefights within the battle. Major Murray Blake told the authors of *Jungle Tracks* that he was concerned that he would be stuck in the village and be surrounded by the enemy. He decided to move his force out to the south and reconsolidate. More tanks also arrived from FSPB Virginia, which allowed Brian Sullivan's troop to disengage and replenish their ammunition.

With the flanks of the village now blocked off by Bravo Company to the east and the Regional Force/Popular Force in the northern arc, Delta Company swept back through Binh Ba from the west. They soon struck determined and courageous resistance by an enemy that was obviously something more than a local guerrilla force. This battle was won by close infantry–tank cooperation with the power of the tank demolishing the hiding places and the infantry mopping up any remaining resistance. In some of the older Australian Army pamphlets, 'mouse holing' was a term used to explain how to blow a hole in common walls that would allow entry to the next house in house-to-house fighting. At Binh Ba, the Centurions' 84 mm mouse holes were very large indeed. Although the Centurions had attracted much of the enemy's heavy resistance, the clearance of a house or the standing rubble that remained required some close face-to-face confrontations. Sergeant Brian London commanded 10 Platoon during the battle and his citation for the award of a Distinguished Conduct Medal for his leadership and gallantry acknowledged the action of the infantry:

Sergeant London commanded 10 Platoon, whose total strength at the time was 15 men. In two days of continuous action, 10 Platoon attacked the enemy in house after house. On at least six occasions, the platoon was held up by enemy rocket and machine gun fire. Sergeant London . . . led assaults into the houses, throwing grenades at enemy firing from windows and from behind walls. In one house, he shot two enemy dead at point blank range.[114]

On 7 June, the two sides had an initially friendly encounter when what looked like a South Vietnamese Regional Force company approached Bravo Company. Both sides waved to each other and then the realisation struck that they were waving at their enemy. In spite of some frantic firing, the enemy force disappeared without trace. Although the village had to be cleared again, this time there was no resistance but the task was gruesome. Bodies were piled in the local square on the directive of the district chief *to encourage the others*. This task was worse than the battle. People were gathered away from their shattered houses while the search continued to ensure that no enemy had switched clothes to mingle with the locals. During the search, the soldiers made the heartbreaking discovery of a young girl's severely damaged body in a tunnel that was watched over by her weeping mother.

The main action then swung to the north in Duc Trung hamlet where 50 to 80 enemy soldiers were seen and 5RAR flew in its Assault Pioneer Platoon to reinforce its reaction force. At first, Major Tran Van Ngo used his Regional Force/Popular Force troops to clear the area, but the enemy had gone again. They reappeared back at Duc Trung a few hours later, overran the Popular Force platoon, killed four of them and wounded another seven. Bravo Company and a troop of tanks were manoeuvred quickly through the southern side of the hamlet to attack the enemy, but due to the number of civilians in the area Major Ngo's troops were used in an effort to avoid civilian casualties. Although his troops found several enemy bodies as well as numerous blood trails the enemy had retreated to the northwest.

By the morning of the third day, 8 June, the enemy's resolve to stay and fight had been broken and later in the day the Australians returned to Nui Dat. The initial enemy tally stood at 43 killed by the Australians: 20 by Delta Company, 5RAR, nineteen by the tanks, and four by Bravo Company. Eight were killed by the Regional Force/Popular Force and a further 21 unattributable bodies were found later for a total of 72 enemy killed.[115] This is another example that contradicts the claims that Australians did not concern themselves with body counts. Eight prisoners were captured and twenty weapons were captured along with a variety of ammunition and equipment, but Senator McKellar—the Minister for Repatriation—adjusted these figures to 110 dead and 29 wounded in reply to a parliamentary question in August 1969. The supporting information for that claim is not known.[116] The Australians had a total of one killed and ten wounded. Colin Khan added in his report that the power of the tanks was a 'battle-winning factor'. Khan also emphasised the lessons of fighting in a built-up area that contained a lot of civilians:

Immediate and continuous liaison with the District Chief is necessary. Civilians must be moved out of the Viet Cong occupied area by all means possible. The District Chief must give the Aust Comd authority to use force to destroy the Viet Cong and property if necessary. If too many casualties may be done by Aust troops to civilians left . . . it may be preferable to get Regional Force/Popular Force troops to complete the task.[117]

Many years later, in May 1985, an Australian Broadcasting Corporation correspondent, Richard Palfreyman, broadcast a claim made by a Vietnamese official that the Australians had attacked the forces of the People's Army of Vietnam—the North Vietnamese Army—at Binh Ba and after the battle committed to massacre the women and children of the village. It was a malicious and false claim. The Australian commanders, Khan and Blake in particular, strongly refuted the charge. In doing so, they did not deny that some civilians had been killed, but they emphasised that strong efforts had been made to get civilians away from the danger. Khan also wrote in his 1969 report that:

Individual soldiers . . . showed remarkable constraint when sweeping through Binh Ba. On several occasions soldiers exposed themselves [to enemy fire] before engaging to determine identity.[118]

There were some niggling disagreements between the fighters and the rebuilders following the battle when the Civil Affairs Unit was cleared to go into Binh Ba to assess the damage. The village had been severely damaged with houses destroyed and the rubble—the result of fighting in a built-up area—was spread all around. Lieutenant Colonel Peter Gration, the Commanding Officer of the Civil Affairs Unit, was not impressed by the magnitude of destruction and he gave Major Blake a bit of serve, as Blake later remembered:

I had had little rest for two days and here was this fresh, cleanly shaven major [lieutenant colonel] standing in front of me and berating me. There wasn't a house that hadn't been damaged; it wasn't wilful destruction on our part. There had been bad guys in every house and it just had to be cleared.[119]

Of more significance, over the following months the Australians rebuilt the village. They worked hard and methodically to provide the necessary basic needs of the people and got them back into their homes within a reasonable time frame. Coupled with the defeat of the enemy, this civil affairs task won the respect of the villagers and they were more receptive to future visits by the Australian soldiers.

Following the battle, the Australian intelligence summaries indicated that a battalion of the *33rd NVA Regiment* was the main enemy force deployed around Binh Ba. Latter-day documents confirm that *Battalion 1* from the *33rd NVA Regiment* was involved in the battle. However, the first plan by the enemy was for *D440 Battalion* to attack Binh Ba in coordination with elements of *33rd Regiment*. That plan was foiled by an attack on *D440* by 'Australian commandoes' on 4 June. The Australian Task Force logs maintained by the operations officer show a series of clashes by Alpha Company 6RAR in an arc of territory to the northwest of Binh Ba on 4 June. It is possible that these contacts disrupted the enemy's main plan for their attack on Binh Ba.

The *33 NVA* plan is explained in a document provided by a former NVA soldier, Xuan Thu:

> The engagement [against *D440*] . . . used artillery and air support. For this reason, even before the first shot was fired, the Battle of Binh Ba was unfavourable, and principally for this reason the Campaign Headquarters [not named] changed the forces for the battle. This involved using part of the 1st Battalion of the 33rd Regiment to take over 440 Battalion's task of attacking Binh Ba. The targets inside Binh Ba included the 664-security post, the police station, the Phoenix spy agency and civilian defence spots. When 1 Battalion replaced 440 Battalion, 440 were told to block enemy reinforcements for a battle on Route 2 that would be supported by 2 Battalion, 33 Regiment commanded by Quach Thai Son. At about 4am on 5 June, 33rd Regiment's combat forces left their base (in the present-day Hac Dich area) and were led through the jungle by liaison cadres to the battle area. At about 6am on 6/6/69 as expected the Australian force came from Nui Dat. They did not enter the ambush and the commander decided not to fight, but to change from attack to defence.[120]

The attack by Blake's force inflicted heavy casualties on the NVA. They admit that they failed in their mission even after the NVA headquarters sent a recoilless-rifle platoon and part of a company from *D440* to reinforce the *1st Battalion*. Although the casualties for *D440* are not mentioned in the

33 Regiment paper, it does highlight the *1st Battalion*'s casualties at 53 killed and goes on to state that only three members of *1/33* survived. They were named as comrades Hung, Phong and Bao, who hid out in the Catholic Church and finally in a rubbish pit.[121] Those figures would mean that the battalion was at a very low strength and when cross-referenced against other enemy documents, it is difficult to establish a truly clear picture of what enemy units were involved and where they were located.[122]

The aim of the *COSVN* military campaign at the time was to eliminate troops of the ARVN 18th Division and to destroy equipment and the enemy's policy of 'urgent pacification'.[123] The operation was planned for the period 5 May to 20 June 1969 and it fell under the command of Nguyen Thanh Liem, chief of the *5th Viet Cong Division*. Liem had the *5th Viet Cong Division* as well as the *29th NVA Regiment* and a company from the *24th Battalion* for the operation. According to the *5th Viet Cong Division*'s history, on 6 June 1969 *33rd NVA Regiment* supposedly attacked the ARVN 2nd Armoured Company on Route 333 and destroyed eleven armoured vehicles. The allies recorded an attack on 7 June in the vicinity of Gia Ray that involved 2/5 ARVN Cavalry, but the enemy unit was identified as the *95th NVA Regiment*. However, in the 2011 document *The Story of the Memorial Area for the Battle of Binh Ba*, not only was *1/33 Battalion* heavily involved in the battle at Binh Ba on 6 June (or certainly elements of the battalion), but *2/33 Battalion* also may have been nearby without getting involved.

This major contradiction between the NVA and Viet Cong records is difficult to explain. For example, a letter from *MR7* dated 29 July 1969 stated that *E33* (*33 NVA Regiment*) was directly subordinate to higher headquarters and only designated to cooperate with *MR7*. The operations of the regiment would be restricted due to difficulties with rice supply and it preferably should be assigned to operations north of Highway 1.[124] Le Van Nhanh, a platoon commander with *D440* who gave himself up, said that the battalion had fought at Binh Ba and had suffered about 60 casualties (both killed and wounded).[125]

In other cases the locations of units and battles can be correlated between enemy and allied reports, but any analysis does require a sifting out of the extravagant successes claimed by the enemy, and occasionally the allies too. Although there is a suggestion that the NVA may have had a plan to ambush

Australians on Route 2 during June 1969, the enemy's main objective was to defeat the South Vietnamese pacification program and that might explain why this enemy force had deployed into the centre of Phuoc Tuy Province.

Without the plans of the Viet Cong *Military Region 7*, any conclusion is no more than a best guess but the available information on enemy activity at the time does indicate that the Binh Ba operation was a side issue to the Long Khanh operation. Perhaps it was a proselytising task with a mission to impress and coerce the people in the area of Route 2 through a brazen display of power and propaganda to show them that neither the ARVN nor the Australians could protect them. This would satisfy the *COSVN* political directive while it also allowed the *Military Region 7* military commander to concentrate on his main combat objectives, which were obviously the more important and continuing battles against the 18th ARVN Division outside of Phuoc Tuy Province.

Operation Lavarack a success story

Operation Lavarack was overshadowed by the battle that had taken place in Binh Ba, which was a 5RAR affair although initially it had been controlled by 6RAR/NZ. Frequent contacts with the enemy during Lavarack continued throughout June and the rain came in torrents just to make the environment that little bit more unpleasant. Even though the Australians had repeated ambush success on the trails throughout their operational area, the enemy kept coming, almost as if the message of danger had not got back to their commanders.

On 12 June, Lieutenant Farland's 1 Platoon, Victor Company, saw the movement of an estimated 200 NVA who had started to cross a clearing 300 metres from their position. Farland's men opened fire with their platoon weapons and helicopter gunships were called to assist, but the enemy had been spooked by another helicopter pilot who apparently wanted to see what a large group of enemy in the open looked like. As a result, the enemy quickly escaped from a potential killing ground. Lieutenant Farland's identification of the enemy from a distance of 300 metres based on the colour of their clothes and some so-called NVA helmets should have been classified as *possibly* NVA troops. Although documents allegedly identified the group as elements of

33 NVA Regiment, once again the *5th Viet Cong Division*'s history disagreed, stating that on this date the regiment was away to the east of Xuyen Loc and to the north of Route 1.[126]

A few days later, on 20 June 1969, Second Lieutenant Rod Chandler's 10 Platoon, Delta Company, ambushed an enemy party of 60. They killed 22 without a friendly casualty. This was probably the most successful Australian force ambush of the war. Remarkably, the platoon had been in the ambush for two days before it was sprung. Although the firepower from the Australians cut down the enemy party with a devastating blast of claymores and small-arms fire, five of the eleven claymores failed to detonate. Rod Chandler was awarded a Military Cross and Corporal Richard Brown, a national service veteran of the Long Tan battle in 1966 who had joined the Regular Army, was later awarded a Military Medal for his alertness and positive action during the 20 June ambush as well as for his leadership and coolness under fire during Operation Burnham in September 1969.

When 6RAR/NZ returned to Nui Dat on 30 June 1969, they had completed a very successful 'nursery operation'. In statistical terms, the battalion had killed 33 enemy soldiers for every one of their three losses—the artillery were only credited with another three—and they had captured 71 weapons as well as food and equipment from a recorded 88 contacts.[127]

Although the enemy's historical documents do not mention that the *33rd NVA Regiment* fought battles in the 6RAR/NZ operational area in June 1969, there was a reference to the 1969 Spring Campaign at Binh Ba on Baria Vung Tau television during a Buddhist ceremony that was broadcast in August 2009:

> The regiment had *3050 martyrs, including 2008 who bravely fell on the Eastern Nam Bo battlefield* [emphasised]. In particular, in the fighting to liberate Binh Ba in the 1969 Spring Campaign, close to 50 cadre and fighters bravely died.[128]

Clearing the scrub

The Task Force went back to tackling the problem of fencing off Dat Do, although the dilemma remained: on which side of the fence were the Viet Cong? As part of an attempt to control the population around Dat Do and Long Dien, the Australians continued with their efforts to clear the land in a general line along Route 326. This road was on the northern side of the Long Hai hills and ran approximately in an east–west direction between Hoi My and Tam Phuoc and then into Long Dien. About 50 per cent of the growth had been cleared under operations overseen by 9RAR. Scrub that stood between 3 and 20 feet—1 and 6 metres—still remained when 5RAR was moved in to replace the 9th Battalion. A 5RAR review of the intelligence for Operation Esso gave this summary, which was a prescient and sombre note on what was to follow.

The land clearing in AO ALDGATE is cutting the enemy in the Long Hai's [sic] off from the population and re-supply centres. He may be expected to avoid contact where possible and use mines, booby traps and attacks by fire to delay and demoralize 5RAR.[129]

On 23 July 1969, an article in The Australian recorded that:

Official figures show that 13 Australian soldiers have been killed and 90 others wounded in the past five weeks. This is well above the monthly average since Australia first sent advisers to the war in the middle of 1962.[130]

During Operation Esso, the 5RAR group suffered eleven killed, including two Americans, and a further 58 wounded. Mines caused most of these casualties and it was obvious from their operational quality that they had come out of the Australian minefield at Dat Do. The 5RAR after action report noted that a Hoi Chanh—the term for an enemy defector—said that 'most mines in the Allied [Australian] Dat Do minefields had been lifted, fuses changed and were now being used by the Viet Cong'.[131] The high number of casualties attracted a lot of attention back in Australia and the 5RAR after action report provided nearly two pages of lessons learnt on mines and booby traps. It also conveyed a subliminal message about how sensitive both politically and militarily these losses were. The report warned that in a known mined area casualties were expected, but active continuous offensive patrolling had to proceed. Commanders at all levels were required to emphasise enemy signs, the wearing of protective clothing and what action to take if a mine detonation happened. At the same time, commanders were advised to keep it all in balance, otherwise some soldiers would be reluctant to move anywhere.[132]

The casualties worried the commanders and the politicians. On 24 July 1969, Major General Hay wrote to Brigadier Pearson that he had received a signal from Mr Bruce White, the highly respected and long-serving Secretary for the Department of Army. Mr White 'informed COMAFV of attitudes in Australia'. Hay told Pearson, 'you can see the Australian reaction to our recent casualties from mines ... There is no doubt that we should both take full account of Bruce White's comments'.[133] Operation Esso was ended soon afterwards, although in subsequent interviews Brigadier Sandy Pearson denied that he was pressured to end the operation because of the mine casualties.

Lieutenant Colonel Colin Khan, who commanded 5RAR, summarised the multi-mission operation with a positive conclusion to his after action report.

The presence of 1ATF forces has produced a considerable and real result in pacification in this previously Viet Cong dominated area and has stopped infiltration by large Viet Cong groups into the populated areas. It is also strongly recommended that further efforts be made to co-ordinate the activities of all military and para military organisations to get a more effective result.[134]

Khan's recommendation showed that the problems of fragmented responsibilities within the province remained. Whilst the efforts of the Australians in and around the main areas of population and the clearing of the scrub-covered approaches to the villages stifled the activities of the Viet Cong, they did not eradicate the National Liberation Force's infrastructure. By way of comparison, General Abrams had commented upon the 1st US Division's efforts at pacification back in 1968. Abrams said:

In terms of body count the ... [Division's] isn't worth a damn ... but the Division stuck with pacification ... and when the [enemy] ... got out ... the people told them [the Americans] and they went out and killed about 85. If that pacification battalion hadn't been there ... we'd be back on our ass.[135]

The people of Dat Do–Long Dien did not provide assistance to the Australians against the Viet Cong. That area was not pacified but rather subdued into an uncooperative and glowering resentment. Pulling out of the operation reopened the gates to the Long Hai hills for the Viet Cong and it certainly wounded the military pride of the Australians after they thought they had finally achieved some success against this enemy stronghold. The Task Force had been put back on its 'ass' through either so-called 'indirect political pressure' or demands by General Ewell that the Australians get out and 'tear the guts out' of the main enemy force. Paradoxically, Ewell had praised the Australian efforts in pacification and the training of the South Vietnamese forces, which impressed him and he considered that the effort would pay real dividends.[136]

A French minefield lesson

There have been many arguments for and against the Dat Do minefield, and much scathing criticism. General Wilton thought the unfavourable judgements were more a case of being 'wise after the event'. He added, 'perhaps the commander concerned was a bit optimistic about the reliability of the Vietnamese allies [to patrol and protect]. I wouldn't criticise any . . . commander for putting out something, which in the end lost its effectiveness'.[137] Come what may, a program of observation and protective firepower was a requirement for a minefield of this type. The Australians could not abrogate their responsibility for at least a half share in those tasks. They simply didn't have the manpower for the task and they paid a high penalty as a result.

When Australian officers prepared themselves for duty in South Vietnam, the *French* [Military] *Lessons of the War in Indochina* might have been appropriate reading. Rarely did anyone in this conflict turn back to the French; they had been the losers. Their observation on the use of mines might have been one valuable lesson, however:

> Mines were more frustrating than useful. They probably caused more casualties in our own ranks than those in the enemy because of the difficulties imposed by their employment. The laying of mines within an obstacle is not recommended. It is better to place mines in readily accessible open areas. However, they must not remain in the same location for too long, for the enemy will find and remove them, and use them against us. The minefield should not become a fixture.[138]

A further point of interest: the North Vietnamese Army and the VC forces that operated in South Vietnam did not establish deliberate minefields. Their mine warfare caused a lot of damage by the targeted laying of mines along roads, tracks and around suitable ambush sites or in random and nuisance patterns with no apparent connection to a given action. The Viet Cong employed mines with imagination and foresight, a MACV paper stated in 1964. The US Army also conducted a comprehensive study on mine warfare in 1968 that reinforced a lot of the information previously published on enemy mines. A snapshot of their deadliness is included in the endnote.[139]

HMAPC Flint & Steele

Australian casualties from mines in the vicinity of the southeastern quadrant of Phuoc Tuy Province demanded that something be done about the Dat Do minefield. The soldiers *knew* that the Viet Cong were taking the mines and using them, but even if their suspicions were wrong the enemy had won a victory against their morale. It did not matter whether the M16 mines caused more casualties or less than other types of mines, or if they really came from the Australian field. Rumour had it to be true, and therefore it was.

If there had ever been any doubts that the enemy had taken large quantities of mines it was erased when enemy bunkers/storage areas were found constructed within the minefield. If that was insufficient proof, a Vietnamese girl named Mai, who had surrendered, gave a 'mine-lifting demonstration to interested Australians', which included bringing live mines out from within the minefield's overgrown foliage.[140] This and the now public criticism by past and present Task Force members helped fuel the political, military and public press criticisms of a tactic thought to have gone horribly wrong.

The majority of Australian field commanders in Vietnam recognised that the minefield needed to be destroyed, but the decision-making process required some finesse. The field's architect was now the Deputy Chief of the General Staff and any suggestion that it was a liability would be an embarrassment to Defence and probably not good for the career health of those involved in such criticism. The puzzle was how to remove or destroy more than 20,000 mines. A variety of methods were trialled and some good successes were achieved, especially the trials and development of a clearing system conducted by Captain Les Power and Major Rex Rowe and the sappers of 1 Field Squadron that used Her Majesty's Armoured Personnel Carriers (HMAPC), nicknamed Flint & Steele in a play on the names of Army chief engineers past and present.[141] In one month, during August 1969, approximately half of the recorded 20,292 mines had been destroyed. But no one knew how many the Viet Cong had lifted.[142]

Clearance problems continued as a result of monsoonal rain and inaccessible overgrowth that made complete removal of the mines virtually impossible. Another effort was made to bury the mines beyond a depth at which they would be dangerous. This was not completely successful, as mines reappeared in the sandy southern area of the field when the soft soil was either washed or blown away. Although a tremendous effort that took remarkable initiative and guts cleared a lot of the minefield, it could not be claimed that 100 per cent of the mines had been destroyed or made inoperative. No more could be done, however.

Mr G. F. Cawsey, the scientific adviser to COMAFV, concluded in his 1969 study on casualties caused by mines that the 'mine battle had been won'. Approximately 45 per cent of 1ATF casualties were due to mines, he added. In the 'broadly comparable' US 9th Division, 52 per cent were mine casualties and the Americal (23rd) Division suffered 110 casualties in a single day, Cawsey noted.[143] To compare 1ATF—*a light brigade*—even broadly with American *divisions* with personnel strengths from 16,000 to 20,000 that fielded three infantry brigades and support battalions was a curious analogy. Furthermore, the areas of operations for the two American divisions were much larger and more diverse than Phuoc Tuy Province. For example, the Americal Division's area of operations was 155 by approximately 35 kilometres in size and covered parts of three provinces in I Corps.

In a minefield postscript, the Baria–Vung Tau Information Office released more information on how the Viet Cong lifted the mines during the war. In the 2006 publication *The Minh Dam Base 1945–1975*, the office recorded how they discovered a method to lift the mines after they had suffered casualties in previous attempts.

A faulty M-16-E3 was found and removed. We studied it and trained all of our forces to neutralize it. From then on our soldiers knew how to neutralize this mine and reopen our supply and communication route. The fence was rendered useless. All the mines we used to fight the enemies. Over 200 were reinstalled into minefields and several times the invaders were killed by their own mines.[144]

Relentless pursuit

Although the efforts by the Australians in the sphere of influence immediately adjacent to Nui Dat had set a solid base for a continuing pacification campaign, the results crumbled. The division of efforts required much more from the Regional Force/Popular Force/PSDF personnel than they were either willing or capable to commit. The Australian Task Force had hurt the guerrilla/local force operations in the southern sector of the province, but the Australians had also been hurt. Regardless of the reason the Australians withdrew from the Long Hai–Dat Do region, the task of providing a protective cover for the people now fell upon the South Vietnamese local forces. In the words of South Vietnamese General Hieu, the hand had been withdrawn from the goldfish bowl, which allowed the Viet Cong 'fish' to return and fill the gap. The American provincial officials were more upbeat in their reports that showed some successes against the grassroots communist infrastructure, but in spite of the improved statistics the general mood of the Australians was pessimistic.

Following the successes of 6RAR/NZ during Operation Lavarack, most of the other activities by the Task Force resulted in fleeting contacts with the enemy. Patrolling continued, as did the training with the South Vietnamese. It was good counterinsurgency work because it kept the enemy off balance, but it frustrated commanders. The chase was on again to hunt down the enemy's main logistics units in their corridors that crisscrossed Phuoc Tuy. This time it was up to 9RAR to hunt for the big fish and they moved out on Operation Matthew at the end of June 1969. The operational area was centred at first approximately 10 kilometres east of the Courtenay rubber plantation and then around the plantation proper, south of Blackhorse. None of the main enemy force or their support elements were there and the operation fizzled out following sporadic contact with a few enemy soldiers. The *5th Viet Cong Division* had ended its 'resounding' 1969 Autumn–Summer campaign, as its records recalled:

Over 40 continuous days of combat on the Long Khanh front . . . we had driven hundreds of enemy from the battlefield. The resounding victories . . . had demonstrated the maturing of the Division in its organization and tactical leadership. Operating independently for the first time . . . the Division had fought continuously and won. From a weak formation, the Division strived to become a strong division. However, after two years of combat . . . the Division's forces, equipment and weapons declined significantly. The 5th Division was given the mission to deploy to Phuoc Long [province, on the Cambodian border].[145]

The last battles recorded before the *5th Viet Cong Division* moved off to the western border with Cambodia were on 18 June 1969 around the streams to the north of Gia Ray and east of Xuan Loc. This left the usual local force suspects spread across Phuoc Tuy Province and the *274 Viet Cong Regiment* as the perennial main force scourge in the western Hat Dich zone. But plans were underway to trap and destroy this regiment. Elements of a South Vietnamese marine brigade blocked areas to the west of the Hat Dich while 9RAR leapfrogged across from the east into the vicinity of the Ca River on 18 July 1969. This movement put the Australian battalion in an area where they operated in three provinces—Phuoc Tuy, Long Khanh and Bien Hoa—simultaneously.

Once again, an enemy bunker system proved dangerous when 7 Platoon, Charlie Company was hit by heavy enemy fire from a well-hidden defensive position, which forced the platoon to withdraw. In the process they had to leave the body of Private Ray Kermode behind, but not before several gallant attempts were made to recover him. Bad weather on 20 July prevented the use of air strikes to cover a move into the enemy bunkers, but they were hit by artillery and Charlie Company got back in without any resistance. The enemy had slipped away; they had used the cover of the foul weather and the night to escape. Ray Kermode's body was recovered, but his watch and dog tags were gone. The enemy had also scavenged any sleeping gear and weapons left when the Australians had withdrawn.[146]

The Hat Dich was a thorn in the side of the allied efforts, not only in Phuoc Tuy but also around the villages in Bien Hoa and Long Khanh provinces. Although the May Tao Mountain darkened the eastern flank, the enemy's activities in that area had been reduced to administrative and resupply tasks.

Even though *D445* was reported to be resting up in the May Tao, a four-day reconnaissance in force operation conducted by two companies from 5RAR, supported by armoured personnel carriers and artillery and a Regional Force company, only found a large cornfield and evidence that the enemy moved through the area but not much else. Notably, the companies did not venture too close to the May Tao Mountain stronghold; had they done so, it might have proved to be a dangerous move. Full attention was now switched to the western side of the province, where a plan was underway to eradicate a large area of jungle and hopefully destroy one of the enemy's longstanding sanctuaries.

Operation Camden

5RAR moved to the western border to replace 9RAR and Operation Camden ran from 29 July to 29 August 1969. The operational area was named Mindy and it was centred on Fire Support Patrol Base Polly. This base was just across the Phuoc Tuy–Bien Hoa border, about 15 kilometres to the northeast of Phu My, which was on Route 15. As already known, the Hat Dich's tangle of jungle and streams provided an ideal environment in which an enemy could hide and fight and get away, especially at night. It was also littered with bunkers that blended with their surrounds so that often they were found only when the soldiers were among them. Fortuitously for the searchers, the enemy occupied only a few of those found, although two involved contacts that had the potential to turn very deadly.[147]

On 8 August, 3 Platoon, Alpha Company and the Tracker Platoon from Support Company struck an estimated enemy company among bunkers but when they withdrew to call in a medical evacuation aircraft, the enemy closed up on the Australians. This 'hugging the belt buckles' tactic was designed by the enemy in an effort to negate artillery and aircraft support fire; if they kept close, the hope was the Australians would be reluctant to fire because of the fear of hitting their own soldiers. In this contact, the gunships fired within 30 metres of the Australians before the enemy broke contact and withdrew.

A more serious contact happened on 21 August when 3 Platoon and the Assault Pioneer Platoon struck a strong enemy position—reportedly an estimated battalion—that cost the Australians one killed and 37 wounded. Two enemy soldiers were killed, but it needed a considerable effort by gunships, air strikes and artillery to get the Australians out of harm's way. Bombardier Gerard Dekker was the artillery forward observer with the infantrymen when the platoon commander was wounded and he displayed gutsy determination in an effort that helped save the small infantry force, as the citation for his Military Medal detailed:

> The force was engaged on three sides by an established enemy company in a bunker system. The commander was wounded and his headquarters and one platoon were pinned down by small arms and rocket-propelled grenade fire. Bombardier Dekker immediately called in artillery fire . . . he attempted to get the wounded . . . commander back to safety. In doing so, he . . . received a head wound. He continued to direct the fire of the guns onto the bunker system for a further thirty minutes . . . that relieved the pressure on the force and it withdrew safely.[148]

Corporal Michael Dench, a section commander with 3 Platoon, was in action on both 8 and 21 August against the bunkers. On both occasions he displayed personal courage of the highest order and during the second battle he took over temporary command of the platoon to reorganise its defence whilst under mortar, rocket and sniper fire. He was also awarded a Military Medal.[149] These clashes again illustrated the dangerous disadvantage that a patrolling force was under when it either unexpectedly entered, or deliberately attacked, a well-prepared enemy defensive position.

Following these contacts, Lieutenant Colonel Colin Khan provided some valuable notes on actions against enemy bunkers that he said consolidated the lessons of previous operations, but Camden also highlighted some major differences to previous encounters. These included the enemy's use of snipers in trees and their willingness to stay and fight even when fired upon by artillery and gunships. Whilst the battalion used its artillery and air support aggressively, the 105 mm howitzer was not a bunker-buster because thickly wooded areas absorbed the blast effects of a 105 mm shell.[150] Gunships, including the mini-gun equipped Spooky, provided excellent support and a strong psychological advantage but there were also tactical limitations that influenced their deployment. Artillery and aircraft do not mix; therefore, clear and concise information had to be passed between the guns, the aircraft and the troops on the ground. This meant that occasionally the guns stopped firing while the aircraft attacked, which was a pause that the enemy could exploit. Additionally, 7.62 mm rounds also lacked the power to penetrate wooded areas, especially when an aircraft was forced by enemy fire to fly higher than 500 metres. Spooky and helicopter gunships were also very vulnerable to 12.7 mm machine-gun fire.

Lieutenant Colonel Khan concluded that not all methods of attacking bunkers worked. He noted, 'we still need a grenade launcher to punch an explosive through foliage to hit enemy outside the bunkers'.[151] This was a most relevant piece of information because not all bunkers were designed for fighting. Many of the dugouts were built for hiding in and to protect the occupants from heavy weapons as well as being storage areas for supplies. The really deadly positions were those with fighting pits that covered possible approaches via a series of defended satellite localities.

The United States Army Vietnam (USARV) had conducted a seminar on attacks against fortified positions in February 1968 and the lessons learnt by them were very similar to those discussed by Colonel Khan and the other Australian commanders. The Americans also questioned whether they should break or maintain contact when bunkers were found, but there was no common answer. Most other lessons learnt mirrored the Australian tactics, even down to the use of artillery and tanks and the challenges of finding and destroying the fortifications.[152]

Operation Camden was a success, not only because the enemy had been harassed in a domain they had dominated for many years, but also because of the intelligence information that was captured, which provided detailed information on the enemy organisations involved. The Australian 5RAR in concert with the US 501 Engineer Company, as well as supporting Australian units, had killed 48 enemy soldiers for the loss of three Australians and 61 wounded. The land clearing operation had also destroyed 1029 bunkers, 379 weapon pits and more than 1000 metres of tunnels and trenches. In spite of all the effort, the general region around Hat Dich remained a base for the enemy, as 6RAR found during Operation Burnham in September 1969.

8

INEVITABLE WITHDRAWAL
1970–1972

---

*There is at least one thing worse than fighting with allies—and that is to
fight without them.*
Winston Churchill

Strategic strings—tactical ramifications

The Australian government and its departmental advisers had been grappling
with the challenges of whether to stay or get out of Vietnam probably from
the day the nation first committed to become involved, figuratively speaking.
Following the first phase of the redeployment that had reduced American
forces in Vietnam by 25,000, President Nixon announced the next step-down
on 15 September 1969. This second redeployment of 35,000 was to be completed by 15 December 1969, but the tranche would total 40,500 and include
the 3rd Marine Division from around the Demilitarized Zone. A note to the
transcript of the announcement explained that the two reductions amounted
to 65,500.[1]

Soon after this, the Australian Prime Minister made a bold statement on
9 October that Australia would not pull its troops out of Vietnam.[2] Gorton's
speech was part of a rally for the federal House of Representatives election,
which was conducted on 25 October 1969. Although the Coalition won, it
was a feeble victory with the government's majority in the House reduced
from 40 seats to seven. Interestingly, a survey about Vietnam held after the

election found that 'the most popular answer, by a large margin, was to have only volunteer troops in Vietnam'. The war apparently would have retained considerable support if only regular troops were used.[3]

Following President Nixon's 'The Silent Majority' speech[4] on 3 November 1969, the Australian Chiefs of Staff Committee met on 1 December to discuss the withdrawal options for Vietnam. Previous considerations concluded with advice that the Australian withdrawal should be *one out, all out*. In other words, taking away parts of the Task Force had the potential to weaken its capabilities and put those who remained at an increased risk. This recommendation held sway, but the defence chiefs understood political reality, adding:

> If, however, for political reasons, the government decides to reduce our Task Force it could be reduced to a two battalion Task Force without undue risk provided that we have a guarantee that a US battalion would be placed under operational control of our Task Force should there be a threat to Phuoc Tuy Province or our force beyond its capability.[5]

The Australians worried about what the Americans might think of them if they withdrew any forces. If anything, the American administration—the president and his closest advisers—were unconcerned, despite statements from some of their senior field commanders who wanted the Australians to fight on undiminished. Defense Secretary Laird had advised the American president on 13 March 1969 that a reduction by Australia and others would not significantly affect matters and President Thieu expected and was ready for a reduction.[6] Nine months later, Gorton spoke for ten minutes with President Nixon in a call placed by Nixon on 14 December (US date). What was said was not recorded, but on 15 December Nixon announced a further decrease of 50,000 US personnel, to be completed by 15 April 1970.[7]

Regardless of the Nixon telephone conversation, the Americans had not kept Australia closely informed on their force reduction plans. The announcements caught John Gorton's government unawares but by 15 December they were not completely unprepared. Gorton had accepted the earlier one out, all out advice provided by his senior military commanders. This was followed by an internal squabble between External Affairs and Defence with each side digging its heels in over partial or full withdrawals. Australia would be forced to follow suit not only to avoid any political backlash at home, but also militarily; Australian forces could not be left in the field while all else were seen to steam across the horizon, heading home. John Gorton announced on 16 December 1969 that some Australian troops would be withdrawn from Vietnam, but the move would be linked to future American redeployments. Arguments reignited over what could or could not safely be sent home from Vietnam, and internal political manoeuvring added fuel to the flames.

The one out, all out decision came under scrutiny, probably instigated by a question asked by Malcolm Fraser at Defence. He wanted to know 'why was it safe for a two-battalion force to enter Phuoc Tuy [in 1966] while additional support is now necessary in an area that should be much safer than it was then?'[8] General Wilton's 1966 boast that the Australian two-battalion task force was worth any three-battalion US brigade was also long forgotten.[9] The Australians refused outright to have a South Vietnamese battalion attached to bolster the Task Force, citing, among other reasons, the longstanding mistrust of South Vietnamese military capabilities. To place an Australian battalion group into a US brigade was also not recommended. That would have meant being 'Americanised, a loss of identity and prestige', the Defence Committee advised.[10]

The inevitable withdrawal of American forces from Vietnam challenged the Australians. As a junior partner in the allied force they had little say, if any, in how the war was to progress and their tactical purpose remained under the operational control of the American II Field Force Vietnam. The spectre of friendly casualties again caused considerable angst at a time when the debate was about coming home. Nine soldiers of 8RAR—who had replaced 9RAR—were killed in February 1970 in the Long Hai area. A further sixteen were wounded; all of which disturbed General Tom Daly, the CGS. He demanded of Major General Robert Hay in Saigon:

Most distressed and concerned at casualties being suffered by 8RAR in Long Hai area. In view of our experience I am at a loss to understand 1ATF undertaking operations in an area in which they have already been costly and of doubtful value. Please let me have a report urgently, including the aims of the operation and the responsibility for its initiation. At the same time examine its scope in the light of the current situation and role of 1ATF.[11]

Hay had already signalled Canberra that the 'losses were hard to justify' and that he would speak with the commander of 1ATF—Brigadier Stuart Weir—on 1 March. The two signals between Daly and Hay had crossed but Daly apparently had not seen Hay's information before sending his enquiry. The other part of Hay's answer placed the blame on the Americans because they had wanted to put Australians into the Long Hai hills over a long period of time, he wrote.[12] If the Australian commanders thought this to be an operational area of dubious value, why didn't they play the national card and excuse themselves from what they considered to be futile and unnecessarily dangerous efforts? Even the US 173rd Airborne Brigade had said that about the Long Hai back in 1966 during Operation Hollandia.[13]

Diplomatic juggling

On 29 March 1970, Major General Colin Fraser, who had replaced Hay as COMAFV, met with General William Rosson, the Deputy Commander of MACV, to discuss topics expected to be raised in a forthcoming visit by Malcolm Fraser and General Wilton. The General Fraser–Rosson discussions covered Australia's potential withdrawal and the possibility of expanded military training, which was to be an offset to Australian troop reduction. Major General Fraser emphasised that any reduction would be a partial withdrawal linked to the next US redeployment announcement. General Rosson stated, 'from a military point of view the stakes warranted a maximum Australian contribution and their long-term security interests in Southeast Asia justified that effort'.[14] That was all a bit hollow now. General Rosson also suggested that Australia might consider expanding its advisory role, which was a separate task to the training previously mentioned. Although the Australians later gave a preliminary concept plan on increased training for the Regional Force/Popular Force in Phuoc Tuy to the Vietnamese Central Training Command, no definite dates or numbers were promulgated by mid-1970.[15] On 22 April—two days after Nixon directed a 150,000-man American drawdown—John Gorton announced that 8RAR would not be replaced when it was due home in November 1970, which would cut the Task Force back to a two-battalion formation.

An interesting side study by MACV into the Vietnamisation of ports had the potential for a more profound influence over Australian operations than any political directives from Canberra. The Vung Tau port was to be turned over to the Vietnamese by 1 July 1970, but they planned to place it on standby status, with only a small housekeeping detachment stationed there.[16] MACV wanted to move the Australians to Phan Rang, where the RAAF Canberra bombers were located. The now fully expanded Saigon port could handle the logistics distribution for the southern regions. According to David Horner in *Strategic Command*, General Wilton had warned Major General Fraser about Australia's possible troop reduction in March 1970, before his takeover of the Australian Force Vietnam and before the prime minister's April announcement. Armed with this advice, General Fraser apparently managed to persuade the Americans not to transfer and/or close Vung Tau.[17]

This decision was probably more diplomatic than military. No mention is made in the *MACV Command History* of any anticipated difficulties that the Australian force might have encountered as a result of the proposal for the Vung Tau port. At the time of the base selection for 1ATF in March 1966, General William Westmoreland had emphasised that forces operating in Phuoc Tuy along Route 15 and the eastern portion of the Rung Sat Special Zone were required in order to protect the Vung Tau–Saigon highway and relieve the pressure on the then underdeveloped Saigon docks. By 1970, the Australian deployment had grown into an immovable settlement at Nui Dat.[18] Perusal of any of the unit routine orders will confirm its small city status. To upset the Australians by making them undertake a costly move at a time when all eyes were focused on troop reductions probably would have caused an unnecessary diplomatic distraction for the Nixon administration. The Australian plan to not replace a battalion but to fight on—whatever fight on might mean at the time—attracted some cynicism and anger from soldiers and the general public along the lines of: whatever the Americans do, so we will follow.

The hunt goes on

Irrespective of the planned withdrawals, the hunt for the enemy continued. Commanders also kept up their efforts to find and implement a winning formula that would bring notable achievements against their elusive foe. 8RAR had had a series of successful actions against local force units using a technique called close ambushing. Lieutenant Colonel Keith O'Neill, the 8RAR commanding officer, had placed his ambushes closer to the local villages rather than in a wider arc in the fields and jungle beyond, based on the simple idea that the enemy must converge as they headed towards a hamlet to gather the resources that they normally demanded of the villagers. It was not a new concept but it was successful as the US 1st Cavalry Division proved earlier in its operations during 1969.[19] There was no overarching Australian Task Force plan that capitalised on this success, however. Each commander wanted a stamp of recognition for his efforts, which meant that in the main the battalions were free to do their own thing under the umbrella of Task Force operational plans.

The battalions searched for the Viet Cong in all of their old hiding places. The two understrength Viet Cong battalions *D445* and *D440* were the main local force units in the province, although they also had their weaknesses. They moved frequently and allegedly did not cooperate well together because of a clash between North Vietnamese personnel and the southern Viet Cong.[20] The badly mauled *274 Viet Cong Regiment* with less than 1000 personnel was generally thought to be in a swathe of territory around the tri-border area at the western edge of Phuoc Tuy. In mid-1969 the *5th Viet Cong Division* had gone back to its Phuoc Long base from where it had operated since 1967 although the *33rd NVA Regiment* had been hived off to eventually operate with *Military Region 7*. It was probably licking its wounds anywhere between the La Nga River north of Xuyen Loc and Binh Tuy Province, to the east of Phuoc Tuy. Intelligence reports and captured documents confirmed that the enemy was suffering from a lack of food, severely affecting their operational capabilities.

The Australians continued to encounter morale-shattering mines as well as bunkers and elements of enemy that fought hard when found. Starving small units did not mean that the battles were any easier. Second Lieutenant Peter Lauder discovered this in a battle in the Long Hai hills for which he was awarded a Military Cross:

> Lauder located his platoon in an ambush at the northeastern extremity of the hill chain. Just after last light, an enemy force of approximately one hundred moved into the ambush area. Once the ambush was sprung, the platoon became involved

in a fierce firefight for the next forty minutes. The enemy force . . . repeatedly attacked from three sides supported by machine gun and anti-tank rocket fire. The platoon repeatedly repulsed the enemy assaults and the enemy force eventually withdrew . . . with an estimated thirty of its number killed. Three soldiers lightly wounded, were the only casualties sustained by Lauder's platoon.[21]

There was little rest between patrols; for many soldiers it seemed to be nothing but endless footslogging that suddenly exploded into an adrenalin-boosted clash of kill or be killed. Differences of opinions between the commanding officers on how to defeat the enemy were also apparent. Colin Khan at 5RAR thought that cordon-and-searches around villages were a waste of time. Ron Grey, who commanded 7RAR, was daring when it came to attacking bunkers; although he agreed that tanks were useful he felt it was wrong to wait for them and hand the initiative to the enemy. Keith O'Neill at 8RAR held a different opinion:

> He concluded that no infantry tactics were likely to be effective against bunkers. He resolved to avoid attacks on them unless tanks were available or to surround them with blocking forces, hit them with air or artillery strikes and ambush on likely escape routes.[22]

O'Neill's doubts were reinforced by an analysis from the Australian Scientific Adviser's Office that showed 13 per cent of contacts were against bunkers—which was not an alarming figure—but during those clashes Australians suffered 44 per cent of their casualties. The main problem associated with tanks was simply time. If they were not with the infantry, delays of between one and three days were experienced in getting the tanks to the battle site. If they were with the infantry their noise spoilt any chance of surprise.[23]

Brigadier Stuart Weir was keen to get his men out to patrol the far-flung reaches of Phuoc Tuy Province. He demonstrated his desire to come to grips with the enemy when he sent a large armoured column supported by Bravo Company, 6RAR/NZ, on what might be impolitely referred to as a grand tour of the province in January 1970. The results were of no consequence in an area around the May Tao Mountain where Brigadier Graham had used similar tactics in 1967. Armoured vehicles that thundered along roads and tracks soon startled any enemy elements into hiding. Although the Viet Cong were basically being starved by being prevented from entering the population centres, this type of tactical activity appeared to have an aim to kill the enemy just to increase the body count.

Trust and battle confidence

Although the 18th ARVN Division at Xuyen Loc had put units through a 1ATF training cycle, the division carried a stigma. It had been one of the worst divisions in the ARVN, but now in August 1969 it was under a new commander and it was improving. Even though the Australian training plan was to concentrate upon the Regional and Popular Forces as part of their troop withdrawal, all of the South Vietnamese needed a display of trust and confidence to prepare them to stand alone. While Australians did train South Vietnamese and conduct some combined operations, the lack of rapport between the forces persisted, and efforts to integrate Australians with ARVN and Regional Force/Popular Force failed.[24] Criticism of the ARVN and the Regional Force/Popular Force was a self-fulfilling prophecy, though. Little was known or understood of their battles, as General Abrams reported to General Earle Wheeler following the August–September 1968 offensive.

> The ARVN killed more enemy than all other allied forces combined. [They] also suffered more KIA, both actual and on the basis of the ratio of enemy to friendly killed in action [because] they get relatively less support . . . than US forces, i.e., artillery, tactical air support, gunship and heli-lift.[25]

Australian newspapers carried articles that implied the South Vietnamese were not fighting or suffering as much as the Free World Military Forces. After President Nixon's withdrawal announcement in November 1969, Bruce Grant wrote for *The Age* under the headline 'Colour change for corpses'. 'If the only effect of an American withdrawal is to transfer the fighting to the Vietnamese . . . US policy will be shown to be impotent.'[26] That comment insinuated that the Americans and everyone else had been fighting and dying but not the South Vietnamese, and it was a seriously incorrect aspersion. The Vietnamese had also objected to the term 'Vietnamisation', which implied that they had not been fighting prior to implementation of that plan. Total American battle deaths during the years 1964–1973 were 47,424.[27] For the period 1964–1970, the Republic of Vietnam armed forces suffered 116,336 killed by hostile action. Australia had lost 302 killed in action for the period 31 July 1962 to 5 December 1969.[28] By the end of the war, 326 Australians had been killed in action. However, the total number of deaths was 500. Australian wounded, injured and ill numbered 3129.[29]

Further afield, in II Corps, an Australian-led Mobile Strike Force battalion was instrumental in the breaking of a siege around the Dak Seang Special Forces camp in April 1970. Ten Australians commanded by Major Pat Beale MC and several Americans led 300 Montagnards into the battle, during which they were joined by a second MSF battalion. It took the force eleven days to break through 3500 metres to the camp while under continual attack from three North Vietnamese Army regiments. Three Caribou aircraft were shot down during attempts to resupply the camp. Pat Beale summed up the feelings of those who had risked all and survived when they got back to Pleiku:

Two nights after coming out of Dak Seang we sat around the pool at Pleiku Detachment B Headquarters and celebrated our victory. In reality we celebrated our survival. Missing from the gathering was John Pettit, killed, three other Australians and five US Special Forces wounded, and nearly one hundred of our Montagnards dead or badly wounded and nearly as many again with light wounds who had kept fighting. Against all odds not only had we survived, but also in achieving our objective we could claim to have won the battle and raised the siege of Dak Seang. When a rocket attack on the city around midnight drove everyone else in their underwear and helmets to their sandbagged bunkers, we continued to sit there. We were immortal and bore the scars to prove it.[30]

This was a distinguished story of success achieved by a sometimes-maligned force that had stood firm and fought to the point of exhaustion. Some trust and confidence, training and support helped to forge the battalion into an effective battle unit. It could be done.

The real backbone of regional security was the Regional Force/Popular Force. The Australians had correctly identified that their training and support efforts should be directed to the 'Ruff-Puffs', as they were known, as a priority.

Unfortunately some of these units in Phuoc Tuy continued to lack the capabilities needed to stand alone in battle. This under-performance needed to be fixed if the Australians were to get out of the province with their dignity intact. The enemy were already trumpeting that the Australians were going and the people were worried.

A separate war in Phuoc Tuy

Was Prime Minister Gorton's April 1970 no-replacement announcement the opportune time for the Australian force to move closer to grassroots security? In Phuoc Tuy Province several disparate enemy groups called battalions, which in reality were hard-pushed to field several hundred personnel apiece, and badly depleted guerrilla force companies continued their efforts to harass the government's administration and pacification programs. The danger of major attacks against Nui Dat and other main facilities had passed. The enemy in Phuoc Tuy had been forced back into an earlier phase of guerrilla warfare. Although the Australians understood that they could not run a separate war in Phuoc Tuy Province outside of the American effort, the Americans only held a loose rein over how the Australian Task Force operated. This created a general impression that Phuoc Tuy was the *Australian province*, which was inaccurate. It was a province in which the Australians conducted their main military operations; nonetheless, the civil guidance and administrative advice and dollars flowed from the US Civil Operations and Revolutionary (later Rural) Development Support organisation (CORDS). The Americans had pushed for the Australians to take over this responsibility on several occasions, but Australia could not afford the cost or the manpower and they rejected the idea.

Australian arguments over the proper method to reduce their troop numbers skirted around the idea that it was not just the size of the Task Force that mattered now. What really counted was the size and power of the remaining American–Vietnamese shield to prevent any major movement of the enemy's main force units and resupply into their eastern base areas that would threaten Phuoc Tuy. In these latter years nothing of significance came by sea through the enemy's old docking ports. Instead the enemy's logistics groups had to undertake an arduous cross-country journey to get sustenance and personnel to the two regiments that remained in the vicinity of Phuoc Tuy. The principal supply routes used by the *86th Rear Services Group* to get men and materiel to *274* and *33* regiments followed two tracks known as Adams and Jolley roads south from Phuoc Long Province along the border between II and III Corps Tactical Zones. *Base Area 300* in the general region of the boundary between Phuoc Tuy and Binh Tuy provinces was the terminus for this route. It also fed supplies to *Base 303*, which was *274 Regiment*'s territory in the tri-border area of Phuoc Tuy, Bien Hoa and Long Khanh. These supply routes were constantly interdicted, forcing the regiments to rely upon the local people and their agriculture to survive—a strategy labelled the Shadow Supply System.

The severities experienced under this system were noted in *COSVN* Directive 13/CT-70. The difficulties continued throughout 1970, which caused NVA Major General Tran Do to broadcast measures to overcome 'ideological problems that lowered combat effectiveness'. General Tran Do said: 'many units have to fight in extremely difficult conditions with a shortage of everything . . . in a number of areas, self-reliance . . . using of the enemy's weapons to fight . . . have become a routine way of life'.[31]

Several Viet Cong party and military committees also reinforced the self-sufficiency message issued by *COSVN*:

> In view of this situation . . . they were told to fully understand the importance of self-sufficiency . . . they should not rely on support from COSVN. If conditions permit, some reinforcements will come, but they will only assist local areas in improving their self-sufficiency. [This meant] that as a result of the critical situation some measures were to be taken to include the establishment of a light and compact organization [and] a decrease in support strength.[32]

Arguments in Australia about the enemy's capabilities and the threat to the Australian force continued after Gorton's announcement. If 1ATF were withdrawn piecemeal, would the enemy take advantage of the lesser numbers and march upon the province? Supposing the claim that MACV wanted to move the Australians to Phan Rang in 1970 was correct, it surely indicated that the province was not in danger of collapse. Although the remnants of the *274th Viet Cong* and *33rd NVA* regiments remained in contiguous territory, they were being hounded by other allied troops and they were in no condition to conduct large-scale attacks. Within *COSVN*'s area of operations—including Phuoc Tuy—the predominant theme of enemy operations was about rebuilding the guerrilla base insurgency with an aim to target Vietnamisation and pacification. The risk of main force units marching upon Phuoc Tuy—or through the province to Saigon—was minimal. Infrastructure support for large units in this region was inadequate, the area lacked reliable external supply and all of *COSVN*'s divisions—*1st, 5th, 7th* and *9th*—were positioned to fight against the allied incursion into Cambodia.[33]

With the Australian force to be reduced, forays into the province's hinterland would achieve little apart from wearying those Australians who remained. Admittedly, active offensive patrolling was a requirement for sound defence but Phuoc Tuy offered an additional challenge: the task of improving the Vietnamese Regional Forces so that they could assume the duty of protecting the people and keep close control over food resources to make sure the enemy continued to starve. It was here that *COSVN* forces in Phuoc Tuy were fighting their battles in accordance with Resolutions 9 and 14 issued in 1969. After July 1969, enemy action against the pacification efforts intensified following the admission by *COSVN* that 'we could not annihilate the enemy's large-sized units and our attacks against fortifications were not successful'. In accordance with Directive 136, the Viet Cong were ordered: 'to kill any hamlet chief, deputy hamlet chief, or village council member possible; they are the target of our attack on the government pacification program'.[34] The 'puppet forces' of the Republic of South Vietnam were the enemy's main targets, not the Australian 'satellite troops'.

In the jumble of the multifaceted total *Indochina* battlefield, tactics that had previously been questionable in Phuoc Tuy Province were now possible. Strong combined action groups had the potential to provide the necessary bedrock of protection and confidence needed to defeat the Viet Cong's attacks against the population but this would require the Australians to willingly integrate their military expertise with the South Vietnamese Regional Forces and to be less contemptuous of South Vietnamese capabilities. There was recognised risk, but the USMC combined action sub-units that operated in I Corps provided plentiful examples of the challenges and the successes that such programs could achieve.[35]

Another cogent example of cooperative battle success came from Lieutenant General Ngo Quang Truong, who wrote about the efforts that involved an American Army airborne battalion in cooperation with Regional Force/ Popular Force units in Thua Thien Province, close to the Demilitarized Zone.[36] In the aftermath of Tet 1968, security in Quang Dien District—a coastal area just north of Hue—was so bad that less than 5 per cent of the territory was under government control. Lieutenant Colonel Leslie Carter joined with Major Tran Tien Dao to fuse the American 1st Battalion, 502nd Infantry with the district's Regional Force/Popular Force units to clear the area of enemy. As General Truong related:

> The successful results from combined operations were invariably those [when] ... forces participated with enthusiasm and dedicated cooperation. The task assigned to each element [at Quang Dien] was designed to match ability ... regardless of nationality.[37]

Care was taken during the link-up stages each day when the local South Vietnamese troops joined with the American forces. General Truong elaborated:

> The Regional Force/Popular Force operated in the lead element ... in areas where their familiarity with the local terrain and people, and their special ability to detect mines, booby traps and secret hideouts could be best employed. US Troops, meanwhile, constituted the main strike elements. The Regional Force/ Popular Force troops enjoyed the same support provided to US troops, including rations, hot food, medical treatment, fire support and ammunition.[38]

The campaign began with small elements of the Regional Force and Popular Force guided and protected by larger American units and increased in size as the capabilities of the South Vietnamese developed. Eventually the operations were completely South Vietnamese with Americans providing only helicopter support. The operation started in April 1968 and by mid-October the American commitment was reduced to a token company-sized force at most. 'The key factor', General Truong said, 'was not merely cooperation ... It was the ability of the 1/502 Battalion to fully grasp the special qualifications and capabilities of the Regional Force and Popular Force and its sympathetic dedication to the ultimate cause underlying the concept of combined operations'. As a result, the Regional Force/Popular Force troops of Quang Dien became more audacious in combat and their morale and self-assurance were greatly enhanced. They continued to keep the district free of enemy until the very last days of the war.[39]

General Truong believed that the major advantage enjoyed by the Regional Force and Popular Force was their undisputed knowledge of the local environment and local people. Their motivation was not artificial; it was a matter of life or death for soldiers who had to defend their own families and villages. They always suffered considerably more losses that the ARVN: for example, during 1970 the Regional and Popular Forces lost 15,783 killed versus the ARVN figure of 5602. The Regional Force and Popular Force remained the largest number of volunteers to serve during the war and their desertion rates were far fewer than those of the regular forces.[40] Too much was demanded of them and too little given in return, General Truong lamented.

A change of command

There were two changes of command in mid-1970 that altered the Australian Task Force's tactical concept of operations. First, Lieutenant General Michael S. Davison assumed command of IIFFV on 15 April. He replaced General Julian Ewell, no doubt to the relief of some Australians. Although Davison had not commanded in Vietnam previously, he had extensive combat and staff experience from World War II. He came to the war with broad background knowledge on Vietnam, having commanded the US Army Pacific after which he was the chief of staff to CINCPAC, the theatre commander. Brigadier William (Bill) Henderson, who took command of 1ATF on 1 June 1970, was the second new appointment. He had not commanded in Vietnam previously either, but he had a good knowledge of what was going on at that stage.

Brigadier Henderson worked hard to establish a strong rapport with senior local Vietnamese officers like Lieutenant Colonel Nguyen Van Tu and his CORDS adviser Lieutenant Colonel John Bacci. American troops commanded by Colonel Joseph Ulatoski from the 2nd Brigade 25th Infantry Division based at Xuan Loc were also included in these provincial meetings. They agreed to get back to keeping the enemy away from the villages. The 199th Light Infantry Brigade with four battalions also fought in conjunction with the 18th ARVN

Division. Brigadier General William Bond commanded the brigade, but he was killed in action on 1 April, 2 kilometres south of Vo Dat. His death was claimed by *33 NVA*. In mid-July 1970, the 199th moved into the Binh Tuy provincial area, to the east of Xuyen Loc, to seek out and attack *33 NVA Regiment* that had been detached from the *5th Viet Cong Division*. Apparently *33 NVA* had been ordered to assist *Military Region 6* and later 'to cooperate' with *Military Region 7* in certain operational campaigns, preferably in the northern area of Route 1 to support guerrilla activities and disrupt pacification.[41]

Although the Australians didn't mind chasing their old enemies *D445* and *D440*, they didn't take kindly to a new directive to go back into the Long Hai hills. Major General Colin Fraser raised his objection with Lieutenant General William Rosson at MACV and they did not operate in the hills again. Brigadier Henderson also baulked at the overwhelming use of combat power by the Americans; the old 'pile on' approach. It was spectacular to watch, but often the results did not justify the expense. Henderson also wanted to assist the South Vietnamese Regional Forces to improve their competence. The aim now was to coax the Regional Forces and the Australians into better performance through closer cooperation and support, similar to what had happened in Quang Dien District with 1/502 Battalion, but not the same as the US Marines combined action platoons with the Popular Force at hamlet level. That program was the father of the subsequent US Army Mobile Advisory Teams. Brigadier Bill Henderson's plan became Operation Together (Cung Chung), a main part of the Task Force's tactical efforts over the next eight months of 1970 into early 1971.

The plan was to operate in close cooperation with the local Vietnamese commanders and to integrate some of the patrols and ambushes, which undoubtedly caused some nervous moments but the Vietnamese Regional Forces showed that they were willing to learn. As the Officer Commanding Alpha Company, 7RAR, wrote on one of Lieutenant Chris Johnson's after action reports: 'It is encouraging to note the positive participation of the Regional Force in this contact'.[42] The 2RAR/NZ report for Operation Dagger also listed several lessons and recommended improvements for the Regional Force Company that they mentored:

772 Regional Force Company's tactical ability and aggressiveness could be improved. It is not considered to be capable of independent company operations

for five days at this stage. With further attention to detail and guidance in training and on operations, it should be capable of reaching this standard quickly.[43]

Another company, 302/2 Regional Force, was judged by Lieutenant Colonel John Church, the CO of 2RAR, as being capable of independent company operations.[44] However, Lieutenant Colonel Ron Grey at 7RAR cautioned, there was not only a requirement for more interpreters but also a need for patience:

A few minor joint operations will not suddenly change military character and habits of the Regional Force/Popular Force soldier. The Regional Force/Popular Force soldier must be encouraged by example and attitude of our private soldiers and junior leaders. Improvement is slow. A regular programme to work with local forces . . . will win more than weeks of talking and drinking tea at comd levels.[45]

Operation Together saturated large areas of the province with patrols and the constant ambush of likely tracks and resupply routes hurt the enemy badly, but the curse for the Australians continued to be mines and booby traps. Lack of food remained the enemy's greatest weakness, but they continued to fight when cornered. In some of the villages, the Viet Cong also managed to stay just ahead of their tormentors, either through the acquiescence of the villagers or simply by brazen resolve. A directive permitting only Vietnamese forces to operate inside villages annoyed Lieutenant Colonel O'Neill at 8RAR because it prevented implementation of an 8RAR plan to flush out possible Viet Cong infrastructure personnel during the day and have them run the gauntlet of their night ambushes.

The 8RAR tactics of surrounding hamlets hurt the enemy badly. *D445 Battalion* recorded: 'the local forces and 445 Battalion were almost never able to slip into the hamlets by night. The numbers of our casualties and those captured increased daily'.[46] The long-running Operation Together also confirmed that the enemy's order of battle in the province was mainly centred upon *D445 Battalion* supported by elements of local force companies, some of which were now in very bad condition with reduced numbers and limited supplies.

Even though the efforts of Operation Together emphasised support for the South Vietnamese, the Australians also continued to improve their own combat skills. The topic of inaccurate shooting was always good for a disparaging remark, whether said of the enemy or of all Vietnamese in general. But criticism could go both ways. A former Viet Cong soldier was asked, 'We [Australians] sometimes say the Viet Cong or NVA are not good shots with rifles. What do the Viet Cong or NVA say about our shooting?' The answer, '[w]ith some laughter and slow smiles ... about the same!'[47] His verdict was borne out by these remarks taken from several Australian contact reports:

> Range of first engagement against 4 enemy – three to four metres, 560 rounds fired – 2 enemy KIA. Three enemy at six metres, 800 rounds fired – 1 KIA. 2 to 3 enemy, range of first engagement 15 metres, 200 rounds fired – no casualties. Comment, there is a requirement for more accurate shooting [!].[48]

Marksmanship, or lack of it, was a frequent subject of discussion in most of the infantry units that served in Vietnam. In September 1970, 2RAR/NZ made the following comments about small-arms fire:

> There is an apparent tendency for soldiers in contact but without enemy in view to point their weapon in the general direction of the enemy and pull the trigger. This may occur because of: The lack of emphasis in training on the need to make every shot an aimed one intended to kill the enemy. This ... *may be due to the reluctance of instructors to inculcate the desire to shoot to kill when such an attitude appears at variance with the general public attitude towards the war in Vietnam* [emphasised].[49]

There were repeated warnings during training about the danger of pointing weapons at other soldiers, which might have gone some way towards explaining why soldiers were reluctant to shoot to kill.

> The soldier is encouraged to add to the realism and noise of battle by firing blank ammunition; on the other, he is warned to aim away from the 'enemy' when firing blank. The result may be to make him reluctant to seek a definite target but convince him that firing is an essential part ... whether he sees the enemy or not.[50]

The potential for psychological resistance to the close-range killing of another person was not addressed. As detailed in Lieutenant Colonel Dave

Grossman's book *On Killing*, learning to kill comes at a psychological cost.[51]

Brigadier Henderson also got himself into political hot water when he told the press that the withdrawal of a battalion would mean the remainder would have to work harder.[52] The implication was that the Vietnamese were not ready to fill the military void, which ran counter to the positive messages being uttered about Vietnamisation. The previous reluctance of the ATF to integrate and prepare the Vietnamese—especially the Regional Force and Popular Force—for their eventual role as the primary security force in the province was undoubtedly a factor.

When the Opposition in the Australian Parliament latched on to statements by the prime minister that the Australian force would require a 'modified and different function' because of the non-replacement of 8RAR, the cat was well and truly out of the bag.[53] No matter how the government attempted to explain away the differences it was patently obvious that the capabilities of a two-battalion task force were less than the larger force and they would either have to do more to cover the same area or reduce their area of responsibility.

Previously the Australian Defence Committee had acknowledged the undesirability of giving the impression that any decision made on an Australian withdrawal would be dependent upon an American plan for their troop reduction. At the same time, the committee recognised the need to garner some detail on Vietnamisation for Phuoc Tuy, as this would influence the future size and role of the Task Force. With only the occasional temporary deployment of ARVN into the province, it must have been obvious that Australian efforts towards Vietnamisation would be linked to the Regional and Popular Forces. American moves were predicated upon a 'cut and try' test: what will the enemy do and will the remaining force be safe? The American decision was also influenced by the speed at which the Army of the Republic of Vietnam could be handed the instruments of war: bases, trucks, guns, helicopters, aircraft, spare parts. This was packaged as Modernisation and Vietnamisation, both of which would need a lot of training.[54]

The Jungle Warfare Training Centre

The idea for an Australian training centre for the South Vietnamese had its beginnings back in the days before the formal commitment of advisers in

1962. Canungra, then known as the Jungle Training Centre, was suggested as an option. It was rejected not only on travel costs but also on the unsuitability of the environment and the fact that the Vietnamese were already using the British Kota Tinggi camp in Malaya. Dr Phan Quang Dan, the Vietnamese Minister of State, who visited Canberra in December 1969, mentioned the potential for an ARVN–Australian Army training complex in Phuoc Tuy Province. Such a facility, he suggested, could offer training in Australian methods of warfare in lieu of the 1ATF combat troops that he surmised would begin to be withdrawn in the future. The suggestion started a series of discussions that were fragmented between External Affairs and Defence. The question of who was to be trained bedevilled the planners; was it to be the Regional Force/Popular Force or the ARVN? Dr Dan had suggested that a facility at Nui Dat could train several hundreds to replace Kota Tinggi where less than 50 ARVN trained per year, but the Australians went ahead with a plan to concentrate on Regional Force/Popular Force soldiers.

In April 1970, Malcolm Fraser and General Wilton visited Saigon where they continued to discuss the training possibilities and the use of Nui Dat, which in the minds of the Australians was the obvious location for a training facility. General Wilton was quite firm in his idea that any Australian training assistance was to be coupled with the special significance that Phuoc Tuy Province had with the main Australian deployment to Vietnam. Consequently, he reasoned that Australian training should be devoted to the pacification and security of that province. This reflected a Cabinet endorsement for the development of a training program for the South Vietnamese forces. What followed in terms of advice, requests and negotiation on which troops to train and where they would do it, was either misunderstood or managed in isolation from the total training package available to the South Vietnamese.[55] Although General Creighton Abrams and General Cao Van Vien approved the general idea of an Australian training centre, the concept soon started to stumble.

Locating a facility at Nui Dat made sense from an Australian point of view. The economy of effort was obvious. Some facilities were already available and security could be balanced with the training base to take the place of the—yet to be announced—withdrawn Australian battalion. At least the students would not have to sleep on the perimeter at night, as happened in other locations because of a lack of barracks space. The Australians continued with their plan to assist the Regional Force/Popular Force in Phuoc Tuy Province through the provision of a senior instructor and ten assistant instructors in an Australian-sponsored Jungle Warfare Training Centre that would be commanded by the South Vietnamese. At this stage, General Wilton thought the administration and logistics of the centre would be a Vietnamese responsibility.

Déjà vu! Australia's first venture into the war in 1962 was to have been at a training centre in Quang Ngai, where the Vietnamese would provide the logistics support while the Australians were to send instructors only. That idea had fallen through because other facilities were available and the Americans objected to paying to replicate an expensive camp recently built at Duc My near Nha Trang.

During the first three months of 1970, agencies within MACV conducted several surveys in conjunction with the Vietnamese Central Training Command to evaluate capabilities and capacities of training centres. Several unfavourable aspects of that inspection noted that there were 'below minimum requirements' of physical conditions in a number of schools and centres and inadequate funds for training support, maintenance and repair.[56] The massive transfer of US facilities to the South Vietnamese throughout 1970 swamped their armed forces, which had a facilities management budget of only $US2.5 million. In contrast, the American budget was almost US$200 million.[57] It was naïve of the Australians to think that all they had to do was provide instructors for the proposed training centre.

A later request by the Department of Army back in Australia for approval of the training concept added that 'we [Australia] should be prepared to make some material contribution'.[58] The Department of External Affairs and Treasury ducked for cover when Major General Colin Fraser in Saigon provided an approximation of costs for the project that totalled $500,000. Nevertheless, General Wilton continued to strongly support the proposal in correspondence to the Minister for Defence in which he highlighted the importance of Australia's reputation.

Although the Australians continued to emphasise the importance of the Regional and Popular Forces to Phuoc Tuy's security as the main reasons for the establishment of the centre, the Vietnamese would not approve it. It was

to be a facility to replace Kota Tinggi and it was to be for the ARVN, the Vietnamese coordinating officer, Colonel Bang, told Australian officers on 18 June
1970.[59] This was not the first time that Kota Tinggi was raised in relation to an
Australian-sponsored site. However, in 1970, there were 33 training centres—
including Regional Force/Popular Force installations—located around Vietnam
that provided instruction in 34 courses on everything from jungle warfare to
divisional operations. One National Training Centre as well as a Popular Force
Training Centre was at Baria, just down the road from Nui Dat.[60]

Further confusion was added to the training plan when President Thieu
abolished the Regional Force/Popular Force on 1 July 1970. The Regional
Forces were re-titled as ARVN units to be located exclusively at the provincial and district level, but the change on the ground was not noticeable.[61] A
second presidential decree signed on the same day renamed corps tactical
zones as military regions; for example, III CTZ became Military Region 3. The
Capital Military District of Saigon and Gia Dinh Province was placed subordinate to MR 3. Other than adding two deputy commanders to each region's
headquarters, there was no real change to a commander's dual military and
political responsibilities. One side of a military region headquarters commanded military operations against the enemy's main force while the other
handled territorial defence, pacification-development and civil defence.[62]

Eventually, even though there was a noticeable coolness to the project by
the Vietnamese, the JWTC at Nui Dat was approved. Major General Fraser
had detected that the Vietnamese didn't want the centre to be at Nui Dat
for similar reasons that later worried Australian commanders: isolation and
security. When Fraser conveyed this to General Wilton he got a reply in a tone
that explained the Vietnamese unwillingness to comment on the subject.
General Wilton wrote, 'the Australian Government approval to go ahead with
the centre related to Nui Dat only. Any Vietnamese objections to that would
have to be stated formally.'[63] General Cao Van Vien had already agreed to the
location because 'that's where Wilton wanted it to be'.[64] Vien was not going to
rescind the decision; to do so would cause him a severe loss of face. Although
Fraser was uneasy, he now accepted that Nui Dat was where the centre was
going to be built.

In consultation with MACV and the Vietnamese, a program of instruction
for the JWTC course was finally approved. Ironically, Major Pat Beale and

some of the MSF team from Pleiku who had been redeployed to Phuoc Tuy assisted in the preparation of the course syllabus from recollections of Beale's days at the British Jungle Warfare School, Kota Tinggi. He also recalled:

> I remember doubting that it would remain there if the TF [Task Force] were to leave. Despite the Australian insistence on Nui Dat we were not made welcome. I constantly had to smooth relationships when provosts would bail up our Vietnamese staff (from the Commandant down) at the front gate and refuse them entry. Difficult times and a great lack of sensitivity displayed. It seemed we were both needed and resented by the TF.[65]

The first class of Vietnamese instructors and cadre personnel started in December 1970. 'A major frustration', Pat Beale remembered, 'was the lack of interpreters. We had developed the syllabus and the training plans but were frustrated in getting them translated into Vietnamese so that we could get the ARVN instructors into the net'.[66] This training was followed by the first six-week student course for 40 Regional Force leaders, which began on 8 February 1971.

Just eight months and 772 students later, on 15 October, the training centre moved to Van Kiep near Baria. JWTC was a very wasteful program that had more to do with diplomatic recognition and observable support for the Saigon regime than essential military need. 'It was a memorable part of my career for its forget-ability', Pat Beale said.[67] There were senior and middle-ranking officers involved in the planning and establishment of the facility at Nui Dat who knew it would not last, but General Wilton had been adamant. He believed that the centre could have defended itself and the training standards would have surpassed the 'sloppy methods' allowed at Van Kiep. He would not have approved a JWTC there, he said after his retirement.[68]

Sloppy methods or otherwise, the many training centres scattered around the country were under the influence of the US Military Assistance Command Vietnam's advice and assistance through the Vietnamese Joint General Staff and Central Training Command. As Des Pryde, an adviser with the 4th Battalion, 2nd ARVN Regiment in I Corps found, even attendance at the Kota Tinggi course did not mould his commanding officer to follow British-influenced Australian tactics. Des wrote:

The ARVN seldom deployed [in this environment] in platoon or section formations. The normal company formation was arrowhead of platoons in file. On a
search-and-destroy operation near My Loc he once put the whole battalion into
Australian type formations just to please me, but you could see that he didn't take
it seriously.[69]

In earlier days, the Viet Cong were more impressed by the Malayan-
trained ARVN who caused them tactical headaches through their use of raids
and ambushes at night and on rainy days. Major Tan, who commanded the
1st Viet Cong Regiment which operated in southern I Corps, wrote a training
note in 1964 on how to counter the enemy plot in which he identified the
new tactics:

These are counter guerrilla tactics, which they (ARVN) have learned from Malaya
and this is the first time they are being used in our area. They were able to win
some victories because of our shortcomings and lack of alertness. The enemy
[ARVN] understands our disciplines and customs. We also did not keep secret
while moving, and they learned this through their reconnaissance personnel.[70]

The Australian sponsored Jungle Warfare Training Centre would also
train at variance with American techniques, an issue that had been identified back in 1962 when the AATTV was sent to the war with the (never
implemented) proviso that the Australians be trained in US Army tactics
before deployment. In addition, a study conducted by MACV and dated
29 September 1970 showed that there were fourteen Popular Force training
centres—not including Nui Dat—across Vietnam and the average capacity
was 1500 students per year. Another analysis of ten selected centres undertaken to gauge the training requirements for 1970–1975 indicated that the
consolidation of facilities as well as improvement and modernisation *would
avoid costly construction programs.* As a result of this study, it was estimated
that the Van Kiep National Training Centre, if it combined with the Phuoc
Tuy Popular Force centre, could train 5000 students per year.[71] Based on the
results of those studies, the Australian forecast throughput at Nui Dat of
4000 trainees per annum was wishful thinking.[72] The Australian plan was not
of financial relevance to the Americans and therefore not of much interest.

The Vietnamese maintained polite agreement because General Wilton had demanded it, and the Australians would wonder with some embarrassment after the event why the centre had opened at all.

The Jungle Warfare Training Centre proposal was to be supplemented by mobile training teams that were first provided by the Task Force and then by redeployment of some AATTV personnel from other provinces. That requirement would push the AATTV establishment from 100 to more than 200 and see the deployment of corporals into Mobile Advisory (later Assistance) Training Teams (MATT).[73] Although it appeared to be paradoxical, the MATT members were required to undergo an eighteen-day US training course at Di An. Even though Dr Dan had said that the Australians were expert in the type of warfare being conducted, and Australians themselves thought they were much better than the Americans, the course was more about coming to grips with a new military environment and impressing upon MATT soldiers the differences to expect in their duties. Corporal Ian Kuring, who had arrived in May 1970 with 2RAR, volunteered to join AATTV. He remembered:

At Vung Tau I joined a group of more than twenty warrant officers and corporals and [we went to] the United States Army Vietnam Advisor School at Di An located about 10 kilometres northeast of Saigon. The 18-day training course was designed to educate and familiarise [us] about the MAT concept and working with South Vietnamese territorial forces. The instruction covered language and culture, weapons, tactics, and aspects of American and South Vietnamese organisation and administration. The course was not difficult or assessed ... it was primarily theoretical [see Notes].[74]

In general, a MATT consisted of six men commanded either by an officer or warrant officer with a mixture of corporals from infantry and specialist corps such as a medic and an engineer. The concept was a watered-down version of the American Marines fifteen-man squads that were paired with Popular Force platoons to form combined action platoons which concentrated upon hamlet protection. The Marines soon learnt that building and staying in a compound invited an enemy attack. They decided to go mobile, to move from hamlet to hamlet but remain within the village precinct so that the Viet Cong could not establish a plan of attack on a fixed point.

The Australian teams undertook a hectic schedule of duties with the Regional Force at the start and later with the People's Self Defence Force. The teams had to be capable of fighting to protect themselves, able to provide medical assistance to the villagers, to advise on defences, minefields, booby traps, and numerous routine tasks associated with helping isolated and often uncared-for units at the bottom of the military totem pole.

Colonel J. A. (Alex) Clark, CO AATTV, told Canberra that eight MATT would be sufficient to cover the province but he was ignored and General Wilton directed that twelve teams be raised. By December there were briefly fourteen in operation with one team at JWTC—there were no American teams left in the province—and as Ian Kuring recalled:

This saturated the province to such an extent that most of the MATT became static rather than mobile. The Australian MATTs were numbered without 10 and 13 because the number 10 was bad to the Vietnamese and 13 was unlucky to the Australians.[75]

Major Ken Phillips, AATTV, also commented on the demands to produce results. 'It should be noted that discussion and implementation can be poles apart if the Vietnamese do not wish to accept the main points. Advisers are not commanders and this is not often appreciated by those not directly involved in the advisory system.'[76] There were 28 Regional Force companies in the province during November 1970 and there had been some progress made with their operational use, but no improvement had been achieved with the Popular Force, who remained at a poor standard. The challenges for the Australian advisers varied from an attempt to stop the Vietnamese using the battalion command post location as a toilet, to advising a disinterested commander that firing weapons indiscriminately while at the halt or on the move was not good for security.

Captain Len Opie DCM, who commanded MATT 3 located around the southern area of the Long Hai Peninsula, remarked on how the Vietnamese had changed the location of a Regional Force group deliberately to show the US who had the final say. Opie also made several wise observations on Vietnamese–US relations when the American provincial adviser attempted to bring pressure to have an inept Vietnamese commander removed. 'This will rebound in the form of obstructionism and procrastination. The CO obviously has friends at court . . . pressure from foreigners will only give him prestige he may not otherwise merit'.[77] Opie also provided a very interesting forecast of future events:

> *While there is no great NVA/Viet Cong threat in province* [emphasised], there is nothing requiring immediate reaction and this condition could prevail indefinitely with talk of a possible Cease Fire in the air, a running down and consequent desire to minimise casualties. It is this very climate that favours operations capable of being undertaken while there is still friendly reaction (i.e. ATF) capability in province.[78]

But, among the seriousness of it all there was some humour, albeit black, as Corporal Dennis Manski recalled:

> One dark night at Binh Ba, one of our ambush parties close to the compound called for mortar illumination so we all raced down, pulled off the canvas tarp covering the 60 mm mortar, tore the charge bags off the bomb and dropped it down the tube. Nothing happened, no bomb on the way, so we did all the necessary drills but still no bomb on the way. The barrel was tipped and the bomb slid out—nothing wrong with it—then down the barrel again without success and by this time the boys at the ambush site were getting a bit annoyed. The next time we slide the bomb out of the tube a very concussed rat followed it out.[79]

A Magpie is missing

On 3 November 1970, a Canberra bomber from 2 Squadron RAAF based at Phan Rang disappeared off the radar screens immediately after a night bombing run in western Quang Nam Province. Flying Officer Michael Herbert was the pilot and his navigator was Pilot Officer Robert Carver. Magpie 91, the aircraft's call sign, had been on a mission known as a Combat Sky Spot. During these missions, a ground-based radar directed the aircraft to the target where the bombs were released on a signal from the radar controller. Magpie 91's target was a recently located enemy headquarters that had foolishly transmitted on a high power radio, which had been detected by electronic warfare techniques. Herbert was under the control of 'Milky', the radar operator near Hue. He massaged the Canberra along a general bearing of 200 degrees (3555 mils) to the target that was nestled in extremely rugged terrain 100 kilometres southwest of Danang and just 25 kilometres east of the border with Laos.

The night was clear, as Herbert told Milky when he was asked if he could work at 20,000 feet (6100 metres):

Should be no problem it's pretty good up here tonight, Herbert replied. Could you make it up to 22 thousand all right, Milky asked. No problem, Magpie 91 answered. I'm levelling 22,000 at 400 knots, Herbert added a little later. Milky [directed] . . . 1 [degree] more left 205, [following several more directions] . . . and you have sixty seconds. Magpie 91, Milky, stand by count down . . . five four three two one, hack. Magpie [advised] . . . six away [six 340 kilogram bombs dropped] breaking left. Milky . . . target number 6736S known enemy location support 1st ARVN. Excellent run sir, it looked real good down here and enjoyed working with you see you again another day.[80]

Six 340-kilogram bombs dropped on the basis of radar calculations may have looked good on the screen, but in reality their power would have been a mere pinprick in this terrain. Mountaintops here ranged up to 1000 metres with corresponding deep valleys and sharp ridgelines that provided excellent protection from bombs. The North Vietnamese Army commanders, nonetheless, would have got the message: don't transmit on high power again.

Herbert then turned towards Chu Lai on the coast as he headed back to Phan Rang base, but the aircraft disappeared from radar and radio contact approximately 18 kilometres away from the target. In spite of search and rescue efforts by both Australian and American aircraft over several days, the Canberra was not found and the crew of two was listed as missing in action. A court of inquiry convened on 8 November 1970 could not determine the cause of the loss. This caused the rumour mill to go into overdrive and stories about black operations into Laos or North Vietnam quickly spread, as did another piece of false information that a SAM-2 had destroyed the aircraft.

Inexplicably, the RAAF inquiry did not tap into the network of Australian advisers who·were sprinkled throughout the tactical region in which the aircraft disappeared. In addition Major Bob Aitken, AATTV, was the Assistant to the Chief of Staff in I Corps (MR 1) and a perfect conduit to all of the operational information that might have assisted with the search and rescue efforts, but he was not contacted. Although using the Australian network might not have changed the outcome of the search, the advisers could have provided current details on friendly units and suspected enemy formations in the area where the aircraft disappeared. Had the court of inquiry asked, the investigators would have been told that the 1st ARVN Division was not operating in the target area at the time. It was only revealed many years later that the target information provided by Milky was designed to mislead. The detail was deliberately disguised so as not to disclose that it had come from an electronic warfare intercept.

The search area had also been severely flooded by Typhoon Kate in late October 1970. Combat activity on both sides tapered off dramatically, as the rains washed away bridges and roads and made many areas inaccessible. More than 250 people drowned and over 25,000 head of stock was lost. The flooding created a frenetic rescue activity during which Vietnamese and American aircraft evacuated 20,000 civilians and more than 1000 troops. All of this was still underway at the time Magpie 91 went missing. Little wonder that attention spans for a missing Australian aircraft were brief, particularly when the Americans numbered their aircraft losses at more than 7000 as at 26 June 1970.[81] They had lost 56 Martin B-57s alone, which was the same type of aircraft as the Australian Canberra that was built under a British design licence. An American Army Mohawk also crashed in the area of the search on 3 November. Even though it was many kilometres to the east of the last known position of Magpie 91, it added to the searchers' difficulties when its distress signals activated.[82]

Ka Tu Montagnard hunters found the crash site of Magpie 91 in 1978. It was about two-thirds up a mountainside, which was later described as very remote by investigator Major Jack Thurgar:

> The heavy engines were at the bottom of the stream at the foot of the mountain. It appeared that the aircraft impacted at a steep angle and exploded. The wings were possibly sheared off as it went through the very tall trees. Those large pieces rolled down the hill and were about 200 metres below the crash site.[83]

Four years later in 1982, woodcutters also found the site and removed large pieces of the wreckage to sell as scrap metal. Australian investigators were led to what remained of the aircraft on 15 April 2009 and found what looked like a junkyard of aircraft pieces. Subsequent tests confirmed that the aircraft was the missing Australian Canberra bomber and not an American Martin B-57. Major Jack Thurgar from the Army History Unit was one of the main investigators to be taken to the aircraft. He remembered:

> The search then shifted to look for evidence that the crew were on board and had not ejected. The detailed search revealed personal items from both the pilot and navigator. Had the crew ejected, then these items would not have been located at depth within the crash site. Former NVA personnel were adamant that they did not capture any Australian aircrew, nor did they discover the bodies of Australian aircrew. They were equally adamant that they did not shoot down the bomber. But they did have a three-man observation post in the vicinity and they did see A84-231 [Magpie 91] crash.[84]

Armed with this information and a cross-reference to information on enemy units described in *The Battle at Ngok Tavak*, the RAAF mounted a full recovery operation.[85] A team of workers and forensic specialists excavated the site over a two-week period and recovered the remains of Michael Herbert and Robert Carver, which were repatriated to Australia on 31 August 2009. This was a remarkable achievement and something that many never expected to see, especially anyone with first-hand experience of the terrain in which the bomber crashed.

Conventional war: Lam Son 719[86]

For many years, the so-called Ho Chi Minh Trail had carried reinforcements and supplies from the Great Rear Area to the battlefields of the South. By 1970, the trail was a sophisticated network of roads, rivers, pipelines, footpaths and storage bases. The network was watched constantly through attempted ground reconnaissance patrols, sensors and all types of aircraft that kept track of movement along the trail. Where the roads traversed the main mountain passes—Mu Gia, Ban Karai and Ban Raving—they were bombed by everything from B-52s to electronically guided fighter-bombers. Anything else that moved was attacked by fixed-wing gunships such as the C-119 Shadow and Stinger and the very deadly C-130 Spectre. Regardless of these efforts, supplies and reinforcements still got through.

At the other end of the country, supplies had been shipped in via the Cambodian port of Sihanoukville/Kompong Som. However, that avenue was now shut off as a result of coastal boat patrols under the long-running US Operation Market Time and the mid-March 1970 ousting of the North Vietnam-friendly Cambodian Prince Sihanouk coupled with the main Cambodian attacks in May–June by ARVN and American forces. As a consequence, Group 559—the trail's logistics organisation—was reinforced to around 42,000 personnel and efforts were increased to bring more supplies through Laos. Group 559 was named for May 1959, the date the trail was established for this war (it had been used previously in 1954). A sea route had also been established in 1959.[87] Roads were repaired, alternative routes were developed and substantial numbers of anti-aircraft weapons were also brought into the region. The Laotian lynchpin was the deserted area of Tchepone at the western end of Route 9 beyond Khe Sanh; the North Vietnamese had at least thirteen NVA Battalions and twenty Pathet Lao (communist influenced) battalions to call on in the region. Base Area 604, a large roughly rectangular tract from Tchepone to the east, and Area 611 to its southeast were rest and refit bases for the enemy's main fighting divisions that threatened Military Region 1 in South Vietnam.

To cut the supply umbilical cord from Hanoi had been a long-held ambition of the Americans and probably some of the senior South Vietnamese generals, too. In June 1968, an operational plan named El Paso was approved by MACV for distribution and further development by component commanders for a corps-size force to go into Laos. This plan was suspended when the Khe Sanh base was evacuated in July 1968. Without that base it was impossible to provide the logistics for the operation. By late 1970 allied intelligence had concluded that the North was in the final stage of preparation for a military offensive against the lowlands of Quang Tri and Thua Thien provinces. As American ground forces were specifically forbidden from entering Laos, US Operation Dewy Canyon II was launched on 30 January 1971 to support a South Vietnamese thrust into what was known as the Panhandle

Area. The ARVN Operation Lam Son 719 followed on 8 February and it was the main pre-emptive strike along Route 9 into Laos against the enemy's resupply lines.[88]

The restriction against American ground troops—but not air support—going into Laos included advisers, such as those of the AATTV. This was a gut-wrenching time, as the advisers stood aside and watched their units fly westward into what was to be a massive clash. AATTV Warrant Officer Des Pryde was one of them:

No advisers were allowed to cross the border. It was hard seeing 'my' battalion loaded onto helicopters without me. The North Vietnamese brought in AA [anti-aircraft] and the helicopter support became virtually impossible. My unit, 4/2 ARVN [battalion], went in with 400 fit troops, but by the end of the operation only 85 fit soldiers returned to Vietnam. The CO was captured and the XO was believed killed. Much later I found out that he had been captured and spent ten years in prison camps before being released and escaping to the US.[89]

Coincidentally, Tran Ngoc Hue—the Hac Bao commander in the Hue Citadel in 1968—was now the commanding officer of 2/2 ARVN Battalion. He was captured on 21 March 1971 and taken to prisons inside the North. He was released in July 1983 and eventually settled in America.[90]

Des Pryde suffered from the loss of trust and respect that had been built up over many years between advisers and their units, but the most humiliating moment came when he visited the wounded:

I accompanied the new CO to visit the wounded in the military hospital in Hue. As we walked along the ward talking to the men in their beds one sergeant who had lost his lower leg said to me, where were you when we really needed you?[91]

The operation ended in controversy and generated numerous articles and analyses, which were mainly papers of condemnation. Most were quick to blame the ARVN command, but it was not as simple as that. Weather and terrain influenced the airmobile operations far more than had been anticipated, and when that was coupled with the enemy's sophisticated anti-aircraft defences it made some missions impossible. The environment also restricted the mobility of the ARVN's M41 light tanks, but the NVA had built tank tracks through the jungle that allowed for the rapid movement of their PT76, T34 and T54 tanks for use as mobile guns. The losses on both sides were high, but the South Vietnamese system crumbled. It was a task too ambitious for their senior command and too much to ask of an army that had not yet become independent of the combat power guaranteed by their advisers. As Major General Nguyen Duy Hinh caustically noted:

> An outstanding feature of Lam Son 719 was the conspicuous absence of US combat troops and US advisers who were not authorised to go into lower Laos. Advisers could provide assistance . . . but only at command posts located on the RVN side of the border. Even division senior advisers were not authorised to fly over lower Laos.[92]

When the force struggled back across the border on 7 April, this summary taken from the *MACV Command History* highlighted the intensity of the battle:

> Enemy soldiers killed, 19,360. Weapons destroyed, 5170 individual and 422 confirmed crew served. Enemy tanks destroyed, 106. Allied losses personnel, 215 US killed, 1549 RVNAF killed, 38 US MIA, 651 RVNAF MIA. Equipment lost, 2470 small arms, 418 crew served, 441 vehicles, 71 tanks, 1577 radios and 37 bulldozers. Helicopter losses, 102 (four others crashed), 601 were damaged by hostile action.[93]

Some old NVA lessons were relearnt when they moved as close as possible to 'hug' ARVN forces located on fire support bases or at landing zones, which afforded them protection from artillery, tactical air strikes and armed helicopters. The North Vietnamese anti-armour tactic was to disperse the infantry that protected the South Vietnamese tanks and to defend critical terrain that restricted the lateral movement of the ARVN armour. The NVA also attacked with tank/infantry teams supported by indirect fire while tank machine guns were used in the anti-aircraft role. A new and effective technique used by the northerners saw them employ small, very mobile combat teams of ten to twelve well-armed men—with machine guns, a mortar and several rocket-propelled grenade launchers—to attack successfully throughout the battle zone.[94]

The Australians adopted a similar practice in Phuoc Tuy by splitting platoons, but they learnt a very harsh lesson following a contact against a bunker system in March 1971, Lieutenant Colonel Peter Scott at 2RAR/NZ recalled.[95] The separated fighting elements of 8 Platoon were too far apart, as were other platoons of Charlie Company, to get to the assistance of the soldiers caught in the heavy fire from the enemy's bunkers. Scott changed his combat rules as a result. He restricted the distance that a group could patrol from a firm base to 250 metres and he only broke the platoons down into smaller groups under exceptional conditions.

The ferocity of Operation Lam Son 719 and its results attracted attention and concern throughout South Vietnam, but in general other regions remained quiet.

Winding down: military dangers

Although some of the senior American commanders in Vietnam had conveyed and continued to maintain that Australia should not reduce its combat force—with similar communications relayed through diplomatic channels—it was an audacious request. The generals and most of the other officials may be excused because President Nixon kept the real decision on the redeployment of American forces very close. Nixon's directive in April 1970 was an example of a withdrawal decision made in isolation, but nevertheless one that meant a great deal to the Australian position in Phuoc Tuy. Henry Kissinger detailed the magnitude of the withdrawal increment in a memorandum to the president on 13 April. In that memorandum, Kissinger noted that the president was to announce the decision but had kept the information from the members of the Cabinet, the bureaucracy as well as 'the *troop contributing countries* [TCC]'.[96]

General Abrams, COMUSMACV, and Admiral John S. McCain, CINCPAC, were questioned frequently by the administration on the effects of withdrawal with regard to security, Vietnamisation and pacification. The only third country forces that would have an impact if they withdrew out of alignment with the American plan were the Koreans, Admiral McCain said. In February 1971 Admiral McCain told the Joint Chiefs of Staff, the 'phase out of Australian, New Zealand and Thai forces appears to have little impact on plans for Vietnamisation'.[97]

As a result of Nixon's redeployment plan the 199th Light Infantry Brigade, who had been hacking away at the *33rd NVA Regiment* and its resupply chain in Binh Tuy Province, stood down from operations in September and returned to America on 14 October 1970. The 25th Infantry Division less its 2nd Brigade was sent home on 30 December 1970. The 2nd Brigade, which was also a four-battalion brigade—like the 199th LIB—stayed on until April 1971 primarily in support of operations against the enemy's *274 Regiment*. They were withdrawn from operations in Phuoc Tuy Province on 31 January 1971. The old 199th area of operations to the east of Xuan Loc and into Binh Tuy had been transferred to the 3rd Brigade (Separate), 1st Cavalry Division (Airmobile) who combined with the 2nd Squadron—an armoured battalion—11th Armored Cavalry Regiment until 16 April 1971 when the squadron was moved west to the Ho Bo woods, near the Cu Chi tunnels.

Although the 3rd Brigade (Separate)—also of four battalions—was responsible for security around the Saigon–Long Binh complex it continued to conduct airmobile operations in a huge area of operations that initially covered most of Long Khanh and all of Binh Tuy provinces. This was later cut into segments of those provinces plus an area of Phuoc Tuy and Bien Hoa provinces.[98] The brigade maintained a heavy forward operating base near Chua Chan Mountain, 15 kilometres east of Xuan Loc, which allowed them to operate out to Binh Tuy Province. That base was dismantled in December 1971, but the brigade kept a battalion area of operations in the vicinity of Chua Chan until March 1972. The brigade then withdrew to its final area of operations around Bien Hoa as it prepared to return to America in June 1972.

Even with the presence of the 3rd Brigade, the reductions were an obvious tactical headache for the Australian Task Force, which was now down to two battalions and support troops. This was effectively reduced to one operational battalion—2RAR/NZ (ANZAC)—during the period 21 February–9 March 1971 when 7RAR handed over to 3RAR. The Australians could not hope to cover the void even with the South Vietnamese Regional Forces who filled in behind them. Nevertheless, security was thought to be of a standard that permitted the Australian Civil Affairs Unit to conduct guided familiarisation tours of Long Dien and Dat Do districts every Friday. Those interested, a notice in Task Force Routine Orders said, were to bring their own drinks and wear clean field dress and carry a long-barrel weapon.[99]

The enemy remained active in large areas, especially the known east–west resupply corridor and base areas, although the enemy's two main force regiments had been kept in check by poor resupply and the presence of the American brigades. The Australians had numerous other small successful contacts scattered across the province from Xuyen Moc to the border area around Courtenay Rubber and Cam My that hurt the enemy's local forces and their rear services group infrastructure. The most successful of these actions was an ambush that had followed a clash at 1113 hours on 30 December 1970 with elements of *D445 Battalion* in bunkers located just to the west of the Kho Mountain, 6 kilometres south of Xuyen Moc.

A quick reaction group of Bravo Company, 7RAR, and armoured personnel carriers from 1 Troop, B Squadron, 3 Cavalry Regiment, moved to cut off the withdrawing enemy force that was trying to escape from the bunker firefight. They set their ambush on a known enemy track about 6 kilometres southeast of Xuyen Moc and approximately 10 kilometres from the bunker ambush. Just before 0400 hours on 31 December, Sergeant Ed Levy, who commanded three armoured personnel carriers, engaged the enemy and 'the fire from his small force was so effective that 21 enemy soldiers were killed'. In addition, seventeen weapons, a radio and a large quantity of documents, food and clothing were captured.[100] There were no friendly casualties although four soldiers had been wounded in the earlier bunker fight, including Private Allan Lloyd who later died of his wounds. Sergeant Levy was awarded a Distinguished Conduct Medal for his calmness, resolution and sound judgement in this action and for another successful engagement on 21 June 1971.

The Viet Cong battalion remembered the ambush with 'grief and pain' in its history published in 1991:

Hai Khanh again asked the political officer of the 2nd Company, you have checked the route carefully haven't you? The political officer angrily responded . . . I'd bet my life on it for you. At 2am the battalion had all reached the open area of [Lang] Ca Thi [village]. The whole battalion was in the middle of the open area when suddenly a ring of fire burst forth followed by a salvo of explosions. The Australian ambush had fired claymores—and this was followed by a thick hail of gunfire. All of the vanguard 2nd Company Headquarters and two-thirds of the leading formation of the battalion were hit by the mines. Nineteen were killed on the spot and 22 were wounded seriously (the personnel strength of a company was only about 20 riflemen at that time) [parentheses in the original document]. *From our founding, the battalion had never suffered such large casualties like that in such a short time* [emphasised]. Those who survived still recall the Ca Thi clearing with grief and pain and our never-before-suffered heavy casualties—brought about by a perfunctory attitude, subjective thinking and underestimating the enemy.[101]

Brigadier Ernie Chamberlain (Retd), who translated the document, observed, 'This passage is quite interesting as it is perhaps the most frank in the whole *D445* history on their casualties'. On the surface, this battalion account contradicted a commonly agreed Australian belief that the battle at Long Tan was the most deadly for the *D445 Battalion*. Chamberlain added that these casualty figures were more believable than some accounts provided by former VC commanders:

I am increasingly of the view that, not surprisingly, the *D445* history has been influenced by the subjective accounts of the *D445* 'survivors' Nguyen Van Kiem [who did not command at Long Tan] and to a lesser extent Nguyen Duc Thu who have 'embroidered' their roles in the unit's history.[102]

But *D445* also managed to bite back when on 6 February they killed six American troopers from the 1st Cavalry Division's 3rd Brigade and wounded ten more in a clash on the slopes of Be Mountain to the east of the May Tao in Binh Tuy Province. A Bushranger gunship was forced to land under fire when troops of 3RAR fought a group in a bunker system 10 kilometres north of Xuyen Moc on 20 March 1971. Second Lieutenant David Paterson was killed, as well as the co-pilot of the helicopter. Captured documents indicated that elements of *D445* were possibly involved in this clash.

A bigger worry was the possible movement of *33 NVA Regiment*. They had been lurking around Binh Tuy and eastern Long Khanh provinces but were generally being kept in check by the presence of the American 3rd Brigade and the lack of supplies getting through from Cambodia. Although the battalions of this regiment were not large—probably less than 200 personnel—they were known to be aggressive fighters.[103] The general intelligence picture based on the *COSVN* directive to *Military Region 7* inferred that the *33 NVA* priority remained counter-pacification and anti-Vietnamisation.

A clash on 14 April 1971 with what was believed to be the *3rd Battalion* of *33 NVA* against the American 3rd Brigade placed the enemy battalion 12 kilometres north of the Phuoc Tuy border and around 20 kilometres east of the Blackhorse base, confirming that the enemy was on the move. A follow-up intelligence summary warned that the enemy was planning a high point of activity in May to coincide with the Dien Bien Phu Battle (7 May 1954) and Ho Chi Minh's official birthday (19 May). That these were perennial warnings was not added to the summary. One part of the warning message suggested that an area around Duc Thanh in Phuoc Tuy Province might be attacked and that part of the attacking force would possibly include soldiers from *33 NVA Regiment*.[104]

As part of the continuing wind-down of American forces, Lieutenant General Davison had proposed in January 1971 that 1ATF be responsible for the whole of Phuoc Tuy Province, which was an unreasonable request. Even though the Australian defence chiefs had agreed to a smaller Task Force, it was on the proviso that an American battalion be placed under operational control should there be a threat beyond the Task Force's capability.[105] That was not going to happen now, but Brigadier Bill Henderson and Major General Colin Fraser did not ask for a change to the 1966 directive that was issued to the Australian force commander.[106] Brigadier Henderson was willing to continue operations unimpeded by qualifications because this allowed him the freedom of movement to attack any perceived security threat before it developed.

Winding down: political dangers

Even the American planners acknowledged that their now rapid withdrawal of combat troops must have an influence upon the decisions of other contributing nations. On 12 March 1971, the US Joint Chiefs of Staff advised the Secretary of Defense:

> As the US withdrew its combat forces . . . the troop contributing countries should be encouraged to continue their support . . . *with a shift of emphasis from combat*

forces ... [to provide] *support to civic action, nation building, and advisory roles* [emphasised].[107]

The secretary then outlined the department's position on 26 March 1971 in which he said that the troop contributing countries should be encouraged to keep 'at least temporarily *a token military force in Vietnam* [emphasised]'. Notably, the Americans thought the only countries that would remain 'if there was no net cost to the US [financial aid]' would be Australia and New Zealand.[108]

By a quirk of fate, it was a disagreement over civic action matters that now engulfed Prime Minister John Gorton, Malcolm Fraser at Defence and Lieutenant General Sir Thomas Daly, the Chief of the General Staff. Daly had warned Major General Colin Fraser, COMAFV, that future likely withdrawals would have an effect on civic action projects and it would be inadvisable to commit to projects that might have to be abandoned. As it was, those involved in the Australian Force Vietnam planning process asked for a budget increase over the previous year, but at the same time recognised that the Vietnamese were now more capable of running certain projects alone. This was a desirable achievement that indicated a program's success. Coincidentally, a report by II Field Force Vietnam on its civil affairs efforts was a mirror image of Daly's suggestion. The Field Force operational report for 1 November 1970 to 1 April 1971 emphasised that civic actions already underway were to be finished and, due to the troop withdrawal program, only projects that could be completed in 90 days were to be initiated.[109]

Colonel John Salmon, the Chief of Staff at AFV, released a message in February 1971 on Australian plans that was misconstrued by some in the military and beyond as meaning that the Australians were to get out of civic action altogether. As a result, several journalists inferred that the force in Vietnam had disobeyed the government. Malcolm Fraser issued rebuttals, but the controversy went on. Fraser's handling of the situation also put him at odds with the highly respected Daly, the CGS.

Subsequently, on 1 March, Gorton called Daly to his office for a briefing without his Defence Minister being present. Malcolm Fraser then submitted his resignation, based on the information contained in an article about the meeting written by *The Australian*'s Alan Ramsey a few days later. Ramsey wrote that Daly had complained to Gorton that Fraser had been disloyal to the Army. Multiple denials flowed from both sides, but the damage was done. When Fraser resigned, he criticised Gorton in a speech to Parliament in which he concluded that John Gorton was unfit to hold the office of prime minister. At a later Liberal Party meeting, a vote of no confidence in John Gorton was tied and Gorton—who held the casting vote—voted himself out of office. William McMahon replaced him. Fraser went to the backbench and Gorton took over at Defence. General Daly retired, as planned, soon after.[110]

Military reality

As the American forces withdrew around them, the small Australian force that remained suffered a further blow to its security and operational capability when Prime Minister McMahon announced on 30 March 1971 that 1000 personnel would be withdrawn. The redeployment was to begin in May and take up to six months. The usual committees and departments in Australia had been involved in the planning considerations and the standard arguments between Defence and External Affairs over military options versus political and diplomatic needs continued. The formal announcement was not to be made until after a planned visit by Gorton to Saigon in March 1971 that did not eventuate. He went to Vietnam in June as the Defence Minister and the Americans warned Gorton that they now had limited resources in Military Region 3, which meant that help from them might not always be readily available.

The difficulty now was to decide which 1000 men would be sent home. To reduce the Task Force to one battalion was rejected because a single battalion could do nothing more than protect Nui Dat. Such a role would be a Catch-22 task: the combat role would be to secure an Australian camp that was there to support the troops that were there to protect the camp. With these restrictions on who could go home, the planners had to scrabble around to get the numbers. The final decision saw the tanks leave, along with the RAAF's 2 Squadron at Phan Rang. Three Caribou aircraft and the small RAN detachments at the 135th Assault Helicopter Squadron and the Clearance Diving Team rounded out the required 1000. This reduced the Task Force to a manpower level almost equivalent to when it arrived, but the loss of the tanks' combat power was underestimated.

The Americans had established a withdrawal template that kept an air-mobile cavalry brigade reinforced with an armoured cavalry squadron as their protective force. They gained from the experience of General Creighton Abrams, who had been a tank battalion commander during World War II in the 3rd Army under the command of the renowned General George S. Patton, Jr. Patton's son had also commanded the 11th Armored Cavalry Regiment in Vietnam.

Corporal Warren Dowell, who served with 4RAR/NZ, recalled that it was a sad day when the Australians were told that their tanks were going:

> Anybody that says that tanks can't operate in the jungle just doesn't know what he is talking about. They did an excellent job and got in there and really sorted it out for us, and it was a sad day when we saw that they were being pulled back to Australia. They did a good job.[111]

Warren Dowell's statement is a robust endorsement of tanks in the jungle, but the deployment of tanks into a jungle environment was much more than crashing through jungle and crushing bunkers. Tanks can only crash through so much jungle before they crash to a halt. During Operation Lam Son 719, the ARVN's light M41 tanks were severely restricted by thick, high grass while the enemy had to build tank tracks to move their PT76, T34 and T54 through the jungle. In dense jungle, the main armament of a tank is generally prevented from traversing, which obviously restricts its field of fire. Tanks also need a fair grade of infrastructure to get them near to a battle site and into a position from where they can start jungle-bashing. All of this meant solid tracks, bridges and access to a logistics tail for fuel, ammunition and spare parts. The move of the Centurions from Nui Dat to FSB Coral in 1968 was a perfect illustration of that requirement. Phuoc Tuy Province was sufficiently well serviced by a topography that suited armour operations and the Australians used their tanks well. They saved lives.[112]

As discussed previously, it was the open spaces that were more dangerous for the tanks than the jungle. There are many examples of open-country anti-armour attacks in the records, such as one classic but little-known ambush that occurred close to Nui Dat in December 1967. The US 3rd Squadron, 5th Cavalry moved into Blackhorse on 28 December and on 31 December sent two cavalry platoons along Route 2 to pick up a convoy at Vung Tau. This is a summary of what happened:

About nine kilometres south of Blackhorse [just south of Courtenay Hill], a rocket-propelled grenade hit the lead tank, killing the driver and stopping the tank in the middle of the road. An ambush then erupted along the entire two-kilometre section of road. Intense small-arms fire killed most of the men riding atop the vehicles. The mortar carrier was hit by a command-detonated mine, exploding mortar ammunition destroyed the vehicle. The last tank was hit by a rocket grenade round, blew up and burned. When individual vehicles attempted return fire, the enemy concentrated on that one vehicle until it stopped firing. Within ten minutes the fight was over. Of eleven vehicles, four ACAV [armoured cavalry assault vehicle] and one tank were destroyed, three ACAV and one tank severely damaged. The two platoons suffered 42 casualties; apparently none [of the unidentified enemy] was killed or wounded.[113]

The ambush force came from *D445 Battalion* and they described the action in their history:

Each company [there were three companies] organised from three to four teams. Each team was armed with B40 or a B41 [RPG2 or 7] (and six rounds) and two AKs. Everyone had parachute grenades. Exploiting broken sections of the sealed road . . . we buried two mines in the middle of the road. In the very first minutes, three American tanks had struck the mines . . . and at the same time, our groups in the groves of trees and undergrowth [50 metres from Route 2] burst forth and split the armoured column in order to destroy it. It was a struggle between men and steel. The whole ambush site was clouded by smoke and dust, and the hulks of tanks and armoured vehicles were scattered in disorder. Many of our soldiers even forgot to support one another . . . thinking only of one thing, pursuing the tanks and destroying them.[114]

Although the battalion misidentified the American unit as 11ACR, that was understandable because the two units had just changed over on 28 December 1967. *D445* also admitted that several of their force had been wounded, but overall it was a deadly successful ambush.

Following Prime Minister McMahon's statement on the force's reduction, the United States invited the foreign ministers of Australia, New Zealand, the Republic of Korea and Thailand to meet in Washington on 23 April 1971. The ministers reviewed the war, but publicly painted a very positive image when they announced that:

> Notable progress [had been] accomplished in bringing an end to the North Vietnamese aggression in South Vietnam, which permitted re-examination of the future combat role of the troops contributing countries [TCC]. They noted . . . the assumption of the South Vietnamese forces of their own self-defence . . . the US redeployments . . . and agreed that it was possible for them [the TCC] to withdraw some of their combat forces. No announcement of actual force reductions occurred . . . but the ministers did note the announced plans of Australia.[115]

The rapid reduction in American manoeuvre battalions from 54 to 33 by June 1971 was a real concern, not only for the Vietnamese but for the protection of American installations, and by association the Australian base. As a consequence a new tactical concept emerged that was titled 'Dynamic Defence'. To make sure that his subordinate commanders understood the new directive, General Creighton Abrams issued 'additional guidance' on 21 June 1971. There was a message in the commander's counsel for all combat troops:

> As combat forces diminished, commanders were to turn from 'combat operations' . . . to 'security operations'. The following definition applied: security operations . . . primarily defensive against enemy incursions . . . if . . . unchecked would threaten US installations, facilities or units. These operations will normally include . . . units of company size and smaller.[116]

Combat operations were defined as: 'those that are primarily offensive in nature and normally involving units of battalion size or larger operating against formations beyond striking distance (35–50 km) of . . . unit bases'.[117]

The Dynamic Defence concept was not to be misconstrued to imply a static garrison-type defence posture, but the reluctance to do more than was absolutely necessary was evident as American battalions were reduced to sixteen by December 1971 and their combat deaths fell to just seventeen in the same month. Even so, Brigadier James Hamlet, the commander of the 3rd Brigade, 1st Cavalry Division, noted in his debriefing that his unit's widely spread area of operations was inconsistent with the mission of Dynamic Defence.[118]

To close with and kill the enemy

During the first six months of 1971, resupply continued to be a severe challenge for the enemy's main force units. As a result of the allied attacks into Cambodia formations like *33 NVA Regiment* had been forced to buy, confiscate, or gather by whatever means they could the supplies necessary to prosecute their military operations. The shortage of rice and other staples combined with the constant harassment by US and ARVN battalions across Long Khanh Province had forced *33 NVA Regiment* to shift its centre of operations to the eastern end of that province and into Binh Tuy where there were good fields of rice. Battalions of the regiment appeared to roam in a broad area south of Gia Ray and out to Tanh Linh village, which was about 40 kilometres north of May Tao Mountain.

In addition to the external resupply difficulties, the NVA/Viet Cong tactical efforts against American targets and other bases had been defeated. Throughout this period, the enemy's activity in Military Region 3 relied more upon local rather than main force units. In the standard language of *COSVN* resolutions, the communist hierarchy had kept their combat options open by not admitting tactical defeat but by emphasising that sapper training and support for guerrilla activity was to be intensified to disrupt the pacification program.

During 1969 several directives distributed by *COSVN* demanded greater efforts of the subordinate military and political agencies and an admission, with the release of its Resolution 14, that past campaigns by the guerrillas had lacked capability. The resolution stated: 'It is obvious that our present guerrilla warfare, due to its big deficiencies, is not yet capable of meeting the requirements for developing the revolutions in the various strategic areas'. The papers intimated a lower profile and dispersed deployment method that was calculated on the withdrawal of US forces—then expected to be in 1970— which meant concentration of combat forces would not be necessary.[119]

The *COSVN* directives—as well as the precarious resupply system—probably had a strong influence on the movement of the *3rd Battalion 33 NVA* to the vicinity of Courtenay Rubber in May–June 1971 to link with and strengthen *D445 Battalion* and local guerrilla units. The mix of North Vietnamese with Viet Cong, however, was often fraught by ethnic dislikes that affected the morale of the soldiers, especially the North Vietnamese cadre who felt being assigned to a local force unit was too lowly for them.

The two widely spread main force regiments—*274 Viet Cong* and *33 NVA*—continually worried the Australians, and the complete destruction of *D445 Battalion* was a goal every Australian commander desired as the feather in his cap. The Australians understood all too well, though, that to seek out and close with the enemy could also come with a sting in the tail. The question now was how to protect Nui Dat with a modicum of support provided to the South Vietnamese Regional Forces in Phuoc Tuy. Cross-border or distant operations that killed Australian soldiers would only exhaust the patience of politicians and senior officers at Defence, even though the commanders' directives permitted such forays. The Australian public was also now more vocal in its criticism of the war. At a time when withdrawal was a prominent story around the world any deaths seen as being unnecessary had the potential to incite more anger towards the Australian government and its generals, and to increase the volume of the cries to get out of the war. That did not bode well for the government, with an Australian election due in 1972. Brigadier Bruce McDonald—who had assumed command of the Task Force on 28 February 1971—nevertheless continued to plan operations with a singular mission in mind, which was to destroy the North Vietnamese Army and VC units in his sphere of operations.

Operation Overlord

Over the period of 5–13 June 1971, the two remaining Australian battalions and supporting arms were despatched by Brigadier Bruce McDonald to conduct Operation Overlord. The American 2/8 Battalion joined the operation 'in cooperation'.[120] Although the American forces were in the midst of major changes in their countrywide redeployments, they maintained a watching interest in what the Australians were doing. II Field Force Vietnam had merged with the US Army Advisory Group, III Corps, on 30 April and

Major General Jack Wagstaff assumed command of the newly titled Third Regional Assistance Command (TRAC) on 1 May 1971.[121] He retained operational control of 1ATF and continued to provide the Australians with combat support, but the withdrawal of American forces and their safety in that process was a more pressing demand. That task also meant he kept a very close eye upon what the ARVN was doing.

Operation Overlord's mission was to destroy the NVA/VC units in the area of the Suoi Nhac, a creek 8 kilometres northeast of Courtenay Hill in an area that spanned Phuoc Tuy's northern border with Long Khanh Province 25 kilometres north of Nui Dat. The border ran in a ragged but generally east–west direction to the May Tao Mountain at its eastern pivotal point. That well-known enemy hideaway was 45 kilometres northeast of Nui Dat. The boundary line also sat in a naturally tough topographical corridor along which the enemy had moved their supplies over many years. The enemy's combat arms had also crisscrossed the regional provincial boundaries frequently and had laid up in base camps, especially in a tract to the east of Courtenay Rubber and around the notorious Hat Dich region over on the western edge of Phuoc Tuy where it joined Bien Hoa Province.

Some of the enemy's provincial units that the Task Force normally fought against were thought to be located in the Suoi Nhac jungle hideaway, along with the *3rd Battalion* of *33 NVA*. In May 1971, according to an Australian intelligence summary, the *3rd Battalion* had an estimated total strength of 185. At this stage, *D445 Battalion* had dispersed its three companies around the province, with *3 Company* located in the Chau Duc, a region a few kilometres southwest of the Overlord area of operations. The company probably had a maximum of 75 personnel and it was directed to coordinate with *33 NVA* and *274 Viet Cong*.[122] In the unlikely event that the two main force regiments massed for battle they might have mustered about 850 and 1000 personnel respectively. In western configurations those numbers would make for two strong infantry battalions. The area was thus operational territory that would almost certainly guarantee a firefight for any allied force that might venture there.

The Australian Task Force established a forward headquarters on Courtenay Hill, which was on the western edge of Route 2 across the road from the old Courtenay airstrip, and the troops went hunting to destroy the enemy. On 7 June at 0645 hours Bravo Company 3RAR found some near the main search area around Suoi Nhac. Tanks from 5 Troop, C Squadron joined the battle as well as American and RAAF gunships. The fight lasted for just over six hours against a well-equipped enemy force with at least two heavy machine guns, which probably accounted for the RAAF resupply helicopter that was shot down and destroyed. Once again, the enemy proved their fighting skills and mobility and withdrew before they could be pinned in place. Although they left behind some items of equipment, and a body was found, their total casualties were unknown. The Australians lost three killed in action and twelve wounded (one accidentally). Captured documents identified the enemy as *3 Battalion, 33 NVA Regiment* and subsequent searches through the bunker system confirmed this when a further four enemy bodies were found.

Five days later, and just 3 kilometres to the west of the Task Force headquarters, 84 Independent Section (APC) commanded by Corporal Kim Brumfield and elements of the Defence and Employment Platoon (D&E) were ambushed. It was a devastatingly effective attack that killed seven immediately and wounded three, one of whom died from his wounds later. The vehicles had stopped to investigate an artillery illumination canister when the enemy fired upon them with rocket-propelled grenades and small arms. One of the rocket-propelled grenades hit a box of claymore mines stowed on the armoured personnel carrier commanded by Corporal Ken Boardman, which virtually blew the vehicle to bits. Major Terry Walker, the squadron commander, and 1 and 3 troops commanded by captains Rod Earle and Barrie Wade respectively, moved within 30 minutes to the ambush scene, where they came across a grisly site of body parts scattered around the destroyed vehicle.

Neil Holbrook was Barrie Wade's driver and he remembered the action many years later.

That was the day we got our arse kicked well and truly by the Nogs [enemy]. It was my old section that had copped it. Memories of that day: making an LZ for the Dustoff choppers to come in and get the bodies; keeping my head down while driving and with my third eye at the back of my head watching that short barrel on the .50-calibre [Barrie Wade's weapon] as it traversed behind my head.[123]

Holbrook's concern about the .50-calibre machine gun was justified as he discovered later when he got out for 'a well-earned smoke'. 'I noticed that the padded driver's hatch had a bloody big furrow in it about 6 inches from the back of my head', he said. Barrie Wade had blasted away but he had depressed the short-barrelled weapon a little too much! When they returned to Nui Dat, the short barrels were quickly replaced with long ones.

Part of the immediate action after the ambush saw Australian Bushranger gunships fly protective cover for the troops and to watch over the casualty evacuation aircraft. Task Force then sent in the 4RAR/NZ Assault Pioneer Platoon as the first reinforcements. Following a minor disagreement between Task Force and 4RAR/NZ over which company was in the best position to react, Bravo Company was told to move but they struggled to get their platoons to positions where they could be picked up by helicopters. As a result, it took four hours for the company to get to the ambush site. Barrie Wade's troop was then ordered to clear to the southwest towards the Suoi Cha Rang, a stream that ran parallel to the southern side of the track on which Corporal Brumfield's section had been ambushed. The enemy had not gone and they welcomed the arrival of the cavalry troop with rocket-propelled grenades and small-arms fire. This action was about 400 metres from the initial ambush. A rocket-propelled grenade hit one of the carriers and wounded Len Cadzow and Dan Handley. Handley was later awarded a Mention-in-Despatches for his 'cool courage and competence' at a time when his crew commander was badly wounded.[124]

Major Terry Walker believed that the enemy had set up or were in the process of setting up a second ambush when Wade's troop disturbed them. Walker wanted to finish the battle with some Cavalry flair and he was not happy when Major Bob Hogarth, OC Bravo Company, his operational controller, stopped him. Walker later wrote in his commander's diary:

> 1 Troop, which had been moved to block and assist 3 Tp, was ordered out by the coy comd as he wanted to move his infantry through. Initially it was a Cavalry battle. I should have insisted to the Coy Comd that [I?] pursue it and let him take over again at say the creek line [Cha Rang].[125]

As a result of the second clash, Task Force ordered strike aircraft into the attack but without warning Terry Walker the aircraft flicked to the squadron's command radio net and virtually blocked the cavalry's conversations. The enemy were undeterred by all of the firepower massed against them and they continued to engage the armoured personnel carriers with small arms and rocket-propelled grenades, one of which wounded Corporal Angus McEwan. Much of the return fire from the armoured personnel carriers was not effective because the enemy, thought to be elements of *274 Viet Cong Regiment*, used the natural protective barrier of bamboo clumps and the creek line to perfection. Fading light and air strikes by American fighters also caused the Australians to withdraw to a safe distance and contact with the enemy was broken. Terry Walker lamented:

Fire and movement is a basic drill and we didn't use it. We met an aggressive enemy in our first major contact for some time and he stopped us cold. Whilst I don't think that he got off scot-free he was better than us on the afternoon.[126]

These were familiar lessons, also learnt from the 3RAR contact on 7 June when Major Ivan Cahill's Bravo Company hit the bunker system occupied by elements of *33 NVA Regiment*.[127] Their saving grace was Centurion tanks coupled with the destructive firepower of American 155 mm howitzers as well as helicopter gunships, American Cobras in particular. As a result, the old argument re-emerged; was it wise to engage infantry against well-constructed defensive positions without heavy help? That heavy help in the shape of Centurions would soon be phased out of action and sent back to Australia. The last tank was taken out of action on 31 August 1971.

Regardless of the explosive firepower that tanks and guns and aircraft provided to break down the jungle barrier and to smash bunkers, the enemy were agile and on familiar territory. If they decided not to fight, any (cautious) pursuit also required an adroit infantry hunter to protect and clear and then kill the enemy. Australian soldiers were cumbersome by comparison, weighed down by 30-kilogram packs and more, which sapped their energy when moving through a close jungle environment even before they engaged in combat. It was not as if this drag upon combat mobility could not be altered. Too much weight was a lesson that was continually ignored, Colonel S. L. A. Marshall wrote in 1950.[128] His study is worth re-reading to remind commanders that excess weight had an impact upon the psychological as well as physical tiredness and that its effects went beyond the immediate battle.

Operation Overlord was costly: ten Australians were killed and 24 were wounded against a meagre number of enemy losses. An American platoon leader with 2/8 Battalion, C. J. Spence, did not have pleasant memories of the operation.

> It was a biggie . . . a battalion size joint operation with the Australians. It was a logistical nightmare. The grunt's question, why were we doing this? My response was, for show. I thought it was a boondoggle [useless] from the get-go. Our insertion took hours; moving off the LZ was slow, noisy and cumbersome. The tall grass was making life miserable. Visibility was non-existent. The grunt description for Overlord was a major F-up! In terms of trapping the enemy, Overlord was a dud.[129]

Once again there were robust discussions between Canberra and the commander Australian Force Vietnam about what was going on in Phuoc Tuy. Brigadier Bruce McDonald at Task Force held to the line that his operation had thwarted a major offensive by the enemy in the province.[130] This was a doubtful assessment. *D445* had been dispersed to assist the local force guerrillas and they had suffered in recent battles, while other allied forces had harassed the elements of the two understrength main force regiments on the fringes of Phuoc Tuy. Their resupply chain had also been severely disrupted. Task Force supplementary intelligence reports produced by Intelligence Officer Major Charles 'Mike' Peters highlighted the possible activities that the enemy units around Phuoc Tuy might have attempted during the first half of 1971. His forecast included small-scale sapper attacks, kidnapping, attacks by fire, and assassinations. Mike Peters also concluded that the enemy campaign was likely to be of a combined political and military nature to achieve a psychological victory over the South's pacification efforts. He did not predict a major offensive, but identified the possible targets as territorial force outposts along northern Route 2 and Xuyen Moc to the east.[131] The enemy looked to the easy prey such as the People's Self Defence Force and to interdict the main roads in the province rather than to engage the more powerful Australian force.[132]

Home for Christmas

On 13 June 1971, *The New York Times* published *The Pentagon Papers*, leaked extracts from a US Defense Department report on the war in Vietnam, in a series of articles that were stopped by a federal court injunction, but were followed by similar releases in *The Washington Post* on 18 June. Although the publication of *The Pentagon Papers* started heated civil and legal arguments in America about US involvement in the Vietnam War, they didn't stir much action in Australia beyond the question of why Australia had sent an infantry battalion in 1965. Greater political pressure in Australia came in the form of three major protests against the war—known as moratoriums—that culminated with a demonstration by about 500,000 people in Melbourne on 30 June 1971. Despite its size, it was a tame affair compared with the earlier two, especially the violence that was associated with the second group of marches in Adelaide and Sydney in 1970. The growing disenchantment with the war following the earlier announcement that Australia would pull out 1000 troops created an expectation that another withdrawal would follow soon.

The presidential elections in South Vietnam were due on 3 October 1971 and the Australian Ambassador in Saigon as well as other advisers to the government recommended that nothing further be said about withdrawals until after that election. At this stage, the Americans and the South Vietnamese thought that Australia would not take out any more troops in 1971. Unbeknown to their allies, this belief also matched a timetable that the Australian Defence Committee had recommended. On 17 June 1971, the committee recorded that the next round of reductions could start in February 1972 and all of the Australian Force Vietnam—except the AATTV—would then be out by August.

This seemingly orderly plan of withdrawal was thrown into disarray when Gough Whitlam, the Leader of the Opposition, visited China in the second week of July 1971. He met with Premier Zhou Enlai and following their meeting Zhou sent a birthday cake to Whitlam on 11 July, which was Whitlam's 55th birthday. It seemed that the Opposition was literally supping with the enemy, and Prime Minister McMahon no doubt thought that Whitlam had made a bad political error. He was stunned a few days later when the world was told that Henry Kissinger had also been in Peking preparing the way for a visit by President Richard Nixon. All civility and order was now abandoned in the scramble to get out of Vietnam.

An Australian Cabinet Decision—319, dated 26 July 1971—followed promptly with an updated analysis on the future of AFV; the decision noted:

In the light of the development ... which the U.S. President's proposal to visit Peking implies ... there could be no assumption that United States would not now speed up its own programme of withdrawal. [Cabinet] took the view that early decision to withdraw the Australian force was inevitable. In the circumstances ... it would be the objective that the first of the ... battalions be withdrawn in October 1971 and the second in December 1971.[133]

Prime Minister McMahon addressed the House of Representatives on 18 August 1971 and told the members that most of the combat troops would be home by Christmas 1971.[134] Ironically, 18 August was the anniversary of the 6RAR battle at Long Tan in 1966, and a commemorative service had been conducted at Long Tan that day not long before the withdrawal news filtered through from Australia to the Task Force. Many of the mainstream newspapers also quickly posted the announcement with published articles and/or editorials printed on 19 August. The news spread quickly, and when the message got out to the troops it was clear that their outpouring of relief would be difficult to contain. This would be a taxing time for commanders and soldiers alike. No one wanted to be the last man killed in Vietnam, or to be the commander who might be held *politically* responsible for that death.

At the same time as the withdrawal decision was made, Prime Minister McMahon announced that the national service obligation was to be reduced from two years to eighteen months, meaning those soldiers in Vietnam whose discharge was due in September, November and December would be returned to Australia not later than four weeks before their discharge. This had the potential to cause operational manning difficulties and to possibly incite some anger between regular soldiers and national servicemen, but that didn't happen in the event. The soldiers had formed a bond of camaraderie that blended their type of service into one. They were an indistinguishable band of brothers.

When all of these movements were put together under a withdrawal umbrella, it was clear that the outcome could be fraught with danger. General Wilton had noted back in 1966 that a common border with the sea would be useful if 'some frightful disaster was impending'.[135] Although a 'frightful disaster' is probably overstating the case, a planned orderly close-down of operations now turned into a phrenetic dash to meet the challenges of reduced deadlines. Thankfully, the gateway for the homeward-bound traffic was just a few kilometres down the road from Nui Dat at Vung Tau.

Getting away from a pernicious enemy

Brigadier Bruce McDonald briefed his principal staff and commanding officers about the withdrawal from Nui Dat during two conferences on 19 August 1971. He called the officers together 'to make them all aware of what is happening'. An outline plan of action was discussed but 'there are a lot of unanswered questions', he told them. There were a lot of question marks against such matters as the handover of Nui Dat, the preparation of stores to go home, the national service dates, and leave for rest and recreation. But the crux of it all was the tactical plan; how were they to defend and get away from 'a pernicious enemy'?[136]

The second conference was told that the withdrawal plan 'will be based on a premise [*sic*] used since the Commander has been in South Vietnam and that was to keep the enemy as far away from our bases as possible'. Security of the force during the withdrawal was paramount and all planning was based on a presumption that the enemy knew what was happening, the conference was told:

[The enemy] is making plans to inflict some damage on us. The intention of the enemy is clear—if he can do something he will. Against all the factors of doing all the administrative things units must ensure we don't end up being clobbered before we leave.[137]

These were sensible warnings that mirrored a sound tactical technique of stepping back with a protective foot on the ground at all times. The ominous warning that the enemy intended to do something bigger than attacking isolated targets of opportunity was questionable, even if *elements* of *33 NVA Regiment* had moved into Phuoc Tuy. Contrary to the statement that the danger posed by the enemy 'was borne out by US operations', enemy initiated activity in Military Region 3 remained low into the fourth quarter of 1971.[138] The *MACV Command History* reports showed that the enemy had confined his activities to scattered attacks by fire, limited ground attacks and sapper operations. In statistical terms, enemy incidents had dropped markedly throughout the military region during 1971. The enemy had also switched their primary target away from the American forces to the Vietnamese pacification efforts.[139]

A possible enemy attack upon his force was an assumption made by the Australian commander, perhaps based upon the logic that a withdrawing force steadily weakened itself to a point when an enemy obtained a combat advantage and would surely attack.

Too much information is not intelligence

As the Australian Task Force started its final countdown, the need for solid intelligence increased and the 1ATF intelligence papers were full of information. Reports ranged in degrees of reliability from not much better than rumour to confirmed details on enemy units, their possible locations and any recent clashes. There were also numerous scraps of detail—sometimes contradictory and inaccurate—from local agents, aerial reconnaissance and sensor devices, interrogations, personal letters, signal intercepts and reports from other allied agencies. Well-meaning intelligence agencies sometimes swamped the units to a point where the amount of information probably clouded their assessment about its usefulness. Commanders who were presented with this plentiful array of details would then have to decide what was relevant.

The enemy had a number of means by which they could cause some damage to the Australians. Three main arms of the enemy force were of concern: *D445 Battalion* (operating as three independent companies), *274 Viet Cong Regiment* and *33 NVA Regiment*. The Australian Task Force was more alert whenever information suggested any of these units—especially the regiments—were on the move. In particular, any detected movement of *33 NVA* towards Phuoc Tuy was a big concern for the Australian commander. Phuoc Tuy was not the regiment's territory of operations and any redeployment here would reinforce the brigadier's worry that its mission was to 'clobber' the Australians before they left the province.

Throughout 1971, numerous intelligence summaries advised on the possible strengths and whereabouts of *33 NVA*. These reports ranged from a low 185 personnel for the *3rd Battalion* and a total regimental strength of about 1000 in May to battalions of 300 for a total of 1245 in July–August 1971. The assessments were qualified with an annotation that 'all figures are approximate'.[140] A more detailed examination of the numbers with an estimate of how many might be available to fight was not provided. A field strength that was 70 to 80 per cent of the book figures was a good guide—but where were they? This question always overshadowed estimates on what the enemy might have planned. During the first six months of 1971, *33 NVA* units were spread in a general pattern to the east of Xuyen Loc and out to Binh Tuy Province, where the regimental headquarters and the *1st Battalion* were thought to be stationed. The *2nd Battalion* was probably in the area of Vo Dat–Nui Chua Chan, with the *3rd Battalion* somewhere in the area of southern Long Khanh or northern Phuoc Tuy.

Concern about *33 NVA*'s activities increased when the Third Regional Assistance Command advised the Australians that the main element of *33 NVA* had moved west from Binh Tuy Province in late August. This report put the group with two battalions—*1* and *3*—somewhere northeast of Courtenay with the *2nd Battalion* still near Nui Chua Chan. But the inclusion of the *1st Battalion* was classified as 'probably co-located', based upon its normal tasking, which was to protect the headquarters. Intelligence Officer Major Peters advised that the threat posed by the movement of *33 NVA* remained one of localised attacks against regional outposts along northern Route 2. He added that a battalion of *274 Viet Cong Regiment* might attack locations further south along that road—like Ngai Giao—to support *33 NVA*'s western movement. No connection was made between the redeployment of *33 NVA* and possible attacks upon the Australian force. Major Peters also linked the general increase in enemy activity to the coming presidential election in his summary for the week of 13 to 19 September:

The move of 33 Regt elements into Phuoc Tuy may be in response to pressure from 3 Bde (Sep) 1 Cav Div, combined with a belief that a vacuum may have been created because of the future withdrawal of 1ATF troops. The general increase in activity [in the main, small-scale attacks against Regional Force/Popular Force] may be related to the coming Presidential elections and is likely to continue.[141]

The enemy's political directives highlighted their *three-pronged attack*—military, political and troop proselytising—that underpinned their military plans and operations. During 1971, for example, *COSVN* directives made counter-pacification a priority and their tactical battle plans returned to 'limited warfare', especially in the Delta, and rural and jungle areas.[142] Resolution 9, released in 1969, and subsequent notes of qualification, heralded the re-emphasis on small unit tactics, reliance upon sappers, terrorism and increased attacks by fire. These were the most efficient tactics of wearing down the Republic of Vietnam (South Vietnam) Armed Forces, the directives said.[143]

COSVN also identified exploitable weaknesses associated with Saigon's security forces: conscription—something that Australia knew a lot about—and taxes. Another identified flaw was the outpost and local security network manned by Regional Forces/Provincial Forces and the People's Self Defence Forces. Whilst main force warfare remained in the enemy's documents, it was considered 'to be an eventual option rather than an immediate goal'.[144] Some analysts also believed that the rhetoric about main force was retrospective, or justification for their costly Tet 1968 efforts.

Although an Australian operational assessment for *33 NVA Regiment* regarded it as the enemy's most capable formation in Military Region 3, that was an overly ominous judgement.[145] Any difference in the level of danger presented by *274 Viet Cong Regiment* and *33 NVA* was debatable, as they had demonstrated in the past and would soon reinforce during Operation Iron Fox. In addition, enemy formations closer to the Cambodian border, such as *101 NVA Regiment*, were better supplied and equipped than *33 NVA Regiment* was. Poor resupply to *33 NVA* was exacerbated by the capture of over 95 tons of supplies around Nui Be—east of May Tao—by the US 3rd Brigade during the first six months of 1971.[146] The regiment was a dangerous foe and the northerners had shown that they were not afraid to stand and fight when it was demanded of them, even in the face of overwhelming firepower.

The enemy, however, had a greater objective to achieve, which was not the destruction of a withdrawing force. If anything, the NVA/VC forces would leave the back door open through which the Australians could go home, with a desultory parting shot or two. In the words of Sun Tzu, 'Do not thwart an enemy returning homewards'.[147] Although the tactical commanders did not know it, this stance was aired during secret meetings at Paris in September

1970. Xuan Thuy, a senior northern negotiator, told Henry Kissinger there would be a 'cease-fire' between US and communist forces while the US withdrew by June 1971, but the war against the South Vietnamese forces would continue.[148] The North's eight-point proposal was not accepted.

COSVN's greater goal was to make the South Vietnamese 'puppet forces' collapse so that the people saw that they would be unable to protect them when the Americans and Australians had gone. *COSVN*'s rural interest was to establish a secure base area for the urban movement where political activity—not sappers and guerrillas—would be used to exhaust the government's local defence programs. Control over the rural population and local supplies were a higher priority than killing the Australian 'satellite troops'.

Searching for danger

Brigadier Bruce McDonald continued to push his two remaining battalions out into the province to find and destroy the enemy. He wished to shield his base against a believed enemy plan of attack to damage the Australian withdrawal. The battalions slogged through the province on their continuing hunt for the enemy. Although the rifle companies were rotated through Nui Dat to get some well-earned rest and to clean up, the operations merged into a continuous cycle of jungle warfare. Operation Iron Fox rolled into Operation North Ward, which later became Operation Ivanhoe. Once again the plan was to disrupt the enemy's northern corridor and to deny them access to a firm operational base from where they could launch an attack or a major offensive, in Brigadier McDonald's words.

Following Operation Overlord, 4RAR/NZ moved its headquarters to Courtenay Hill, which was to be its operational base for the remainder of the battalion's tour. 3RAR phased through Nui Dat and out northeast and then back to join with 4RAR for Operation Iron Fox. This operation was a two-battalion mission to destroy an enemy force suspected to be elements of *274 Viet Cong Regiment* probably based near two streams, Suoi Ca and Suoi Soc, with a centre of operational area approximately 7 kilometres west of Courtenay. Suoi Ca marked part of the borderline here with Long Khanh Province.

The plan was for 3RAR and Alpha Squadron, 3 Cavalry Regiment to provide a blocking force while the enemy base area would be hammered by artillery and air strikes. When the block was in position, 4RAR would advance along the axis of Suoi Ca supported by tanks from C Squadron. The first clash happened on 29 July 1971 when Charlie Company, 4RAR, hit enemy ensconced in bunkers. Once again the enemy used their defences to advantage and elements of a platoon commanded by Lieutenant Paul Andrews were hit by heavy fire and unable to move out of a re-entrant. Sergeant Garry Chad, the platoon sergeant, regained the initiative through his aggressiveness and quick reaction that allowed the forward elements to withdraw with light casualties. Chad was awarded a Mention-in-Despatches for his actions.[149] Delta Company, supported by tanks commanded by Second Lieutenant Bruce Cameron, was directed to reinforce Charlie Company but their arrival was delayed by the extremely difficult terrain and that allowed the enemy once again to use the night and escape.

The fight was not over yet. The next day Delta Company struck another bunker system. The tanks had gone off to refuel, but they smashed their way back into the battle where they were met by rocket-propelled grenades that were fired at them and also into the trees to create additional shrapnel. The battle was now a quick lesson in infantry–tank cooperation that saw the infantry locate the bunkers and the tanks destroy them. Although wounded, Bruce Cameron pressed on with the attack. When a target was found, several methods were used to 'talk' to the tanks. Soldiers used radios, smoke, the telephone at the back of the Centurion—with a very close eye on which way the tank was moving—to bravely climbing on board to yell at the commander. Lieutenant Cameron was awarded a Military Cross for his courage and leadership during this battle and another bunker attack in July.

The two platoons in contact—10 and 12—ran short of ammunition and 11 Platoon, commanded by Second Lieutenant Gary McKay, gathered a replenishment that had been delivered by armoured personnel carriers to the rear of the battle. McKay's platoon then fought their way forward to resupply the other two platoons.

The battle lasted nearly four hours before the Australians captured the bunker system from a tenacious and tactically smart foe. The Viet Cong soldiers had used well-sited fire lanes when they joined the battle with a heavy volume of fire from their arsenal that also included captured GPMG-M60 machine guns and claymore-style mines in the trees. Then they once again used the cover of night to get away, leaving twelve bodies among the 23 bunkers in the system. Although one Australian was killed and three others were wounded, the infantry commanders agreed that the tanks had made all the difference.[150]

Another earlier recommendation was revisited in the after action comments; the infantry needed a bunker-busting weapon that they could carry. The M-72 Light Anti-Armour Weapon had been withdrawn because of malfunctions and there was nothing else in the Australian armoury that met the demand. The LAW could also detonate prematurely in thick under-growth, which meant it would not penetrate a bunker screened by vegetation. Surprisingly, some Viet Cong said that the weapon they disliked the most was the M-79 because of its small fragments, but it was not a bunker-buster. Its round also exploded when it hit vegetation. Rocket-propelled grenades used by the enemy had the same problem as the M-72, which the enemy often used to their advantage by deliberately firing into the undergrowth to create an area fragmentation effect.[151]

In comparison to Iron Fox, Operation North Ward—5 August to 18 September—was a tame affair. In the early part of September the potential danger to the Australians increased when intelligence reports suggested that elements of *33 NVA Regiment*—possibly the headquarters and a battalion—had been detected to the east of the Blackhorse base. This base was just 6 kilometres north of Courtenay Hill. Major Peters' assessment dated 6 September concluded that should a high point of enemy activity happen, the most likely form of attack would be harassing fire and sapper probes. He also noted that eight government officials had been assassinated recently—three in Phuoc Tuy Province and five across the border in Xuan Loc District—which confirmed the importance the enemy now placed on counter-pacification.[152] It was dangerous to be a South Vietnamese government official. Across Vietnam during January to July 1971, twelve village chiefs and 54 hamlet chiefs were murdered, as were 69 national policemen, 55 development officials and 344 PSDF.[153]

During the main period of Operation North Ward, 4RAR/NZ patrolled an area to the southwest of Courtenay and to the west of Route 2. Victor Company (NZ) covered the eastern side of the main road, just north of Cam My village. On 9 September the New Zealanders were relieved by Delta Company, who then pushed further to the east to patrol about 1 kilo-metre northeast of the Nui Le feature and around the southeastern fringe of

Courtenay Rubber. On 16 September, the company headquarters moved onto Hill 265, which was connected by a northwestern saddle to Nui Le. The 265-metre feature was in a string of prominent hills that curled about 4 kilometres in a southeasterly direction between Nui Le and the southern Nui Sao.

Major Jerry Taylor, who commanded Delta Company, then spread his platoons in a wide patrol pattern to cover a northeasterly arc from the north of Nui Le around to the northern slope of Nui Sao. One platoon was on the northern side of Nui Le, a kilometre away from company headquarters. The other two were also a kilometre apart, with one on the high ground to the southeast of Taylor's 265 position and the other further south near Nui Sao. This meant that the company was spread over an irregular-shaped 4 kilometres of jungle. Charlie Company was 14 kilometres away to their northwest—due west of 4RAR/NZ headquarters on Courtenay Hill—and the two other companies of the battalion were back at Nui Dat.

The Delta Company platoons remained separated from company head-quarters by at least a kilometre when they set up their defensive positions for the night of 16–17 September. The only sign of enemy activity had been

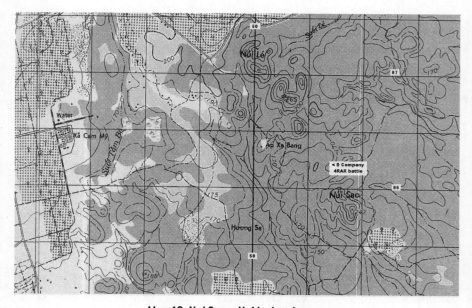

Map 10: Nui Sao – Nui Le battle area
The last major engagement by the Australians was fought on the northern slope of Nui Sao on 21 September 1971. D Company 4RAR clashed with *9* (aka *3*) *Battalion, 33 NVA Regiment*, in a deadly series of firefights that also included B Company 4RAR.

the discovery of two Bangalore torpedoes. Second Lieutenant Kevin Byrne's 10 Platoon settled into its night routine at grid reference YS516855, 500 metres due north of Nui Sao. On 17 September, the Delta Company patrols moved to the western side of the Nui Le–Nui Sao hill line without incident but enemy signal shots were heard around the platoons that night.

The next day, the company regrouped on high ground a kilometre west of the 265 feature to take a resupply, during which Jerry Taylor had a radio briefing discussion with Lieutenant Colonel Jim Hughes, the battalion commander. They discussed a concern that more elements of *33 NVA* might have moved south from Long Khanh Province into a base area to the southeast of Courtenay Rubber. Taylor planned to search within artillery range to the southeast of his position, back down towards Nui Sao and in the general direction of where the enemy might be. They were all a little more cautious because of the intelligence summary and at this stage, owing to company rotations, only Delta Company was in the immediate vicinity of Nui Sao.

Deploy ASAP to search-and-destroy

During the early hours of 19 September, Regional Force Company 626 located at Xa Bang hamlet—2 kilometres southwest of Cam My on Route 2—was attacked by fire when six 75 mm recoilless rifle rounds and fifteen 82 mm mortar bombs were fired at the hamlet. Only two of each hit inside the compound, but they wounded three of the Regional Force soldiers. The compound was a little over 5 kilometres to the west of Nui Sao. The attack coincided with another attack by fire, thought to be either rocket-propelled grenades or 60 mm mortars, against Ngai Giao, 6 kilometres south of Xa Bang.

These harassing attacks probably had a compounding influence over Brigadier McDonald's decision to commit to a search-and-destroy mission in the Nui Sao area, a plan probably reinforced by a comment from his intelligence officer that the *C17 Recoilless Rifle Company* of *33 NVA* was 'clearly in the area' and had been involved in the Xa Bang attack. As a consequence of that assumption, the intelligence officer also advised that the headquarters of *33 NVA Regiment* was also 'probably' in the Xa Bang area because *C17 Company* often moved with the headquarters. The report added that the *1st Battalion, 33 NVA* normally protected the headquarters; therefore, some elements of that battalion might also be located with the regimental headquarters group. Other documents captured by the Americans contradicted that information with additional details that suggested the *1/33 NVA Battalion* was possibly located north of Xuyen Loc.[154]

The Australians also had earlier intelligence summaries that indicated at least two battalions of *274 Viet Cong Regiment* might also be operating in the northern–northwestern region of Phuoc Tuy with a mission to harass and disrupt the South Vietnamese pacification process. *274 Viet Cong Regiment* also had a *C17 Company* and they carried the 75 mm recoilless rifle, too. *D445 Battalion* who also carried the same weapon had deployed its *3rd Company* to coordinate with the two main force regiments in an effort to control Route 2.[155] Task Force was aware from captured documents that *274 Viet Cong Regiment* had several storage sites holding an ample supply of 75 mm rounds as well as 82 mm mortar bombs located to the west of Blackhorse.[156] In addition, intelligence had suggested that there was a possible connection between the operations of *274 Viet Cong Regiment* and the redeployment of *33 NVA*, although the latest movements by the NVA unit appeared to be forced by the pressure of operations by the US 3rd Brigade.

Over the period of 12–16 September, six enemy soldiers were killed by the US 3rd Brigade near Nui Hot. After that contact, the Americans found documents that identified, among others, the *Recoilless Rifle Company* of *33 NVA*.[157] This action was at least 25 kilometres away from where the firing position against Xa Bang was found on 19 September. The countryside in between was strongly contested territory. As a consequence, the possibility that a large group—more than a battalion—of *33 NVA* was in the immediate vicinity of Xa Bang and Nui Sao came from a jumble of assumptions. These had started with bad advice on the ownership of the 75 mm recoilless rifle that had fired on Xa Bang. As a result, this very important intelligence summary was no better than a wild guess.[158]

More meaningful information came from Australian reconnaissance pilots who reported on track usage in the area. When this detail was linked with radio intercepts it painted an intelligence picture of enemy troop movement south out of Long Khanh Province and into the Australian area of operations. Some of the *33 NVA* headquarters group may have also been detected in the Suoi Tam Bo area, which was a well-known enemy base area southeast of Nui Sao.[159] As a result, on 19 September, the Australian Task Force issued Operation Order 9/71—Operation Ivanhoe—with the mission 'to search-and-destroy enemy elements [not *33 NVA* specifically] in the Nui Sao/Cu My area'. Cu My was a hamlet 6 kilometres to the east of Nui Sao. Companies from both 3RAR and 4RAR/NZ and supporting arms were ordered to deploy ASAP and commence searching.[160]

The last big battle: Operation Ivanhoe

Delta Company, 4RAR, was near Nui Sao and ready to go. Major Jerry Taylor moved his company off at 0800 hours on 19 September to begin the hunt when, after a few minutes, he received the first of two coded radio messages that told him:

A Task Force signals intelligence intercept put the company within 500 metres of an enemy radio set. Twenty minutes later a second message was received . . . D Company, it said, were within 500 metres of *two* enemy radio sets.[161]

Although there was later disagreement about the number of radios, Taylor assumed that: 'The presence of two radio sets might indicate the presence of *two enemy battalions* [emphasised]'. That meant there was a possible enemy force of nearly 600 nearby.[162] Taylor noted later that:

He did not discuss his assumption with Courtenay Hill [4RAR HQ], but based on it he kept the company more concentrated than usual. As might be expected . . . D Company was tightly wound and all their senses were focused forward . . . when at 0900hr the leading scout of 11 Platoon saw an armed black figure.[163]

The forward scout of 11 Platoon immediately opened fire and a firefight erupted, but it was stopped quickly when two platoon commanders—Byrne (10) and McKay (11)—reported that they were in simultaneous contact. The error had killed one soldier and another was slightly wounded. Although McKay felt a lot of the responsibility for what had happened, he was concerned for the scout 'knowing that this kind of thing would be with him for a long time to come'. He was also worried that the platoon would become 'over cautious and lack the aggression of our previous contacts'.[164] Delta Company's movement was stopped because Task Force had ordered an immediate inquiry, which concluded that: 'no one was to blame for this terrible event . . . caused by a series of adverse circumstances . . . the leading scout . . . was completely exonerated'.[165]

Jerry Taylor now had to get his men focused back on the search for an enemy force that in his mind outnumbered him by about five to one. Although he had been told that an enemy radio set had been detected within 500 metres of his company, he continued to spread his platoons over a wide front. Two platoons, 11 and 12, actively searched a kilometre apart along his selected axis southeast towards Nui Sao. The area remained quiet, although Second Lieutenant Graham Spinkston's 12 Platoon found signs that indicated a nearby track had been used within the last hour. At 1510 hours, Delta Company, 3RAR, who had been placed under operational control of 4RAR/NZ, landed immediately to the east of Courtenay Rubber and moved to block off an area northeast of Nui Le. The day ended without further incident.

The next day, 20 September, started literally with a bang with an explosion 1000 metres south of 12 Platoon that was thought to be an artillery mission for the South Vietnamese military at Duc Thanh. The artillery fire was followed by an ambush of a section of armoured personnel carriers commanded by Second Lieutenant Philip Lawrence. The carriers were on the way towards Courtenay Hill from Nui Dat along Route 2 when they were hit in what was described as a rather neat trap. The enemy had established a position that was 100 metres long just to the east of the road about 1 kilometre south of Xa Bang near Ap Hean. The ambush was set around a small cutting with a rocket-propelled grenade pit at its northern end. There were positions for six to ten enemy in the middle of the site and pits for another six to ten at the southern end of the ambush.

The enemy sprang the contact with a rocket-propelled grenade fired from the northern pit; it missed the lead carrier although its explosion splashed the vehicle and slightly wounded Corporal Ike Robin, the crew commander. Several more rocket-propelled grenades—either four of five—were fired, but they all missed and this allowed the carriers to engage the enemy with their machine guns. Unfortunately, the armoured personnel carriers were hampered by radio problems and that disrupted their immediate pursuit of the enemy, who escaped.

A little later, Lieutenant Grant Steel, a Kiowa helicopter pilot, guided the armoured personnel carriers to a dead soldier 1 kilometre to the east of the initial firefight. The soldier carried an AK-47 and 174 rounds of ammunition, all of which was in good condition. He also wore a new North Vietnamese Army belt buckle but 'he carried no identifying documents which is characteristic of 33 Regt', Major Mike Peters wrote in his report dated 20 September.[166] To conclude that the soldier came from *33 NVA* because he did not have documentation was inconsistent with previous recent reports in which *33 NVA* soldiers were identified by the papers that they had on them. The possibility that elements of *274 Viet Cong Regiment* might have been in the area and that northern soldiers now served in many of the VC units was not entertained in the intelligence reports. Delta Company, 4RAR, was told about the action because the enemy apparently withdrew in an easterly direction, which was towards their patrol path about 5 kilometres away northeast of the contact.

A later summary of the attempted ambush written by Phil Lawrence showed that the enemy had a mixture of six main pits and seventeen sleeping bays scattered around the site. Although the subsequent notes implied that the enemy were well prepared for offensive action, their reaction during the firefight did not support that assessment.[167]

Meanwhile, Major Jerry Taylor's Delta Company continued its search in a southerly direction towards Nui Sao. Taylor maintained a wide separation between his platoons when 11 Platoon reported at 0840 hours a 'one time effort' track that had been used 'by 5–6 persons' in the last 24 hours. By 1030 hours, the three platoons were spread in a general southwest–northeast line about 1 kilometre northwest of Nui Sao. Company headquarters was a kilometre away to their northwest. Bravo Company, commanded by Major Bob Hogarth, had also been lifted back into the area by armoured personnel carriers and they established a position 2 kilometres to the east of Xa Bang and just north of the track on which the remnants of the attack by fire against that outpost had been found. Major Hogarth intended to patrol slowly east with the track as a general axis. He later told Jerry Taylor:

> I don't recall expecting to meet North Vietnamese regular soldiers. We may have been so briefed but in most operations the threat always seemed to be painted more severely than it actually transpired. It seemed to me to be a routine operation.[168]

Delta Company continued their search under conditions that now 'started to look decidedly spooky', Gary McKay wrote.[169] Not long after, at 1303 hours on 20 September, McKay's 11 Platoon contacted a 'large enemy force ... that appeared to be 12 enemy [later reported as in excess of fifteen]' at grid reference YS514854. This was in the immediate vicinity of 10 Platoon's overnight position on 16–17 September, which was on the little hill north of Nui Sao. Kevin Byrne's 10 Platoon immediately moved toward the contact and got within 500 metres to the west of McKay's position. Graham Spinkston's 12 Platoon was about a kilometre away to the southwest but they now headed for the battle area, too.

Gary McKay and his opposing commander had similar thoughts; both sides wanted to kill the other. McKay remembered:

> I noticed that the enemy was using fire and movement just as we did. We could hear the enemy commanders shouting commands just before they fired and then they would rush to their next fire position.[170]

Eleven Platoon killed two enemy soldiers, but the remainder fought on aggressively and tried to outflank the Australians. The arrival of some additional firepower provided by American gunships and the Australian artillery convinced the enemy to break contact. A forward air controller known as Jade 07, which reportedly was the call sign for Lieutenant Rodriguez, provided essential assistance during this clash. The firefight and follow-up manoeuvring had lasted about an hour and the Australians got through without a casualty. During the firefight an American gunship, Fox 26, also found a heavily used track a little over a kilometre northeast of the action. It had been used recently and it was in the general direction of where Delta Company 3RAR was deployed.

Taylor now drew his platoons closer together and established a defended locality for the night on a ridgeline 1 kilometre northwest of Nui Sao, almost 2 kilometres due south of Nui Le. Early the next day, 21 September, McKay's platoon found signs on a track that indicated ten people had moved on it in the last 24 hours. This track was less than 100 metres away from the location of the contact on the twentieth. Soon after this report, 12 Platoon was in contact against what Spinkston thought was a bunker system. Gary McKay moved his platoon up on the right flank, but the enemy continued to hit

12 Platoon with rocket-propelled grenades until Jade 07 brought RAAF Bush-rangers and Fox 26 into the action and the enemy started to break north. The Australians suffered one killed—whose body could not be recovered—and three were wounded.

The two platoons then advanced towards the enemy position, but true to their previous tactics the enemy kept close and hugged the Australians in an almost face-to-face battle with the combatants at times no more than 20 metres apart. Fortuitously more American Cobra gunships, ground attack jets and Australian artillery came on line and the respite that this support gave Delta Company allowed Taylor to consolidate his position. But to complicate matters Bravo Company—to the southwest—contacted two enemy soldiers who appeared to be following a telephone line north, which Bravo believed was something big. Nevertheless, all of the heavy attention remained with Delta Company as aircraft laden with bombs, bullets and napalm swarmed to the battle, creating an attendant identification problem for the ground troops as they began to run out of smoke grenades and water for inflating marker balloons. Lieutenant Rodriguez and Captain Merle Shields, Jade 01, his relief, were also flat out coordinating the attacks so that the fast jets didn't mingle with the helicopters or the artillery.

By 1300 hours, even with all of the firepower used against them, the enemy had not relented and Fox 26 reported a heavy concentration of enemy troops—who had now been identified as NVA—to the rear of a bunker system. The gunships were not having it all their own way; they were fired upon with extensive bursts of .30-calibre and AK-47 assault rifle fire from enemy located on the southern knoll of Nui Le and the 265 feature. Although the gunships were forced to pull away, neither of the forward air controllers was hit and Jade 07, Lieutenant Rodriguez, got approval to hit the enemy position with 225- and 340-kilogram bombs and napalm.[171] While the air pounded the Nui Le area the enemy also made moves to encircle the Australian position but Taylor pulled his platoons back to establish a stronger defended locality. This lull in the fighting also allowed him to replenish ammunition and evacuate his wounded. The body of Private James Duff, the 12 Platoon soldier who had been killed earlier, was also recovered.

Major Taylor now decided that if the enemy appeared to be withdrawing due to the pounding that their position had received—which was an almost continuous bombardment from either artillery or aircraft—the company would assault through the bunkers. The plan was to attack with 12 Platoon on the left and 11 Platoon on the right with a company tactical headquarters in the centre. Kevin Byrne's 10 Platoon was to secure a firm rear base at what was called the 'Winch Point' on the high point of the little hill just north of Nui Sao. The soldiers would wear their large packs in the assault, just in case they had to pursue the enemy. This was an unusual directive and it would have unintended—but predictable—consequences. As Colonel S. L. A. Marshall had noted back in 1950, the combination of unnecessary weight and fear fatigued soldiers and reduced their tactical capabilities. Another lesson about weight came from a French battalion commander who had fought in Indochina and who noted, '[in the jungle] the advantage lies with the well trained and lightly equipped rifleman'.[172] To wear large packs while attacking and then possibly chasing after this modern enemy renowned for fighting withdrawals was fraught with danger.[173]

Lieutenant Rodriguez reported that people were running out of the area and at 1540 hours Delta Company attacked the bunkers. Fifteen minutes later, 6 Platoon, Bravo Company was mortared—probably by a 60 mm—that initially caused 'a couple of casualties' (actually 12). They were about 4 kilometres southwest of Delta Company. Soon after the enemy also hit 4 Platoon, who had gone to assist them and Rodriguez was requested to hive off some gunships to help out. Within the hour, the Delta Company attack had stalled and they had taken more casualties. The enemy had used one of their well-known tactics, which was to leave a fighting group behind to protect the main withdrawal. The Australian assault was now on dangerous ground and it was forced to extract back to its start line at the Winch Point. This movement was hindered by the soldiers' packs, which snagged in the thick and damaged undergrowth, and they were ordered to drop them. Delta now reported to battalion that they had had one killed and three wounded, and one was in need of urgent evacuation. At the same time, Bravo Company requested a Dustoff for seven wounded.

Delta Company then reported three dead—who were unable to be recovered—with four wounded. They had hit an enemy position that was well dug-in with good fire lanes and the enemy had targeted the company's machine guns. Private Kevin Casson recovered one of the guns in a display of courage and steadiness that contributed to the successful extraction of the remaining wounded. He was awarded a Mention-in-Despatches that was upgraded in 1999 to a Medal for Gallantry.[174]

Jerry Taylor knew he was in trouble when the enemy moved to close on his position—the hugging the enemy tactic—which stopped the air strikes. He managed to move away to the southwest of Nui Sao, but at 1851 hours he reported 'we are completely surrounded and we need more ammo'. Seven minutes later, he requested 'every available support the enemy are getting bad'.[175] It got worse two minutes later when Second Lieutenant Gary McKay was wounded badly by what the medic, Corporal Michael O'Sullivan, thought was shrapnel that hit him below the rear of his left shoulder. Corporal O'Sullivan was worried and requested radio advice from the battalion doctor on how to stop the bleeding. Gary McKay would write later that he was told at the hospital an X-ray had revealed he had been shot. They were both correct; McKay had been shot once and also hit by shrapnel. O'Sullivan had also run out of morphine. A medevac helicopter could not get into the position and McKay would have to bite on his dog tags throughout the night in an effort to ease his pain and not make too much noise.[176]

By late in the evening, around 2115 hours, the enemy activity had quietened down and although an air of trepidation remained, it seemed that the worst was over. In the early hours of 22 September, the gunships and Dustoff gathered again and Victor Company was ordered to marry up with Delta before moving into the 'target area'. Things now looked a bit brighter. Gary McKay's wound had stopped bleeding and although some enemy movement was seen on their northeastern perimeter the Dustoff was completed at 0840, nearly fourteen hours after McKay had been wounded. The medevac then went down to Bravo Company to collect their wounded. That included another platoon commander, Second Lieutenant Dan McDaniel. The two companies had now had three platoon commanders evacuated as well as a platoon sergeant.

Victor Company met up with Delta in the evening of 22 September and a plan of action for the following day was discussed with Lieutenant Colonel Jim Hughes. He approved an attack by Victor Company with two platoons. Two platoons remained in reserve with Delta Company to secure the line of departure. Both companies moved back into the contact area during the morning of 23 September, but it was difficult going among shattered trees and heavy rain. Delta got to the Winch Point while Victor readjusted from being slightly off-track and then they headed towards the bunker system at 1225 hours, but it was very slow going. During an intense rainstorm they veered too far northwest and had to return to the start point.

Eventually two sections from 10 Platoon and Victor Company found the sixteen packs dropped during the assault. Then at 1802 hours, much to everyone's relief, they found the three Australian bodies that Delta had been forced to leave behind during the battle. The enemy had not disturbed them. The bodies were immediately lifted out by Dustoff and the two assault platoons from Delta Company confirmed that their packs, equipment and claymores were all intact, but they were unsure about their radio codes.

Lieutenant Colonel Hughes now established a priority of search and destruction of the enemy bunkers. There was plenty to find, but thankfully none of the positions was occupied. A stream of reports came in from the airborne controllers who spotted freshly used tracks around the area. Bravo Company also found a well-prepared main track with blazed trees that they believed had been prepared for a very large force to move quickly with heavy loads. One of the platoons reported that they had found and were following a recent blood trail. A little later, a no doubt embarrassed commander advised that they had followed a bleeding forward scout.

As the two reinforcement companies—Delta Company 3RAR and Victor 4RAR—cleared the battleground, more and more bunkers were found around the Nui Sao features. Remarkably, numerous bunkers were found in areas where the Australians—10 Platoon in particular—had patrolled without incident three days before the main battle.

A much more experienced and battle-weary Delta Company, 4RAR/NZ, was lifted out of the operation and returned to Nui Dat at 1424 hours on 26 September. This had been a savage fight and the awards that were approved later reflected the company's gallantry on an extremely dangerous battlefield. There were no further clashes with the enemy and Operation Ivanhoe concluded at 2400 hours on 2 October.[177]

The aftermath

Although there were enemy in a broad circle around Delta Company's position—including those to the southwest fighting Bravo Company—the main ground battle had been fought on the small hill 500 metres north of Nui Sao. Jerry Taylor had taken a calculated gamble with an attack, although the assault was more a reconnaissance in force. He did not know the extent of the bunkers or if they were still occupied and even though he had eyes in the sky he was blind on the ground, which meant that there were no clear objectives to attack. He was aware of the danger that a dug-in enemy represented from his recent experience during Operation Iron Fox. All of this was practical proof of the lessons highlighted by the Australian Army Training Information Letter 4/70, *Viet Cong/NVA Bunker Systems*. Without tanks and infantry-carried *bunker-busting* weapons, the risk to his company would be high if the enemy had not withdrawn as expected under the bombardment of artillery and attack air. The forward air controllers had fed him constant information that the enemy appeared to be fleeing, which was supported by a fortuitous pause in the fighting. That prompted Major Taylor to implement his plan and to go back in, although the assumption was it would be more of a pursuit than an assault. The battle had been misread.

'The moment the company commander said that we were going into the system, my guts turned over ... for some reason I didn't feel too good about going into this system', Gary McKay wrote.[178] The misgiving was prophetic. The Australians suffered during this operation with five Delta soldiers killed and 25 wounded between both Bravo and Delta companies. The number of key personnel—'platoon leaders and a platoon sergeant'—who were wounded during the battle concerned the Third Regional Assistance Command. However, the Australians advised TRAC that the casualties were coincidental and that the enemy had not specifically targeted the commanders. Delta claimed nine enemy soldiers killed, which was remarkably few considering the pounding the area took, and Bravo killed at least two. All of those killed were probably northern soldiers. Task Force recorded a total for Operation Ivanhoe of fourteen enemy soldiers killed and a further nine who had been killed by air strikes, but there were no enemy captured or any known wounded.[179]

Although it was considered odious by some to count the dead, a comparison of the numbers killed in this battle was cause to question the necessity of searching for danger at a time when the Task Force had lost its tanks and the Australian troops were on the verge of leaving the province. In general the search-and-destroy operation was explained away as a dammed if you do, damned if you don't mission, but the questions about tactical relevance remained. While the Army scrambled to explain the operation's purpose in terms of necessary security, Gough Whitlam, the Leader of the Opposition, hit them with an acrimonious barb: 'these casualties were needless and the operation pointless'.[180] There was no doubt that without American close air support to supplement the artillery, the Australians would have been in a very nasty jam with an increased likelihood of loss of life. That would have answered the question about tactical relevance without equivocation.

After the action

On 22 November 1971, Tran Van Cot, an assistant platoon leader with *C9 Company, 3 Battalion, 33 NVA Regiment* was captured near Suoi Luc in southern Long Khanh Province. He told his interrogators that the original intention of their being near Nui Sao on 21 September was to ambush the Australians. He said:

> The 2nd Battalion and Regimental Headquarters had occupied a bunker system [assumed to be near Nui Sao] while 3 Battalion moved into an ambush position along a logging trail. They were told that the Australians would probably move along this trail to attack the Regt. The battalion waited in ambush for three days . . . on the third day they were told that the Australians had somehow evaded the ambush and contacted 2 Bn and the Regt HQ. The [3rd] battalion . . . withdrew north . . . *without incident* [emphasised].[181]

An Australian Task Force summary of his statement noted that the information 'is quite interesting and possibly reveals details of enemy plans for a large ambush of 1ATF troops'. The author—assumed to be the recently arrived Intelligence Officer Major James Graham—also surmised that the attack by fire against the Regional Force Company at Xa Bang on 19 September, and the failed ambush against the Australian armoured personnel carriers were probably intended as bait to lure an Australian force into the ambush. The enemy was surprised when the Australians came from the north and hit the position on Nui Sao because they expected them to come from the *southeast*.[182]

Tran Van Cot's story is questionable. The *33rd NVA Regiment* had been hounded by the US 3rd Brigade, forcing the enemy battalions to be deployed into self-supporting regions to obtain supplies, especially food. They were in no condition to conduct a deliberate battle against the Australian Task Force. *COSVN* had also directed counter-pacification to be a priority target in 1971. An attempt to lure an Australian force into an ambush would be to disobey that directive and to engage in an unnecessary battle.[183] Any detection of the regimental headquarters—intentional or not—and its support echelons carried great risk for the enemy. The US 3rd Brigade and deadly American air power were just over the horizon and always ready to pounce—in concert with the Australians—on such a lucrative target.

The NVA/Viet Cong were also known to plan battles with great attention to detail. Even the most ignorant of NVA commanders would have known that the Australians had been operating north and northwest of the proposed ambush site for several months before this battle. Task Force headquarters had sat on Courtenay Hill and then the position was occupied by 4RAR after they went back to Nui Dat. Australian platoons had patrolled around and through the middle of the little hill north of the Nui Sao feature on 16–17 September; one had remained on it that night. Delta Company then moved to the west and northwest of that feature for several days before the first contact on 20 September—at the same time, supposedly, that a large group of enemy moved into and prepared a major defensive position on the little hill, including bunkers with overhead protection and well-prepared fire lanes. All of this was to have been done without any telltale signs of construction. Tran Van Cot added that the enemy ambush force had moved into its location *late on 18 September* and remained there for three days before moving north *without incident*. It is difficult to believe that an enemy battalion would withdraw without incident while a regimental headquarters was threatened, especially if *3 Battalion* was to the rear of Delta Company who was engaged—according to Tran Van Cot—with its sister *2nd NVA Battalion*. They were in a position to create a great deal of havoc and to accomplish their alleged ambush by another means.

According to the commander of the *3rd Battalion*, Captain Trieu Kim Son, his unit did not arrive in the area until 1700 hours on 20 September. Who then was the force that clashed with the Australian armoured personnel carriers and fought the subsequent skirmishes with Bravo Company in the operational area along the track on which the alleged ambush was sited? The attack against Bravo Company did not bear the hallmark of *33 NVA*. Their ambushes were aggressive, generally over a long distance and set on both sides of the road. When the trap was sprung they used a high volume of fire that included small arms, rocket-propelled grenades and sometimes mortars and heavy machine-gun fire.[184] Was the contacted group an element of *274 Viet Cong Regiment* that had been included in the Operation Ivanhoe brief as possibly operating in the area? The Australian reliance upon unit identification that was based on uniforms and some documents was weakened by the influx of northerners—following Tet 1968—into VC units and the frequent cross-assignments between NVA and Viet Cong formations.[185]

The attack against the Australian armoured personnel carriers on 20 September smacked of a half-hearted attempt to make travel along Route 2 more dangerous: a tactic that threatened pacification efforts and obeyed *COSVN*'s overall objective. The layout of this ambush had the weapon pits between 200 and 300 metres away from the eastern edge of the road—beyond effective rocket-propelled grenade range—and masked by grass 1.5 metres high. The area around the pits was covered with a lot of sleeping bays, with one very close to the road from which the ambush was initiated. Furthermore, the number of enemy soldiers involved in the ambush was not confirmed. No one reported seeing 20 to 30 enemy soldiers running through the long grass and there were no trees for approximately 300 metres to the east of Route 2. This attack was neither a well-planned decoy nor a deadly ambush and it is extremely doubtful that Tran Van Cot—an assistant platoon leader—would be privy to a detailed regimental plan.

The tenacity of the enemy's defence indicated that at least a battalion from *33 NVA Regiment* was located around the Nui Le–Nui Sao hills. NVA tacticians had also developed the mobile fighting squad of approximately 15–20 men who were well equipped and who moved rapidly around a battlefield. In a well-prepared position this tactic made less appear to be more, allowing defenders to cover numerous arcs of responsibility and protect the evacuation of the position as well as stop any quick follow-up of a main withdrawing force. This was a well-known enemy tactic.[186]

Although the Australian reports and later writings marked this battle as significant, it only rated a single sentence entry in the Third Regional

Assistance Command intelligence report for the period 19 September to 22 October 1971.[187]

When two former NVA soldiers were asked in 2011 to explain the 1971 battle, they said that it was just another fight against the enemy. The battle was not a major firefight, according to them. They referred to the 1969 battle at Binh Ba as a memorable clash with the Australians and used it as a battle benchmark. Captain Trieu Kim Son commanded the *3rd Battalion* (aka *9th*) during the Nui Sao battle. The regiment had changed the identities of the battalions to *7, 8* and *9* sometime around early 1969. He finished the war as a senior colonel (brigadier) and he kept a diary in which he recorded the following notes:

[The information has been edited for clarity.] In the afternoon of the 20/9 at 1700 hrs, the whole of the main formation of 9 Battalion got to the stipulated position. The Battalion had 245 comrades, three infantry companies (C9, C10, C11) and a support company (C12).[188]

From 1730 hrs to 1900 hrs all of the troops had arrived and started digging the trench positions. From 1900 hrs to 2000 hrs the companies finished digging and the communication system were clear. At this stage 9 battalion reported to the Regt HQ that all the tasks had been completed and were waiting for the order. At 5.30 a.m. [21 September] the observation tower reported that they discovered one Australian platoon about 25–30 people had divided into two groups, each of them were about 5–10 meters apart. The battalion reported to the Regt and asked for opinions. The Regt ordered to let the enemy get close then open fire. Obeying that order the battalion allowed the enemy to get into the battlefield, the troops only opened fire when ordered. At 1905 hrs the first enemy group arrived at the point where the up front company was. The majority of the enemy were entering very, very fast as we expected. The enemy got very close to the front point (where to stop the enemy) and the back point (where to lock them in). The whole battalion assaulted nearly face to face to fight the enemy. They [the Australians] organised to pull backward. They called in helicopters for support. Also, their artillery fired to assist continually.[189]

They were ordered by regiment to withdraw to the *observation line*, to reinforce the defence works, settle the force, supplement the ammunition and bring out the injured troops to the back, Trieu Kim Son wrote. He continued:

> The battle occurred the whole day on 21/9 until 1.00 a.m. The enemy could not break into our defence line and we waited so we could counter attack. In the battle the enemy got airplanes and artillery to assist them. At this point, one group of the enemy was close to us. We all fired. They again called artillery and we took advantage and assaulted closely to limit the casualties by the bombs from the airplanes.[190]

The battalion suffered seven killed, including a platoon commander. A further 25 comrades were wounded. The bodies were taken to a 'stipulated hill' and the battalion withdrew 'safely and secretly' to avoid discovery by 'spies' (reconnaissance patrols). Trieu Kim Son claimed his battalion destroyed nearly two platoons of the enemy (Australians) and that the *9th Battalion* had '*broken off the raid toward our logistic base* [emphasised]'.[191]

Trieu Kim Son was definite that only his battalion was involved in the 21 September battle. Vo Xuan Thu also emphasised that only the *9th Battalion* was involved in the battle. In a subsequent email to the author, Thu identified the two officers who had commanded *33 NVA Regiment* during the 1971–1972 period:

> Hoang Cao Hy, he was the regional commander at the time [of the battle on 21 September]. Hy was posted to the Division and Nguyen Van Thuong replaced him. I know that Hy retired and nowadays lives in the North. Nguyen Van Thuong lived in Long Thanh, Dong Nai province, and died about three years ago. As for the regiment's base at that time, it was near Bien Hoa. The base didn't stay at one fixed place for long. The 9th Battalion was an independent mobile unit. As for the battle, Son has given you that information already.[192]

Although Trieu Kim Son did not say so directly, the inference gleaned from his communication was that the elements of *33 NVA Regiment* had come to the area to rest and recuperate. This matched discussions with other former NVA soldiers who said that the battle was a result of the Australians getting too close to a base or a headquarters camp. It was not as a result of a planned deliberate ambush or attack against the Australian force.

9

AN INGLORIOUS END

'You never defeated us on the battlefield,' Colonel Summers said.
'That may be so, but it is also irrelevant,' Tu replied.

Colonel Tu retort to his US counterpart, Colonel Harry G. Summers,
Hanoi, 1975

Homeward bound

On 1 October 1971, 3RAR returned to Nui Dat, where they were restricted to local defence duties in preparation for their return to Australia. Even at this stage in the war, the Australians needed the generous assistance provided by the US 3rd Brigade in the form of Chinook helicopters to extract part of the force from Fire Support Base Maree. The battalion was farewelled on 5 October at a parade reviewed by Major General Lam Quang Tho, the Commanding General of the 18th ARVN Division, after which they boarded HMAS *Sydney* on 6 October and sailed off to Port Adelaide the next day.

The much-reduced Task Force then folded back onto Nui Dat with Phuoc Tuy Province split into two unequal tactical parts. ARVN and American forces were responsible for an arc of territory in the north but their *real* priority was above Route 1 in Long Khanh Province. South Vietnamese territorial forces took over most of the southern area of the province; however, they continued to have a low status for combat support and logistics. The American provincial advisory teams remained, but the Australian MATTs were withdrawn until only two remained, based at Van Kiep. During their final months of deployment they would provide training support to the Jungle Warfare Training Centre and Baria Sector.[1] Two Australian majors, Paul Webb and Barry O'Neill, were deployed as district senior advisers at Duc Thanh and Xuyen Moc respectively and Major Bob Musgrove was located at Baria as the Regional Force/Popular Force adviser.

On 5 October the Courtenay Hill base was handed over to an ARVN officer from the 18th Division following a quick tidy-up after most of the facility had been dismantled or destroyed. The ARVN officer was accompanied by 3 Platoon, 177 Regional Force Company who occupied the hill when 4RAR/NZ withdrew in a final convoy to Nui Dat later that day. When 3RAR flew out to Vung Tau, 4RAR/NZ occupied their old position and grouped to the northern side of the total area previously filled by the Task Force. Luscombe Airstrip divided the battalion position into two distinct halves, with Delta Company and 104 Field Battery on the southern side and the remainder fanned out to the north. The rest of the base was now off limits to Australians as 2/43 ARVN Battalion moved into the area previously occupied by C Squadron, 1 Armoured Regiment. The Jungle Warfare Training Centre retained its location but it was in the process of moving out to Van Kiep, which it did on 15 October although it didn't clear Nui Dat until the sixteenth.

The Australian force in Vietnam was now to get out as quickly as possible, which was made clear by Amendment No. 3 to the Australian Force Vietnam General Staff Instruction 7/71, Operation Interfuse—a plan for the complete withdrawal of the Australians. When the drawdown of troops had reduced the Task Force to no more than a battalion group, the previously discussed limited operational capability of a single battalion became a reality. It could do no more than circle its wagons and keep a close eye over its immediate surrounds, which in tactical terms was useless. The Nui Dat base was accordingly handed over to the South Vietnamese and the 4RAR/NZ (ANZAC) Battalion Group moved to Vung Tau. When the Australians moved out on 7 November, the South Vietnamese immediately tore the base apart. Major Brian McFarlane, the Task Force GSO2 (Operations), watched it all disappear:

There were lines of people going in and out carrying sheets of iron, chairs, office chairs, filing cabinets, curtains, beds. You name it they were carrying it away. So within a day of us leaving, the whole thing was being dismantled.[2]

The Australian convoys moved out, protected to the last by 1 Troop, A Squadron, 3 Cavalry Regiment. There was no action by the enemy and at mid-afternoon—1445 hours—the withdrawal from Nui Dat was finished. What remained of the Task Force was now located at Vung Tau, but 40 members of the AATTV stayed on in Phuoc Tuy Province. They were split between JWTC at Van Kiep and Baria Sector duties.

Although a wary watch was kept over operational matters in Phuoc Tuy, the Australians now had no tactical obligation within the province and the Third Regional Assistance Command also relinquished its operational control of the Australian force. Major General Donald Dunstan, COMAFV, assumed those responsibilities on 9 November 1971. The enemy continued to worry the Australian commanders, but nothing of any significance was detected to suggest that a major effort would be launched against the Vung Tau enclave. The pilot of Possum A20 may have had a different opinion on the enemy's activities when they hit him with a burst of automatic fire on 15 November. The helicopter was hit twelve or thirteen times and Lieutenant Grant Steel was forced to land just south of Phu Hai, 6 kilometres west of Baria.[3] He had been a little too nosy about checking a possible bunker opening on the edge of the Rung Sat. There were no casualties and the aircraft was secured soon after by the 4RAR ready reaction platoon and recovered to Vung Tau.

With the main attention focused on the return of the Task Force to Australia, the deployment of the AATTV was not forgotten but it remained a background issue. From the middle of 1971, the changes to the countrywide MACV advisory effort had begun to bite as personnel were not replaced and basic equipment needs were not filled. Paradoxically, the AATTV reached its maximum strength of 224 briefly in August with 125 of those deployed in Phuoc Tuy.[4] Then the Team was gradually reduced, but in November they remained sprinkled around the country with nine advisers in Military Region 1, twelve instructors in Military Region 2 at Phu Cat in Binh Dinh Province and thirteen still in the Delta, Military Region 4. Fifty-eight others were located in Saigon, Vung Tau, the JWTC and the MATTs in Phuoc Tuy. These figures included four New Zealand infantrymen who had followed Sergeant Limo Karaka, the first Kiwi to join AATTV in May 1970 and add a little Anzac tradition to the Team.

The reduction was soon completed when all of the AATTV advisers were removed from Military Regions 1, 2 and 4 by 15 December 1971 and concentrated at Vung Tau. Soon after, the Team was directed to train and select a group of 30 to be attached to the United States Army Vietnam–Individual Training Group. This small team would assist in the training of Cambodian light infantry battalions at two training centres known as Long Hai and Phuoc Tuy. To confuse the issue, the Long Hai camp was at the old B-36 Special Forces camp about 10 kilometres south of Long Dien on the western side of the Long Hai hills The Phuoc Tuy camp was at Long Hai, a further 3 kilometres south along Route 44. In addition to the two mobile assistance teams and Baria Sector, there were now three distinct AATTV field locations: JWTC at Van Kiep and the two USARV camps.

Waiting to go home

One of the bigger worries now for 1ATF was how to fit all of the Australians into their Vung Tau camp without causing aggravation between the combat arms and the logistics units. Movement outside the wire now meant avoiding clashes with the local bar owners and the Vietnamese 'cowboys' of Vung Tau. There were also warnings about possible booby traps being sold as souvenirs such as lacquered dolls and poisoned cigarettes. It all sounded a bit melodramatic; there was even an apocryphal story that some prostitutes had concealed razor blades in a most inappropriate part of their body. No reports surfaced of a check on this danger by the military police, however.

Getting the main part of the force out of Vietnam inside the political time frame set by the prime minister—home by Christmas—placed an enormous administrative burden on the planners and the force as a whole. Cleaning, packing and sitting around waiting are the devils of an army on the way home from war and the Australian commanders watched the wind-down carefully. There were plenty of vehicles to wash, containers to stuff, boxes to pack, documents to be labelled and ready-reaction drills to be planned that kept the men active, even if they were bored with the mundane work. Frustration affected all ranks, as Staff Sergeant Bob Langley discovered when he failed to salute Lieutenant Colonel Keith Kirkland, who berated him. Kirkland was somewhat peeved by not getting a phone call connected to his family in Australia.

On a more serious note, although it sounded somewhat ludicrous a *company contingency force* commanded by Major E. F. Fred Pfeitzner from 9RAR at Brisbane was placed on *seven days'* notice to move to provide an emergency reinforcement of AFV in the event of a serious threat developing. The contingency force would arrive with one full magazine for each of their individual weapons and although the group was allocated two 90 mm recoilless rifles it was possible that there would not be any trained operators with the company. Marked maps would be issued when the orders group assembled after arrival. It was a well-intentioned plan, but its size and capability surely raised doubts about its usefulness should a major threat be identified. It also said a great deal about Australia's capabilities.[5]

The need for security, and getting rid of stores and equipment either by back-loading or giving them away—included the proposal to deep-sea dump carbon tetrachloride—as well as providing support for the remaining troops created a continued logistics balancing act. As well as the logistics of loading the ships correctly and making sure that they were safe while at anchor, there was an almost mind-boggling relentless administrative demand. The forgotten administrative details of a peacetime army gained importance and created more work: applications for leave and associated travel requirements, married quarter paperwork and household removals, along with numerous other sundry queries and requests.

In a repetition of events around 1RAR's arrival seemingly a lifetime earlier in 1965, a parade was organised, but this time to say goodbye. General Creighton Abrams, COMUSMACV, and Lieutenant General Nguyen Van Minh, the Commanding General of Military Region 3, both attended the farewell parade on 1 December 1971 at which General Minh presented South Vietnamese awards, but some of the 64 'approved recipients' had already left Vietnam.[6] Following a visit to HMAS *Sydney* by President Nguyen Van Thieu on 8 December, a heavy contingent of infantry, artillery, the RAAF helicopters and assorted support groups sailed for Townsville on the ninth. The New Zealand Victor Company flew out to Singapore on 9 and 10 December to rejoin their parent battalion, 1 Royal New Zealand Infantry Regiment.

All that remained now of a previously bustling military city was a reduced Headquarters 1ATF, Delta Company 4RAR, a detachment of cavalry from the recently redesignated B Squadron 3 Cavalry Regiment and elements of the support echelons such as personnel from movement control, engineer workshops, military police, the signal squadron and the field ambulance.[7]

Going, going, gone

Ostensibly Delta Company 4RAR and the detachment of armoured personnel carriers that remained had a principal duty to protect the ever-shrinking Task Force. They were also used as stevedores, forklift operators and security pickets during the loading of the ships through to the end of February 1972. Noticeable niggling administrative and base security matters now stretched the patience of those waiting to go, as one duty officer recorded in several log entries in January 1972:

> Strongpoint Bravo reports 3 Vn inside 600 metres extension and want to know what to do. After no effect on the telephone . . . Ops scrambled Cav Reaction Force . . . incompetent cretin manning emu switchboard could not get any numbers we asked for, so stopped answering our calls. Total of 20 children chased out of the area and back to the dump. OC HQ Coy blasted me for not knowing the net [radio] procedures. My compliments to the OC . . . will he reread his own copy of SOs [Standing Orders].[8]

A more unusual incident baffled Colonel Phillip Greville, who now commanded the Task Force that had amalgamated with the Logistics Support Group on 16 October. Private Charles Carstairs had been wounded when an Australian Land Rover was ambushed near Cam My in northern Phuoc Tuy. A group of six soldiers had taken an unserviceable vehicle supposedly to drive into Vung Tau, a few kilometres away. They left the Australian camp at 1230 hours on 30 January and were ambushed several hours later at Cam My, 30 kilometres to the north and beyond Nui Dat. Colonel Greville advised AFV that the enemy were probably as mystified as he was about why the soldiers were travelling north along Route 2. Unfortunately the interesting details of their journey were not recorded.

A by-product of this extraordinary incident was the admission by the commander that 'the area near Cam My cannot be considered secure' and he recommended that the vehicle not be recovered.[9] Major Bob Musgrove, the Baria Regional Force/Popular Force adviser, assessed the enemy's activities in the province more likely to take the form of harassment and attacks by fire, which he experienced first-hand when he and Bombardier Pat Gallagher were slightly wounded in a convoy ambush just east of Long Dien on 9 February. That ambush was part of the continuing effort by the Viet Cong to demoralise the South Vietnamese. It was a message to the people that the South Vietnamese government could not protect the rural localities without the support of the allied troops. They continued to deliberately target the Popular Force more than the Regional Force, but the major sufferers were the members of the People's Self Defence Force, who were being kidnapped or recruited by the Viet Cong at an unacceptable rate. During November and December 1971 and January 1972, across South Vietnam 138 had been assassinated and 184 abducted. Musgrove considered the PSDF to be the key to pacification: if they became effective they would make it extremely difficult for the Viet Cong to operate with a large degree of freedom.

Activity around the Vung Tau base now concentrated upon the pending arrival of HMAS *Sydney* on 28 February and its planned final sailing home the next day. The ongoing closing down of the facilities created expected disruptions and annoyance as less and less became available to the force that remained. Among the serious decisions there were also the annoyingly pernickety matters, like sorting out a stamp account, that took up planners' time. As the containers were packed and locked, the AATTV would soon have to depend upon their scrounging abilities and the good graces of the Americans in order to operate and live in reasonably secure surrounds at their training camps.

Given the extremely challenging timetable and associated difficulties both in Vietnam and Australia, the extraction of the Australian force went very well. The Chief of the General Staff, Lieutenant General Mervyn Brogan, recognised the dedication and hard work that had made it possible and in a personal message to all ranks, he wrote:

I wish to express my sincere thanks and congratulations to the commanders and staffs involved . . . Operation Interfuse will go down in our records as another 'job well done'. But I am well aware that it has only been achieved by the dedication, forethought and sheer hard work of those concerned. All ranks responded splendidly to the challenge and proved their worth. Thank you.[10]

A final parade commanded by Captain Paul Green that assembled near the Vung Tau Soldiers' Memorial at 1000 hours on 25 February presented a last lucrative target of 100 unarmed Australians to the enemy, but it passed without incident. Following the farewell by the Vung Tau City Council, refreshments were taken at the mayor's house, where some of the Australians now felt remorseful as they detected some dismay—albeit mostly well concealed under an impassive façade—among the Vietnamese. What would happen to them now? Although most Australians were just pleased to be getting out, there were those who felt they had betrayed the confidence of the people in Phuoc Tuy Province and the South Vietnamese in general. They were saddened by it all.

The phrenetic clean-up of the buildings and facilities continued and the final embarkation papers were prepared, listing 454 personnel to sail on *Sydney*'s final run home. Lieutenant General Brogan inspected the camp on 29 February and the 'Australian flag [was] struck—[an act of submission]—at [the] Vung Tau base' at 1225 hours and the Task Force finally vacated the base at 1230 hours.[11] Then they were gone. A few Australians remained to finalise the paperwork, but they left within a few days and flew out of Saigon about a week later.

The headquarters of AFV at Saigon also closed and the Australian Army Assistance Group Vietnam (AAAGV) replaced it on 6 March 1972. Brigadier Ian Geddes was appointed the commander and he controlled the AATTV, an Embassy Guard and Escort Platoon, the 198 Royal Australian Engineers Works section, a signals detachment and a cash office.[12] Mr David Fairbairn, the Minister for Defence, announced on 1 March that the AAAGV was not to have a combatant role.[13]

Year of the Rat

Major General Donald Dunstan had warned General Creighton Abrams on 30 October 1971 that:

A small training and advisory element, with a strength of no more than 132, will remain in Vietnam after the main force has completed its withdrawal in February 1972. *I am unable to forecast how long this residual element will remain in country* [emphasised].[14]

An inevitable sequence of events overtook this advice, as the Australian government committed to assist in the training of light infantry battalions (consisting of about 500 men per battalion) from the Cambodian Army. They were known by the acronym FANK, for Forces Armées Nationales Khmer.[15] A reorganisation of AATTV on 1 February 1972 saw its headquarters move from Saigon to Van Kiep, where Lieutenant Colonel Keith Kirkland assumed command from Lieutenant Colonel Jim Stewart. Several New Zealanders also remained with the AATTV, but the New Zealand Army established their own nineteen-man training group with the USARV at the Dong Ba Thin base near Cam Ranh Bay in March 1972. The Australian advisers were now located at training centres only, mirroring the first deployment of AATTV back in July 1962; the Team had come full circle.

Regardless of the 'non-combatant role' announcement by Minister Fairbairn, with the experience of training the Vietnamese at the JWTC under their belts, the Australian commanders were aware that clashes with the enemy were likely to happen. Although not highlighted in the monthly reports, the potential menace was obvious. As one part of the fourfold FANK mission noted, they were 'to conduct local security operations in assigned TAOR [tactical area of responsibility]'.[16] Whilst most of the FANK training was conducted in the area close to the two camps, the local training areas at the Phuoc Tuy camp were pushed out into the Long Hai foothills to gain more space. Not exactly a benign close training area. In addition the *field training exercises* were to be completed around the Long Hai and in the Xuyen Moc District, locations that were akin to a two-way rifle range.

An article by Alan Dawson headed 'Reports Berets [US Special Forces] Training Cambodians in Vietnam', published in late 1971 by United Press International, alerted the outside world that training in this environment also included combat.[17] Dawson wrote:

Lt. Col. Edward S Rybat's somewhat shadowy training group . . . have taken over former secret training bases . . . to train their 35,000 mercenary soldiers in Vietnam

... two of them are at Long Hai, a sleepy district capital 48 miles southeast of Saigon. The other is at Dong Ba Thin, 195 miles northeast of the capital.[18]

Dawson continued:

The training includes 18 days in the field, trying to find an increasing number of Viet Cong in northern Phuoc Tuy Province. In one case, contact was made, resulting in one Viet Cong killed and several Cambodians wounded.[19]

The Australians joined this group under a Memorandum of Understanding that included the requirement for the operational deployment of the Team to be arranged with the concurrence of the Commanding Officer AATTV.[20] That memorandum did not prevent the Australians from accompanying the Cambodians on *field exercises*, but there was an alleged caveat. Australians were permitted to go into the field with the FANK battalions in an *exercise* capacity; they were not to attempt to initiate contacts with the enemy.[21]

Brigadier Ian Geddes—the AAAGV commander—was adamant that orders from Australia directed that the Training Team's operational role had concluded. He told the US commanders this and issued a written directive to the senior Australian officer in each area, which they were required to initial.[22] Captain Terry Smith, who served at the Phuoc Tuy camp from July 1972, confirmed that he had initialled such a document.[23] The directive was a naïve attempt to control an uncontrollable aspect of the war in the province.

Sixty-five thousand Cambodians were trained in Vietnam across all of the USARV camps during 1972.[24] With eight battalions in training between the two camps near Long Hai in February and more to follow on rotation, the chances of Australians remaining non-combatant in the field were very slim. Even the base camps lacked good defences. Being so close to the Long Hai hills didn't help, as Terry Smith outlined:

I have just been posted to Phuoc Tuy Training Battalion ... at Ap Long Hai. It is ... built around an old Vietnamese training camp. The place is very much like an old fort and is surrounded by a berm [protective ledge] into which are set bunkers and firing bays of somewhat dubious value. It is ... manned by 130 round eyes [US and Australian] and 1500 Cambodian troops. However, I feel the bad guys could come down and take it any time at all if they wanted to. About 1000 metres to the north are the Long Hai Mountains which are very steep and tangled. Chuck (Viet Cong) lives up there so we don't annoy him and so far he hasn't annoyed us.[25]

Major Bob Musgrove at Sector Headquarters also warned about increased enemy activity in the Xuyen Moc District in February. Territorial forces had repeatedly engaged a battalion from one of the old Viet Cong warhorses, the *274 Viet Cong Regiment*, in that area. Eventually the 18th ARVN Division got involved and sent its 2nd Battalion, 52nd Regiment down to do battle. Both sides fought with great tenacity, Musgrove reported. He added that the ratio of killed was more in the enemy's favour during the month than it had been for some time: the South Vietnamese had lost 34 killed against 19 enemy soldiers.[26] MACV reported that the 18th Division had encountered enemy forces on several occasions, but most of the contacts were recorded as insignificant.[27]

The dangers of the Long Hai hills, well known to Australians, were reinforced when a reconnaissance patrol from the Long Hai Training Battalion, the previous B-36 camp, was ambushed 4 kilometres north of the camp between Nui Hon and Nui Dien on 25 March. The patrol had four killed and four wounded, which was added to when a 25-man reaction force tripped a mine that killed one more and wounded two others. The patrol and their reinforcements eventually got out with the support of some heavy ARVN 155 mm artillery, the mortars based at Long Hai and helicopters supported by American Cobra gunships. No Australians were involved in this clash.

On 30 March 1972, the North Vietnamese Army launched an explosive assault against South Vietnam. The North committed at least eight divisions at first and up to 26 separate regiments plus substantial armour and artillery forces to the onslaught.[28] The invasion started in Quang Tri Province and was followed by two other main thrusts on 5 and 14 April. The first of these hit the Loc Ninh–An Loc region just 100 kilometres north of Saigon, which was followed by attacks against Kontum and Pleiku in the Central Highlands. Quang Tri City was lost on 1 May and a few days later the whole province was in enemy hands. As the people fled south towards Hue, they were caught up in the battle, along what was to become known as the Highway of Horror. Quang Tri City would not be retaken until 15 September 1972.

The redeployment of the US manoeuvre battalions continued unabated and by the end of June 1972 only two were planned to remain in Vietnam— the 1st Battalion, 7th Cavalry (MR3) and the 3rd Battalion, 21st Infantry (MR1). The South Vietnamese now carried the burden of stopping the invading army, which now fielded modern tanks, artillery and other weapon systems like the Strela SA-7 anti-aircraft missile. These were serious conventional battles, not previously experienced in the conflict, and they challenged the much-argued training wisdom of the past about how to train and for what threat. Both sides suffered. The northerners were struck with an incredible concentration of air power supported by resilient American advisers and an outstanding system of massive logistics replenishment to the ARVN. Some South Vietnamese commanders and units failed, but no one was prepared for such a dramatic switch in tactics. Vo Nguyen Giap's conventional invasion also cost him dearly. This was exactly the war the Americans had wanted to fight all along, and their air power exacted a heavy toll.

North Vietnamese Lieutenant General Tran Van Quang told how badly they had been hurt in a 1972 interview in Moscow. Quang admitted that the Nixon approved bombings of the North were successful. They were much more so than the four years of air war under Johnson, he said, adding that their leaders at the tactical and strategic levels had made some mistakes in the battles inside South Vietnam. He listed their combat losses:

We have lost 140,000 personnel from *regular forces* [emphasised] . . . these were heavy losses for us. We lost . . . trucks, armor personnel carriers and prime movers – 872 pieces; 67 tanks in Quang Tri; 93 in Binh Long and Tay Ninh and 104 in Tai Nguyen [Central Highlands]. In infantry and artillery armaments, we lost more than 3000 pieces. We lost more than 100,000 tons of food.[29]

Strong fighting also broke out in Phuoc Tuy Province in April 1972 with clashes in Xuyen Moc and Duc Thanh districts where South Vietnamese Regional Force troops fought against elements of *274 Viet Cong Regiment* and a mixture of local force that included *D445*, the old guard battalion. The Long Hai camp was also mortared from the Long Hai hills in an attack that wounded twenty Cambodians, four of them seriously.[30] The other usual suspects from *33 NVA* clashed with an ARVN battalion around the Binh Ba

In September 1967, 3000 incoming shells from NVA artillery hit the Gio Linh outpost close to the DMZ. This is a direct hit by a 122 mm shell on a US Marine ammunition bunker. The NVA 122 mm artillery could outshoot the American artillery by several kilometres. *AP Photo*

The heartbreak of the Tet Offensive. All that remains of a block of housing near the An Quang Pagoda (top of the photograph), Saigon, 5 February 1968. *AP Photo/Johner*

South Vietnamese soldiers operating in the paddy fields of the Mekong Delta, 14 November 1969. This company was moving to the U-Minh forest, a large marshy and swamp forest area at the southern tip of Vietnam. The Mekong Delta was considered as a likely area of deployment for the first Australian troops, but rejected because of the topography. *AP Photo/Godfrey*

A pamphlet—front and back covers—published by the Ministry of Information and Chieu Hoi of the Republic of (South) Vietnam. Dr R. Wyllie was an Australian physician in Vietnam in 1966.
Courtesy NVV Museum

VIETNAM THROUGH FOREIGN EYES

> **UNSUITABLE FOR CHILDREN**
> This pamphlet contains pictures of the unfortunate victims of Viet Cong brutality. It should not be placed in the hands of children.

The Truth
Of Viet Cong Terror

By Dr. R. G. Wyllie, of the
Baker Medical Research Institute,
Alfred Hospital, Melbourne.

In this poignant story, Dr. R. G. Wyllie, an Australian physician who worked as a volunteer in Vietnam for six months, relates his experiences and tells the truth of Viet Cong terrorism as he actually saw it.

The Vietnamese among whom we work have no doubt the war is necessary. After seeing the alternative, I have no doubt. The war is brutal and necessary. It may be repulsive, but it is not pointless.

Published by the Ministry of Information and Chieu Hoi of the Republic of Vietnam. For additional copies, write to 19 Ky Dong St., Saigon.

167-30
TT-ST-01

```
      (14)  "Little girl" mine.  This mine consists of a little
Vietnamese girl with approximately twenty pounds of explosives
concealed under her clothing.  Attached to the explosives is a
friction-pull firing device which the little girl pulls when a
group of G̶I̶'s are near her.  This is just one example of the Viet
Cong's little regard for human life.

Allied soldiers
```

A lesson from a Viet Cong mine warfare pamphlet produced by the US Army portrays a 'suicide bomber' from the Vietnam era. *Pamphlet Lesson Reference file: Viet Cong Mine Warfare, July 1968, US Army Engineer School, Virginia*

The 33 NVA Regiment Museum located near Binh Ba. On 6 June 1969, the Australians clashed with elements of 33 NVA Regiment in Binh Ba village in a costly battle for the North Vietnamese soldiers. *Courtesy Noel de Grussa*

Senior Colonel (brigadier) Trieu Kim Son, commander 9th (aka 3rd) Battalion, *33 NVA Regiment*. The NVA battalion fought the last battle against the Australians in September 1971 at Nui Sao (Nui Le). *Courtesy Xuan Thu*

Hoang Cao Hy (rank not known) commanded the *33rd Regiment* in September 1971. Hy returned to the North in 1972 where he retired in 1977. *Courtesy Yen Bai Online*

In Northern Quang Tri Province, the PLAF (Viet Cong) continually pressed their attacks from 11 to 18 August 1971. *Courtesy Douglas Pike Collection, Texas Tech University Vietnam Center and Archive (TTUVC&A)*

Captured Viet Cong photograph (no date) showing Viet Cong porters' imaginative use of bicycles. *Courtesy Donald Jellema Collection, TTUVC&A*

Captured Viet Cong photograph (no date) showing a Viet Cong soldier approaching a destroyed allied tank. *Courtesy Donald Jellema Collection, TTUVC&A*

Captured enemy photograph (no date) showing a Viet Cong soldier firing over what appears to be the body of an allied soldier (possibly Special Forces or Ranger). *Courtesy Donald Jellema Collection, TTUVC&A*

An enemy soldier coming out of a tunnel to surrender, July 1971—location not known. *Courtesy Ben G. Crosby Collection, TTUVC&A*

Water Point
red
AEME

Road South to Hoa Long & Vung Tau

1 ATF HQ   Sigs   Artillery   3 Cav
Engineers   Pearly Gates
        Kangaroo Pad   SAS Hill
RAASC   Quarry

Battalion Lines   Ordnance   Force Flt
    Anzac   PO   Battalion Lines

        Battalion Lines

Rubbish dump

Road to Long Tan

1 ATF base at Nui Dat, circa 1971, looking southwest. *Courtesy NVV Museum*

A typical bombing run by a B-52 Stratofortress dropping 340-kilogram bombs, 5 November 1965. The B-52 raids were closely monitored within the Johnson administration, with targets only approved after high-level analysis of the target's military value. *AP Photo/USAF*

B-52 strikes were feared by the NVA/Viet Cong forces. The strategic bombers were first used inside South Vietnam on targets near Ben Cat, 40 kilometres north of Saigon, 18 June 1965. *AP Photo/Henri Huet*

Lieutenant General Peter Cosgrove MC, Chief of the Australian Army, presenting a slouch hat to his Vietnamese counterpart during an official visit, 2001. *Courtesy WO1 Jeni Chiron*

rubber plantation, all of which brought the following comment from Captain Adrian Roberts, now based at Long Hai. 'It was for all the world to me as it had been in 1966 at the very beginning ... as if we had never really been there.'[31] Roberts had commanded the APC reaction force at Long Tan in August 1966.

During May, the major NVA thrust in Military Region 3 had concentrated around the districts in Binh Long Province on the Cambodian border. In Phuoc Tuy Province, the two enemy main force regiments hit at targets near Duc Thanh as well as Dat Do, where one-third of the village was occupied, possibly by troops from *33 NVA Regiment*. On 17 May, an ARVN task force of six companies killed 92 enemy soldiers 6 kilometres southwest of Duc Thanh for the loss of six of their own. Although the situation around Dat Do was dire, a battalion from the 18th ARVN Division fought through to the east of the village where they killed 31 enemy soldiers. They reported that the dead possibly came from *33 NVA Regiment*, but they were probably soldiers from *274 Viet Cong Regiment*. This clash was followed by a 5th Ranger Group deployment on 24 May that saw fierce firefights to the west of Dat Do on 28 and 29 May, during which the Rangers reported that they had killed 106 enemy whilst their own casualties were light.[32]

D445 Battalion reported that they had entered Dat Do on 19 May and established fighting positions around the police compound. They also established blocking positions against any movement into Dat Do from Phuoc Hoa Long on the western side, while elements of *274 Viet Cong Regiment* defended to the northwest. Following eleven days of fighting, the *3rd Company* of *D445* was reduced to 'six comrades' from an initial 70. On the thirteenth day, their history noted, the battalion was ordered to block Route 23 to Xuyen Moc, but it had been reduced to '17 comrades ... who were fit enough to undertake their task'. A few days later their troop strength increased as men who had been lightly wounded or exhausted rejoined the fighting. In the second phase of their attacks, *D445* combined with local force guerrillas to hold Route 23 and to continue the fight around Dat Do, Long Hai and Phuoc Hai.[33]

The lack of sufficient discipline and a low level of recognition of combat duty was a subject broached by northern General Quang with the Soviet Army Intelligence Directorate in June 1972. He said that it explained the reasons for some heavy losses of their forces. Although his comments were not specific to Phuoc Tuy, they mirrored a number of criticisms expressed over the years by senior North Vietnamese and Viet Cong officers. Quang also noted a lack of high quality tactical training and combat experience among a number of their commanders.[34] The comments sounded like an echo of some of the complaints lodged by the Americans and the Australians against the ARVN.

Although Duc Thanh and Xuyen Moc headquarters were isolated during this period of heavy fighting, they were resupplied by air and not lost to the enemy. Nonetheless, all that was held at Xuyen Moc was the small Regional Force compound. On 16 June, American aircraft used an air resupply system known as high velocity delivery to hit the compound with an extremely accurate drop of one ton of canned meat. In what can only be described as a farcical sequence of events, the load landed on top of the district headquarters and collapsed the building. A second load landed next to the ammunition warehouse and caught fire. This detonated a load of 60 mm mortar bombs and trip flares. That explosion set off a small arms detonation in an adjacent warehouse, which resulted in the loss of 60,000 rounds of M-16 rifle and M-60 machine-gun ammunition. In spite of this friendly 'help', the ARVN held the position![35]

During this Easter offensive, the poor performance of the territorial forces, especially their lack of battle preparation, was good cause for the South Vietnamese province chief to be replaced. On 21 May, Lieutenant Colonel Tran Dinh Bich took charge and most hoped it would be a change for the better. Colonel Bich faced a demanding task. Much of the outer ring of the province had suffered damage and a lot of the gains made over the past few years lay in ruins. Although the battles around many parts of the province were tactical failures for the Viet Cong, they were an operational success that had been underpinned by the post-1969 *COSVN* directives. The people had lost faith in their government's capability to protect them and most thought the Viet Cong would win when the Americans had gone.

This serious deterioration of security prompted a visit by Brigadier Geddes to the provincial headquarters at Baria after the May battles. He discussed intelligence advice with Mr Raymond Perkins and Lieutenant Colonel John Kwasigroch, the senior American provincial advisers, that a further attack was anticipated but this time against Baria. Geddes was concerned for the security of the AATTV members, especially at Van Kiep on the outskirts of the town. There was little he could do other than rely upon the efforts of the South Vietnamese, or withdraw the Australians completely.

The fighting in Phuoc Tuy continued into June, but the ARVN more than held their own against VC forces in several battles around the province. On 11 June, with American strike aircraft in support, they killed 54 soldiers probably from the *274 Viet Cong Regiment*. South Vietnamese Rangers had another successful clash on 16 June when they killed a further 43 enemy. On 29 June, a battalion from the 52nd ARVN Regiment engaged an enemy force 10 kilometres east of Dat Do and killed 63 of them for a loss of two dead and 23 wounded. These were commendable efforts by the South Vietnamese and a far cry from their past poor performance. Brigadier General Le Minh Dao had assumed command of the 18th ARVN Division mid-stream on 4 April 1972 and his command ability had obviously steadied them.

The combat performance by the territorial forces throughout the worst of the Easter offensive had worried Ian Geddes and probably increased his concern about the AATTV soldiers who were frequently going into harm's way. In fairness to the Regional Force, they were capable and could hold their own in a local battle but their senior commander had been tested and found to be deficient. Subsequent to his visit, Brigadier Geddes wrote the following directive to Lieutenant Colonel Kirkland, the CO of AATTV, 'Request you keep this HQ advised by names and dates of Australian personnel accompanying FANK battalions on field training exercises'. AATTV repeated the demand to the two training battalions and insisted that a minimum number of two Australians be allocated to each *field exercise*.[36] Surprisingly, although it appeared that a lot of fuss was applied to checking on where the advisers were, no one commented that the Cambodian battalions were *training* in what was the old area of 1ATF operations—with all of its associated dangers—in a supposedly non-combatant role.

FANK training covered areas that were within the operational responsibility of the South Vietnamese territorial forces. This was an extraordinary arrangement of tactical cooperation—for very pragmatic reasons—between the two historic enemies: Cambodia and Vietnam.[37] For the South Vietnamese, the Cambodian training deployment must have been an operational godsend. Lieutenant General Nguyen Van Minh and his staff at III Corps appreciated that Phuoc Tuy Province was not critical to *COSVN*'s current plans, but they could not leave the province bare. It needed sufficient force to at least provide an impression of security with adequate strength to delay any unanticipated major attacks. The Cambodian battalions would also be seen in the field while the South Vietnamese Regional Forces—occasionally reinforced with ARVN battalions—protected the main villages. Although the FANK battalions were not deployed to provide that security, their presence in association with American trainers—who could get ground attack aircraft quickly—would be sufficient to create some tactical doubt in the minds of the enemy. As Terry Smith recalled:

> Between February and November 1972, with the exception of June [*sic*, the May battles discussed above], the FANK battalions were the only allied units conducting extended operations [supposedly training] outside the population centres in Phuoc Tuy Province. The province's three small Regional Force battalions and four Regional Force inter-company groups ... were deployed defensively to secure the population centres.[38]

The critical battle during this offensive was at An Loc City and the Quan Loi airfield, 100 kilometres away to the west of Phuoc Tuy. The besieged An Loc defences shrank into an area of no more than 3 square kilometres and 78,000 rounds of artillery, of which 10,000 hit the defenders on 11 May alone, pounded the enclave. General Minh had ordered the 18th ARVN Division to move Task Force 52 to reinforce the ARVN defences there in late March 1972. Lieutenant Colonel Nguyen Ba Thinh commanded Task Force 52, which was named after the 52nd Regiment that he commanded. TF52 consisted of two battalions and two sections of guns, both 105 mm and 155 mm. The third battalion of the regiment remained at Xuyen Loc, but operated in Phuoc Tuy during May and again in late June until 9 July. Lieutenant Colonel Tran Ba Thanh's 48th Regiment of the 18th Division followed Thinh's TF52 on 13–14 June and then the entire 18th Division deployed to Binh Long Province from 11 July until 20–29 November 1972, although AATTV reported that six 105 mm and four 155 mm guns from the division remained in Phuoc Tuy. When it was relieved in November by ARVN Ranger battalions, the 18th Division moved from An Loc to cover a northern arc around Saigon with a regiment each in Binh Duong, Bien Hoa and Long Khanh provinces.[39]

North Vietnamese Lieutenant General Tran Van Quang corroborated the assessment made by the South when he implied that the eastern approach to Saigon had no priority in the Northern High Command's campaign plans during 1972–1973. Quang Tri, Hue (a symbolic target), Danang, the Central Highlands and the Tay Ninh–Loc Ninh approach to Saigon were the primary strategic thrusts of the Supreme High Command, he told the Soviets, to which he added a point of interest: Khe Sanh was to be 'a launching pad' for the liberation of Hue.[40] General Westmoreland's 1968 Khe Sanh judgement may have been more accurate than many of his critics would admit.

Fierce counteroffensive fighting continued on and off for the remainder of the year to retake and secure the areas occupied during the Easter offensive. Fighting in the Phuoc Tuy region calmed to occasional and scattered contacts until October. During the week of 19–25 October, *33 NVA Regiment* attempted to cut Route 1 near the border between Long Khanh and Bien Hoa to the west of Xuan Loc, but they were defeated by the ARVN. Another battle by 36 Ranger Battalion 15 kilometres southwest of Xuan Loc caused heavy casualties to an enemy force when the Rangers killed 50 while they sustained only nine wounded.[41]

A brief ripple of relief came with Henry Kissinger's late October 1972 announcement of an impending cease-fire but it was soon overtaken by the actions of both sides to make a 'land grab' in an attempt to mark out their territorial boundaries. This caused another burst of fierce fighting in Phuoc Tuy, especially in Dat Do where about 80 Viet Cong were killed.[42] *D445 Battalion* had barely recovered from their losses in June, which meant that the district guerrillas probably bore the brunt of this battle.[43] It was a testing time for the South Vietnamese territorial forces—some of whom had been trained by Australian mobile teams—but with the extra firepower now available to them they defeated the Viet Cong. The enemy then withdrew to their old hiding places and military activity in the province calmed down once again.

Although the Australians remained deployed at Van Kiep and active with the mobile assistance training teams, their tasks at the JWTC were few and their time there was drawing to a close. Discussions were already underway to plan reduction at all of the camps—including FANK—with a view that AATTV would phase out by the end of 1972. Once again there was a military plan for an orderly and sensible close-down of a military commitment, countered by a political agenda that required the Australian soldiers to stay in country regardless of their usefulness. Irrespective of the government's internal brawling, the 'non-combatant' trainers fought on. Terry Smith recalled:

Eighteen FANK battalions were deployed into the field between August and November and ten of those definitely had Australian advisers with them. These so-called training exercises resulted in 44 incidents against the enemy in which eight Viet Cong were killed. The Cambodian battalions suffered a minimum of fourteen killed and 54 wounded while one American adviser was killed and eight others were wounded.[44]

The so-called training continued when, during the night of 20–21 November 1972, three Australian warrant officers—James Thorburn, Robert Mackenzie and Anthony Ling—took part in what was to be the last recorded combat action by Australians in Vietnam. The three went out with a Popular Force platoon of 28 soldiers and three interpreters from Xuyen Moc to conduct reconnaissance training that ended in a very interesting ambush. Almost immediately after the ambush was set, three unarmed people walked into the killing ground but they were not engaged. A few minutes later, they re-emerged with a weapon and the ambush was sprung. Control of the ambush party then collapsed. An argument between the Australian senior adviser and the platoon commander over leaving the position ensued, during which elements of the platoon moved out. The advisers were obliged to follow, or be left alone.

Not long after moving away from the ambush site, the leading squad was hit by intense enemy fire that caused the rear elements to scatter. Some of them threw away their equipment and probably some weapons. The platoon commander disappeared, but the advisers managed to control a group of fourteen Vietnamese and withdrew to a defensive position, where they avoided contact with the enemy soldiers who searched for them. The next day the advisers got the group to go back and recover the bodies of four who had been killed, but no enemy dead were found. When the group was extracted by vehicle, at Hoa Long they found some of the platoon that had run away during the night.[45] What happened between them when the deserters were discovered also might have made an interesting after action report.

This last combat action, which took place on the road to Long Tan, just

2 kilometres east of Hoa Long, was an inglorious end to the Australian war.[46] The FANK program closed down on 29 November and the Australians were relocated to Van Kiep. As Terry Smith wrote at the time:

> Well, this place is just about fini now and we will go to Van Kiep tomorrow and see if we can get a job. The original plan to send some fellows home has been quashed and there are some pretty unhappy people about.[47]

An air of frustration and some anger permeated the activities around the AATTV when the government refused permission for the surplus instructors to go home. Although the Minister for Defence soon changed his mind, it was of no consequence because the government was defeated at the 2 December 1972 elections. Following this, on 11 December, Prime Minister Whitlam— only he and his deputy Lance Barnard had been sworn into office at that time—publicly released his order of 8 December that the Australians were to get out of South Vietnam by 18 December 1972. The Embassy Guard could stay, but no rear party was to remain for a final handover. It was simply, just get out. The final number of Australians to be withdrawn is difficult to determine; estimates range between 127 and 179.[48]

Many of those involved at the time were embarrassed and angered by the obscene haste of it all. Several advisers were on their third tours; Geoff 'Derby' Munro at FANK was on his fourth. Most of those who worked closely with the Vietnamese or the Cambodians had some empathy with their plight, even if they despaired of their military standards. Many of them spoke about the guilt they felt when they left Vietnam. The job had not been finished and there was definitely no withdrawal with honour. When Terry Smith came home it was with a feeling that he has never forgotten:

> I do not know if I will ever really forget the shame that I felt as an Australian soldier, nor my distaste for a system, which would allow it to happen, when we left two platoons of South Vietnamese in the scrub west of Nui Dat. The reason we were there . . . was part of a deception plan for AATTV's withdrawal from Phuoc Tuy to Saigon. We were picked up by two or three vehicles led by the 2IC of AATTV. We just left these two platoons to carry on without us. There was a hurried explanation and a quick farewell . . . we jumped in the rovers and we were off—gone.[49]

During the weekend of 16–17 December 1972, the final journey home began with a parade at Van Kiep. The Sunday was taken up with the usual administrative details of cleaning and handing back equipment and packing up. The next day, they were gone.

In the years to follow, the Australian people and their veterans argued and stumbled through the fog of the Vietnam War. The war's many contradictions have puzzled the nation as it searched for the merit in Sir Basil Liddell-Hart's maxim: 'War is always a matter of doing evil in the hope that good may come of it'.

> Where was the good, we had left part of ourselves in the jungles and the paddy fields and in the hearts and minds of those who had dared to follow and we had abandoned them to the ruins.[50]

EPILOGUE

———————

The US has a population of 200 million, but it cannot stand wars.
Mao Zedong to Pham Van Dong, 17 November 1968

On 2 December 1972 the conservative Coalition government of William McMahon lost the general election and the Australian Labor Party took office. Prime Minister Gough Whitlam immediately cancelled conscription and directed the small Australian contingent that remained in South Vietnam to leave the country. When the last 35 members of the AATTV departed on 18 December, only the Guard and Escort Platoon were permitted to stay to protect the Australian Embassy. They were withdrawn in June 1973.

Whitlam's government, however, was to be relatively short-lived and beset by controversy. The Coalition-controlled Senate refused to pass essential supply bills in October 1975, leading to the government's dismissal by the Governor-General, Sir John Kerr, on 11 November. Malcolm Fraser, who had served as the Minister for the Army and the Minister for Defence during the Vietnam War, now replaced Whitlam as caretaker prime minister. In the double dissolution election that followed on 13 December, the Coalition parties gained a majority of 54 seats in the House of Representatives and retained control of the Senate.

The end of America's war

In December 1972, President Richard Nixon authorised a massive bombing campaign against all significant military targets in the Hanoi–Haiphong region. Although the specific targets were the industrial infrastructure that provided arms and materiel support to the NVA and the VC forces in the South, its true object was a political and psychological attack upon the Politburo. Contrary to many popular reports of the day, the cities of Hanoi and Haiphong were not 'carpet bombed'. North Vietnamese officials said that 1318 civilians were killed around Hanoi and that 305 died in Haiphong.[1] The December air campaign, known as Operation Linebacker II, was designed 'to shock the North Vietnamese back to negotiations [that had stalled at Paris] in a frame of mind to end the war before the newly elected and anti-war [US] Congress convened in January [1973]'.[2] In President Nixon's words, 'the bastards have never been bombed like they're going to be bombed'.[3]

From 18 to 29 December 1972 the Americans launched 729 B-52 sorties and 724 tactical fighter sorties against 59 targets, some of which were hit several times. The B-52 bombers dropped 15,000 tons and the tactical fighters another 5000 tons on the closely monitored military targets in an effort to achieve maximum destruction.[4] These were dire times for the North Vietnamese and the intense bombing campaign forced them back to the negotiating table. It was a successful but controversial American tactic that the international press condemned with editorials like that of the *Washington Post*, which described it as 'the most savage and senseless act of war ever visited, over a scant ten days, by one sovereign people upon another'.[5] However, it mirrored a previous strategy of the North Vietnamese, which was to fight to gain strength while negotiating.

The heavy bombing effort was not without cost to America with the loss of 27 aircraft including fifteen B-52s.[6] Recorded crew casualty figures vary between 43 missing and/or killed in action, 41 prisoners of war and 33 rescued in some reports to 33 POW, 25 MIA and 26 rescued and 8 KIA in other documents.[7] Although the loss of B-52 aircraft in particular caused a press frenzy in America, the losses overall represented a little less than 2 per cent attrition, lower than the 3 per cent factored in by the planners.[8] Also, the North had fired off most if not all of their surface-to-air missiles—reportedly 1250 were fired—as well as their heavy anti-aircraft artillery, meaning that in the final days, or if the bombing had continued, the target areas were as good as being defenceless.

On 23 January 1973, on prime time television President Richard Nixon announced to the American people that the Paris Peace Accords had been signed.

It was 'peace with honour', Nixon said. The White House staffers referred to the event as 'VV Day', a label reminiscent of World War II victory slogans. The governments of the Democratic Republic of Vietnam (North Vietnam), the Republic of Vietnam (South Vietnam), and the United States, as well as the Provisional Revolutionary Government (PRG) of South Vietnam signed the Agreement.

The PRG appeared on the diplomatic scene in 1969 with a published Manifesto to provide an alternative (revolutionary) government in South Vietnam. Hanoi understood that the NLF's association with North Vietnam and communism was a weakness in the propaganda stakes and worked against it obtaining the voluntary and much-needed support of the peoples in the South. The PRG façade continued through the peace talks but Hanoi pulled all the strings through *COSVN* to the NLF and surreptitiously to the PRG.

In essence, the Paris peace agreement guaranteed that South Vietnam would have free and fair elections and other western democratic rights such as freedom of the press, religion and speech. The agreement also demanded the return of all captured military personnel and foreign civilians, to be completed within 60 days of the signing. A significant part of the agreement retained the 17th parallel demarcation line that was written into the 1954 Geneva Accords. In effect, two distinct regions were to remain while the reunification of Vietnam was to be 'carried out through peaceful means . . . discussions and agreements . . . without coercion or annexation by either party'.[9]

The Paris agreement also stated that a cease-fire was to be observed throughout South Vietnam as of 2400 hours Greenwich Mean Time on 27 January 1973. Within 60 days of the signing, America and associated foreign countries were to withdraw totally from South Vietnam. There was no such requirement demanded of the North Vietnamese Army. In a manner similar to the 1954 Geneva Accords that saw America restock the fledgling forces of South Vietnam, Article 7 of the Agreement permitted periodic replacement of armaments, munitions and war materials that had been destroyed, damaged, worn out, or used up *after the cease-fire* on the basis of piece-for-piece.

But the fighting continued. The South Vietnamese recaptured some territory against an exhausted northern war machine that had an estimated 150,000 men in the South. The NVA had not recovered from their hammering during their early 1972 attempted invasion of the South. However, the North understood that the ARVN would eat up its resources without the aid of America, and they rightly predicted that the dreaded B-52s would not return. Although President Nixon continued to hint that America would re-enter the war, politically it was unthinkable. On 4 June 1973, a bill passed through the Senate that blocked any funds for US military activities in Indochina. The House of Representatives endorsed the legislation, locking the Americans out of the renewed fighting.

North Vietnam seized the opportunity and the General Staff prepared a strategic plan titled Combat Directions for 1973–1975. Following extensive preparatory training and pre-position of logistics, four army corps were formed for a major offensive against the South. They remained cautious, however, and the northern political leaders conservatively marked 1976 as the year of victory. Before this, General Tran Van Tra at COSVN lobbied Le Duan with his proposal that an attack against Route 14 in Phuoc Long Province would provide an essential pathway to Saigon. He got his approval and on 6 January 1975 they overran Phuoc Binh, the province capital. This success emboldened the North to begin their invasion in earnest. During March, the Central Highlands fell in ignominious circumstances when the senior ARVN commanders ineptly abandoned the main highland cities. President Thieu then directed the military to retreat from the northern areas and consolidate into the southern region. The retired Australian colonel Ted Serong—former AATTV commander and honorary brigadier—had also tried to influence the ARVN staff to cut away the northern provinces. Frank Snepp, however, was not complimentary about Serong's efforts when he wrote in Decent Interval:

> Realising that truncation was a live consideration he [Serong] quickly latched onto it as an entrée. Neither Thieu nor the Americans ever took Serong very seriously. Murray [US major general, defence attaché] considered him a 'fake' and the rest of us in the Embassy were advised explicitly to stay away from 'that kook'.[10]

American Ambassador Graham Martin was more praiseworthy, however. The Americans had been prohibited by the 1973 Peace Agreement from providing military assistance/advice, as Martin explained: 'The Vietnamese (in Saigon) did not seek our advice about this plan. The small Vietnamese group involved did utilize the services of a brilliant retired Army officer of another country [Serong] who strongly urged its early implementation'.[11] The subsequent dithering by Thieu saw the northern provinces abandoned in panic, as troops and civilians fled the communist assault. No doubt the slaughter of civilians during Tet 1968 by the NVA/Viet Cong remained a vivid prompt for self-preservation.

The rapid demise of the units defending the northern part of South Vietnam surprised everyone, including the NVA. It allowed Senior General Van Tien Dung—the NVA Commander-in-Chief—to launch his final attack against Saigon in April. The operation, named Ho Chi Minh, had the aim of capturing Saigon before 1 May to avoid the coming monsoon season. By 7 April, three North Vietnamese divisions attacked the Xuan Loc region. This was a defensive block on Highway 1, 65 kilometres east of Saigon. Other major NVA assaults streamed in across the western provinces from Cambodia towards Saigon. The battle-hardened men of the 18th ARVN Division, who were commanded by the resilient Brigadier-General Le Minh Dao, defended Xuan Loc. They were later reinforced by elements from the 25th ARVN Division and the 1st Airborne Brigade.

The odds were never in favour of the South Vietnamese. They were heavily outnumbered, with estimates ranging as high as six to one. For two bloody weeks, severe fighting raged around the city as the ARVN defenders made a last stand to try to block the North Vietnamese advance. But it was a lost cause without further relief, which was not available, and at great loss the 18th ARVN Division was finally ordered to withdraw to defend Bien Hoa. A North Vietnamese source has said that an estimated 2036 South Vietnamese soldiers were either killed or wounded and another 2731 were captured.[12] The numbers of ARVN losses recorded in allied documents are generally expressed in percentages. For example, James Willbanks wrote that the ARVN suffered 30 per cent casualties in all units that fought in the battle, except for the 52nd Task Force that suffered 70 per cent losses. The enemy reportedly had 5000 men killed and 37 tanks destroyed.[13] The defeat at Xuan Loc severely depleted the ability of the ARVN to resist the North Vietnamese Army's onslaught that was to follow.

In his radio broadcast of resignation on 21 April 1975 President Thieu fought back tears as he declared that the United States had betrayed South Vietnam. In a scathing attack, he suggested US Secretary of State Henry Kissinger had tricked him into signing the Paris peace agreement in 1973. They had promised military aid that failed to materialise, Thieu said. The presidency passed briefly to Tran Van Huong, a politician, and Thieu left for

Taiwan on 25 April. Huong resigned after one week and handed power to General Duong Van Minh—'Big Minh'—on 28 April.

By now North Vietnamese tanks had reached Bien Hoa, only two hours' drive north on Highway 1 and headed toward Saigon. Isolated ARVN units along the way provided little resistance. The general populace was in panic and thousands of refugees streamed away from the fighting, ahead of the main communist onslaught. By 27 April, 100,000 North Vietnamese troops encircled Saigon, which was protected by 30,000 desperate ARVN troops. When the main airport, Tan Son Nhut, was closed owing to savage fighting and persistent shelling and rocketing, the city was doomed. Within three days cinematographers captured the moment when NVA T54 tanks flying Viet Cong (NLF) flags smashed through the gates of the Presidential Palace to end the war.

Save the children

In April 1975, only a month before Saigon was to fall, there was a last-minute attempt to evacuate the defenceless from the war zone. Operation Babylift was initiated in South Vietnam, to relocate Vietnamese children, many orphans and those of mixed American–Vietnamese parentage, to adopting families in the United States and other countries (including Australia, France and Canada). Although the actual number of orphans and escorts flown out of South Vietnam is probably not known, US Pacific Air Force documents show that 2894 orphans had been brought out during Operation Babylift. According to an American Embassy (Canberra) message, 496 Vietnamese orphans were accepted for adoption in Australia.

However, this operation was not without incident. On 2 April, a World Airways DC-8 took aboard a total of 84 orphans, children and adults and, disregarding an air traffic control directive, took off and flew to Oakland, California via Yokota in Japan. The first *official* flight, a USAF C-5 Galaxy, ended in tragedy. Not long after take-off, the pilot reported a problem and told controllers he was attempting to return to Tan Son Nhut. Soon after, the aircraft was reported as down and burning 5 to 7 miles from the airport. The pilot survived, and he told investigators that during the climb out at about 23,000 feet (7000 metres), the aft bulkhead door had blown out and struck the tail, rupturing hydraulic lines. Although he retained some control over the aircraft he could not govern the rapid rate of descent on approach to landing and the aircraft crashed. No one knew precisely how many orphans and others were on the aircraft. The Defence Attaché's Office in Saigon reported that 77 US passengers and crew had been on board and on 6 April the DAO listed a death toll of eight US citizens with a further 32 unaccounted for. Of the 29 members of the crew, three dead had been identified and seven were missing and many of the others were injured. Mortuary staff based at the Central Identification Laboratory in Thailand also requested assistance from embassies to provide identification media if the remains of an Australian, a Malaysian and three German nationals who were on the manifest were recovered. Two days after the crash a death toll of 76 children was released, which had a profound emotional impact upon all of the personnel involved in the operation.[14] After a brief hiatus, Operation Babylift continued and the children were flown on to America and other destinations without further mishap.

Concurrently, Operation New Life (4 April to 3 September 1975) was initiated, which was the evacuation of South Vietnamese families seeking political asylum. These operations were just the start of what were to be successive waves of refugees as Vietnamese domestic and foreign policy swayed in the uncertain political climate that swept through Southeast Asia. Immediately after the war there would be a mass exodus, mainly in boats, followed by ethnic Chinese being forced to leave the country. They were followed by a second wave of refugees who fled following the programs of repression and re-education of former 'enemies' by the communist regime. The catalyst for all of this was the absorption of the South by decree. The PRG disappeared, as did the Viet Cong. There was no free and fair election on unification.[15]

The exodus

In 1977 the world began to witness a mass exodus from Vietnam, one of the largest in history. Some people would depart as refugees, escaping what they saw as their personal persecution. Others, mainly ethnic Chinese, were driven out of the country to China and elsewhere in Asia in a crude but relatively bloodless form of ethnic cleansing. At the time, many of those fleeing Vietnam were improperly labelled economic refugees but the reality was much different. For example, a former South Vietnamese Army officer or previous government official may have had his house ransacked at any time and any items of value 'confiscated'. Government jobs in the new Socialist Republic of Vietnam (SRV) were limited to those who were Party members or could prove that they were pro–Viet Cong during the American War. Capitalists or anyone possessing the slightest wealth were considered to be bourgeoisie who must have 'robbed the poor'. Consequently their property was seized.

Escapees-cum-refugees were not a new problem for the Vietnamese. In a report released on 25 June 1965, the 89th Congress of the United States observed:

> The dramatic flow of terrorized refugees from Communist-dominated areas of South Vietnam reflects the great variety of problems confronting the United States in Asia. The subcommittee believes that adequate assistance, including resettlement, to those refugees is an integral part of the effort to safeguard the independence of South Vietnam—for humanitarian, as well as political, military and economic reasons.[16]

While this investigation covered internal movement of terrorised people, the report acknowledged that immediately following the 1954 Geneva Accords 'nearly 7 per cent of the population of North Vietnam, some 1 million persons, sought refuge from Communism'. Many more would have fled, but they were prevented from leaving by the communist authorities when the 300-day free departure permission elapsed, the report noted. In almost a mirror image of the 1975 exodus:

> The refugees ... fled largely for political reasons. A substantial number were Roman Catholic, often led into exile by their religious leaders. But all who left chose to abandon their homes and most of their possessions, and by foot and by oxcart made the long trek ... to the free republic in the south.[17]

For most, the new escape would be by boat.

The boat people

Immediately after the fall of Saigon, 125,000 Vietnamese fled the country. Once people wishing to escape the tyranny of communism in the South were able to gather enough funds they embarked on perilous journeys, usually by sea. It is estimated that between 1 and 1.5 million people fled between 1975 and 1982. Refugees faced dangers from overcrowded boats, pirates, and the perils of the South China Sea and the Gulf of Thailand.[18]

To gain a passage the average price was around 7 ounces of gold per head, although it was often quoted in taels—37.5 grams—of gold leaf.[19] At that time the price of an ounce of gold was between $240 (May 1979) and $520 (December 1979) per ounce, which was big money for those wishing to make a quick dollar from the plight of refugees. For example, the *Huey Fong* sailed into Hong Kong harbour in December 1978 with 3318 on board who had paid nearly $3000 per head in gold.[20]

Many Vietnamese left because of their involvement with the former South Vietnamese government or armed forces. Others left because they were seen as enemies of the new socialist society, as Cao Lu, then a sixteen-year-old young man from the Mekong Delta region, explained:

My family owned a tobacco business in the heart of Can Tho. It was successful but only because of the sacrifices my mother and father had made over the years . . . But life became more and more difficult. In 1976, the year after the war ended, the local government imposed restrictions on the business of suspected capitalists. Not only was it harder and harder to make a living but also our home was continually ransacked for money and gold. When, finally, the government closed the marketplace where our shop was located, we knew it was time to leave . . . We knew it was for the best. There was no future for us in Vietnam.[21]

In late 1975 David Thuc Tran was seven years old and one of six children. His father was serving seven years in jail for being an ARVN lieutenant colonel. David recalls that SRV officials 'confiscated our belongings, forced us out of home and deprived all of us children of the chance to attend school'. Fearing that the two eldest boys would be conscripted to fight in Kampuchea (Cambodia), David's mother was determined to get the family out of Vietnam. It was an often-repeated refugee story.[22]

The Australian Prime Minister, Gough Whitlam was unsympathetic, reportedly saying around the time of the fall of Saigon, 'I'm not having hundreds of fucking Vietnamese Balts coming into this country with their political and religious hatreds against us'. Clyde Cameron, the Minister for Immigration, wrote 'I could have hugged him for putting my own view so well'. Foreign Affairs Minister Don Willesee pleaded for the former local embassy staff to be given passage to Australia, but Whitlam rejected his request peremptorily.[23]

This initial wave of refugees and asylum-seekers became a tsunami of 'boat people'. The main impact of the exodus was felt in Hong Kong as well as various landing sites in the Philippines, Malaysia and Indonesia. The number became so great and the death toll at sea so high that the UN had to act. Under the auspices of the United Nations refugee agency, the UNHCR, a Memorandum of Understanding was signed with the government of the Socialist Republic of Vietnam that established a program of legal emigration. This was known as the Orderly Departure Program (ODP).

Carina Hoang was sixteen years old when her family fled Vietnam in 1979 when the Orderly Departure Program became disorderly. Her story is a window to the experience of thousands of others who endured terrible suffering during their exodus. Carina wrote in her book *Boat People*:

> After the fall of Saigon, life became extremely difficult for my mother. My father was in a political prison and our house had been confiscated. She had to take care of seven young children, her mother and her mother-in-law all by herself. Because of my father's military background we children were not permitted to attend high school, and so there was no hope for our future. Add to that the tremendous uncertainty of the situation: people were living in the constant fear of what might happen tomorrow.[24]

Anthony Nguyen's father had been an ARVN officer incarcerated in Katum re-education camp in Tay Ninh Province. During a visit Anthony made to the camp, his father asked him why he was still in Vietnam, more or less telling him to leave the country. Despite two failed attempts, Anthony persevered. He was determined to leave. His family was continually harassed; he couldn't secure a well-paying job and two of his children died because he couldn't afford medicine. As he said, 'Things were really, really bad. Escape was on everyone's mind, and a popular saying in Saigon at the time was that if a power pole could escape it would do so'. The trouble was it was hard getting hold of a boat or getting a passage and not being turned into the police. So, Anthony built his own boat. He bought the materials on the black market, found a friend who could help him construct a sea-worthy vessel and started his own great escape. Boldly he painted the boat grey for camouflage, got hold of uniform styled clothing, and with a former naval officer recently released from re-education, Anthony, his wife, two children and 80 others set off down the Saigon River at midnight. A few very close shaves, deception, and a lot of luck eventually saw Anthony Nguyen and his family rescued and ultimately sent to Kuku Island in Indonesia.

Kuku Island in Indonesia became home for thousands of Vietnamese refugees during the great exodus, but the first group had to slash, hack and chop a camp out of the bush to make an area in which to survive. The huts were very basic with palm frond roofs and rudimentary sanitation. Luu Thich, on Kuku Island with his eighteen-month-old grandson, described his experience:

> After a violent two-week journey at sea we were dumped on Kuku Island like rag dolls. We had nothing but our hands, and with those hands we built huts out of trees we chopped down. But until we had the strength to do that we had to sleep on the sand underneath a blanket of stars . . . I saw people die from starvation and illness every single day. Yet there were still thousands of us on the island, grappling with the harsh reality that we were still as lost as ever . . . Our days were spent collecting water, dates and firewood, while conjuring up as a much hope as possible that we would be rescued once and for all.[25]

At least 200 refugees died on Kuku. Carina Hoang described how 'we were stranded for nearly three months before aid came . . . initially we survived on coconuts, jungle fruit and vegetables, seafood or anything we could find in the jungle or in the ocean'.[26] Others spent six months and longer waiting to be transferred to established UNHCR refugee camps like the Indonesian Galang Island.

Taking to the sea in riverboats not designed or equipped for ocean travel was extremely perilous. Most skippers were more than competent on their rivers but navigating on the open sea would test many who would be found seriously wanting, often with fatal consequences. And then there was the added danger of open sea piracy.[27]

Refugee David Lee recalled the pirate attacks and one especially terrifying day. The engine on their 24-metre boat had broken down on the fourth day of their escape and they were drifting helplessly at sea when pirates attacked them a second time, David recalled:

> On this occasion, the pirates, who numbered about twenty, forced all of the men off the escape boat onto their own vessel; then in full view of the women and children, they stripped the men naked at gunpoint, lined them up and forced their jaws open. When they found gold teeth, they yanked them out with pliers. After this grisly work, a few pirates kept guard over the men while their cohorts returned to the escape boat and herded the women and children down into the lower deck, where, to their horror, the pirates harassed and repeatedly raped the young women for hour after hour.[28]

Norman Aisbett, a reporter for the *West Australian* newspaper, covered the exodus with photographer David Tanner. Norman was on board the West German rescue-cum-hospital ship the *Cap Anamur*, which intercepted fleeing refugee boats in an effort to prevent the mounting loss of life at sea. The refugees were desperate and determined to escape Vietnam, but Norman was not prepared for what he witnessed.

When they came alongside a 14-metre boat they initially thought it was empty until they looked into its forward hold. Norman said, 'I wrote for my newspaper, "that it was like peering into a mass grave", and that is surely what the boat would have become for 103 people, including 35 children, had we not found it'.[29] Ships like the *Cap Anamur* performed outstanding feats of humanitarian aid. In just a few weeks, it picked up 695 people and in total the organisation that funded the rescue ship saved about 10,000 people. At one stage the *Cap Anamur* even drove off a blockade of Thai pirate boats preying on escape boats.

Hong Kong

The boat people had several choices: take the shorter journey north towards Hong Kong or risk traversing the South China Sea and enter the Pacific and head towards Malaysia, Indonesia or even Australia.

In 1979 Talbot Bashall was appointed as Controller of the Refugee Control

Centre in Hong Kong. Bashall noted that there seemed to be a deliberate policy by the SRV to expel the ethnic Chinese as a flood of humanity swept towards Hong Kong. From his diary of Sunday 6 May, he wrote: 'they are coming and keep on coming. Vietnam's policy is to expel all Ethnic Chinese'.[30] Many of the Chinese fled Vietnam by road into mainland China or took to the seas and headed for Hong Kong.

Theresa Carino describes China–Vietnam dealings during this period in her paper on the politics of Sino-Vietnamese relations:

> For the Chinese businessmen in the South, business had continued as usual after liberation and their capitalistic ventures continued to flourish under a socialist regime. Saigon had always been the economic powerhouse of the country and it was maintaining that position, much to the chagrin of the central government. A series of currency reforms meant to break the grip of the private sector on the economy in the South failed to achieve its goal mainly as a result of the ingenious and swift tactics of the Chinese businessmen . . .
>
> Not only in the South but in the North as well, both economic and political pressures began to build up on the Chinese. The gap between China and Vietnam's attitude towards the Soviet Union had visibly widened after 1975 and their differences grew increasingly antagonistic with China's continued support of the Pol Pot regime in Kampuchea. In Vietnam, the hostility towards China and the Chinese grew correspondingly as the conflict between Kampuchea and Vietnam intensified. As early as February 1978, the on-off border dispute between China and Vietnam in the North had begun to affect the lives of Chinese communities strung along the common border as well as in the Hanoi-Haiphong area. As thousands of ethnic Chinese streamed across the border into China, the Chinese government accused the Vietnamese of systematically and forcibly driving the Chinese out of Vietnam.[31]

Hanoi accomplished this by directing that the 'bourgeois trade' be abolished in the South. This was achieved by the mobilisation of a large police and military force to surround Cholon.

> Cholon was the habitat of 80 per cent of South Vietnam's Chinese. Thousands of Vietnamese youth, accompanied by soldiers, were then sent to make an inventory of assets and goods in shops and houses in the area. These raids produced large amounts of

goods, money and gold bars. While the element of anti-Chinese politics was evidently present in these raids, the Vietnamese authorities justified their actions by citing the necessity to break 'bourgeois' (read 'Chinese') control over food prices and the rice trade and to persuade the unproductive population of Ho Chi Minh City to leave for 'New Economic Zones' in order to further the socialist transformation of Vietnam.[32]

This was ethnic cleansing Asian style and the SRV was diligent in its wholesale approach to cleaning out the Chinese.

Regardless of the dangers, the refugees continued to move across Asia. Bashall's diary of Monday 21 May 1979 recorded 'a long day with over 30,000 in Hong Kong (ashore in camps) and 9,000 odd in Dockyard (still afloat and awaiting processing). The conditions are simply abominable'. In 1980, 75,000 boat people sailed into Hong Kong harbour and in total, 195,833 people made it to Hong Kong.[33]

The Vietnamese diaspora

Many countries in the region had a policy (official or otherwise) of simply giving what they saw as illegal immigrants water and food and pushing them back out to sea. They were to become the Asian flotsam and jetsam.

Australian comedian Hung Lee was nine years old when Saigon fell and his family fled on a boat heading for anywhere out of Vietnam. In an interview with George Negus he related how the boat they were on ran out of fuel and what happened next:

We were just floating. But the American Navy was waiting to pick up refugees. The (US) 1st [sic; 7th] Fleet were waiting there. So they picked us up and took us to the Philippines for a night, to Subic Bay, and then took us to refugee camps on Guam. We were on Guam for about four months.[34]

Hung Lee had an uncle attending RMIT in Melbourne and after borrowing money he was able to sponsor the family to live in Australia. However, to get to a refugee camp was not an automatic pass to freedom. Refugees were processed on arrival at a UNHCR centre, where their claims were examined. For those who had fled and lost their documentation or had it lost at sea or stolen by pirates, this was an impossible demand. Following initial screening, they then had to apply for, and be accepted by, a country willing to take them as a suitable immigrant. Stane Salobir, who worked for the UNHCR on Galang Island, spoke of the difficulties in determining refugee status and the potential awful consequences:

> It was a very hard period for many because of the screening process. Most of those who were there at that time (Galang) had to prove they were genuine refugees when screened; otherwise they were repatriated back to Vietnam. Many of them stayed in the Galang Camp as long as six years, and then they were repatriated. Sadly, this often led to tragic outcomes as refugees chose to take their own lives rather than return. Many of these were young.[35]

Don Hardy, a US Congressional staffer, provided an example on the flow of Vietnamese from the Indonesian camp on Galang Island:

> As of my visit in 1991 [to Galang], Canada became home to 13,516 people, followed by Australia's acceptance of 6470. Other countries had not stretched their arms as widely. Japan accepted only 113 people. Spain, Italy, Argentina and Ireland took fewer than 20 each.[36]

These more detailed figures come from Carina Hoang's *Boat People*:

Between 1975 and 1995 there were approximately 764,478 *refugees and emigrants* resettled outside Vietnam:

Australia	110,996
Canada	103,053
France	27,071
Germany	16,848
Netherlands	7,565
United Kingdom	19,355
United States	424,590
Others (estimated)	55,000[37]

On 30 July 1989, Robert Lloyd Funseth, Senior Deputy Assistant Secretary of State and Acting Director of the Bureau for Refugee Programs, negotiated with

the government of the Socialist Republic of Vietnam to allow emigration to the United States of former re-education camp prisoners to be included in the Orderly Departure Program. A surge of applications followed until 1994. Gary McKay recalls driving past the US Consulate in Ho Chi Minh City in 1993 and seeing half-kilometre long queues of Vietnamese civilians waiting to submit their applications for emigration. From the program's beginning in 1979 until its closure in 1994, the Orderly Departure Program helped over 500,000 Vietnamese to enter the United States. A Humanitarian Resettlement Program was opened in 2005 for a two-year period to cover soldiers or officials of the former South Vietnam who were unable to apply before the 1994 close of the ODP. A modification to that program—known as the McCain amendment—allowed adult single children of former re-education camp prisoners to be considered for resettlement and that was extended to cover the humanitarian program. A previous interpretation of the refugee resettlement provisions had not permitted children to accompany an ex-political prisoner during emigration to the United States. The McCain amendment expired on 30 September 2009.[38]

Saigon's defeat

When most allied veterans heard the news about the fall of Saigon in mid-1975 it was as if a close relative had finally succumbed to terminal cancer. It was not unexpected, yet still sad. They had been hoping for a miracle cure that they knew deep inside would never happen. When the South fell the communists immediately appointed their own Party people into positions of power and authority in the cities and districts. Local People's District Committees were formed but always overseen by a northerner positioned to ensure that everyone toed the Party line. This in itself was to be expected and probably unremarkable if it wasn't for the southerners who held power and influence within the communist hierarchy. Le Duan, who was born in Quang Tri Province, had been the de facto head of the DRV and the real power in the North during the 1960s. When Ho Chi Minh died in 1969, Le Duan held absolute power as the Secretary General of the Lao Dong Party. Pham Van Dong, another southerner, who was born in Quang Ngai Province, served as prime minister of the DRV for 25 years. Another example is Madame Nguyen Thi Binh, a long-serving revolutionary. She was the highly publicised face of the NLF at the attempted peace talks in Paris when Lyndon Johnson was US President. Madame Nguyen was a member of the Central Committee for the National Front for the Liberation of the South and later, in 1969, she served as Foreign Minister of the Provisional Revolutionary Government. Nguyen Thi Binh was elected Vice-President of the Socialist Republic of Vietnam in 1992. She was re-elected in 1997 and served until 2002. Madame Binh was born in Sa Dec in the Mekong Delta.

But at much lower levels of provincial government, it didn't matter if one had fought for the Viet Cong for a decade—there was still a party member in control who had been appointed from the North. Anyone who had served the South Vietnamese in the armed forces, police, or who had worked for the allies in any capacity during the war was denied any opportunity to be gainfully employed. The best a former soldier could hope for if he lived in Saigon was to be a cyclo-driver. Basic human rights were denied those who fell into this category, including the right to vote, although that right was probably irrelevant in the immediate post-war communist environment.

In a miserable example of communist fervour immediately post-war, most South Vietnamese military cemeteries were bulldozed in the name of 'progress' but impressive structures honouring the martyrs of the war against the American invaders were built to dominate most large towns and cities the length and breadth of the nation. Quite remarkably, Australia has been permitted to establish a memorial at Long Tan to commemorate the battle fought there in 1966. The Vietnamese post-war literature almost always refers to a war against the Americans and hardly ever mentions the South Vietnamese. To the Vietnamese hierarchy, the war, known as the American War, was a struggle against imperialists. This matched the nationalistic French War label for the First Indochina War. The ready acceptance of the title American War is another example of a successful propaganda plan by the Northern Politburo. The North's Great Invasion may be closer to the truth, however; the West has accepted the American War prevarication as readily as most use PAVN for the invading North Vietnamese Army.

The aftermath

The communists were victorious but they also had a problem in that almost 20 million people in the South had not actively supported them and they would need to be controlled. In addition, the country was in dire straits; about 16 per cent of the entire population had been killed or wounded and a large number had been rendered homeless.

The newly declared Socialist Republic of Vietnam introduced a series of measures designed to maintain control of the country. The *Vietnam Courier*, an official government publication in the SRV, described Vietnam in December 1975 as being a country of two distinct, incongruent societies. The North was naturally viewed as a 'progressive environment ... imbued with patriotism, proletarian internationalism and socialist virtues'. On the other hand the South was suffering from 'the neo-colonialist influences and feudal ideology of the United States'.[39] The South was seen as fractured into various class groups, none of which were good for the country and would need strong measures to overcome. Those measures varied from repressive to extremely harsh and were most usually conducted with coercion and direct violation of the most basic of human rights, all of which was at odds with the Paris peace agreement of 1973 and the sentiments expressed by Prime Minister Pham Van Dong: 'How could we have the stupid, criminal idea of annexing the South', he told various foreigners. Le Duc Tho went one better: 'We have no wish to impose communism on the South', he declared to the international press at Paris.[40] Tho was the real power at the Paris peace talks and he was an active member of the Communist Party Central Committee. He was also a part of the planning team located in the South that directed the final campaign in 1975.[41]

In the event, the SRV had a multi-pronged assault plan to deal with the southerners and northern-based dissidents: summary justice that included execution, population relocation and 're-education'. To instil the system, specific groups of Vietnamese were required to register with the new regime. Thus began several decades of population control, which to the people often meant terror.

Subjugation of the dissidents

Human rights activist Jacqueline Desbarats has claimed that approximately 100,000 political executions took place in the SRV, mostly in the first two years after the fall of Saigon.[42] The Hanoi government explained the reasons for the summary executions to Amnesty International in a 1981 aide memoir.

Hanoi said that 'the laws of the Democratic Republic of Vietnam had been applicable to all citizens of South Vietnam from 1945 onward'. Ho Chi Minh initially espoused this decree in 1967 and the Provisional Revolutionary Government repromulgated the order in 1976 prior to 're-unification'.[43]

That probably meant whatever any person did in South Vietnam during the 'American' (Second Indochina) War could be considered to be traitorous and therefore deserved extreme punishment: execution. The SRV gave themselves carte blanche to remove the perceived threats to their control and maintenance of power, all in the name of 'national interests'. The re-issued decree listed the 'counter-revolutionary' crimes with a regime of punishments that ranged from execution to short-term (three years) imprisonment. The accused had no legal protection, and the tribunals set up for judgement had no legal experience.[44]

The people allegedly executed, according to a study conducted by Jacqueline Desbarats, were government officials of the former regime, province chiefs, district chiefs, mayors, police, senior military officers and anyone with any connection to the intelligence community.[45] Desbarats' study found that two-thirds of the executions took place in 1975 and 1976 and then tapered off. By far, the most widespread alleged reason for execution was acts of 'anti-government resistance', Desbarats found. The SRV records indicate that 49 per cent of the executions were for both armed and passive resistance, such as a refusal to register for re-education. The remaining 51 per cent of deaths were not explained.

Mr Phan Quang, the Vice-Minister of the Ministry of Information in the SRV, repudiated the claims that military officers and officials of the former Saigon puppet regime had been executed. In a statement made on 11 February 1988, he said:

> The Socialist Republic of Vietnam decided to set free or reduce prison term for detainees or convicts who have shown repentance and made progress during the course of their re-education on the occasion of the Tet of the Dragon Year. The number of beneficiaries of our humanitarian and lenient policy on this occasion is 9,174 in total. The so-called blood bath has never taken place. No one among those who had served in the puppet army or puppet administration has been executed. Over the past years [releases] have been gradually completed . . . the last was on National Day 1987 in which 480 people were granted amnesty.[46]

Re-education camps

Secret re-education camps were first used in North Vietnam in 1961, according to Hoang Son, a North Vietnamese spokesman, but the camps attracted world attention after the South surrendered in 1975. Detailed information on what happened and how many were sent off for 'educational reform, but not punishment' is difficult to ascertain and often contradictory. First, the number of people re-educated varies markedly from 'hundreds of thousands' to 'two and a half million'. What is clear, however, is that a structured system of punishment was enacted for those 'who collaborated with the other side during the war' and for people 'who have been arrested in the years since 1975 for attempting to exercise democratic freedoms mentioned in Article 11 of the 1973 Paris Agreements'.[47]

Amnesty International reported in 1978:

There were four categories of re-education camps in Vietnam: (a) detention centres in towns where the initial enquiries were held; (b) second category camps which held both criminal and political prisoners; (c) third category . . . prisoners held according to their alleged past offences and (d) camps for former senior officers and members of intelligence services who have been judged to be 'ac on' (wicked).[48]

The Library of US Congress *Country Study: Vietnam* (1987) corroborated that assessment:

The re-education camp system fell into three broad categories: short term re-education, long-term re-education and permanent incarceration. Short-term re-education was split into two types. One was a study camp where attendees were taught socialism and to unlearn their nasty old way and were allowed to return home at night. These 'day' camps lasted 30 days. These level one camps probably processed about half a million people and were the most common kind of camp. The second short term camp was one that required full time attendance for a period of three to six months, but where one had to bring their own food or go hungry. During the 1970s it was estimated that about 200,000 people were subjected to this type of re-education. The long-term camps were the level three centres and termed by the SRV as 'collective reformatory'. The processes inside the camps were now tougher, and decidedly more physical and psychological. The system considered those attending level three to be 'salvageable' but detainees would need a lot longer to be re-educated. The camps existed in every province of southern Vietnam in which about 50,000 inmates were processed. The third type of camp designed for permanent incarceration at level four involved forced labour and political indoctrination. The forced labour varied from building the indoctrination camps to tree felling, mine field sweeping, agriculture including jungle clearing and civic projects such as well drilling. Inmates were told that they would be required to undergo re-education that would last three years for level four and five years for level five. These camps were where those with senior rank or positions within society were treated and held until the SRV central government considered that the situation was stable enough to permit their release.[49]

Gary McKay's personal experiences with men who were incarcerated in level four and five re-education camps have confirmed to him that re-education was nothing short of brutal indoctrination and brainwashing. A refusal to accept communist ideology would result in floggings, beatings, and torture. Some men interviewed (but who wished to remain anonymous) have stated that because they were ARVN officers their re-education lasted between five and seven years. Lower ranking soldiers were usually released after two years. Recalcitrant subjects were initially sentenced to five years' incarceration and at the end of that period were re-sentenced, again summarily and with no recourse of appeal or trial. In 1987 at least 15,000 inmates were still held in level four and level five camps.[50] The number of deaths in the re-education camps from disease, malnutrition or torture was extremely high.

The imprisonment of former officers had many ramifications. One former officer who worked closely with Gary McKay related how he had been arrested immediately after the fall of Saigon and was sent to several different camps. He believed this was to prevent his family (wife, son and daughter) visiting him in order to punish his 'recalcitrance'. He was entitled to one 30-minute visit a month but he never saw his family. When he was released after seven years of re-education, he returned to Bien Hoa but was unable to locate his wife and children. All attempts at establishing what had happened to his family failed and he began a new life and to this day does still not know if his wife and children escaped the tyranny of the SRV, perished on the high seas or were 'disposed of'.[51]

Resettlement program

Another form of population control, which was also a form of political repression, was the forced relocation of people to rural areas that were called New Economic Zones (NEZ). This style of population control is not new and it is sometimes employed to avoid ethnic or religious strife among a nation's populace. However, in Vietnam there is evidence that the SRV population redistribution program involved extensive coercion.

There were three programs within this policy; the first was a southern de-urbanisation program designed to repatriate war refugees out of Saigon and back to their native places. Some observers believe that this was simply a method of ridding the former capital of South Vietnam of 'undesirable' elements. The second tier in this relocation policy was a North–South program, ensuring more pro-North people settled in the South to shore up the SRV regime. The third tier of the relocation program involved resettlement of the 1.5 million hill tribes of the Central Highlands: the Montagnards. This group relied on slash-and-burn agriculture and were shifting constantly to grow their crops and eke out a living. The Montagnards have had a long-running dispute with governments going back before the French over their oppression and desire for ethnic recognition and self-rule.

Above all else, the SRV wanted to avoid a civil uprising because there was no shortage of weapons in the country. The problem was that the NEZ areas were not conducive to new settlement: their location in the outer areas away from plentiful water sources made crop-growing difficult. The central government tried disincentives to prevent people staying in the major cities by introducing programs like food rationing through 'mouth registration'. The near-famine conditions that existed in 1977 after a catastrophic attempt at commune farming accompanied by nationwide drought brought all of that undone. As a final attempt to coerce people to move out of the cities, education was denied to those families who didn't relocate.[52]

The government issued the following public policy directive on who *must* take part in the building of the new economic areas:

1. Those who do not have a job and are in economic difficulty;
2. Those who, though employed, are in temporary difficulty and have no assurance for the future;
3. Families of government and army members having undergone or now undergoing re-education and who are in difficulty; and
4. Those who have production means and equipment.[53]

In other words, almost everyone the local authorities decided they needed to move. The final threat was that if one refused to relocate, it would be viewed as a counter-revolutionary crime (read active anti-government resistance), which was punishable by life imprisonment or death.[54]

By 1978 the government would simply confiscate the house and property of anyone refusing to move and expel them from the city. Official statements on the relocation indicated that about half a million people left Saigon in one year (1976) and of those some 80 per cent did so voluntarily. This would mean that approximately 100,000 people were coerced into leaving. In the Second Five Year Plan of the SRV (1976–1980) estimates are that 1.3 million people relocated to NEZs (but this figure includes many northerners who went to the South). Under the Third Five Year Plan (1981–85) a little less than one million people were relocated, but again they were virtually all northerners. The southerners were resisting the government's plan to relocate them—albeit passively—and eventually the SRV gave up on the policy.[55]

The Kampuchean war and economic pragmatism

A Vietnamese invasion of Kampuchea (Cambodia) in December 1978 further drained the resources of the nation. With approximately 200,000 troops deployed, the Vietnamese drove the murderous Khmer Rouge from Phnom Penh and established a surrogate government propped up by their occupation force that would remain for ten years. Although the invasion was a tale worthy of the Churchill quote 'a puzzle inside a riddle wrapped in an enigma', there is little doubt that Hanoi saw the Khmer Rouge as a Chinese-backed flanking of Vietnam. The Vietnamese held no moral compunction to take action against the Pol Pot regime's slaughter of Cambodians; they were age-old enemies. Their paranoia saw the Cambodians making a military grab at retaking the lands lost to Vietnam in the early part of the 19th century. Other nations in the region also became nervous when the Vietnamese push extended to the Thai border. International pressures plus the USSR's reduction in monetary and materiel support eventually forced them to withdraw.

Soviet leader Mikhail Gorbachev had unleashed new reforms within the USSR and although they strongly backed Vietnam as a counter-foil to China, Vietnam would now have to make its own way and undertake some serious economic changes. When Nguyen Van Linh succeeded Le Duan as head of State in 1986, he started a renovation program known as 'Doi Moi'. The plan was to move the country to a socialist oriented market economy that allowed for privately owned commodity production with an overarching, but more relaxed state control. Collective farming or 'agricultural cooperatives' that had proved to be disastrous were mostly dismantled. A quasi-form of capitalism was their saving grace, but it was more successful in the South and much of the country still struggled with inflation, rural famine and rising urban unemployment. All of this led to a surge of boat people in 1989–90, mainly to Hong Kong; however, large numbers of refugees (principally ethnic Chinese) were forcibly repatriated to mainland China.

Economic reform continued under party leader Mr Do Muoi, Nguyen Van Linh's 1991 replacement as general secretary. Prime Minister Vo Van Kiet—a southerner—and President Le Duc Anh—also a southerner—also continued the economic reforms. Vietnam had turned to a hybrid economy with strong communist political overtones, but it functioned more as a capitalist society with the normal freedoms associated with that type of market economy. Bureaucracy ruled, sometimes overpoweringly; however, economic growth was strong between 1990 and 1997 and reached an enviable 8 per cent.

In 2006 Nguyen Minh Triet was elected president and Nguyen Tan Dung was elected prime minister; they were both southerners.

The Australian aftermath

The Australian experience in South Vietnam divided the nation more than any other conflict. What some considered in 1962 to be an expedition to support democracy against communism became a drawn-out war that seemed to have no end. Was it really, as the dissidents were saying, a civil war and one in which Australia should not be involved? The war arguments percolated throughout the country and they generally centred on conscription, Australian casualties and Vietnamese nationalism. Nevertheless, the leaders of western democracies during the 1950s held a sincere belief that because of Vietnam's geographic location its loss to a communist-inspired expansion would damage the stability of Southeast Asia. That instability would then have a detrimental influence over economic development and the recovery of other nations after World War II. In strategic terms, Australia would suffer through its isolation. The recommendations arising from these strategic analyses continued into the 1960s, as discussed in the main part of this book.

The conclusion that the falling domino theory—a euphemism for the subjugation of Southeast Asia by a communist bloc—was false appears to be explained by a judgement that it didn't happen, therefore it was never feasible. This conclusion assumed a military confrontation only and not coercion through military posturing combined with an ideological invasion. There were always two strands to the strategic planning issues that affected Vietnam. The strand that grabbed the headlines and created fear was the threat of a war in which the communist bloc—later fractured—smashed its way south. Another strand, less overt and possibly more disturbing for western leaders, was the threat posed by any socialist–communist hindrance to post-World War II rebuilding. Restrictions on economic development, access to raw materials and emerging markets had worldwide implications. That perceived threat underpinned the philosophy of engagement and protection, which carried a strong influence among the democratic–capitalist decision-makers. US president Truman drew the first communist containment line during the Greek Civil War (1946–49), a theme reiterated in later years by presidents Eisenhower, Kennedy and Johnson. We know that China, who held sway over Vietnam during the mid-1950s, did have a falling domino plan. That is evident in the exchange of telegrams between Mao Zedong and Zhou Enlai at Liuzhou, southern China, on 7 July 1954:

The Indochina issue was different from the Korean issue in that Indochina could affect all Southeast Asia (including Burma, Thailand, Malaya, Indonesia, the Philippines), Pakistan, India, Australia, New Zealand and Ceylon. 'If we are not

careful, we will affect 600 million people in ten countries. We should make necessary concessions. In this way, we can isolate the minority (the United States), win
over the majority' and reach a final agreement.[56]

Another conversation that also involved Zhou Enlai took place much
later, in March 1971. Le Duan, the North Vietnamese leader, told the Chinese
Foreign Minister that weapons being provided to the Thai Communist Party
were shipped through Vietnam and Laos. 'It [Thailand] also knows that
China has a road that runs to the Sino-Lao border. Therefore, it faces the
threat of the war expanding all over Southeast Asia.' Le Duan added: 'We want
to smash the US–Japan alliance as well as the alliance between the US, Japan,
and the regional Bourgeois class'.[57]

The Soviet Union also expressed a broader strategy to follow a victory in
Vietnam. Soviet diplomats at Hanoi believed in 1971, 'when the DRV [Demo-
cratic Republic of Vietnam] has become the leading force in the struggle of
the peoples of Indochina, we will possess comparatively more possibilities for
establishing our policy in this region. It is not excluded that Indochina may
become for us a key to all Southeast Asia'.[58]

Furthermore, in 1979, the Ministry of Foreign Affairs, Socialist Republic
of Vietnam, released this statement about a Chinese Communist Central
Committee meeting in August 1965:

> We must by all means seize South-East Asia including South Viet Nam, Thailand,
> Burma, Malaysia and Singapore . . . This region is rich in raw materials it is worth
> the costs involved. After seizing South-East Asia, we can increase our strength in
> this region. And we shall be strong enough to confront the Soviet-East European
> bloc; the East wind will prevail over the West wind.[59]

A more subtle result was that under the darkness of defeat, America's
global credibility was damaged and the country also lost its political will to
challenge Soviet revolutionary missions into the Third World: in a broad
sense, falling dominoes on a different board. The previously strategically
important South Vietnam was now a discarded Cold War battleground, and
Australia could do no more than slink away in the shadows.

Regardless of the international strategic climate, when the men who had served their tour of duty returned home it was often into an atmosphere of either apathy or disdain. Some veterans deliberately avoided mentioning that they had been in South Vietnam on return to Australia. Even the military hierarchy sensed the public mood and service personnel working in the national capital were told to avoid wearing uniform on public transport. It was no wonder the veterans felt as if their blood, sweat and tears had been in vain.

The nation's political division—with the Australian Labor Party vehemently opposed to Australian involvement in the war—led to feelings of betrayal and suspicion of politicians, especially those to the left of the political spectrum. Gary McKay recalls his feelings of anger and betrayal in hospital in Australia recovering from war wounds in 1972 when he watched television footage of Bob Hawke, then the leader of the Australian Council of Trade Unions, escort a North Vietnamese Trade Union delegation up the steps of the Sydney Town Hall. Even the bastion of returned soldiers, the Returned and Services League of Australia (RSL), let down the veterans through the attitude of some clubs that spurned the returned veterans. Thankfully, such cases were isolated but they should never have arisen at all. Some Vietnam veterans found that it was better to keep quiet about their recent war service to avoid possible verbal and physical confrontation with opponents of the war.

Following a battle against perceived indifference by the government to health problems and disagreements with the RSL that the League was not proactive in its aid to Vietnam veterans, the veterans turned to each other and formed organisations like the Vietnam Veterans' Association in 1979, and the Vietnam Veterans' Federation in 1981. These bodies carried the fight to government departments such as the Department of Veterans Affairs regarding the special circumstances under which Australia's soldiers, sailors, and airmen had fought. Years later, further concerns on the RSL's attitude towards Vietnamese matters were raised in October 2011 when the national president of the RSL attempted to sign a Memorandum of Understanding with his counterpart in Hanoi. He did this without proper consultation with the membership of the RSL. The reaction was intense and the issue was cancelled.

There was no post-war counselling in the late 1960s and early 1970s. National servicemen were discharged within weeks of returning to Australia and sent back home into a climate that was far from conducive to resettlement and repatriation. Suicides among the Vietnam War veteran population were alleged to be higher than the remainder of the male population. In the United States, studies showed that once a veteran got past the first five years after returning home his likelihood of suicide was lessened. In a report to the American Congress it was noted that:

> The US CDC (Centers for Disease Control and Prevention) Vietnam Experience Study Mortality Assessment showed that during the first 5 years after discharge, deaths from suicide were 1.7 times more likely among Vietnam veterans than non-Vietnam veterans. After that initial post-service period, Vietnam veterans were no more likely to die from suicide than non-Vietnam veterans. In fact, after the 5-year post-service period, the rate of suicides is less in the Vietnam veterans' group.[60]

The Australian Centre for Posttraumatic Mental Health (ACPMH), however, found that 'contrary to much previous research, a large prospective US study found that veterans were in fact twice as likely as civilians to die from suicide' (although, interestingly, they were no more likely to die of other causes).[61] In Australia the rate of suicide was found not to be greater, but this was from a study of national servicemen and did not include regular soldiers.[62]

If any good could be said to have come out of the poor post-war treatment of Vietnam veterans it is that there is now a better understanding of the hidden impacts of combat. Today's warriors in Iraq and Afghanistan have a better chance of recovering from the stressors of conflict. Nevertheless, the rate of suicide among the children of Australian veterans is worthy of mention. In a media release on 7 August 2000, Bruce Scott, the Minister for Veterans' Affairs, confirmed that children of Vietnam veterans have three times the suicide rate of the general community.[63] The reasons for this remain unsolved; however, the suicides are part of a detailed and long-running analysis by the Department of Veterans' Affairs Family Study Program that is yet to report at the time of this book's production.

Agent Orange and other chemicals

One of the more contentious issues of the Vietnam War was the use of herbicides and pesticides. Defoliants were used for killing off jungle foliage that might provide cover for an enemy camp, and around allied camp perimeters to open up defensive fields of view. Enemy crops or crops in remote areas were also sprayed. It is estimated that the US military sprayed more than 76,000,000 litres of herbicides over Vietnam in the air force operations known as Ranch Hand and Trail Dust.[64]

Australian troops were also involved in the use of herbicides and insecticides, the latter being widely sprayed in Phuoc Tuy Province, particularly around Nui Dat. Spraying programs tended to concentrate on areas where it was considered likely that enemy troops might congregate or move through the thick vegetation while attempting to avoid aerial reconnaissance. The most heavily used of these herbicides was Agent Orange, contaminated with 2,3,7,8-tetrachlorodibenzo-p-dioxin, a known toxic agent. Other chemicals used widely in Vietnam included herbicides (Paraquat and dimethyl-arsenic acid), pesticides (picloram and DDT), antimalarial drugs (dapsone) and solvents (toluene).

The debate over the use of chemicals and their effect on servicemen in South Vietnam has been longstanding and acrimonious. Comprehensive studies have been completed in both the United States and by the Department of Veterans' Affairs in Australia. It is a complex subject and one that goes beyond exposure to chemicals, as the conclusions to an Australian study completed in 2005 explained:

> This study provides good evidence that Australian male veterans of the Vietnam War have an increased rate of cancer overall. There was an excess of 613 cancers; 88% of this excess consisted of lung cancers, oral cavity, pharynx and larynx cancers, prostate cancers and melanomas. Rates of melanoma, and to a lesser degree prostate cancer, were consistently elevated across Navy, Army and Air Force veterans, although patterns of other cancers were not consistent across the three groups. The reasons for these increases are unclear. In addition to exposure to known carcinogens, lifestyle changes, including alcohol and tobacco consumption may play a role. For several other malignancies, this study provides evidence suggesting that Australian Vietnam veterans may have rates lower than the rate in the Australian population.[65]

Another difficulty was identified by a House Oversight Committee in the US Congress, which noted, 'it is impossible to determine from records which Vietnam veterans were exposed to the toxic chemical [Agent Orange]'.[66]

A further expression of the 'horrors endured by soldiers in the Vietnam War' is found in Eric Dean's analysis, *Shook Over Hell*. One of his central premises is that for the last 30 years Vietnam veterans have been portrayed by the media, politicians, and a cottage industry of mental health professionals as tragic actors in a flawed opera who have experienced Post-Traumatic Stress Disorder, unlike those of veterans of other American wars.[67]

Dean asserts that PTSD amongst Vietnam veterans was low (12 per 1000) when compared against Korea (37 per 1000) with the World War II figures being higher again. Although PTSD was a new name, 'neuropsychiatric impairment', previously known as 'shell shock', could be traced back to the American Civil War.[68] Vietnam veterans have not cornered the market on battlefield-related PTSD. To the contrary, Dean provides irrefutable evidence that the Vietnam veteran has been perhaps the most adaptive of all veterans and has fared better in all respects than veterans of other wars.[69]

Welcome home

In 1987 a 'Welcome Home Parade' was held in Sydney to recognise the service in Vietnam of those men and women who never had a homecoming parade. It was almost as if the nation sensed the guilt of the treatment of its Vietnam veterans. Many veterans who had not attended Anzac Day services or unit reunions found their long-lost mates and began the slow process of rehabilitation. However, it is a common misperception that soldiers returning from the war were not welcomed home. In fact there were fifteen battalion-contingent parades through Adelaide, Sydney, Brisbane and Townsville between June 1966 and December 1972. Nevertheless there were many who missed out. In 1970, HMAS *Sydney* was in dry dock and 6RAR came home in piecemeal contingents by air. Those soldiers who served in smaller units and 'trickled' across to South Vietnam did not receive a welcome home. For those who came home by air, it was deplane, and then demob or dismiss.

The parade in Sydney on 3 October 1987 was the precursor to another Welcome Home parade and unveiling of the Australian Vietnam Forces National Memorial in Canberra on 3 October 1992. The Long Tan battle that was commemorated by some veterans on 18 August became a politically anointed national Vietnam Veterans Day to record the nation's apology and to acknowledge that the veterans deserved greater recognition.

The economy of Vietnam

The country of Vietnam was devastated by the war. As well as the huge death toll and the ongoing trauma of the wounded and homeless, many of the hamlets and villages throughout the land had suffered war damage or were in a state of disrepair. The nation was now a net importer of rice where once rice had been one of its most valuable exports. Failed attempts at agricultural reform through communes and poorly executed socialist programs in the initial Five Year Plan instituted by the SRV put the country in a precarious situation. In 1978 Vietnam joined the Soviet-controlled Council for Mutual Economic Assistance (COMECOM) and began to obtain investment benefits, especially from the Soviets, who had a strategic interest in Vietnam's US-built naval and air bases. The former Australian rest centre at Vung Tau served as a barracks for Soviet personnel during this period. The good times didn't last, however. The Soviet power within the Council was too great and there were doubtful economic benefits to a widely divergent membership. In the late 1980s with the political changes in Europe and the 1998 approval for individual COMECOM countries to negotiate their own trade treaties, the money flow to Vietnam began to dry up. An American trade embargo and other boycotts by various nations protesting at Vietnam's stance and policy on refugees and asylum-seekers had made conditions even worse. In 1978 the SRV was paying dearly for invading Kampuchea. Nature also stepped in to wreak her vengeance with floods in the central coastal region in 1978 submerging over 1 million hectares (2.5 million acres) and killing over 20 per cent of the nation's cattle.

More money was spent on military operations when China attacked northern Vietnam in a 29-day clash during February and March 1979. In China's eyes, Hanoi had become too close to the Soviet Union. That, and the expulsion of ethnic Chinese from Vietnam, and the perceived Vietnamese dreams of controlling Southeast Asia were cause for China to teach them a lesson. Some analysts considered, however, that the real intent was to test the Soviet Union's military allegiance with Vietnam. Although the Soviet Union contributed an immense quantity of defence support to North Vietnam between 1964 and 1974, including some advisers who fought in South Vietnam, they did nothing to thwart the Chinese attack.[70] This strengthened Chinese confidence in their belief that the Soviet 'friendship' amounted to little and they need not concern themselves with their northern border if the Chinese continued to needle the Vietnamese.

In Hanoi's eyes, almost the reverse was true. The Vietnamese feared encirclement on their western flank by the hated Chinese surrogate and heavily supported Khmer Rouge army. They were reminded of China's expressed 1965 desire to capture Southeast Asia, including South Vietnam. Some of the elder Hanoi leaders from the Viet Minh era never forgave China for pressuring them to give up the territorial advantage they had gained before the 1954 Geneva Accords, when the DRV leaders were *advised by the Chinese* to sign off on a demilitarised zone, in effect a quasi-border, at the 17th parallel when they really controlled much more of the country below that line.

Heavy Vietnamese resistance to the 1979 Chinese attack and an unsatisfactory Chinese logistics system stalled the Chinese incursion, which had advanced— without air power—about 8 kilometres into Vietnam. Although the Chinese eventually got to Lang Son at the intersection of Routes 4 and 1A approximately 15 kilometres south of the border, the attack had run out of steam. China declared that a lesson had been taught, and withdrew; however, they moved about 28 divisions to the border while Vietnam responded with a deployment of 32 (light scale) divisions. This was a cost that the country could ill afford, even with Soviet backing. Interestingly, a 2011 biography by Ezra F. Vogel on Deng Xiaoping claims that 'the US provided tacit support for the China attack'.[71]

Following the Doi Moi reforms, industrial output grew along with the expansion into other trade markets and the economy began to flourish. By 2010 exports totalled US$71.6 billion through such principal products as crude oil, garments, seafood, rice, pepper, coffee and rubber. But the SRV, along with many other countries, is not without economic challenges. The nation's GDP had been in a steady climb and strong in the Asian region with a growth of between 6 and 8 per cent (1990–1997), which dropped down to 6.5 per cent (1998–2003) before climbing back to 8 per cent during 2004– 2007. The global financial crisis saw that growth stripped back to 5.3 per cent in 2009 and then recover to 6.78 per cent in 2010.

Although average per capita yearly income has improved from US$220 during 1994 to US$1168 in 2010, inflation increased to 11.75 per cent in the same year. In October 2011, international exchange rates against the Vietnamese dong were heading towards the unmanageable range at 22,500 to one Australian dollar. Unemployment remains low at 2.88 per cent (approximately 2,600,000), but it is on the rise with urban unemployment registered at 4.43 per cent versus rural figures of 2.27 per cent. Another factor in Vietnam's economic stability is its dramatic population growth: the population has more than doubled in 35 years to 90 million in 2011.[72] *The Global Competitiveness Report 2011–2012* rated Vietnam's competitiveness strengths as a fairly efficient labour market and innovation potential; however, future challenges include a strained infrastructure and frequent and pervasive corruption.[73]

Tourism is one sector that has expanded, from yearly arrival figures of 300,000 in 1991 to over 1.3 million by 1995. The country has vastly improved the quality of tourist accommodation and transportation, and raised the standards of service across the entire spectrum in the hospitality industry. There were some setbacks caused by the 1998 Asian economic crisis and the SARS outbreak in 2003. Nevertheless, the industry bounced back with some assistance from the Southeast Asian Games held in Hanoi during December 2003. The number of visitors to Vietnam increased markedly between 1999 and 2004 when 2.9 million tourists travelled through the country. This was an increase in annual visitors of 63 per cent over five years. According to one tourism study, 'Most of the visitors in 2004—27 per cent [783,000]—came from China, with 8–9 per cent [232,000] from the United States, Japan, and South Korea'. Tourism is encouraged because it brings much-needed foreign exchange into the country and by 2002 the industry contributed 5.8 per cent to Vietnam's GDP.[74]

Once were enemies

Australia has played a large part in helping Vietnam regain its feet after the crippling effects of a very costly war. The Gillard government has signed agreements with Vietnam and following a meeting on 7 September 2009, the Australian Department of Foreign Affairs and Trade announced that:

> Encouraged by Viet Nam's ambition to become an industrialised country by 2020, Australia and Viet Nam resolve to deepen and expand cooperation on public policy

planning and development through a range of activities including information exchanges, exchanges of personnel, training and human resource development.[75]

The My Thuan Bridge in the Mekong Delta is an excellent example of Australia's assistance to Vietnam. Not only is the bridge a magnificent structure, it has cleared a major bottleneck to development of trade and tourism into the Mekong Delta. A clean water project to supply water to five major provincial towns was completed in 2005. The Australian government in partnership with the Government of Vietnam funded the program, in which Australian companies were awarded contracts worth $30 million. Australia has also assisted Vietnam in a program to eliminate dengue fever, which had killed 1000 people a year in Vietnam over the past 25 years. An $80 million water and sanitation project funded by AusAID and the Vietnamese government in the lower Mekong Delta brought clean water to more than 280,000 people in the southern provincial towns of Ha Tien, Sa Dec and Bac Lieu. Australian Army advisers had been active in these villages during the war. Education assistance is another cooperative project that is growing rapidly. The Royal Melbourne Institute of Technology opened RMIT University Vietnam in 2000 as the first and as-yet only 100 per cent foreign-owned university in Vietnam. It operates campuses in Hanoi and Saigon South.

The Australian Department of Foreign Affairs and Trade Country Brief stated on its website in August 2011:

Australia's total overseas development assistance to Vietnam in 2010–11 is expected to reach $119.8 million, making Vietnam Australia's sixth largest development assistance partner. Among 40 donor countries and agencies in Vietnam, Australia consistently ranks among the top ten bilateral donors. During her visit to Vietnam in October 2010, Prime Minister Gillard announced that Australia would be making an additional $148 million contribution towards the construction of the Cao Lanh bridge [across the Mekong River].[76]

Wars and consequences

At what point do we consider a review of the validity of the war and its cost in lives and dollars? Looking back upon that period, many people today would question the sanity of the leaders from both Vietnams and their allies and ask: how could they not have seen how the region would grow in peace? Their answers to the questions on the cost of war would probably be that it was not worth one death or one cent.

Few analyse the dark days of post–World War II and the conclusions drawn by eminent generals and renowned politicians about communist-inspired dangers. A Southeast Asia dominated by communism would be to the detriment of the region's peoples and the opportunity to build and prosper following the war, they said frequently. It was not complete altruism of course; raw materials, trade and emerging markets for the developed nations meant increased prosperity for them, too.

To cost the war in dollars and cents would be to quote unimaginable numbers, if the real expenditures could ever be assembled.[77] The impossible figures can be imagined in terms of the expenditure on manpower, munitions, aircraft, ships, armoured vehicles and the other accoutrements of war. Fairly accurate figures can be promulgated on the numbers of allied troops that were killed, wounded or went missing in action. Losses for the former NVA and Viet Cong are not so apparent—they will not tell—but they were extremely heavy. The numbers of civilians killed or who suffered debilitating injuries in both the North and the South are emotionally overwhelming.

In addition, the war extended beyond the borders of Vietnam into the contiguous territories of Laos and Cambodia. Laos is said to be the most heavily bombed nation per-capita ever. The legacies of warfare in those countries remain evident to this day, an often deadly environment caused by the illegal movement of troops and supplies by the NVA in an effort to obtain sanctuary against American air power. North Vietnamese tactical use of this territory eventually attracted powerful retaliation by both America and South Vietnam. Unfortunately the Democratic Republic of Vietnam disobeyed UN Treaty number 6564, dated 23 July 1962, signed by fourteen countries and supposedly guaranteeing the neutrality of Laos. Although America and South Vietnam were not blameless, the North Vietnamese instigated this undeclared war.

Beyond the combat zone, the costs to the societies of the countries who bore the brunt of providing combat forces are probably immeasurable. Expenditures in terms of social upheaval, family breakdowns, cancelled government programs and health and repatriation issues to name a few examples, would be incalculable. Incongruously, other areas of nations grew with war. Tonnes of bombs were manufactured; thousands of aircraft were replaced; food and equipment was needed; huge construction projects were needed to build ports, airports and barracks in South Vietnam. The prosperity from such industry also fed into other Southeast Asian economies.

People are perplexed, however. Constant—almost plaintive—questions continue to be asked about the Vietnam War and its causes. Some of the answers can be found in an examination of the period 1975–1986, which provided cogent examples of the dangers that the western leaders feared most about a communist-controlled region. That Vietnam evolved economically is testament to the failure of communism—after the Vietnam War—and a growing realism that the nation's survival depended upon an improved market economy and better relations with the capitalist West: the Vietnamese Doi Moi program. The great tragedy is that it took many years of warfare to reach that point.

Australia was willing to pay the price of the war for the improved strategic security it obtained through the deployment of American military forces into the Pacific Theatre of operations. Not only did they provide a Southeast Asian shield, but they also defused any perceived potential threat to Australia from Indonesia. Tunku Abdul Rahman, the Malaysian prime minister, also saw winning in Vietnam as a screen against communism for his country when he told renowned counterinsurgency expert Sir Robert Thompson that 'you must go to Vietnam and help hold my front line'.[78]

Furthermore, the war provided a bulwark that allowed the peoples of the nearby Southeast Asia dominoes to prosper and to develop into mini economic powerhouses. Singapore's Lee Kuan Yew believed that it had been his country's saving grace when he said in 1998:

> In 1965, when the US military moved massively into South Vietnam, Thailand, Malaysia and the Philippines faced internal threats from armed communist insurgents and the communist underground was still active in Singapore. Standards of living were low and economic growth slow. America's action enabled non-communist Southeast Asia to put their houses in order. By 1975 (when the Vietnam war ended) they were in better shape to stand up to the communists. Had there been no US intervention, the will of these countries to resist them would have melted and Southeast Asia would have most likely gone communist.[79]

The changes to Southeast Asia's fortunes were manifold. First, the communist military powers were overly occupied with their support for North Vietnam and that provided at least a veneer of security for the region. Following the end of the war and after the nervous Kampuchean invasion period, the fundamentals of the Marxist–Leninist state systems began to unravel in the mid-1980s. Deng Xiaoping also changed China in the 1980s. Doi Moi followed in Vietnam and some say it is a mirror of China's transformation. The changes stunned the international community. The old communist regimes appeared to be moving towards more liberal economic programs and less restrictive but not completely free political and social systems. Support for armed confrontation was exhausted, for the time being. Although the Vietnam War attracted more than its fair share of criticism as a ruinous and unnecessary conflict, Lee Kuan Yew's assessment affirmed Australia's own strategic studies, dating from 1953, on Vietnam's importance.[80]

However, to scroll forward to 2011, a new terminology has emerged, known as the 'billiard table'. The billiard table is the geographic space out of which China will knock all of the balls (other interests) to gain complete control of the area's resources. The table is Southeast Asia and the South China Sea. The assessment seems very close to a return to the 'discredited' Domino Theory, which cautioned about loss of the natural resources and potential markets that would drive post–World War II construction and regional development. It might even be seen as a carbon copy of the strategic theory underpinning Australia's willingness to fight in a land that was to become a deadly domino.[81]

ACKNOWLEDGEMENTS

Former publisher Ian Bowring and Gary McKay discussed the concept for this book many years ago. Ian retired after establishing a framework for the manuscript that he passed to Foong Ling Kong. However, the challenges of a difficult research regime struggled over the years to a point where it was almost an archive too far. Comprehensive reviews of files and publications required the help of friends and professionals that included Gus Pauza who assisted with files in Canberra. In America, Amy Mondt and Sheon Montgomery, two polite and professional assistant-archivists at the Texas Tech University, Vietnam Center and Archive were very helpful. Veterans of Vietnam, in Australia, America and Vietnam assisted enormously, especially Ernie Chamberlain who provided incalculable assistance as a translator. In Vietnam, Xuan Thu, a 33 Regiment veteran, supplied detailed information on that regiment's wartime activities. Ms Tran Thi Tuyet Thu (no relation) also added valuable guidance on obtaining Vietnamese books on wars over the ages. A special thank you goes to the Vietnam Veterans' Museum (Phillip Island) for access to many of its records and photographs. Without the support of Foong Ling Kong, along with Angela Handley and her team of editors, the book would not be on the shelf. Nevertheless, Bruce Davies as the principal researcher and author holds the final responsibility for the content.

GLOSSARY OF TERMS AND ACRONYMS

———

2IC	Second-in-command
III MAF	III Marine Amphibious Force
AAAGV	Australian Army Assistance Group Vietnam
AAFV	Australian Army Force Vietnam
AATTV	Australian Army Training Team Vietnam
ACR	(US) Armored cavalry regiment
ACTIV	US Army Concept Team in Vietnam. Established to test tactics, techniques and materiel
AFV	Australian Force Vietnam
AHQ	Army Headquarters, Canberra
Air America	An airline wholly owned by the CIA that supported its diverse and widespread operations throughout Vietnam, Laos and Cambodia
AK	VC/NVA automatic assault rifle, e.g. AK-47, AK-54. Manufactured in Communist Bloc countries
ALSG	Australian Logistical Support Group
Americal	US 23rd Infantry Division, associated with My Lai massacre
ANZAC	Australian and New Zealand Army Corps, a combined Australia–New Zealand unit
ANZUS	Australia, New Zealand and United States of America security treaty
AO	Area of operation
APC	Armoured personnel carrier, the M113, a 10-tonne, tracked vehicle
Arc Light	B-52 operations
ARU	Australian Reinforcement Unit
ARV	Armoured recovery vehicle
ARVN	Army of the Republic of Vietnam, the South Vietnamese Regular Army
ASIS	Australian Secret Intelligence Service

ATF	Australian Task Force, located at Nui Dat
Attack by Fire	Enemy mortar, recoilless rifle and RPG attacks, used to describe indirect fire from the enemy
AWM	Australian War Memorial
B-40	Also known as the RPG-2, a rocket-propelled grenade. The RPG-7 (B-41) was more powerful with longer range and a larger explosive head
B-52	US strategic 8-engine jet bomber
B-57	US light jet bomber, RAAF Canberra equivalent, built under licence from UK
BOQ	Bachelor Officer Quarters, US forces
British Advisory Mission in Vietnam	A small counterinsurgency advisory team headed by Sir Robert Thompson
Browning Automatic Rifle	A .30 calibre, 20-round, magazine-fed, light machine gun
C-130 Hercules	A four-engine combat transport aircraft capable of using unprepared airstrips. Used in a variety of roles from carrying troops, paratrooper drop, cargo and as a gunship
CAB	The Covert Action Branch was a section of the CIA's Combined Studies Division. A small number of the AATTV served in these activities
Canberra Bomber	A light twin jet-engine bomber that carried a bomb load of 3628 kg. Flown by the RAAF in Vietnam as well as by the USAF, see B-57
CAP	Combined action platoon, a mix of allied and South Vietnamese soldiers particularly the USMC and Vietnamese in I Corps
Caribou Aircraft	A short-range, twin-engine, tactical transport aircraft. Flown by the RAAF, also by the US Army; later transferred to the USAF
CGS	Chief of the General Staff, Australia
Charlie	Viet Cong, taken from the phonetic-sounding 'VC', or 'Victor Charlie'
ChiCom	Chinese Communist
Chieu Hoi	Enemy soldiers who defected
ChiNat	Chinese Nationalist force, Taiwan
Chinook	US Army (CH-47), twin-rotor, heavy-lift helicopter
CIA	The American Central Intelligence Agency. A small number of AATTV operated with the CIA
CIDG	Civilian Irregular Defense Group, a project started in 1961 through the recruitment of Rhade Montagnards. Trained and operated under American Special Forces teams that included Australians. See Mike Force
CINCPAC	Commander in Chief Pacific, a four-star appointment who commanded the Pacific Theatre that included Vietnam. Based in Hawaii
Civil Affairs or Civic Action	Projects to assist the local populace and gain their support to lessen the terror and influence of the Viet Cong/NVA. Initially minor in scope but developed in scale with the arrival of the Civil Affairs Unit. An adjunct to pacification
Civil Guard	A South Vietnamese military force, generally restricted to provincial operations. Later known as the 'Regional Force'

Claymore	Anti-personnel mine
CMF	Citizen Military Forces, militia
CO	Commanding Officer, usually a lieutenant colonel in rank. ARVN battalions generally commanded by a major or captain
Cobra	AH-1, attack helicopter armed with cannon, machine gun and rockets
Cochin China	The southern half of South Vietnam that was a French colony pre-1954. Tonkin and Annam (northern and central regions) were protectorates of France
COMAFV	Commander Australian Force Vietnam, Saigon
Combined Document Exploitation Center	An intelligence centre that examined captured enemy documents
COMUSMACV	Commander United States Military Assistance Command Vietnam. The senior American (four-star) general in South Vietnam
Contact	To engage in a battle with the enemy
CORDS	Civil Operations and Revolutionary Development Support, the organisation that coordinated all civil and military pacification effort under MACV
COSVN	Central Office of South Vietnam, main enemy headquarters for South Vietnam. It was located in the western region of Tay Ninh Province and eastern Cambodia. Arguments persist over its size, but claims that it was a small and lightly manned headquarters are questionable. It received its directives from Hanoi
Crew-served weapon	A weapon requiring more than one person to operate and fire, e.g. mortars and heavy machine guns
CSD	Combined Studies Division, a paramilitary organisation. A department of the CIA located in Saigon
CTZ	Corps Tactical Zone. South Vietnam was divided into zones I–IV from the DMZ to the Mekong Delta, later known as Military Regions (MRs). The zones were commonly called 'corps', e.g. I Corps. A Vietnamese general commanded each corps zone and was responsible for military as well as political control of the allocated geographic region
DCGS	Deputy Chief of the General Staff, Australia
DCM	Distinguished Conduct Medal, a gallantry award second only to the Victoria Cross. Awarded to non-commissioned ranks
DFC	Distinguished Flying Cross, a decoration awarded for valour, courage or devotion to duty while flying in active operations
DFM	Distinguished Flying Medal, as for the DFC but awarded to non-commissioned ranks
District	A subdivision of a province
DMZ	Demilitarized Zone, a 10-kilometre buffer zone around the 17th parallel (5 kilometres either side)
Domino Theory	A strategic plan based on the concept that the fall of one country would create instability in a region to the point that other countries would also topple (like dominoes) to communist pressures
DRV	Democratic Republic of Vietnam (North Vietnam)

DSO	Distinguished Service Order, a distinguished service award for officers, initially intended for actual combat. Awards to ranks below lieutenant colonel were for a high degree of gallantry just below a Victoria Cross
Dustoff	Helicopter casualty evacuation, medevac. Taken from a call sign used by ambulance helicopters early in the war and retained throughout the conflict
FAC	Forward air control, generally airborne, strike aircraft controller
FANK	Forces Armées Nationales Khmer, Cambodia's Army
FARELF	Far East Land Forces, a UK command that included Australians. Based in Singapore
FFV	Field Force Vietnam, a corps-size US headquarters that commanded US operations. IFFV controlled operations in II CTZ and IIFFV was responsible for III CTZ, which included the Australian Task Force under its operational control. Commands named 'FFV' so as not to be confused with the ARVN Corps Tactical Zones
FGA	Fighter Ground Attack, tactical strike aircraft
Free Fire Zone	An area into which weapons could be fired without prior approval
FRUS	*Foreign Relations of the United States*
FSB	Fire support base, a base that included artillery or mortars to support patrolling forces. Fire Support Patrol Base also used generally to indicate a temporary base
FWMAF	Free World Military Assistance Forces. Forces from those countries that provided military units to support South Vietnam
Geneva Agreement	An armistice agreed at Geneva on 20 July 1954 to cease hostilities between the Viet Minh and the French Union Forces. Only the military commanders of the French forces and the PAVN (Viet Minh) signed the document. No country signed the Agreement. Also called Geneva Accords
Guerrilla Warfare	Mao Tse Tung divided guerrilla warfare into three phases. Phase 1 planned to gain the support of the population through propaganda. Phase 2 included increasing (hit-and-run) military attacks that were to culminate in conventional fighting (Phase 3) that would seize and hold territory
Gunship	A helicopter, normally an Iroquois, mounted with rockets and machine guns. Aerial Rocket Artillery is also included in the generic term 'gunship'. See Cobra. Fixed-wing gunships also used, see Spooky
H&I	Harassment and Interdiction, e.g. artillery fired on to a suspected enemy area of movement and/or camp. Most H&I was unobserved
HMAS	Her Majesty's Australian Ship, Royal Australian Navy
Ho Chi Minh Trail	A series of trails from North Vietnam through Laos and Cambodia into South Vietnam. Initially, they were no more than foot tracks that eventually developed into roads with linked fuel pipelines. First used in the war against the French and resurrected in May 1959 (Unit 559). The Trail at Sea was also established in 1959 under the guise 'Gianh River Fishing Group'

Hoi Chanh	Former enemy soldiers who had defected and then worked with the allies
HQ	Headquarters
HQAFV	Headquarters Australian Force Vietnam, Saigon
Huey	Iroquois helicopter, its first nomenclature was HU-1 (helicopter utility), later UH-1
In country	To be within South Vietnam; 'up country' was to be in the northern provinces of the South
INTREP	Intelligence report
INTSUM	Intelligence summary
JCS	Joint Chiefs of Staff, USA
JPC	Joint Planning Committee
JTC	Jungle Training Centre, Canungra, Qld
JWTC	Jungle Warfare Training Centre located at Nui Dat then Van Kiep in Phuoc Tuy, South Vietnam
KBA	Killed by Air (aircraft)
KIA	Killed in action
LAW	Light Anti-Armour Weapon
LIB	Light Infantry Brigade
Light Fire Team	Two helicopter gunships, Heavy Fire Team three helicopters. Although USAF considered all helicopters to be 'light fire teams'
LLDB	Vietnamese (ARVN) Special Forces, Luoc Long Dac Biet
LOH	Light observation helicopter, a Sioux or Bell OH-58 Kiowa or Hughes OH-6 Cayuse
LRRP	Long Range Reconnaissance Patrol, sometimes shown as LRP
LZ	Landing zone, an area in which a helicopter could land
M-48	US medium tank (Patton)
M-50A1	Ontos, tracked chassis that mounted six 106 mm recoilless rifles
MAAG	US Military Assistance and Advisory Group, absorbed by MACV May 1964
MACV	US Military Assistance Command, Vietnam
Market Time	Navy patrols designed to intercept the enemy along the Vietnamese coastline
MAT	Mobile Advisory Team, US forces
MATT	Mobile Assistance Training Team, sometimes referred to as 'Advisory', Australian forces
MC	Military Cross, equivalent to the US Silver Star
Medevac	Medical evacuation
MGF	Mobile Guerrilla Force. US Special Forces–led attempts to operate as guerrilla units. A few AATTV were assigned
MIA	Missing in Action
MID	Mention-in-Despatches
Mike Force	Multi-purpose reactionary-reconnaissance units also used in conventional combat operations manned by Montagnard and Nung soldiers led by US and Australian soldiers. The formal title was Mobile Strike Force

Military Medal (MM)	For non-commissioned ranks, equivalent to the US Bronze Star (V)
Military Region	There were four military regions (1–4), from the DMZ to the Delta. Previously called CTZs
Montagnards	Hill tribes of indigenous people throughout Vietnam. Also known as 'Yards'. Recruited into the CIDG
MSF	Mobile Strike Force, see Mike Force
Napalm	Firebomb of petroleum jelly
NAT	Night assistance teams
NCO	Non-commissioned officer
NLF	The National Front for the Liberation of South Vietnam. An organisation controlled by North Vietnam, divided into political and military (Viet Cong) arms
NOAT	Night Operations Advisory Team
NOTT	Night Operations Training Team
Nungs	Chinese mercenaries resident in Vietnam, allegedly descended from Chinese warrior class
NVA	North Vietnamese Army, also PAVN
OC	Officer commanding, usually a sub-unit commander and major in rank (Aust.) or captain (US) or lieutenant (ARVN)
OPORD	Operation Order
OSS	Office of Strategic Studies planned and executed covert operations during World War II. A forerunner to the CIA
Pacification	Pacification was the military, political, economic and social processes of establishing or re-establishing local government responsive to and involving the participation of the people. It included the provision of sustained, credible territorial security, to include the destruction of the enemy's underground government
PATs	People's Action Teams supported local infrastructure; designed to counter VC operations. A CIA-funded project
PAVN	People's Army of Vietnam, the military arm of North Vietnam; more commonly and correctly known as 'NVA'
PERINTREP	Periodic intelligence report
PFF	Vietnamese Police Field Force
Phoenix Program	Allied action against the NLF infrastructure, very effective but also controversial because it carried a tag of assassination squads, kidnappers and extortionists
Popular Force (PF)	South Vietnamese military force used for local village protection, formerly Self Defence Corps
Protocol States	Three states (Cambodia, Laos and South Vietnam) were added to the SEATO Treaty by protocol that provided the benefits (upon request) of the alliance without full membership. Sometimes referred to as 'protectorates'
Province	A political region administered mainly by military offices within South Vietnam. There were 44 provinces in the country. CTZs administered provinces that sometimes answered directly to Saigon. See Sector and CTZ

PRU	Provincial Reconnaissance Units, the enforcement arm of the Phoenix Program. Their original name was Counter Terror Units, but that changed in 1965. Although a very controversial program, senior ranking NVA/VC officers said after the war that the program severely damaged the VCI
PSDF	People's Self Defence Force, a village or hamlet protection program
PX	Post Exchange, a duty free store and commissary for soldiers
RAAF	Royal Australian Air Force
RAE	Royal Australian Engineers
RAN	Royal Australian Navy
Ranch Hand	US defoliation projects, missions known as Trail Dust
RAND Corporation	An influential research and analysis organisation based in the United States
Rangers	Infantry forces trained in conducting reconnaissance and surveillance operations and lightly equipped for ground mobility operations
RAR	Royal Australian Regiment, infantry
RD Cadre	Revolutionary Development cadre. Forces designed to bolster the defence of hamlets and villages as the leading edge of pacification
Regiment	Army formation generally of three battalions with a total strength of about 3500. ARVN and enemy formations were smaller, around 1500
Regional Force	Formerly Civil Guard
Regroupee	Individual who moved from South to North circa 1954 and later infiltrated back into the South
RPG	Rocket-Propelled Grenade, see B-40
R&R	Rest and Recuperation, also known as Rest and Recreation
Ruff-Puffs	A facetious nickname for Regional/Popular Forces
RVN	Republic of (South) Vietnam
RVNAF	Republic of Vietnam Armed forces
S2	Captain, intelligence (US Army) at battalion, G2 at division and J2 at MACV
S3	Captain, operations (US Army) at battalion, see above
SAM	Surface-to-air missile
Sappers	VC/NVA commandos who specialised in attacks against installations using mines and satchel charges. Also an Australian engineer
SAS	Special Air Service, generally operated in small groups as long-range reconnaissance patrols
SDC	Self Defence Corps (Sometimes 'Force'). Later known as Popular Force
SEATO	South East Asia Collective Defence Treaty (Organisation). A treaty signed by Australia, France, New Zealand, Pakistan, the Philippines, Thailand, the United Kingdom and the United States. The aim of the treaty was to resist armed attacks and to counter subversion aimed at the overthrow of their governments
Secondary	An explosion or fire caused by an initial blast, e.g. by a bomb or artillery fire
Sector	South Vietnamese military operational area that overlaid a province

SF	Special Forces and Special Forces Group, the US 5th Special Forces Group (Airborne), headquartered at Nha Trang. Other groups provided temporary duty teams in the early years of the war to provide training and advice to the South Vietnamese
Sigint	Signals intelligence, information gathered by listening in on enemy electronic transmissions. Both sides used counter measures in efforts to foil the other
Skyraider	Propeller-driven, single seat, fighter ground attack aircraft
Slick	Troop-carrying helicopter, usually an Iroquois (Huey) that did not have external weapons systems, thus it was 'slick'
SLR	7.62 mm, self-loading rifle (semi-automatic), carried by Australians
SOG	Studies and Observation Group. Highly secret Special Forces cross-border patrols
SOIC	Sector Operations and Intelligence Center
Sortie	A single aircraft
Spooky	C-47 fixed-wing close air-support gunship (also known as 'Puff the Magic Dragon') that evolved through several types: Shadow, Stinger, and Spectre in C-119 and C-130 airframes
SRV	Socialist Republic of Vietnam
Strategic Hamlet	A program to group rural people into defendable localities
Sub-sector	Equivalent to a district within a province
SUPINTREP	Supplementary intelligence report
SVNLA	South Vietnam Liberation Army, another name for the Viet Cong. Also People's Liberation Armed Force
Tactical Air	Generally all aircraft sorties other than B-52. Tactical air strikes against ground targets
TAOR	Tactical area of responsibility
Tet	Chinese New Year, a movable date based on a lunar calendar
Third-country Nationals (TCN)	Any third group other than Vietnamese and American
TOC	Tactical Operations Centre, command post
Tri-Border Area	To the west of Dak To where Cambodia, Laos and South Vietnam converge
Uc Da Loi	Vietnamese term meaning people from the great southern land (Australians)
USAID	United States Agency for International Development
USARV	United States Army, Vietnam. Answered to MACV but also commanded by General Westmoreland
USIS	United States Information Service, a department of the US Embassy, Saigon
USMC	The United States Marine Corps
USOM	United States Operations Mission, a department of the US Embassy, Saigon
USS	United States Ship
USSR	Union of Soviet Socialist Republics. Although technically incorrect, the term 'Russian' equipment was often used in reports instead of 'Soviet'

VC	'Viet Cong', from 'Viet Nam Cong San'. The term 'Viet Cong' (communists) was invented by President Diem or USIS in the late 1950s to rename the 'Viet Minh', a term they thought was too close to nationalism. See NLF
VCI	Viet Cong Infrastructure, the communist 'political cell' system
VDAT	Village Defence Advisory Team
Viet Minh	A contraction of 'Viet Nam Doc Lap Dong Minh Hoi'. The term applied to Vietnamese resistance fighters from the First Indochina (French) War
WIA	Wounded in action
WO1	Warrant Officer Class One, usually a regimental sergeant major, the senior NCO in a battalion
WO2	Warrant Officer Class Two, a rank below WO1, usually a company sergeant major
WP	White phosphorus, 'willie-pete'
XO	Executive Officer, the second-in-command of a military unit

NOTES

Chapter 1

1   Peter Cochrane, 'History, Imagine all the people', a review of *Uses and Abuses of History* by Margaret MacMillan and other titles, *Australian Literary Review*, 3 February 2010, p. 8. MacMillan retells a story originally told by American author Susan Jacoby.

2   Donald Lancaster, *The Emancipation of French Indo-China*, Oxford University Press, London, 1961, p. 15.

3   Bernard B. Fall, *The Two Viet-Nams: A Political and Military Analysis*, Pall Mall Press, London, 1963, p. 12.

4   Lancaster, *The Emancipation of French Indo-China*, p. 15.

5   Jean Chesneaux, *Contribution à l'histoire de la nation vietnamienne* (Contribution to the History of the Vietnamese Nation), Editions Sociales, Paris, 1955 (1956); Georges Maspero, *Le Royaume du Champa* (The Champa Kingdom), G. van Oest, Paris/Brussels, 1928.

6   Lancaster, *The Emancipation of French Indo-China*, p. 20.

7   Lam Quang Thi, *The Twenty-five Year Century*, University of North Texas Press, Denton, TX, 2001, p. 62.

8   Lancaster, *The Emancipation of French Indo-China*, p. 27.

9   Attributed to journalist James Reston, following President Kennedy's meeting with Soviet leader Nikita Khrushchev, in Vienna in 1961.

10 Lancaster, *The Emancipation of French Indo-China*, p. 72.

11 Sophie Quinn-Judge, *Ho Chi Minh: The Missing Years 1919–1941*, Hurst & Company, London, 2003, p. 75. William J. Duiker, *Ho Chi Minh*, Allen & Unwin, Crows Nest, NSW, 2000, p. 127. Pierre Brocheux, *Ho Chi Minh: A Biography*, trans. Claire Duiker, Cambridge University Press, 2007, Notes p. 216.

12 Phan Boi Chau, *Overturned Chariot: The Autobiography of Phan-Boi-Chau*, trans. Vinh Sinh & Nicholas Wickenden, Shaps Library of Translations, University of Hawai'i Press, Honolulu, 1999. p. 26.

13 The Department of State, *United States Relations with China*, released August 1949, p. 438.

14 J. G. Latham, 'Australian Eastern Mission: Report', in Australia, House of Representatives, *Debates*, 6 July 1934, p. 328.

15 Letter addressed to Mr President of the Republic, Marseilles, 15 September 1911, and signed by Nguyen Tat Thanh (Ho Chi Minh).

16 Alexander B. Woodside, *Community and Revolution in Modern Vietnam*, Houghton Mifflin, Boston, 1976, p. 171. Also, ibid.

17 Lancaster, *The Emancipation of French Indo-China*, p. 79.

18 Quinn-Judge, *Ho Chi Minh*, p. 27.

19 Duiker, *Ho Chi Minh*, 2000, p. 48.

20 The Office of Strategic Services (OSS) was the predecessor to the Central Intelligence Agency (CIA).

21 'Atlantic Charter, August 14, 1941', The Avalon Project, Yale Law School: <www.yale.edu/lawweb/avalon/wwii/atlantic.htm> [18 June 2008].

22 *Times*, 11 November 1942.

23 *Foreign Relations of the United States [FRUS]*, vol. IV, 1940, 'Southward Advance of Japanese Expansionist Movement: The Netherlands East Indies; French Indochina; British Hong Kong and Burma; Thailand'.

24 Ibid., pp. 15, 16. A minister, not an ambassador, headed Australia's mission at this stage in Australia's diplomatic development.

25 *FRUS*, vol. IV, 'The Far East 1940', p. 29.

26 Fall, *The Two Viet-Nams*, p. 45.

27 Ibid., p. 46.

28 *FRUS*, 'The Tehran Conference: The President's Log at Tehran', 27 November – 2 December 1943, p. 485.

29 Fall, *The Two Viet-Nams*, p. 453.

30 *FRUS*, vol. IV, 1940, p. 157.

31 *FRUS*, vol. V, 1941, 'The Southward Advance of Japanese Expansionist Movement', p. 390.

32 Graham Freudenberg, *Churchill and Australia*, Pan Macmillan, Sydney, 2008, p. 447.

33 John Curtin, 'The Task Ahead', Melbourne *Herald*, 27 December 1941.

34 Letter from British prime minister to Mr Curtin, marked Personal and Secret, 29 December 1941. Original held by UK Public Records Office Prem 4/50/15.

35 Memo from Churchill to Lord Privy Seal and Dominions Secretary, 2040Z/29 [December 1941].

36 *FRUS, The Conferences at Washington (Arcadia), 1941–1942*, 'The First Conference [December 1941–January 1942]', p. 110.

37 Vice-Admiral Milton E. Miles, USN, *A Different Kind of War*, Doubleday, New York, 1967, pp. 181–2.

38 *FRUS, The Conferences at Cairo and Tehran, 1943*, 'The Tehran Conference', p. 485.

39 *FRUS, Europe 1942*, vol. II, p. 416.

40 *FRUS, Diplomatic Papers, 1944, The British Commonwealth and Europe*, vol. III, 1944, 'Australia', p. 183.

41 *FRUS, The British Commonwealth and Europe*, vol. III, 1944, pp. 168–209.

42 *FRUS, Diplomatic Papers*, 1945, 'General: The United Nations', vol. I, p. 122.

43 *FRUS, Conferences at Malta and Yalta,* 'The Conference at Yalta 4–11 February 1945', references throughout.

44 Sir Keith Waller, *A Diplomatic Life: Some Memories,* Centre for the Study of Australia–Asia Relations, Griffith University, Nathan, Qld, Asia Series No. 6, July 1990, p. 15.

45 *FRUS, Diplomatic Papers, 1945, French Indochina,* p. 307.

46 Stanley Karnow, *Vietnam: A History,* Penguin, 1984, p. 149.

47 *FRUS, Diplomatic Papers: The Conference of Berlin (the Potsdam Conference), 1945,* vol. I, 1945, p. 1319.

48 Philip Ziegler, *Mountbatten: The Official Biography,* Collins, London, 1985, pp. 331, 332.

49 Ibid., p. 303.

50 Fall, *The Two Viet-Nams,* p. 101.

51 Bruce Davies & Gary McKay, *The Men Who Persevered,* Allen & Unwin, Crows Nest, NSW, 2005, p. 2.

52 The Australian Commissioner for Malaya, Departmental Despatch No. 11/49, 4 April 1949.

53 US Senate, Committee on Foreign Relations, 14 January 1965 (Washington), p. 137.

54 *FRUS, 1949,* vol. VII, Part II, East-Asian Pacific Area, Policy Planning Staff Paper 51, pp. 1128–33.

55 Extract from Richard Casey's diary, dated 11 August 1951: <dfat.gov.au/historical publications>.

56 Australia, House of Representatives, vol. V, October 1954, p. 2382.

57 *FRUS, 1952–1954,* General United States Policies with respect to the East-Asian Pacific Area, vol. XII, Part 1, p. 76.

58 ANZAM was initially established for the defence of sea and air communications for the British Territories in Malaya and Borneo (probably around 1948). It was later extended (1954) to cover the defence of Malaya. See Kin Wah Chin, *The Defence of Malaysia and Singapore,* Cambridge University Press, New York, 1983.

59 *FRUS, 1952–1954,* General United States Policies with respect to the East-Asian Pacific Area, vol. XII, Part 1, p. 214.

60 *Strategic Basis of Australian Defence Policy,* January 1953, a paper endorsed by the Defence Committee, 8 January 1953.

61 *FRUS, 1952–1954, Indochina,* vol. XIII, Policy of the United States with respect to Indochina, Part 1, p. 385.

62 Ronald H. Spector, *Advice and Support: The Early Years 1941–1960,* Center of Military History, United States Army, Washington DC, 1983, p. 173.

63 *Strategic Basis of Australian Defence Policy,* January 1953, Part V, 'Main Conclusions'.

64 Indochina Political File, Part 1 December 1948 – December 1952, File 25/23/1, NAA, Canberra.

65 Military Equipment for French Forces Indochina, NAA A5954 (A594/69). Live sheep procurement is mentioned in the *French Lessons of the War in Indochina,* The RAND Corporation 1967.

66 Martin Windrow, *The Last Valley: Dien Bien Phu and the French Defeat in Vietnam,* Weidenfeld & Nicolson, London, 2004, book cover, p. 624.

67 Jung Chang & Jon Halliday, *Mao: The Unknown Story,* Jonathan Cape, London, 2005; Qiang Zhai, *China & The Vietnam Wars, 1950–1975,* University of North Carolina Press, 2000.

68   Sherman Adams, *Firsthand Report: The Story of the Eisenhower Administration*, Harper & Bros., New York, 1961, p. 122.

69   Windrow, *The Last Valley*; Jules Roy, *The Battle of Dien Bien Phu*, Harper & Row, 1963. Dien Bien Phu 1954; <http://orbat.com/site/history/> [accessed 20 February 2012]; <www.dienbienphu.org/english/> [accessed 7 April 2011].

70   United Nations S/PV.603-para 66 S/2760 [Security Council official record]. Application for Membership (Vietnam), 18 September 1952.

71   Zhou Enlai zhuan, *The Biography of Zhou Enlai*, vol. 3, Beijing, 1998, pp. 1131–2. There is further reference to this partition plan in Chang & Halliday, *Mao*.

72   Vietnamese Press Agency Broadcast, Saigon, 7 July 1954.

73   Pham Van Dong statement quoted in P. J. Honey, *Hanoi and the Vietnam War*, p. 259 footnote, RAND study.

74   Melvin Gurtov, *Negotiations and Vietnam: A Case Study of the 1954 Geneva Conference*, Part II, The RAND Corporation, Springfield, July 1968.

75   Ibid., p. 143.

76   *FRUS, 1952–1954, Indochina*, vol. XIII, pp. 1420–1.

77   *FRUS, 1952–1954, General United States Policies*, East-Asia and the Pacific, vol. XII, Part 1, ANZUS powers; five-power military consultations, throughout; Radford's statement, p. 192.

78   An initiative by the US Secretary of State, General George C. Marshall, was a large-scale economic program for the rebuilding and recovery of Europe post–World War II.

79   *FRUS, 1952–1954, General United States Policies*, East Asia and the Pacific, vol. XII, Part 1, p. 193.

80   Dang Phong (ed.), *Lich Su Kinh Te Viet Nam 1945–2000, Tap II: 1955–1975* (Vietnamese Economic History 1945–2000, vol. 2: 1955–1975), Hanoi Social Science Publishing House, 2005, p. 85. I am most thankful for my discussions with Nathalie Huynh Chau Nguyen who provided this information. Nathalie Nguyen, *Memory is Another Country*, Praeger ABC-CLIO, Santa Barbara, CA, 2009.

81   Robert Manne, *The Petrov Affair*, Permagon Press, Sydney, 1987, p. 87.

82   Australian Bureau of Statistics, 1301.0 *Year Book Australia 1957*, 'Defence'.

83   Ibid.

84   *Strategic Basis of Australian Defence Policy*, January 1959, pp. 2–5, NAA A2031/8.

85   Attributed to Nikita Khrushchev at the Polish Embassy in Moscow, November 1956.

Chapter 2

1   SEATO-MPO [Military Planning Office] Plan 5C/59.

2   *The History of the (US) Joint Chiefs of Staff: The Joint Chiefs of Staff and the War in Vietnam 1960–1968*, Part 1, p. xxv. Historical Division, Joint Secretariat, Joint Chiefs of Staff, Washington.

3   Ibid.

4   Ibid., Chapter 1, p. 8.

5   Ibid., Chapter 1, p. 6.

6   United Press International article, Saigon, 13 February 1962.

7   Edward Geary Lansdale, *In the Midst of Wars*, Fordham University Press, New York, 1991, p. 338.

8   'The Impracticability of Increasing the Australian Army Training Team in South Vietnam', CGS 7/1965, 29 January 1965.

9   *US Joint Chiefs of Staff*, Part 1, Chapter 1, pp. 1–11.

10   Ibid., Chapter 1, pp. 1–12.

11   US Embassy Saigon, message no. 624 to State, 16 September 1960.

12   Draft, undated copy with handwritten notes, signed by Mr Blakeney. Paper addressed to The Australian Embassy Saigon, 'Counterinsurgency – Possible Australian Contribution', Your file V201/2/7 memorandum 663/61. Australian counterinsurgency techniques were heavily influenced by the Malayan campaign and training techniques evolved through methods detailed in pamphlets such as *Anti Guerrilla Operations in South East Asia*, produced by GHQ FARELF, Singapore. In 1962, Brigadier Frank Hassett led a study team that obtained assistance from British experts on the subject; the results of this work became Australian military doctrine in 1965.

13   Department of External Affairs, Outward cablegram O.17924 to Australian Embassy Washington, 27 November 1961.

14   Record of discussions on 'Possible Forms of Assistance to South Vietnam', held at the Department of External Affairs, 14 December 1961.

15   *A Threat to the Peace: North Viet-Nam's Effort to Conquer South Viet-Nam*, Department of State, Publication 7308, December 1961. US National Security Memorandum No. 29, March 1961, and associated documents.

16   Discussions on 'Possible Forms of Assistance to South Vietnam', 14 December 1961.

17   Department of External Affairs, Inward cablegram I.30715, from Australian Embassy Washington, 20 December 1961.

18   *Foreign Relations of the United States 1961–1963 [FRUS]*, vol. I, entry 159, letter from the Chief of the MAAG in Vietnam (McGarr) to the Chairman of the Joint Chiefs of Staff (Lemnitzer), 12 October 1961.

19   Notes on the meeting with Mr R. G. K. Thompson, British Advisory Mission to Saigon, 28 March 1962, NAA File 3014/10/15/1.

20   Colonel F. P. Serong, letter to General Reginald Pollard, 20 February 1962, Rangoon, NAA A1945, Colonel Serong-Burma series.

21   *FRUS, 1961–1963*, vol. I, *Vietnam, 1961*, various entries in item 159.

22   *The History of the Joint Chiefs of Staff . . . Vietnam 1960–1968*, Part 1, Chapter 4. *FRUS, 1961–1963*, vol. II, Vietnam 1962, Document 16, p. 67.

23   Athol Townley to Hon. Sir Garfield Barwick, QC, MP, Minister for External Affairs, March 1962.

24   Lieutenant General Pollard, CGS, to Secretary [Department of Army?], 19 March 1962, pp. 1–6.

25   In February 1962, General McGarr (MAAG) defined a concept that he called the 'Secure Village' that included several hamlets. Both Robert Thompson and McGarr saw the village protected as a single complex and the name changed to 'strategic village'. The term 'strategic village' tended to be replaced by 'strategic hamlet' and then it disappeared from use. A hamlet was the smallest population unit in the civil government organisation. In 1962, there were approximately 16,000 hamlets and 2000 villages in South Vietnam. *The History of the Joint Chiefs of Staff . . . Vietnam 1960–1968*, Part 1, Chapter 4, pp. 16–17.

26   For example, C. V. Sturdevant's 1962 research for *The Border Control Problem in South Vietnam*, The RAND Corporation, Santa Monica, CA, 1964.

27   War Diaries: HQ 6 Australian Division, November 1942; Advance HQ New Guinea Force, November–December 1942; HQ 7 Australian Division, February–March 1943; HQ 8

Australian Infantry Brigade August 1945. Diaries: 4 and 35 Australian Infantry battalions, June, July and September 1945. Daisy Force–Patrol Report, HQ 4 Aust Infantry Battalion (AIF), 30 June 1945. Service records and efficiency reports held by Central Army Records Office on F. P. Serong.

28   Burma, Cambodia, Canada, People's Republic of China, Democratic Republic of Vietnam (North), France, India, Poland, Republic of Vietnam (South), Thailand, USSR, UK and the USA signed the agreement. Laos signed a statement of neutrality that entered into force as an international agreement on 23 July 1963.

29   Notes of Agenda items 4, 5 and 6, ANZUS meeting, Canberra, 8–9 May 1962.

30   Ibid.

31   Ibid.

32   Notes of Discussions with US Secretary of State (Dean Rusk), 9 May 1962. Those in attendance: (US) Dean Rusk, Mr Belton, Mr Nitze, Admiral Felt; (Aust.) Sir Garfield Barwick, Mr Townley, Air Marshal Sir Frederick Scherger, Sir Arthur Tange, Mr Hicks, Sir Howard Beale.

33   ANZUS Council Meeting, News Conference given by Minister for External Affairs, Parliament House, Canberra, 10 p.m., 9 May 1962, pp. 1–10.

34   Ibid.

35   Sir Garfield Barwick, *A Radical Tory: Garfield Barwick's Reflections and Recollections*, Federation Press, Annandale, NSW, 1995, p. 189.

36   Annex to Joint Planning Committee Report (not numbered), 1962: 'Brief for Discussions—Proposed Australian Aid to Vietnam', p. 3.

37   Decision No. 241, Cabinet Minute, Canberra, 15 May 1962, pp. 1–4.

38   Agenda item 5, ANZUS meeting, 8–9 May 1962.

39   Statement by the Hon. Athol Townley MP, Minister for Defence, 24 May 1962.

40   David Horner, 'From Korea to Pentropic: The Army in the Early 1950s and 1960s', paper presented at Chief of Army's History Conference, 1997.

41   Ian McNeill, *To Long Tan*, Allen & Unwin, St Leonards, NSW, 1993, p. 23. See also, David Horner, 'From Korea to Pentropic'.

42   For RAN strength, see Jeffrey Grey, *Up Top: The Royal Australian Navy and the Southeast Asian conflicts, 1955–1972*, Australian War Memorial, Canberra, 1999, p. 8, notes.

43   Air Board, Agendum No. 12814, 10 July 1959.

44   Merle Pribbenow (trans.), *Victory in Vietnam: The Official History of the People's Army of Vietnam, 1954–1975*, University Press of Kansas, 2002. See Chapter 'South Vietnam Defeats the American Special War', p. 134.

45   Garfield Barwick, personal letter to the Hon. A. C. Townley, MP, Minister for Defence, 1 June 1962, pp. 1–2.

46   Keith Brennan, personal note to Ambassador Brian Hill, 29 May 1962.

47   Ambassador Hill, Saigon, personal handwritten note to Keith Brennan, 5 June 1962, pp. 1–2.

48   Mai Elliott, *RAND in Southeast Asia: A History of the Vietnam War Era*, RAND Corporation, Santa Monica, CA, p. 39.

49   F. P. Serong to General Pollard, 20 February 1962, p. 5.

50   Colonel F. P. Serong to Chief of the General Staff, 5 June 1962.

51   Lieutenant General Reginald Pollard to the Secretary, Department of Defence, 2 July 1962, CGS 46/62.

52 Appointment of Commander, Australian Army Component, Vietnam, letter, Department of Army to Department of Defence, 5 July 1962. Department of External Affairs, Outward cablegram O.10957 to Australian Embassy Saigon, 23 June 1962. Department of External Affairs, Inward cablegram I.15648 from Australian Embassy Saigon, 27 June 1962.

53 Bruce Davies & Gary McKay, *The Men Who Persevered*, Allen & Unwin, Sydney, 2005, p. 18.

54 Australian Army Headquarters 41/441/69, 21 June 1962, authorised the unit to be raised against establishment VIII/492/1 (TE).

55 Davies & McKay, *The Men Who Persevered*, p. 19.

56 CGS letter 42/62 to Secretary, 2 July 1962. Directive to Commander, AATTV, July 1962, and Australia, House of Representatives, *Debates*, 18 October 1962, p. 1663.

57 *Commonwealth Gazette*, No. 65, 2 August 1962. Dallas Brooks, Administrator, declared 'that the persons subject to military law serving in Vietnam or on their way from Australia . . . or on their way back . . . after so serving shall be on active service'. The declaration was dated 13 July 1962. Also, AMR&O–Active Service, State Library of Victoria. Later documents such as the *Repatriation (Special Overseas Service) Act 1962* used the term 'allotted for special duty'. Although special duty was not defined, its significance was that a person so allotted rendered operational service. MBI 216-1, 22 April 1966, defined special duty, special area and special service. The Vietnam (Southern Zone) date of effect was 31 July 1962, the day Colonel Serong arrived in Saigon. Contrarily, the Letters Patent for the GSM with clasp South Vietnam authorise an entitlement for the GSM with clasp South Vietnam from 24 December 1962.

58 Commander and a commanding officer were the formal appointments necessary to satisfy a military law requirement. Each officer had different powers at law.

59 Department of External Affairs, Outward cablegram O.13727, message 266 to Saigon, 6 August 1962. Department of External Affairs, Inward cablegram I.19264, message 303 from Saigon, 7 August 1962. Cablegram, Hill to Brennan, 13 November 1962, NAA 221/1/4/5.

60 Department of External Affairs, Outward savingram O.14680, 21 August 1962. This was addressed to South Asian and Southeast Asian posts as well as London, Washington, Ottawa and the Australian post at the UN–New York.

61 *The History of the Joint Chiefs of Staff . . . Vietnam 1960–1968*, Part 1, Chapter 1 'The Counterinsurgency Plan', throughout.

62 Ibid.

63 Thomas L. Ahern, Jr., *CIA and Rural Pacification in South Vietnam*, Center for the Study of Intelligence—Central Intelligence Agency, Washington DC, 2001, p. 41.

64 AATTV Report No. 2, September 1962, signed by Colonel Serong.

65 *The Joint Chiefs of Staff . . . Vietnam 1960–1968*, Part 1, Chapter 16, p. 42.

66 Commander AATTV, A36/1, Personal & Top Secret letter to General Pollard, 19 October 1962.

67 *The Team*, video, 2001, produced by Training Technology Centre for Training Command-Army, Australia.

68 Directive to Commander, AATTV, 25 July 1962, signed by Deputy Chief of the General Staff.

69 President John Kennedy approved the Bay of Pigs invasion of Cuba by a CIA paramilitary force. The force members were mainly Cuban exiles but they were discovered immediately on landing and over 1000 were taken prisoner. Four Americans were killed. The president

sacked the director and deputy director as well as the deputy director of operations at the CIA as a result.

70 National Security Action Memorandum 57, 28 June 1961.

71 Neil Sheehan, *Washington Post*, 4 January 1963.

72 Australia, House of Representatives, *Debates*, 23 May 1963, p. 1820.

73 The circumstances of Sgt Hacking's death are explained in Davies & McKay, *The Men who Persevered*, p. 33.

74 Certificate of Death signed by Captain Allison J. Berlin, 1 June 1963. The Court of Enquiry documents, HQ AATTV Saigon, Vietnam, 12 November 1963.

75 Ibid.

76 Department of External Affairs, Inward savingram No. 49 (I 12222) from Australian Embassy Saigon, 6 May 1963, pp. 1–4.

77 Outward savingram No. 49 from Australian Embassy Saigon, 6 May 1962? [1963], NAA File 221/1/4/1/5.

78 Ibid.

79 Don Dalton to author, 21 July 2004.

80 President John F. Kennedy's diary: <www.jfklibrary.org>.

81 Minutes of a meeting of the Special Group for Counterinsurgency, Washington, 23 May 1963 at 2 p.m. David Halberstam, *The Best and the Brightest*, Ballantine Books, New York, 1992, p. 276.

82 'The Tide has Turned', *Times of Vietnam*, 18 March 1963, cited in Elliott, *RAND in Southeast Asia*, p. 39.

83 Memorandum no. 573/63, Australian Embassy Washington to The Secretary, Department of External Affairs, 29 May 1963.

84 Anne Blair, *Ted Serong*, Oxford University Press, Melbourne, 2002, p. 96.

85 External Affairs, Outward cablegram O.18729, 26 August 1963, to Washington and London.

86 Department of External Affairs, Inward cablegram I.22136, 20 August 1963, from Australian Embassy Rome.

87 AATTV Commander's Diary, September 1963, AWM 1/2/16.

88 Special Assistance for Counterinsurgency and Special Activities (SASCA), Chronology, August 1963 (S). *CIA and the Vietnam Policy Makers: Three Episodes 1962–1968*, Harold P. Ford Center for the Study of Intelligence, CIA, 1998. Dr William C. Gibbons, *The U.S. Government and the Vietnam War, Part II, 1961–1964*, U.S. Government Printing Office, Washington, 1985, pp. 148–59. National Security Archive posting by John Prados, 11 December 2009: <www.gwu.edu/~nsarchiv/> [accessed December 2009].

89 Reference MACJO1 signed by Paul D. Harkins, 18 December 1963. The Reference was Australia/United States Document on Command and Administrative Arrangements, 27 July 1962, Annex Number 1. Serong's handwritten letter of explanation is signed and dated, 18 December 1963.

90 Interview II, Brigadier [Honorary] Francis Philip 'Ted' Serong and Anne Blair, 3 June 1994, p. II–9, Lyndon Baines Johnson Library.

91 Ambassador Anderson to Tange, External Affairs, 29 April 1964.

92 Colonel Do Cao Tri to the Senior Adviser, 1st Infantry Division: Assignment of Australian Officers, copy to Lt Col A. S. Mann, Australian Military Advisory Group [*sic* AATTV], 17 May 1963.

93   Barry Petersen with John Cribbin, *An Australian Soldier's Secret War in Vietnam: Tiger Men*, Macmillan, 1988. Frank Walker, *The Tiger Man of Vietnam*, Hachette, 2009.

94   Anderson to Tange, 29 April 1964.

95   F. P. Serong, 'Project Paper: Formation of a Federation—Vietnam, Laos & Cambodia. Purpose: To Gain Fighting Room', Saigon, April 1964, pp. 1–17.

96   Ibid.

97   Serong to Major General Hassett, 25 May 1964.

98   In the first encounter, a detachment of naval torpedo boats commanded by Le Duy Khoai 'chased Madoc [*sic*] . . . from the region', according to *The History of the Resistance War against America 1954–1975*, vol. 1, 1996, National Politics, n.p. *The History of the Joint Chiefs of Staff . . . Vietnam 1960–1968*, Part 1, Chapter 11.

99   *The History of the Joint Chiefs of Staff . . . Vietnam 1960–1968*, Chapter 11, 'The Pentagon Papers', throughout 1964.

100 Ibid. Gibbons, *The US Government and the Vietnam War*, Part II, Chapter 5.

101 Ambassador H. D. Anderson, 215/4/1, to The Secretary, Department of External Affairs Canberra, 14 September 1964.

102 Enemy forces were *761* and *762* regiments, battalions *500* and *800*, various mortar and recoilless-rifle 'artillery' units and local militia that included *445 Company*. *Operations in the US Resistance War*, The Gioi Publishers, 2009.

103 Commonwealth Department of Veterans' Affairs, *Mortality of National Service Vietnam Veterans*, 1997, Chapter 1.

104 Sue Langford, AWM Encyclopedia Appendix: 'The National Service Scheme, 1964–72', <www.awm.gov.au/encyclopedia/conscription/vietnam.asp>.

105 The 1st Recruit Training Battalion (1RTB) was located at Kapooka, near Wagga Wagga, in southern NSW. The 2nd Recruit Training Battalion (2RTB) was at Puckapunyal, Vic., and the 3rd RTB was at Singleton, inland from Newcastle, NSW.

106 Gordon Hurford, interview with Gary McKay, Alice Springs, NT, 1988.

107 Ibid.

108 David Chanoff & Doan Van Toai, *Portrait of the Enemy*, Random House, New York, 1986, pp. 43–4.

109 See, for example, Garry Woodard, *Asian Alternatives: Australia's Vietnam Decision and Lessons on Going to War*, Melbourne University Publishing, 2004.

110 Cabinet Minute Decision No. 195, Canberra, 30 April 1962, and Decision No. 241, 15 May 1962.

111 Minutes of the Defence Committee, 20 April 1965, 'Possible Australian Force Contribution to South Vietnam', para. 2 (c).

112 Department of External Affairs, Inward cablegram I.40959, Waller to Acting Minister, 4 December 1964, message no. 3365.

113 Lyndon B. Johnson, letter to Prime Minister Menzies, 14 December 1964.

114 Prime Minister, letter to President Johnson, 18 December 1964, NAA.

115 'Aid to South Vietnam', Report by the Chiefs of Staff Committee. 'United States Proposals for further Action in South Vietnam', 16 December 1964, NAA A1945/39.

116 *The History of the Joint Chiefs of Staff . . . Vietnam 1960–1968*, Part 2, Chapter 19 'Limited Deployment of US Forces', p. 23.

117 Anatoly Dobrynin, *In Confidence: Moscow's Ambassador to America's Six Cold War Presidents*, University of Washington, 2001, p. 140.

118 *The History of the Joint Chiefs of Staff . . . Vietnam, 1960–1968*, Part 1, Chapter 18.

119 Ibid.

120 Ibid.

121 Ibid.

122 Bob Breen, *First to Fight*, Allen & Unwin, Sydney, 1988, p. 13.

123 Jung Chang & Jon Halliday, *Mao: The Unknown Story*, Jonathon Cape, London, 2005, p. 597.

124 Douglas Valentine, *The Phoenix Program*, iUniverse.com, Lincoln, NE, 2000, pp. 92–3. Although none of Colonel Grieves' personal papers were found, the author's telephone conversation with his son in 2008 reinforced the information that Grieves was extremely anti–Colonel Serong.

125 Bill Robertson, email to author, 27 October 2008.

126 Papers of Federal Parliamentary Labor Party (Caucus), NLA, MS 6852, Box 10.

127 CGS 7/1965, 29 January 1965.

128 This was released as National Security Action Memorandum 328 on 6 April 1965.

129 *The History of the Joint Chiefs of Staff . . . Vietnam 1960–1968*, Part 2, Chapters 21 and 22. Dr William C. Gibbons, *The U.S. Government and the Vietnam War, Part III*, January to July 1965. (See note 90.)

130 Department of External Affairs, Inward cablegram I17570, 29 April 1965 [time 1736] from Australian Embassy Saigon.

131 Phan Huy Quat premier (prime minister), document 511-TTP/VP/M, addressed to the Australian Ambassador at Saigon, 29 April 1965.

132 'Vietnam – Defence Assistance', NAA A1838 TS696/8/4, Part 8.

133 Cablegram 1281, from Australian Embassy Washington, 13 April 1965.

134 Neil McInnes, interview with Gary McKay, 26 March 1991.

135 Bob Breen, *First to Fight*, p. 23.

136 Ibid., Chapter 2, 'The Deployment'.

137 Pat Burgess, *Sun-Herald*, 27 June 1965, p. 27.

138 US Joint Public Research Service 29,284, 25 March 1965. Madeleine Riffaud, 'Two months with guerrilla forces in South Vietnam', 14, 17, 18, 19, 23, 24, 25, 26 February and 2, 3, 4 March 1965. See also Stephen Crittenden, interview with Wilfred Burchett, ABC Radio National, 3 November 2005.

Chapter 3

1   Madeleine Riffaud, 'Two months with guerrilla forces in South Vietnam', *L'Humanité*, Paris, 14, 17, 18, 19, 23, 24, 25, 26 February and 2, 3, 4 March 1965. Also, see 'The Battle of Binh Gia', pp. 49–51, US Joint Public Research Service 29,284, 25 March 1965. The North referred to the South Vietnamese as puppets of the USA, but in this case, Riffaud probably tried to distinguish between local units and the ARVN.

2   David Chanoff & Doan Van Toai, *Portrait of the Enemy: The Other Side of the War in Vietnam*, Random House, New York, 1986, pp. 159–61 (told through interviews with North Vietnamese, former VC and Southern Opposition Leaders).

3   AAP report, 17 June 1965.

4   *MACV Command History 1965*, prepared by the Military History Branch, Office of the Secretary, Joint Staff, p. 361. David Horner, *Australian Higher Command in the Vietnam War*, ANU, Canberra, 1986, p. 11.

5   Note by Sir James Plimsoll, 20 April 1965, NAA 1838 696/8/4, Part 8.

6   Alexander V. Preece, telephone conversation with author, 15 March 2009.

7   *Sun News Pictorial*, Melbourne, 10 June 1965.

8   Ibid., 16 June 1965.

9   Alan Ramsey, *Sun*, 28 June 1965, p. 2.

10   Don Petersen, *Sun*, 28 June 1965, p. 1.

11   Adrian Roberts, draft notes, recorded by Gary McKay, ca September 2006.

12   Bob Breen, *First to Fight*, Allen & Unwin, Sydney, 1989, p. 66.

13   Patrick Shaw, note to the Minister for Defence, 7 April 1965, NAA A1838 696/8/4, Part 8.

14   Inward cablegram from Australian Embassy Saigon, I.18058, 4 May 1965. Top Secret message on courtesy calls made by the ambassador on Defence Minister Thieu and Acting Commander-in-Chief Minh.

15   Gerry Stone, *Sunday Mirror*, 27 June 1965, p. 3.

16   *Sun*, 18 June 1965, p. 6.

17   Presidential letter transmitted to the prime minister through the US Chargé d'Affaires, Jack Lydman, 26 July 1965.

18   G. A. Jockel, First Assistant Secretary, Division I, Defence Liaison Branch, 696/84/, 16 August 1965.

19   Lieutenant General Stanley R. Larsen and Brigadier General James L. Collins, Jr, *Allied Participation in Vietnam*, Department of the Army, Washington DC, 1985, p. 89.

20   Foreign Affairs and Defence Committee, Canberra, 17 August 1965, Decision No. 1153 (FAD).

21   Department of External Affairs, Outward cablegram to Saigon, O.25528, 17 August 1965.

22   Department of External Affairs, Outward cablegram to Washington, London, Wellington and Saigon, O.25549, 17 August 1965.

23   Breen, *First to Fight*, pp. 49–50.

24   'Blue' O'Reilly, interview with Gary McKay, Brisbane, 21 May 1999.

25   Defence Committee Cabinet Submission No. 970, July 1967, NAA A1838696/8/4, Part 9.

26   'Regular Army' refers to those who enlisted voluntarily. 'National Service' is used for those who were conscripted into the army as members of the Regular Army Supplement.

27   Defence Committee Submission No. 970; see the Army chapter.

28   John Essex-Clark, *Maverick Soldier*, Melbourne University Press, 1991, p. 112.

29   Ibid., pp. 126–7.

30   Preece, telephone conversation, 15 March 2009.

31   Eugene Jordan, personal correspondence with author, 12 December 2006. This correspondence is a detailed explanation of the course of events prior to Scott's death and the aftermath.

32   *Defence Instructions (General)* PERS 20-4, 15 August 1997.

33   Lieutenant General Hoang Phuong, Director of Contents, *History of the Resistance War against America 1954–1975*, National Politics, vol. 1, 1996, note 1 to discussion about Operation Crimp (Cu Chi tunnels), January 1966, n.p.

34   'Chicom' is an abbreviation for weapons and military paraphernalia of Chinese Communist origin.

35   George Wilson to Gary McKay, 15 March 1999.

36   Ibid.

37   John Hooper & 'Sandy' MacGregor, 'Operation "CRIMP": The First Penetration of Vietcong Tunnels', *Duty First*, n.d. (copy held by author).

38   Lex McAulay, *Blue Lanyard – Red Banner*, Banner Books, Maryborough, Qld, 2005. Australian Army commanders' diaries [Vietnam], Infantry units, 7/1/57, 1RAR [1–31 January 1966], AWM95. Sandy MacGregor as told to Jimmy Thomson, *No Need for Heroes*, CALM, Lindfield, NSW, 2006.

39   'Faces and Places', *Alfred Hospital Journal*, 1967. For a full account of the civilian surgical teams, see Gary McKay & Elizabeth Stewart, *With Healing Hands*, Allen & Unwin, Crows Nest, NSW, 2009.

40   Bob Gray, interview with Gary McKay, 24 May 2006.

41   This deadly battle is described in Lieutenant General Harold G. Moore & Joseph L. Galloway, *We Were Soldiers Once . . . and Young*, Random House, New York, 1992.

42   *MACV Command History 1965.*

43   Merle Pribbenow (trans.), *Victory in Vietnam: The Official History of the People's Army of Vietnam, 1954–1975*, University Press of Kansas, 2002, pp. 141–2.

44   Ibid.

45   *MACV Command History 1965*, 'ARVN Operations'.

46   *MACV Command History 1970*, vol. I, pp. V14–15.

47   Robert S. McNamara, *In Retrospect: The Tragedy and Lessons of Vietnam*, Vintage, New York, 1996, p. 265.

48   *Foreign Relations of the United States 1964–1968 [FRUS]*, vol. III, Vietnam June–December 1965, McNamara Document 222, 7 December 1965, and Harriman Document 240, 23 December 1965.

49   Essex-Clark, *Maverick Soldier*, p. 129.

50   PROVN, Prepared by the Office of the Deputy Chief of Staff for Military Operations, Department of the Army, March, 1966.

51   David Horner, *Strategic Command*, Oxford University Press, Melbourne, 2005, p. 246.

52   Essex-Clark, *Maverick Soldier*, p. 147.

53   Ibid., p. 161. See also, Australian Army commanders' diaries [Vietnam], Infantry units, 7/1/61, 1RAR [1–31 March 1966], entry for 18 March 1966, AWM95.

54   The author was the company signaller in the ambush that night. He passed the messages from the ambush commander to the company commander, Major Ian Fisher, and relayed all the information to the battalion command post.

55   In February 1943 the area in which CMF conscripts were permitted to serve was extended to cover Japanese-held islands south of the equator. See <john.curtin.edu.au/manof peace/homefront.html>.

56   The reasons for selecting Phuoc Tuy Province are explained in publications like Ian McNeill, *To Long Tan*, Allen & Unwin, St Leonards, NSW, 1993, and Ian McNeill & Ashley Ekins, *On the Offensive*, Allen & Unwin with AWM, Crows Nest, NSW, 2003. There were strong considerations both for and against the decision.

57   Horner, *Strategic Command*, p. 248.

58   *MACV Command History 1966*, 'RVNAF Deployment', p. 122. The Capital Military Region was changed on 7 June 1966 to the Capital Military District under the command of III Corps, although the area is often referred to as a separate military tactical area.

59   *MACV Command History 1966*, Chapter III 'Free World Military Assistance Force', p. 93.

60   Ibid.

61   Directive by the Chiefs of Staff Committee to Commander Australian Force Vietnam, signed by Air Chief Marshal F. R. W. Scherger, Chairman, 17 May 1966.

62   Ibid.

63   Horner, *Strategic Command*, p. 249.

64   Alan Stretton, *Soldier in a Storm*, Collins, Sydney, 1978, p. 213. Stretton was Chief of Staff at HQ AFV, April 1969–April 1970, for which he was awarded a CBE.

65   Michael O'Brien, *Conscripts and Regulars with the Seventh Battalion in Vietnam*, Allen & Unwin in assoc. with 7th Battalion, The Royal Australian Regiment Association Inc., 1995, p. 17.

66   Trevor Roderick, email to author, 12 February 2010.

67   Chanoff & Doan Van Toai, *Portrait of the Enemy*, p. 104.

68   Ibid., p. 105. Trinh Duc was Chinese by birth; he was born on Hainan Island. At this time he was a member of the Xuan Loc District Party Branch.

69   Pribbenow (trans.), *Victory in Vietnam*, Chapter 'The Summer 1965 Campaign in South Vietnam'.

70   Horner, *Strategic Command*, p. 250.

71   A summary of Annex A to 1RAR Operation Order 7/66, 29 March 1966.

72   1st Infantry Division Combat Operation After Action Report, Operation Abilene, [30 March 1966 – 15 April 1966], pp. 17, 33. *MACV Command History 1966*, 'Operations in III Corps', p. 380. Spencer Tucker (ed.), *Encyclopaedia of the Vietnam War: A Political, Social & Military History*, ABC–CLIO, Santa Barbara, CA, 1998, p. 1.

73   AP wire from Saigon, 18 April 1966.

74   *FRUS*, vol. IV, Vietnam 1966, Document 117, 8 April 1966.

75   Frank Amy, interview with Gary McKay, Sydney, 8 July 1991. QANTAS was the only airline to buy the Boeing 707-138, a longer range version of the aircraft.

76   Ibid.

77   Roger Wainwright, interview with Gary McKay, 15 February 2005.

78   *MACV Command History 1966*.

79   HQ AFV OO J1 (Operation Hardihood), 20 April 1966.

80   Harry Smith, draft manuscript, held by Gary McKay, ca September 2006.

81   Peter Schuman, interview with author, 4 September 1997.

82   1 Aust Reinforcement Unit, *Raising of 1 AUST RFT UNIT* paper, 28 April 1966, AWM95-17-16-1.

83   1 Field Regiment, 1–30 June 1966, Item 3-6-4, AWM95.

84   Trevor Roderick, email to author, 12 February 2010.

85   Lieutenant General Julian J. Ewell & Major General Ira A. Hunt, Jr, *Sharpening the Combat Edge: The Use of Analysis to Reinforce Military Judgement*, Department of the Army Washington DC, 1995, pp. 18–19.

86   Ron Shambrook, interview with Gary McKay, 14 July 2005.

87   1 Field Regiment, 1–30 June 1966, Item 3-6-4, AWM95.

88   Draft ms, Gary Mckay, 'Long Tan The Commanders', ca September 2006.

89   1ATF, Commander's Diary Narrative, July 1966, AWM95-1-4-4.

90   This chapter uses information from the Australian Army commanders' diaries [Vietnam], [June, July 1966], AWM95.

91   Detachment C-3, 5th Special Forces Group (Airborne), INTSUM No. 27, 6 August 1966.

92   *FRUS*, vol. IV, Vietnam 1966, Document 2375, Lodge telegram to President, item 47, 10 August 1966.

93   There are two Lo O streams, approximately 10–12 kilometres northeast of Nui Dat.

94   *The Heroic D445 Battalion: Its History and Tradition*, trans. Brigadier Ernest Chamberlain CSC (Retd), Military Headquarters of Dong Nai Province, Dong Nai, 1991, pp. 62–5. Also, Pham Quang Dinh, Colonel, *The History of the 5th Infantry Division 1965–2005*, The People's Army Publishing House, Hanoi, 2005, pp. 18–20. The author thanks Brigadier Chamberlain for translation of Vietnamese copies.

Chapter 4

1   *The History of the Joint Chiefs of Staff: The Joint Chiefs of Staff and the War in Vietnam 1960–1968*, Part 1, Chapter 29, Joint History Office, Joint Chiefs of Staff, Washington DC, 1970, p. 1.

2   Killed in action, *MACV Command History 1970*, vol. 1, pp. V14–15. Costs: Major General Leonard B. Taylor, *Financial Management of the Vietnam Conflict 1962–1972*, Department of the Army, Washington DC, 1974, p. 24.

3   *Foreign Relations of the US [FRUS] 1964–1968*, vol. IV, Vietnam, 1966, telephone conversation between President Johnson and Secretary of Defense McNamara, 17 January 1966.

4   The fourteen points were: the United States accepted the 1954 and 1962 Geneva Agreements as an adequate basis for peace; the United States would welcome a conference on Southeast Asia or on any part of Southeast Asia; the United States would welcome 'negotiations without pre-conditions' as proposed by the 17 non-aligned nations; the United States would welcome unconditional discussions as proposed by President Johnson; a cease-fire could be the first order of business at a conference or could be the subject of preliminary discussions; Hanoi's four points (announced in April 1965) could be discussed along with points that others might wish to propose; the United States wanted no bases in Southeast Asia; the United States did not want a continued military presence in South Vietnam after peace was assured; the United States supported free elections in South Vietnam; the reunification of Vietnam should be determined by the free decision of the Vietnamese people; the nations of Southeast Asia could be 'non-aligned or neutral' if that was their choice; the United States was prepared to contribute $1 billion to a regional development program for Vietnam, including North Vietnam; the Viet Cong would have no difficulty in having their views represented at a conference after hostilities had ceased; the United States 'could stop the bombing of North Vietnam as a step toward peace although there has not been the slightest hint or suggestion from the other side as to what they would do if the bombing stopped'. *The History of the Joint Chiefs of Staff*, Part 2, Chapter 29.

5   *FRUS, 1964–1968*, vol. IV, Vietnam 1966, notes on a meeting, 24 February 1966, between president, vice-president and Congressional leaders.

6   *The History of the Joint Chiefs of Staff*, Part 2, Chapter 29, p. 6.

7   *MACV Command History 1964*, Chapter 8.

8   *FRUS, 1964–1968*, vol. IV, Vietnam 1966, McGeorge Bundy memorandum to President Johnson, 'The Peace Offensive—Where We Are Today', 3 January 1966.

9   Ibid., Memorandum, from the President's Special Assistant (Valenti) to President Johnson, 25 January 1966.

10 Ibid., Memorandum from Secretary of State Rusk to President Johnson, 29 January 1966.

11 *The History of the Joint Chiefs of Staff*, Part 2, Chapter 25, p. 2.

12 A lot of information is available on the bombing in the North. See US Department of Defense, *United States–Vietnam Relations, 1945–1967* (a chapter of *The Pentagon Papers*), vol. 1 'The Air War in North Vietnam'. *The History of the Joint Chiefs of Staff*, Part 2. Admiral Ulysses S. Grant Sharp, *Strategy for Defeat: Vietnam*, Presidio Press, San Rafael, CA, 1979.

13 *The History of the Joint Chiefs of Staff*, Part 2, Chapter 29, p. 9. Slightly different figures are shown in *MACV Command History 1966*, Chapter 1, p. 3. A manoeuvre battalion is defined as an infantry battalion.

14 Seven nations provided military aid: USA, Australia, New Zealand, the Philippines, the Republic of China, South Korea and Thailand. The main contributors to economic and technical assistance were: Argentina, Belgium, Brazil, Canada, Costa Rica, Denmark, Ecuador, France, West Germany, Greece, Guatemala, Honduras, Iran, Ireland, Israel, Italy, Japan, Liberia, Luxembourg, Malaysia, Morocco, Netherlands, Norway, Pakistan, South Africa, Spain, Switzerland, Tunisia, Turkey, Uruguay and Venezuela. In total, 40 countries provided military, economic and technical assistance to South Vietnam.

15 *The History of the Joint Chiefs of Staff*, Part 1, Chapter 16, p. 44.

16 *MACV Command History 1966*, pp. 3–4.

17 Ibid.

18 The trial that ended in 1985 collected 20,000 pages of transcripts, 30,000 pages of depositions and affidavits and 30,000 pages of documentary exhibits. For a reading list about this case, see <www.clemson.edu/caah/history/faculty pagesEdMoise/ob.html>.

19 *The History of the Joint Chiefs of Staff*, Part 2, Chapter 29, p. 10.

20 Bruce Davies & Gary McKay, *The Men Who Persevered*, Allen & Unwin, Sydney, 2005, pp. 91–2.

21 *The History of the Joint Chiefs of Staff*, Part 1, Chapter 31 and US MACV, *Command Histories*, see 1965 Chapter 1.

22 Barry Rust, correspondence with author, 9 April 2004.

23 *MACV Command History 1966*, p. 21.

24 Ibid., p. 20.

25 The numbering of the military regions changed several times between the pre-1954 French colonial period and the post-1954 era. In Nam Bo, the regions went from 7, 8, 9 to 1, 2, 3, and then back to 7, 8, 9. Different references do not always agree on designations for the regions. *MACV Command History 1966*; David W. P. Elliott, *The Vietnamese War: Revolution and Social Change in the Mekong Delta, 1930–1975*, Pacific Basin Institute, 2006; papers from the MACV Combined Intelligence Center, Vietnam, in particular paper no. 001205, study 1966 through 1973. Tran Van Tra, *Vietnam: History of the Bulwark B2 Theater*, Vol 5: 'Concluding the 30-Years of War', Joint Publications Research Service, 2 February 1983.

26 Zones and base areas were generally named after prominent features such as villages, streams and hills.

27 In early 1956, a communist cadre joined a Binh Xuyen unit in the Rung Sat that was in revolt against the Saigon regime. By 1958, through the efforts of Nguyen Quoc Thanh, the unit had evolved into a communist company called *C40*. After the attack on Binh Ba in March 1960, a second communist company titled *C45* was formed with Nguyen Quoc

Thanh as its commander. In 1962, *C40* and *C45* were combined as *C445 Company*, which was led by Tu U. In early 1963, *C445* was reportedly 120-strong and comprised three platoons. In early 1964, *C440 Company* was raised and commanded by Nam Danh. Tu Chanh was the *C445* commander. Both were involved in the attacks on Binh Gia in late 1964 when the *C445* strength was reportedly 140. In February 1965, the two companies combined to become the *Baria Province Concentrated Battalion* and, on 19 May, Ho Chi Minh's (official) birthday, it was formally designated *D445 Provincial Mobile Battalion*, which was made up of four companies and had a strength of 350. This summary was provided by Brigadier Ernie Chamberlain (Retd). *D440 Battalion* was established in early 1968 by the arrival of recruits from North Vietnam to reinforce Baria Province.

28   Truong Son (an alias for General Nguyen Chi Thanh), *The Winter 1966 – Spring 1967 Victory and Five Lessons Concerning the Conduct of Military Strategy*, Foreign Languages Publishing House, Hanoi, 1967.

29   Pham Quang Dinh, Colonel, *Lich su Su doan bo binh 5 (1965–2005)* [*The History of 5 Infantry Division (1965–2005)*], The People's Army Publishing House, Hanoi, 2005, p. 10.

30   These figures are estimates based on the study of many intelligence papers and books written about the NVA and Viet Cong. Although some intelligence papers provide slightly higher figures than shown here, the higher figures in general were the authorised establishment numbers that did not take into account battle losses, illness and the lack of reinforcements. Studies indicate that the *5th Viet Cong Division*'s personnel strength was at the lower end of the scale in its early years. The strength of *275 Regiment* in May 1966 is quoted in Pham Quang Dinh, *The History of 5 Infantry Division (1965–2005)*, pp. 13–17, translator's notes.

31   Pham Quang Dinh, *The History of 5 Infantry Division (1965–2005)*, p. 14.

32   Subsequent references to the eastern Nui Dat will show it as (2); the Australian base is shown as Nui Dat unless it is necessary to avoid confusion when Nui Dat (1) is used.

33   Detachment C-3, 5th Special Forces Group (Airborne), INTSUM No. 24 16 July 1966.

34   *MACV Command History 1966*. Detachment C-3, 5th Special Forces Group (Airborne) INTSUM No. 24, 16 July 1966. HQ, 1ATF 5th Viet Cong Division, R569-1-16, 15 November 1967. Pham Quang Dinh, *The History of 5 Infantry Division (1965–2005)*.

35   1ATF INTSUM No. 47, 18 July 1966.

36   The 10th ARVN Division was later renamed the 18th Division because the number '10' was considered to be a bad number, much the same as the number '13' for Australians.

37   1ATF INTSUM No. 54, 25 July 1966.

38   Pham Quang Dinh, *The Heroic D445 Battalion*, pp. 31–2.

39   1ATF INTSUM No. 55, 26 July 1966.

40   1ATF INTSUM No. 58, 29 July 1966. Australian Army commanders' diaries, HQ, 1ATF, July 1966, AWM95.

41   1ATF INTSUM No. 58, 29 July 1966.

42   Mike Wells, emails to author, 25 May 2009.

43   Operation Jack Stay (Operation Order 328-66), 19 March 1966, was conducted by USMC Battalion Landing Team 1/5 from USS *Princeton* (LPH-5). Operation Jack Stay After Action Report, 12 April 1966, to CO Special Landing Force (CTG 79.5).

44   *US Naval Forces Vietnam Monthly Historical Summary: July and August 1966*, pp. 25–7, 15–16. See also their preceding monthly summaries for 1966.

45 I Field Force Vietnam (IFFV), formed in November 1965, was headquartered at Nha Trang and exercised operational control over the US Army and allied units in II CTZ. II Field Force Vietnam (IIFFV), formed in March 1996, was first at Bien Hoa and then Long Binh. It exercised operational control in III CTZ. A lieutenant general commanded each Field Force Vietnam. A major general commanded IIFFV from July 1967 to April 1969 and IFFV in 1971. IFFV deactivated on 30 April 1971 and IIFFV closed on 2 May 1971.

46 Ian McNeill, *To Long Tan: The Australian Army and the Vietnam War 1950–1966*, Allen & Unwin, Sydney, 1993, pp. 286–9.

47 Information available in Australian Army commanders' diaries [Vietnam], July and August 1966, AWM95.

48 A 'slick' was a helicopter without external armaments; it was clean or slick.

49 'Warrant officer' was an old US Army rank brought back into service. Warrant ranks were also seen in administrative duties and similar tasks. An interesting adjunct to the warrant rank system saw Australian warrant officers (sergeant major) being permitted entry into officers' clubs.

50 The following example of Australian emplaning drills as practised in the early 1960s shows that a peacetime regulation could become ridiculous in operations: On receipt of the thumbs up signal from the pilot the stick leader will lead his stick smartly to the starboard door and open. Members must watch the following: muzzle of weapon as they pass through the door, muzzles horizontal until inside; crouch low so the pack will clear the door sill; move smartly to their seat, first man sits behind crewman in the farthest single seat, next five sit along the rear wall, stick leader sits behind the pilot; pick up the two halves of a seat belt, be sure to look where they are before they sit; hold rifle between knees and fasten seat belt; indicate they are ready by holding up one hand, fist clenched; After entering the stick leader will close the door and fasten his seat belt. When ready the leader will tap the pilot's shoulder and the aircraft will depart. There will be no smoking except by a member of the crew.

51 1ATF INTSUM No. 60, 31 July 1966. 1ATF OPORD 1-6-66 (Op Holsworthy), 310800H July 1966. 5RAR OPORD 11-66 (Op Holsworthy), 062230H August 1966, Annex A.

52 5th Special Forces Group (Airborne), INTSUM No. 27, 6 August 1966.

53 Notes on the Interrogation of Le Xuan Chuyen, Assistant Chief of Staff and Chief of Operations of the *5th Viet Cong Division*. Captive Interrogation Section, Military Intelligence Centre, 5 August 1966. Chuyen turned himself in to South Vietnamese authorities on 2 August 1966.

54 Ang Cheng Guan, *The Vietnam War from the Other Side*, Taylor & Francis (Routledge), 2006. MACV Office of the Assistant Chief of Staff, Intelligence Order of Battle Reference Manual-Strength, February 1967. 1ATF R569-1-16, April and November 1967.

55 Notes on the Interrogation of Le Xuan Chuyen.

56 Ibid.

57 US Bureau of Intelligence, undated 9-page report from Department of State files, in document held by the author. See Battalion 70, 2nd NVA Division. Bruce Davies, *The Battle at Ngok Tavak: A Bloody Defeat in South Vietnam, 1968*, Allen & Unwin, Sydney, 2008, p. 3. Also, Merle Pribbenow (trans.), *Victory in Vietnam: The Official History of the People's Army of Vietnam, 1954–1975*, University Press of Kansas, 2002, p. 51.

58 US MACV MACJ261 *Bulletin 3975*, Enemy Documents, 19 April 1966. *Group 605* was probably the cover for an infiltration group that included more reinforcements than the

4th Battalion. The strength of the group therefore would not equal the size of the battalion that became the *3rd Battalion* of *275 Viet Cong Regiment.* Captain Tran Van Tieng, Assistant Political Officer, *275 Viet Cong Regiment,* said in his 1969 interrogation that the battalion arrived in May 1966.

59   United States Mission in Vietnam, Viet-Nam Documents and Research Notes: Document Nos. 43–44, September 1968. Australian Army, *Training Information Letter No. 14/70,* November 1970, Chapter 4, p. 11. See also general comments in Douglas Pike, *People's Army of Vietnam,* Presidio Press, Novato, CA, 1986. Also, information based upon personal experiences of the author in Quang Tin and Quang Ngai provinces, I Corps, 1967–68 and 1969–70. Viet-Nam Research Notes: Friction between Northern and Southern Vietnamese, September 1968.

60   Combined Military Interrogation Center, Special Report, 'Le Xuan Chuyen', 26 December 1966.

61   Major General Spurgeon Neel, *Vietnam Studies, Medical Support of the U.S. Army in Vietnam 1965–1970,* Department of the Army, Washington DC, 1961, Chapter III. Ashley Ekins with Ian McNeill, *Fighting to the Finish: The Australian Army and the Vietnam War, 1968–1975,* Allen & Unwin, 2012. Australian Service Casualties Appendix G, Table 1.

62   USMC Battalion Landing Team 1-26, Command Chronology for the period 2–31 August 1966.

63   Department of the Army, Headquarters 173rd Airborne Brigade (Separate), Combat Operations After Action Report, 15 December 1966. Operation Toledo, 10 August – 7 September 1966.

64   Combined Intelligence Center (English edn), 'NVA/Viet Cong Electronic Warfare Capability', 1 July 1967.

65   Report of *Deckhouse III,* Phase II/Operation Toledo, 2 September 1966.

66   173rd Airborne Brigade (Separate): Operation Toledo Report. II Field Force Vietnam Operational Report for Quarterly Period Ending 31 October 1966, dated 15 November 1966.

67   Interview with Tran Van Tra, 23 November 1990, at the Vietnam Mission to the UN. Interviewer John M. Carland, US Army Center for Military History.

68   Pham Quang Dinh, *The History of 5th Infantry Division,* p. 19.

69   1ATF INTSUM No. 69, AWM95-1-4-6, Part 2.

70   Douglas Pike, *PAVN: People's Army of Vietnam,* Presidio Press, Novato, CA, 1986. See also, MACV Office of the Assistant Chief of Staff, Intelligence Order of Battle Reference Manual-Strength, 2 February 1967.

71   Combined Military Intelligence Center: Special Report–Radio Intercept Capability, Prior Warning of Airstrikes, Air Defence Tactics and Weapons. Danang Interrogation Centre: Date of information 1960 to February 1967. *MACV Command History 1967,* 'Viet Cong Intelligence Operations', pp. 102–03.

72   6RAR, Duty Officer's log, serial 52, 17 August 1966, AWM95-7-6-5.

73   Ashley Ekins, 'Not one scintilla of evidence?', *Australian Journal of Politics and History,* vol. 42, no. 3, 1996, pp. 345–64.

74   *MACV Command History 1967,* 'Viet Cong Electronic Warfare', p. 106.

75   See, for example, *273 Viet Cong Regiment* and *9th Viet Cong Division* in *History of the 273 Viet Cong Regiment July 1964–December 1969,* United States Army, 5 February 1970, p. 32.

76   Australian Army commanders' diaries, HQ, 1ATF, Commander's summary for 17 August,

Part 1, AWM95-1-4-6. Also, 6RAR After Action Report Operation Smithfield, 18–21 August 1966, p. 3, sub-para. 7 (7), AWM95-7-6-5.

77 Australian Army Commanders' diaries [Vietnam], Item 7/6/5, 1966, AWM95. Annex C to 6RAR After Action Report – B Company's report.

78 Ian McNeill, *To Long Tan: The Australian Army and the Vietnam War 1950–1966*, Allen & Unwin, Sydney 1993. Australian Army commanders' diaries, HQ, 1ATF, 1966, AWM95.

79 Pham Quang Dinh, *The History of 5th Infantry Division*, p. 19.

80 6RAR Narrative, Duty Officer's log, Maps, Annexes, [1–31 August 1966], D Company After Action Report, Operation Smithfield, AWM95-7-6-5.

81 *War Materiel Used by the Viet Cong*, a publication released by Brigadier General J. A. McChristian, Assistant Chief of Staff, J2 [Intelligence] MACV, February 1966. Chicom Type 53 (Soviet 82mm Mortar Model M1937) Range 3040 metres (3320 yards).

82 Bob Grandin, *The Battle of Long Tan: As told by the commanders to Bob Grandin*, Allen & Unwin, Sydney, 2004, p. 114.

83 6RAR, Duty Officer's log, Australian Army commanders' diaries [Vietnam], Item 7/6/5, August 1966, 0635 hours, p. 18, AWM95. Also, Annex C to 6RAR After Action Report – B Company, p. 2. Serial 11.

84 D Company, 6RAR After Action Report: Operation Smithfield.

85 *Review of Recognition for the Battle of Long Tan March 2008*, Department of Premier and Cabinet, Canberra, 2008, p. 9.

86 Terry Burstall, *The Soldiers' Story: The Battle at Xa Long Tan, Vietnam, 18 August 1966*, University of Queensland Press, 1986, p. 51. See also, *Australian*, 23 November 2009, in which Allen May repeated his claim.

87 6RAR, Duty Officer's log, 18 August, at 1556 and 1557 hours.

88 Douglas Fabian, telephone conversation with author, 16 December 2009.

89 Grandin, *The Battle of Long Tan*, p. 121.

90 Lex McAulay, *The Battle of Long Tan*, Century Hutchinson, Hawthorn, Vic., 1986, pp. 48–9.

91 See Buick's explanation in Bob Buick with Gary McKay, *All Guts and No Glory*, Allen & Unwin, St Leonards, NSW, 2000, pp. 89–90, and Burstall, *The Soldiers' Story*.

92 Headquarters US MACV, MACJ233, Serial No. 0192, 10 February 1965: Orientation Material, p. 15.

93 Spencer C. Tucker (ed.), *Encyclopedia of the Vietnam War*, ABC CLIO, Santa Barbara, CA, 1998, p. 1.

94 The following books provide accounts of the Long Tan battle: Buick with McKay, *All Guts and No Glory*; Burstall, *The Soldiers' Story*; McAulay, *The Battle of Long Tan*; McNeill, *To Long Tan*; Grandin, *The Battle of Long Tan*; Paul Ham, *Vietnam: The Australian War*, Harper Collins, Sydney, 2007, Chapter 18.

95 Headquarters US MACV, MACJ233, Serial No. 0192, 10 February 1965: Orientation Material, p. 9.

96 Tucker (ed.), *Encyclopedia of the Vietnam War*, p. 1. See also, US 1st Infantry Division After Action Report, Operation Abilene, p. 17.

97 HQ, 1ATF, Commander's Diary Narrative, May 1966, AWM95-1-4-1.

98 One American publication that came too late for the veterans of Long Tan was Brigadier S. L. A. Marshall (Retd) and Lieutenant Colonel David Hackworth's *Military Operations: Vietnam Primer*, US Department of Army pamphlet 525-2, 1967. The pamphlet

summarised the lessons learnt during the fighting operations of 1966. The information contained in the pamphlet came as a result of interrogation of the men who had done the fighting in the months May 1966 to February 1967. From the questioning, the authors were able to reconstruct most of the combat actions in that period.

99 Pham Quang Dinh, *The History of the 5th Infantry Division*, p. 20. The *2nd Company*, *D445 Battalion*, suffered 3 dead and 20 wounded. No figures are known for the other two companies, but they admit getting caught in the artillery fire; see *The Heroic D445 Battalion: Its History and Tradition*, Military Headquarters of Dong Nai Province, Dong Nai, 1991.

100 6RAR, Duty Officer's log, 18 August, Serial 89,90, and 6RAR Commanding Officer's Orders, Operation Smithfield, 19 August 1966.

101 McNeill, *To Long Tan*, p. 44.

102 Ernest Chamberlain, *The Viet Cong D445: Their Story*, self-published, Geelong, Vic., 2011, p. 43, note 142.

103 *The Heroic D445 Battalion*, pp. 62–5.

104 *The History of the 5th Infantry Division*, p. 19. Trenches, see Annex E to 6RAR After Action Report, Operation Smithfield, paras 9 and 30.

105 Ibid.

106 *The Heroic D445 Battalion*, pp. 30–2.

107 Unit strengths are impossible to determine exactly. The numbers used here come from calculations made after considering a wide range of information in US, Vietnamese and Australian documents. Battlefront figures also take into account that not everyone in a formation or unit was at the front line.

108 Ang Cheng Guan, *The Vietnam War from the Other Side*, Routledge Curzon, New York, 2002, p. 109. Pribbenow (trans.), *Victory in Vietnam*, p. 192.

109 Annex B (Intelligence) to OPORD 5-66 (Denver), HQ 173d Abn Bde (Sep) 9 April 66. Pribbenow (trans.), *Victory in Vietnam*, p. 464, note 22.

110 See McNeill, *To Long Tan*, p. 365, for an inference that Kiem commanded during the battle. He did command *D445* later in 1966, but in August 1966 he was the commander of the *Chau Duc Company*. Bui Quang Chanh signed a 'six-monthly political report' as commanding officer of *D445* on 18 July 1966. Document provided by Brigadier Ernie Chamberlain (Retd). Chamberlain, *The Viet Cong D445 Their Story*, p. 41, note 130.

111 James W. Wirtz, *The Tet Offensive: Intelligence Failure in War*, Cornell University Press, Ithaca and London, 1991, Chapter 'The Communist Debate over Strategy'.

112 MACV Office of the Assistant Chief of Staff, Intelligence Order of Battle Reference Manual-Strength, February 1967. *MACV Command History 1966*.

113 Annex F to 6RAR After Action Report: 3 TP 1 APC SQN, serial 7.

114 *MACV Command History 1967*, 'Enemy Operations in RVN, NVA/Viet Cong Weapons', p. 88.

115 Pribbenow (trans.), *Victory in Vietnam*, pp. 214, 177.

116 Ibid., p. 464, note 18. Following the battle of Binh Gia in December 1964, the VC force wrote: 'operation Binh Gia taught us to draw the enemy into our ambushes'. Op cit. *Operations in the US Resistance War*, The Gioi Publishers, Hanoi, 2009, p. 5.

117 Buick & McKay, *All Guts and No Glory*, pp. 112–13.

118 Ibid., pp. 114–15.

119 Ibid., pp. 116–17. Sergeant Buick's recollections on the body count are not corroborated by the information recorded in the 6RAR after action reports.

120 World War II commanders' diaries and HQ, 1ATF, Duty Officer's log, August 1966, p. 37, AWM 95-1-4-7.

121 Burstall, *The Soldiers' Story*, p. 136.

122 This total is the combination of casualties for the *2nd Company, D445 Battalion* and *275 Regiment*, but numbers are not used to explain the term 'heavy casualties'. *The Heroic D445 Battalion.*

123 Douglas Pike Collection: Unit 05 – Fifth PLAF Regiment, WS-5: 1965-69, Captain Tran Van Tieng, Assistant Political Officer, p. 8.

124 6RAR After Action Report, Operation Smithfield.

125 A guess factor is applied here. The guess being that not every wounded man needs assistance and the equivalent number of labourers could be reduced by a factor equal to the number of trips per recovery group. Also, the movement of the dead probably required less labour than for moving wounded men. There are anecdotal reports from other battles of one man using a butcher's hook to drag a body away.

126 MACV Office of the Assistant Chief of Staff, Intelligence Order of Battle Reference Manual-Strength, February 1967. *MACV Command History 1966.*

127 S. G. Spring, K. Harris & J. R. Lind, *Fast-Val: Case Study of a Two-Company NVA Attack on a Marine Company in a Defensive Position on Foxtrot Ridge*, RAND, Santa Monica, CA, 1971.

128 See pp. 30–1 of the interview with Major General S. C. Graham in the Army Office transcripts of military history interviews with senior officers concerning the Australian Army in Vietnam, AWM107. Contents date range 1972–1973. None of the papers from Ut Thoi's diary have been produced to corroborate the translation.

129 The Combined Documentation Exploitation Center (CDEC), located in Saigon, was organised on 1 October 1965. When there were important documents to be examined, teams were sent to translate and photograph on the spot and to distribute immediate information to units while the originals were taken back to the CDEC.

130 US 1st Infantry Division Combat Operations After Action Report, Operation Abilene, 30 March – 15 April 1966. Undated paper, Phuoc Tuy Province Information Brief, held by author. Vung Tau had a population of 38,000 but it was a separate municipality and its population is not included in these figures.

131 MACV, Intelligence Order of Battle Reference Manual, February 1967. *MACV Command History 1966.* Signal General Westmoreland, COMUSMACV–General Wheeler, CJCS 26 August 1967, re battle at Suoi Long. See also Merle Pribbenow, *COSVN* directive to the 5th Division to conduct operations in October 1966 in Baria and Long Khanh. In Pribbenow's previously cited work, see above.

132 1ATF Commander's Diary Narrative, 1–28 February 1967, AWM95-1-4-30.

133 Major Noel Ford, B Coy Action Report, Operation Smithfield 23 August 1966, serial 7.

134 Dave Sabben's novel, *Through Enemy Eyes*, Allen & Unwin, Sydney, 2005. Harry Smith, 'The Battle of Long Tan' <www.hotkey.net.au/~marshalle/harry/harry.htm> [accessed 21 December 2009]. Harry Smith, 'The Battle of Long Tan', *Commando*, vol. 10, no. 74, March 2009. Buick with McKay, *All Guts and No Glory*. Lieutenant Colonel Colin Townsend After Action Report, Operation Smithfield, 18–21 August 1966. Major Noel Ford, B Coy Action Report, Operation Smithfield, 23 August 1966. Major Harry Smith, D Coy After Action Report Operation Vendetta—changed to Smithfield (undated). HQ, 1ATF, INTSUM No. 77 for 170001H to 172400H, August 1966.

135   D Company After Action Report, Operation Smithfield.

136   Richmond Cubis, personal letter, 2 October 1974. A copy is held by the author.

137   Ibid.

138   See commanders' diaries for 1ATF and 1 Field Regiment, November 1966.

139   See Directorate of Military Training, *Training Information Bulletin Number 11*: Lessons from Operations in Vietnam by 1RAR, Army Headquarters, Canberra, 1966. See also, 1RAR R569-1-50, 29 May 1966, a paper submitted by officers of 1RAR on operations in Vietnam. The papers covered Airmobile Assault, Viet Cong tactics and suggested methods of countering them, Viet Cong tactics encountered by 1RAR, Tactical lessons learnt in Vietnam, Battalion patrol planning, Notes on establishing and operating an A Echelon, Health problems, Communications, Fire support, and a summary of lessons learnt from operations with APCs in Vietnam.

140   A good example of the later increases is seen in the 3RAR 1971 scales: SLR 100-150 rounds, M16 200-250, M60 750-1000. Minutes of a Battalion Group Debrief, 21 June 1971, AWM95-7-3-77.

141   6RAR after action reports, Operation Smithfield.

142   HQ, 1ATF, Diary Narrative, August 1966.

143   Grandin, *The Battle of Long Tan*, p. 145.

144   See McNeill, *To Long Tan*, p. 322.

145   Grandin, *The Battle of Long Tan*, pp. 145–6.

146   Adrian Roberts, correspondence with author, 29 December 2009.

147   See the after action reports in the 6RAR diary for August 1966, AWM95, 7/6/5.

148   Ibid.

149   Ibid.

150   'Foreword', in *Armor on Leyte, Sixth Army Operations, 17 Oct – 26 Dec 1944*, US Armored School, research report, May 1949.

151   Pamphlet on Military Honours and Awards, [UK] War Office 12922, 1960.

152   *London Gazette*, Supplement, 30 September 1966.

153   Recommendations for honours and awards for Army personnel serving in Vietnam, NAA A1945, 133/3/26.

154   Major General (Retd) Peter Abigail AO, Chairman, *Review of Recognition for the Battle of Long Tan, March 2008*, Department of Prime Minister and Cabinet, 2008. Professor Dennis Pearce AO, Chair, *Inquiry into Unresolved Recognition Issues for the Battle of Long Tan*, Australian Government, Defence Honours & Awards Tribunal, 3 September 2009.

155   *Inquiry into Unresolved Recognition Issues for the Battle of Long Tan*, 2009.

156   See Report of the *Independent Review Panel of the End of War List 1999*, pp. 48–9. See also the narrative for US Presidential Unit Citation, 28 May 1968.

157   *MACV Command History 1966*, Annex K–1966 Chronology, 18 August 1966, p. 842. See also, p. 386—Australians destroyed a VC reinforced battalion which contained a large number of NVA troops.

158   Foreign Office 1954, *Regulations concerning the Acceptance and Wearing of Foreign Orders, Decorations and Medals by Persons in the Service of the Crown: United Kingdom and Dependent Territories*. These regulations were extant in the early 1960s and should not be confused with the wording in later editions.

159   Davies & McKay, *The Men Who Persevered*, pp. 52–3.

160   *Foreign Office Regulations* 1954, Order 1. Orders for insignia also applied to medals.

161 Abigail, *Review of Recognition for the Battle of Long Tan*, p. 30.

162 Recommendations for honours and awards for Army personnel serving in Vietnam. See detailed discussion note of the Vietnamese Campaign Medal to Mr Flanagan, 19 May 1966, NAA A1945, 133/3/26.

163 1ATF Message A221 dated 220645Z August 1971 to List A and C: Honours and Awards.

164 Remarks of Welcome to Prime Minister Holt of Australia on the South Lawn at the White House, 29 June 1966. <http://en.wikipedia.org/wiki/Harold_Holt> [accessed 14 February 2012].

165 *FRUS, 1964–1968*, vol. IV, Vietnam 1966, Memorandum from Senator Mike Mansfield to President Johnson, 29 June 1966, with attachment dated 28 June 1966.

166 *United States–Vietnam Relations, 1945–1967*, Book 12, Part VIB, pp. 218–19.

167 President Lyndon B. Johnson, Daily Diary, 21 October 1966.

Chapter 5

1   1ATF, Commander's Diary Narrative, 1–31 January 1967, AWM95-1-4-24.

2   *The Division in Battle*, Pamphlet No. 11, 'Counter-Revolutionary Warfare', Army Headquarters, Canberra, 1965, p. 25.

3   Ibid., p. 36.

4   5RAR, Message LOG, 19 February 1967, 1ATF to B, C Coy at 0905, AWM95-7-5-13.

5   1ATF, Commander's Diary Narrative, 1–31 January 1967.

6   Bruce Davies & Gary McKay, *The Men Who Persevered*, Allen & Unwin, Sydney, 2005, pp. 98–9.

7   George Mansford, email to author, 12 February 2010.

8   Ibid.; also 13 February 2010.

9   Davies & McKay, *The Men Who Persevered*, pp. 88–9.

10 Ibid.

11 Clarry Rule, telephone conversation with author, 11 February 2010.

12 Mike Wells, correspondence with author, 19 February 2010.

13 Ibid.

14 Peter Samuel, 'The task force role: A critique', *Vietnam Digest*, no. 2, Friends of Vietnam, Canberra, August 1969, p. 35.

15 Annex I to Colonel P. A. Roy, 'Staff Memorandum: Integration of Allied Forces', Caserta, Italy, 6 June 1944.

16 As an example, see USMC, 3rd Marine Division, 'Concept of Operations to Operation Order 325-65, July 1965. Phase I: Security of Base Area; Phase II: Deep Patrolling and Offensive Operations that contribute to the security of the base … to prevent massing of enemy for surprise attack; Phase III: Reserve and Reaction Forces in Coordination with RVNAF'.

17 *MACV Command History 1967*, vol. I, 'Free World Military Assistance Forces, General', p. 247.

18 Ibid.

19 See 'The McNamara Line', later in this chapter.

20 Directive by the Chiefs of Staff Committee to Commander Australian Force Vietnam: para. 13, March 1967.

21 *MACV* Command *History 1967*, vol. II, Chapter VI, 'Pacification and Nation Building', p. 577.

22 *MACV Command, History 1967*, vol. I, 'Combined US/RVN Strategy', p. 317.

23 *MACV Command, History 1967*, vol. II, Chapter VI, p. 577.

24 Ibid.

25 See Ian McNeill, *The Team: Australian Army Advisers in Vietnam 1962–1972*, Australian War Memorial, Canberra, 1984, pp. 94–5.

26 Robert K. Brigham, *ARVN: Life and Death in the South Vietnamese Army*, University Press of Kansas, 2006, p. 83.

27 Ted Gittinger, interview with General Samuel T. Williams, 2 March 1981, at General Williams' residence, San Antonio, TX. Transcripts held by Lyndon Baines Johnson Library, Austin, TX.

28 General William E. DePuy (US Army, Retd), *What We Might Have Done and Why We Didn't Do It*, Army, February, 1986. DePuy was a former commander of the US Army Training and Doctrine Command. He spent over six years in direct, close contact with the evolution of counterinsurgency doctrine and large-unit operations in Vietnam.

29 Edward Geary Lansdale, *In the Midst of Wars*, Fordham University Press, New York, 1991, p. 573.

30 Ian Teague to author, October 2004.

31 Thomas L. Ahern, Jr, *CIA and Rural Pacification in South Vietnam (U)*, Center for the Study of Intelligence, 2001.

32 Office of Assistant Secretary of Defense (SA), March 1967, 'South East Asia Analysis Report'.

33 United States Marine Corps, *Small Wars Manual 1940*, United States Government Printing Offices, Washington, 1940. This publication of 15 chapters and 446 pages covered everything from strategy, psychology, military and civil relationships to force composition, training and operations.

34 Lieutenant General Victor Krulak, Commanding General Fleet Marine Force Pacific, *First to Fight: An Inside View of the US Marine Corps*, Naval Institute, Annapolis, Chapter 12.

35 Mai Elliott, *RAND in Southeast Asia: A History of the Vietnam War Era*, RAND Corporation, Santa Monica, CA, p. 39.

36 *The Pentagon Papers*, Gravel edn, vol. 2, Chapter 7 'Re-Emphasis on Pacification: 1965–1967', pp. 515–623. Jim Tennison, 'Vietnam', *Herald Sun*, 22 April 1995. See also Paul Ham, *Vietnam: The Australian War*, HarperCollins, Sydney, 2007, p. 85. This entry refers to a thesis by Martin Hamilton-Smith, p. 65, held at the AWM MSS01082. The thesis mentions an interview given by William Colby, former Director of Central Intelligence (CIA), for the 1983 ABC documentary *Allies*. In the interview Colby said 'President Johnson, I think, received him a couple of times as I recall'. Original transcripts of *Allies* held by the author, courtesy of Sylvie Le Clezio, Producer. See also, RAND Corporation reports written by Serong in 1968 and subsequent years. List of US Invited Contractors Operating in Vietnam 1973, copy held by author. Former CIA agents spoke only on the guarantee of anonymity. A freedom of information application to the CIA to release a file on Serong was refused. Digital copy of President Johnson's daily diary is available from the Johnson Library. President Nixon's diaries are available at <www.nixonlibray.gov/virtuallibrary/documents/dailydiary.php#Diary>. President Kennedy' diary is available at <www.jfklibrary.org>.

37 Lieutenant General Ngo Quang Truong, *RVNAF and US Operational Cooperation and Coordination*, Indochina Monographs, US Army Center of Military History, Washington DC, 1980, p. 60.

38 Ibid., Chapter ' Combined Action Program'.

39 Rule, telephone conversation, 11 February 2010.

40 Roy, Memorandum.

41 Truong, *RVNAF and US Operational Cooperation and Coordination*.

42 Roy, Memorandum.

43 *Foreign Relations of the United States 1964–1968*, vol. V, Vietnam 1967, item 197, memorandum from the President's Special Counsel (McPherson) to President Johnson, Washington, 13 June 1967.

44 A. H. Tange, High Commissioner, India, personal letter to Sir James Plimsoll, Secretary, Department of External Affairs, 10 August 1967.

45 Ibid., p. 2.

46 Ibid., p. 3.

47 Ibid., pp. 2–3.

48 Peter Edwards, 'Defence Policy Making: A Close-Up View, 1950–1980', Chapter 1, <express.anu.edu.au> [16 February 2010].

49 Ibid., Preface, pp. ix–x.

50 See <www.navy.gov.au/Naval_Operations-in_Vietnam#Clearance_Diving_Team_3>.

51 *MACV Command History 1967*, vol. I, 'Free World Military Assistance Force', 'Australia', p. 248.

52 Ibid.

53 Gary McKay, *Vietnam Fragments: An Oral History of Australians at War*, Allen & Unwin, St Leonards, NSW, 1992, pp. 75–6.

54 *MACV Command History 1967*, vol. I, 'Free World Military Assistance Force', Australia, pp. 248–9.

55 Ibid., p. 249.

56 McKay, *Vietnam Fragments*, p. 89.

57 Ibid.

58 1ATF, GS Instruction 8/67, Civil Affairs, 23 June 1967, AWM95-17-1-2.

59 Ibid.

60 Ibid., para. 15.

61 Stuart C. Graham, 'Observations on operations in Vietnam', *Army Journal*, no. 235, Dominion Press, Canberra, 1968, pp. 5–32.

62 6RAR, Operation Bribie Combat Operations – After Action Report, 22 May 1967, AWM95-7-6-11.

63 *Australian*, 30 March 2010. The article quoted AWM sources.

64 16646 Private Richard Beverley Odendahl MM, citation.

65 HQ, 1ATF, [1–28 February 1967], Operation Bribie, AWM95-1-4-30.

66 Ibid.

67 6RAR, Operation Bribie Combat Operations – After Action Report, 22 May 1967, AWM95-7-6-11.

68 Ibid.

69 Chris Coulthard Clark, *Australian Encyclopedia of Australia's Battles*, Allen & Unwin, Crows Nest, NSW, 2001, p. 286.

70 6RAR, Operation Bribie, Combat Operations – After Action Report, 22 May 1967, AWM95-7-6-11.

71 Commander's Daily Situation Report (SITREP): From 180001H to 182400H, February 1967, para 1. a. (6), AWM95-1-4-30.

72 *The Heroic D445 Battalion: Its History and Tradition*, trans. Brigadier Ernest Chamberlain

CSC (Retd), Military Headquarters, Dong Nai Province, Dong Nai, 1991, pp. 34–5.

73   Detachment 1 Division Intelligence Unit, 16-1-2 (19), 29 March 1967: Preliminary Interrogation Report – PW (prisoner of war). The details provided by the two captured soldiers of the *2nd Battalion* differ from the information provided by Captain Tran Van Tieng who did not mention this battle in his 1969 interrogation.

74   Interrogation of Le Tan Dat, B-23 Medical Company, captured by 3/43 ARVN Battalion on 4 May 1967, 135th Military Intelligence Group paper.

75   Ian McNeill & Ashley Ekins: *On the Offensive: The Australian Army in the Vietnam War, January 1967 – June 1968*, Allen & Unwin, Crow's Nest, NSW, in assoc. with the Australian War Memorial, 2003, pp. 270, 148.

76   Captain Tran Van Tieng (captured in 1969) stated that *275 Viet Cong Regiment* suffered 150–200 casualties, both killed and wounded.

77   Annex A to 1ATF Op Instruction 8/67 (Op Kirribilli), 22 February 1967.

78   6RAR, Operation Bribie, Combat Operations – After Action Report, 22 May 1967, AWM95-7-6-11.

79   Australian Army, *Training Information Letter No. 4/70* [undated], 'Viet Cong/NVA Bunker Systems'.

80   Tactical lesson taught to the author in his role as an Australian adviser in 1967.

81   Pham Quang Dinh, Colonel, *Lich su Su doan bo binh 5 (1965–2005)* (The History of 5 Infantry Division (1965–2005)), The People's Army Publishing House, Hanoi, 2005.

82   1ATF, Commander's Diary Narrative, February 1967, AWM95-1-1-30.

83   Graham, 'Observations on operations in Vietnam', pp. 5–32.

84   Hoang Ngoc Lung, Assistant Chief of Staff Intelligence, Joint General Staff, *Intelligence*, Department of the Army, Washington DC, 31 October 1976. *MACV Command History 1967*, 'Viet Cong and NVA Forces in South Vietnam'.

85   Greg Lockhart, *The Minefield: An Australian Tragedy in Vietnam*, Allen & Unwin, Crows Nest, NSW, 2007, p. 73.

86   Ibid., p. 107.

87   See the AWM95 series 1ATF commanders' narratives, for the period mid-1967 to the departure of Brigadier Graham in October.

88   Lockhart, *The Minefield*, p. 95.

89   The base was named after Bui Cong Minh and Mac Dinh Dam, secretary and deputy secretary of the Long Dien District Committee, who were killed on 17 November 1948. Phan Chi Than, *The Minh Dam Base 1945–1975*, Baria-Vung Tau Province Information and Cultural Office, Vietnam, 2006.

90   Major L. Telfer, Lieutenant Colonel Lane Rogers, and V. Keith Fleming, Jr, *US Marines in Vietnam, 1967*, Headquarters and Museums Division, US Marine Corps, 1984, Washington DC, p. 94. See also extensive information on this subject in *MACV Command History 1967*, 'Annex A: The Anti-Infiltration Barrier'.

91   5RAR, 6RAR and 7RAR paraded; 5RAR was in the process of going home.

92   McNeill & Ekins, *On the Offensive*, p. 202.

93   Ibid.

94   1ATF, Commander's Diary Narrative, July 1967, AWM95-1-4-47.

95   11ACR had strength of around 4000. Their armoured vehicles were a mixture of M113, its derivative the Armoured Cavalry Assault Vehicle, and M48 Patton tanks. General George S. Patton's son commanded 11ACR during 1968–69. 11ACR got a few Sheridan

tanks around 1969. A squadron was approximately equivalent to a battalion in size. The regiment had 50 tanks, 300 APCs and 50 helicopters.

96 Annual Historical Summary (RCS CSHIS—6 R2), 3rd Squadron, 11ACR, 1 January 1967 – 31 December 1967. Also, HQ 1ATF, Ops Log, [19 June1967], AWM95-1-4-43. Pham Quang Ding, *The History of 5 Infantry Division (1965–2005)*, pp. 27–9.

97 The Hydra was well known to Australian soldiers as the symbol of the Jungle Training Centre at Canungra in Qld. In Greek mythology a Hydra was a many-headed serpent that grew two more heads for each one that was cut off.

98 Operational Report—Lessons Learned for Quarterly Period Ending 31 July 1967, submitted by 9th Infantry Division, 7 November 1967, p. 21.

99 HQ, 1ATF, Ops Log, serials 1059, 1060, 1067, 1070, 1072, AWM95-1-4-49.

100 1ATF, Commander's Diary Narrative, July 1967, AWM95-1-4-47.

101 HQ, 1ATF Narrative, Duty Officer's log [1–31 July 1967], Commander's Diary Narrative, AWM95-1-4-47.

102 1ATF, *Troops Information Sheet, no. 52*, 9–15 July 1967, p. 4, AWM95-1-4-50. There is a noticeable gap in the information released by the AWM for July 1967. The INTSUM and daily SITREP pages for the period of Operation Paddington are missing.

103 Ibid., p. 5.

104 Operational Report—Lessons Learned for Quarterly Period Ending 31 July 1967, submitted by 9th Infantry Division, 7 November 1967, p. 37.

105 Department of the Navy, Judge Advocate General and Chief of Naval Operations: Investigation of Forrestal Fire. CNAL 012, Serial 0863, USS *Forrestal* (CVA-59) Fire Investigation, 26 September 1967.

106 Jack Shulimson et al., *US Marines in Vietnam: The Defining Year 1968*, 'The 3D Marine Division and the Barrier', History and Museums Division, US Marine Corps, 1997, p. 19. Also, Major Gary L. Telfer et al., *US Marines in Vietnam. MACV Command History 1967*, vol. I, Chapter V.

107 Pham Quang Dinh, *The History of the 5th Infantry Division 1965–2005*, p. 31.

108 7RAR, Commander's Diary, November 1967, AWM95-7-7-15.

109 HQ, 1ATF, *Troops Information Sheet no. 69*, 5–11 November 1967, p. 7, AWM95-1-4-69.

110 Operational Report—Lessons Learned for Quarterly Period Ending 31 July 1967, submitted by 9th Infantry Division, 7 November 1967, p. 8.

111 Brigadier Graham interview, p. 34, AWM 107, AHW file 707/R2/38(2).

112 Save our Sons flyer, undated, authorised by Mrs J. Golgerth, Mrs P. Ashcroft and Mrs A. Gregory.

113 February–June 1967, Australian Gallup Polls.

114 *FRUS, 1964–1968*, vol. V, Vietnam 1967, Serial 238, Notes of meeting, Washington, 12 July 1967.

115 Ibid., notes for 20 July.

116 Ibid., notes for 5 August, president's meeting with Clark Clifford and General Maxwell Taylor.

117 Clark M. Clifford, 'A Viet Nam reappraisal: The personal history of one man's view and how it evolved', *Foreign Affairs*, vol. 47, no. 4, July 1969, pp. 606–07.

118 Ibid.

119 See Clifford's discussion on this in his article 'A Viet Nam reappraisal'. Also *FRUS* papers discuss strategic matters throughout.

120 *FRUS*, vol. 47, July 1969, p. 613.

121 *FRUS, 1964–1968*, vol. V, Vietnam 1967, Serial 238, Notes on weekly luncheon with Secretaries Rusk and McNamara, Walt Rostow and George Christian (General Johnson was also present), 12 September 1967.

122 Clark, 'A Viet Nam reappraisal', p. 607.

123 *FRUS* notes for meeting with President Johnson, Secretary Katzenbach, CIA Director Helms, Walt Rostow and George Christian, 26 September 1967. See also president's daily diary, 25 September 1967.

124 *FRUS, 1964–1968*, vol. V, Vietnam 1967, Serial 341, meeting, 3 October 1967.

125 *FRUS, 1964–1968*, vol. XXVII, Mainland Southeast Asia, Regional Affairs, Serial 31, Memorandum of conversation between President Johnson and Paul Hasluck, 10 October 1967.

126 Ibid, Serial 30, Memorandum of conversation between Secretary of Defense, Robert McNamara, and Minister for External Affairs, Paul Hasluck, 10 October 1967.

127 Ibid.

128 Ibid, Serial 31, Memorandum of conversation between President Johnson and Paul Hasluck, 10 October 1967.

129 Ibid.

130 *FRUS, 1964–1968*, vol. V, Vietnam 1967, Serial 341, meeting, 3 October 1967.

131 *U.S. Army Mechanized and Armor Combat Operations in Vietnam*, Department of the Army, Headquarters United States Army Vietnam, 28 March 1967.

132 General Donn A. Starry, *Mounted Combat in Vietnam* (MACOV), Vietnam Studies, Department of the Army, Washington DC, 1989, p. 79.

133 *MACOV*, Section 3, 'Antitank Techniques'.

134 McNeill & Ekins, *On the Offensive*, pp. 247–9.

135 A US tank company had 17 tanks. C Squadron's tanks arrived in February 1967: 12 gun tanks, two dozer tanks, two bridge layers, two armoured recovery vehicles plus the Forward Delivery Troop's vehicles. Commanders Diaries, C Squadron, 1 Armoured Regiment, AWM95-2-3-5 1968.

136 McNeill & Ekins, *On the Offensive*, p. 249.

137 Lieutenant General Daly interview, p. 62, AWM 107 AHQ File 707/R2/38(5).

138 McNeill & Ekins, *On the Offensive*, p. 257.

139 *MACV Command History 1967*, vol. I, 'The Enemy Situation at the Year's End'.

140 Bernard O'Riordan, *Guardian*, 24 August 2005.

Chapter 6

1 Ian McNeill and Ashley Ekins, *On the Offensive: The Australian Army in the Vietnam War, January 1967 – June 1968*, Allen & Unwin, Sydney, NSW, in assoc. with the Australian War Memorial, 2003, p. 270.

2 See commanders' diaries for 1ARU and 1ATF Logistics Company, 1966, AWM95-17-6 and sequential numbers.

3 See commanders' diaries for 1ARU, 1966, AWM95-17-6-8 and sequential numbers.

4 AWM95-2-3-5: C Squadron 1 Armoured Regiment Narrative Annexes 1–29 February 1968; see the entry for 16 February 1968.

5 Ibid., see the entry for 24 February 1968. The first tank was 169099. For those who may wish to set a Trivial Pursuit style question, Sergeant Neville Calliss drove the first Centurion into South Vietnam and Captain Bernard Sullivan commanded it.

6   Major General R. N. L. Hopkins, *Australian Armour: A History of the Royal Australian Armoured Corps 1927–1972*, Australian War Memorial and the Australian Government Printing Service, Canberra, 1978, p. 251.

7   This number was gleaned from all of the Armoured Regiment reports. It may not be precise but it would be a very close approximation.

8   AWM95-2-36: C Squadron 1 Armoured Regiment, 1–31 March; see the entry for 6 March 1968.

9   The Russians supplied the more powerful RPG-7 in 1967. *MACV Command History 1967*, vol. 1, p. 21. In September 1967 an RPG-7 was used against a Mobile Riverine Assault Craft in IV Corps. See MACV report in the same publication, p. 91. In January 1968, USARV conducted test firings of RPG-2 and RPG-7 against bunkers to determine an effective barrier, which was decided to be chain link fence. See *MACV Command History 1968*, vol. 1, p. 673. At this stage there had not been a report of an RPG-7 attack against a tank. During Tet 1968, the B-40 and B-41 (RPG-2 and 7) were considered by the Viet Cong to be too heavy and have no serious effect when fired into upper stories of buildings. Weapons that should be used included the anti-tank French Tromblon and Basdor bullet. From a Viet Cong 'lessons learnt' pamphlet, quoted in the same volume.

10 See *Mechanized and Armour Study Combat Operations in Vietnam*, United States Army, 28 March 1967, p. 67. Mines were the tanks' greatest threat, a point that was stressed by tank crews to a US Army 1970 study group. US Army Concept Team in Vietnam (ACTIV) Project No. ACG 69F Annex L.

11 Colonel Pham Quang Dinh, *The History of the 5th Infantry Division (1965–2005)*, The People's Army Publishing House, Hanoi, 2005.

12 Ibid., p. 163. At this stage, the *5th Viet Cong Division* reportedly had 75–80 per cent NVA, with many conscripted under eighteen years of age.

13 David Chanoff and Doan Van Toai, *Portrait of the Enemy*, Random House, New York, 1986, p. 108.

14 Lewis Sorley, *Vietnam Chronicles: The Abrams Tapes 1968–1972*, Texas Tech University Press, 2004, p. 68.

15 Ibid., p. 278.

16 McNeill & Ekins, *On the Offensive*, p. 89.

17 Ibid., p. 126.

18 Patrick J. McGarvey, *Visions of Victory: Selected Vietnamese Communist Military Writings, 1964–1968*, Hoover Institution Publications 81, Stanford, CA, 1969, p. 8.

19 James J. Wirtz, *The Tet Offensive: Intelligence Failure in War*, Cornell University Press, Ithaca and London, 1991, p. 47. See also Patrick McGarvey *Visions of Victory*.

20 Don Oberdorfer wrote in *Tet!* Johns Hopkins University Press, Maryland, 2001 that Thanh had died as a result of a B-52 attack. Hoang Van Hoan disagreed in his *A Drop in the Ocean: Hoang Van Hoan's Revolutionary Reminiscences*, Foreign Language Publishing Press, Beijing, 1988. Hoan discussed assassination by Le Duan on page 420. Bui Tin wrote that Thanh died of a heart attack; see *Following Ho Chi Minh: Memoirs of a Vietnamese Colonel*, Hurst & Co. Publishers Ltd, United Kingdom, 1994. Nguyen Thi Cuc, Thanh's widow, wrote in 2006 that he became ill inexplicably after a full day of meetings. 'Love Stories of Vietnamese Statesmen', footnotes to Lien-Hang T. Nguyen's article, 'The War Politburo: North Vietnam's Diplomatic and Political Road to the Tet Offensive', *Journal of Vietnamese Studies*, vol. 1, nos 1–2, 2006, pp. 4–58.

21 Jung Chang and Jon Halliday, *Mao: The Unknown Story*, Jonathon Cape, London 2005, p. 597. Also, John W. Garver, 'The Chinese Threat in the Vietnam War', *US Army War College Quarterly*, vol. XXII, no. 1, Spring 1992.

22 McNeill & Ekins, *On the Offensive*, p. 256.

23 Ibid., p. 257.

24 Army Office Transcripts: Military history interviews with senior officers concerning the Australian Army in Vietnam. Commanders Australian Force Vietnam Major General A. L. MacDonald interview, AWM 107, AHQ file 707/R2/38(1), p. 17.

25 Directive by the Chiefs of Staff Committee to Commander Australian Force Vietnam, signed by Air Chief Marshal F. R. W. Scherger, Chairman, on 17 May 1966.

26 A horoscope for monkeys might have carried a message on what would soon happen: 'Monkeys are curious and clever people and they can generally accomplish any given task. They appreciate difficult or challenging work. Monkeys can run circles around other people with ease.' The words are from a summarised generic horoscope.

27 Wirtz, *The Tet Offensive*, p. 93.

28 Bruce Davies, *The Battle at Ngok Tavak*, Allen & Unwin, Sydney, 2008, p. 7.

29 Stanley Karnow, *Vietnam: A History*, Penguin Books, New York, 1984, p. 536.

30 Wirtz, *The Tet Offensive*.

31 Ibid., pp. 260–1.

32 Ibid., p. 13.

33 William Childs Westmoreland, *A Soldier Reports*, Doubleday, Garden City, New York, 1976, p. 142.

34 Lieutenant General Bernard William Rogers, *Cedar Falls–Junction City: A Turning Point*, Department of the Army, Washington, DC, 1989.

35 Westmoreland, *A Soldier Reports*, p. 83.

36 Lieutenant General Phillip B. Davidson, *Vietnam at War: The History 1946–1975*, Sidgwick & Jackson, London, 1988, p. 450.

37 Wirtz, *Tet Offensive*, p. 55.

38 Karnow, *Vietnam*, p. 548.

39 Klaus Knorr and Patrick Morgan (editors), *Strategic Military Surprise: Incentives and Opportunities*, National Strategy Information Center, New York, 1983, p. 161.

40 Ibid.

41 Merle Pribbenow (trans.), *Victory in Vietnam: The Official History of the People's Army of Vietnam, 1954–1975*, University Press of Kansas, Lawrence, 2002, p. 214.

42 *Vietnam, The Anti-US Resistance War for the National Salvation, 1954–1975*, translated and published by the Foreign Broadcast Information Service, (Joint Publications Research Service) Arlington, Virginia, 1982, p. 100.

43 *Phillip B. Davidson, Jr. and Army Intelligence Doctrine*, an interview with Jeanette D. Lau, *INSCOM Journal*, March–April, 1996; *Reports of General MacArthur*, Prepared by his General Staff, Center for Military History, Washington, DC, January 1966. Davidson also served in General Patton's 3rd Army during World War II as the commander of a reconnaissance squadron in the 3rd Cavalry Reconnaissance Group.

44 Peter Young, personal papers provided to the author. In particular, a paper headed 'The Military Situation in South Vietnam', dated 9 July 1967.

45 Denis Warner, *Not With Guns Alone: How Hanoi Won the War*, Hutchison, Richmond, Vic., 1977, p. 1147.

46   Denis Warner, *Not Always On Horseback: An Australian Correspondent at War and Peace in Asia 1961–1993*, Allen & Unwin, Sydney, 1997, p. 128.

47   Ibid., p. 127.

48   Ibid.

49   Peter Young papers.

50   Paul Ham, *Vietnam: The Australian War*, HarperCollins Publishers, North Ryde, 2007, p. 344.

51   Anne Blair, interview with Brigadier Francis Phillip 'Ted' Serong, Melbourne, 13 April 1994, P. Serong – II – 17, Lyndon Baines Johnson Library, Austin, Texas, 1995. Who Serong was making his estimates for is not clear. He was not a senior CIA agent, as claimed by Paul Ham in his book.

52   Ham, *Vietnam: The Australian War*, p. 344.

53   This speculation is supported by an entry in *The History of the Resistance War against America 1954–1975*, National Politics (publisher) Vietnam, vol. 1, 1966 that linked the date change with the disruption to the attack date in the Central Highlands.

54   Nguyen Huu An, Senior Lieutenant General, *The New Battlefield (A Memoir)*, The Gioi Publishers, Hanoi, 2006, p. 80.

55   Peter Young papers.

56   Ibid.

57   Ham, *Vietnam: The Australian War*, p. 344.

58   In a document attached to Peter Young's July 1967 papers, the late Colonel Fitzgerald indicated that he had worked for Colonel Kenneth Houghton when he moved to the senior intelligence position at III MAF. Houghton did not take up that position until 10 July 1967; Fitzgerald said that he had returned to MACV in March 1967. See *Command Chronology III MAF July 1967*: Staff Officers. Also, Colonel Fitzgerald's statement that he had provided information about the enemy involved in the hill fights around Khe Sanh in April and May 1967 is considered to be unreliable. Fitzgerald said he had told the USMC about NVA divisions around the base, which allegedly was ignored. The III MAF PERINTREP [Periodic Intelligence Report] No. 17–67 dated 30 April 1967 does not support the Fitzgerald statement. In January 1968, General Davidson and Colonel Houghton had a discussion with Colonel Lownds who commanded Khe Sanh at the time and they told him about the NVA divisions in the area, which Lownds did not believe. See Phillip Davidson, *Vietnam at War*, p. 554. Inside the North Vietnamese leadership in 1967, there were two main factions that squabbled over what to do about the stalemate in the South. On 27 July, a series of arrests took place in Hanoi and this was followed by a further purge in October when even members of Vo Nguyen Giap's staff were arrested. At the date of Young's paper, July 1967, there was no clear directive or intimation about what course of action was to be followed regarding the 'liberation of the South'. See Lien-Hang T. Nguyen, *Journal of Vietnamese Studies*, vol. 1, nos 1–2, 2006, pp. 4–58.

59   Contribution by Richard Betts in Klaus Knorr and Patrick Morgan, *Strategic Military Surprise: Incentives and Opportunities*, National Strategy Information Center, New York, 1983, p. 161.

60   See the briefing suggestion in Ham, *Vietnam: The Australian War*, p. 344.

61   Wirtz, *Tet Offensive*, p. 128.

62   Betts in Knorr and Morgan, *Strategic Military Surprise*, p. 162.

63   Westmoreland v CBS exhibit 831, p. 23, as quoted in Wirtz, *Tet Offensive*, p. 172.

64 *The History of the Joint Chiefs of Staff: The Joint Chiefs of Staff and the War in Vietnam 1960–1968,* Part 1, The Tay Ninh Incident, Historical Division Joint Secretariat, Washington, 1970.

65 Senior editor Lieutenant Colonel Pham Van Son, *The Viet Cong Tet Offensive (1968),* Military History Division – Joint General Staff VNAF, Printing and Publication Centre, 1969.

66 Combat After Action Report, Tet Offensive After Action Report: Reporting Officer: LTG Frederick C. Weyand, CG II Field Force Vietnam – undated, p. 2.

67 Ibid., pp. 2–4.

68 *MACV Command History 1968,* vol. 1, p. 120.

69 McNeill & Ekins, *On the Offensive,* p. 289. The 10 January date is too conveniently matched to the US change of plan; it does not match the activities of the enemy at the time.

70 According to the prisoner of war Captain Tran Van Tieng, the *5th Viet Cong Regiment* was located around Bu Gia Map in Phuoc Long Province with the divisional headquarters camped along the Cambodian–Vietnam border. According to Captain Tieng's interrogation, the units had arrived in the area from the end of August 1967. Detachment 1 Div Int Unit, 16-1-2 (19), 29 Mar 67: Preliminary Interrogation Report – PW.

71 Ted Gittinger, interview with Phillip Davidson, 30 March 1982, Davidson – I – 48, Lyndon Baines Johnson Library, Austin, Texas, 1982.

72 *Report on the War in Vietnam (As of 30 June 1968),* Section II: Report on Operations in South Vietnam January 1964 – June 1968, General W. C. Westmoreland, USA, Commander, US Military Assistance Command, Vietnam (as of 30 June 1968), US Army Military History Institute, p. 157.

73 Tet Offensive After Action Report: Reporting Officer: LTG Frederick C. Weyand, CG II Field Force Vietnam, Texas Tech Vietnam Archives, undated, p. 5.

74 AWM95-1-4-79, Annex A to 1ATF OPO 4/68 dated 23 January 1968. AWM95-1-4-86, Headquarters, 1 Australian Task Force—Operation Coburg After Action Report shows that 27 rifles, one RPG 2 and one RPG 7, were captured in the week 25–31 January 1968. The weapons were a mixture of American carbines, SKS Russian carbines, a US Garand, one Mosin-Ngant bolt-action rifle, four unidentified rifles, twelve AK-47 and two AK-50 assault rifles.

75 Tet Offensive After Action Report: Reporting Officer: LTG Frederick C. Weyand, CG II Field Force Vietnam, Appendix 1.

76 Tran Minh Tam was appointed the commander of the *Front* when it was formed on 14 December 1967. He had been the acting commander of the *5th Viet Cong Division.* A front was equivalent to a corps.

77 Information in this chapter was gleaned from several main references: IIFFV Tet Offensive After Action Report; the *5th Viet Cong Division's* history; *MACV Command History 1968; 199th Infantry Brigade After Action Report TET Campaign;* and AWM files.

78 *199th Brigade TET Campaign,* p. 11.

79 Colonel Pham Quang Dinh, *The History of the 5th Infantry Division (1965–2005),* pp. 34–6, translator's notes.

80 *MACV Command History 1968,* vol. 1, p. 391; IIFFV Tet Offensive After Action Report, p. 23.

81 Colonel Pham Quang Dinh, *The History of the 5th Infantry Division.*

82 McNeill & Ekins, *On the Offensive,* pp. 303–4.

83 *The Australian*, 8 February 1968; Commonwealth Parliamentary Debates, House of Representatives, vol. 45, 26 March 1968, p. 458.

84 *The Heroic D445 Battalion: Its History and Tradition*, Military Headquarters of Dong Nai Province, 1991, pp. 38–9.

85 Ibid., p. 39.

86 IIFFV Tet Offensive After Action Report, p. 17.

87 3RAR Combat After Action Reports 22 March 1968, AWM95-7-3-56.

88 Ibid.

89 Lieutenant Colonel Pham Van Son (ed.), *The Viet Cong Tet Offensive (1968)*, p. 34.

90 Tet Offensive After Action Report: Reporting Officer: LTG Frederick C. Weyand, CG II Field Force Vietnam, p. H-2-2.

91 General William C. Westmoreland *A Soldier Reports*, Doubleday, New York, 1976, p. 83. *MACV Command History 1968*, vol. 1, Chapter V, p. 371. 1ATF directed that the terminology was to change on 24 January 1968 in a signal released on that date. AWM95-1-4-79, p. 115.

92 *Foreign Relations of the United States [FRUS], vol. VI, 1964–1968, Vietnam*, January–August 1968, Serial 64, Notes of the President's Meeting with the Joint Chiefs of Staff, Feb 9, 1968, 11:02 a.m. – 12:43 p.m.

93 'Fixated on crime and cricket, Australia not ready for war, said LBJ', *The Australian*, 13 February 2012.

94 *FRUS, vol. VI, 1964–1968, Vietnam*, January–August 1968, Serial 64.

95 Lewis Sorley, *Vietnam Chronicles: The Abrams Tapes 1968–1972*, Texas Tech University Press, 2004, p. 241.

96 Fleet Marine Force Pacific, Special Category Exclusive Marine Corps Eyes Only for MAJGEN Robertson info LTGEN Cushman from LTGEN Krulak signal dated 281937Z February 1968.

97 Davidson, *Vietnam at War*, p. 556.

98 Lewis Sorley, *Thunderbolt: General Creighton Abrams and the Army of His Times*, Simon & Schuster, New York, 1992, pp. 208–9.

99 Graham A. Cosmas, *MACV The Joint Command in the Years of Withdrawal, 1968–1973*, Center of Military History, United States Army, Washington, DC, 2006, pp. 47–8. Also included in the series of Special Category USMC–FMFPAC signals in January 1967. CG III MAF told the Commandant of the USMC that the move was prompted to get USMC out of the corps command business and by a lack of confidence in Cushman and his staff and concern for the coming battle on which many careers rode.

100 Wirtz, *Tet Offensive*, p. 205.

101 Translation of a captured enemy document, Combined Document Exploitation Centre, MACV: Bulletin 439, Document Log 04-2244-68 on 29 February 1968.

102 John M. Carland, interview with Tran Van Tra for the *Vietnam Magazine*, December 2002.

103 Davidson, *Vietnam at War*, p. 444.

104 Sorley, *The Abrams Tapes 1968–1972*, pp. 33–4.

105 Top Secret/LIMDIS/NOFORN/MCEO [limited distribution/no foreigners/Marine Corps eyes only] message on Khe Sanh from General Westmoreland [COMUSMACV] to General Wheeler [CJCS Committee] information Admiral Sharp [CINCPAC], dated 032223Z Feb 68. A copy of the message was sent to Lieutenant General Victor Krulak, CG FMFPAC, from MAJGEN Frank Tharin, USMC.

106 *FRUS, 1964–1968, vol. VI, Vietnam,* January–August 1968, Serial 158, Notes of Meeting Washington, 26 March 1968. Also, there was a nuclear reactor at the Vietnamese city of Dalat that was cause for concern if it was damaged. The reactor was to be shut down in late 1968.

107 See restrictions on killed in action information throughout, David Chanoff and Doan Van Toai, *Portrait of the Enemy,* Random House, New York, 1986.

108 SPECAT message from Krulak to General Chapman, dated 23 January, reported the defection of an NVA lieutenant from the *14th Anti-Aircraft Company, 2nd Regiment, 325C Division* who alleged the campaign was being controlled directly by the NVN Defence Minister.

109 Peter Brush, 'The Battle for Khe Sanh, 1968' in Marc Jason Gilbert and William Head (eds), *The Tet Offensive,* Greenwood Publishing Group, Westport CT, 1996. The 37th ARVN Ranger Battalion was flown in to the base in late January. The Special Forces camp at Lang Vei was overrun on 6 February by NVA troops who used PT76 tanks in the assault. John Prados, Ray W. Stubbe, *Valley of Decision: The Siege of Khe Sanh,* A Marc Jaffe Book, 1991, p. 453.

110 *Victory in Vietnam,* trans. Pribbenow, p. 229.

111 At certain times of the year the river carries the aromas of tropical flowers, which gave it the name Perfume River.

112 The Reconnaissance Company commander's name is shown as Nguyen Thi Tan in a number of publications. However, Thi is female and in personal correspondence with the author dated May 2006 he signed his name as Tan Tri Nguyen. He had westernised Nguyen Tri Tan by placing his name Tan before his family name Nguyen.

113 Nguyen Tri Tan, email to the author, 2 May 2006.

114 Ibid. The battalions of the *5th NVA Regiment* were 815 and 818 plus some sapper units.

115 Ibid. See also the correspondence on 3 May 2006.

116 Jack Etzle, email to the author, 16 May 2006. Fred Ferguson, email to the author, 18 May 2006.

117 Jim Coolican to the author, May 2010.

118 Tran Ngoc Hue, telephone interview with the author, 31 May 2010.

119 Ibid.

120 Ibid.

121 Ibid.

122 *The 1968 Tet Offensive Battles of Quang Tri City and Hue,* US Army Center of Military History/Erik Villard, 2006; Excellent accounts of the battle can be found in the following books and records: George W. Smith, *The Siege at Hue,* Ballantine Publishing Group, 1999; Jack Shulimson et al., *US Marines in Vietnam: The Defining Year 1968,* History and Museums Division, US Marine Corps, 1997; The Battle of Hue, After Action Report 1st Infantry Division, Advisory Detachment, Advisory Team 3, Department of the Army, 45th Military History Detachment, 19 March 1968; The Australian War Memorial record: The Battle of Hue, AWM R723-10-8.

123 Truong Nhu Tang with David Chanoff and Doan Van Toai, *A Viet Cong Memoir,* Vintage Books New York, 1986, p. 154.

124 Correspondence from Donald Killion to the author, 5 April 2004.

125 Paul Ham, *Vietnam: The Australian War,* p. 356. The reference was found in the unaltered first edition in hardback ISBN 9780732382370.

126 The author was in I Corps during Tet 1968. Whilst he was not at Hue, he feels sure that any rumours or information on such claims would have quickly spread through the advisers network. Furthermore, during comprehensive research for his and Gary McKay's book *The Men Who Persevered*, which is a detailed history of the AATTV, not one suggestion was uncovered that would support the mutilation claim. Subsequent contact with American advisers and also Vietnamese commanders elicited replies of disbelief that such a claim could be aired without a shred of evidence. A former commanding officer of the Team in 1968 replied, 'What nonsense'. See Captain D. H. Campbell's letter in AWM files The Battle of Hue, R723-10-8. In this letter, Captain Campbell wrote about the atrocities committed by the Viet Cong that included to 'strangle military types with wire and decorate the walls [of houses] with the bodies'.

127 *FRUS, 1964–1968, vol. VI, Vietnam, January–August 1968*, document 159, editorial notes.

128 See numerous newspaper articles on this trial such as *The Australian*, 24 and 25 January 1968, *Canberra Times* and *Sydney Morning Herald* January 1968.

129 The downside to the American system was the mix and match of personnel within units. A platoon, for example, could have some men who had recently arrived, a group who had months of experience and others who were near going home. Each group carried different sentiments about how to conduct an operation; as a result the groups might not have melded into one cohesive fighting team.

130 AWM95-1-4-74, Minutes of the Commander's Conference held at Nui Dat at 1030 hrs, 21 December 1967.

131 McNeill & Ekins, *On the Offensive*, p. 269.

132 O. D. Jackson had previously served as Commander of AAFV and the AATTV and he commanded 1ATF from 4 May 1966 and handed over to S. C Graham in January 1967. Graham relinquished command to R. L. Hughes in October 1967. Hughes stayed until 20 October 1968. C. M. Pearson, who commanded until 1 September 1969, replaced him. S. P. Weir then served until he handed over to W. G. Henderson on 1 June 1970. B. A. McDonald was the last commander from 28 February to 3 December 1971. General Cao Van Vien and Lt. Gen. Dong Van Khuyen, *Reflections on the Vietnam War*, US Army Center of Military History, Washington, DC, 1980, p. 153.

133 Walter Cronkite CBS evening news broadcast for 27 February 1968.

134 George W. Smith, *The Siege at Hue*, The Ballantine Publishing Group, New York, 1999, p. 151.

135 See the *Sydney Morning Herald* 15 February 1968, and the directive to the Commander of AFV by Chiefs of Staff Committee.

136 Peter Samuel, *The Bulletin*, 25 May 1968; AWM 107, AHQ file 707/R2/38(2), Brigadier Hughes interview.

137 Lieutenant Colonel Pham Van Son, *The Viet Cong Tet Offensive (1968)*, pp. 56–7.

138 Viet-Nam Documents and Research Notes: Document No. 27, fighting at *TET: A Viet Cong After Action Report*, United States Mission in Vietnam, February 9, 1968.

139 *FRUS, 1964–1968, vol. XXIX*, Part 1, Korea, document 213.

140 *FRUS, 1964–1968, vol. VI, Vietnam*, January–August 1968, document 26.

141 W. Joseph Campbell, *Getting it Wrong: Ten of the Greatest Misrepresented Stories of American Journalism*, University of California Press, Berkeley, 2010. The 'wise men' were senior statesmen and generals: Dean Acheson, McGeorge Bundy, Douglas Dillon, Cyrus

Vance, Arthur Goldberg, George Ball, Matthew Ridgway, Omar Bradley, Maxwell Taylor, Abe Fortas, Robert Murphy, Henry Cabot Lodge, John McCloy and Arthur Dean.

142 *FRUS, 1964–1968, vol. VI, Vietnam*, January–August 1968, document 156.

143 Ibid., document 169.

144 Headquarters 173D Airborne Brigade (Separate) report on Operation Hollandia conducted 9–17 June 1966.

145 See the citation for 1730824 Second Lieutenant Gordon Warrington Hurford, MID.

146 AWM95-2-3-8, Routine Orders Part 1, C Squadron 1 Armoured Regiment RAAC.

147 *The Minh Dam Base*, Phan Chi Than, 2006; *The Heroic D445 Battalion: Its History and Tradition*.

148 Operation Hollandia report, p. 24.

149 McNeill & Ekins, *On the Offensive*, p. 341.

150 *FRUS, 1964–1968, vol. VI, Vietnam*, January–August 1968.

151 Messrs Harry Ashmore and William Baggs of the Center for the Study of Democratic Institutions. See *FRUS, 1964–1968, vol. VI, Vietnam*, January–August 1968, document 184.

152 Ibid.

153 *FRUS, 1964–1968, vol. VI, Vietnam*, January–August 1968, document 185.

154 Ibid., document 155.

155 Ibid., document 187.

156 AWM95-1-4-94 part 3, HQ 1ATF: Minutes of Commander's Conference Nui Dat 1030 hours 20 April 1968.

157 *The Guardian*, 4 May 1968, p. 8.

158 Richard Halloran, *Strategic Communication*, <http://www.carlisle.army.mil/usawc/parameters/Articles/07autumn/halloran.pdf> 2007, p. 4. Colonel Harry Summers found out it was a false premise when he met Colonel Tu in 1975 at Hanoi. 'You never defeated us on the battlefield', Summers said. 'That may be so, but it is also irrelevant', Tu replied.

159 *The Guardian*, 6 May, 1968, p. 9. The journalists were Bruce Pigott and Donald Laramy from Reuters, Michael Birch from Australian Associated Press, John Cantwell of Time-Life and Frank Palmos, a freelance writer.

160 Gary McKay, *Vietnam Fragments: An Oral History of Australians at War*, Allen & Unwin, Sydney, 1992, pp. 118–19.

161 Matt Dunn, interview with his father Vince Dunn, *Herald Sun*, 23 April 2008, p. 37.

162 Ibid.

163 Ibid.

164 Kevin Meade, 'Courage under fire in Battle of Coral', *The Australian*, 10 May 2008.

165 Ibid.

166 Correspondence between Brian Cleaver and the author, May 2010. Also paraphrased article from *Sunday Times*, Perth, 30 May 2010.

167 Ibid.

168 AWM95-2-3-9, C Squadron 1 Armoured Regiment Narrative, Annexes 1–31 May 1968, After Action Report 28 May 1968 by 2LT Michael Butler, p. 2.

169 Bob Buick with Gary McKay, *All Guts and No Glory*, Allen & Unwin, Sydney, 2000, p. 113.

170 'Poppies and Flowing White Rubber', *Viet Bao*, 18 November 2007, courtesy Ernie Chamberlain email 5 June 2010.

171 AWM95-1-4-103, Headquarters, 1ATF, Annexes 1–30 June 1968, Commander's Daily Situation Report 2 June 1968.

172 American support included medium lift helicopters (CH-47), added heavy artillery-like firepower provided by 155 mm and 175 mm guns, fixed and rotary wing gunships and tactical airstrikes.

173 Senior Colonel Tran Xuan Ban (Chief Editor), *The History of the 7th [NVA] Infantry Division 1966–2006*, Peoples Armed Forces Publisher, Vietnam, 2006, pp. 25–6.

174 The bodies were recovered and identified in 1999. See Bruce Davies, *The Battle at Ngok Tavak: A Bloody Defeat in South Vietnam, 1968*, Allen & Unwin, Sydney, 2007.

175 Lieutenant General W. Peers, Memorandum for the Secretary of the General Staff dated 3 February 1970.

176 Brigadier General John Chaisson to Mrs Chaisson, 14 May 1968, Chaisson Papers, Hoover Institute Archives, Stanford, California.

177 IFFV Combat After Action Report, Battle for Duc Lap, 24 September 1968; 5th Special Forces Group (Abn), After Action Report, Relief of Duc Lap SF Camp, September 1968.

178 Annex D to AATTV report for August 1968.

179 *FRUS, 1964–1968, vol. VI, Vietnam*, January–August 1968, document 253.

180 Harry Lovelock, correspondence with the author, 18 March 2004.

181 *FRUS, 1964–1968, vol. VII, Vietnam*, January–August 1968, document 3.

182 Ibid., document 68.

183 Andrew J. Birtle, 'PROVN, Westmoreland, and the Historians: A Reappraisal', *Journal of Military History*, 72 (October 2008), pp. 1213–47. PROVN: A Program for the Pacification and Long-Term Development of South Vietnam was commissioned by US General Harold K. Johnson, Army Chief of Staff and completed in March 1966.

184 Sorley, *The Abrams Tapes*, p. 12.

185 Ibid., p. 16.

186 Ian McNeill, *The Team*, Australian War Memorial, Canberra, ACT, 1984, pp. 254–5.

187 Defence Minute Paper DM 84/12619, SPP 515/88 dated 23 June 1988. *MACV Command History 1968*, vol. I.

Chapter 7

1 *FRUS, 1952–1954, General United States Policies . . . East-Asian Pacific Area, vol. XII*, Part 1, ANZUS powers; five-power military consultations throughout, Radford's statement, p. 192.

2 *The History of the Joint Chiefs of Staff*, Part 2, Chapter 19, 'Limited Deployment of US Forces', p. 3.

3 A statement based upon casualties inflicted upon the allied forces. The most dangerous provinces and (CTZ) were Quang Tri (I), Quang Nam (I), Binh Dinh (II), Quang Ngai (I) and Dinh Tuong (IV). The next most deadly were Tay Ninh (III), Thua Tien (I), Kontum (II), Kien Hoa (IV) and Quang Tin (I).

4 An article broadcast by Radio Hanoi, 4–7 July 1966. The comments are attributed to Truong Son, an aka for General Nguyen Chi Thanh, and are taken from Chapter IV of an undated translation.

5 Ibid.

6 AWM98, MacDonald (COMAFV) demi-official letter to Daly (CGS), 10 March 1968, p. 2, as cited in McNeill & Ekins, *On the Offensive*.

7   David Horner, *Australian Higher Command in the Vietnam War*, Australian National University, Canberra, 1986, p. 64.

8   *MACV Command History 1969*, vol. 1, Chapter II, The Strategy and the Goals.

9   Frank Frost, *Australia's War in Vietnam*, Allen & Unwin, Sydney, 1987, p. 131.

10   Horner, *Australian Higher Command in the Vietnam War*, pp. 35–8.

11   Minutes of the Commander's Conference held at Nui Dat, 20 March 1968, Item 2.

12   The squadrons changed nomenclature when the new squadron commander arrived. Troopers moved through the unit in the trickle flow replacement system.

13   Routine Orders Part 1 by Commander 1st Australian Task Force Nui Dat, 26 December 1968, Order 118.

14   Eugene Linden, 'Fragging and Other Withdrawal Symptoms', *Saturday Review*, 8 January 1972, p. 12. A detailed discussion on fragging is available in *A Study of Strategic Lessons Learned in Vietnam*, The BDM Corporation, Virginia, 28 April 1980, Chapter 3.

15   McNeill & Ekins, *On the Offensive*, p. 201.

16   Ibid., p. 392.

17   AWM95-1-4-139, Exercise Lifesaver, HQ 1ATF Nui Dat, 17 February 1969.

18   Horner, *Australian Higher Command in the Vietnam War*, p. 34.

19   Ibid., p. 38.

20   Lieutenant General Julian J. Ewell and Major General Ira A. Hunt, Jr., *Sharpening the Combat Edge: The Use of Analysis to Reinforce Military Judgment*, Department of the Army, Washington, DC, 1995, pp. 227–8.

21   Ibid., p. 228.

22   *FRUS, 1969–1976, vol. VI, Vietnam*, January 1969 – July 1970, Document 38, Memorandum from Secretary of Defense Laird to President Nixon.

23   Horner, *Australian Higher Command in the Vietnam War*, p. 41.

24   *FRUS, 1969–1976, vol. VI, Vietnam*, Document 38.

25   Ibid.

26   Ibid.

27   Ibid.

28   Ibid.

29   Ibid.

30   Nguyen Ngoc Linh (ed.), *The Armed Forces of the Republic of Viet Nam*, The Vietnam Council on Foreign Relations, Saigon, Republic of Vietnam, n.d., p. 8.

31   Horner, *Australian Higher Command in the Vietnam War*, p. 58.

32   Alan Stretton, *Soldier in a Storm: An Autobiography*, Collins, Sydney, 1978, p. 215.

33   *The Third Australian Vietnam Veterans Mortality Study*, Department of Veterans' Affairs, Canberra, 2005, Chapter 5.3, 'Nature of Service'.

34   Senior Officer Debriefing Report: Lieutenant General Julian J. Ewell, CG, II Field Force, Vietnam, Period 2 April 1969 through 15 April 1970, Department of the Army, 15 June 1979, p. 14.

35   The 1st and 2nd ARVN divisions were in I Corps; 22nd and 23rd ARVN divisions were in II Corps; III Corps had the 5th, 18th (originally the 10th) and 25th divisions; IV had the 7th, 9th and 21st divisions. In 1971, the 3rd ARVN Division was constituted and located in Quang Tri Province. There was also a Marine Division located in Saigon and an Airborne Division, which was in Saigon, as well.

36   The title 1st Air Cavalry Division was used from 1 July 1968 to 26 August 1968 when the unit was formally named 1st Cavalry Division (Airmobile).

37 Office of the Assistant Division Commander, AVDB-ADS, 1 September 1969, Memorandum for Record, Discussion with General Hieu concerning Dong Tien operations. See also <www.generalhieu.com/pacification-2.htm> [accessed 9 July 2010].

38 Stephen T. Hosmer, Konrad Kellen & Brian M. Jenkins, *The Fall of South Vietnam: Statements by Vietnamese Military and Civilian Leaders*, Crane, Russack and Company, New York, 1980, p. 36.

39 1ATF report: Statistics—Operation Goodwood.

40 *MACV Command History 1969*, vol. 1, Chapter V, Military Operation, p. V-95.

41 *T7* was a Viet Cong geographic command that answered to *COSVN*. It was an intermediate headquarters between *COSVN* and sub-regions 4 (part of Bien Hoa and all of Gia Dinh), sub-region 8 or U-1 (an area surrounding Bien Hoa City) and sub-region 9 (Phuoc Tuy and Long Khanh aka Ba Long or Ba Bien). Albert E. Palmerlee, *Viet Cong Political Geography*, United States Mission in Vietnam, Document No. 23, March 1968.

42 Colonel Pham Quang Dinh, *The History of the 5th Infantry Division*, pp. 45–7.

43 Ibid.

44 See AATTV Monthly Report for May 1968.

45 Bruce Davies & Gary McKay, *The Men Who Persevered*, Allen & Unwin, Sydney, 2005, p. 132.

46 There were various acronyms used for these teams such as: Night Operations Advisory Team, Mobile Assistance Training Team and Mobile Advisory Training Team. In general use, MAT was American and MATT Australian.

47 See AATTV reports through 1968, 1969 and 1970. See also Davies & McKay, *The Men Who Persevered*.

48 Horner, *Australian Higher Command in the Vietnam War*, p. 40.

49 Ibid.

50 *FRUS, 1969–1976, vol. VI, Vietnam,* Document 7, Telegram from the Embassy in Vietnam to the Department of State. See also *FRUS, 1964–1968, vol. VII,* Document 285.

51 *FRUS, 1964–1968, vol. VII, Vietnam,* Document 140 Notes of Meeting 29 October 1968; (US) Department of Defense: Report on Selected Air and Ground Operations in Cambodia and Laos dated 10 September 1973. The bombing by B-52s was approved from 17 March 1969 through to 26 May 1970. Further strikes were authorised by tactical (fighter-bomber) aircraft from May 1970 to August 1973.

52 Ibid.

53 Letter and background by Mr Ron Ridenhour, 29 March 1969, at <www.digitalhistory.uh.edu/learning_history/vietnam/r_ridenhour.cfm [accessed 27 July 2010].

54 Lieutenant General W. R. Peers, *The My Lai Inquiry*, W.W. Norton, New York, 1979, p. 279.

55 The author, Bruce Davies, adviser to 2nd Battalion, 5th ARVN Regiment, September 1967 somewhere to the east of Hill 29 and across Highway 1. Hill 29 was 10 km north of Tam Ky and 1 km west of Highway 1.

56 <en.wikipedia.org/wiki/The_Times_They_Are_a-Changin'_> (song) [accessed 28 July 2010].

57 Professor Murray Goot & Rodney Tiffen, 'Public Opinion and the Politics of Polls' in Peter King (ed.) *Australia's Vietnam*, Allen & Unwin, Sydney, 1983, pp. 129–64.

58 Singapore's Lee Kuan Yew believed it was part of their saving grace, as did Tunku Abdul Rahman, the Malayan Prime Minister, when he told Sir Robert Thompson, the renowned

counterinsurgency expert, 'You must go to Vietnam and help hold my front line'. Robert Thompson KBE, CMG, DSO, MC, *Make for the Hills: Memories of Far Eastern Wars*, Leo Cooper, London, 1989, p. 121.

59   Frost, *Australia's War in Vietnam*, p. 26.

60   *Background Information relating to Southeast Asia and Vietnam* (7th rev. edn), Committee on Foreign Relations, United States Senate, December 1974, 8 October 1969, p. 82; *The Australian*, 9 October 1969.

61   In numerous studies conducted by MACV and agencies such as the RAND Corporation, security was the main concern of rural South Vietnamese. A successful pacification program generally revolved around security, village administration, village economy, health services and education.

62   A Vietnamese village consisted of a grouping of hamlets that could be spread over several kilometres.

63   AWM95-7-5-29, Report of MAT Team at Phuoc Hoa and Long Cat, 8 July 1969.

64   Ibid., B Company MAT Team Hoa Long 609 RF Company.

65   Ibid., Report for Hoa Long 4.

66   AWM95-1-4-156, Letter Julian J. Ewell to Brigadier Pearson (undated), but distributed under covering letter dated 12 June 1969.

67   AWM95-7-5-29, Deployment of 5RAR Mini-MAT 4–9 June 1969.

68   AWM95-1-4-152, Q Instruction NO 7/69 ARVN Training—*Horseshoe* Feature, May 1969.

69   General William C. Westmoreland, *A Soldier Reports*, Doubleday, Garden City, New York, 1976, pp. 150–1.

70   Ibid.

71   12840 WO2 Alec Henry Morris, citation Distinguished Conduct Medal.

72   Jay Scharbutt, an AP account of Hill 937 Battle, *The Washington Post*, c. 24 May 1969.

73   Ibid.

74   Ibid.

75   Ibid.

76   Hamburger Hill report by WO2 M Kelly, 2/3 ARVN Battalion, 13 June 1969, Annexure 3 to Annex D, AATTV Report, June 1969.

77   Ibid.

78   Headquarters 101st Airborne Division, Office of the Commanding General, 24 May 1969: Subject: News Release, Vietnam–Zais (Filed by Les Santorelli).

79   Headquarters 101st Airborne Division, Subject: Dong Ap Bia as at 24 May 1969.

80   Ibid.

81   This statement is based on Imperial Awards only.

82   Although many of the division's reinforcements came from North Vietnam it continued to be known as a Viet Cong division.

83   Colonel Pham Quang Dinh, *The History of the 5th Infantry Division*, pp. 45–51.

84   The geographic changes by the communist regime were frequent and often inexplicable. Ba Long/Ba Bien encompassed Bien Hoa, Long Khanh and Phuoc Tuy.

85   See HQ 1ATF Vietnam Digest for May and June 1969.

86   *Victory in Vietnam*, trans. Pribbenow. See the chapter entitled 'Growing Difficulties in the South', p. 244.

87   See various reports in *MACV Command History* for 1968 and 1969 as well as MACV

monthly summaries. See also *Victory in Vietnam* chapters on the 1968–69 period; Colonel Pham Quang Dinh, *The History of the 5th Infantry Division*, pp. 40–5.

88 AWM95-1-4-152, Vietnam Digest Issue 18-69, pp. 2–3.

89 Colonel Pham Quang Dinh, *The History of the 5th Infantry Division*, p. 47.

90 Ibid., p. 48.

91 Ibid., p. 49.

92 HQ 1ATF Vietnam Digest for May and June 1969, see details of major enemy-initiated attacks.

93 This narrative is a summary of events as recorded in Colonel Pham Quang Dinh, *The History of the 5th Infantry Division*, pp. 45–51.

94 Ibid., p. 49.

95 AWM95-1-4-156, Vietnam Digest Issue Number 22–69 (period 1–6 June 1969).

96 Senior Officer Debriefing Report: Major General Julian J Ewell 9th Infantry Division, Period 25 February 1968 to 5 April 1969, Department of the Army, Office of the Adjutant General, Washington, DC, 24 November 1989, pp. 11–12. See also the debriefing of Lieutenant General Ewell for his period as CG, IIFFV, 2 April 1969 through 15 April 1970, p. 4.

97 Ibid., p. 8.

98 Ibid., p. 5.

99 Ibid., p. 8.

100 Lieutenant General Julian J. Ewell and Major General Ira A. Hunt, Jr, *Sharpening the Combat Edge*, p. 228.

101 Ashley Ekins with Ian McNeill, *Fighting to the Finish: The Australian Army and the Vietnam War, 1968–1975*, Allen & Unwin, Sydney, 2012, p. 188.

102 Ibid., p. 139.

103 Ibid., p. 279.

104 Len Johnson, 'Operation Lavarack: Phuoc Tuy province, Vietnam, 1969', *Australian Army Journal*, vol. VII, no. 2, p. 90.

105 AWM95-1-4-151, Enemy Situation—AO *Vincent*, Annex A to 1ATF Op Instruction No 49-69.

106 S. L. A. Marshall & David Hackworth, *Vietnam Primer*, US Department of the Army, PAM 525-2, 21 April 1967, p. 7.

107 COSVN Resolution No. 9, July 1969; COSVN A Preliminary Report on Activities During the 1969 Autumn Campaign and the Central Committee (North Vietnam) Missions and Guidelines for Operation and Strengthening of the SVN (NVA/Viet Cong) Armed Forces, Texas Tech University, Vietnam Center and Archive.

108 The Viet Cong geographic region known as *T7* was renamed *Military Region 7* mid-1968. *MR7* retained the status of an intermediate headquarters between *COSVN* and sub-regions *4, 8* or *U-1* and sub-region *9*. See *Viet Cong Political Geography* by Albert Palmerlee.

109 AWM95-7-5-25, Operation Hammer report dated 11 June 1969, para. 8.

110 Hosmer, Kellen & Jenkins, *The Fall of South Vietnam: Statements by Vietnamese Military and Civilian Leaders*, p. 83.

111 Citation 2783093 Second Lieutenant Brian John Sullivan, MC.

112 See AWM95-1-4-153, HQ 1ATF Commander's Diary, June 1969, sheets 40 and 46. Time command structure to change was recorded at 1242H; 5RAR reported HQ at Duc Thanh

at 2145H. Although the timings in sheet 40 run in numerical sequence the times jump from 1045H to 1250H and back to 1010H between serials 561 and 571. Also, at 1603 hours both B and D Company were recorded as under command the 2IC of 5RAR who was at Duc Thanh.

113 The term RF/PF is used because the reports do not make clear which of the South Vietnamese forces were used in the different phases of the battle. The No 39 PF platoon at Duc Trung had a listed strength of 39. The 655 RF Company that was nearby was just over 100 personnel and it is the most likely to have been the main part of the South Vietnamese reaction group. See Annex F to 6RAR Operation Order 1 (Operation Lavarack).

114 Citation 214650 Sergeant Brian Kent London, DCM.

115 5RAR Combat After Action Report 6/69 Operation Hammer dated 11 June 1969; AWM95-7-5-25, 5RAR operations Log June 1969, see entry 8 June.

116 See Ekins, *Fighting to the Finish*, Chapter 7, note 118.

117 5RAR Operation Hammer report.

118 Ibid. Richard Palfreyman broadcast on ABC 'The National' 2 May 1985.

119 Gary McKay & Graeme Nicholas, *Jungle Tracks: Australian Armour in Viet Nam,* Allen & Unwin, Sydney, 2001, pp. 211–12.

120 The Story of the Memorial Area for the Battle of Binh Ba on 6/6/69 by 33 Regiment at Binh Ba Village, Chau Duc District, Baria–Vung Tau Province, 2011. This reference was provided by Xuan Thu.

121 Ibid.

122 CDEC document December 1968 translated a notebook entry by Bui Van Hien (possibly) from *12th Company, 9th Battalion* (aka *3rd*), *33rd NVA Regiment*. The notebook showed a company assigned strength of 37 men.

123 *Operations in the US Resistance War*, Operation Long Khanh (5 May – 20 June 1969), The Gioi Publishers, Hanoi, 2009, pp. 87–90.

124 CDEC document Log No: 1-1611-69 from the US 199th Light Infantry Brigade.

125 Initial Interrogation Report Le Van Nhanh: 1 ATF INTSUM No 198/69 dated 17 July 1969.

126 AWM95-7-6-22, Contact After Action Report Lieutenant M. R. Farland, 12 June 1969. The dress of the enemy was reported as black uniforms, assorted civilian clothing and NVA helmets. Both Viet Cong and NVA soldiers wore a style of pith helmet (although not exclusively).

127 AWM95-7-6-22, see the annexes and appendices to After Action Report Operation Lavarack.

128 <brt.vn/6/26654/Le-cau-sieu-va-dang-huong-tuong-nho-cac-anh-hung-liet-sy-Trung-doan-33.htm> (A Buddhist Mass and Ceremony to Remember the Heroic Martyrs of the 33rd Regiment.) Baria Vung Tau television [accessed 18 August 2010].

129 AWM95-7-5-26, Review of the Intelligence and Friendly Forces Situation for Operation Esso, dated June 1969. AO Aldgate was a slab of land in an arc that covered the space between the Long Hai hills and the southern edges of Long Dien and Dat Do.

130 *The Australian*, 23 July 1969 as cited in Frost, *Australia's War in Vietnam*, p. 127. There were only two Australians killed between July 1962 and June 1965.

131 AWM95-7-5-30, 5RAR Combat After Action Report 9/69 Operation Esso dated 6 August 1969.

132 Ibid.

133 Horner, *Australian Higher Command in the Vietnam War*, pp. 41–2.

134 AWM95-7-5-30, Operation Esso.

135 Lewis Sorley, *Vietnam Chronicles: The Abrams Tapes 1968–1972*, Texas Tech University Press, 2004, p. 166.

136 AWM95-1-4-156, attachment to Brigadier Pearson letter dated 12 June 1969.

137 David Horner, The Australian Army and the Vietnam War 1962–1972, Chief of Army Conference, 2002, p. 7.

138 *The French Lessons of the War in Indochina*, vol. 2, RAND Corporation, May 1967, pp. 139–40.

139 MACV Lessons Learned No. 42: Viet Cong Employment of Land Mines, 7 October 1964. In 1967, enemy mines caused 4237 casualties that represented a personnel loss of five infantry battalions. The 1968 casualties through May amounted to three infantry battalions and 65 per cent of APC losses and mines caused 70 per cent of tank losses. US Army Concept Team in Vietnam, *Study and Evaluation of Countermine Measures*, vol. I, Department of the Army, September 1968.

140 Lockhart, *The Minefield*, p. 148.

141 Her Majesty's Armoured Personnel Carriers Flint and Steele were the humorous titles applied to the mine clearing test bed APC used to demonstrate a proposed clearing technique. Brigadier Flint was the army's Engineer in Chief and Major General Steele had held the position during World War II.

142 AWM95-4-2-51, 1 Field Squadron Commander's Diary, September 1969.

143 AWM103, 723/1/91, Headquarters 1ATF Mine Casualty Study in 1ATF, June–August 1969, para. 18. Also quoted in Ekins, *Fighting to the Finish*, pp. 381–2.

144 *The Minh Dam Base 1945–1975*, Baria-Vung Tau Province Information and Cultural Office, 2006. Translated excerpt provided by Brigadier Ernie Chamberlain (Retd) and Ann Pham.

145 Colonel Pham Quang Dinh, *The History of the 5th Infantry Division 1965–2005*, p. 51.

146 AWM95-7-9-21, 9RAR Combat Operations After Action Report, Operations Matthew and Hat Dich.

147 See Annex B to 5RAR Combat After Action Report 11/69, Operation Camden—Sequence of Events. The Australian patrolling elements found bunkers on 54 occasions, but only six areas involved a clash with an enemy group.

148 Citation 1200814 Gunner (T/Bombardier) Gerardus Cornelius Dekker MM.

149 Citation 55159 Private (T/Corporal) Michael Allan Dench MM.

150 5RAR After Action Report, Operation Camden, para. 15; Major General David Ewing Ott, *Vietnam Studies Field Artillery 1954–1973*, Department of the Army, Washington, DC, 1975, p. 172; Jack S. Ballard, *Development and Employment of Fixed-Wing Gunships 1962–1972*, The United States Air Force in Southeast Asia, 1982.

151 5RAR After Action Report, Operation Camden, para. 16.

152 USARV Seminar Report: Attack of Fortified Positions in the Jungle, dated 2 January 1968. Copies were sent to CO, Australian Forces Vietnam.

Chapter 8

1 *The History of the Joint Chiefs of Staff and the War in Vietnam, 1969–1970*, Chapter 4, p. 124.

2 *United States Senate, Background Information, Southeast Asia and Vietnam* (7th rev. edn), December 1974, 8 October 1969; *The Australian*, 9 October 1969.

3   Peter Edwards, *A Nation at War*, Allen & Unwin in assoc. with the Australian War Memorial, Sydney, 1997, p. 235.

4   President Nixon addressed the nation on the war in Vietnam. Nixon spoke about the government's policy and answered questions that he knew were on the minds of many people listening to him that day. The full address can be read at http://watergate.info/nixon/silent-majority-speech-1969.shtml.

5   David Horner, *Strategic Command*, Oxford University Press, Melbourne, 2005, p. 337.

6   *FRUS, 1969–1976, vol. VI*, Document 38: Memorandum from Secretary Laird, 13 March 1969.

7   President Nixon's daily diary, 14 December 1969, entry 1055 to 1105, detail of the conversation is not included. *MACV Command History 1969*, vol. I, Chapter 1.

8   David Horner, *Strategic Command*, p. 339.

9   Ibid., p. 248.

10 Report of the Defence Committee Withdrawal from Vietnam, 5 December 1969, p. 17.

11 Ibid., p. 344.

12 Ibid., p. 413 and p. 344.

13 See the section entitled 'The Long Hai' and Note 143 of Chapter 6 in this book.

14 *MACV Command History 1970*, vol. I, Chapter IV, 'US and Other Free World Forces', p. 34.

15 Ibid.

16 *MACV Command History 1970*, vol. II, Chapter IX, 'Logistics—Transfer of Port Facilities', pp. 41–2.

17 Horner, *Strategic Command*, p. 347.

18 *MACV Command History 1966*, Chapter III, 'Free World Military Assistance Force', p. 93.

19 IIFFV Operational Report: Lessons Learned Period ending 31 October 1969, p. 30.

20 AWM95-1-4-183 part 2, HQ 1ATF INTSUMS [intelligence summaries].

21 Citation 1731459 Second Lieutenant Peter John Lauder MC.

22 Ekins, *Fighting to the Finish*, pp. 466, 530.

23 AWM95-7-7-50, 7RAR notes on NVA/Viet Cong Bunker Systems, July 1970. See also USARV seminar notes in Chapter 7.

24 AWM98, File R176/1/31(B), Joint AFV-Embassy Group Pacification Situation in Phuoc Tuy province, meeting 17 November 1969.

25 MAC 13555, 071007Z October 1968, message Abrams to Wheeler and [Admiral] John McCain [CINCPAC].

26 Bruce Grant, *The Age*, 'Public Affairs' column, 27 November 1969, p. 4.

27 *American War and Military Operations Casualties: Lists and Statistics*, Congressional Research Service updated 14 May 2008, p. CRS-3. Prepared for Members and Committees of Congress, Washington, DC.

28 *MACV Command History 1970*, vol. I, pp. V-14-V15. Report of the [Australian] Defence Committee withdrawal from Vietnam dated 5 December 1969, Annex A: Force Comparisons.

29 Ekins, *Fighting to the Finish*, Appendix G, Table 1.

30 Pat Beale DSO, MC, *Operation Orders*, Australian Army History Unit and Australian Military History Productions, 2003, p. 94. Eight of the Australians received awards for this battle: Pat Beale DSO, Peter Shilston MC, Des Cochrane MM, Ray Barnes DCM, Aleck McCloskey DCM, Alan White DCM, John Pettit (KIA) MID and George Jamieson MID.

31 Ideological Problems within the People's Liberation Armed Forces, Document 94 Viet-Nam Documents and Research Centre, p. 4.

32 Ibid., p. 5.

33 *MACV Command History 1970*, vol. I: The Enemy; Merle Pribbenow (trans.), *Victory in Vietnam*, Chapter 10: Maintaining Our Main Force Elements in South Vietnam; Chapter 11: Increasing Our Ability to Conduct Combined-Arms Operations.

34 *MACV Command History 1970*, vol. I, NVA/Viet Cong Military Operations, pp. III94–III97.

35 USMC Command Histories Combined Action Groups, III Marine Amphibious Force, see example 2nd CAG, Quang Nam Province, April 1970. The CAG had fourteen officers and just over 600 enlisted men. The CAG was broken down into seven combined action companies. Graham A. Cosmos and Lieutenant Colonel Terrence P. Murray USMC, *US Marines in Vietnam: Vietnamization and Redeployment 1970–1971*, Chapter 8: The Struggle for Security, History and Museums Division, Headquarters, US Marine Corps, Washington, DC, 1986.

36 General Truong commanded the 1st ARVN Division 1966–1970 and later MR 4 1970–1972 and MR 1 1972–1975.

37 Lieutenant General Ngo Quang Truong, *Territorial Forces*, US Army Center of Military History, Washington, DC, 1981, pp. 119–20.

38 Ibid., p. 122.

39 Ibid., p. 123.

40 Ibid., p. 128; *MACV Command History 1970*, vol. II, Chapter VII: Desertion.

41 CDEC document Log 10-1611-69. A letter dated 29 July 1969, captured on 9 October to the north of Gia Ray.

42 AWM95-7-758, 7RAR After Action Report by Lieutenant C. Johnson, 6 September 1970.

43 AWM95-7-2-61, 2RAR/NZ (ANZAC)/772 RF Coy After Action Report: Operation Dao Cam, September 1970.

44 Ibid.

45 AWM95-7-7-58, 7RAR After Action Report: Operation Cung Chung II and Cung Chung III (Phase 1), September 1970.

46 *The Heroic D445 Battalion: Its History and Tradition*, trans. Brigadier Ernest Chamberlain, CSC (Retd), Military Headquarters of Dong Nai Province, Dong Nai, 1991, p. 50.

47 Interview with recruit Bushman Scout Nguyen Ming Ky by Sergeant Rung. (See following note.)

48 The references are excluded to protect the bad shooters!

49 AWM95-7-2-60, 2RAR/NZ (ANZAC) Battalion: After Action Report Operations Nathan/Cung Chung II, 22 September 1970.

50 Ibid.

51 Dave Grossman, *On Killing: The Psychological Cost of Learning to Kill in War*, Little, Brown, Canada, 1995.

52 There are many references to this period in the press, such as *Four Corners*, ABC TV, 7 November 1970; *The Australian*, 10 November 1970.

53 External Affairs outward cablegram 2638 to Embassy in Saigon 15 October 1970.

54 Report of the Defence Committee Withdrawal from Vietnam 5 December 1969, p. 9; *MACV Command History 1970*, vol. II, Chapter IX, Logistics.

55 A detailed discussion of this period is in Ian McNeill, *The Team*, Australian War Memorial Canberra, 1984, Chapter 16.

56 *MACV Command History 1970*, vol. II, Chapter VII, RVNAF Training Capability, p. VII-35.

57 Ibid., Chapter IX, Transfer of Excess Real Property to RVNAF, p. IX-36.

58 McNeill, *The Team*, p. 433.

59 Ibid., p. 438.

60 Brigadier General James Lawton Collins, Jr., *The Development and Training of the South Vietnamese Army, 1950–1972*, p. 10; *MACV Command History 1970*, vol. II, Chapter VII, Training, pp. VII33-VII56.

61 HQMACV: MACJ3, 5 July 1970, Subject: RVNAF/JGS Reorganization.

62 There were four CTZ numbered from north to south inside South Vietnam: I, II, III and IV. They became MR 1, 2, 3 and 4. The geographic areas of responsibility remained unchanged. The MR commander became the overall authority for both ARVN and Regional Force activities. The aim was to streamline command from the Joint General Staff to the front line for both combat and pacification. A further plan was floated to divide MR 2 and 4 to create six regions, but that did not eventuate. See *MACV Command History 1970*, vol. II, Reorganisation of the RVNAF pp. VII-16-17.

63 McNeill, *The Team*, p. 440.

64 Ibid.

65 Beale, email to the author, 15 October 2010.

66 Beale, email to the author, 31 October 2010.

67 Ibid.

68 McNeill, *The Team*, pp. 440–1.

69 Davies & McKay, *The Men Who Persevered*, p. 183.

70 Office of the Senior Adviser, Advisory Team 2, Memorandum: Captured VC Document, dated 20 April 1964. Author's copy.

71 MACV Training Plan 1-70, 29 September 1970, Subject: Support of Consolidated RVNAF Improvement and Modernisation Program (CRIMP).

72 *MACV Command History 1970*, vol. II, Chapter VII, Training, pp. VII-37-40.

73 There are differences in the titles among the AATTV files; some used 'Advisory' others 'Assistance' and others used the shorter title, MAT. A MACV review of advisers in December 1969 mentioned that the term 'Adviser' might be changed, as it implied 'superiority'. MACV established province Mobile *Assistance* Teams during the latter half of 1971. See *MACV Command History 1970* and *1971*. In February 1971 the AATTV numbers were 26 officers, 109 WO, 7 sergeants, and 63 corporals (205). It reached a peak of 224 all ranks in August 1971. Davies & McKay, *The Men Who Persevered*, p. 196 and commanders' diaries, AWM 103 and 293 series.

74 Davies & McKay, *The Men Who Persevered*, pp. 174–5. United States RV established the course in 1968 to train personnel who had in-country experience of four to six months for duty with MAT. The course was 125 hours, broken into general advisory subjects 38 hours, weapons training 29 hours, tactics 21 hours and language 37 hours. In October 1970, the US had 487 MAT throughout Vietnam. Robert D. Ramsey III *Advising Indigenous Forces*, Combat Studies Institute Press, Fort Leavenworth, Kansas, n.d. [2006?].

75 Davies & McKay, *The Men Who Persevered*, pp. 174–5.

76 Report by Major K. Phillips, Senior Australian Advisor, Phuoc Tuy Province, November 1970.

77 Report by Captain Len Opie, MATT 3 Team Leader, November 1970.

78 Ibid.

79 Correspondence, Manski to the author, 2 April 2004.

80 Excerpts from transcript of the log for Milky controller attached to Court of Inquiry report concerning loss of Canberra A84-231 and crew in Vietnam on 3 November 1970.

81 MACV news release, dated 26 June 1970, reported that losses of US aircraft from all causes in connection to the war in Southeast Asia surpassed the 7000 mark.

82 *USMC 5th Marines Command Chronology*, November 1970, p. 3.

83 Personal correspondence, Thurgar to the author, 8 October 2009.

84 Ibid.

85 Report on the Finding of A84-231 and her crew in Vietnam, by Major Jack Thurgar. The 1968 battle at Ngok Tavak was to the south of the crash site, but information gleaned from the records of that battle assisted with enemy unit identification and allied locations.

86 Lam Son is a mountain and village in Thanh Hoa Province of North Vietnam renowned as the resistance base of Le Loi, who expelled the Chinese Ming Dynasty invaders in the period 1418–27. It was a name chosen by the South Vietnamese for many of their operations.

87 Under a cloak of secrecy, the trail at sea was also established in 1959. It was called the Gianh River Fishing Group. The South's demand for arms and personnel exceeded the North's supply capabilities and the challenges of how to pass the borderline were not simple. Nguyen Tu Duong, *The Trail at Sea*, The Gioi Publishers, Hanoi, 2011.

88 *MACV Command History 1971* vol. II Annex E Cross Border Operations; Major General Nguyen Duy Hinh, *Lam Son 719*, US Army Center of Military History, Washington, 1979; 101st Airborne Division (Airmobile), Final Report, Airmobile Operations in Support of Operation Lam Son 719, vol. II, 1 May 1971 and 101st Airborne Division report dated 5 November 1973.

89 Davies & McKay, *The Men Who Persevered*, p. 189.

90 Telephone conversations between Hue and the author, May and June 2010.

91 Davies & McKay, *The Men Who Persevered*, p. 189.

92 Hinh, *Lam Son 719*, pp. 42–3, in which he quotes an after action report by Colonel Arthur W. Pence.

93 *MACV Command History 1971*, vol. II, Annex E.

94 Ibid., Enemy Tactics.

95 AWM107, AHQ707/R2/38(4), Colonel P. Scott interview, p. 16.

96 *Foreign Relations of the United States, 1969–1976*, vol. VI, Vietnam, January 1969 – July 1970, paper 228, p. 806.

97 *MACV Command History 1971* Supplement, p. TSS-12; also *History of the JCS and the War in Vietnam, 1971–1973*, pp. 59–60.

98 In late 1971, the 3rd Brigade (Separate) had four battalions (1/7, 1/12, 2/5 and 2/8) and also operational control of the 2nd Squadron, 11 ACR. The brigade had a forward base near Nui Chua Chan in Binh Tuy Province. Brigadier General James F. Hamlet, Commander, 3rd Brigade (Separate) 1st Cavalry Division, Senior Officer Debriefing Report (13 Dec 71 – 20 June 72), Dept of the Army, Washington, DC, 4 December 1972.

99 1ATF Routine Orders Part 1 dated 6 June 1971.

100 Citation: 37178 Sergeant Edmund S. Levy DCM; AWM95-7-7-65, 7RAR Commander's Diary Narrative December 1970.

101 *The Heroic D445 Battalion*, p. 106.

102 Ernie Chamberlain, email to the author, 10 December 2010, and a discussion on the command structure of the *D445 Battalion* on the same date.

103 The average size of an enemy infantry battalion in MR3 in early 1971 was 111. There were thirteen listed infantry battalions in the Military Region. Local force battalions averaged 79 men. IIFFV Operational Report for the period ending 30 April 1971.

104 1ATF SUPINTREP [Supplementary Intelligence Report] 18/71 (Period 26 April – 2 May 71) dated 3 May 71.

105 Horner, *Strategic Command*, p. 337.

106 AWM95, 1ATF R579/1/59: Defence of Vietnam with particular reference to Phuoc Tuy province, January 1971.

107 *History of the JCS and the War in Vietnam, 1971–1973*, p. 60.

108 Ibid.

109 To shift more of the civic action effort to the Vietnamese was a recommendation made by the US 25th Infantry Division in their area of responsibility back in April 1970. To not do so was considered to be detrimental to the US disengagement effort and impede the projection of the Vietnamese government's image throughout the countryside. 25th Infantry Division, Operational Report and Lessons Learned for the period ending 30 April 1970. See also, HQ IIFFV Operational Report—Lessons Learned: 1 November 1970 – 1 April 1971, Civil Affairs.

110 A detailed explanation of this matter is given in Peter Edwards, *A Nation at War*, Allen & Unwin, Sydney, 1997; Frank Frost, *Australia's War in Vietnam*, Allen & Unwin, Sydney, 1987; Ekins,, *Fighting to the Finish*.

111 Corporal Warren Dowell in Gary McKay, *Delta Four*, Allen & Unwin, Sydney, 1996, p. 212.

112 General Donn A. Starry, *Mounted Combat in Vietnam*, Department of the Army, Washington, DC, 1989, pp. 101–2; Michael Evans and Alan Ryan, Working Paper No. 122, Land Warfare Centre, July 2003.

113 *Mounted Combat in Vietnam*, pp. 109–10.

114 *The Heroic D445 Battalion*, pp. 34–5.

115 *History of the JCS and the War in Vietnam, 1971–1973*, p. 61.

116 *MACV Command History 1971*, vol. I, Chapter IV, 'Plans and Operations—Dynamic Defense', p. IV–10.

117 Ibid.

118 Brigadier Hamlet debriefing report 25 June 1972.

119 IIFFV Operational Report—Lessons Learned period ending 30 April 1971; *MACV Command History 1971*, vol. I, Chapter III, 'Enemy Military Operations in the RVN': COSVN Resolutions 9, 10 and 14 dated July 1969 and 30 October 1969.

120 Operation Order 6/71 (Operation Overlord) dated 3 June 1971. Until May 1971, 2RAR/NZ (ANZAC) and 3RAR, who had replaced 7RAR in February, were operational. 4RAR became operational in June 1971, replacing 2RAR who returned to Townsville, Qld.

121 General Davison's IIFFV was redesignated the Third Regional Assistance Command on 30 April 1971. 1 Field Force Vietnam became Second Regional Assistance Command on 30 April and then Second Regional Assistance Group on 16 May. Mr John P. Vann was its director, but he was killed in a helicopter crash in June 1972 when SRAG reverted to SRAC. The First Regional Assistance Command replaced XXIV Corps on 19 March 1972. The Delta Military Assistance Command was established in late 1969 when US combat forces

withdrew from IV Corps and it was redesignated Delta Regional Assistance Command on 30 April 1971. See *MACV Command History 1969* and *1972.*

122 For *3/33 NVA* see Annex F to 1ATF INTSUM 122/71 dated 2 May 1971. *D445* had rifle companies of 20 men in December; see the Sergeant Levy ambush para.

123 Email correspondence between Neil Holbrook, Barrie Wade and the author, 30 November 2010.

124 Citation 1203040 Trooper Daniel John Handley, Mention-in-Despatches.

125 AWM95-2-4-33, A Squadron 3 Cavalry Regiment Narrative 1–30 June 1971.

126 Ibid.

127 Ivan Cahill commanded the USMC Company E in I Corps from November 1967 to February 1968.

128 Colonel S. L. A. Marshall, *The Soldiers' Load and The Mobility of a Nation,* The Marine Corps Association, Quantico, Virginia, from a United States Army publication dated 1950, p. 5.

129 C. J. Spence, *Blackfoot Platoon Vignettes 1971,* 11 March 2003. Copy held by author.

130 AWM103, HQ 1ATF R569/2/291, Operation Overlord report.

131 See 1ATF SUPINTREP for the period January to June 1971.

132 *The Heroic D445 Battalion,* p. 54.

133 Cabinet Minute Canberra, 26 July 1971, Decision No. 319: Withdrawal of Australian Force from Vietnam.

134 Australia, House of Representatives, *Debates,* vol. 73, 18 August 1971, pp. 226–50.

135 Horner, *Strategic Command,* p. 249.

136 Headquarters 1st Australian Task Force Nui Dat, 20 August 1971: File R579/1/57, minutes of two conferences held at Nui Dat on 19 August 1971.

137 Ibid.

138 Ibid. Also, see *MACV Command History 1971,* vol. I, 'The Enemy'.

139 *MACV Command History 1971,* vol. I, 'The Enemy'.

140 Annex F to 1ATF INTSUM 137/71 dated 17 May 1971; 1ATF SUPINTREP 28/71 (5 Jul–11 Jul 71); Annex F to 1ATF INTSUM 179/71 dated 28 June 1971; SUPINTREP 35/71 30 August 1971.

141 1ATF SUPINTREP 38/71 (Period 13–19 September 1971) dated 20 September 1971.

142 Limited warfare meant smaller scale guerrilla-type activity rather than main force attacks.

143 1ATF INTREP 38/71. See also *COSVN* resolutions 9, 10, 14 and Directive Number 01/CT 71.

144 *MACV Command History 1971,* vol. I, 'The Enemy'.

145 Annex A to 1ATF Op O 9/71 dated 19 September 1971.

146 1ATF SUPINTREP 28/71 (5–11 Jul 71).

147 Samuel B. Griffith, *Sun Tzu: The Art of War,* Oxford University Press, 1963, p. 109.

148 Henry Kissinger, *Ending the Vietnam War,* Simon & Schuster, New York, 2003, p. 183. Also, see *History of the Resistance War against America 1954–1975,* para. for 17/9/1970. Madame Nguyen Thi Binh was the public chief negotiator while Xuyen Thuy was more powerful but both answered to Le Duc Tho, a so-called adviser to the Mission.

149 Citation 216372 Sergeant Gary J. Chad, Mention-in-Despatches.

150 1ATF SUPINTREP 31/71 (Period 26 July–1 August 71), para. 15.

151 The Australian Army, *Training Information Letter No. 4/70, Bunker Systems.* Prepared and issued under the direction of the Director of Military Training, Army Headquarters, Canberra.

152 1ATF SUPINTREP 36/71 (30 August–5 September 71), para. 30.

153 Army Activities Report: SE Asia (U), as of 1 September 1971, United States of America War Office.

154 1ATF INTSUM 262/71 (19 September 1971); 1ATF SUPINTREP 38/71 (13–19 September 1971). Annex A to 1ATF Op O 9/71.

155 *The Heroic D445 Battalion*, pp. 54–5.

156 AWM95-1-4-232, Annex B to 1ATF INTSUM No 232/71 dated 20 August 1971.

157 1ATF SUPINTREP 38/71 (13–19 Sept 71); Headquarters 1st Australian Task Force file R569/2/301, Op 9/71 (Op Ivanhoe) dated 19 September 1971.

158 AWM95-1-4-232/235, 1ATF Intelligence Summaries for August and September 1971.

159 1ATF, Op 9/71 (Op Ivanhoe) dated 19 September 1971: SUPINTREP 38/71.

160 Ibid.

161 Jerry Taylor, *Last Out*, Allen & Unwin, Sydney, 2001, p. 212.

162 Third Regional Assistance Command, Periodic Intelligence Report [PERINTREP] Number 14-71, Period covered 5–18 September 1971, Annex A.

163 Taylor, *Last Out*, p. 212.

164 Gary McKay, *In Good Company*, Allen & Unwin, Sydney, 1987, pp. 142–4.

165 Taylor, *Last Out*, p. 213.

166 1ATF SUPINTREP 38/71 (13–19 September 1971).

167 AWM95-1-4-233, HQ 1ATF Log Sheet for 20 September 1971; AWM95-7-4-50, 4RAR/NZ Operations Log for 20 September 1971; AWM95-1-4-247, Summary of Contact 20 September 1971.

168 Taylor, *Last Out*, p. 213.

169 McKay, *In Good Company*, p. 145.

170 Ibid., p. 147.

171 Although Lieutenant Rodriguez is identified in several reports as the FAC Jade 07, he could not be identified during the research for this book. No Rodriguez is recorded as receiving a Navy Cross during the time frame of this battle, which Taylor mentioned in *Last Out*, p. 229. No Navy or USMC pilots flew with Detachment 5, 19th Tactical Air Support Squadron in September 1971. None of the squadron's aircraft was hit by ground fire during September according to the 19th TASS history for July–September 1971, contrary to Taylor's statement in *Last Out*, p. 229.

172 Marshall, *The Soldier's Load; The French Lessons of the War in Indochina*, p. 162.

173 The enemy's withdrawal tactics were promulgated in lessons learnt papers and training information letters, specifically Australian Army *Training Information Letter No. 8/70: Contents Viet Cong Withdrawal Tactics*, Prepared and issued under the direction of the Director of Military Training, Army Headquarters, Canberra, May 1970.

174 Citation 511381 Private Kevin Casson: *End of War List—Vietnam*, dated 25 August 1999.

175 4RAR/NZ Operations Log for 20 September 1971.

176 4RAR Operations Log 21–22 September sheets 29, 31, 32 and 33 record that the medic had discussed the shrapnel wound with the doctor via radio. McKay wrote in *In Good Company*, p. 167, that at first he didn't know he had been hit by bullets and the bang that he first heard was not an RPG but the shock and impact of bullets hitting him. However, there were two wounds, one caused by gunshot to the left shoulder and a second caused by RPG shrapnel to his left back: 1 AFH In-Patient records 22 September – 4 October 1972. The notification of casualty record sent by AFV did not report the gunshot wound and only stated 'sustained depp [*sic*] frag wound left side of chest posterial'. Signal Aust

Force Vietnam PA13935 211920Z September 1971 and CARO Non Fatal Casualties Action Sheet 2789609 2LT G. J. McKay.

177 Major Taylor and 2nd Lieutenant McKay were awarded the Military Cross for command competence, bravery and courage respectively. 2nd Lieutenant Michael Sonneveld was awarded a DFC for quiet determination, courage and skill for his flying efforts during the battle. Privates Kevin Casson and Colin Kemp as well as Corporal Doug Melrose and Sergeant Daryl Jenkin were awarded a Mention-in-Despatches. (Casson's award was later upgraded to a Medal for Gallantry.)

178 McKay, *In Good Company*, p. 159.

179 AWM95-1-4-247, After Action Report Operation Ivanhoe: Own troops 5 KIA and 30 WIA included four from A Sqn 3 Cav and 1 NZ. If the enemy suffered badly, as was claimed later, their clearance of the battlefield was extraordinary. During the night the area was bombarded incessantly by artillery and the damage impeded the allied search next day during daylight.

180 Ekins, *Fighting to the Finish*, p. 623.

181 1ATF Intelligence Report 5/71 dated 2 December 1971: Interrogation Report Tran Van Cot. Also, Interrogation Report Private Nguyen Van Hung—AWM95-7-4-56—who was captured by US 3 Brigade on 7 November 1971. Nguyen Van Hung's report included the claim that eight *3/33 NVA* had been killed and seventeen wounded, but his information was second-hand, something that he had heard.

182 Ibid., but see also AWM95-7-4-58, the 4RAR Commander's Diary December 1971 that elaborated on the Xa Bang attack and contact with B Company that reportedly killed eight and wounded thirteen members of *3/33 NVA*.

183 See also *The Heroic D445 Battalion*, p. 54: 'the *3rd Company* [*D445*] coordinated with the *33rd Regiment*, the *4th* [*274*] *Regiment*, and the local forces of Chau Duc District [an area around Xa Bang] to take control along Route 2'.

184 Annex F to 1ATF Intelligence Summary 264/71 dated 21 September 1971. See also *The Heroic D445 Battalion*, p. 60: 'the soldiers of the *7th Company*—a unit of the *33rd Regiment* whose forté was the mobile ambush'.

185 As an example, see 1ATF INTREP 5/71 where Tran Van Cot's company was detached to the *Chau Duc District*, but operated with guerrillas from Ngai Giao for twenty days when they failed to find the *Chau Duc group*.

186 *Training Information Letters 4/70* (undated) and 6/70 April 1970. See also *MACV Command History 1971*, vol I, Annex E; lessons from *Lam Son 719*, Enemy Tactics, p. E36.

187 Third Regional Assistance Command, SUPINTREP 15-71 Period 19 September– 22 October 1971.

188 The battalion's weapons were: two tubes 82 mm mortar, three tubes 60 mm mortar, two 75 mm recoilless rifles, six machine guns, nine B40/B41 RPG and 215 AK (AK 47).

189 Email correspondence between Vo Xuan Thu and the author, October–November– December 2011 that included excerpts from Trieu Kim Son's diary.

190 Ibid.

191 Ibid.

192 Email correspondence between Vo Xuan Thu and the author, 24 March 2012.

Chapter 9

1 AWM293 R579/2/1 Part 2, AATTV Organisation, 27 September 1971: MATT1 Duc Thanh, MATT2 Horseshoe, MATT3 Horseshoe, MATT4 Long Dien, MATT5 Dat Do, MATT6 Hoa Long, MATT7 Ong Trinh, MATT8 Xuyen Moc.

2   Ashley Ekins with Ian McNeill, *Fighting to the Finish: The Australian Army and the Vietnam War, 1968–1975*, Allen & Unwin, Sydney, 2012, p. 819.

3   AWM95-1-4-241, sheets 38 and 39 record thirteen hits and twelve bullet holes respectively, with considerable damage. AWM95-8-1-63, 161 Recce Flt recorded thirteen holes in the aircraft.

4   Colonel G. J. Leary, End of Tour Report, Annex B to AATTV Report, November 1967; AATTV Report, August 1971.

5   AWM95-1-4-246, 1ATF General Staff Instruction 9/71 dated 19 November 1971, Operation Sharpener, the emergency reinforcement of AFV.

6   General Minh held the dual title of CG III Corps, an army formation, and MR3.

7   The remaining units were: HQ Company 1ATF, Det B Sqn 3 Cav Regt, Det 11 MC Gp, Det 30 Term Sqn, 55 EWPS, 110 Sig Sqn, D Coy 4RAR, 5 Coy RAASC, 8 Fd Amb, 2 AOD, 102 Fd Wksp, AFV Pro Unit. HQ AFV was in Saigon and AATTV was still deployed.

8   AWM95-1-4-252, 1ATF Duty Officer's Log for January 1972.

9   1ATF to AFV signal Ops 2646 dated 31 January 1972, Reference Unusual Incident 30 January 1972.

10   AWM95-1-4-255, General Brogan's message at 1ATF Commander's Diary Annex 1–29 February, signal SD 2767, R553/1/10 dated 22 February 1972.

11   AWM95-1-4-254, 1ATF Log Sheet No 3 29 Feb 72.

12   Davies and McKay, *The Men Who Persevered*, pp. 201, 399. Although the AAAGV commanded AATTV, the units were raised on separate establishments and the senior AATTV officer at Van Kiep was the unit CO, not Brigadier Geddes.

13   Troop withdrawals from Vietnam, statement by Minister for Defence, 1 March 1972; Interview Brigadier I. A. Geddes, AHQ 707/R2/38(1), pp. 4–8.

14   AFV R579-1-93, Dunstan to Abrams, 30 October 1971.

15   FANK was operational from 24 February 1971 to 14 December 1972. The unit was administered under the auspices of MACV, now redesignated Army Advisory Group, FANK Training Command (15 May 1972). Later it was known as Field Training Command. After the March 1972 Offensive the FANK Command was tasked to train some ARVN units, which expanded into a major training effort at over eighteen sites around the country.

16   AWM95-1-2-80, AATTV Monthly Report January 1972: Report by Major S. R. Hearder.

17   Alan Dawson, published by UPI in late 1971, exact date unknown, quoted in Bowra's study in Note 20 below.

18   Ibid.

19   Ibid.

20   Lieutenant Colonel Kenneth R. Bowra, *An Historical Study, The US Army Vietnam Individual Training Group (UITG) Program, 1971–1973*, US Army War College, Carlisle Barracks, Carlisle, PA, 1991. An interim copy of the Memorandum of Understanding was signed on 11 January 1972.

21   Ian McNeill, *The Team: Australian Army Advisers in Vietnam 1962–1972*, Australian War Memorial, Canberra, 1984, p. 469.

22   Ibid.

23   Included in correspondence from Terry Smith to the author between 2004 and 2011.

24   Army Activities Report: SE Asia (U) 20 December 1972: Khmer Training.

25   Terence J. Smith, 'Training the "Bodes"', (papers) later published by Big Sky Publishing Pty Ltd, Newport, NSW, 2011; letter to author 8 July 1972.

26 AATTV Monthly Report, February 1972.

27 *MACV Command History 1972*, vol. I, Combat Operations, January–March 1972.

28 General Cao Van Vien and Lieutenant General Dong Van Khuyen, *Indochina Monographs: Reflections on the Vietnam War*, US Army Center of Military History, Washington, DC, 1980. See also Lieutenant General Ngo Quang Truong, *The Easter Offensive of 1972*, US Army Center of Military History, Washington, DC, 1980. See also Tran Van Quang's discussions in note 30, below.

29 Report of the Deputy Chief of the General Staff of the NVA, LT GEN Tran Van Quang at the Politburo meeting of the USSR General Staff, Main Intelligence Directorate (GRU), 15 September 1972, TTU Vietnam Center and Archive.

30 Smith, 'Training the "Bodes"'. The Long Hai Training Battalion was hit twice on 6 April 1972 by 82 mm mortar fire.

31 McNeill, *The Team*, p. 470.

32 *MACV Command History 1972*, vol. I, Combat Operations, April–June 1972.

33 *The Heroic D445 Battalion*, pp. 55–7.

34 Report of Tran Van Quang at USSR Main Intelligence Directorate.

35 The high velocity method was to drop from a high altitude with just a drogue chute deployed; this meant the load hit the ground at 115 km/hr. Airlift to Besieged Areas 7 Apr – 31 Aug 72, HQ PACAF, 7 December 1973.

36 AWM 293, R810/1/4, Australian personnel engaged in FTX July–December 1972.

37 Lam Quang Thi, *The Twenty-five Year Century*, University of North Texas Press, Denton Texas, 2001.

38 Smith, 'Training the "Bodes"', Chapter, 'Contact with the Enemy'.

39 *The Battle for An Loc 5 April – 26 June 1972*, Project CHECO Report, Department of the Air Force, 31 January 1973; *MACV Command History 1972–1973*, vol. I, Ground Operations, November 1972 – January 1973 & vol. II Annex J An Loc; Lt. Gen Ngo Quang Truong, *The Easter Offensive of 1972*, pp. 112, 134–5; Lieutenant Colonel James H. Willbanks, US Army Retired, *Thiet Giap! The Battle of An Loc, April 1972*, US Army Command and General Staff College, Kansas, 1993, pp. 19, 21, 58–9. See also the AATTV reports May to November 1972: AWM 293, R723/2/16 Part 1.

40 Report of Tran Van Quang at USSR Main Intelligence Directorate.

41 *MACV Command History 1972*, vol. I, Ground Operations, July–October 1972.

42 AWM98, 723/R5/128 Annex A. See also CORDS Team 89, Lt Col Gia P. Modica's province Report, Phuoc Tuy for the period ending 31 October 1972.

43 There is a brief mention in the *D445 History* about this without details of the battle and also in *The History of the Revolutionary Struggle in Long Dat District*, Dong Nai, Vietnam, 1986.

44 Terry Smith to the author, 28 February 2011.

45 AWM293 R723/1/3, After Action Report of Ambush Conducted by Xuyen Moc Recon Platoon night 20/21 November 1972. This explanation is a summary of that report. The assistance of Terry Smith with this research is greatly appreciated.

46 In Davies & McKay, *The Men Who Persevered*, the last contact is shown as 31 October 1972; this error was corrected by Terry Smith when more information was found in AWM files.

47 Ibid.

48 The lower figure is listed in the US Army Activities Report: SE Asia, 20 December 1972:

Australia Actual Strength as 14 December 1972. The higher figure is quoted in *The Men Who Persevered*, but it should indicate before the 18 December withdrawal.

49   Davies & McKay, *The Men Who Persevered*, p. 210.

50   The author, personal observation, April 2011.

Epilogue

1   Mark Clodfelter, *The Limits of Air Power: The American Bombing of North Vietnam*, University of Nebraska Press, Lincoln, 2006, p. 195.

2   *FRUS, 1969–1976, Vietnam, October 1972 – January 1973*, Preface VI.

3   C. James Novak, 'Linebacker II', *The Retired Officer Magazine*, November 1992, pp. 11–12.

4   *Linebacker Operations September–December 1972*, CHECO, Dept of the Air Force, Headquarters Pacific Airforces, San Francisco; Lieutenant Colonel Phillip S. Michael, *The Strategic Significance of Linebacker II*, USAWC Strategy Research Project, 2003. Tonnage of bombs dropped varies across several references.

5   Nigel Hamilton, *American Caesars*, Vintage Press, UK, 2011, p. 241.

6   There was one non-combat loss that was caused by engine failure, two F-111 were lost to unknown causes, three aircraft were shot down by MIG-21, seventeen were hit by SAM, three were hit by AAA and a Jolly Green Giant (rescue) was downed by small arms. HQ PACAF/OA: Linebacker II Air Operations Summary (18–29 December 1972).

7   C. James Novak, 'Linebacker II'; Lieutenant Colonel Phillip S. Michael, *The Strategic Significance of Linebacker II*.

8   Admiral U. S. Grant Sharp, *Strategy for Defeat*, Presidio Press, San Rafael, California, 1978, p. 254.

9   Articles: Agreement on Ending the War and Restoring Peace in Vietnam, Paris, January 1973.

10   Frank Snepp, *Decent Interval*, University of Kansas Press, 2002, pp. 109–10.

11   *The Vietnam-Cambodian Emergency, 1975, Part III—Vietnam Evacuation*, US Government Printing Office, Washington, 1976, p. 539.

12   Wikipedia: Battle of Xuan Loc [accessed 25 October 2011]. The article cites Pham Ngoc Thach and Ho Khang, *History of the War of Resistance against America*, National Politics Publishing House, Hanoi, 2008, pp. 392–3.

13   *Xuan Loc: The Final Battle, 1975*, a paper by Lieutenant Colonel James Willbanks (Retired), 19–22 April 2000.

14   *Commander in Chief Pacific Command History*, Appendix III: Babylift, Carl O. Clever, CINCPAC Hawaii, 1976.

15   Truong Nhu Tang with David Chanoff and Doan Van Toai, *A Viet Cong Memoir*, Vintage Books, USA, 1986.

16   *Report made by the Subcommittee to Investigate Problems connected with Refugees and Escapees*, US Government Printing Office, Washington, 1965, p. 2.

17   Ibid., p. 11.

18   Horrible Statistics of Thai Pirates vs Vietnamese Refugees, Viet Ka—Archives of Vietnamese Boat People, October 2010, <http://www.vietka.com>.

19   A tael is an ancient Chinese unit of weight. Its exact weight is imprecise, but it is within a few decimal points of 3.7 grams.

20   Carina Hoang, *Boat People: Personal Stories from the Vietnamese Exodus 1975–1996*,

Fremantle Press, North Fremantle, WA, 2011, p. 126. See also Carina Hoang website: <carinahoang.com>.

21 Hoang, *Boat People*, p. 70.

22 Ibid., p. 122.

23 Clyde Cameron, *China, Communism and Coca-Cola*, Hill of Content, Melbourne, 1980.

24 Hoang, *Boat People*, p. 126.

25 Ibid., p. 198.

26 Ibid., pp. 126–8.

27 Ibid., p. 38.

28 Ibid., p. 56.

29 Ibid., p. 184

30 Ibid., p. 27.

31 Theresa C. Carino, Vietnam's Chinese Minority and the Politics of Sino-Vietnamese Relations, <www.ibiblio.org> [accessed 27 October 2011].

32 Ibid.

33 Hoang, *Boat People*, pp. 27, 207, 244.

34 Interview George Negus, *George Negus Tonight*, ABC TV, 15 September 2004.

35 Hoang, *Boat People*, p. 83.

36 Don Hardy, <VietKa.com> [accessed 27 October 2011]. Also Fate of the Boat People, <boatpeople75.tripod.com>.

37 Hoang, *Boat People*, p. 224.

38 United States of America *Congressional Record, Proceedings of the 107th Congress, First Session*, p. 20980. The repeal was approved by the 11th Congress, P.L. 111–117 (Division F. Title VII).

39 Ronald J. Cima (ed.), *Vietnam: A Country Study*, GPO for the Library of Congress, Washington, 1987.

40 Tang, *A Viet Cong Memoir*, p. 284.

41 Le Duc Tho was a powerful member of the politburo. A protégé of Le Duan, he served in the South on a number of occasions, in particular when Le Duan headed *COSVN* in the 1950s. He was also involved in the invasion of Kampuchea (1978) and on the Chinese border in 1979.

42 Jacqueline Desbarats, 'Repression in the Socialist Republic of Vietnam: Executions and Population Relocation', in J. N. Moore (ed.), *The Vietnam Debate: A Fresh Look at the Arguments*, University Press of America, Maryland, 1990. The source for the number is copied from E. Kaufman & P. Fagen, 'Extrajudicial Executions: An Insight into the Global Dimensions of a Human Rights Violation', *Human Rights Quarterly*, vol. 3, no. 4, November 1981, p. 81.

43 Jacqueline Desbarats & Karl D. Jackson, *Political Violence in Vietnam: The Dark Side of Liberation*, Executive Publications, Singapore, 1986.

44 Ibid.

45 Ibid.

46 A Statement by Mr Phan Quang, Vice-Minister of the Ministry of Information, at the 11 February 1988 Press Conference. Copy kindly provided by Brian and Nhung Day. Gary McKay was approached by a Vietnamese woman in Vung Tau in 1994 who claimed that her husband had been arrested in Vung Tau in 1975 and taken to Back Beach where he and several other ARVN officers were machine-gunned to death and their bodies pushed into

the South China Sea. When questioned why this occurred she replied that it was because her husband, an ARVN captain, 'had worked with the Americans'. No proof was offered of this murder but the sincerity of the informant was highly evident and palpable.

47 Ginetta Sagan & Stephen Denney, 'Re-Education in Unliberated Vietnam', *The Indochina Newsletter*, October–November, 1982; Jacqueline Desbarats, in Moore, *The Vietnam Debate*, pp. 193–201.

48 Sagan & Denney, 'Re-education in Unliberated Vietnam'.

49 The Library of Congress Country Studies, *A Country Study: Vietnam* (Library Call Number DS556.3.V54 1989). See <icweb2.loc.gov/frd/cs/vntoc.html> [accessed 30 October 2011].

50 Ibid.

51 The former officer wishes to remain anonymous for obvious reasons.

52 A summary of Jacqueline Desbarats writing on the New Economic Zones is given in Desbarats, 'Repression in the Socialist Republic of Vietnam'.

53 *Saigon Giai Phong* newspaper article, 10 October 1975, copied from Jacqueline Desbarats essay, first published in Moore, *The Vietnam Debate*, 1990.

54 Decree Quang Doi Nhan Dan issued 27 June 1977, from Desbarats, 'Repression in the Socialist Republic of Vietnam'.

55 Desbarats, 'Repression in the Socialist Republic of Vietnam'.

56 Dick Wilson, *Zhou Enlai zhuan, the Biography of Zhou Enlai*, Viking Press, New York, 1984. See also Jung Chang and Jon Halliday, *Mao: The Unknown Story*, Jonathan Cape, London, 2005. Yang Kuisong, Working Paper No. 34, *Change in Mao Zedung's Attitude toward the Indochina War*, Woodrow Wilson International Center for Scholars, Washington, D.C., February 2002.

57 Odd Arne Westad, Chen Jian, Stein Tonneson, Nguyen Vu Tungand, and James G. Hershberg, *77 Conversations between Chinese and Foreign Leaders on the Wars in Indochina, 1964–1977*, Working Paper No. 22, Woodrow Wilson International Center for Scholars, p. 35.

58 Ilya V. Gaiduk, *The Soviet Union and the Vietnam War*, Ian R. Dee, Chicago, 1996, p. 217.

59 *The Truth about Vietnam–China Relations over the Last 30 Years*, Ministry of Foreign Affairs, Socialist Republic of Viet Nam, 1979, p. 10.

60 Testimony by Dr Houk, Oversight on Post-Traumatic Stress Disorder, 14 July 1988, p. 17, Hearing before the Committee on Veterans' Affairs, United States Senate 100th Congress second session.

61 ACPMH website, Summary of the Military Mental Health and Traumatic Stress Literature: 2007, 21 April 2008, <www.acpmh.unimelb.edu.au>.

62 P.J. Crane, D.L. Barnard, K.W. Horsley and M.A. Adena, A report of the 1996 retrospective cohort study of Australian Vietnam Veterans issued by the Department of Veterans' Affairs, Canberra, 11 November 1997.

63 VVAA website report into the incidence of suicide in children of Vietnam Veterans, Media Release, 7 August 2000, <www.vvaa.org.au>.

64 William A. Buckingham, Jr, *The Air Force and Herbicides in Southeast Asia 1961–1971*, Office of Air Force History, USAF, Washington, DC, 1982.

65 *Cancer Incidence in Australian Vietnam Veterans Study 2005*, Department of Veterans' Affairs, Canberra, 2005.

66 House Oversight Committee, Subcommittee to review the Centers for Disease Control's study on the defoliant Agent Orange, 11 July 1989, <http://www.archive.org.details/org. c-span.8342-1>.

67 James O. Pittman, review of *Shook Over Hell: Post-Traumatic Stress, Vietnam and the Civil War* by Eric T. Dean, Jr., *Journal of Military History*, October 1998, p. 896.

68 Eric T. Dean, *Shook Over Hell: Post-Traumatic Stress, Vietnam and the Civil War*, Harvard University Press, Cambridge, Mass., 1997, p. 40.

69 James O. Pittman, review.

70 The author recalled in 1967 being asked by a South Vietnamese farmer if he was a Russian. When the farmer was asked why he thought the author was a Russian, he answered that it was because of his rifle (SLR), which was not a common weapon in the area and it looked like a Russian rifle.

71 John Garnaut, review of *Deng Xiaoping and the Transformation of China* by Ezra F. Vogel, Belknap Press, 2011, *Saturday Age*, 5 November 2011.

72 Economic data from US Department of State, Bureau of East Asian and Pacific Affairs, <http://lcweb2.loc.gov/frd/cs/vntoc.html>.

73 Professor Klaus Schwab (ed.), *The Global Competitiveness Report 2011–2012*, World Economic Forum Geneva, Switzerland, 2011, Vietnam, p. 31.

74 John Tribe, *The Economics of Recreation, Leisure and Tourism*, Elsevier Press, 2004, pp. 295–6; Library of Congress—Federal Research Division, Country Profile: Vietnam, December 2005, <http://lcweb2.loc.gov/frd/cs/vntoc.html>.

75 DFAT website: Vietnam Country Brief and Vietnamese Embassy Australia website, <http://www.dfat.gov.au/geo/vietnam/vietnam_brief.html>.

76 DFAT website: Vietnam Country Brief. The bridge is part of a central Mekong Connectivity project. The bridge was begun in 2008 and should be completed in 2015.

77 According to the Center for Defense Information, Washington, the total US military spending for the years 1965–1973 was $2886.7 billion (in 1996 dollars). Vietnam cost $738 billion (2010/2011 dollars) for military operations only. The figure does not include such things as veterans' benefits or assistance to allies. The cost is only for war-related activities over and above the regular non-wartime costs of defence. Stephen Daggett, *Costs of Major US Wars*, Congressional Research Service, 29 June 2010.

78 Robert Thompson KBE, CMG, DSO, MC, *Make for the Hills: Memories of Far Eastern Wars*, Leo Cooper, London, 1989, p. 121.

79 Lee Kuan Yew, *The Singapore Story: Memoirs of Lee Kuan Yew*, Prentice Hall, College Division, 1998.

80 Stephen Fruhling, *A History of Australian Strategic Policy Since 1945*, Defence Publishing Service, Dept of Defence, Canberra, ACT, 2009, throughout.

81 Michael Auslin, 'China plays its own games as US treads water', *The Australian*, 11 July 2011.

INDEX

Page numbers in *italics* refer to maps; please see the Glossary for abbreviations